CW00801966

ALL SOULS AND THE WIDER WORLD

All Souls and the Wider World

Statesmen, Scholars, and Adventurers, c.1850–1950

Edited by
S. J. D. GREEN
PEREGRINE HORDEN

OXFORD
UNIVERSITY PRESS

OXFORD
UNIVERSITY PRESS

Great Clarendon Street, Oxford OX2 6DP

Oxford University Press is a department of the University of Oxford.
It furthers the University's objective of excellence in research, scholarship,
and education by publishing worldwide in

Oxford New York

Auckland Cape Town Dar es Salaam Hong Kong Karachi
Kuala Lumpur Madrid Melbourne Mexico City Nairobi
New Delhi Shanghai Taipei Toronto

With offices in

Argentina Austria Brazil Chile Czech Republic France Greece
Guatemala Hungary Italy Japan Poland Portugal Singapore
South Korea Switzerland Thailand Turkey Ukraine Vietnam

Oxford is a registered trade mark of Oxford University Press
in the UK and in certain other countries

Published in the United States
by Oxford University Press Inc., New York

© All Souls College 2011

The moral rights of the authors have been asserted
Database right Oxford University Press (maker)

First published 2011

All rights reserved. No part of this publication may be reproduced,
stored in a retrieval system, or transmitted, in any form or by any means,
without the prior permission in writing of Oxford University Press,
or as expressly permitted by law, or under terms agreed with the appropriate
reprographics rights organization. Enquiries concerning reproduction
outside the scope of the above should be sent to the Rights Department,
Oxford University Press, at the address above

You must not circulate this book in any other binding or cover
and you must impose the same condition on any acquirer

British Library Cataloguing in Publication Data

Data available

Library of Congress Cataloging in Publication Data

Data available

Typeset by SPI Publisher Services, Pondicherry, India
Printed in Great Britain
on acid-free paper by
MPG Books Group, Bodmin and King's Lynn

ISBN 978–0–19–959370–5

1 3 5 7 9 10 8 6 4 2

Preface

This book is the product of Chichele Lectures on the history of All Souls delivered in the College over a number of years. It forms the final part of a trilogy of such volumes that also includes Jeremy Catto et al., *Unarmed Soldiery: Studies in the Early History of All Souls College, Oxford* (Oxford: All Souls College, 1996), and S. J. D. Green and Peregrine Horden (eds), *All Souls under the Ancien Régime: Politics, Learning, and the Arts, c.1600–1850* (Oxford: Oxford University Press, 2007). As before, the present editors are grateful to the Warden and Fellows for the hospitality that they afforded speakers and guests on the occasion of the original lectures, and for their support of this publication. The editors are no less indebted to the contributors for their patience. They would also like to thank Sarah Holmes of Oxford University Press for her commitment to the project, Norma Aubertin-Potter and Gaye Morgan of the Codrington Library, All Souls, for their indefatigable archival labours and expert advice, Leen Van Broeck for valuable editorial assistance, Humaira Erfan Ahmed for her characteristically unstinting help in preparing the collection for press, and Malcolm Todd for sympathetic yet ever vigilant copy-editing.

S.J.D.G.

J.N.P.B.H.

Contents

Abbreviations   ix

Contributors   x

Introduction: Anson's Legacy – All Souls and
the Wider World, *c.*1850–1950   1
S. J. D. Green and Peregrine Horden

1. Prizes, Fellowship, and Open Competition in All Souls,
   *c.*1850–1950   13
   Adrian Wooldridge

2. 'Government by Mallardry': The Golden Age of the
   Prize Fellows, *c.*1875–1925   43
   S. J. D. Green

3. Simon: A Lawyer in Politics   73
   Stephen Cretney

4. Government by a Mallardian: On the Possibility
   of Public Service in the Political Thought of R. H. Brand   101
   S. J. D. Green

5. Have Brain, Will Travel: W. K. Hancock and
   the Idea of Public Service   135
   Jim Davidson

6. All Souls and 'The Round Table'   155
   Michael Howard

7. All Souls and the War of the Professors   167
   John Clarke

8. All Souls and India: The 1920s   193
   Sarvepalli Gopal

9. All Souls and India: The 1930s and After   207
   Sarvepalli Gopal

10. Appeasers and Anti-Appeasers: All Souls and the
    International Crisis of the 1930s   223
    S. J. D. Green

11. Leo Amery and the Post-War World, 1945–55   263
    Wm. Roger Louis

12. All Souls and Suez   281
    Wm. Roger Louis
13. G. M. Young: The Last Victorian?   295
    J. Mordaunt Crook

Index   321

Abbreviations

Hist. Univ. Oxf.	*The History of the University of Oxford*, general editor T. H. Aston, 8 vols (Oxford: Oxford University Press, 1984–94), cited by editor and volume number.
ODNB	*Oxford Dictionary of National Biography*
TNA	The National Archives

Contributors

John Clarke, University of Buckingham

Stephen Cretney, All Souls College

J. Mordaunt Crook, Brasenose College, Oxford

Jim Davidson, University of Melbourne

†Sarvepalli Gopal, Jawaharlal Nehru University

S. J. D. Green, University of Leeds and All Souls College

Peregrine Horden, Royal Holloway, University of London, and All Souls College

Michael Howard, All Souls College

Wm. Roger Louis, University of Texas at Austin

Adrian Wooldridge, *The Economist*

Introduction

Anson's Legacy – All Souls and the Wider World, c.1850–1950

S. J. D. Green and Peregrine Horden

By the time of his death in June 1914, Sir William Anson, Warden of All Souls since 1881, was widely acknowledged as one of the pre-eminent public figures of Edwardian England. This was for good reason. His individual achievements were unusually diverse; the extent of his broader service was, if anything, more considerable still. Elected a fellow of All Souls in 1867, he was appointed Vinerian Reader in English Law at Oxford just seven years later, at the age of 31. The *Principles of the English Law of Contract*, first published in 1879, firmly established his scholarly reputation. It survived for nearly a century after, into a twenty-sixth edition. This appeared in 1975, some sixty years after its author's passing. Anson's three-volume treatise on *The Law and Custom of the Constitution*, issued sequentially in 1886, 1892, and 1898, made him into a national figure. Catapulted late into politics, first as Liberal Unionist then as Unionist MP for Oxford University between 1899 and 1914, he was also briefly a government minister. A leading figure in the Electoral Reform Society, he simultaneously served as Oxford's Vice-Chancellor and evinced a life-long commitment to university extension.[1]

Yet it was for none of these distinctions – in law, politics, and education – that Anson was chiefly commemorated in 1914. Edwardian England feted him still more as the 'second founder' of All Souls College. In the words of Oxford's pre-war Chancellor – his protégé, Lord Curzon – Anson's truly enduring achievement had been to transform All Souls from an inert academic backwater into a 'recognised citadel for the studies of History and Law'; no less, from a nominal instrument of

---

[1] There is no modern *Life* of Anson. His All Souls career will be covered in S. J. D. Green, 'The Impact of Anson', in idem, *The Exceptional College: All Souls c. 1850–1950* (forthcoming). There is a succinct summary of his achievements in H. C. G. Matthew, 'Anson, Sir William Reynell, Third Baronet (1843–1914)', *ODNB*. Much of value can still be gleaned from H. H. Henson (ed.), *A Memoir of the Right Honourable Sir William Anson, Baronet: Warden of All Souls College, Burgess for the University of Oxford* (Oxford, 1920), see esp. chs 3–10.

the Church into a vital source for the 'flow of eminent public servants to the state'.[2] Curzon's was, of course, a somewhat self-regarding view. But it was widely corroborated beyond the College's walls. When Hensley Henson published a *Memoir of the Right Honourable Sir William Anson*, a laudatory reviewer in *The Spectator* took great pains to praise the 'wise rule' of one who had turned a 'refuge for dilettantes' into an 'invaluable ... promoter of research ... in the [new] schools of History and Law'.[3] A rather more reflective notice in *The Times Literary Supplement* no less insistently identified a 'subtly pervasive influence' in national life – an influence that it dated to the moment when Anson assumed leadership of the College. This was 'the turning point [in] his career'; it was also the instant when All Souls emerged from the doldrums as both a 'specialist ... centre ... in education' and a valuable mediator between 'Oxford and the outside world'.[4]

Such a combination – of significant academic work and reputation for distinguished public service – accounts in large part for the prestige enjoyed by All Souls in English society more generally during the years immediately prior to the First World War. Certainly, it was then celebrated as a *national* institution to an extent that would be scarcely imaginable today. Yet that was, in many ways, an ironic achievement. For Anson's College – the core subject of this book – with its balance of 'pure' scholarship and public 'impact', came about as much by default as by design. The Royal Commission of 1850–2 had initially conceived of the reformed All Souls as a centre for the theory and practice of modern statesmanship. It envisaged a wholly recast institution, staffed by a phalanx of professors and dedicated to the systematic teaching of the new (and practical) subjects of law and history. This would turn out lawyers and diplomats by the dozen, all dedicated to the good counsel and wise administration of the commonweal.[5]

All Souls manfully resisted so drastic a reformation of its traditional ways for the next decade or so. But the success of its recalcitrance owed more to corporate poverty than to collective guile.[6] It was also necessarily short-lived. Oxford was reformed again barely a generation later. As one of the College's two leading advocates to the Selborne Commission in 1877, Anson skilfully promoted the College as a future centre for research in (rather than teaching of) law and history in the University. All Souls promised the authorities that its existing professors would

    [2] 'Sir William Anson: An Appreciation by C', *The Times*, 5 June 1914, 10.
    [3] Anon., 'A Memoir of Rt. Hon. Sir William Anson', *The Spectator*, 124, no. 4793 (8 May 1920), 624.
    [4] Anon., 'Sir William Anson', *Times Literary Supplement*, 956, 13 May 1920, 294.
    [5] *Report of Her Majesty's Commissioners Appointed to Inquire into the State, Discipline, Studies and Revenues of the University and Colleges of Oxford, Together with Evidence and an Appendix* (1852) (hereafter *RCO*), 'All Souls College', 215–20. For a modern interpretation of the Commission, see W. R. Ward, 'From the Tractarians to the Executive Commission, 1845–1854', in M. G. Brock and M. C. Curthoys (eds), *Hist. Univ. Oxf.*, vii, 1, ch. 10. For particular reference to All Souls, see S. J. D. Green, 'The "Fremantle Affair" and the Destruction of the *Ancien Régime* in All Souls, 1857–1864', in S. J. D. Green and Peregrine Horden (eds), *All Souls under the Ancien Régime: Politics, Learning, and the Arts, c.1600–1850* (Oxford, 2007), ch. 15, esp. pp. 349–55.
    [6] Green, 'The "Fremantle Affair"', 349–55; J. S. G. Simmons, 'All Souls', in Brock and Curthoys (eds), *Hist. Univ. Oxf.*, vii, 2, ch. 8.

be supplemented by Research Fellows, all increasingly committed to the ever more academic ends of a new house of secular learning. The agricultural depression of the 1880s put paid to this ambition, if such it ever truly was. Anson's All Souls did indeed become a great home of legal and historical scholarship. But no more than two such Research Fellows were ever resident in the College at any one time before the outbreak of European hostilities.[7] To that degree, the most striking feature of All Souls during the period 1850–1914 is what it did *not* become. It did not become a school of government. It did not become an institute of advanced study. It did not become an ancillary of the Indian Institute or an adjunct of the Bodleian Library. *Faute de mieux*, partly through luck, partly through both principled and unprincipled opposition to organic change, it became what Anson always secretly wanted: an exceptional college, a curious amalgam of university professors and Prize Fellows – especially Prize Fellows.[8]

The College that nurtured so many scholars, statesmen, and adventurers in the first half of the twentieth century was defined – to a greater degree than by any other factor – by the peculiar history of the All Souls 'prize' fellowship after 1881. Yet this was an ironic development too. Prize Fellowships – that is, fellowships allocated by genuinely open competition – constituted one of the truly great innovations of the 1852 Commission. More than any other institution, they had been responsible for the elimination of kinship, locality, and even profession as the principal criteria for the allocation of academic rewards in the post-1850 University. More than any other institution, they permitted the transformation of Oxford from a gentleman's seminary into a secular university.[9] But more than any other institution they were also the principal victims of the Selborne Commission. This was because Selborne demanded above all that Oxford become a teaching university – a place where the fellows taught the undergraduates – and the colleges responded by electing ever more 'official', that is, tutorial, fellows to perform this task. They also tried to convert their 'prize' fellows into teaching fellows as quickly as possible. So 'prize fellowships' were effectively abolished or transformed. As a result, the number of 'prize' fellows elected throughout the University declined precipitously. Between 1878 and 1914, the whole of Oxford (outside All Souls) elected just 128 of them; of those, 62 – very nearly half – eventually assumed academic responsibilities within the University. At the same time, All Souls (alone) accounted for sixty-three such elections. Amongst these, just nineteen, less than one-third, dedicated their lives to scholarly pursuits thereafter.[10]

---

[7] Green, 'The Impact of Anson'; Simmons, 'All Souls', 218.

[8] To be considered at length in Green, 'The Years of the Constituent Assembly', *The Exceptional College*. For now see C. Grant Robertson, *All Souls College* (London, 1899), ch. 10, esp. pp. 199–208.

[9] *RCO*, 'Removal of Restrictions on the Election to Fellowships', 149–68; Ward, 'From the Tractarians to the Executive Commission', 308ff.; also W. R. Ward, *Victorian Oxford* (London, 1965), ch. 9.

[10] See Green, this volume, ch. 2; A. J. Engel, *From Clergyman to Don: The Rise of the Academic Profession in Nineteenth-Century Oxford* (Oxford, 1983), ch. 4.

All this rendered the Oxford 'prize fellowship' increasingly rare. Other developments made it prestigious. For a lucky few, the All Souls Prize Fellowship was a bonanza: £200 per annum – a respectable bachelor's income – for seven years, with no obligations attached: indeed, no academic obligations of any kind, prior to 1911. Not everyone approved, even at the time. Some thought it wasteful. Others believed it pointless. It is at least worth noting that it actually enabled many young men from relatively modest backgrounds to pursue careers that might otherwise have been closed to them. The fellowship did not become simply the preserve of the privileged, as many later presumed. The major public schools did not predominate amongst successful applicants, *c*.1881–1914. Many remarkably talented scholars won a first foothold on the professional ladder, including Hensley Henson in the Church and John Simon at the Bar.[11]

The Prize Fellowship was a leg-up that enabled many young men to do what they wanted to do, at least for a while. Most rejected the contemplative, or at least the academic, life. For all that, experiments in scholarship were far from frowned upon. The future Lord Halifax published a biography of Keble before going into politics – both whilst still a Prize Fellow. The more creative, for instance Frederick Trench, even tried their hands at poetry. Those of robust constitution usually travelled. Some did so to good effect. Curzon virtually initiated the twentieth-century practice of visiting distant parts of the world in order to become expert on them; thereby to gain the first-hand experience that might equip a future statesman for imperial administration. Others went straight into the business of running the Empire. Some of the most famous – like Perry and Brand – became prominent members of Milner's famous Kindergarten in South Africa following the Boer War.[12] Near contemporaries, such as Dawson and Amery, followed them as journalists. Each in his own way would make a profound contribution to *Pax Britannica* after 1918.

The outcome of all this effort was to turn Anson's All Souls into both a beacon of public spirit and an icon in national life. This was at least in part because Anson so carefully cultivated that collegiate reputation through his own person. Considerable scholar that he continued to be, he increasingly turned his learning towards practical ends, from reform of the House of Lords to the status of women in the universities.[13] He also encouraged others in the College – even amongst its professors – to do the same. Thus Albert Venn Dicey, under the Warden's tutelage, moved from theorist of public opinion to apologist for Irish Union.[14] Others, less ostentatiously but no less influentially, devoted their talents to the broader improvement of English law. Recall, in this respect, the career of the Master

---

[11] For more detail on this and what follows, see chs 2 and 3 below; also Simmons, 'All Souls', 216ff.

[12] See Howard, this volume.

[13] Henson (ed.), *Memoir of Anson*, chs 6–9.

[14] R. S. Rait (ed.), *Memorials of Albert Venn Dicey, being chiefly Letters and Diaries* (London, 1925), ch. 8.

of the Rolls, Wilfred Greene.[15] Their collective achievement was never reducible to mere kudos-seeking. Anson naturally sought to send ambitious young men out into the world. But he also wanted to bring them back and set them to painstaking labour in the world's best interests. The Round Table was at least in part a product of that continuing and altruistic ambition.[16] Moreover, his sense of the world and its needs was not limited to obviously great things, nor indeed to the interests of the great. So Warden Anson became one of the earliest patrons of the Workers Educational Authority. Albert Mansbridge remembered how

[t]his keen little man, conservative to his finger-tips, was ever ready to welcome working-class students to Oxford. All Souls took at the outset a real and unflagging share of the work. He loved to meet the men and fraternise with them. The dignified fellows of an earlier day would have rubbed their eyes in disapproving astonishment at the sight of a Warden, near to midnight, keeping time to 'Auld Lang Syne' with hands clasping those of burly trade unionists on either side of him ... not every Warden, however well-disposed, could have managed it with his entire absence of self-consciousness.[17]

Indeed not. That self-conscious – and perhaps peculiarly late-Victorian – harmonization of abstract ethical and immediate practical concerns, similarly of grandiose and benevolent ends, captured the imagination of many of Anson's compatriots. It also enthused many beyond these shores. In this way, Anson's All Souls became famous. Its Prize Fellows were annually announced on the news pages of *The Times*. It also found itself the subject of idolizing imitation abroad. Some were captivated by the idea of an institution that supported clever young men, freed to pursue whatever (intellectual) interest took their fancy. This notion served as a model for Harvard's Society of Fellows. It offered three years of endowed leisure to carefully selected bright graduates – provided they did *not* succumb to the 'Ph.D. octopus'.[18] *Mutatis mutandis*, the College of Müller, Edgeworth, and Dicey, also of Gardiner and Pollard, served as an inspiration for the Institute of Advanced Study at Princeton. This august society was established by Abraham Flexner at much the same time. It was conceived as neither a teaching nor a research school, but as a 'wedge between the two – a small university in which a limited amount of teaching and a liberal amount of research are both to be found'.[19]

---

[15] Once again, there is no modern *Life*. The best summary of Greene's achievements can now be found in J. Lever, 'Greene, Wilfred Arthur, Baron Greene (1883–1952)', *ODNB*.

[16] See again Howard, this volume.

[17] A. Mansbridge, *The Older Universities of England* (London, 1923), 262.

[18] The phrase is that of William James. There is a short account of the Society's origins in Andrew Schlesinger, *Veritas: Harvard College and the American Experience* (Chicago, 2005), 174. The All Souls connection is explicitly brought out in A. M. Schlesinger, Jnr, *A Life in the Twentieth Century: Innocent Beginnings, 1917–1950* (Boston, 2000), 221.

[19] Cited in K. Bird and M. J. Sherwin, *American Prometheus: The Triumph and Tragedy of J. Robert Oppenheimer* (New York, 2005), 371–2, which again brings out the All Souls connection.

But a place ever more admired in the wider world became increasingly alien to Oxford's academic village after 1918. So far from rejoicing in the achievement, much local opinion increasingly came to see All Souls as a domestic abuse. To this way of thinking, the post-war College was just a very rich institution whose vast endowments 'were used [neither to the advantage of] higher education generally nor the University [of Oxford] particularly'. It remained an idle community, of 'non-resident fellows' illogically freed from otherwise universal obligations to 'literary...study or scientific endeavour'. Still worse, it sustained a perverse society, pointlessly dedicated to 'augmenting the income of prosperous' men pursuing 'non-academical vocations' in each and every part of the wider world – except in Oxford.[20]

These were not just the isolated ravings of a few disaffected dons. They also constituted the 'considered opinions of the Oxford Reform Committee'. This suitably damning judgement was formally submitted by the group as evidence to the Royal Commission that investigated the finances, government, and organization of the ancient universities between 1919 and 1922. In fairness, its various objections to all of the supposedly long-standing, and many of the apparently more recent, abuses of All Souls actually represented one of the saner examples of that 'special criticism' for which the College was repeatedly singled out in both public and private memorials to that Royal Commission.[21] The aim of such condemnation was to effect organic transformation. That is to put the point politely. Twenty years later, Llewellyn Woodward (then a young Prize Fellow) remembered the situation rather differently. In his own words, 'after the war, various groups of reformers in the University wanted to abolish us'.[22]

What most stirred the reformers' ire was All Souls' desultory contribution to the formal teaching strength of the University. This became even more apparent after 1919, as the post-war influx of demobilized undergraduates stretched existing resources to the limit. It was brought into still sharper relief by the recent emergence of natural sciences as important academic disciplines within the University: a departure to which All Souls then made little obvious contribution.[23] Underlying these real but contingent difficulties lay an altogether broader divergence of purpose. This was increasingly defined by the very nature of the Prize Fellowship itself. Selborne had slowly converted Oxford's other prize fellows into teaching dons. But Anson's manipulation of the 1881 Statutes had enabled All Souls not only to retain its non-academic element amongst the

[20] Oxford, Bodleian Library, M/5, Top. Oxon, b. 104/29, Memoranda with Regard to Reforms at Oxford: Professor E. B. Poulton, 'The Position of All Souls College', 28 September 1920.

[21] M/5, Top. Oxon, b. 109/9, Oxford Reform Committee, represented by Mr W. D. Ross, 4 June 1920. This question will be investigated at length in Green, 'Affluence and Anxiety: The Significance of the Asquith Commission', *The Exceptional College*, ch. 8.

[22] E. L. Woodward, *Short Journey* (London, 1942), 156.

[23] M/5, Top. Oxon, b. 104/29, Poulton, 'The Position of All Souls College', notes this point at length. Substance is offered by J. B. Morrell, 'The Non-Medical Sciences, 1914–1939', in B. Harrison (ed.), *Hist. Univ. Oxf.*, viii, ch. 6.

younger members of the College, but also to maintain a phalanx of so-called '£50 fellows': 'extraordinary' fellows deemed capable of contributing to the continuing life of the College in some generally undefined and invariably unscholarly manner. Still more skilful manoeuvring through the murkier waters of the existing by-laws had permitted the bachelor Warden effectively to limit this class of increasingly anomalous Oxonians to the increasingly anomalous category of unmarried men.[24] His successor, the happily married Francis Pember, guilelessly followed suit. Indeed, he went so far as to describe such men as essential to the 'continuity... and effectiveness' of Chichele's College: this in 1919. Many, outside its walls, had by then come to doubt that view.[25]

None of which would probably have mattered very much had All Souls remained a respectably impecunious society during the interim. For a long time this was not as improbable a fate as it has subsequently come to seem. All Souls was a relatively poor college, right down to the 1890s. Indeed, such poverty constituted a crucial component in its preservation, as late as 1914.[26] During the 1850s its miserably under-endowed fellowships had proved poor pickings for a radical Royal Commission, otherwise keen to turn the College into a concentration of professorial Chairs. Even during the 1880s, a simple lack of funds had prevented the College from fully implementing an earlier promise to promote higher scholarship at All Souls by the appointment of more Research Fellows. This was true even in the face of otherwise ingenuous goodwill. Warden Anson furnished the stipend for the great historian, S. R. Gardiner, out of his own pocket.[27]

But from around the turn of the twentieth century, All Souls grew rich. In part, this was the result of simple good fortune. The College had long owned large estates in what a century of suburbanizing had turned into north-west London. These were now ripe for further development. To be sure, they did not transform themselves. The riches they brought were the product of unprecedented entrepreneurial initiative. A policy of running down agricultural leases and letting out buildings permitted a huge increase in revenue – perhaps thirty times greater from this source alone – between 1889 and 1909. Overall College income rose considerably with it: from around £27,000 per annum in 1888 to perhaps £35,000 in 1914; then to something closer to £40,000 by 1919. This represented a rise of nearly fifty per cent in little more than twenty years. That was remarkable enough in itself. It was also very atypical of early twentieth-century Oxford.[28]

Yet very little of this increased income went into the appointment of more Research Fellows. That was not least on account of the College's long-standing obligations towards more general university purposes, whether in the form of

[24] Green, 'The Impact of Anson', will deal with this murky question.
[25] M/5, Top. Oxon, b. 109/10, F. W. Pember, 'Memorandum on All Souls College', 29 September 1920.
[26] Simmons, 'All Souls', 213.
[27] Ibid., 218.
[28] For this and what follows see Green, 'Affluence and Anxiety'.

grants to the Bodleian Library or salaries for new professors. These had been cut back between 1887 and 1898 during the worst of the agricultural recession. They were vigorously increased thereafter. To that degree, at least, the College's failure to supplement its academic element by 1918 was (and is) perfectly explicable. Yet it would be idle to deny that such a bias – even in scholarship, towards the practical rather than the theoretical – eventually came to represent the result of preference as well as of exigency. Moreover, by 1918, All Souls was not just a rich society in the midst of poor neighbours. It had also become a College made up almost entirely of Prize Fellows and professors, cast adrift in a university ever more populated by college tutors and university instructors. And it continued to flaunt within (or rather, without) its walls the luxurious anomaly of non-residence – amidst a community of desk-bound dons.[29]

Even in Oxford the various resentments that such contrasts inevitably inspired could scarcely be articulated in the language simply of envy. So they were expressed as the imperatives of contemporary academic urgency. The post-war University was expanding both literally and metaphorically. It was getting bigger: taking up more space, incorporating more colleges and private halls, housing more students. It also taught more subjects, especially in the natural and social sciences. Finally, it taught them not just to greater numbers of undergraduates but to different kinds of pupil – both postgraduates and women. To cope with that increase, the University needed – and increasingly, demanded – more posts, more funds, indeed more of everything. Yet neither expansion nor increase had been accompanied by greater non-collegiate income. Worse still, the ancient universities received no government grant.[30]

Hitherto, they had neither required nor sought such public support. But the impact of slack agricultural revenues and general inflation taken together ensured that the real purchasing power of university and college incomes was lower in 1918 than it had been before the war. Forlornly trying to do more with less, the ancient universities finally turned to the government for help. They swallowed their pride and asked for a subsidy. With that, the question of how Oxford University, collectively conceived, consumed its available resources assumed a previously unrecognized importance. In the face of so many seemingly novel and all too obviously burdensome impositions now placed upon the University, Anson's All Souls, long regarded as something of an anomaly, came to seem more of an institutional abuse. Up to this point, there had been no one, and nothing, to which the hostile might profitably turn. Suddenly, there was. This was the aforementioned Royal Commission, appointed to inquire into the finances, government, and organization of the Universities of Oxford and

---

[29] M/5, Top. Oxon, b. 104/32, Dr H. Rashdall, 'University Reform', n.d., *c.* June/July 1920, captures the spirit of this resentment nicely. Rashdall, by then Dean of Carlisle, made a point of speaking to the Commission 'as a former fellow of New College'.

[30] For a detailed account, see J. P. D. Dunbabin, 'Finance Since 1914', in Harrison (ed.), *Hist. Univ. Oxf.*, viii, ch. 24.

Cambridge on 14 November 1919. It has come down to us as the Asquith Commission.[31]

The history and politics of that much maligned investigation merit separate treatment.[32] What matters here is simply to understand the impact of the Asquith Commission on All Souls generally, and on the Prize Fellowship in particular. This has been much misunderstood. The significance of Asquith for the general administration of the ancient universities may have been disappointingly slight to some. But its importance for the particular development of All Souls after 1923 was very considerable indeed. No small part of that effect lay in the subtlety of the attack that Asquith mounted against Anson's citadel. Much of his report, even indeed much of that part of the report specifically devoted to the peculiar case of All Souls, read superficially like an exquisitely balanced defence of a falsely traduced society. The devil lay in the details. Denying any intention of seeking punitive transformation, Asquith nevertheless pushed the College in the direction of broader change. First, he stipulated that the prize element of the Prize Fellowship be limited to two years. He also suggested that continuing financial support of the College should be dependent upon the pursuit of recognizable academic interests. Secondly, he recommended that the '£50-er' element should, in effect, be phased out; at an absolute minimum, such fellows were to be deprived of any strategic role in the administration of the College. Thirdly, he encouraged All Souls to make further appointments to Research Fellowships, and to endow new Chairs. All of this, he insisted, must come from its existing resources.[33]

Perceptive onlookers appreciated the implications of these proposals at once. Most endorsed them. But a few, even some outside All Souls such as Sir Herbert Warren, now mourned the 'passing of the Prize Fellow' in post-war Oxford.[34] For with his demise, they feared, went that union of active and contemplative life that so many had for so long valued. With it also went the generalist, the clever young man as scholar *in* the world. This proved a bit premature. Prize Fellows did not pass away at All Souls (though, to a great extent, they did elsewhere). Nor did young men cease to flow between Oxford and the wider world. But Warren's concerns were not entirely misplaced, even at All Souls. The Prize Fellowship was never quite the same again after 1923. Nor did the College remain the society that Anson had wrought. Young men turned increasingly to academic pursuits. Their seniors, both Professorial and Research Fellows, devoted themselves to ever more ethereal ends. All Souls slowly ceased to influence the world. Not entirely but largely so: certainly, the College had become a very marginal body in the

[31] Parliamentary Papers (hereafter *PP*), *Reports from Commissioners, Inspectors and Others*, 4 vols (1922), *Royal Commission on Oxford and Cambridge Universities: Report (RCO)* (cmd. 1588).
[32] A general account can be found in J. Prest, 'The Asquith Commission, 1919–1922', in Harrison (ed.), *Hist. Univ. Oxf.*, viii, ch. 2.
[33] *PP, RCO* (1922), 'All Souls College', 108–13.
[34] Sir Herbert Warren, 'Comment', *The Times*, 29 March 1922, 5.

bosom of the British 'establishment' by the time of Sampson's famous survey conducted in 1962.[35]

What follows is a multi-authored account of All Souls and the wider world during the years of the College's greatest influence. Its chapters describe the context and offer an interpretation of the public careers of some of those who were elected to the College, principally over the period 1878–1923. These are traced from around the mid-1880s to the early 1950s. Thus it is largely a story of the doings of Anson's Prize Fellows in the world. But it is not exclusively so; public-minded professors make their appearances too. Nor are the chronological boundaries of this history confined to those elected before Asquith's intervention. Our aim is not to discount scholarly activity: far from it. But the focus is on non-academic activity outside the College: mostly public service in some form. The underlying purpose is to come to a view of what precisely Anson's College did: what it stood for, what it attempted to achieve, and the extent to which it succeeded (or failed).

The collection begins with a general investigation of the post-1850 Prize Fellowship itself as the tides of 'open competition' and 'meritocracy' washed over it; an investigation, that is, of the many (and various) reforms to which it was subject between 1854 and 1923 and of the kinds of men that it did (and did not) add to All Souls society. It continues through a consideration of the Prize Fellows themselves: who they were, how they got there, and what they made of their peculiar good fortune, at least during their bachelor years. It then offers a number of case studies, delineating both the public careers and political beliefs of some of the most representative examples of the breed. This culminates in an account of the life and times of the first non-British Prize Fellow, W. H. Hancock, elected in 1924.[36] The volume proceeds with a series of studies detailing some of the best known contributions of groups of All Souls fellows, even of a supposed All Souls connection, during the first half of the twentieth century – in times of war and international crisis; in the formulation and implementation of British governmental, foreign, Imperial, and Commonwealth policy. It is rounded off with an account of one fellow who moved in the other direction from that of many previously described, from public service to the republic of letters.

The result is thus a complicated story, crafted from the conclusions of a number of scholars, working quite independently, over many years. The editors have attempted neither to impose a simple definition of subject matter nor to arrive at some final overall judgement. Such judgements as emerge will do

---

[35] A. Sampson, *Anatomy of Britain* (London, 1962), 214–15.

[36] Davidson, this volume. Hancock's own account can be found in W. K. Hancock, *Country and Calling* (London, 1954), 95ff. and ch. 9; also idem, *Professing History* (Sydney, 1976).

precisely that: they will emerge. They will be the product of collective, but not of uniformly directed, effort. They are also, for the most part, for the reader to discern. The point is neither to praise nor to condemn. Since All Souls College and its Prize Fellows still exist, it is perhaps only to observe how very different such fellows' contributions to, and impact upon, the wider world once were.

1

Prizes, Fellowship, and Open Competition in All Souls, *c.*1850–1950

*Adrian Wooldridge**

In 1860 an editorial writer for a leading liberal newspaper subjected All Souls to the twin tests of fairness and efficiency. Did the College select its fellows fairly and exploit their talents wisely? And did it contribute to the progress of the University and the prosperity of the nation? Predictably enough, he concluded that the College failed – and failed abysmally – on both counts. The leader went on to thunder for reform:

In truth, long before the middle of this nineteenth century a place founded for the noble purposes of religion and learning had become a pleasant club – the perfect counterpart of the institutions of Pall Mall, only that the mode of admission was somewhat more exclusive. The essential qualifications of the candidates were reduced to a formula – *bene nati, bene vestiti, et mediocriter docti*. The questions put to the young men concerned their genealogy and their tailor – neither their learning nor their morals. The examination room was not the schools but the dining-room ... The college was for everything but learning. It was a hunting-box for the hunting-man; a card-room for the whist-player; a betting-room for the betting man; a restaurant for the *gourmet*; a place of gossip for the quidnunc ... The society was a genuine family party – a band of brothers, who took care to admit no one but their private friends or relations. In a word, it was the closest of boroughs.[1]

Sixty-two years later another anonymous journalist turned his gaze to All Souls. (He was, in fact, C. W. Brodribb, a *Times* stalwart and a crony of Geoffrey Dawson.) His conclusions could hardly have been more different. In a privately printed pamphlet, *Government by Mallardry: A Study in Political Ornithology*, he presented the College as a super-charged think tank dedicated to guiding the

* I am most grateful to the late John Simmons and the late Charles Wenden for their invaluable help in preparing the lecture on which this chapter is based. Any remaining errors of fact or perversities of interpretation are my own.

[1] I found the press cutting among the Geoffrey Faber papers in the All Souls College archives. Faber speculates that the leader is from *The Morning Advertiser.*

affairs not just of the nation but of the Empire.[2] He found All Souls men clustered at the top of Britain's most powerful institutions, domestic and Imperial. The fellows of the College constituted a sort of establishment mafia – or, to use his more homely analogy, a 'Rotary condensed to its quintessence and raised to the nth power of efficiency.'[3]

The really remarkable thing seems to be that an institution, so small and so close, so self-contained and so self-contented, should of late years have felt and responded to some latent instinct for expansion and participation in almost every branch of public life and national activity.[4]

How did this striking transformation come about? How did a den of indefensible abuses turn itself into a nest of omnipotent mallards? The simple answer is that All Souls revitalized itself – albeit with a good deal of help from its enemies – by adopting the utilitarian devices of open competition and written examinations.

The unreformed College recruited its fellows largely on the basis of family connections and personal habits. True, all the candidates had to endure a three-day examination. But intellectual ability was regarded as only one among a number of qualifications in an aspiring fellow, and not necessarily the most important one. In his evidence to the 1852 Royal Commission on Oxford, Warden Sneyd (Warden 1827–58) produced an all too lucid explanation of how All Souls went about the business of selecting its fellows:

In some colleges it is believed that the first and principal qualification for a fellowship is academical distinction acquired and proved by the test of public and collegiate examination.

Such a proof of talent is always looked upon with great respect in this College. A candidate so distinguished seldom fails to obtain a Fellowship, if he is found in all other respects to be well-qualified. Every candidate submits to the examination for three days enjoined by Archbishop Whitgift. But this is by no means the only scrutiny. Temper, condition, general habits of life, religious principle, moral conduct, future prospects and present need, and all the various aspects particularly expected to form the character of a gentleman, are carefully inquired into and considered before a selection is made from among the many candidates who offer themselves.

Surely then it may be stated that the Fellowships are disposed of according to merit.[5]

The College gathered information about the candidates from a variety of 'distant sources'. The candidates were also free to bring whatever testimonials they chose.[6] The election was decided in an informal meeting in Common Room.

---

[2] C. W. Brodribb, *Government by Mallardry: A Study in Political Ornithology* (London, 1932), 6.
[3] Ibid., 4.
[4] Ibid. A rather different view of the genesis and significance of Brodribb's tract can be found in Green, this volume, ch. 2.
[5] Evidence of the Warden, Lewis Sneyd, in *Report of Her Majesty's Commissioners Appointed to Inquire into the State, Discipline and Revenues of the University and Colleges of Oxford* (London, 1852) (hereafter *OUC Report*), 329.
[6] 'Rejoinder of the College to the Reply of the Petitioners', in *All Souls College Case: A Collection of Documents relating to the 'Fremantle Affair'* (a bound volume of contemporary printed papers, foliated, kept in the Codrington Library, All Souls), f. 151.

(The Warden was barred from the meeting, but allowed to nominate a candidate of his own whenever there were three vacancies.) The Common Room discussion focused not so much on the results of the examination – most of the absentee fellows had not even had time to glance at the papers – but on the personal habits and social connections. Did the candidate dress well? Did he possess friends in high places? What were his manners like? Was he an agreeable companion? In short, would he make a suitable member of a refined and aristocratic society?[7] Particular attention was paid to the opinions of those younger fellows who might have known the candidates at college or school.

One question overshadowed all others: could the candidate claim kinship with the Founder? The original statutes gave preference to candidates who could prove that they were related to Archbishop Chichele – a provision which effectively turned educational selection into educational genealogy.[8] (Kinsmen were also spared the statutory year as a non-voting probationer fellow.)[9] Sir Charles Oman nicely compared the unreformed fellowship to a sort of loose family confederation which at election time took careful stock of all its younger relatives in the University before it thought of looking outside for a new fellow.[10] The fellows periodically ignored their statutes and rejected kinsmen on the grounds that their learning was deficient or their character questionable. In the 1720s the College exhausted its ingenuity in raising objections to kinsman-candidates: genealogical objections (their relationship to the Founder was too remote, or their proof of pedigree too shoddy), academic objections (they had poor Latin and worse Greek), or moral objections (they had been seen consorting with women of ill repute).[11]

But in two test cases in which rejected kinsmen appealed to the Archbishop of Canterbury – Wood versus All Souls (1723) and Spenser versus All Souls (1762) – the decision went against the College. Both Archbishop Wake (1723) and Archbishop Secker (1762) ruled that the Founder's Kin provisions must be obeyed to the letter.[12] The archiepiscopal rulings had such a dramatic impact on the composition of the College – between 1762 and 1777, thirty-two of the forty-three fellows elected were kinsmen – that Archbishop Cornwallis issued an injunction to limit their proliferation. All Souls was no longer under an obligation to favour kinsmen so long as there were ten of them in fellowship.[13]

---

[7] Lushington et al., 11, in *All Souls College Case*, f. 43.

[8] G. D. Squibb, *Founders' Kin: Privilege and Pedigree* (Oxford, 1972), 4. For what follows see also J. Davis, 'Founder's Kin', in S. J. D. Green and P. Horden (eds), *All Souls under the Ancien Régime: Politics, Learning, and the Arts, c.1600–1850* (Oxford, 2007), 233–67.

[9] J. S. G. Simmons, 'All Souls', in M. G. Brock and M. C. Curthoys (eds), *Hist. Univ. Oxf.*, vii, 2, 209.

[10] H. H. Henson (ed.), *A Memoir of the Right Honourable Sir William Anson, Baronet* (Oxford, 1920), 69.

[11] Squibb, *Founders' Kin*, 114.

[12] Ibid., 43.

[13] Ibid., 45–6.

The College responded to this liberating injunction a little perversely – by upping its intake of kinsmen. In 1809, nineteen of the forty fellows were kinsmen. In 1856 – a year in which the universities were being subjected to the intense scrutiny of a reforming government – the tally stood at about thirty fellows plus the Warden.[14] Between 1815 and 1857 no fewer than 78 of the 113 fellows elected were kinsmen.[15] No wonder our editorial writer dismissed the College as 'a genuine family party – a band of brothers, who took care to admit no one but their private friends and relations'.

Why did a College which had once spurned Founder's Kin now embrace them? The reason is that All Souls used a little genealogical sleight of hand to redefine a kinsman to mean a member of the upper classes. No sooner had Archbishop Secker ruled against All Souls than an anonymous fellow got to work to prove that most of the leading families in the country could claim descent from the Chichele family.[16] In 1775 Benjamin Buckler estimated that more than 120 English peers, and many more in Scotland and Ireland, were descended from Archbishop Chichele's father.[17] In 1852 Warden Sneyd (himself an aristocrat and a kinsman) proudly told the Royal Commission that consanguinity is so widely interpreted that there is scarcely a family of any antiquity that it does not include.[18]

Two predictable results flowed from this ingenious system of affirmative action. The first was that All Souls was much the most aristocratic foundation in Oxford. The Warden belonged to an ancient county family – the Sneyds of Keele – and delighted in presiding over a refined and exclusive society. In 1856, thirteen of the forty fellows were sons of noblemen – an extraordinary score at a time when the rest of the University boasted only two noblemen (both Founder's Kin) among its fellowship.[19] Eighteen of the forty had been undergraduates at Christ Church, the most socially exclusive undergraduate college in the University. The second result was that the College's academic reputation was as dismal as its social standing was elevated. Warden Sneyd took no part in University business and declined to act as Vice-Chancellor.[20] In 1850 only three of the fellows had first-class degrees and twenty-six had pass degrees. Many had little interest in learning. Bathurst was elected a fellow while still an undergraduate

[14] Evidence of the Warden, Lewis Sneyd, in *OUC Report*, 329.

[15] G. Faber, 'The Examination Row at All Souls: A Study of Reform in Action, as exemplified by the controversy over the election to fellowships between 1857 and 1864', unpublished MS in the All Souls College archives: Faber Papers, box I, items 10, 14, 23. See also Davis, 'Founder's Kin', 243, 245 (fig. 11.2).

[16] Squibb, *Founders' Kin*, 46.

[17] Ibid., 48.

[18] *OUC Report*, 329.

[19] 'Lushington and Others versus All Souls College: Short-hand Writers' Notes of Arguments before the Visitor', College archives c. 260–1. Lord Salisbury perversely believed that the fact that he was a peer – and a wealthy one to boot – would count against him in the election. See G. Cecil, *Life of Robert Marquis of Salisbury*, vol. 1 (London, 1921), 38.

[20] C. Grant Robertson, *All Souls College* (London, 1899), 198.

because he was of Founder's Kin. On one occasion he tried to escape from dinner – the fellows then dined at 3 p.m. before retiring for a protracted dessert – in order to do some reading. The request was denied: 'Books. Books. The ruin of young men.'[21] To add to its dismal reputation All Souls was a relatively populous institution – only New College, Christ Church, and St John's had more fellows – yet imposed no educational functions whatsoever on its members.[22]

Such an exotic institution, powerfully connected but socially exclusive, generously endowed but divorced from the humdrum business of university life, was scarcely designed to appeal to the utilitarian temper of the times. For mid-Victorian England was gripped by a passion for institutional reform. The reformers were determined to refashion the establishment to meet the demands of a commercial and expanding society, doing away with jobbery and corruption and opening up official appointments to individual talent, wherever it might be found. Their chosen method for identifying and promoting individual talent was open competition regulated by objective examination.

Open competition was first turned into a political creed by the 'intellectual aristocracy' – a powerful connection of families who owed their pre-eminence to intellect and education and who hoped to advance their social position by abolishing patronage and opening educational and administrative positions to men of talent.[23] The intellectual aristocracy found its most articulate spokesman in Thomas Babington Macaulay, the doyen of Whig historians. As a student, Macaulay had been much impressed by the capacity of a handful of Prize Fellowships to excite youthful ambition and galvanize general education:

At Trinity College, the largest and wealthiest of the colleges of Cambridge, about four fellowships are given annually by competition. These fellowships can be held only on condition of celibacy, and the income derived from them is a very moderate one for a single man. It is notorious that the examinations for Trinity fellowships have, directly and indirectly, done much to give a direction to the studies of Cambridge and of all the numerous schools which are the feeders of Cambridge.[24]

From the 1820s onwards Macaulay devoted a good deal of energy to reforming the system of selection into the Indian Civil Service by abolishing patronage and introducing competitive examinations to select the able.[25] In the process he

---

[21] L. F. Rushbrook Williams, 'All Souls College in the Early Twentieth Century', in College archives.

[22] Simmons, 'All Souls', 209.

[23] N. Annan, 'The Intellectual Aristocracy', in J. H. Plumb (ed.), *Studies in Social History: A Tribute to G. M. Trevelyan* (London, 1955), 241–87. See also Annan, *Leslie Stephen: the Godless Victorian* (London, 1984), 1–7, and K. W. Black, 'Clapham to Bloomsbury: Life-Course and Analysis of an Intellectual Aristocracy', *Biography*, 5 (1982), 28–52.

[24] *Macaulay Report on the Indian Civil Service*, Nov. 1854, signed by T. B. Macaulay, Lord Ashburton, Henry Melville, Benjamin Jowett, John George Shaw Lefevre, as reprinted in J. S. Fulton, *The Civil Service: Reports of the Committee, 1966–68* (Cmnd 3638), i, appendix B (London, 1968), 120.

[25] K. Hope, *The Political Conception of Merit* (London, 1998), esp. chs 1–3, emphasizes Macaulay's role in the development of the meritocratic ideal. I owe a great debt to this work. See also G. Sutherland, *Ability, Merit and Measurement: Mental Testing and English Education, 1880–1940* (Oxford, 1984),

developed a sophisticated theory of examinations. He distinguished between 'ability' and 'mere learning', suggesting that 'the object of the examiners should be rather to test the candidate's powers of mind than to ascertain the extent of his metaphysical reading',[26] and argued that examinations could accurately predict 'what men will prove to be in life', since the qualities required for professional success were precisely those tested in the examination room. He felt that the subject of the examination was irrelevant: the man with the most general ability would always triumph. 'If, instead of learning Greek, we learned the Cherokee', he mused, 'the man who understood the Cherokee best, who made the most correct and melodious Cherokee verses, who comprehended most accurately the effect of the Cherokee particles, would generally be a superior man to him who was destitute of these accomplishments.'[27] Anyone who could do best what all the ablest and most ambitious of his contemporaries were trying to do well was guaranteed success; and his peculiar powers of mind, when properly trained and directed, might do notable service to the state.[28] As if all this was not enough, he argued that examinations were highly successful tests of moral character. 'Early superiority in science and literature generally indicates the existence of some qualities which are securities against vice – industry, self-denial, a taste for pleasures not sensual, a laudable desire for honourable distinction, a still more laudable desire to obtain the approbation of friends and relations.'[29] He also employed his talents as an historian and rhetorician to persuade the establishment that his reforms were in keeping with tradition, transmuting the aristocratic concept of honour into the democratic concept of merit.

Under the influence of these arguments, Sir Stafford Northcote and Sir Charles Trevelyan presented a compelling case for open competition in the permanent Civil Service. Patronage and job-security, they argued, attracted dull, lazy, and feeble-bodied recruits into the profession:

Those whose abilities do not warrant an expectation that they will succeed in the open professions, where they must encounter the competition of their contemporaries, and those whom indolence of temperament, or physical infirmities, unfit for active exertions, are placed in the Civil Service, where they may obtain an honourable livelihood with little labour, and with no risk.[30]

97–111. In what follows I have drawn on A. Wooldridge, *Measuring the Mind: Education and Psychology in England, c.1860–c.1990* (Cambridge, 1994), ch. 7, esp. pp. 166–71.

[26] *Macaulay Report*, 122. Macaulay had been reiterating these arguments since at least the 1830s.

[27] T. B. Macaulay, 'Government of India. Speech Delivered in House of Commons on 10 July 1833', in *The Works of Lord Macaulay*, Albany edn (London, 1898), xi. 572–3.

[28] *Macaulay Report*, 123.

[29] Ibid., 127.

[30] *The Northcote-Trevelyan Report on the Organization of the Permanent Civil Service*, 23 Nov. 1853, as reprinted in Fulton, *Civil Service*, 108. The picture of the existing system was, of course, exaggerated. Several departments already instituted examinations and promotion by merit. See 'Competitive Examination and the Civil Service', *The Quarterly Review*, 133 (1872), 243, and E. Hughes, 'Civil Service Reform 1853–5', *History*, 105 (1942), 55–7.

In the open professions, they noted, 'the able and energetic rise to the top, the dull and inefficient remain at the bottom. In the public establishments, on the contrary, the general rule is that all rise together.'[31] Their solution to the problem was to borrow the principle of open competition from the other professions, admitting candidates on the basis of merit and promoting them on the basis of achievement:

The public service should be carried on by the admission into its lower ranks of a carefully selected body of young men, who should be employed from the first upon work suited to their capacities and their education and should be made constantly to feel that their promotion and future prospects depend entirely on the industry and ability with which they discharge their duties.[32]

They hoped to select recruits by examination, and they insisted that the examinations should be as open as possible, and that they should be designed 'to test the intelligence, as well as the mere attainments, of the candidates'.[33] 'The great advantage to be expected from the examinations', they argued, 'would be that they elicit young men of general ability.'[34]

Why were these reformers so enthusiastic about open competition? In a phrase, because they regarded it as an instrument of institutional efficiency and moral reform. Free trade in commodities had already galvanized a moribund economy. Surely free trade in talent would do the same for a moribund establishment. Patronage had allowed the aristocracy to use the public service as a foundling hospital for the waifs and strays of their families: for 'the idle and useless, the fool of the family, the consumptive, the hypochondriac, those who have a tendency to insanity' and for their bastards. Competition, on the other hand, would promote the rule of the able and energetic,[35] natural gentlemen such as 'well-educated young men who depend for their advancement upon their own exertions, and not upon their wealth and connections' and 'well-educated poor men' who are 'notoriously those who throw themselves into their work with the greatest energy and perseverance'.[36] Open competition, they argued, would also bring moral benefits, promoting the virtues of self-reliance, just as surely as patronage had encouraged the 'moral disease' of dependence.[37] By transforming administrative offices from freeholds, bestowed by patronage, into trusts, awarded for merit, competition would ensure that 'the Government and the

---

[31] *Northcote-Trevelyan Report*, 109.
[32] Ibid., 111.
[33] Ibid., 112.
[34] Ibid., 114.
[35] See, for example, Trevelyan's *Thoughts on Patronage* (17 Jan. 1854), reprinted in E. Hughes, 'Sir Charles Trevelyan and Civil Service Reform 1853–5', *English Historical Review*, 64 (1949), 69.
[36] Cf. C. E. Trevelyan, *The Purchase System in the British Army*, 2nd edn (London, 1867), 2–3.
[37] Cf. Trevelyan's letter of 15 Jan. 1848, quoted in J. Hart, 'Sir Charles Trevelyan at the Treasury', *English Historical Review*, 75 (1960), 99. However, Trevelyan was himself a nepotist, thinking that his own exertions justified the appointment of his relations and connections. See Hart, 'Trevelyan at the Treasury', 97–8.

Governing class would cease to be on the side of corruption',[38] and would set an example to the people. J. S. Mill looked forward to 'the great and salutary moral revolution, descending to the minds of almost the lowest classes, which would follow the knowledge that Government (to people in general the most trusted exponent of the ways of the world) would henceforth bestow its gifts according to merit, and not to favour'.[39]

In particular, the reformers hoped that open competition would reinvigorate English education. (Lord Robert Cecil felt that open competition was 'from beginning to end, a schoolmasters' scheme'.[40]) By abolishing one of the most valued resources of the idle – patronage – and by multiplying the rewards to be earned by academic success, it would encourage parents to send their children to school and the children, once there, to persevere with their studies. Macaulay felt that an annual competition for forty places in the Indian Civil Service – every one of which 'is nothing less than an honourable social position, and a comfortable independence for life' – would galvanize the British universities.

This opinion was enthusiastically endorsed by a group of University reformers – Benjamin Jowett, Frederick Temple, Mark Pattison, A. P. Stanley, and Disraeli's 'wild man of the Cloister', Goldwin Smith. In the 1840s, the Universities started to abolish inconvenient restrictions and to open appointments to individual merit, as measured by competitive examinations;[41] and the results had been spectacular. Open competition rapidly transformed Balliol from an obscure college with dingy buildings into the academic powerhouse of the University. In 1851 its ten open fellowships were held by men who had obtained between them twelve first-class degrees, five University prizes, and five Ireland or Hertford Scholarships; and in the years from 1841 to 1850 its students had gained, in all, twenty-five firsts and three University scholarships. In the same year, 1851, Christ Church's seventy Student fellowships, which were encrusted with restrictions, were held by men who had obtained between them thirteen first classes, two prizes, and three Ireland or Hertford Scholarships; and between 1841 and 1850 Christ Church Students had gained, in all, no more than fifteen first classes and no University scholarships.[42]

The reformers used the Royal Commissions into Oxford and Cambridge, established by Lord John Russell in 1850, to reiterate and reinforce the case for

---

[38] Hart, 'Trevelyan at the Treasury'; Hughes, 'Trevelyan and Civil Service Reform', 70.

[39] J. S. Mill, 'Reform of the Civil Service', *Essays on Politics and Society*, Collected Works of John Stuart Mill, vol. 18 (London, 1996), 207; originally printed in 'Papers relating to the Re-organisation of the Civil Service', *Parliamentary Papers* (1854–5), 20, 92–8. For the circumstances surrounding Mill's paper see the textual introduction, p. lxxx.

[40] Quoted in Hughes, 'Civil Service Reform', 62. The academic bias of the examinations also aroused the opposition of radical reformers, notably Edwin Chadwick. See R. A. Lewis, 'Edwin Chadwick and the Administrative Reform Movement 1854–6', *University of Birmingham Historical Journal*, 2 (1949–50), 186–7.

[41] J. Roach, *Public Examinations in England, 1850–1900* (Cambridge, 1971), 20–1.

[42] *OUC Report*, 152. Christ Church did not even acknowledge the Commission's request for information.

open competition. The Oxford Commission found that only 22 of the University's 542 fellowships were open to general competition: the rest were restricted to candidates from particular districts, schools, or families.[43] These restrictions, the Commission argued, damaged both learning and teaching, diminishing incentives to effort, and populating the colleges with dullards. (The term 'founder', derived from 'founder's kin', was commonly used to mean 'fool'.)[44] 'The effect of these restrictions', Temple argued, 'is most mischievous. Men who are naturally well fitted to be country Clergymen are bribed, because they are born in some parish in Rutland, to remain in Oxford as Fellows, until they are not only unfit for that, but for everything else.'[45] Hayward Cox put the point equally bluntly:

They crowd the colleges with inferior men, often without either the power or the inclination to promote the interests of education, withdraw many who might be useful in their appropriate spheres, hold out incentives to indolence, selfishness and self-indulgence, and engage persons in the work of instruction who are without zeal in the pursuit.[46]

The Commission insisted that restrictions should be abolished and fellowships opened 'to merit, and to merit only'.[47] From this single reform, it argued, all other reforms would naturally follow.

The Fellows are so completely the governing body of the University, that, if no other change were made than to throw all the Fellowships open, and secure that the elections were honest, all other reforms would follow spontaneously.[48]

[43] Ibid., 149. The open fellowships were at Balliol and Oriel. On the Commission see, in particular, E. G. W. Bill, *University Reform in Nineteenth-Century Oxford: A Study of Henry Halford Vaughan 1811–1885* (Oxford, 1973), 88–116, and A. J. Engel, *From Clergyman to Don: The Rise of the Academic Profession in Nineteenth-Century Oxford* (Oxford, 1983), 33–43. The report was mainly the work of A. P. Stanley.

[44] E. Chadwick, *A Lecture on the Economical, Social, Educational and Political Importance of Open Competition for Admission to the Public Service* (London, 1857), 31. Squibb, *Founders' Kin*, 115, points to the Winchester proverb 'as thick as a founder'. According to school lore, a kinsman would be identified by hitting him on the head with one of the wooden trenchers used in place of plates. If the trencher broke, the head was that of a kinsman.

[45] *OUC Report*, 149. See also G. Smith, *Oxford Essays* (London, 1858), 275. For some amusing vignettes of the men who dominated Oxford under the system of closed fellowships see M. Pattison, *Memoirs* (London, 1885), 217–18.

[46] Chadwick, *Open Competition*, 149.

[47] *OUC Report*, 152. For evidence in favour of competition from within the university, see *OUC Evidence* (appendix to *OUC Report*): N. W. Senior, 17; Benjamin Jowett, 30–40; Mark Pattison, 44; H. H. Vaughan, 90; Hayward Cox, 97; Frederick Temple, 123–34; Henry Wall, 150; R. Congreve, 153; A. H. Clough, 214. For evidence in favour of restrictions, see E. A. Freeman, 141, and also *Report and Evidence upon the Recommendations of Her Majesty's Commissioners for Inquiring into the State of the University of Oxford presented to the Board of Heads of Houses and Proctors* (Oxford, 1853), 94–5. Henry Wall warned that 'the evil would not be cured, but rather aggravated, by simply destroying the limits of eligibility. The power of election should not be allowed to be in the hands of a few senior members of society, else you would be but increasing their sphere of patronage. Statutes and wills are not the only hindrances to the benefits of a foundation being bestowed according to merit.' *OUC Evidence*, 150.

[48] *OUC Report*, 149. The Commission is quoting from Frederick Temple's evidence.

The Oxford Commissioners picked out All Souls for particularly vigorous criticism. Much to the surprise of many reformers they resisted the temptation to denounce the College for non-residence. But they endorsed the prevalent opinion that 'proficiency in study, which in colleges of high character is the chief requisite for election to Fellowships, has comparatively little weight in the election to Fellowships at All Souls'.[49] This damning judgement inspired their most dramatic recommendation: that twenty-four fellowships should be suppressed in order to fund four chairs. (This was later bargained down so that ten fellowships were suppressed to fund two chairs.)

In August 1854 the House of Commons appointed Executive Commissioners to implement the recommendations of the *Report*. Three years later, on 3 April 1857, the Commissioners imposed a far-reaching Ordinance on All Souls. Two recommendations were crucial to the future of the Prize Fellowship. The Ordinance abolished the privilege of Founder's Kin and demanded that candidates for an examination fellowship should have either won a University prize or else taken a first class in Honour Moderations or in one of the final honour schools. And, in a bid to link the College with the University's revised syllabus, it stipulated that the fellowship examination should be in subjects 'recognised in the School of Jurisprudence and History'.[50]

The reforms attracted enthusiastic support inside as well as outside All Souls. In the wake of the publication of the *Report*, Warden Sneyd and his fellow conservatives had tried to head off wholesale reform by suggesting some rather more palatable innovations. Robert Cecil (who was elected in 1852) suggested that the College should create fourteen fellowships for undergraduates who would be elected at the end of their first year. James Ryder (who was elected in 1850) suggested that the College should welcome the creation of professorships but preserve its preference for kinsmen. But a College meeting in January 1855 rejected both (half) measures. The conservatives had also contemplated getting up a College petition against the Commissioners. But Robert Cecil wisely warned the Warden that such a move might backfire: more than a third of the fellows were on the Commissioners' side.[51]

Why did an institution which had become a byword for abuse admit such a formidable fifth column of reformers? The rapid turnover of fellows – All Souls habitually elected two or more young men a year but forced them to resign their fellowship on marriage – kept the average age of fellows at under thirty-five and thus ensured that the College was in touch with the latest intellectual and political fashions. (It is a nice irony that the more middle-aged institutions created by the reformers had a tendency to preserve the passions of an earlier generation.)

[49] *OUC Report*, 218. See also 168.
[50] The full text of the Ordinance can be found in the *All Souls College Case*, ff. 17–26.
[51] Faber, 'Examination Row'. Cecil may have been alerted to this by the fact that his twin, Watson, was an ardent reformer.

Warden Sneyd was also right when he argued that the College usually elected candidates who happened to be academically outstanding – just so long as they could excel at the dinner table as well as in the examination room. This tendency became much more pronounced after 1850. Only eight of the nineteen fellows elected between 1850 and 1855 could claim kinship with the Founder; and three of the four elected in 1854 boasted either a first or a University prize or both.

The rapid turnover of fellows combined with this mounting weakness for able candidates ensured that mid-century All Souls was peculiarly vulnerable to colonization by the most academically powerful and politically progressive college in the University – Balliol. In the eighteenth and early nineteenth centuries All Souls had been almost an adjunct of Christ Church. Then the election, in 1839, of Samuel Waldegrave (a kinsman as well as a Balliol man) signalled the decline of Christ Church and the rise of Balliol as the main recruiting ground for the College. Between 1839 and 1855 the College elected twenty-one candidates from Balliol. In 1854 seventeen fellows were Christ Church men (Warden Sneyd was also a Christ Church man) and nine were Balliol men; three years later the Christ Church toll had dropped to fifteen and the Balliol toll had risen to fourteen.[52]

This fifth column played a vital role in forcing the College to do more than pay lip service to the 1857 Ordinance. Three fellows in particular took it upon themselves to harry their alma mater into obedience: William Fremantle, Godfrey Lushington, and Arthur Watson.[53] The three were natural apostles of open competition and moral reform. They hailed from well-connected and self-confident families. Watson and Lushington had been educated at Rugby under Dr Arnold and Fremantle had been at Eton. All three fell under the spell of Jowett at Balliol before being elected to All Souls in 1853–4. They all went on to pursue conventionally successful careers: Fremantle became Dean of Ripon, Lushington Permanent Secretary at the Home Office, and Watson a much-respected schoolmaster at Harrow.

The three were worried that the College would, despite the Ordinance, carry on much as before. In August 1857 they appealed to the Executive Commissioners to confirm that the fellowship examination was a competitive one in which the prizes went to the candidate(s) who performed best in the examination.[54] The Commissioners naturally agreed. But three months later the three were once again up in arms – and this time they added a new complaint to their list. The College was failing to give priority to the new school of Law and History. In the November election the College had rejected

[52] Faber, 'Examination Row'.

[53] For various accounts of the examination row see G. C. Faber, *Jowett* (London, 1957), and Faber, 'Examination Row'; W. R. Ward, *Victorian Oxford* (London, 1965); and, most recently, S. J. D. Green, 'The "Fremantle Affair" and the Destruction of the *Ancien Régime* at All Souls 1857–1864', in Green and Horden (eds), *All Souls under the Ancien Régime*, 343–71.

[54] Lushington et al., in *All Souls College Case*, ff. 33–4.

three candidates with firsts in the Law and History School and chosen instead to elect a man with a first in Greats. Their appeal to the Visitor, the Archbishop of Canterbury, J. B. Sumner, fell flat in October 1859.[55] But they remained undeterred. The three then took the matter to the Queen's Bench. The affair became something of a *cause célèbre* in the battle between the ancients and the moderns. Thanks to generous donations from liberal patrons such as Frederick Temple and Lord Landsdowne, the three managed to hire some of the most expensive legal talent in the land.[56] And *The Times* did its best to ensure that a domestic quarrel was played out before a national audience. The affair dragged on until 1864 when the court ruled in favour of the rebels.

This seven-year war between the Balliol three and All Souls was exceedingly complicated. But two issues are perhaps worth isolating and contemplating at some length – partly because they illuminate the contemporary debate about open competition and partly because they determined the future direction of the Prize Fellowship.

The first is the issue of the importance of the written examination. Did the result of the examination *determine* the election? Or was it just one of a number of factors which the College could take into account? Lushington et al. argued that the examination was all-important. Examinations could produce an object-ive measurement of intellectual merit; but any attempt to test other qualities – moral excellence for example – inevitably degenerated into a system of personal predilection and social prejudice.[57] No other college imposed anything other than an intellectual test on candidates for fellowships. Why should All Souls? To ensure that the examination was all-important Lushington et al. proposed that a committee of examiners should rank the candidates in strict order of merit and that the fellows should be bound to elect them accordingly. This would put an end to what they regarded as the most intolerable abuse in the College: the fact that so many absentee fellows (most of whom knew nothing about Law and History) failed to read the papers and yet felt happy to pontificate on the social qualities of the candidates – on whether they would contribute 'to the happiness, the pleasure, the ease, and pleasant habits of society'.[58]

The All Souls establishment preferred a more catholic conception of merit. Examination marks mattered of course – but then so did a whole range of other qualities. True merit should be measured not by a pedantic system of examin-ation marks but by a more generous estimation of the personal habits and moral worth of a candidate. The Attorney-General lampooned the College philosophy in a splendid passage during the court case:

[55] 'The Judgment of the Visitor, October, 1859', *All Souls College Case*, f. 66.
[56] W. H. Draper (ed.), *Recollections of Dean Fremantle, Chiefly by Himself* (London, 1921), 64.
[57] The three also echoed Macaulay in insisting that 'the cases are indeed rare in which intellectual superiority is not conjoined with moral', 'Lushington and Others', 17.
[58] Ibid., 17. The phrase is the Attorney-General's.

What means merit at All Souls? Why, it means that the candidate shall be one comprehending in himself all the various particularly expected to be united in the character of a gentleman – that his general habits of life shall be such as will be acceptable to the community in which he is to work – of aristocratic birth, of elegant manners, of the habit of moving in society where a particular description of refinement is expected.[59]

The College defended its position by pointing out that it was not just concerned with awarding prizes for past exertions. Its main interest lay in future promise. Examination success provided some indication of future promise – but then so did general talent and moral character.[60] Why limit yourself to just one piece of evidence when so many others were available?

The College had in fact found an ingenious way of ensuring that its conception of merit triumphed over the one proposed in the Ordinance. On receiving the 1857 Ordinance it passed a by-law to treat the examination not as a competitive one but as a pass/fail examination. The examiners usually deemed that *all* the candidates had passed the examination.[61] The real business of choosing between rival candidates could thus be left to the Common Room meeting. By redefining merit to mean manners, and turning the examination into a qualifying examination, the College hoped to proceed much as it had always done, undisturbed by the pesky Ordinance.

The second issue is the priority to be given to Law and History. Lushington et al. argued that fellowships should primarily be rewards for proficiency in Law and History, pointing out that the price the Commissioners had demanded for allowing All Souls remain a non-tutorial college was to oblige it to use its resources to advance the cause of the new joint school. The new subject could hardly hope to establish itself in a university dominated by the classics unless it could offer some guarantee of rich rewards. Anyone who excelled in the classics was more or less certain of a fellowship somewhere. An outstanding lawyer/historian faced a much less certain career unless All Souls played its allotted part in the great scheme of things. On the other hand, the College establishment continued to be rather sniffy about the new school – anyone with a first in Classics could mug it up in a month and still carry off the fellowship.[62] Even after the Ordinance the examination still included a Latin prose paper and a *viva* on classical books.

The rebels won their case. In 1864 the Court ruled that All Souls should reform its fellowship examination so that, from now on, it elected the candidates with the most marks in Law and History. The College was only given leeway if the best candidate was an atheist or a rogue – or else if he displayed 'course [sic]

[59] Ibid., 85. Bovill nicely pointed out that All Souls had only elected one nobleman since the Ordinance – and he had a first in Law and History.
[60] 'Lushington and Others', 9 Jan. 1861, 42–3, Bovill on behalf of the College. See also the Warden to the Visitor, *All Souls College Case*, f. 58.
[61] Draper, *Recollections*, 63.
[62] 'Lushington and Others', 9 Jan. 1861, 54, Bovill on behalf of the College.

and rude habits; a quarrelsome and overbearing temper; an obstinate and perverse intellect'.[63] The result was an inflexible and, for Oxford, idiosyncratic system of selection. The examiners allocated a maximum of 200 marks for each of the six papers which made up the annual examination: two law papers, two history papers, a translation paper, and an essay. They then drew up a report which listed the candidates in strict order of the number of marks they had managed to accumulate. The fellowship election did little more than rubber-stamp the examiner's report.[64] This system gave no room for the candidates to display their idiosyncratic abilities or for the fellows to exercise their individual judgements. It also clashed sharply with the method of examining prevalent in the rest of the University. Examiners in the Cambridge Mathematics tripos and in the Indian and Home Civil Service might rank candidates on a linear scale according to the number of marks they totted up. But in Plato-obsessed Oxford the examiners preferred to divide candidates into three or more broad classes determined not so much by their raw knowledge as by their supposed qualities of mind.

For all its rigidity, the Lushington system prevented the College from resorting to its ancient vices. And as election by examination ceased to be a novelty and became instead a routine so the College slowly loosened and refined its procedures. As early as 1862 it had added a general paper to an examination which had hitherto been dominated by subject papers.[65] The mass of the fellows weakened the tyranny of the assistant examiners. Increasing weight was given to broad intellectual abilities, with the College interesting itself less in the number of marks a candidate managed to amass and more with the quality of mind he succeeded in displaying.

The construction of the Prize Fellowship was finally completed in the 1880s. The College frittered away a great deal of time and energy in the 1870s in discussing various narrow-minded and self-interested schemes for reform. But it was once again prodded into taking definite action by an external agency: the Selbourne Commission of 1877. This time All Souls sensibly choose to cooperate with official opinion: two fellows (Montague Bernard and Mathew Ridley) served on the Commission – a fact which bears testimony to the beneficial workings of the 1857 Ordinance – and the College readily helped to redraft its Statutes in the light of the Commission's recommendations. The College also lobbied the Commission about the manifold virtues of the Prize Fellowship, explaining how it encouraged effort among undergraduates and provided a link between Oxford and the great world.[66] Yet the most important decision

---

[63] 'Report', *All Souls College Case*, f. 188.

[64] All Souls College archives, 'Minute Book, 1858–1875', 45, 76–7.

[65] See Green, 'The "Fremantle Affair"', 369.

[66] 'Minute Book, 1875–1888', 'Report of Committee appointed November, 1877 (consisting of Ridley (Subwarden), Anson, Buchanan, Burrows, Compton, Holland, Mowbray, Wakeman)', inserted between 104 and 105.

of the era owed nothing to outside prompting. In November 1881, following a strenuous contest, the College elected Sir William Anson to the Wardenship.[67]

Anson was the ideal man to complete the transformation of All Souls into a unique institution, meritocratic but cultivated, academically selective yet worldly. Educated at Eton and Balliol, where he got a double first in Classics, and elected to All Souls in 1867, he went on to pursue an amphibious career, part academic, part practical. He read for the Bar and practised on the Home Circuit before returning to Oxford in 1874 as Vinerian Reader in English Law. There he divided his energies equally between teaching his pupils in the University – Dicey regarded him as 'the best teacher of English law in Oxford' – and cultivating contacts in the wider world. He was not yet forty when he was elected Warden and was to hold the position for thirty-three years.

Anson was a Whig and a reformer – but he was also an aristocrat (a third baronet since 1873) with a well-developed respect for ancient privileges and traditional practices. Hensley Henson captured his cast of mind in a perceptive passage:

Sir William Anson shared to the full that devotion to the historic society which redeemed the dislike of change felt by the older fellows from mere obstructiveness. No man felt more deeply the subtle fashioning of power of the institutions into which he had been brought. Eton, Balliol, All Souls were far more than stages in his life to be traversed, and left behind. They seized his heart, stirred his imagination, and commanded his lifelong service. At the same time he was both an able and an eminent lawyer, and an accomplished man of the world. He was also a convinced Liberal in politics. He could perceive the defects of All Souls and, at the same time, offer proposals of change which should remedy them without doing violence to the essential character of the College.[68]

He set himself the task of guiding the College between the Scylla of blind reaction and the Charybdis of vulgar liberalism. He realized that public opinion could no longer tolerate the old order, but decried the self-interest of people like Max Müller (who wanted to turn the College into an annexe of the Indian Institute) and the vulgarity of the more extreme liberals (who regarded ancient colleges as if they were bubble companies or universal warehouses 'where every element of a liberal education could be obtained for a minimum of time, money, and perhaps application').[69] To him it seemed axiomatic that an increasingly democratic and commercial society could only avoid social disintegration and cultural debasement if it was guided by a powerful but enlightened élite. His ideal was to cooperate with the new order while doing his utmost to preserve what was permanently valuable in the old. Commercial society needed to be civilized by ancient institutions.

---

[67] Henson, *Memoir of Anson*, 70–5.
[68] Ibid., 70.
[69] Ibid., 15.

Anson immediately set about refashioning the Prize Fellowship in the light of the new statutes. Prize Fellowships for life were abolished. In future there were to be twenty-one seven-year fellowships: fourteen were to be awarded to Oxford graduates after examination in law and history (separate schools since 1872) and the other seven were to be Research Fellowships. The College was now so confident in its ability to judge merit that it dropped the requirement of the 1857 Ordinance that all candidates must have a first or a University prize.[70] A dozen £50 Fellowships (so-called because they carried a stipend of £50 a year) were reserved for ex-Prize Fellows whose first seven years had expired. The aim of this novel device (to which Anson attached particular importance) was to retain as members of the College some senior non-academics who had become familiar with its business, interested in its special work and devoted to its corporate welfare.[71] To avoid invidious competition for 'fifty-pounderships' the College decided to allot them by seniority among those former fellows who were unmarried, resident in Great Britain, and willing to take a regular part in College business.[72] The 'fifty-pounders' did much to produce the unique tone of future College meetings.

Anson brought to his Wardenship more than just a lawyer's ability to tidy up statutes. He brought a vision. He wanted to use the Prize Fellowship to create (or perhaps to preserve) a unique institution – a college which bestrode the worlds of academia and affairs. In the first Prize Fellowship meeting over which he presided the College elected Charles Oman (who became a distinguished historian) and Nathaniel Curzon (who became an illustrious man of the world), and throughout the rest of his Wardenship Anson promoted the two great departments of college life with equal vigour.

He encouraged London fellows to visit the College at the weekend in order to preserve their contact with academic life and to remind the academic fellows of the great issues of the day. He followed the careers of the fellows with an almost parental solicitude, advising them if they had any doubts and pulling strings to help them get jobs or promotion. Most of his protégés went on to pursue successful or even glittering careers in academia or affairs. John Simmons calculates that only five of the seventy-one fellows elected between 1881 and 1914 who reached middle age were unrecorded in *Who's Who*.[73] But the true measure of his achievement only emerged between the wars, when the College colonized the establishment, religious as well as secular, with breathtaking success.

The All Souls of Warden Anson was half a world away from the All Souls of Warden Sneyd. The College attracted able candidates and subjected them to a

---

[70] 'Minute Book, 1858–1875', 325. The College had considered dropping the requirement in 1874 but decided to keep it: ibid., 292 (motion), 297 (rejected).

[71] Henson, *Memoir of Anson*, 79.

[72] 'Minute Book, 1875–1888', 'Rochfort Maguire to Warden', between 302 and 303. Rochfort Maguire coined the term 'fifty-pounder'.

[73] J. S. G. Simmons, 'Chronological List of Fellows', in College archives.

searching intellectual test. Prize Fellows and ex-Prize Fellows scrambled rapidly up the establishment ladder. The College flourished socially as well as politically – at least at weekends. In the 1850s most fellows had turned up only two or three times a year. Under Anson many London fellows came up to College every weekend during term. Sir Charles Oman recalled that 'we often dine four strong on a Friday night, and 30 strong on a Sunday'.[74]

The Ansonian Prize Fellows looked back on the unreformed College with a mixture of horror and self-congratulation. Or rather they looked around them at the dinner table at the unreformed College. For a number of life-fellows survived to serve as living, if decaying, monuments to an age when fellowships were awarded by genealogy and terminated only by marriage or death. Oman, hardly a wild-eyed radical, recalled in his memoirs his shock on meeting two survivors from the *ancien régime*. The Honourable Charles Wrottesley was a fox-hunting squire with no interest in book-learning. He took his full measure of port in Common Room and bullied his companions into playing whist with him after dinner. He had once been a Major in the Staffordshire militia and his military exploits – which were confined to garrisoning Corfu during the Crimean War – were the sole subject of his small talk.[75] Even more demanding was Dr Henry Bertie. Bertie had been elected in 1836 as Founder's Kin and spent the next forty years as an obscure Essex clergyman. Then on retirement he decided to move back into All Souls, bringing with him his rather drunken and querulous old butler. He was a simple-minded conservative with no intellectual interests or academic aspirations. He was also half-deaf and partly paralysed. Every night he was carried into hall in his chair by two College servants. Most of the conversation he could not hear; and what he could hear he could not understand. In Common Room (whither presumably he was carried by the unfortunate servants) he always insisted on drinking port out of a claret glass.[76] He was obsessed by the fear that he would be forced into Catholicism and took elaborate precautions against letting a priest into his rooms.[77]

Still, for all the evident satisfaction with the Prize Fellowship the prevalence of non-residence continued to worry the College. The apocryphal question ascribed to an American tourist – are these ruins inhabited? – found a sympathetic echo both inside and outside All Souls. The fact that a college which occupied the choice site in the wider University was so often almost empty – the number of residents seldom exceeded four or five – inevitably created disquiet in the College and antagonism in the wider University. This disquiet and antagonism grew by the decade as the College estates generated an ever larger financial surplus.

---

[74] C. W. C. Oman, *Memories of Victorian Oxford and of Some Early Years* (London, 1941), 116.
[75] Ibid., 123.
[76] R. Prothero, *Whippingham to Westminster: The Reminiscences of Lord Ernle* (London, 1938), 68. Prothero is rather kinder to Bertie than Oman.
[77] Oman, *Memories*, 122.

The result was that every decade or so the College pondered novel ways of supplementing or expanding the Prize Fellowship. In 1867 Warden Leighton and sixteen fellows signed a motion in favour of admitting undergraduates. The vote was tied.[78] In the mid-1870s the College pondered, among other schemes, offering accommodation to ten or more candidates for the Indian Civil Service (proposed by Max Müller) and electing ten or more undergraduates who had done well in Mods as junior fellows or Chichele students (proposed by Montagu Burrows and supported by Warden Leighton).[79] The Selborne Commission put an end to the debate.

In 1929 the College once again turned its mind to reform, partly because its growing wealth was becoming an embarrassment and partly because, in 1927, the number of resident fellows had fallen to just one. The fellowship was sharply divided between two rival schemes for filling its rooms and soaking up its surplus: expanding the Prize Fellowship and turning the College into an Imperial Institute.

Geoffrey Faber, Charles Grant Robertson, and Llewellyn Woodward argued that the College should create a third Prize Fellowship for scientists. This innovation would allow the College to tap a new stream for talent in the University. It would also ensure that All Souls exercised the same sort of influence over the new scientific élite as it had long done over the established administrative and legal élites.

We submit that the extension of the range of our studies in such a direction would encourage, rather than decrease, the identification of the typical All Souls fellow with the practical as well as the theoretic life; would enormously widen the contact of the College with contemporary affairs; and would prevent it from falling out of touch with a changing interpretation of national service.[80]

The examination for the scientific Prize Fellows would consist of an essay paper, a general paper or two, perhaps a translation paper, and a *viva*. The College would rest its decision 'on the quality of the candidates' papers, on the character of their testimonials, on their University record, and on their bearing at the *viva voce* examination'.[81] A. L. Rowse endorsed the principle of creating a third Prize Fellowship but suggested that it should be open to candidates from all universities in the country.[82]

---

[78] 'Minute Book, 1875–1888', 'Separate Report by Professor Montague Burrows', inserted between 106 and 107.

[79] 'Minute Book, 1875–1888', 'Selected Indian Civil Service Candidates', inserted between 12 and 13, and the report by Burrows. The Burrows suggestion was defeated by fourteen to seven votes.

[80] 'Minute Book, 1926–1946', vol. 1: 'Documents privately printed for the consideration of the Committee on the College revenues', bundle inserted between 57 and 58: 'Memorandum No. 3: Faber, Robertson and Woodward', 14.

[81] Ibid., 27. John Foster added his support with the reservation that research should not play too large a part in the scheme.

[82] Ibid., 33, letter from A. L. Rowse.

No fewer than eight fellows put their names to a rival proposal to turn All Souls into an Imperial Institute. The eight argued that, at a time when the business of running the Empire had never been more demanding, the old Imperial tradition in the College was dying, thanks to the lamentable preference of so many Prize Fellows for the academic life. Their solution was to pack All Souls with Professorial and Research Fellows dedicated to studying and teaching international relations and 'problems connected with the government of subject races'. This arrangement would fill an important gap in University studies, and restore the vital link between All Souls and the outside world.

The subsequent debate was a delicious one – not least because it converted so many London fellows into champions of research (albeit research of a peculiarly narrow kind) and so many research-minded fellows into champions of a flexible Prize Fellowship.[83] The result of the prolonged wrangle was a qualified victory for Faber et al. (The Imperial faction had to content itself with a single professorship of social anthropology.[84]) They failed to get enough support for a Prize Fellowship dedicated to the sciences. The College feared that it would have to rely too much on outside experts in making such elections – and that scientists would alter the tone of the College. But in March 1932 the College resolved to increase its annual intake of Prize Fellows in the humanities from two to three. It produced plans for an additional building to house the expanded fellowship and proceeded to elect three Prize Fellows in 1932.[85]

In the next couple of years, however, the College mood mysteriously turned against expanding the Prize Fellowship. In 1933 it elected only one Prize Fellow, J. L. Austin. In February 1935 it decided to convert the third examination fellowship into a thesis fellowship.[86] In June 1936, E. L. Woodward – once a champion of the triple Prize Fellowship and now Subwarden – summarized his reasons for resisting further expansion. The College was changing too quickly: eighteen of the fellows, or more than a third of the governing body, had been in College for less than seven years, and eleven for less than four years. The numbers dining frequently exceeded thirty-five. Six Prize Fellows lived in College for all or part of the year. The weekend fellows were busy men and needed to be housed in reasonable comfort.[87] In the late 1930s the College dropped the thesis fellowship. After a spate of elections just after the war the College resorted to its old

[83] Ibid., 'Additional documents privately printed for the consideration of the Committee on the College Revenues', bundle inserted between 69 and 70: 'Supplementary Memorandum signed by Robertson, Faber and Woodward and dated February 5th, 1930', 15.

[84] 'Minute Book, 1926–1946', vol. 2, 'A Professorship of Social Anthropology', inserted between 165 and 166.

[85] Ibid., 'Report of the Financial Committee to the Stated General Meeting on March 5th, 1932', inserted between 107 and 108.

[86] Ibid., 'Report of the Joint Meetings of the Financial and Research Fellowship Committees on the method of election to a third fellowship under Statute III, Clause I', inserted between 155 and 156.

[87] Ibid., 'Statement submitted by the Subwarden to the Joint committee on 28 June 1936', inserted between 175 and 176.

practice of electing two Prize Fellows a year unless the field proved to be particularly distinguished – a practice which, with occasional exceptions, it has preserved since.

What sort of people became Prize Fellows of All Souls? The simplest way to answer the question is to glance at a list of schools and colleges they attended.[88] The Prize Fellows were overwhelmingly drawn from a small number of élite public schools and prestigious Oxford colleges. Before the Great War, Eton and Balliol dominated the field. Between 1860 and 1914 All Souls elected thirty-nine fellows from Balliol and twenty-six from Eton. The other colleges and schools which scored significant numbers were Christ Church (12), New College (10), and Magdalen (7); Harrow (11), Winchester (9), and Rugby (5). (Harrow's score was to fall to just one in 1918–1950.) Lushington et al. had clearly succeeded in turning a college which had once been an annexe of Christ Church into an annexe of Balliol. After the Great War, Winchester and New College successfully challenged Eton and Balliol. Between 1918 and 1950, the College elected seventeen Prize Fellows from New College and twelve from Winchester. Balliol produced just fourteen Prize Fellows and Eton eight. The other Colleges and schools to score significant numbers were Christ Church (7), Magdalen (4), and Rugby (4). Eighty-seven of the 145 Prize Fellows elected between 1860 and 1948 had been educated in one of the nine Clarendon public schools.[89]

These networks were self-reinforcing. Hesitant candidates decided to stand for All Souls because a tutor with All Souls connections told them that they were in with a chance or else because a friend (or rival) from school or college had succeeded in a previous year. H. W. C. Davis (elected in 1895) and Kenneth Bell (elected in 1907) were both long-standing history fellows at Balliol. Keith Feiling was keen to get Christ Church historians into All Souls. Richard Pares, E. L. Woodward, and Isaiah Berlin were all lecturers at New College. The All Souls connection sometimes reached back to schooldays: A. T. P. Williams (1911) taught history at Winchester and was responsible for introducing Richard Pares to the subject.[90]

The extraordinary success of public-school-educated men in the examination ensured that All Souls preserved its unique and exclusive social *cachet*. Warden Sneyd had been wrong to fear that open competition would fill the College with proletarians. He would have been better off listening to Gladstone on the probable impact of open competition:

I do not hesitate to say [Gladstone wrote to Lord John Russell in January 1854] that one of the great recommendations of the change in my eyes would be its tendency to

[88] The following figures are based on Simmons's list of fellows.

[89] The Clarendon Public Schools were those investigated by the Clarendon commission of 1861 as being the nine leading schools in England at the time. Throughout the entire period Merton produced only two Prize Fellows – something which is presumably explained by the fact that the College possessed a generous internal system of senior scholarships and junior research fellowships.

[90] A. L. Rowse, 'Richard Pares', *Proceedings of the British Academy*, 48 (1962), 346.

strengthen and multiply the ties between the higher classes and the possession of administrative power. As a member for Oxford, I look forward eagerly to its operation. There, happily, we are not without some lights of experience to throw upon this part of the subject. The objection which I always hear there from persons who wish to retain restrictions upon elections is this: 'If you leave them to examination, Eton, Harrow, Rugby, and the other public schools will carry *everything*.' I have a strong impression that the aristocracy of this country are even superior in natural gifts, on the average, to the mass: but it is plain that with their acquired advantages, their *insensible* education, irrespective of book-learning, they have an immense superiority.[91]

John Simmons calculates that in 1914 the fellowship included two Privy Council-lors, two baronets, four knights, and one honourable – at a time when elsewhere in the University only Magdalen could boast a single knight in its fellowship.[92]

Yet not all the Prize Fellows were toffs. The gradual construction of a scholarship ladder regulated by examinations and intended to link the village school with the University inevitably forced the products of Eton and Harrow into competition with able children from more modest backgrounds.[93] From the 1870s the College recruited a rising number of men from grammar schools and the Scottish academies – many of them via Balliol.[94] Hensley Henson (elected in 1884) was brought up in a dogmatic Plymouth Brethren household and could only afford to attend Oxford as a non-collegiate student – 'living in lodgings and terribly poor'.[95] A. L. Rowse was educated at a Cornish grammar school. Goronwy Rees was the product of Welsh Nonconformity and Cardiff Grammar School. When Harold Wilson failed to get a fellowship, he was beaten not by an Etonian but by a fellow Northern grammar school boy, Arthur Brown.

Etonians and autodidacts shared one thing in common: an immense skill in passing and appetite for taking examinations. The College classicists had usually taken three public examinations before sitting for All Souls: 'Mods', 'Greats', and a degree in history or law. Most of them had also competed incessantly for school and University prizes. No sooner had they arrived in All Souls than many Prize Fellows immediately buckled down to taking Civil Service or Bar Exams. Harold Butler, who regarded All Souls as 'the haven of my dreams',[96] nevertheless spent the first six months of his fellowship cramming for the Home Civil Service exam at Wren's tutorial college. To amass the necessary number of marks he had to spend three weeks writing desperately against the clock.[97]

---

[91] Quoted in Hughes, 'Civil Service Reform', 63. J. S. Mill made a similar point. See his 'Reform of the Civil Service', 209. Many subsequent historians of University and Civil Service reform have also echoed Gladstone's judgment. See Hart, 'Trevelyan at the Treasury', 110.
[92] Simmons, 'All Souls', 216.
[93] S. Rothblatt, *Revolution of the Dons* (London, 1968), 46–7, 75–86.
[94] Simmons, 'All Souls', 216; S. M. Burrows (ed.), *The Autobiography of Montagu Burrows* (London, 1908), 217.
[95] H. H. Henson, *Retrospect of an Unimportant Life*, vol. 1 (London, 1942), 5.
[96] H. B. Butler, *Confident Morning* (London, 1950), 27–8.
[97] Ibid., 44.

This examination culture may have imposed a certain narrowness of vision and conventionality of thought on some of its initiates. It also imposed a terrible strain. Harold Butler felt so stuffed with facts and theories that he compared himself with a goose destined for *pâté de fois gras*. Patrick Reilly briefly contemplated abandoning his plan to go into the diplomatic corps because he could not face doing another examination. (He soon buckled down to it and passed top into the Foreign Office.)[98]

The College imposed few duties or restrictions on its initiates. In their first year new fellows had to pernoctate – that is, spend a certain number of nights each term sleeping in College. They also had to perform certain menial duties which went under the general heading of 'screwing': mixing the mayonnaise for Sunday dinner (a tradition which was dropped in 1924 when John Foster refused to do it) and decanting the port (a tradition which survives in the rather less demanding form of ringing a bell for refills). Apart from screwing, the new fellows were left pretty much to their own devices. They could spend their time reading and writing (like Rowse) or hunting and shooting (like Makins). Reading and hunting fellows were all paid the same salary (£300 between the wars) in their first two years. Thereafter they had to choose between becoming an academic fellow or leaving academia and seeing their stipend fall to £50.

Most new Prize Fellows found College life pleasant – rather like living in a first-class club. (Only one has committed suicide while still in fellowship.) It was not without its drawbacks however. The most obvious of these was that some of the more ancient fellows could be rather demanding. Spencer Wilkinson was constantly trying to tell an anecdote which was so long and boring that no fellow had heard the end of it. Patrick Reilly found his company at College breakfast as inescapable as it was undesirable.[99] Sir Erskine Holland was nearly blind and had the disconcerting habit of pouring his port into a non-existent glass.[100] His dinner table conversation frequently began with the phrase 'I remember that Metternich once said to me...'[101] Holdsworth was notorious for keeping the junior fellow waiting in dessert while he consumed formidable quantities of port. He also infuriated the young Roger Makins by insisting on describing himself as a Wykehamist despite the fact that he had not been to Winchester.[102] To make things more difficult still, the resident fellows (most of them young Prize Fellows) had to bear the cost of all the drink consumed in the evening, even those of

[98] Reilly to his father, 8 Nov. 1932, All Souls College archives, 11 letters, 1932–33; 'My Election to All Souls', Oxford, Bodleian Library, MS Eng. c. 6916. f. 326. I am indebted to Jane Reilly for permission to use and quote from her late father's papers.
[99] Reilly to his mother, 11 Nov. 1932, All Souls College archives, letters 1932–33.
[100] Dermot Morrah, 'An All Souls Notebook', 83, All Souls College archives.
[101] K. Hancock, 'All Souls 1923–82: Recollections and Reflections', 2, All Souls College archives. See also Davidson, this volume.
[102] Roger Makins' diary, 16 and 18 Nov. 1925, All Souls College archives.

guests, a convention which neatly imposed the cost of collegiate entertainment on those least able to bear it.[103]

The positive side of all this was that the College preserved a tradition of equality among its fellows. Election ensured equality of status and abolished prefixes in names. Cosmo Gordon Lang recalled 'a family life in which we were all on equal terms and there was no respect of persons'.[104] Some young fellows perhaps took the presumption of equality a little far. Patrick Reilly was shocked to see Goronwy Rees ribbing John Simon, the Foreign Secretary.[105] Roger Makins was bemused by A. L. Rowse's habit of giving senior fellows long lectures on their own specialist subjects.[106]

The Empire provided many Prize Fellows with high-profile and often distinguished public careers. Curzon (elected in 1883) was Viceroy of India from 1899 until 1905. Thesiger (elected in 1892) and Wood (elected in 1902) were Viceroys (as Lords Chelmsford and Irwin respectively) in the 1920s. F. Perry (elected in 1896) served as Imperial Secretary in South Africa before becoming a Canadian representative for Lazards. Maurice Gwyer (elected in 1902) was Chief Justice of India from 1937 to 1945. Rushbrook Williams (elected in 1914) worked on the Montagu–Chelmsford reforms and created the Indian Bureau of Public Information.[107] Leo Amery (elected in 1897) fell under the spell of Milner in South Africa in 1900. He later served under Milner for several years – as one of his two political secretaries in 1916–19 (a post which gave him an intimate view of the working of the Imperial War Cabinet) and as his parliamentary under-secretary at the Colonial Office in 1919–21. He was secretary of state for dominion affairs in 1925–9 and head of the India Office in the Churchill administration. Geoffrey Dawson (elected in 1898), Dougal Malcolm (elected in 1899), and Robert (later Lord) Brand (elected in 1901) were all members of Milner's Kindergarten in Johannesburg. Malcolm and Brand later decided to pursue their imperial interests in the private sector: Malcolm through the British South Africa Company and Brand through Lazard Brothers. Malcolm and Brand helped to found the Round Table, an influential mouthpiece of Imperial opinion.[108] Dawson ensured that *The Times* covered Imperial affairs in a depth which might be expected of a paper edited in the Dominions – and that it covered European affairs with a detachment which might be expected from a newspaper edited in the Dominions as well.

The last five fellows on the list formed the hard core of the College Empire builders. They formed a tightly knit coterie: friends from their school and undergraduate days who had been elected to All Souls within a year or two of

---

[103] Reilly to his father, 18 Nov. 1932, All Souls College archive, letters 1932–33.
[104] J. G. Lockhart, *Cosmo Gordon Lang* (London, 1949), 60.
[105] Reilly to his father, 8 Nov. 1932, All Souls College archives, letters 1932–33.
[106] Makins' diary, 18 Nov. 1925.
[107] Rushbrook Williams, 'All Souls College in the Early Twentieth Century'.
[108] See further Howard, this volume.

each other and remained close throughout their lives. They were all heavily and permanently influenced by the New Imperialism which so hypnotized political commentators, Fabian as much as Tory, in the late Victorian and Edwardian period. This New Imperialism – a much tougher and more sophisticated doctrine than the somewhat mushy paternalism of the mid-Victorians – rested on two powerful ideas: federalism and *dirigisme*. Britain needed to draw its Empire into a closer union, political and economic, cultural and spiritual, if it was to survive in a world dominated by super-states and competing trading blocks. The nation's most vital interests lay in the Empire rather than Europe. The state needed to intervene in the economy (through import controls) and in the wider society (though expanded welfare provisions) in order to produce a prosperous and efficient population.

This group did its utmost to enlist the College in support of its imperial mission. A College joke had it that Amery was so keen on recruiting Imperialists that he would 'elect even an emu or a giraffe'.[109] The Imperialists kept a sharp eye out for sympathetic candidates in the annual examination. They also encouraged the College to invest in subjects which might be useful to the Empire. In 1905 Amery persuaded the College to endow a readership (converted into a professorship four years later) in military history.[110] As political fashion turned against the Empire in the aftermath of the Great War, the Imperialists found it harder to find able but sympathetic Prize Fellows. One of the few Prize Fellows to go into Imperial administration, Penderel Moon, became an ardent anti-imperialist. They consequently turned increasingly to their second strategy: packing the College with like-minded research fellows or with professorial fellows who specialized in subjects with an Imperial flavour. They got Lionel Curtis a research fellowship in 1928 and made an energetic but doomed bid to turn the College into an Imperial *école*. They also helped to sway the College in favour of endowing a chair in social anthropology rather than psychology.[111]

Several fellows pursued successful careers in Fleet Street – hardly a surprising choice given that writing fluent examination answers is such perfect preparation for writing fluent newspaper editorials. A fellow of the College sat in the editorial chair of *The Times* for nearly sixty years after 1882. In May 1880 the newspaper's proprietor sent word to Oxford that he was looking for a recent graduate to act as deputy editor. Warden Anson replied that he had the perfect man – a 25-year-old Prize Fellow who had shone at Winchester and New College and was just about to be called to the Bar.[112] George Buckle was made editor two years later and held the post until 1912. In the 1900s *The Times* recruited another generation from All Souls. Robert Brand became a *Times* trustee. Leo Amery was appointed Colonial Editor in 1900. Shortly after his appointment, Amery persuaded the

[109] S. Morison et al., *The History of the Times*, vol. 1 (London, 1935), 10.
[110] L. S. Amery, *My Political Life*, vol. 1 (London, 1953), 221.
[111] See now J. Davis, 'How All Souls got its Anthropologist', in P. Rivière (ed.), *A History of Oxford Anthropology* (New York and Oxford, 2007), 62–82.
[112] Morison et al., *History of the Times*, vols 2 (London, 1939), 418, and 3 (London, 1943), 1–2.

paper to take on another Prize Fellow, Arthur McDowall. A colleague recalled how it happened: 'I remember very well how Amery, who was then with us and had just been examining for All Souls, came in to Buckle's room at about 1.30 a.m. one night to say they had just elected an extraordinarily wise young man, and that we must not on any account miss him.'[113] In 1906 Amery exercised his influence again, persuading the paper to recruit Geoffrey Dawson – then editor of the Johannesburg *Star* – as its South African correspondent. In 1912 Northcliffe invited Amery to succeed Buckle as editor. (He evidently rated Amery: four years earlier he had offered him the editorship of *The Observer*.) But Amery declined – he was too intent on a political career – and instead nominated Dawson. Dawson got the job, much to Buckle's delight,[114] and edited the paper from 1912 to 1918, when he fell out with Northcliffe, and again from 1923 to 1940.[115]

Throughout his editorship Dawson kept close contact with the All Souls circle. In his 1918–23 interregnum he returned to the College as Estates Bursar. Thereafter, he kept a lookout for talented young fellows, sounding out, for example, Patrick Reilly, and used *The Times* to puff College grandees such as Halifax and Simon.[116] His relationship with Halifax was particularly close. He stayed with Halifax (then Irwin) in India in the winter of 1928–9, and the two discussed a subject which they had first dwelt on a couple of decades earlier when they were with Milner in South Africa: how to reconcile a burgeoning national consciousness with the preservation of the Empire.[117] Dawson provided Halifax with unstinting support when he became Foreign Secretary. Halifax used to invite his friend over to the Foreign Office to give him a private briefing or hand him a sensitive internal memorandum. Dawson could then write his leaders and headlines in good time – and make sure that the news coverage was given a suitable spin.[118] By the late 1930s *The Times* degenerated into little more than a propaganda sheet for the Chamberlainite faction.

The reformed College also preserved its close links with politics and affairs. Open competition may not have thrown up a statesman quite as distinguished as the third Marquess of Salisbury. But it did produce a succession of professional politicians who almost climbed to the top of the greasy pole: Tories such as Halifax and Hailsham, Liberals such as Anson and Simon,[119] and socialists such as Douglas Jay. The College's legal tradition remained unbroken. Thanks to the 1857 Ordinance, law was one of the two core subjects in the fellowship

[113] M. McDowall (ed.), *A Detached Observer: Essays and Sketches by the late Arthur McDowall* (London, 1934), vi.
[114] *History of the Times*, iii. 620.
[115] Ibid., i. 3.
[116] Ibid., ii. 798.
[117] A. Roberts, *The Holy Fox: A Biography of Lord Halifax* (London, 1991), 25.
[118] Ibid., 109.
[119] See Cretney, this volume.

examination. A guaranteed income of £200 or £300 a year for the first two years of the fellowship provided the less well heeled fellows with invaluable support during their early careers. And Law, like the College, bestrode the twin worlds of academia and practical affairs. Number 2 Hare Court almost turned into an annexe of All Souls in the Inns of Court.

Still, for all this apparent continuity, the reformed college did break with one important part of the old establishment: the Church of England. For a while in the 1880s it looked as if open competition would not lead automatically to secularization. Between 1882 and 1888 the College elected three Prize Fellows who went on to become princes of the Church: Hensley Henson, A. C. Headlam, and Cosmo Gordon Lang. These three elections are evidence in themselves of the immense success of the short-lived intellectual revival of the Church of England in the 1880s.[120] But thereafter hardly any Prize Fellows chose holy orders. A college which was founded as a purely ecclesiastical society rapidly became the least ecclesiastical of all academic corporations.

Before the Great War only a minority of Prize Fellows chose to stay in academia. Compared with Germany and the United States, the British universities possessed only a rudimentary career structure; and the career structure in All Souls was more rudimentary still. Many non-academic fellows made no secret of their contempt for what Lord Curzon called 'that state of resentful coma which is dignified by the universities with the name of research'.[121] The College failed to develop a systematic scheme for retaining promising Prize Fellows as research fellows or else slotting them into jobs elsewhere. In 1914 the College had just one research fellowship (held by A. F. Pollard).[122] An early career in a College without undergraduates did not necessarily equip a Prize Fellow to compete for tutorial fellowships in other Colleges; taking a job in a provincial university usually involved moving to an obscure part of the country. G. M. Young decided to leave academia for the Civil Service because the career structure was ramshackle and the remuneration so uncertain.[123]

After the War academia became a rather more popular choice. Manchester and London pioneered the professionalization of university life. All Souls began to build an internal ladder of opportunity. In 1919 the College had become so worried about the under-supply of University-based Prize Fellows that it contemplated creating five All Souls tutorial fellowships. It decided instead to create five research fellowships which could be renewed every seven years.[124] Promising

---

[120] R. W. Southern, *A Sermon preached in All Souls Chapel, 8 November 1987* (privately printed, All Souls, 1987), 11–12.

[121] Quoted in K. Rose, *Superior Person: A Portrait of Curzon and his Circle in Late Victorian England* (London, 1969), 106.

[122] Simmons, 'All Souls', 218.

[123] G. Kitson Clark, 'G. M. Young: A Biographical Memoir', in G. M. Young, *Portrait of an Age: Victorian England* (London, 1977), 3, with Mordaunt Crook, this volume.

[124] 'Minute Book, 1915–1925', 'Report of the Statutory Purposes Committee, 16 March 1919', after 209. Sir Erskine Holland violently objected to bribing young fellows to stay in academia.

Prize Fellows could thus win internal promotion after the end of their first seven years.[125] Political fashion reinforced the effect of an improved career structure. Many of the fellows elected from the mid-1920s onwards had no sympathy with the politics of their more worldly College seniors.

The fact that an increasing number of Prize Fellows subsequently chose a career in research encouraged others to emulate them. It would be an exaggeration to say that Pares begat Rowse and Rowse begat Hill. Or that Berlin begat Austin and Austin begat Hampshire. But from the mid-1920s the College clearly accumulated a critical mass of young academic Prize Fellows who began to shift the balance of power away from the world and towards the University.

Whether they pursued careers in academia or affairs, most fellows professed a remarkable degree of affection for their alma mater. Even men who went on to the highest public offices persisted in regarding their election to All Souls as the high point of their lives. Hensley Henson looked upon All Souls as 'a several headed substitute for a father'.[126]

I was welcomed with a generous kindness which made me feel immediately at home. I formed friendships which have enriched my life. I loved everybody from the Warden to the Scout's boy, and even now, after more than half a century, I never enter the College without emotion. It would be difficult to overstate the importance of All Souls in my life.[127]

John Simon described it as 'the nicest club in Europe'.[128] Leo Amery recalled that 'of many cheerful evenings the most joyous I can recall is an All Souls Gaudy' he celebrated in Johannesburg in 1907 along with Dawson, Brand, and Perry.[129] Patrick Reilly writes that 'of all the many blessings that I have enjoyed in a long life, after that of my marriage and my family, the greatest has undoubtedly been my election – and my re-election – to All Souls'.[130]

Enthusiasm for the Prize Fellowship within the College was perhaps only equalled by antagonism outside it. The most important reason for this antagonism is that the College failed to elect candidates who went on to make distinguished careers in Oxford or the outside world. The list of the rejected includes such famous names as Aldous Huxley, Lewis Namier, Hugh Trevor-Roper, Freddie Ayer, and Harold Wilson. For some of these people failure at All Souls was the only academic failure they had ever known and they continued to resent it for the rest of their lives. To compound the injury some successful candidates went on to live humdrum lives. Keith Hancock tells the story of Scottish crofter

---

[125] Reilly to his father, 8 Nov. 1932, All Souls College archives, letters 1932–33.

[126] O. Chadwick, *Hensley Henson: A Study in the Friction between Church and State* (Oxford, 1983), 23.

[127] Henson, *Retrospect*, i. 5. See also iii. 343, for his impressions of how the College changed between 1884 and 1946.

[128] Rushbrook Williams, 'All Souls College in the Early Twentieth Century'.

[129] Amery, *My Political Life*, i. 321.

[130] Reilly, 'My Election to All Souls'.

parents who were sorely disappointed in their two promising sons: one ran away to sea, the other became a fellow of All Souls and was never heard of again.[131] This personal antagonism was compounded by a more dispassionate feeling that All Souls was an anachronism and an anomaly.

The College is certainly unusual in preserving non-academic fellows. Yet judged from a distance the intriguing thing about the Prize Fellowship is not how anomalous it is but rather how typical it is of the British approach to educational selection. In his classic comparative study of American and British education Ralph Turner distinguished between two kinds of educational mobility, contest and sponsored:

Contest mobility is a system in which élite status is the prize in an open contest and is taken by the aspirants' own efforts. While the 'contest' is governed by some rules of fair play, the contestants have wide latitude in the strategies they may employ. Since the 'prize' of successful upward mobility is not in the hands of the established élite to give out, the latter are not in a position to determine who shall attain it and who shall not. Under *sponsored* mobility, élite recruits are chosen by the established élite or their agents, and élite status is *given* on the basis of some criterion of merit and cannot be *taken* by any amount of effort or strategy. Upward mobility is like entry into a private club, where each candidate must be 'sponsored' by one or more of the members. Ultimately, the members grant or deny upward mobility on the basis of whether they judge the candidate to have the qualities that they wish to see in fellow members.[132]

The sponsorship system was the product of a unified élite which knew precisely what it was looking for in an aspirant member. The élite distinguished sharply between those who possessed merit and those who lacked it, and made its decision as early as possible in order to introduce aspirant members into the complicated rules of the club. To retain its legitimacy the selection process was kept as secret as possible.

The English system of educational selection which emerged in the 1880s and survived until the 1960s was sponsored mobility writ large. Selection was more often than not an all-or-nothing affair based on an examination which claimed to test general promise and future ability. At a stroke it separated eleven-year-olds into grammar-school sheep and secondary-modern goats. Schools specialized in introducing children to a way of life as well as instructing them in basic subjects. Grammar schools recruited more than their 'fair' share of middle-class children, but they also proved to be powerful engines of social mobility for able children from obscure backgrounds. A school of English psychologists produced a sophisticated theory to justify this system of sponsored mobility, arguing that individuals differ in their innate abilities, that these differences are inherited rather than

[131] Hancock, 'All Souls 1923–82', 2.
[132] R. H. Turner, 'Modes of Social Ascent through Education, Sponsored and Contest Mobility', in R. Bendix and S. M. Lipset (eds), *Class, Status and Power: Social Stratification in Comparative Perspective* (New York, 1966), 450.

acquired, and that intelligence is a general and unitary quality, ensuring that someone who excels in one subject is also capable of excelling in another. The 11-plus is thus justified as an accurate predictor of future distinction.

The charge that the Prize Fellowship is an anomaly slowly gained substance in the 1960s and 1970s. The new comprehensive schools pursued equality rather than upward mobility. The rapidly expanding university sector became at once more self-absorbed and more anti-establishment. An institution which was both elitist and worldly struck many as combining two vices. Many Prize Fellows elected in that era must have wondered if they would be the last in their line.

2

'Government by Mallardry'

The Golden Age of the Prize Fellows, c.1875–1925

S. J. D. Green

Sometime during the autumn of 1932, Geoffrey Dawson, long-standing editor of *The Times* and distinguished fellow of All Souls, publicly disclosed the existence of a short treatise devoted to a peculiar variation on the gentle art of bird-watching.[1] But this was no hobby-book. It was directed to the doings of human beings rather than their feathered friends. And it pointed to potentially far-reaching conclusions about the nature of modern British democracy. *Government by Mallardry: A Study in Political Ornithology* depicted what its author, C. W. Brodribb, took to be one of the most important – yet least understood – aspects of contemporary life.[2] For it revealed how His Majesty's Government, unbeknownst to 'the common run of the king's subjects who [were] under the impression that they govern[ed] themselves', was in fact 'led and guide[d] by a peculiar flock of "Mallards"'.[3] Brodribb coyly refrained from revealing the

---

[1] Geoffrey Dawson (1874–1944); born Geoffrey Robinson; assumed by royal licence the name and arms of Dawson in 1917 via his mother's elder sister, Margaret Jane Dawson, the family being descended from a long line of landowners of Langcliffe Hall, Settle. Educated at Eton and Magdalen College, Oxford; 'firsts' in Classical Moderations (1895) and 'Greats' (1897); fellow of All Souls, 1898–1944; Assistant Private Secretary to Joseph Chamberlain at the Colonial Office and then Alfred Milner, High Commissioner of South Africa, 1901–6. A leading member of the 'The Round Table' (on which see Howard, this volume) from the time of its formation until his death; briefly editor of the *Johannesburg Star*; journalist on *The Times* from 1906; editor 1912–19 and again 1923–41. Few, perhaps, can have believed more than Dawson in the merits of 'Government by Mallardry' during the twentieth century. Subsequently vilified as an 'arch-appeaser' of Nazi Germany and a generally malevolent influence in British foreign policy. See Green, this volume, ch. 10.

[2] C. W. Brodribb, *Government by Mallardry: A Study in Political Ornithology* (London, 1932), privately printed at *The Times*. Just how many copies of this booklet were ever distributed remains uncertain. The original, now deposited in the Codrington Library, All Souls, contains an explanatory introduction by Dawson, dated All Souls Day, 1932. The first paragraph reads: 'The enclosed was written two or three years ago for his own amusement by C. W. Brodribb, a colleague on the staff of *The Times*, and an Oxford man, but not otherwise connected with All Souls.'

[3] Brodribb, *Government by Mallardry*, 3.

precise identity of these strange birds. However, he offered tantalizing clues for
the partial enlightenment of those not already in the know. These 'Mallards' were
habitués of the 'most exclusive [society] in Europe'. They were also members of
'an unofficial committee [dedicated to] running of the destinies of the Empire';
finally, they were volunteer workers in a kind of 'rotary club raised to the nth level
of efficiency', which had taken 'all political, economic and administrative life into
its province'.[4]

Curiously, perhaps, Brodribb insisted that 'Government by Mallardry' was a
novel development. Indeed, his account repeatedly emphasized how, for much of
the nineteenth century, 'the Mallards' had achieved little more than 'a steady-
going [collective] existence'. Not until the 1860s and 1870s had they 'woken up
and truly taken stock of themselves as a truly [influential] organisation'.[5] Only
towards the end of the nineteenth century did they become properly represented
in all 'branches of public life'. Their seemingly hereditary claim to the position of
'Viceroy of India' was actually the product of an interest nurtured in 'quite recent
years'. Similarly belated efforts had enabled like-minded brethren to secure
comparable positions in 'cabinet . . . government offices, administrative posts
abroad, banking and industry'.[6] Just to be on the safe side, three Mallards sat
on the Episcopal Branch 'at the present moment'.[7]

In 'divulging' such 'salutary' truths to the public, Brodribb meant to expose no
malevolent conspiracy against the British people. To the contrary, he believed
that the 'public at large' might draw considerable comfort – indeed, 'derive some
benefit' – from a closer knowledge of 'the Mallards and their influence'. As such,
he was at pains to emphasize the wisdom, honour, and public spiritedness of
Britain's new and surreptitious governing class.[8] So much so that Dawson, on
discovering this precious document, quickly had it 'privately printed for the
entertainment of members of the College'.[9] They can scarcely have failed to be
flattered by its contents. Brodribb portrayed them as nothing less than a body of
philosopher-kings.[10] New members were elected to its society only after 'the
most careful scrutiny of their [intellectual] qualifications'. They were both
presumed to possess, but also required to augment, an elevated interest in
'historical, legal and constitutional studies'.[11] As a result, modern Mallards

---

[4] Brodribb, *Government by Mallardry*, 3–7.
[5] Ibid., 5.
[6] Ibid., 6–7.
[7] Ibid., 6.
[8] Ibid., 3–8.
[9] Dawson, 'Introductory Letter', *Government by Mallardry*, 1.
[10] Brodribb, *Government by Mallardry*, 7–8. An ancient concept, of various usages, particularly
associated at that time – anyway in England – with the educational writings of Sir Cyril Norwood. See,
in particular, his contemporary work, *The English Tradition in Education* (London, 1929), and also
Religion and Education (London, 1932). For a modern account, consult G. McCulloch, *Philosophers
and Kings: Education for Leadership in Modern England* (Cambridge, 1991), chs 2 and 4.
[11] Brodribb, *Government by Mallardry*, 5.

boasted representatives 'in all branches of knowledge (except possibly the phys-ical sciences)'.[12] But this was not just armchair knowledge. They were also 'diligent travellers, familiar with all the languages, constitutions and legal systems of Europe . . . [also] the dominions and America'.[13] Finally, they communicated this 'extraordinar[ily] rich and deep fund of information' to each other: usually at the 'many dinners' they enjoyed together. In that way, they succeeded in leaving 'no department of public activity, no school of thought, no moment of the hour, unmallarded'.[14]

Still, nothing sinister shadowed their efforts. To be sure, 'these were birds of a feather'. They were recruited from amongst the young. Few became members 'past the prime of their manhood'.[15] As a result, they invariably retained a profound sense of 'loyalty . . . to the club' that had first recognized their talents. But 'they were not a party'. Their 'very method of election', that is, by intellectual attainments alone and strictly according to merit, 'precluded the possibility of their being alike'. They were also, for the most part, biologically unrelated. There were both radicals and conservatives amongst them. All the same, a 'pronounced [practical] ethos' grounded each in generally sensible political teachings, at once preoccupied with 'the urgent' and committed to 'the possible'. This not only ensured that theirs was a 'singularly disinterested creed'. It also guaranteed that they never became 'a collection of cranks or axe-grinders'. Consequently, their influence and example were not only compatible with democracy. They invari-ably acted to its greater – if generally unacknowledged – advantage.[16]

It is important to remember that such poppycock was once widely believed. All Souls no more presided over the British Empire than it ran indigenous English administration in 1932. Indeed, the sort of 'Mallardians' that Brodribb had in mind had effectively ceased even to rule All Souls by that date.[17] But it was

---

[12] Ibid., 6. This was generally true of their *formal* education, at least; though note the exception of Somervell, documented below. Legend has it that Warden Pember (1914–32) or, anyway, Warden Pember's wife, insisted to Frederick Lindemann, shortly after his appointment to the Chair of Experimental Philosophy at Oxford, in 1919, that 'anyone who has a "first" in "Greats" could get up science in a fortnight'. To which Lindemann (rather wittily) replied that 'your husband has [seemingly] never had a fortnight to spare'. I owe this account to A. Fort, *Prof: The Life of Frederick Lindemann* (London, 2003), 74.

[13] Brodribb, *Government by Mallardry*, 6. See A. L. Rowse, *All Souls and Appeasement: A Contribution to Contemporary History* (London, 1961), which specifically refers to Brodribb on p. 2, and pointedly denies that the leading 'Mallards' then displayed much knowledge of Europe generally, or Germany particularly, on pp. 6, 64–5, and 108–9. Yet the surviving evidence more readily supports Brodribb's vicarious boast than Rowse's damning judgement.

[14] Brodribb, *Government by Mallardry*, 6–7.

[15] Ibid., 5–6.

[16] Ibid., 7–8.

[17] As a result of the revolution in All Souls achieved by the statutory reforms of 1931, which effectively reorientated the College as a modern research institute, devoted to the humanities and social sciences. By implication, it (and they) also rejected the idea of All Souls becoming a centre for the study of Imperial government generally, and British imperial problems more particularly. I shall discuss this pivotal decision at length in Green, 'Imperialists and Commonwealthsmen', *The Exceptional College: All Souls c.1850–1950* (forthcoming).

a conceit still widely believed during the years between the wars. That was never more true than at the very moment of Brodribb's sycophantic celebration of its supposed influence. This found as much credence amongst those who then derided the College's continuing national and international importance as within the ever smaller body of opinion that continued to defend it.[18] It had other ingenuous apologists too. Perhaps nothing else quite explains why the election that very year of the first (openly acknowledged) Jew to All Souls provoked a major story in the *Jewish Chronicle*, a letter of congratulations from the Chief Rabbi, and an invitation to the young Isaiah Berlin to spend the next weekend with Baron Rothschild at Waddesdon.[19] Even his lionization was not an isolated incident. Happily recalling his receipt only the previous winter of what he immodestly described as 'one of the greatest gifts [that] Oxford had to bestow... in those days', Goronwy Rees could not entirely hide his embarrass-ment at the orgy of 'national self-congratulation' that it provoked in his native Wales.[20] A. L. Rowse's similar success had much the same effect, throughout Cornwall, in 1925.[21]

To that degree, there may have been *something* to all the fuss. Yet Brodribb spoke truer then he knew when he located the fame of the Mallardians to the closing years of the nineteenth century. He also alluded to one aspect of their surviving distinction that was distinctly double-edged. This was that theirs was not merely a novel influence but also a decidedly recent kudos. Young men elected to All Souls right up to the turn of the twentieth century had been painfully aware of an altogether more ambiguous collegiate inheritance. Put another way: they understood that theirs was a prize which had, in the not so distant past, been almost as much shunned as sought after. In 1863, there were just three candidates for All Souls fellowships.[22] Even the reforms of the so-called ordinance era – roughly, those undertaken during the decade after 1857 – did not entirely dispel a powerful, residual, sense that extraneous, that is, illegitimate criteria were still essential for their award.[23] This explains Leo Amery's remarks

---

[18] For a wide-ranging, and balanced, contemporary view, see G. Martel (ed.), *The Times and Appeasement: The Journals of A. L. Kennedy, 1932–1939* (Cambridge, 2000), esp. 29–30, 40–1, 48, 51–3, 92–5, 101, 126, 142–3, 167–73, 205–9, 255–7, 274–5, and 284–6.

[19] Cited in M. Ignatieff, *Isaiah Berlin: A Life* (London, 1998), 61: 'Berlin had been plucked from Jewish obscurity and elected to what was then the most select club in English life, a college where cabinet ministers, editors of *The Times* and the leading intellectual figures of the day mingled on equal terms.' Shades of Brodribb!

[20] G. Rees, *A Chapter of Accidents* (London, 1972), 104–5. This event is still more fulsomely described in Jenny Rees, *Looking for Mr Nobody: The Secret Life of Goronwy Rees* (London, 1994), 47–8.

[21] A. L. Rowse, *A Cornishman at Oxford* (London, 1965), 240ff.

[22] J. S. G. Simmons, 'All Souls College: A Chronological List of Fellows, 1438–1988, with Additional Lists, Tables and an Index', unpublished, 90. They were T. B. Garnier, Esq. of Balliol and W. H. Gladstone and C. H. Roberts, both of Christ Church. Garnier was elected. For some of the reasons why, see S. J. D. Green, ' "The Fremantle Affair" and the Destruction of the *Ancien Régime* in All Souls, 1857–1864', in idem and Peregrine Horden (eds), *All Souls under the Ancien Régime: Politics, Learning, and the Arts, c.1600–1850* (Oxford, 2007), esp. 369–72.

[23] Green, ' "The Fremantle Affair" ', *passim*; also Wooldridge, this volume.

about the 'legends' that 'still lingered' around the society at the time of his election in 1896. These alluded to fellowships being bestowed upon those '*bene nati, bene vestiti, mediocriter docti*'; similarly, of success in the examination best guaranteed by 'disposing of the [cherry] stones . . . at dinner . . . like a gentleman'.[24] However 'little justified' in practice, such stories remained the stuff of ordinary Oxford conversation in 1932. To some degree, they still do.[25]

More strikingly still, those rare birds that Brodribb slavishly spotted – superior specimens such as Amery himself – were products of a selective system that, though it had been substantially purified during the 1880s, was by then in general eclipse. The truly creative moment for the 'prize fellowship' system in Oxford had been the third quarter of the nineteenth century. In the wake of the University Commission of 1877–81, the institution fell increasingly into abeyance.[26] Even the ideal that had once inspired it came to seem increasingly disreputable.[27] Everywhere, that is, except All Souls: there, it achieved both a unique and a belated success. It also became something of a paradoxical prize. Ostensibly a fellowship awarded 'after examination in . . . subjects connected with the studies of Law and History', it was valued less as a reward for excellent performance in those specialized studies than as the mark bestowed on those who had passed the ultimate 'test of all-round ability'.[28] Perhaps as a result, it generally preferred men more likely to govern British outposts of the globe than to push back the frontiers of mankind's collective ignorance. These gilded youths – prizemen and pioneers – grew up to become Brodribb's 'Mallardians'. His guileless panegyric described them at the climax of their careers. It also depicted the type in what proved to be the twilight of its prestige. To understand how they got there, it is necessary first to imagine them at the moment when they first began to stalk the world. This happened during the golden age of the Prize

[24] The Rt Hon. L. S. Amery, C. H., *My Political Life*, 3 vols (London, 1953–5), i. 55; cf. D. Faber, *Speaking for England: Leo, Julian and John Amery – The Tragedy of a Political Family* (London, 2005), 25.

[25] For a celebration thereof, see L. Gregoriadis and S. O'Neill, 'Mallard Leads Oxford Fellows on a Merry Dance', *Daily Telegraph*, 1 Jan. 2001; for the opposite view, consult R. Stevens, 'Eviscerating Oxford', *The Spectator*, 14 July 2001, 22. Some sense of the surviving myths, clunkily captured, can be found in J. Thynne, 'Life at All Sins by the Man from All Souls', *The Independent*, 27 Mar. 2006. This article celebrated the appointment of Matthew d'Ancona, Quondam Fellow of All Souls, to the editorship of *The Spectator* that year.

[26] For an overview, see C. Harvie, 'From the Cleveland Commission to Statutes of 1882', in M. G. Brock and M. C. Curthoys (eds), *Hist. Univ. Oxf.*, vii, 2, ch. 2. For the specific effects, see A. J. Engel, *From Clergyman to Don: The Rise of the Academic Profession in Nineteenth-Century Oxford* (Oxford, 1983), 158–67, 175, 194, 218, and esp. 257–62.

[27] Engel, *From Clergyman to Don*, 100 and 174; W. R. Ward, *Victorian Oxford* (London, 1965), 299ff. Both, in this context, cite Ch. Ch., Salisbury Mss., Petition of Resident Member of Congregation to Lord Salisbury, 17 Mar. 1875. For a bit of contemporary flavour, see Anon., 'Young Oxford in 1870', *Belgravia: A London Magazine*, 2nd series, ii, no. 8 (1870), 44ff.

[28] Lord Curzon of Kedleston, *Principles and Methods of University Reform: Being a Letter Addressed to the University of Oxford* (Oxford, 1909), 97.

Fellows at All Souls. That began in the years immediately after Selborne's seminal report. It lasted little longer than the outbreak of the First World War.[29]

I

That, anyway, was how *they* remembered it. Charles Oman depicted Chichele's fabled society during the last twenty years of Queen Victoria's reign in a positively glowing hue:

> It is hard to exaggerate the splendid spirit of College patriotism that prevailed [between] 1880 and 1900, or the pride of the lucky juniors who found themselves absorbed into this very abnormal society.[30]

These were the fond reminiscences of an old man. Still, they reflected a broader truth. This was indeed a very good time to be a Prize Fellow of All Souls. In part, that was simply because of the increasing scarcity of prize fellowships in late Victorian Oxford. So-called 'ordinary fellowships' did not entirely disappear after Selborne. But they were progressively marginalized in its wake. New College specifically established a new class of 'tutorial fellows', created for the purpose of college teaching.[31] Magdalen's new statutes explicitly directed all 'future system[s] of examination' to take cognisance of 'every branch of knowledge recognised . . . in the University'; similarly, to make due allowance for the 'specific requirements of the College for tutorial purposes'.[32] Those for Merton offered the possibility of re-election, in effect tenure, only to Professorial Fellows, College Officers, and those 'appointed . . . Lecturer[s] of the College'.[33]

These actions represented particular responses to a more general need. Later nineteenth-century Oxford became, to a degree that it had never been before, a teaching university. That meant the dissemination of secular learning to ever greater numbers of world-destined laymen. With this change came a still broader alteration of attitude. Tutorial instruction increasingly constituted not simply the essential fact of local life, but also its principal justification.[34] After Selborne,

---

[29] For a general account, see J. S. G. Simmons, 'All Souls', in Brock and Curthoys *Hist. Univ. Oxf.*, vii, 2, ch. 8.

[30] C. Oman, *Memories of Victorian Oxford and of Some Early Years* (London, 1941), ch. 10, esp. p. 116.

[31] *Parliamentary Papers [PP]*, 1882, *Accounts and Papers [AP]*, vol. 51, 439–40 (135–6), 'Statutes of the College of Saint Mary of Winchester in Oxford, Commonly Called New College', II, clauses 1 and 6–11.

[32] *PP*, 1882, *AP*, vol. 51, 481–94 (105–110), 'Statutes of Magdalen College, Oxford', IV, clauses 6 and 18.

[33] *PP*, 1882, *AP*, vol. 51, 424–8 (120–4), 'Statutes of Merton College, Oxford', III, clauses 3 and 8.

[34] Engel, *From Clergyman to Don*, ch. 6, appendices 1 and 3. For example, see J. W. Mackail, *James Leigh Strachan-Davidson, Master of Balliol: A Memoir* (Oxford, 1925), 31–52; also M. F. Smith, *Arthur Lionel Smith, Master of Balliol: A Biography and Some Reminiscences by His Wife* (London, 1928).

even *The Spectator* commended the passing of so-called 'idle fellowships' in the university.[35] Once set in regulatory stone, this process proved irresistible. Ordinary fellowships were not so much explicitly abolished as subtly altered at every available opportunity. More and more, they were offered only on the promise of 'the performance of University...related...work'.[36] The long-term effect was that by 1907, of 315 Fellows associated with Oxford colleges, perhaps 220, or some 70 per cent, were either accredited as collegiate staff, or judged to be engaged in 'university or college work'.[37] Put another way: by that date over one-third of all these remaining so-called 'unencumbered fellowships' within the University were based at All Souls.[38] There, they remained profoundly unencumbered, throughout this period. Not until 1911 were post-probationer fellows required even to identify a putative subject for research during the remaining six years of their stay.[39] In the years that followed, many managed little more than that. Small wonder that for some in Oxford – especially amongst those outside Chichele's hallowed walls – general distaste for the prize system and its products had, by the outbreak of the First World War, 'all but resolve[d] itself into criticism of [a] single institution'.[40] By contrast, young men attracted by its allure now looked in just one direction to satisfy their selfish cravings.[41]

In truth, the road to All Souls had never proved an easy path. Now the College made the path to its pleasures more onerous still. This was significant too. No small part of the modern standing of All Souls lay in just how much harder the way to its favours became during the last quarter of the nineteenth century. To some extent, this development simply reflected the inexorable laws of supply and demand. As the availability of ordinary fellowships diminished elsewhere, so the attractiveness of those on offer at All Souls correspondingly increased. For all that, the speed of such change may have been slower than some of the Mallards subsequently remembered. The average number of candidates for the examination rose from just over twelve in the period 1864 to 1881, to around sixteen during the years of Anson's wardenship.[42] One reason that it did not rise higher was that the test itself became demonstrably tougher. The actual content of the examination changed relatively little after 1869.[43] Allowances were made for the formal division of the previously joint School of Law and History

[35] Anon., 'Oxford after the Commission', *The Spectator*, no. 2803 (18 Mar. 1882), 352–3.
[36] Curzon, *Principles and Methods*, 95.
[37] Ibid., 95–6. For a modern analysis, see Engel, *From Clergyman to Don*, 257–62, and Appendix 3.
[38] Author's calculations; for comment, see Engel, *From Clergyman to Don*, 261–2.
[39] All Souls College archives, 'Minute Book, 1905–1914', 5 June 1911, 85. For other examples and a relevant discussion, see Engel, *From Clergyman to Don*, 260–1.
[40] Curzon, *Principles and Methods*, 97.
[41] That said, only one College, Brasenose, actually *abolished* prize fellowships, so called, prior to 1914. See Engel, *From Clergyman to Don*, 260–1, for a useful discussion.
[42] Author's calculation; Simmons, 'Chronological List of Fellows', 'Chronological Lists of Candidates, 1698–1914', 90–4.
[43] 'Minute Book, 1858–1875', 23 Oct. 1869, 165. This established the so-called 'English Essay' paper, later, better known as the 'Essay Question'.

throughout the university in 1872. But the initial alterations were both grudging and minimal. From 1874, three papers were set in both Law and History. Yet for long after, examinees were required to offer a minimum of two in each. A third paper was deemed optional.[44] Only from 1884 did the college deign to distinguish between its Law and History *candidates*.[45] Only after 1895 was it finally established that a full range of 'ancient' questions would be set in all the relevant History papers.[46] The General Paper, the English Essay, and the translation exercise continued largely as before.[47] So too did the way in which the ancient examination as a whole, and also each part of the exercise, was marked.[48]

What really changed was prevailing understanding of the appropriate system for the assessment of this award. College radicals fought during the 1860s to eliminate all extraneous, qualitative, judgements from the published order of merit in elections at All Souls. They succeeded. This transformed the significance of the ancient examination itself out of all previous recognition. Once little more than the preliminary process – in effect, a pass/fail hurdle – to a competition governed more by connection and manners, peculiarly examined *merit* became the sole criterion of selection.[49] Yet even, in fact especially, in the wake of the so-called 'Fremantle Affair' such, specifically academic, judgement still retained a simple, cardinal, principle in its understanding of such 'merit'. Put simply, the college continued to elect what it judged to be the most worthy candidates who presented themselves each year to its fellowship. It never entertained the possibility that, in any given year, even the best of these might not meet an impersonally defined intellectual 'standard' for a fellowship. This institutional straitjacket held sway for so long as the College considered itself legally bound to fill all available vacancies in its fellowship: in effect, to make one or more elections regardless of the overall quality of the candidates.[50] There was nothing odd about this. That was the norm in mid-Victorian Oxford. Even with the advent of so-called 'prize fellowships', most colleges continued to observe this, ancient, convention. At a time when there were often twice as many candidates seeking

---

[44] Ibid., 27, Oct. 1874, 345.

[45] Simmons, 'Chronological List of Fellows', 56.

[46] 'Minute Book, 1888–1905', 4 June 1895, 156–8.

[47] Ibid. The specific rubric actually read:

5. That six hours shall be allowed for the composition of the essay.

6. That two general papers shall be set: that one general paper should consist of passages for translation, shorter and more numerous than heretofore, on which candidates should be invited to write notes or *short* essays arising out of the passages set.

No 'single word' was set in 'English Essay' until 1887 and the practice did not become annual until 1932. It was abolished in 2010.

[48] That is, they were marked separately and given equal weight. The assistant examiners only ever came to a view about a candidate's *overall* performance. For the significance of this, see Green, 'The "Fremantle Affair"', 369–71.

[49] See Wooldridge, this volume.

[50] Simmons, 'Chronological List of Fellows', 'Chronological List of Candidates', 53–4 and 89. Thus, there were no elections in College in 1856 and 1861; but this on the grounds that there was 'no vacancy' in the fellowship for either of those years.

fellowships as men boasting 'firsts' in schools, it might even be argued to have made much sense.[51] But in the years leading up to Selborne, some of the younger fellows began to urge the College surreptitiously to exploit the financial uncertainties of its position in order – so the euphemism had it – to 'postpone' such annual elections, if only candidates that it deemed of insufficient merit presented themselves around November time. So considerable a legal innovation required explicit explanation, indeed justification. This, the Young Turks suggested, should henceforth take the form of 'written statements'. These would be forwarded by the assistant examiners, in addition to their numerical marks, outlining 'their opinions as to the general merits of such candidates as they may think it desirable to report on specifically'.[52]

This, parallel, mechanism was first deployed to real purpose in 1876. That year, the examiners' report established a customary order of merit. But it was accompanied by another document. It set out

their opinion... [that] only one of the candidates showed... sufficient excellence to entitle him to a fellowship for his intellectual qualifications... therefore [they] recommend[ed] that only one of the vacant fellowships should be filled.[53]

The recommendation was unprecedented. To afford it proper statutory cover, Compton and Stanford proposed that 'leave be given to Sir William Anson to [table] a resolution affecting the filling up of one of the vacant fellowships'. Leave was duly granted. Thus prompted, Anson advised 'that the election to one of the fellowships now vacant be postponed until... 1877'. The motion was carried by twenty votes to five.[54] Only one election – that of Raleigh – was made. With it, the notion of 'fellowship standard' was invented.[55] This became the norm after Selborne. It still is. To be sure, the new convention worked within certain limits. At All Souls as elsewhere, the revised statutes laid down maximum and minimum provisions for the allocation of fellowships from corporate revenues.[56] But within those limits, they permitted the College – along with other Oxford societies – considerable room for manoeuvre. This the College gratefully

[51] See *The Oxford University Calendar, 1850* (Oxford, 1850), 117ff. and 246ff. This publication lists all classifications in the Lit. Hum. and Maths and Physics Schools for 1840–49. They show that in no year during that decade (save 1846, p. 19), were more than eleven 'firsts' awarded in the Lit. Hum. School. In no year were more than eight 'firsts' awarded in Maths and Physics. Yet Oxford boasted more than 500 fellowships in 1850. Terminations through resignation on receiving a living, or marriage or whatever, were common. Most colleges had statutory limits to their fellowships. This meant the fellowships were sometimes vacant. That was true of four colleges (Merton, Exeter, St John's, and Pembroke) in 1850. But the emphasis was then firmly on filling fellowships with 'suitable persons'. For these reasons, purely academic standards were not, and could not have been, especially high. For the most subtle contemporary account of all of this, see M. Pattison, *Memoirs*, ed. J. Manton (Fontwell, 1969), 74–5, 77–8, 156–7, and 182–4. See also H. S. Jones, *Intellect and Character in Victorian England: Mark Pattison and the Invention of the Don* (Cambridge, 2007), 19–24.
[52] 'Minute Book, 1858–1873', 17 Dec. 1873, 289–91.
[53] 'Minute Book, 1875–1888', 3 Nov. 1876, 52–3.
[54] Ibid.
[55] Ibid.
[56] *PP*, 1882, *AP*, vol. 51, 305–12 (1–8), 'Statutes of All Souls College, Oxford', ix, *passim*.

accepted. All Souls made no election in 1882 and 1894; and only one in 1878, 1880, 1885, 1887, 1888, 1892, and 1893. From 1895, two elections became the norm, with 1913 the only exception. But there was no instance of three elections to Prize Fellowships until after the First World War.[57]

That made the 'prize' that was embodied in an All Souls fellowship more valuable still. But there was something else. Its fellowships were awarded in either History or Law. Had they been realistically open only to graduates of those schools, it is inconceivable that they would have achieved the standing that marked Brodribb's Mallardians. The era between the Selborne and Asquith Commissions coincided with 'the zenith of Greats'.[58] Never before (or since) had Oxford's classical and philosophical training boasted such intellectual prestige.[59] This was not a matter of numbers. The School of Modern History graduated more men (and women) than that of *Literae Humaniores* no later than the turn of the twentieth century. By 1914, the History and Law Schools taken together accounted for nearly twice the number of 'Greats' men.[60] It was a question of quality. Post-reform Oxford may have ostensibly dedicated itself to the pursuit of modern studies.[61] For all that, the new regulations of 1853 also encouraged the emergence of a uniquely wide-ranging course in Literae Humaniores. This encompassed both ancient history and contemporary philosophy, even rudimentary politics and economics.[62] It was a demanding and comprehensive offering, and it unfailingly attracted the majority of the most able

[57] In 1919, partly in order to make up for the war-time deaths (there were no elections between 1915 and 1918), the College elected three 'History' fellows, namely Lionel Abel-Smith, Humphrey Sumner, and Llewellyn Woodward; also one 'Law' fellow, Geoffrey Faber. In 1920, it elected two 'History' Fellows, Reginald Harris and Dermot Morrah, plus one 'Law Fellow', Eric Beckett. Thereafter the convention reverted back to the pre-war norm, until 1932. See Simmons, 'Chronological List of Fellows', 59.

[58] W. H. Walsh, 'The Zenith of Greats', in Brock and Curthoys (eds), *Hist. Univ. Oxf.*, vii, 2, ch. 11.

[59] Ibid., 317ff. See also A. N. Whitehead, *Essays in Science and Philosophy* (London, 1948), 33ff. and H. Lloyd-Jones, *Blood for the Ghosts: Classical Influences in the Nineteenth and Twentieth Century* (London, 1982), ch. 1. For a subsequent indictment, consult Rees, *A Chapter of Accidents*, 77ff.

[60] See the *Oxford University Calendar, 1915* (1915), 212–16, for details. This same source also reveals that Modern History overtook Literae Humaniores as the most popular school for 'finals' as early as 1901; see ibid., 132–5.

[61] *PP,* 1852 (1482), vol. 22, *Royal Commission Appointed to Inquire into the State, Discipline, Studies and Revenues of the Universities of Oxford and Cambridge, and of the Colleges and Halls Therein*; see especially the section on 'Studies' and 'Proposed Improvements'. For some of the early results, consult the remarks made in P. Gordon (ed.), *The Political Diaries of the Fourth Earl of Carnarvon, 1857–1890: Colonial Secretary and Lord Lieutenant of Ireland* (London, 2009), 171, entry for 29 Nov. 1867 (Oxford): 'The educational system . . . seems to have become inverted since my day. Then classical authors . . . formed the basis of instruction and were illustrated by Christian writers: now modern . . . writers . . . are the textbooks . . . illustrated by heathen writings'. Carnarvon may have been old-fashioned. He was not a fool. He had taken a 'first' in 'Greats' in 1852 and remained a lifelong devotee of the classics. Some of the broader effects can be found in C. Harvie, *The Lights of Liberalism: University Liberals and the Challenge of Democracy, 1860–1886* (London, 1976), chs 1–3.

[62] Walsh, 'The Zenith of Greats', 313ff.; for another perspective, see N. Chester, *Economics, Politics and Social Studies in Oxford, 1900–1985* (Basingstoke, 1988), 1–2.

students in pre-war Oxford.[63] It may have continued to do so right up to 1945, even beyond.[64]

The very breadth of this course prepared its more intelligent recipients uniquely well for a test ostensibly set beyond their grasp. Local developments compounded their advantage. Resistance to the hectoring demands of first the joint and then the separate modern Schools ensured that the All Souls examination had been, from the first, notably eclectic in scope.[65] It remained so, even in the face of continual demands to the contrary.[66] An experiment, effectively to reserve fellowships, by attaching 'special weight' to 'proficiency in law' one year (1887) and then in history the next (1888), was quickly abandoned. Indeed, it was reversed on the revealing grounds that it had 'adversely affected' both the quantity and quality of candidates.[67] Warden Anson then suggested that a

Committee be appointed to report . . . on the character of the question and the arrangement of papers set in the Fellowship Examination, with a view to the better encouragement of postgraduate study of Law and History.

This, similarly, came to nothing.[68] For once, the great man was out-manoeuvred. Thenceforth, the examination was still nominally split between law and history. But the history prize was explicitly kept open to 'Greats' men. Questions in ancient history were set in every 'relevant' paper. Candidates were merely 'warned that some modern history questions should be attempted'. Moreover, the papers as a whole – law fellowships included – were constructed so as to include questions 'the answers to which would require a knowledge of both ancient and modern history'.[69] Consequently, 'Greats' men often sat for the 'Law' fellowships too. The results spoke for themselves: of sixty-three elections to the Prize Fellowship between 1878 and 1914, more than two-thirds, forty-three, were of men who had taken their sole or first degree in *Literae Humaniores*. A further eight first grounded themselves in Classical Moderations before moving on to other academic pastures. Just nine succeeded during those years with a degree in modern history alone. Only one was similarly successful in Jurisprudence. He was Canadian.[70] The numbers were made up by a mathematician with a second degree in Law (Maguire, 1879) and the wholly extraordinary Somervell. He took a 'first' in

[63] See the *Oxford University Calendar, 1915*, 132–85. This source reveals that between 1901 and 1910 no fewer than fifty-eight 'Greats' men were elected to 'examination' and/or 'prize' fellowships throughout the university; just fourteen 'Modern Historians' and seven out of Jurisprudence. See Walsh, 'The Zenith of Greats', *passim* for a more general discussion.

[64] Green, 'The "Fremantle Affair" ', 369–71.

[65] Ibid., 362ff.

[66] 'Minute Book, 1875–1888', 31 May 1887, 332–6.

[67] 'Minute Book, 1888–1905', 14 May 1895, 505–6.

[68] 'Minute Book, 1888–1905', 7 Mar. 1895, 103–4.

[69] Ibid., 14 May 1895, 105–6.

[70] Simmons, 'Chronological List of Fellows', 56–9. The exception was J. G. Archibald, of McGill and New College, in 1908.

Chemistry in 1911. He won a Law fellowship in 1912. No one else has achieved quite such a remarkable intellectual self-transformation, so quickly, since.[71]

But were these really the most brilliant men of their generation? Definitely, Lord Copper![72] Let us ignore the question of the missing sciences.[73] A number of qualifications are still advisable. First, it is important to recall that whilst the quantity and quality of other 'ordinary' fellowships were fast diminishing elsewhere in Oxford, the species was far from extinct by 1914. Many of the very best men simply chose to go elsewhere. Some did so because they genuinely did not have a high regard for All Souls. Think of Asquith senior.[74] Other obvious academic stars just never countenanced the possibility. This seems to have been true of Milner.[75] Then there were those who were committed to their undergraduate colleges. Such men often wished to remain where they first belonged. Ironically, of no one was this more true than Oman. He never forgave New College's negligence in this respect.[76] In a different way, specialists in non-college subjects sometimes rated their chances more highly at Magdalen or Christ Church. These societies rotated their fellowships and studentships by subject, according to a regular cycle.[77] Finally, there was the simple matter of timing. Examinations at Merton were set in September; those at All Souls in October. That did for a few.[78]

[71] Simmons, 'Chronological List of Fellows', 59; Cecil Northcott, 'Somervell, Donald Brierley, Baron Somervell of Harrow', *ODNB*, esp. p. 600.

[72] E. Waugh, *Scoop: A Novel about Journalists* (Harmondsworth, 1977, first published 1938), 14. Lord Copper (after Lord Beaverbrook) was the (lightly) fictionalized owner-editor of the *Daily Beast*: Mr Salter, his foreign editor. As Waugh continued: 'Mr Salter's side of the conversation was limited to expressions of assent. When Lord Copper was right he said, "Definitely, Lord Copper," when he was wrong, "Up to a point" '. Later passages make it clear that enthusiastic assent from Mr Salter required only the most minimal degree of accuracy on Lord Copper's part.

[73] For informed discussions of their pre-war fate, see K. C. Hannabuss, 'Mathematics'; J. Howarth, '"Oxford for the Arts": The Natural Sciences, 1880–1914'; and W. R. Chapman, 'The Pitt Rivers Collection', in Brock and Curthoys, *Hist. Univ. Oxf.*, vii, 2, chs 19–21.

[74] Herbert Henry Asquith, First Earl of Oxford and Asquith (1852–1928): educated at City of London School and Balliol College, Oxford; Classical Scholar; taught by Jowett and Green; 'firsts' in classical moderations (1872) and Literae Humaniores (1874); *proxime accessit* for the Hertford (1872) and Ireland (1874) scholarships; fellow of Balliol, 1874–1882; subsequently barrister and politician; Home Secretary, 1892–5; Chancellor of the Exchequer, 1905–8; Prime Minister, 1908–16.

[75] Alfred Milner, Viscount Milner of St James's and Capetown, KG, GCB, GCMG (1854–1925), classical scholar at Balliol, taught by Jowett and Green; 'firsts' in 'Classical Moderations' (1874) and 'Greats' (1875); Hertford Scholar (1874), Craven Scholar (1877), Eldon and Derby Scholar (1878), fellow of New College, 1877–84; subsequently barrister and politician. See John Marlowe, *Milner: Apostle of Empire* (London, 1976). See also Howard, this volume.

[76] Oman, *Memories*, 109. There, Oman pointed to 'liberal ... modernist' political prejudices amongst the fellowship as the cause for the exclusion (as a 'Conservative ... Churchman ... of rather combative tendencies').

[77] M. D'Ancona, L. W. B. Brockliss, R. Darvall-Smith, and A. Hegaty, '"Everyone of us is a Magdalen Man": The College, 1854–1928', in Brockliss (ed.), *Magdalen College, Oxford: A History* (Oxford, 2008), ch. 5, esp. pp. 418–39; E. G. W. Bill and J. F. A. Mason, *Christ Church and Reform, 1850–1867* (Oxford, 1970), ch. 6.

[78] Possibly including F. E. Smith, later Lord Chancellor and First Earl of Birkenhead, Fellow of Merton, 1896–1899. See J. Campbell, *F. E. Smith, First Earl of Birkenhead* (London, 1983), 66–9.

What can be concluded is that the All Souls fellowship examination was a general test. It invariably rewarded those of general intellectual attainments. We cannot be entirely sure what this actually amounted to. Examiners' reports survive back only as far as 1933.[79] But analysis of the papers themselves, and of arguments about those papers which raged in the College throughout the 1890s, allows for some sort of educated guess. It seems likely that success in the specialist papers was best secured through demonstrated breadth of learning and power of pertinent comparison. True, candidates answering questions in English Law were specifically instructed to 'cite... decided cases' in their answers, from 1884 onwards. But those in History were discouraged from regurgitating large amounts of arcane knowledge in their answers.[80] In the same way, general examinees were invited to roam freely around what for many of them would have been the largely untaught disciplines of political science, political economy, the history of literature, the history of art, and even languages.[81] It must be reasonable to conclude that examiners were credited with a certain ability to do the same. Beyond doubt, the English Essay was accorded a central role in the proceedings. Six hours were permitted for its composition after 1895, a luxury perhaps wisely reduced to just four, in 1897.[82] The kind of range, polish, and even sparkle that this sort of challenge demanded should not be underestimated. It was certainly beyond the compass of many distinguished scholars. Hence the otherwise disturbing roll-call of subsequently famous historians who sat unsuccessfully for the Prize Fellowship. It includes most of the leading representatives of the Oxford-educated branch of the English historical profession during the first half of the twentieth century. These include: Tout, Pollard, Ensor, Powicke, Stenton, Namier, Galbraith, Edwards, and Jolliffe.[83] Compare that list with the nine who were elected as modern historians, during this period: Henson, Knox,

---

[79] They also remain under a one-hundred-year curfew to researchers (author's information). See, however, the remarks (perhaps candid, perhaps flippant) made by the Subwarden to a recently successful candidate in R. Knox, *Patrick Shaw-Stewart* (London, 1920), 75: 'the form of my papers was better than the matter'. These, perhaps, offer some clues as to what was generally sought.

[80] All Souls College archives, 'Examination Paper for fellowships in All Souls College, 1881–1890', Law I, for 1884, 1.

[81] Ibid., *passim*.

[82] 'Minute Book, 1888–1905', 23 Oct. 1897, p. 145.

[83] T. F. Tout (1855–1929): failed candidate, 1878; Professor of History, Owens College and the University of Manchester, 1890–1926. A. F. Pollard (1869–1948): failed candidate, 1892; Professor of Constitutional History in the University of London, 1903–24. R. K. Ensor (1877–1958): failed candidate 1901: journalist; Senior Research Fellow of Corpus Christi College, Oxford, 1937–46. F. M. Powicke (1879–1963): failed candidate, 1903; Professor of History, University of Oxford, 1928–47. F. M. Stenton (1880–1967): failed candidate, 1902; Professor of History, University of Reading, 1912–46. L. B. Namier (1888–1960): failed candidate, 1911; Professor of History, University of Manchester, 1931–53. V. H. Galbraith (1889–1976): failed candidate, 1914; Professor of History, University of Edinburgh, 1937–44; Director of the Institute of Historical Research, 1944–7; Regius Professor of Modern History at Oxford, 1947–57. J. G. Edwards (1891–1976): failed candidate, 1914; Director of the Institute of Historical Research and Professor of History in the University of London, 1948–60. J. E. A. Jolliffe (1891–1964): failed candidate, 1914; tutor then fellow of Keble College, Oxford, 1919–54.

Trench, Diblee, Brand, Wood, Feiling, Bell, and Williams. Good reasons could be furnished to suggest why the latter should have been preferred to the former. They will surely take little cognisance of any argument about peculiarly academic potential.[84]

One final observation: this was a College examination and the College judged as it saw fit. Opinion within All Souls had long insisted that the 1857 ordinance, specifically its instruction that eligible candidates should have secured either a 'first' in Schools, or a University Prize, was unduly restricting.[85] After 1881, the College effectively ignored it. Over the next thirty years, it elected nine men who had previously been awarded only a 'second' in finals.[86] Some of these decisions may subsequently seem difficult to justify. A few provoked astonishment, even at the time. Raymond Asquith was especially scathing that Philip Baker, with 'two seconds... the brain of a schoolboy – and an Harrovian at that', should have been preferred to John Buchan, in 1899.[87] It is difficult at the distance of a century to disagree. But this otherwise benighted category also included a handful of the most intellectually creative men to emerge out of late Victorian Oxford. They included Ker, Curzon, and Young.[88] Perhaps a different set of examiners, charged with a different test to which they applied different criteria, got the judgement right in these instances.[89]

What of the beneficiaries themselves? It should come as no surprise to learn that they were invariably very young men. The average age of those elected up to 1914 was just a fraction over 23 years. This was, interestingly, a full year *younger*

---

[84] H. H. Henson (1863–1947): elected 1884; turned down the Regius Chair of Ecclesiastical History in Oxford. E. F. V. Knox: elected 1886. F. H. Trench (1865–1923): elected, 1889; civil servant and notable poet; his *Ode from Italy in Time of War* (London, 1915) became quite famous. G. B. Diblee: elected 1890. R. H. Brand (1878–1963): elected 1901; see this volume, ch. 4. Edward Wood (1881–1959): elected 1904; Viceroy of India, 1926–9; Foreign Secretary, 1938–1940; British Ambassador to Washington, 1940–6. Sir K. Feiling (1884–1977): elected 1906; Chichele Professor of Modern History, Oxford, 1946–50. Kenneth Bell: elected 1901; later Fellow of Balliol. L. F. R. Williams: elected 1914.

[85] For the reasons behind its initial imposition, and the College's response, see Green, 'The "Fremantle Affair"', 349–55.

[86] Simmons, 'Chronological List of Fellows', 55–9. They were: Curzon (1883), Perry (1896), Cunliffe (1898), Baker (1899), Gwyer (1902), Barrington-Ward (1904), Young (1905), Archibald (1958), Radcliffe (1916).

[87] J. Jolliffe (ed.), *Raymond Asquith: Life and Letters* (London, 1980), 62: Asquith to H. H. Asquith, 12 Nov. 1899. Interestingly, young Asquith failed in his bid to become a fellow of Merton in 1901, but succeeded at All Souls in 1902.

[88] It is, perhaps, worth noting that in each case the candidate had secured a 'first' in Classical Moderations before succumbing to a 'second' in 'Greats': Ker, in 1879, Curzon in 1883, and Young in 1905. The compulsory philosophical element in Greats did for a number of otherwise gifted historians in this respect. Most famously of all, inattention to *both* ancient history and philosophy accounted for A. E. Housman's spectacular failure at this level. See S. J. Heyworth, 'Housman and Properties', in D. J. Butterfield and C. A. Stray (eds), *A. E. Housman: Classical Scholar* (London, 2009), ch. 1, esp. p. 26, n. 2.

[89] Though see the remarks by A. L. Rowse, 'All Souls (1945)', in idem, *The English Past: Evocation of Persons and Places* (London, 1951), 1–5, at 6.

than the average age of the candidates.[90] Only two men, Bain (1889) and Liddell (1891), were elected when as old as 26; only two more, Brierley (1906) and Radcliffe (1910), at 25. Yet very nearly 20 per cent of the candidates, so far as can be judged, were aged 25 or over.[91] But if the system was brutal to the passing years, it was relatively kind to youthful experience. Sixteen hopefuls, that is, more than a quarter of those preferred between 1878 and 1914, were successful at the second attempt.[92] Where did these happy few came from? They were all Oxford graduates, of course. But late Victorian Oxford was a place of many colleges in which only a few really mattered. Certainly, the All Souls fellowship proved something of a competitive sport for Balliol men. Jowett's Chichelian legacy was 26 Prize Fellows. This was fully 42 per cent of the total, down to 1914.[93] Such success reflected well on the intellectual standing of that august institution: for liberal education generally, and in 'Greats' particularly.[94] But it was perhaps also a function of Lady Devorguila's continuing poverty and/or meanness, at this time. Her society's statutes had provided for 'not less than 12 nor more than 16 fellowships... of [which] not fewer than seven nor more than 11 shall be... tutorial fellowships'.[95] That figure might be compared with contemporary provision for up to thirty-six fellowships at New College, also somewhere between thirty and forty at Magdalen, and nineteen to twenty-six at Merton.[96] In the event, even this much smaller quota was seldom actually filled at Balliol. There were never more than fourteen fellows on the foundation during the whole period – and usually fewer. Indeed, Balliol only made twenty-eight fellowship elections in total between 1878 and 1914. Of these, the vast majority were for specific, teaching, positions.[97] *That* was the most important reason why the college passed on two dozen of its best and promoted fully 144 candidates, or around 20 per cent of those who put in for All Souls, prior to the outbreak of the First World War.[98] Seen in this way, 'effortless superiority' was more like the decent drapery in which enforced exile was artfully wrapped.[99]

[90] Author's calculations; see Simmons, 'Chronological List of Fellows', 55–9; also 'List of Candidates, 1873–1914'.

[91] Author's calculations; Simmons, 'Chronological List of Fellows', 55–9 and 90–4; 'List of Candidates, 1873–1914', 1–70.

[92] Author's calculations; Simmons, 'Chronological List of Fellows', 90–4.

[93] Author's calculations; Simmons, 'Chronological List of Fellows', 55–9; and for a subsequent commentary, Rowse, 'All Souls (1945)', 7.

[94] J. Jones, *Balliol College: A History, 1263–1939*, 2nd edn, revised (Oxford, 2005), chs 15 and 16; for some contemporary flavour, see Mackail, *James Leigh Strachan-Davidson*, 80ff., and (albeit of a great History tutor), Smith, *Arthur Lionel Smith*, chs 7, 12, and 15.

[95] *PP*, 1882, *AP*, vol. 51, 315–21 (11–17), III, clause 1.

[96] Ibid., 439–43 (135–9), III, clauses 1, 2, 6, and 13; 409–16 (105–112), IV, clauses 1 and 22 and VI, clause 1; finally, 424–8 (121–5), III, clauses 1 and 7.

[97] Jones, *Balliol College*, 329–30.

[98] Author's calculations; for the evidence, see Simmons, 'Chronological List of Fellows', 'List of Candidates', 90–4; also 'List of Candidates, 1873–1914', 1–70.

[99] Jones, *Balliol College*, 226, n. 4. Anon., 'Political Notes', *The Times*, 23 July 1908, 12: 'A dinner was given to the Prime Minister by Balliol men who are present members of the House [of Commons]...last night...[T]he Chairman proposed the health of the Prime Minister, said

Only a handful of other colleges even got so much as a look in. New College furnished seven 'prize fellows' during those years, Magdalen and Christ Church, six each. These four societies together accounted for nearly three-quarters of all those men elected between 1878 and 1914.[100] Yet curiously, they sponsored fewer than six in ten of all candidates. This discrepancy is best explained – at least to the extent that simply to state the fact is to understand the result – by the dismal performances of St John's, Lincoln, and Corpus men in the contest. These three colleges between them sponsored no fewer than fifty-eight, or around 15 per cent, of candidates during these years. They boasted not one single instance of success.[101] Three colleges effectively took no part in the proceedings: Worcester, with just four candidates; Pembroke, with three, and finally St Edmund Hall. Its sole failure, if that is how he should be described, was one J. M. S. Hunter. He was 28 years of age and unsuccessful in the 'history only' competition of 1888.[102]

More interesting was the social background of the successful. This was surprisingly broad. The decline in Chichele's ancient aristocratic associations continued apace after 1878. Perhaps as many as one-third of those elected from 1850 had been titled. Only seven of sixty-three from Anson's College were similarly privileged.[103] The domination of a very few schools similarly declined. Old Etonians constituted very nearly half of all those elected between 1864 and 1877, but barely one-fifth down to 1914.[104] The three great schools, that is, Eton plus Winchester and Harrow, accounted for two-thirds of all successes in the earlier era, but just one-third later on.[105] Extend the net to Rugby, Marlborough, and Westminster, and the relevant proportions fell from just over four-fifths to barely more than half, respectively.[106] This last figure may still seem high. If so, it is worth nothing that it was actually *lower*, as indeed was the corresponding fraction for the great schools, than the equivalent proportion for those Prize Fellows elected between 1919 and 1939.[107] Inconclusive as this

some newspapers had apparently discovered that what marked off Balliol men from others was their intellectual pre-eminence...Mr Asquith, in response, referring humorously to the Chairman's opening remarks, suggested that the bond which united them, if their critics were to be believed, might be a tranquil consciousness of effortless superiority.'

[100] Author's calculations; Simmons, 'Chronological List of Fellows', 55–9.
[101] Author's calculations; Simmons, 'Chronological List of Fellows', 'List of Candidates', 90–4; 'List of Candidates, 1873–1914', 1–70.
[102] Author's calculations; Simmons, 'Chronological List of Fellows', 'List of Candidates', 90–4; 'List of Candidates, 1873–1914', 1–70.
[103] Author's calculations; Simmons, 'Chronological List of Fellows', 53–9; for a discussion of this change, see the remarks in Green, 'The "Fremantle Affair"', at 355–62.
[104] Author's calculations; Simmons, 'Chronological List of Fellows', 55–9. For some background, see C. R. L. Fletcher, *Edmond Warre, DD, CB, CVO; Sometime Headmaster and Provost of Eton College* (London, 1922), chs 1–3 and 8–10. More recently, consult T. Card, *Eton Renewed: A History from 1860 to the Present Day* (London, 1994), chs 4–6.
[105] Author's calculations; Simmons, 'Chronological List of Fellows', 55–9.
[106] Ibid.
[107] Author's calculations; Simmons, 'Chronological List of Fellows', 59–62.

information is, it points to the intriguing possibility that the educational origins of the Prize Fellows were actually more wide-ranging during the age of Anson than they had been for at least a century previously, or were to be again, until well after the Second World War.[108]

To be sure, the so-called 'public schools' still predominated.[109] But this unremarkable conclusion conceals more than it reveals. Some amongst the Prize Fellows supposedly so advantaged were actually drawn from backgrounds better defined as barely more than 'respectable' by any other social criteria. Oman was the son of an indigo manufacturer in India who had sold up his business to return to what he had hoped would be a comfortable retirement in Cheltenham. Unfortunately, he lost everything in a damages award made against the shipping concern in which he had invested his savings. As a result, the young Charles attended Winchester only as a result of numerous scholarships.[110] John Simon gained his education at Fettes on a similar basis. His father, a Congregationalist Minister in Bath, could not otherwise have afforded the fees.[111] Others derived from stock so humble as to induce the necessity of – anyway, the desire for – concealment. G. M. Young, an old Pauline, reluctantly admitted to a father who was a Thames pilot. He revealed so little else about his immediate family circumstances that one of 'those who . . . knew him in later years found it difficult . . . to picture a congruous youth or childhood for [this] enigmatic figure'.[112]

A few triumphed in the face of genuinely daunting odds. Academic legend still has it that Leslie Rowse was the first young man from a working-class background to win a fellowship at All Souls. Perhaps this was so.[113] But only the most capacious definition of the bourgeoisie would include the boyhoods of Alexander Grant and Hensley Henson amongst its number. Consider Grant first. Born in Bolton on 5 September 1866, he attended Bank Street British School between 1870 and 1878: for the last two years only as a half-timer. He then managed to obtain a Thomason Exhibition, providing for three years' education plus an allowance for maintenance, at Manchester Grammar School. This was converted by distinguished achievement

[108] Author's calculations; Simmons, 'Chronological List of Fellows', 53ff.; Rowse, 'All Souls (1945)', 6–7.

[109] 'Public' as in private, i.e. fee-charging. The economic significance of the characteristic levels of fees, effectively excluding all but 5% of the population from *c*.1815 at the latest, is carefully brought out in T. J. H. Bishop, with the assistance of Rupert Wilkinson, *Winchester and the Public School Elite: A Statistical Analysis* (London, 1967), 84–6.

[110] Oman, *Memories*, 9–11 and 24–7.

[111] Viscount Simon, *Retrospect* (London, 1952), 24–5. See also Cretney, this volume.

[112] W. D. Hancock, 'Introduction', in G. M. Young, *Victorian Essays* (London, 1962), 1–12; J. Sparrow, 'Pietas Chicheleana', in P. Fraser (ed.), *Memorial Addresses of All Souls College, Oxford* (Oxford, 1989), ch. 6, at p. 37; with Mordaunt Crook, this volume.

[113] On which see especially A. L. Rowse, *A Cornish Childhood* (London, 1942), chs 1–32; also Rowse, *A Cornishman at Oxford*, ch. 7; largely corroborated in R. Ollard, *A Man of Contradictions: A Life of A. L. Rowse* (London, 1999), chs 2–5. Some of the subtleties of Rowse's background are perhaps better brought out in R. Payton, *A. L. Rowse and Cornwall: A Paradoxical Patriot* (Exeter, 2005), chs 1–3.

into Foundation and Langworthy Scholarships there three years later. These, in turn, helped him to secure the Lawson Gold Medal at School and a Postmastership at Merton. Then, after 'firsts' in Classical Moderations, 'Greats', and the Law, he won a Prize Fellowship at All Souls in 1890. Called to the bar in 1894, he ended his life as a Bencher and Treasurer of Inner Temple.[114]

Now consider the case of Henson. His background was not perhaps so much poor as deprived. His father, a moderately successful draper, intended all of his sons for trade. He also instructed them in Baptist theology. His suspicion of the sinfulness of the world was so extreme that he did not consent to send young Herbert Hensley to school at all until he had reached the age of fourteen. Even then, he allowed him only to attend the painfully inadequate Broadstairs Collegiate. The independent-minded young man ran away, disgusted at the philistinism of the headmaster and the inadequacy of his staff, two years later. To avoid going back to live with his disagreeable father, Henson applied through an agency for a teaching post. The (presumably desperate) headmaster of Brigg Grammar School in Lincolnshire hired him as an assistant. He was sixteen years old at the time. This may well have been an illegal undertaking, and that on both sides. But Mr Flower also discerned Henson's potential, encouraged him in his studies and, more remarkably still, persuaded old Thomas Henson to send his clearly gifted son to Oxford. The reluctant patriarch agreed on the grounds that the boy earn part of his keep, remain only for the minimum necessary period of three years, *and* be a non-collegiate student, or 'tosher'. This last provision was enforced to ensure that he avoided the otherwise distinct possibility of religious – still worse of irreligious – contamination. To some degree anyway, it worked. Henson chose to study modern history because he lacked the Greek necessary for 'Greats'. He got a 'first'. Elected at All Souls, in 1884, he continued to dabble in historical study for many years afterwards. Partially as a result, he was later offered the Regius Chair of Ecclesiastical History in Oxford.[115] He turned it down. Instead, he became Bishop of Durham at a time when that position was still of national significance.[116]

II

The importance of these stories is that they point to a vital dimension of the Prize Fellowship, as experienced by the Prize Fellows during the golden years. This was

---

[114] There is no biography. He rates no mention in the *ODNB*. But his was, nonetheless, a remarkable career. It can be followed, in outline, in Anon., *Who Was Who, 1941–1950* (London, 1967), 458. Grant died on 21 Mar. 1941.

[115] H. H. Henson, *Retrospect of an Unimportant Life*, vol. 1: *1863–1920* (London, 1942), 1 and 4, which offers only the sketchiest account of the events, perhaps understandably so. O. Chadwick, *Hensley Henson: A Study in the Friction between Church and State* (Oxford, 1983), chs 1 and 2, tells a fuller story.

[116] Henson, *Retrospect*, chs 4 and 5; Chadwick, *Henson*, ch. 11.

the unprecedented diversity in the origins of its beneficiaries. That profoundly altered its nature and purpose, anyway after 1878. The Prize Fellowship may once have been an Oxford plum reserved for the well-born and neatly turned out. It now emphatically ceased to be so. It became a mark of the clever and the polished; at least, to the degree that this kind of examination performance displayed such qualities. It may once have been intended for those heading towards the Church. Now it prepared men for the professions. But it did not train them for these vocations. Indeed, it did not train them for anything at all. The fellowship offered successful candidates income, lodging, and board. But it made effectively no demands of its charges. As a result, it became so flexible as almost to become self-defining. Even to the extent that it tried to stamp some part of its own authority on the Prize Fellows, it usually did so without ever attempting to bind their souls. For the most part, these remained remarkably outward-looking, even open-minded. Certainly, they were strikingly different from one another. It was not just that there were relatively few bona fide aristocrats amongst them. The Prize Fellowship drew little succour from contemporary intellectual cliques either. The Souls, that legendary menagerie of the self-consciously superior that twittered around the Tennant sisters from the mid-1880s, accounted for just one member of Anson's college: George Curzon.[117] More remarkably still, their literal and figurative progeny, the Coterie, later contributed just two more: Raymond Asquith and Patrick Shaw-Stuart.[118]

If the Prize Fellows were, for the most part, institutionally unconnected either to sophisticated or even fashionable society, they seldom withdrew into a brotherhood of the determinedly detached either. In this respect, they were noticeably *unlike* the Cambridge Apostles of the same generation. Once again, the differences are worth considering. That famous West Anglian society was a self-selecting body. Largely as a result, it derived its membership from an extremely narrow band of the educated classes. Over 60 per cent of its number between 1860 and 1914 attended Eton. A startling 92 per cent went on to Trinity, anyway up to the 1870s; Kings got a bit of a look in thereafter.[119] The Apostles also developed into a community explicitly dedicated not merely to the pursuit of intellectual

---

[117] Now most fully chronicled in A. Lambert, *Unquiet Souls: The India Summer of the British Aristocracy, 1880–1918* (London, 1984), part 1; see the list of Souls on pp. xv–xxi. The example of Curzon can be followed in the Earl of Ronaldshay, *The Life of Lord Curzon, Being the Authorised Biography of George Nathaniel, Marquis Curzon of Kedleston, K. G.*, vol. 1: *1859–1918* (London, 1928), ch. 10, esp. pp. 162–72; also K. Rose, *Superior Person: A Portrait of Curzon and his Circle in Late Victorian England* (London, 1969), 14, and D. Gilmour, *Curzon* (London, 1994), ch. 8.

[118] On which, see Lambert, *Unquiet Souls*, ch. 9; the list of the 'Coterie', on pp. xxi–xxiv. For details, consult J. Mackenzie, *Children of the Souls: A Tragedy of the First World War* (London, 1986), pt. 1. Some of the flavour can be gleaned from Knox, *Patrick Shaw-Stewart*, ch. 4; also M. Jebb, *Patrick Shaw-Stewart: An Edwardian Meteor* (London, 2010), 138ff.; finally, Jolliffe (ed.), *Raymond Asquith*, ch. 3.

[119] W. C. Lubenow, *The Cambridge Apostles, 1820–1914: Liberalism, Imagination, and Friendship in British Intellectual and Professional Life* (Cambridge, 1998), 102–12, and ch. 2 more generally; also P. Allen, *The Cambridge Apostles: The Early Years* (Cambridge, 1978), ch. 12.

excellence but to very specific ideals concerning personal friendship. That was why its members largely defined themselves against the world.[120] According to this understanding, *they* were what was real. *It* was merely phenomenal. Moreover: only in their reality was truth revealed and comradeship made possible. Outside was a world of delusions and instrumental relationships, respectively compromised by deception and ambition.[121] The Prize Fellows never made that kind of distinction. Nor, by extension, did they make such claims for themselves, or even of their mutual association. With few exceptions, they generally took themselves to be men of this world. Most, indeed, quite happily chose to make their way in it. That kind of ambition demanded a certain pragmatism. But it did not preclude the possibility of high ideals. It might even be suggested that it better sustained them.[122]

There was something else. Effectively divorced from the system of family networks that sustained the Souls, Prize Fellows developed virtually few if any of the hospitable institutions that generally marked out such peculiar social territory. Reciprocal entertainment was simply not required of, or by, them. Such socialization as ever thrived in All Souls extended little beyond the fellows' 'Sunday Walk', something of an institution before the Great War.[123] Fun and games accounted for even less. Some Prize Fellows were good athletes; Amery was perhaps something more than that. But specific – and certainly exclusive – amusements played a very minor part in communal life. Oman wistfully recalled some decent 'sport' after the annual bursar's dinner. This amounted to nothing much more than an *impromptu* steeplechase around the hall.[124] That was small beer compared to the elaborate charades, complex parodies, and even cruel diversions that kept the Souls amused on similar occasions.[125] In a different way, nothing in College life approached the intellectual intensity of the Apostles' Saturday evening essay. This was read out loud by a so-called 'moderator',

---

[120] Lubenow, *The Cambridge Apostles*, chs 1, 3, and 4; and more generally, see P. Levy, *Moore: G. E. Moore and the Cambridge Apostles* (London, 1979), Book 2.

[121] Best appreciated through the original sources. See, *inter alia*, L. Strachey, *The Really Interesting Question and Other Papers*, ed. P. Levy (London, 1972), pt. 2; L. Woolf, *Sowing: An Autobiography of the Years 1880 to 1904* (London, 1960), esp. 148–56; and, for a devastating auto-critique, J. M. Keynes, 'My Early Beliefs', in *The Collected Works of John Maynard Keynes*, vol. 10: *Essays in Biography* (London, 1972), ch. 39, 435–52, esp. 435–8, and 447–52.

[122] For what remains the best account of what that then consisted in, see H. H. Henson (ed.), *A Memoir of the Right Honourable Sir William Anson* (Oxford, 1920), ch. 3. The 'worldliness', even of the scholars amongst them, is nicely brought out in J. A. Hawgood, 'Charles Grant Robertson (1869–1948)', *University of Birmingham Historical Journal*, 1 (1948), 350–9, esp. 353.

[123] It seems to have been led during these years by W. R. Ker, anyway as revealed by (the then) Viscount Simon, in *Retrospect*, 39. For another account, see R. W. Chambers, 'W. P. Ker, 1855–1923', *Proceedings of the British Academy*, 11 (1924–5), 1–14, at 7.

[124] Oman, *Memories*, 129–30.

[125] A. James, First Earl of Balfour, *Chapters of Autobiography*, ed. Mrs E. Dugdale (London, 1930), 231–3; J. Ridley and C. Percy (eds), *The Letters of Arthur Balfour and Lady Eldon, 1885–1917* (London, 1992), 15–19 and 39–41. See p. 41, Balfour to Lady Eldon, 6 Oct. 1887: 'The Glen Party... Everyone in great form... playing Abstract and Concrete occupied most of the time'. No doubt this was captivating for the participants.

standing on the hearth-rug, before each of the assembled brethren took to their feet in an order chosen by lot and offered ingenious criticisms of its arguments.[126] There was no Chichelian equivalent. Finally, absolute candour in personal relations was never required of Anson's young men. 'Good manners' were generally deemed quite sufficient.[127]

Perhaps as a result, these Prize Fellows developed very little in the way of a collective ethos and almost nothing that amounted to a private language. Verbal games, nicknames, and words meaning something quite different from their ostensible definition, similarly arcane jargon, even a characteristic tone of voice, were critical to the very existence of the Souls.[128] Such conventions simultaneously kept them together and set them apart. The same was true, *mutatis mutandis*, of the Apostles.[129] Even such an otherwise worldly Soul as John Maynard Keynes unapologetically separated the 'real' from the 'phenomenal'. He also distinguished stumps, or philistines, from 'embryos', or potential 'apostles'. He was happy to identify the otherwise unremarkable chest in which the society kept its records as its 'Ark'. And he enjoyed eating a 'whale', that is, anchovies on toast, with his coffee. The Prize Fellows had no equivalent of this exclusive vocabulary. They were too numerous, too diverse, and (dare one say it?) possibly also too sensible to sustain so complex an alternative universe. In their, altogether more informal, world few 'bother[ed] much about what "anyone else . . . did" '. Even 'talk[ing] at meals' was something other than compulsory.[130]

That difference was more important than it may initially appear. It certainly wrought one clear consequence. The prize fellowship may have been the 'blue-riband' of Victorian and Edwardian Oxford. But it was not necessarily of life-transforming significance for all of those who won it. Some, for perfectly honourable reasons, were scarcely changed at all. Hardinge, elected in 1881, had already by then begun a Foreign Office career. As it prospered, so he was required to resign; in his own words, 'propter profectionem in Libyam'. This he did without any rancour or even obvious regret.[131] From a later generation, Harold Butler acted in much the same way. His memoirs contain precisely two,

---

[126] Most fully described in R. Skidelsky, *John Maynard Keynes*, vol. 1: *Hopes Betrayed, 1883–1920* (London, 1983), 115–21, esp. 116–17.

[127] Keynes, 'My Early Beliefs', 435–6; Knox, *Shaw-Stewart*, 75–6. Something of the price paid can be gleaned from Jolliffe, *Raymond Asquith*, 139; entry for 29 Oct. 1905.

[128] Perhaps most fully brought out in E. A. M. Asquith, *The Autobiography of Margot Asquith*, vol. 1 (London, 1922), 139–40 and 173–95. This latter section also includes George Curzon's famous poem of 10 July 1889, celebrating the clique, *en masse*; see 176–81.

[129] Again, best elucidated in Skidelsky, *Keynes*, i. 115–16.

[130] Ibid.; Jebb, *Shaw-Stewart*, 142.

[131] Sir Arthur Hardinge, *A Diplomat in Europe* (London, 1927), 33–5, at 35. G. H. Mungeam, 'Hardinge, Sir Arthur Henry (1859–1933)', *ODNB*, 176–7, notes however that '[Hardinge] had a lasting affection for Oxford, timing home leave whenever possible to attend College meetings and gaudies at All Souls, and corresponding on College business with Warden Anson until he reluctantly relinquished his fellowship in 1894'.

passing, references to All Souls; both were polite, neither was fulsome.[132] Other motives may have been less pure. Patrick Shaw-Stewart trampled on good form by moving straight from his Prize Fellowship into Barings Bank without any intervening effort in penurious public service. In so doing, he demonstrated all too clearly his dependence more on Ettie Desborough's charms than Warden Anson's example.[133]

These were striking cases. They can be matched by equally extreme counter-examples. Henson, for reasons all too obvious, regarded his election at All Souls as 'the beginning' of his 'Oxford life'. His recollections still bear repetition:

> I was not quite twenty-one when I became Fellow of All Souls, still young enough to form friendships and dream dreams. The society into which I found myself so unexpectedly introduced gave me just what I wanted, an atmosphere of vivid and varied culture...I was welcomed with a generous kindness which made me feel immediately at home...I loved everybody from the Warden to the Scout's boy, and even now, after more than half a century, I never enter the college without emotion.[134]

Lang, through imperatives scarcely so immediate but possibly not less binding, was equally enthralled. His subsequent account may or may not bear repeating:

> Balliol [was] my [nursing] mother...Magdalen, my mistress...[but] All Souls, my [lawful] wedded wife.[135]

But most were neither noticeably indifferent nor metaphorically betrothed. The overwhelming majority was sincerely bound but not emotionally enslaved. Their relationship with the College is perhaps best conceived in a balance of calculation and conscience. Such calculation, at its most trivial, involved the additional labour required to sit the examination and the potential ignominy of failure. More importantly, it also weighed the advantages and limitations of College life: above all, those concerning the question of marriage.[136] Conscience exerted its force over their choices of career and in a more general attitude to the commonweal. Every man judged its requirements differently. But three responses predominated. They may be called those of: the public servants, the *litterateurs*, and the adventurers.

---

[132] Sir Harold Butler, *Confident Morning* (London, 1950), 28 and 45. Ironically, Sir Harold's son, Rohan Butler, was continuously a fellow of All Souls (and in residence there), from 1938 to 1984.

[133] Knox, *Shaw-Stewart*, 71ff.; Shaw-Stewart's pressing need of, and desire for, money is intriguingly explored in Jebb, *Shaw-Stewart*, 73, 115–16, 140, and 211. See also R. Davenport-Hines, *Ettie: The Intimate Life and Daunting Spirit of Lady Desborough* (London, 2008), esp. 122, 143, and 225.

[134] Henson, *Retrospect*, vol. 1; Chadwick, *Henson*, 22ff.

[135] J. G. Lockhart, *Cosmo Gordon Lang* (London, 1949), 55; also ch. 8. See A. L. Rowse, 'Archbishop Lang of the Abdication', in idem, *Friends and Contemporaries* (London, 1989), 157–82, for an altogether less discrete portrait.

[136] From around 1885, College conventions were interpreted (in particular, were interpreted by Warden Anson) to prefer 'unmarried men' in the election of £50 fellows. This rule was generally – though not invariably – applied for nearly a century thereafter. This is a murky area of College history which I intend to explore at length in Green, 'The Impact of Anson', *The Exceptional College*.

III

The public servants included men like Liddell (elected 1891), Gwyer (1902), and Greene (1907).[137] They attracted least attention to themselves. This often involved quite deliberate self-denial. Most were practising lawyers, gently persuaded to turn their talents to wider purposes. For some, like Gwyer, this constituted a permanent decision. He became a Treasury Solicitor. That choice bore its finest fruit in what became the Statute of Westminster.[138] Yet he probably most wished to be remembered as Anson's posthumous editor.[139] For others, like Greene, unwilling to abandon their first calling, it necessitated massive additional labour, *pro bono*. A busy silk, he became the unpaid chairman of the committee which laid the foundation of the 1929 Companies Act. A dedicated Master of the Rolls, he also served as President of the British Records Association and saved innumerable collections of documents from possible destruction. But it was a lawyer after Anson's heart who served as President of the Classical Association, in 1947.[140]

The men of letters varied from exacting scholars of early metre, such as Ker (1879), to occasional versifiers, like Medd (1901).[141] For the most part, they pursued their vocation sporadically. More remarkable was the fact that they thrived in this way at all. Trench combined glorious incompetence as an educational administrator with lasting ambitions as a poet and playwright. Not everyone will agree that these were entirely fulfilled.[142] McDowall (1900) passed via a nervous breakdown at *The Times* to fruitful employment at its new *Literary Supplement*. There he became a champion both of Hardy and of Lawrence, the

---

[137] Sir Frederick Francis Liddell (1865–1950): ed. Eton and Christ Church, first class, Lit. Hum., 1888; private secretary to Lord Stanmore, Governor of Ceylon, 1888–90; fellow of All Souls, 1891–1906; Eldon Scholar, 1892; called to the Bar, 1894; First Parliamentary Counsel, 1917–1928; Counsel to the Speaker, 1928–1943; an Ecclesiastical Commissioner for England, 1944–8; see Anon., *Who Was Who, 1941–1950*, 684.

[138] Sir Maurice Gwyer (1878–1952): elected 1902; called to the Inner Temple, 1903; Legal staff of National Health Commission, 1912; Legal Advisor and Solicitor to Ministry of Health, 1919; Treasury Solicitor, 1926; Parliamentary Counsel to the Treasury, 1934; also key adviser on Government of India Act of 1935 and during Abdication Crisis of 1936; Chief Justice of Federal Court of India, 1937; Vice-Chancellor of University of Delhi, 1938.

[139] Douglas Veale, rev. by S. M. Cretney, 'Gwyer, Sir Maurice Linford', *ODNB*, refers to 'Gwyer's profound learning'. He had edited *Sir William Anson's Law and Customs of the Constitution: Parliament* (1922) and between 1910 and 1923 taken responsibility for four editions of Anson's *Law of Contract*. For a beguiling contemporary pen-portrait, see A. P. Herbert, *The Ayes Have It* (London, 1937), 106.

[140] J. Lever, 'Greene, Wilfred Arthur Baron Greene', *ODNB*; elected 1907. Lever notes that 'half a century after Greene's death his judicial reputation stood fully as high as it did in his lifetime, with his judgement cited daily in the courts' (p. 585).

[141] Chambers, 'W. P. Ker'. Arthur Cuthbert Medd was not in the same league.

[142] H. Granville-Barker, rev. K. Mullin, 'Trench (Frederic) Herbert (1865–1923)', *ODNB*, 293; *Poems, with Fables in Prose* (1918) was largely ignored.

latter long before he became more widely fashionable.[143] Young, as J. Mordaunt
Crook shows elsewhere in this volume, eventually emerged, ironically *out* of
public service, to become a great historian – arguably the greatest historian the
Prize Fellowship produced in this generation – and a considerable *litterateur*.

Perhaps the essence of calculation tempered by conscience was best expressed
in the lives of the adventurers. For theirs was an existence that typically embodied
respectable idealism, ruthless ambition, and surreptitious opportunism, often in
exquisitely balanced proportions. Recall the case of Amery. In his own words:

I had no desire to become a college don and devote myself to teaching. But the thought of
belonging to a society like that of All Souls, where the world of intellectual and that of
active life came together in the happiest intimacy, attracted me greatly.[144]

So much for the idealism. Now consider his ambition and the opportunism. He
continued:

Nor was the attraction diminished by the prospect of an income of £200 per year for
seven years – a starting point in the task of earning a livelihood, and a helpful factor in the
choice of one's immediate occupation.[145]

No one lived the dream more fully. To be sure, there was nothing strange about
its pursuit at that time. No secular 'grail' absorbed the late Victorian mind more
intensely than the potential union of the active and contemplative lives. The
contemporary growth of a secular intelligentsia, taken together with the extension of government both domestic and Imperial, simultaneously suggested both
the necessity, and also the possibility, of rule by the wise. This was true for British
democracy. It was still more assuredly the case beyond the shores of European
civilization.[146] Scarcely less significant was the peculiar development and subtle
integration of the liberal professions. For the fortunate few, this had consequences so agreeable – above all, so flexible – that their later bureaucratization
and commercialization would make Ronald Knox openly 'pity' those who had
never known the 'golden age' of these vocations during the years before 1914.[147]
At the same time, the reformed universities' encouragement of new forms of
learning, particularly in the human sciences, pointed to great gains in human
welfare that might be made through the informed application of theory to public
policy. The best 'Greats' men needed little additional stimulus to appreciate its

[143] L. H. Myers, 'Preface', in M. McDowall (ed.), *A Detached Observer: Essays and Sketches by the
late Arthur McDowell* (London, 1934), pp. v–xvi, esp. pp. xi–xii.

[144] Amery, *My Political Life*, i. 55; cf. Faber, *Speaking for England*, 23ff.

[145] Amery, *My Political Life*, i. 55. It might however be noted that, well into the 1920s, this sum
was paid annually, and for those without generous private incomes these arrangements could
sometimes prove embarrassing; see E. L. Woodward, *Short Journey* (London, 1942), 146.

[146] See, above all, G. O. Trevelyan, *The Competition Wallah* (London, 1866), at almost any
point. The classic interpretation remains that of Noel Annan, 'The Intellectual Aristocracy', now
most easily consulted in idem, *The Dons: Masters, Eccentrics and Geniuses* (London, 1999), Annexe.

[147] Knox, *Shaw-Stewart*, 6.

broader possibilities. So far from being held back by an anachronistic immersion in a 'classical' past, their surprisingly relevant education pointed to the ways in which the truly learned and the well disposed could beneficially determine the future of mankind.[148]

For these sorts of men, All Souls offered a most promising start. First, it gave them a period of real, if temporary, leisure. That did not necessarily mean luxury. Bathrooms made no appearance in the college until 1921.[149] But there were many compensations for Spartan lavatorial arrangements. Not least that the Prize Fellowship effectively entailed no obligations whatsoever. True, probationers were supposed to pernoctate during their first year. But even this minimal requirement could be, and often was, postponed.[150] The junior fellow in residence was also charged with the awesome responsibility of making the mayonnaise for the salad at dinner on Sunday nights, similarly with decanting the port in Common Room. Halifax's memoirs recalled all of these onerous obligations in suitably grave terms.[151] They neglect to mention that the young Edward Wood also wrote a biography of Keble during his Prize Fellowship.[152] Those who insisted on pursuing a career, whether academic or (more likely) at the bar, were naturally free to do so. But the adventurers could look forward to a few years of interesting travel, some opportunity for literary experiment, and the ideal conditions for the pursuit of a young man's fame. The shrewdest put all three of these possibilities together.

Contemporary fashion helped them. The British political classes may have travelled little, anyway for the purposes of political intelligence, for three generations after Waterloo.[153] But everything changed with the advent of steam shipping and the 'new imperialism'. From the mid-1880s, it became positively de rigueur for a budding young statesman to undertake what became, in effect, the modern grand tour.[154] This characteristically took in North America and the

[148] Walsh, 'The Zenith of Greats', 318ff.; R. M. Ogilvie, *Latin and Greek: A History of the Influence of the Classics on English Life from 1600 to 1918* (London, 1964), 91ff.
[149] Woodward, *Short Journey*, 147. The word 'leisure' is understood here in its ancient sense. The best modern restatement can be found in J. Pieper, *Leisure: The Basis of Culture*, trans. by A. Dru, with an introduction by T. S. Eliot (Indianapolis, 1998; first published London, 1952), see esp. 1–53.
[150] See, for instance, J. Barnes and D. Nicholson, *The Leo Amery Diaries*, vol. 1: *1896–1929* (London, 1980), ch. 1. Amery was far from alone in being so indulged.
[151] The Earl of Halifax, *Fulness of Days* (London, 1957), 54.
[152] Hon. E. F. L. Wood, *John Keble* (London, 1909). The young Wood modestly claimed 'not . . . to have contributed much that is original to the existing knowledge of the subject' (p. ix). Still, his (as it turned out) 'only attempt at historical scholarship' was published in an eminently respectable series on 'Leaders of the Church, 1880–1900', edited by George Russell, and issued by A. N. Mowbray, between 1905 and 1909. Other volumes covered Dean Church, Bishop Wilberforce, Dr Liddon, Bishop Westcott, Dr Percy, Frederick Denison, and Mr Gladstone. Short accounts are offered in the Earl of Birkenhead, *Halifax: The Life of Lord Halifax* (London, 1965), at 78, and A. Roberts, '*The Holy Fox': A Biography of Lord Halifax* (London, 1991), 7.
[153] A point – which may or may not be sound – made in Halifax, *Fulness of Days*, 57.
[154] Halifax, *Fulness of Days*, 57–8, where the, by then retired, statesman referred to the revivifying influence of Kipling in these matters. A fuller account, also referring to the specifically modern 'Grand Tour', is furnished in Birkenhead, *Halifax*, 77ff.

colonies, possibly also India and the Eastern approaches. Contemporary convention demanded that such coming stars also write up their travels, thereby announcing themselves to the world as suitably fit for public office. So much so that the genre of the so-called 'political odyssey' had become something of a cliché by the time Anthony Hope satirized it in his swashbuckling story of *The Prisoner of Zenda*. But then Anthony Hope's real name was Anthony Hope Hawkins. And he was a Prize Fellowship candidate in 1885.[155]

The finest flower of this kind of 'political odyssey' was probably George Curzon's *Persia and the Persian Question*, published in two volumes, in 1892.[156] It was not even its author's first foray into this kind of production. His *Russia in Central Asia*, also based upon extensive and arduous travel within and beyond that enigmatic empire, had appeared three years earlier.[157] That later work was the product of still more lengthy and hazardous journeying. Six months of it: covering two thousand miles on horseback and reaching into places so remote there were no consuls to greet him when he got there.[158] The book was grounded in considerable reading, in all the relevant European languages. And it was very long: adding up to something like 1,300 closely-printed pages, and running to more than half a million words.[159] Curzon was just 33 years old at the time. Few contemporaries doubted that in writing it he was also staking a claim to be Viceroy of India. He had his reward just six years later.[160] This is not to say that the Prize Fellows really became Viceroys quite so easily. Indeed, it is not to say that All Souls *produced* Viceroys at all. The historian too easily tempted to assume that causal connection should be reminded of the wise words of Cecil Spring-Rice: 'one might as well talk of P & O boats breeding viceroys as of Eton

---

[155] A. Hope (Anthony Hope Hawkins), *Memories and Notes* (London, 1929), chs 4 and 5 give a full account of Hope. The All Souls episode is mentioned only obliquely, on 88: 'I also (for it is only fair to record my failures as well as my achievements) stood twice for fellowship – in both cases without success or, as I think, any new approach thereto.' The purposes and fate of *The Prisoner of Zenda* are rather more fully set out on 119–23.

[156] Hon. George N. Curzon, *Persia and the Persian Question*, 2 vols (London, 1892). Curzon was identified as 'MP' and 'Late Fellow of All Souls College, Oxford'; in fact, by the time of the publication of this work, he was back in fellowship.

[157] Hon. George N. Curzon, *Russia in Central Asia in 1889* and *The Anglo-Russian Question* (London, 1889). Curzon was identified as 'Fellow of All Souls College', though no obligations to the College were acknowledged in his 'Preface' (pp. vii–xiv). Shorter versions of these tracts can be found in P. King (ed.), *Travels with a Superior Person* (London, 1985).

[158] Curzon, *Persia*, 'Preface', p. vii.

[159] Ibid. Hence perhaps its author's 'not, I hope, vainglorious hope that, until superseded by a better it may be regarded as the standard work in the English language on the subject to which it refers'.

[160] Yet further enhanced by his later work, *Problems of the Far East: Japan–Korea–China* (London, 1894). Curzon famously dedicated *this* book: 'To those who believe that the British Empire, under Providence, the greatest instrument for good that the world has seen and who hold, with the writer, that its work in the Far East is not yet accomplished' (p. v). Curzon's broader purposes for the British Empire were never more eloquently set out than in his speech, prior to leaving for India in a 'Dinner given by Old Etonians in London, 28 Oct. 1898'; see Sir Thomas Raleigh (ed.), *Lord Curzon in India: Being a Selection of His Speeches as Viceroy and Governor-General of India, 1898–1905* (London, 1906), 1–6. For an interpretation, see Gilmour, *Curzon*, chs 6 and 7.

breeding governor-generals: it was the only route for them to go by'. *Mutatis mutandis*, this salutary truth applied to All Souls too.[161]

There is another point. The true privilege of All Souls was that it pointed not merely to the possibility of short-term excitement but also to a path back into theoretical life. Thus doubly blessed, some of the adventurers slowly became something else. Indeed, what is most striking about the Prize Fellows after 1878 is less the supreme distinction that a few of them achieved in particular fields than the more extraordinary variety of achievements subsequently displayed within so many of their individual lives. It is possible to break down their adult lives into recognizable career patterns. The result reads something like this:

Lawyers	17
Journalists	3
Scholars	10
Writers	3
Politicians	4
Public Servants	8
Bankers	2
Churchmen	5
Others	8

Plus three killed in action, too young to have pursued a career.[162]

Yet whilst this kind of categorization is possible, it is also profoundly misleading. This list defines Maguire as a lawyer. He could equally have been considered as a businessman or a politician: ditto, Harrison. Simon might plausibly have been designated as lawyer rather than politician. Many of his contemporaries thought so.[163] Amery is identified here as a politician. But for much of his life he made his living as a journalist and a writer. The principal protagonist for Imperial preference in the quarter-century up to the Ottawa Conference was decidedly all three. And just how are we to characterize the man who (re)wrote at least part of the Balfour Declaration?[164] This is not logic-chopping. It points to a vital aspect of pre-1914 England professional life. This was its remarkable amphibiousness. It also identifies the social type that found its happiest home in Anson's All Souls. This was the young, educated, virtuoso. He was most frequently and vividly celebrated in the novels of John Buchan.[165]

---

[161] Cited in Rose, *Superior Person*, on plate 23, between 288 and 289. Spring Rice was often Curzon's companion on these travels; see Gilmour, *Curzon*, 89–91. His (not inconsiderable) pique at Curzon's later preferment is recorded in S. Gwynn (ed.), *The Letters and Friendships of Sir Cecil Spring Price*, 2 vols (London, 1929), i. 257–9.

[162] Author's calculations.

[163] See D. Dutton, *Simon: A Political Biography* (London, 1992), 324–5 and 327–8 for the evidence.

[164] Amery, *My Political Life*, ii. 117; W. R. Louis, *In the Name of God Go! Leo Amery, and the British Empire in the Age of Churchill* (London, 1992), 73; M. J. Cohen, *Churchill and the Jews* (London, 1985), 52–3; with Louis, this volume, ch. 11.

[165] A vision that can now be most conveniently consulted in *The Best of John Buchan: The Thirty-Nine Steps, Greenmantle and Mr Steadfast* (Prion, 2010). For a serious consideration of Buchan's broader political thought, see J. P. Parry. 'From the Thirty-Nine Articles to the Thirty-Nine Steps', in M. Bentley

These – highly influential – tales projected the image of the ideal, young, Englishman. For Buchan, this was (of necessity) a very loosely defined category. But whatever his origins, he was supposed to be supremely intelligent, also learned, indeed cultured. He was also presumed to be worldly and practical-minded. Finally, he was understood to be mentally tough and even physically brave; he was invariably also single, indeed celibate, almost indeed pre-erotic.[166] That last notion can be subjected to endless historical psychologizing. It is still figuratively a million miles away from the 'higher sodomy' of Edwardian Cambridge.[167]

It was also more than just a fantasy. Indeed, it is easily recognizable in the world of Milner's Kindergarten. Buchan may have been a failed Prize Fellowship candidate. But he knew the Kindergarten well. He was there. So too were five contemporary All Souls men: Perry, Amery, Dawson (then Robinson), Malcolm, and, above all, Brand. Moreover, in Brand, the theoretical and practical lives really did come together.[168] He was an historian who taught himself economics to a level of expertise that gained the respect of Keynes. He was also an international banker whose career culminated at Bretton Woods. He began as a minor functionary in Milner's bureaucracy. More remarkably, he gained the trust of Smuts and became secretary of the Transvaal delegation to the Constitutional Convention. Quickly becoming its *eminence grise*, he wrote the blueprint for the new republic virtually single-handed (aged 30). He did so anonymously, of course. Still, modesty had its rewards. His account of the *Union of South Africa* reads like an austere treatise in political science. It is really an exercise in disguised autobiography.

IV

It was also a period piece. This is because it described a world that did not survive the First World War. That is why Brodribb was so wrong. He was out of date. To the extent that the world he described had *ever* existed, it had passed away by the time he wrote. There were many reasons why this was so. The most important were those changes in Imperial and domestic administration that followed the great conflict of 1914–18. But some of the causes can be traced to an altered idea of Oxford, indeed to the All Souls Prize Fellowship itself, at this time. The Prize Fellowship may have largely escaped the professionalization of the University

(ed.), *Public and Private Doctrine: Essays in British History Presented to Maurice Cowling* (Cambridge, 1993), ch. 10. Much of value can still be derived from consulting G. Himmelfarb, 'John Buchan: The Last Victorian', in idem, *Victorian Minds* (London, 1968), ch. ix.

[166] J. Buchan, *Memory Hold the Door* (London, 1940). For his background, see chs I and II. For his ideal (loosely disguised in portraits of Raymond Asquith and Auberon Herbert), see ch. III.

[167] Most thoughtfully interpreted by P. Levy, 'The Bloomsbury Group', in M. Keynes (ed.), *Essays on John Maynard Keynes* (London, 1975), ch. 8, esp. pp. 63–4.

[168] The case of Brand is considered at greater length in ch. 4, this volume.

after 1881. But it was not indefinitely immune to the criteria of those professions thereafter. Demands for reform in Oxford generally were invariably accompanied by calls for the abolition of so-called idle fellowships, in particular.[169] Post-war poverty, which reduced once proudly independent institutions to (partial) state subsidy, allowed the government to do (some) of the radicals' work for them. The results of these labours became ever more obvious during the years after 1923.

Oxford was widely thought to have survived the Asquith Commission largely unscathed – alternatively, too little transformed. This is a serious misreading of the text. Hidden away in the details of that otherwise innocuous document lay sufficient, putative, provisions designed to bring Prize Fellowships, even at All Souls, into line with ordinary academic appointments elsewhere in the University. Naturally, the idea of 'abolition' was never mentioned. 'Assimilation' was the contemporary watchword. Few were fooled. On reading the report, Sir Herbert Warren, President of Magdalen observed that:

All Souls will remain but Prize Fellowships will disappear; [there] and everywhere else [too]. This is more of a change than many... realise or will be realised for some years.[170]

He was right on both counts. Lucky beneficiaries of Oxford's most famous prize after 1919 may scarcely have noticed. Few probably would have much cared if they had. But what might without too much nostalgia be described as the 'pure freedom' their predecessors had once enjoyed passed away forever. The fellowship retained much of its erstwhile prestige. This was true down to 1945, and even beyond. But it pointed if not to poorer then to fewer practical possibilities than had previously beckoned. It no longer opened each and every door, even in the minds of those who still sought its laurels. It did not become merely a job for many more years to come. But it had lost some of its metaphorical sheen all the same.

---

[169] See, for instance, E. B. Poulton, *John Vivien Jones and other Oxford Memories* (London, 1911), ch. 10, which directed partial fire at All Souls, from 260ff.

[170] Sir Herbert Warren, 'Comment', *The Times*, 27 Mar. 1922, 5.

3

Simon: A Lawyer in Politics

*Stephen Cretney**

If this were television, the screenplay for the opening scene would be easy to write.[1] The camera zooms in past the familiar police constable standing guard on the black door with its polished brass ornaments. In the lobby, discreet but agitated murmuring amongst the morning-coated men gathered round the telephone (an authentic instrument of the period, of course). The door into the Cabinet Room quietly opens. A note passes from hand to hand. More agitated but sympathetic muttering – 'oh dear, of course, of course'. We cut to the tall, athletic, albeit prematurely balding, figure slipping from the room. The camera closes in on the calendar: it is 4th June 1914. Sir John Simon, the Attorney-General, has left his cabinet colleagues to their discussion of the military dispositions judged necessary by the red-tabbed Generals as the country moved ineluctably to war – not, you understand, war in continental Europe but civil war in Ulster, a prospect all the more appalling because of the further strains which such a conflict would place on the loyalty of the armed forces of the Crown. Sir John Simon, Subwarden of All Souls College, is on his way to Paddington station and the train to Oxford in order to discharge – with the impeccable efficiency for which he was already noted – the duties falling on him in consequence of the death of Warden Anson.

---

* The text of a lecture delivered in All Souls College on 31 May 2002 in a series entitled 'All Souls and the Tradition of Public Service in the Twentieth Century'. Footnotes have been added but these do not seek to take full account of events – notably the enactment of the Constitutional Reform Act in 2005, of which Simon would not have approved – in the interval between the delivery of the lecture and delivery of copy to the printer. The extent to which I have drawn on David Dutton's excellent *Simon: A Political Biography of Sir John Simon* (London, 1992) will be apparent. The forty-five pages devoted to Simon in R. V. F. Heuston's *Lives of the Lord Chancellors 1940–1970* (Oxford, 1987) succeed in giving a vivid picture of Simon's legal, political, and personal life, informed by a wide knowledge of the source material and illuminated by many insights into a complex personality.

[1] This opening paragraph is a device, hopefully justified by the circumstances, to remind the audience of some of the background. Sources confirm that Simon missed a Cabinet meeting to travel to Oxford in order to carry out his duties as Subwarden (see H. H. Henson (ed.), *A Memoir of the Rt Hon Sir William Anson* (Oxford, 1920), 231), but the Downing Street scene is a product of the author's imagination.

It would be difficult to find a more appropriate point of reference for any discussion of 'All Souls and the public service' than Anson's funeral[2] at the end of the week, conducted by the Archbishop of York[3] and the Dean of Durham[4] (both fellows of the College) in the presence of a great congregation[5] including Curzon (Chancellor of the University, sometime Viceroy of India and a Quondam Fellow), Edward Prince of Wales (in whom Anson had, not altogether successfully, tried to instil an understanding of the British Constitution),[6] and Prime Minister Asquith (father of a college lawyer,[7] one of the six fellows and Quondams soon to be killed in action during the Great War). Perhaps it was Curzon who wrote the tribute to Anson, published in *The Times*[8] above the single initial 'C', and recording Anson's achievement in changing the character of the fellowship: the 'learned professor and the research student' had replaced 'the cultivated scion of an aristocratic order' but the College continued to 'contribute an unarrested flow of eminent public servants to the state'. Certainly the past, present, and future Cabinet ministers,[9] viceroys, ambassadors, civil servants, editors of *The Times*,[10] headmasters of the great public schools,[11] judges and other distinguished lawyers[12] must have shared the emotion apparent in

---

[2] A memorial service (evidently intended for those prevented by official duty from travelling to the funeral) was held at the same time in St Margaret's, Westminster.

[3] Cosmo Gordon Lang; subsequently Archbishop of Canterbury.

[4] Herbert Hensley Henson; subsequently Bishop of Hereford, and thereafter Bishop of Durham.

[5] Lists of those attending the funeral in the University Church are to be found in *The Times*, 10 June 1914. H. H. Asquith noted that the congregation in St Mary's was 'rather remarkable' and assessed Anson as 'a very cultivated and agreeable man'. But he also thought Anson to be 'a teaching example of the futility of the don in politics. Lord Palmerston once defined dirt as "matter in the wrong place", and equally misplaced is an Oxford or Cambridge jurist...in the House of Commons'. Asquith to Stanley, 9 June 1914, as printed in M. Brock and E. Brock (eds), *H. H. Asquith, Letters to Venetia Stanley* (Oxford, 1982).

[6] P. Ziegler, *King Edward VIII: The Official Biography* (London, 1990), 40. He estimates that Anson probably taught the Prince everything which he retained from his time as an undergraduate at Magdalen College. However, in 1936 Simon (as Home Secretary) sarcastically told the Cabinet that the instruction the King had received in constitutional law from Anson should have disabused the King of his expressed belief that the sovereign had a right 'by ancient custom' to address his subjects; and the Cabinet unhesitatingly refused to allow the King to broadcast to the nation on the subject of his intended marriage: S. M. Cretney, 'The King and the King's Proctor: The Abdication Crisis and the Divorce Laws 1936–1937', *Law Quarterly Review*, 116 (2000), 583, 591.

[7] Raymond Asquith (1878–1916), killed in action on the Somme whilst serving in the Grenadier Guards: see C. Clifford, *The Asquiths* (London, 2002), 365–71, and generally J. Jolliffe, *Raymond Asquith: Life and Letters* (London, 1980).

[8] 6 June 1914.

[9] Curzon, Amery, and Halifax were all to hold Cabinet office (Curzon and Halifax both having claims to the premiership).

[10] G. E. Buckle and Geoffrey Robinson (who assumed the name Dawson by Royal Licence in 1917).

[11] Edmund Warre and Cyril Alington were both Headmasters of Eton. Alington had previously been Head of Shrewsbury, and was subsequently Dean of Durham.

[12] The association between All Souls and the public service was particularly strong amongst the College lawyers. Three of them (Frederick Lidell, William Graham Harrison, and Maurice Gwyer) successively held the office of First Parliamentary Counsel between the years 1917 and 1937. Others – Walter Phillimore, Wilfrid Greene, and Donald Somervell – were to hold high judicial office after successful careers at the bar.

their Subwarden's silky, musical voice as he read the great passage from Ecclesiasticus in praise of famous men. This congregation could readily identify with the 'leaders of the people by their counsels, and by their knowledge of learning meet for the people, wise and eloquent . . . honoured in their generations and . . . the glory of their times'.[13]

A LONG WAY FROM MOSS SIDE

Simon, elected to a Prize Fellowship in law in 1896 (with the presidency of the Union[14] and a first in Greats[15] behind him) had come a long way – a very long way – from what he described as the 'poky, uninteresting house . . . in the rather grimy' Moss Side district of Manchester[16] where on 28 February 1873 he was born, the only son of the Congregational Minister of the Zion Chapel in Hulme.[17] And Simon was to go further – much further. The brilliant career at

[13] Ecclesiasticus 44: 4.

[14] In Hilary Term 1896. The closing years of the nineteenth century can fairly be described as the 'golden age' of the Union: C. Hollis, *The Oxford Union* (London, 1965), 141. Simon preserved links with the Union throughout his life: in 1933, on the invitation of Michael Foot, Simon spoke in support of the continuance on grounds of principle of the National Government and 'particularly impressed [the audience] by speaking entirely without notes': D. Walter, *The Oxford Union: Playground of Power* (London, 1984), 95; and in 1947, he spoke on the invitation of Anthony Wedgwood Benn, and complained that the Attlee government's socialist policies were cramping 'the springs of energy and enterprise', urging the restoration of the 'real enjoyment of the liberties of ordinary citizens': Walter, *The Oxford Union*, 130.

[15] But only seconds in Mathematical and Classical Moderations. Simon had also overcome the disappointment of rejection in the Balliol entrance scholarship, but Wadham was more discriminating and he evidently enjoyed a stimulating undergraduate career. (F. E. Smith, Lord Chancellor 1919–22, and Secretary of State for India 1924–8, was on the same staircase.)

[16] 16 Yerburgh Street. The house, in common with most of its neighbours, has been demolished, but the street still marks a divide between a large estate of 'social housing' and the more spacious roads and substantial houses of Whalley Range immediately to the south, now apparently mostly occupied by students and others connected with one or other of Manchester's institutions of tertiary education. Although there may have been, as Simon put it, 'little *rus in urbe*' in the immediate neighbourhood, the house was within walking distance of the Lancashire County Cricket Club's ground at Old Trafford; and in 1926 Simon told the visiting Australian cricket team that there was 'hardly any holiday afternoon when the Lancashire team was playing at home' that he and his father did not watch the game 'sitting in the sixpenny stand': *Comments and Criticisms, by the Rt Hon. Sir John Simon*, ed. D. Rowland Evans (London, 1930), 274.

[17] Edwin Simon, one of the six sons (four of whom became Congregationalist Ministers) of John Simon, a tenant farmer in Stackpole Elidor, South Pembrokeshire. Simon's mother, Fanny Allsebrook (1846–1936) was the daughter of an evidently prosperous Worcestershire farmer and was said to be descended from Margaret Countess of Salisbury. It appears that the family's move in 1883 to Bath (where Simon attended King Edward's School) was prompted in part by concern for her health. In 1887 Simon won a £60 scholarship to Fettes College, Edinburgh, his father paying the other half of the fees from savings he had made out of his £300 annual stipend. Simon would not have been able (even had he wished to do so) to dispute A. L. Rowse's claim to be the first 'working class' fellow of All Souls; but it is clear that his social background was comparatively modest. Indeed Rowse classified Simon as a 'Liberal Nonconformist Little Englander from the lower-middle-class' whose 'personality was inhibited, if not crippled, by his Nonconformist origins': A. L. Rowse, *All Souls in My Time* (London, 1993), 60–3.

the Bar. A member of the House of Commons for thirty years.[18] Solicitor-General,[19] Attorney-General with a seat in the Asquith Cabinet[20] (often said to be one of the most talented administrations of the twentieth century), twice Home Secretary,[21] Foreign Secretary,[22] Chancellor of the Exchequer;[23] then, finally, Lord Chancellor throughout Churchill's wartime governments.[24] And this record of high ministerial office (virtually unparalleled in the twentieth century) is not all. There is, for example,[25] the monumental 750-page report

[18] Simon was MP for Walthamstow, Essex, from 1906 until 1918 (when he was defeated by a coalition Liberal) and for the Spen Valley from 1922 to 1940.

[19] 1910–13. Simon unsuccessfully resisted the knighthood for long conventionally granted to the Law Officers: see Simon, *Retrospect: The Memoirs of the Rt Hon Viscount Simon* (London, 1952), 75. However, Simon's role in 1911 in the prosecution of Edward Mylius for criminal libel (in claiming that King George V, whilst serving as a Naval Officer in Malta, had in 1890 contracted a marriage with the daughter of an Admiral with the result that his marriage in 1893 to Princess Mary of Teck had been bigamous and its issue illegitimate) won the monarch's gratitude; and Simon was made KCVO. In 1936 Simon's learned Opinion in the *Mylius* case on the position of the monarch as litigant and witness was treated as definitive in the discussions about possible action to set aside the decree nisi of divorce obtained by Mrs W. W. Simpson: see Cretney, 'The King and the King's Proctor', 583, 599. But Simon (recording in his diary the King's sincere gratitude for the conduct of the *Mylius* case) noted that the authorities had been 'very lucky... If M, instead of justifying, had pleaded guilty and explained that he was only repeating what thousands of reputable people had said for years without being prosecuted for it, we could never have established the falsity of the lie so effectually. Winston Churchill as Home Secretary has been absolutely resolved to prosecute from the beginning – and the result justifies him': Oxford, Bodleian Library, MS Simon 2, 3 Feb. 1911.

[20] 1913–15: the offer of a seat in the Cabinet is some indication of the prominence Simon had achieved in the Parliamentary Liberal Party. But Simon came to share the conventional view that it was a mistake for the Attorney to be a member of the Cabinet (as distinct from attending it when that was considered appropriate) since membership could make it difficult to maintain the appropriate degree of distance and objectivity on aspects of policy on which the Law Officers' opinions and advice were sought: see Simon, *Retrospect*.

[21] 1915–16; 1935–7: see below.

[22] 1931–35: see below.

[23] 1937–40.

[24] 1940–5. However, as Lord Chancellor, Simon was not a member of the War Cabinet; and although he retained his office in Churchill's 'Caretaker' administration he was excluded from the cabinet, 'a unique exclusion for the Lord Chancellor in twentieth century history': Dutton, *Simon*, 309.

[25] Simon also chaired a Departmental Committee on Street Trading in 1909, and served as a member of the *Royal Commission on the Selection of Justices of the Peace*, Cmd 5250, 1910 (having first obtained an assurance from the Prime Minister that absence from the Commission's meetings 'for professional reasons' would be excused: MS Simon 47). Much more important was Simon's role in chairing the *Royal Commission into the Arrest and Subsequent Treatment of Mr Francis Sheehy Skeffington...*, Cmd 8376, 1916 – a painstaking investigation into the circumstances in which three entirely innocent Irishmen were shot on the orders of one Captain Bowen-Coulthurst. (Bowen-Coulthurst was found guilty of murder but insane by a speedily concluded court martial and apparently thereafter made a rapid recovery.) Simon also conducted an *Inquiry into the loss of the R101 Airship on its maiden voyage to India* (when all but eight of the fifty-four on board 'perished instantly in the flames'): Cmd 3825, 1931. The Report contains a detailed examination of the technical and other facts and identified the cause of the disaster; but Simon abstained from allocating any blame, pointing out that airship travel was still in an experimental stage and that it was for others to determine whether it should proceed. Finally, Simon was appointed to chair the *Royal Commission on the Population* in March 1944, but withdrew in 1945 because of pressure of work as a Lord of Appeal. (The Commission was reconstituted under the Chairmanship of Sir H. Henderson, Warden of All Souls College, 1951–2, and reported in 1949.)

on the government of India,[26] the product of three years' discussion and negotiation, much of it in the subcontinent. And after 1945 he remained active both as a Law Lord (sitting in nearly sixty cases reported in the Law Reports)[27] and also, almost to the day of his death at the age of 80, as an extremely effective[28] 'working' peer.[29] Nearer home, he was Standing Counsel to the University,[30] served on the Royal Commission on the Universities of Oxford and Cambridge,[31] and was subsequently High Steward.[32] He was a fellow of All Souls for more than fifty years.[33]

[26] *Report of the Indian Statutory Commission*, i, *Survey*, Cmd 3568 (p. 409), ii, *Recommendations*, Cmd 3568 (p. 344). The Commission's terms of reference required an inquiry into the 'working of the system of government, the growth of education, and the development of representative institutions, in British India' and the making of recommendations on the extent to which it would be desirable to 'establish the principle of responsible government, or to extend, modify, or restrict the degree of responsible government . . . existing therein'. Simon was appointed Chairman on the recommendation of the Secretary of State Lord Birkenhead (who had been advised by the Viceroy, Lord Irwin, fellow of All Souls, 1903–59, better known as the Earl of Halifax). The *Report*'s masterly analysis of what Simon had described as the 'stupendous constitutional issues' justifies R. F. V. Heuston's description of the *Report* as a 'great state paper of which [Simon] was justly proud' (Heuston, *Lives of the Lord Chancellors 1940–1970*, 47). But the Commission's unanimous recommendations were overtaken by rapid shifts in informed opinion in the United Kingdom and by events. A good account can be found in P. E. Roberts, *History of British India*, 3rd edn (London, 1952).

[27] See below.

[28] But sometimes bitterness also seems close to the surface: see for example Simon's speeches on the Married Women (Restraint on Anticipation) Act 1949 (a measure removing one of the legal disabilities affecting married women but clearly prompted by the particular concerns of Countess Mountbatten). Simon said that 'as a former Chancellor of the Exchequer' and also as 'someone who, lacking inherited wealth, had never had a marriage settlement' he could not 'remain silent . . . as to the effect upon the Revenue of this wholesale cancellation of a provision in past marriage settlements': *Official Report* (*HL*) 19 July 1949, vol. 164, col. 182.

[29] Simon was certainly effective in questioning decisions taken by the 1945–51 Labour governments. Sir Harold Kent records that when Simon gave in his name as an intending speaker in a House of Lords debate 'alarm and despondency' would come upon Lord Chancellor Jowitt: ' "Does anyone know what Simon is going to say?" he would ask anxiously. "What points is the old so-and-so going to raise?" We none of us knew. Simon was not one to give away his hand in advance. I only knew that with a sure touch he would prod the sorest spots, would proceed unerringly to the places where the ice was thinnest. His tall, gaunt figure rising in his place, the acid voice addressing the Woolsack with words of deceptive courtesy, could still strike a chill. He may have been a pacifist and an appeaser, but he was an old warrior none the less.' H. Kent, *In on the Act: Memoirs of a Lawmaker* (London, 1979), 151.

[30] In his letter of acceptance Simon wrote: 'I realize that the appointment is, for a loyal son of Oxford, the choicest of professional honours as well as a very serious responsibility, and I will serve . . . with all the devotion of a man who knows well that he owes everything to the good fortune which took him to Oxford': Simon to Warren, 21 Feb. 1909, MS Simon 47.

[31] Cmd 1588 (1922).

[32] From 1948. It appears that Simon had been passed over when a vacancy arose in 1930 because of his unpopularity: see Heuston, *Lives of the Lord Chancellors 1940–1970*, 57.

[33] Playing an important part on a number of occasions, not least in 1952 when Warden Henderson's serious illness caused uncertainty and difficulty. According to Rowse, Simon 'set himself to clarify' the 'awkward situation', and his 'resolution was surprising: he went up to see Henderson and came back with the resignation in his pocket': Rowse, *All Souls*, 162. Rowse believed that Simon wanted him to stand in the ensuing election but that he 'went over to the other side' when he saw which way the majority lay: ibid., 163.

You might infer from all this that Simon would be an exemplar to be held up as a model of professional achievement and public service. And what I have said about him and his career is indeed the truth, and nothing but the truth. But I am afraid it is very far from being the whole truth. There are three notable, and to some extent related, omissions to be filled if we are to complete the picture.

First, the account I have given is distinctly short on chronology: I have not reminded you that Simon resigned from the government in 1916 and was not to hold office again until appointed Foreign Secretary in Ramsay MacDonald's national government in November 1931. I have not reminded you that he became Chancellor of the Exchequer in 1937 in Neville Chamberlain's administration. And here, of course, is the second omission: if Simon is remembered at all today it is as a 'Man of Munich', one of the 'Guilty Men' excoriated in the tract of that name written by Michael Foot and other journalists[34] – a huge publishing success in July 1940 and more recently republished as a Penguin Modern Classic.[35] Our imaginary screenplay would certainly include the dramatic scene in the crowded House of Commons on 28 September 1938:[36] the Prime Minister at the dispatch-box explaining the meetings at Berchtesgaden, the telegram passed to Simon who, choosing his time, hands it to Chamberlain. The whispers, 'shall I tell them? – yes'. The almost universal hysterical cheers at the news of the invitation to meet Hitler for the third time the next day at Munich (the final meeting, at which Czechoslovakia was betrayed). And there is my third omission: what today would be described as Simon's 'image'. From the half-mocking Asquithian 'the impeccable'[37] through the 'cold fish or something worse',[38] to the 'sly fellow eaten up with ambition', the 'egotistic intriguer'[39] with his 'petty and sneaky spite',[40] his 'lamentable reputation as a twister',[41] 'snakiest of them all',[42] covered with the 'slime of hypocrisy',[43] his name 'despised

[34] At the time Foot (another former President of the Oxford Union) was a working journalist and in 1942 became acting editor of Lord Beaverbrook's *Evening Standard*. Elected to Parliament as Labour MP for Plymouth Devonport he was to hold Cabinet office between 1974 and 1979, and was Leader of the Labour Party from 1980 until 1983.

[35] The book was published by Victor Gollancz in 1940, the authors concealing their identity under the pseudonym 'Cato'. The 1998 Penguin Edition contains an informative preface by Foot (whose co-authors had been Peter Howard and Frank Howard) and a useful introduction by John Stevenson.

[36] The official record is in *Official Report* (*HC*) vol. 339, col. 26; but some details have to be taken from the recollections of observers and participants (including Simon himself: see Simon, *Retrospect*, 239).

[37] See e.g. Brock, *Asquith, Letters to Venetia Stanley, passim*.

[38] Sir Maurice Bowra (as quoted by Heuston, *Lives of the Lord Chancellors 1940–1970*, 56).

[39] D. Margesson, Conservative chief whip 1939: Dutton, *Simon*, 287.

[40] See Heuston, *Lives of the Lord Chancellors 1940–1970*, 46 (citing D. Marquand, *Ramsay MacDonald* (London, 1977), 52).

[41] Lord Balcarres to Irwin (1929), as cited in Dutton, *Simon*, 91.

[42] Hugh Dalton, *Diary* (London, 1986), as cited in Dutton, *Simon*, 275.

[43] *Official Report* (*HC*), 3 July 1931, vol. 254, col. 1667 (D. Lloyd George, who is often also credited, perhaps incorrectly, with the jest that Simon had 'sat on the fence for so long that the iron had entered into his soul': Dutton, *Simon*, 337).

throughout the world'.[44] Simon inspired strong feelings, mostly hostile, not allayed by his marble smile or by all the 'soapiness and flattery'[45] and the false bonhomie:[46] 'God', Harold Nicolson exploded in his diary,[47] 'what a toad and a worm Simon is . . .' And to those under him – his officials, for example – there wasn't much bonhomie, whether false or genuine. Simon took pride in not (as he put it) suffering fools gladly.[48] The experience of the young Treasury civil servant who found his careful minute returned by the Chancellor with no comment but torn neatly into two pieces[49] seems to have been not untypical.[50] No doubt the official understood the unwritten message.[51] (Happily he overcame this setback. He was Burke Trend, subsequently Cabinet Secretary and, as Lord Trend, Rector of Lincoln College.) Even in All Souls Simon apparently upset the staff: he loved the College, Rowse tells us,[52] but nobody loved him.

SIMON THE ADVOCATE

It is, I am afraid, not a happy story. But at least nobody can deny Simon's unalloyed success at the bar. His success in the law Prize Fellowship in 1896 was

[44] Aneurin Bevan (as cited in Dutton, *Simon*, 290).

[45] Sir Thomas Inskip (subsequently, as Lord Caldecote, Lord Chancellor 1939–40 and thereafter Lord Chief Justice of England 1940–6) as cited in R. F. V. Heuston, *Lives of the Lord Chancellors 1885–1940* (Oxford, 1964, reissued with corrections 1987), 593.

[46] L. E. Jones, *An Edwardian Youth* (London, 1956), 182, records a sadly not untypical incident: a young barrister is greeted effusively and for a time treated by his eminent senior (believed to be Simon) with unexpected warmth. But all changed when Simon discovered that the barrister was unable to assist Simon in his election campaign: the 'next time we met he nodded and passed by; in a few weeks even the nod was omitted . . . He . . . pursued his bleak, unswerving way to the very highest positions open to a political lawyer. He achieved all his ambitions save getting colleagues to call him by his Christian name.' I am grateful to the late John Simmons for this reference.

[47] H. Nicolson, *Diaries and Letters 1939–1945* (London, 1967), 11 January 1954.

[48] See the remarkable account of his interviewing a young Parliamentary draftsman in Kent, *In on the Act*, 85–7.

[49] J. Colville, *The Fringes of Power: Downing Street Diaries 1939–1955* (London, 1985), 34. Colville (at the time Assistant Private Secretary to the Prime Minister) also records that Simon was 'friendly, forthcoming and often agreeably witty' with those who did not work under him, and claims to have been one of 'a sadly restricted company who actually liked him'.

[50] Note also the experience of Heuston: 'In 1953, Simon attended Encaenia: there was some problem at the door over tickets for his companions, and a Pro-proctor went forward to help. He was rebuffed with a withering snarl': Heuston, *Lives of the Lord Chancellors 1940–1970*, 44, n. 7.

[51] But Simon did have the respect of officials dealing with legislation: Sir Harold Kent describes his abrasive behaviour at a conference on the drafting of the Factories Act 1937; but notes that the official in charge of the Home Office Factories Division remained 'fresh and unperturbed', commenting 'He's always like this. But he listens to what you say, and then next day uses it beautifully, especially when he's on his feet, and you forgive him everything': Kent, *In on the Act*, 89.

[52] Rowse, *All Souls*, 97. Simon recorded in his memoirs that over many years he found 'Saturday night at All Souls the choicest of his experiences'; and that nothing in his life has meant so much to him 'as the comradeship . . . of the fraternity of All Souls'. The present author's conversations with those who were in fellowship in the early 1950s confirm that Simon was friendly and approachable to the younger fellows.

founded on a few months' 'furious reading' of legal texts, for (so he tells us) at that time a budding barrister often succeeded if he could do well in the general papers and translations.[53] Supported by writing obituaries for the *Manchester Guardian*,[54] teaching Greek history,[55] and by the income from the Barstow Scholarship he won in 1898 (the year in which the highlight for Simon's near contemporary and long-time ministerial colleague, Winston Churchill, was thundering across the Sudanese desert with the 21st Lancers' in the cavalry charge at Omdurman, personally accounting in a few desperate minutes for five or more dervishes),[56] Simon joined the Western Circuit.[57] In his first year he earned all of 27 guineas (perhaps £1,700 in modern values).

Simon was soon to establish himself as an immensely successful jury advocate. Some years later he defended a man on a murder charge. The story was very simple. Simon's client, Lieutenant Dougal Malcolm, armed with a horse-whip and an automatic pistol, left his wife at their home in Cadogan Square. Twenty minutes or so later, by pretending to be a policeman, he gained access to the Bayswater flat where the man with whom his wife had fallen in love lived. Four shots rang out. As you may think, to make matters worse, Simon's client had written to the deceased: if 'ever I hear of you trying to see or even talk to my wife again, I will . . . hunt you out and give you such a thrashing that even your own mother will not know you again. I will thrash you until I have maimed you for life. This I swear before God in whom I believe . . .'

Simon did not put his client into the witness box, nor did he call any witnesses. He addressed the jury for perhaps an hour and a half. The judge (McCardie J) then summed up strongly for a conviction. Twenty-five minutes later the jury returned: the accused was not guilty of any criminal offence. Of course, you may think it helped that the accused was a subaltern on active service on the Western Front; whereas the deceased was (in Simon's words) 'Russian by nationality, with the worst of records, passing under a false name, flaunting a bogus title, the associate of some infamous German woman, a man without honest occupation, without apparent means of support, one of those pieces of human refuse that are carried along in the tide of great cities, living no one knows how, lunching at the best restaurants, sleeping in a cheap lodging, maintaining an existence with the

---

[53] Simon, *Retrospect*, 37.

[54] Which had sought to recruit him as a full-time journalist.

[55] Simon, *Retrospect*, 37.

[56] See R. S. Churchill, *Winston S. Churchill*, vol. 1: *Youth 1874–1900* (London, 1966), 414. R. Jenkins, *Churchill* (London, 2001), 41, views Churchill's claim with some scepticism.

[57] Simon was called by the Inner Temple on the same day in January 1899 as Rayner Goddard (subsequently Lord Chief Justice of England). He undertook the customary pupillage with A. J. Ram (father of the legendary First Parliamentary Counsel, Sir Granville Ram) and joined the chambers of Sir Richard Acland. In his early years in practice Simon (who made his first appearance at the Bristol Quarter Sessions) seems to have spent much of his life on the Western Circuit: see his speech to the Western Circuit Bar Mess, Winchester, 24 Feb. 1942, printed as Appendix B to *Retrospect*.

help of such women as had his acquaintance'.[58] And some of you may think this a classic, indeed perhaps a disgraceful, example of the abuse of trial by jury by an advocate indulging the jury's xenophobic prejudices. For what defence could the accused – long before Parliament created that of diminished responsibility – possibly have had? And of course Simon did remind the jury of the 'peculiar glory of our English law that in these dread matters of life and death it leaves the final decision not to the pedantic application of some written code, not even to the learning and impartiality of our judges, but to the sense of justice and the sense of duty of twelve citizens chosen by lot to represent the community as a whole, relying upon them that they will preserve and that they will apply that law which is the foundation of all our liberties'. And Simon with great skill insists that the jury must apply the law. The basis of this defence is, curiously, the letter I have quoted. Where (asks Simon) 'is there in that message, written to this cur, any indication of murderous intent?' Quite the contrary: 'I will not murder you, I will not shoot you in cold blood, I will not deal with you as one would deal with some mad dog, but I will thrash you . . . I will leave you, not a dead man, but marked for life.'[59] It is, you see, a simple matter of construction, which we lawyers can explain to you. And earlier Simon had indirectly but very clearly conveyed to the jury the message that none of the soft options for which they might have settled (the recommendation for mercy, the conviction of manslaughter) would have provided a satisfactory or even a lawful answer. So, Simon succeeds in convincing them that, even though there is no evidence of any struggle, this man who fired four shots into the body of the unarmed fellow human being his wife wished to marry must have been acting in self-defence.[60]

Old Bailey trials were not of course typical of Simon's professional practice (although he did hold the even then unfashionable view that the barrister should not become too much a specialist, and for example made a point of accepting one brief each year in the Divorce Court).[61] He soon had a practice of the highest

[58] The text of Simon's speech was privately printed: *Rex v. Malcolm. Speech of Sir John Simon for the Defence* (London: Stevens and Sons, 1917). Remarkably, Lieutenant Douglas Malcolm and his wife resumed married life, and a son, Derek (who became a distinguished journalist and film critic), was born in 1932. His autobiographical memoir *Family Secrets* (London, 2004) is of great interest.

[59] In this respect Simon came close to misleading the jury: the mental element required to found a conviction for murder is not restricted to an intent to kill but extends to an intent to cause grievous bodily harm: see Sir J. Fitzjames Stephen, *Digest of the Criminal Law*, 3rd edn (London, 1883).

[60] The trial judge's biographer described Simon's closing speech as 'one of the greatest speeches in the classical style ever delivered in a British Criminal Court': G. Pollock, *Mr Justice McCardie: A Biography* (London, 1934). Perhaps surprisingly Simon himself claimed not to 'believe in forensic eloquence. Advocacy is the art of persuasion, and English judges and juries are suspicious of flamboyant oratory': Simon, *Retrospect*, 48; and note also his speech 'The Vocation of an Advocate' to the American Bar Association in 1921: Rowland Evans (ed.), *Comments and Criticisms*, 207.

[61] See Dutton, *Simon*, 9. Simon's most celebrated appearance in the divorce courts was as leading counsel for the husband petitioner in the case of *Russell v. Russell and Mayer* (1922). Simon failed to convince all members of the jury that the wife had committed adultery and was not available at the subsequent retrial; but he evidently played some part in persuading Sir Edward Marshall Hall – probably the most fashionable advocate but by no means the greatest lawyer of the time – to present

class:[62] a general retainer for nearly every Railway Company,[63] a large practice before the Privy Council and elsewhere in intergovernmental boundary and other disputes.[64] It seems that he could hold the Lords of Appeal in his hand as effectively as he had held the jurors who acquitted Lieutenant Malcolm: Sir Harold Kent (subsequently, as Treasury Solicitor, Head of the Government Legal Service) observed him, called in on the final appeal against a particularly powerful judgment of the awesome Lord Justice Scrutton. Kent describes the way that Simon went along with each of the Law Lords as they developed their own line of argument, 'showing appreciation... but turning [the argument] gently and tactfully in the desired direction' as 'a lesson in the highest kind of advocacy'.[65] And the cases were always meticulously prepared with a wealth of learning. One of the most intriguing features about Simon's career is why it was that this marvellous sensitivity to the feelings and understandings of such very different bodies as an Old Bailey jury on the one hand, and the most intellectually sophisticated judicial tribunal in the land on the other, seems to have been so conspicuously absent in other areas of his public life.

THE BAR, THE PUBLIC SERVICE, AND PRINCIPLE

Some of you may ask what these tales of yet another lawyer's, possibly well deserved, ascent to the millionaire class – I refer to the annual earnings, you understand[66] – have to do with 'the public service'? Simon had a clear answer to this question. '[I]n my... case the Bar has been regarded as offering a career which may enable a man without private fortune to enter public life and do his best there.'[67] And the evidence that for Simon the law was no more than a means

the husband's case and a decree was granted. Correspondence in MS Simon 57, f. 72, indicates that Simon's efforts were well appreciated by the husband's family; but the House of Lords ultimately held that the divorce court (and the Court of Appeal) had been wrong to admit evidence from the husband about his intimate relationship with the wife: *Russell v. Russell* [1924] AC 687. See S. M.Cretney, *Law, Law Reform and the Family* (Oxford, 1998), ch. 4.

[62] Simon claimed that his first substantial brief came from the Government of Siam which, 'having no one else to consult', sought the advice of Simon's All Souls colleague, Professor Max Müller: Simon, *Retrospect*, 51.

[63] See Simon's letter to the solicitor R. L. Hunter, reproduced in Heuston, *Lives of the Lord Chancellors 1940–1970*, 40.

[64] Simon gave an interesting account of the Labrador boundary dispute in a lecture delivered in 1927 to 'the University I love': see Rowland Evans (ed.), *Comments and Criticisms*. Simon also accepted the role of editor of what became the standard encyclopaedic work on personal taxation, *Simon's Taxes* (still in print, albeit in a much amended and now loose-leaf format); and he apparently made real contributions to the text: see Heuston, *Lives of the Lord Chancellors 1940–1970*, 62.

[65] Kent, *In on the Act*, 87.

[66] It seems that Simon's fees amounted to more than a million pounds (in modern values) annually throughout the 1920s. He gave up practice when appointed Chairman of the Indian Statutory Commission, having been advised by his clerk that he would easily earn fees at this level when he subsequently resumed: Heuston, *Lives of the Lord Chancellors 1940–1970*, 47–8.

[67] Simon, *Retrospect*, 11.

to an end is overwhelming: appointed Solicitor-General, aged only 37, in 1910 he tells Asquith[68] that it was the political rather than the legal side of things which interested him, his real heart was in policy; in 1913 Asquith has to persuade him that accepting office as Attorney-General with a seat in the Cabinet will not prejudice a political future;[69] in 1917, out of office and enlisting in the Royal Flying Corps, Simon offers as his 'only military qualification . . . a willingness to do what I am told as well as I can . . . so long as you do not turn me on to a lawyer's job'.[70] Most telling of all is his refusal in 1915, aged 42, to accept office as the youngest Lord Chancellor in history (in place of Haldane who, notwithstanding his record as perhaps the most successful reforming war minister of modern times, had to go because his interest in Hegel and Kant made him unacceptable to the more xenophobic Unionists invited into the government).[71] 'Better the sack than the woolsack', Simon said.[72]

What, then, was the 'end' which Simon sought to achieve? Simon liked to boast that the whole of his youth was spent in the very midst of the tradition of Welsh Nonconformity[73] – four of his father's six brothers were Nonconformist Ministers – and in politics he was a cradle Gladstonian liberal:[74] the 22-year-old telling the electors of Frome of his passionate belief in free trade,[75] speaking in

[68] See his letter to Asquith quoted in Heuston, *Lives of the Lord Chancellors 1940–1970*, 41; Simon, *Retrospect*, 86.

[69] See Asquith's letter to Simon of 15 October 1913, as quoted in Dutton, *Simon*, 18.

[70] Simon to Charteris, 24 Sept. 1917, MS Simon 53.

[71] On this episode, see Heuston, *Lives of the Lord Chancellors 1885–1940*, 221–6; D. Sommer, *Haldane of Cloan: His Life and Times, 1856–1928* (London, 1960). Clifford, *The Asquiths*, 276, quotes some interesting correspondence between Haldane and the Prime Minister's wife, Margot Asquith.

[72] Simon to Buckmaster, 18 May 1915, as quoted in Heuston, *Lives of the Lord Chancellors 1885–1940*, 265.

[73] For example, in 1914 (speaking in support of the disestablishment of the Church in Wales) he emphasized that he was himself 'half a Welshman, and the whole of my youth was spent in the very midst of the tradition of Welsh Nonconformity'. In the 1927 Parliamentary debates on reform of the Book of Common Prayer he claimed to speak for the 'great mass' of quiet, simple people 'in the sort of home from which I come' who acquiesced in the Establishment of the Established Church 'precisely because they hold the fundamental view expressed by saying that the Church is a Protestant and Reformed Church': *Official Report (HC)* 15 December 1927, vol. 211, cols. 2571, 2575; and see Rowland Evans (ed.), *Comments and Criticisms*, 274. Simon admitted that his own religious convictions were 'not of a very orthodox character' (ibid.); and left specific instructions in his will that there be no religious service at his funeral.

[74] See Simon, *Retrospect*, 16, claiming that children in liberal families 'learned to admire [Gladstone] with an unqualified devotion which nothing could stale. He was our political idol, not least for his "sledgehammer mind".' Simon also evidently admired Gladstone's view of life as a 'call to ceaseless endeavour and an opportunity for public service': *Retrospect*, 19. But he did not allow his sympathy for Gladstone's politics to descend to hero worship: in 1892 the undergraduate Simon preferred to go down to the river to train for Torpids rather than fighting for a place with the huge crowd seeking admission to Gladstone's Romanes Lecture. By an interesting coincidence Claud Schuster (subsequently the long-serving Permanent Secretary in the Lord Chancellor's Department) did prefer the lecture to other attractions, and gave an account of the event in his own Romanes Lecture, 'Mountaineering', delivered in the Sheldonian Theatre on 21 May 1948. Oral tradition within the Lord Chancellor's Department has it that Schuster and Simon were mutually antipathetic to the extent that they took measures to avoid being in the same room together.

[75] There are interesting papers relating to the campaign in 1895 in MS Simon 47, 'Correspondence etc. 1894–1909'.

the Union in support of striking miners,[76] opposing the claims of powerful monopolies (whether the brewers[77] or the Church of England[78]), became, a decade later, front bench spokesman for the Asquith administration with special responsibility for some of the great issues of the day, such as disestablishment of the Welsh Church and above all Home Rule (a 'tardy measure of justice [to effect] a real reconciliation between the British and Irish people').[79] Over and over again he expresses his commitment to the social policies of the 1906 Liberal government: individual liberty must be protected from erosion by the state but it is the duty of the state to come to the help of those who needed it most; and to humanize industry using legislation to correct the rigours of unrestricted selfishness and putting public needs and human rights before private interests.[80]

But it was pacifism (or at least an aversion to war as an instrument of policy) which first caused Simon serious trouble. The Cabinet, confronted for the first time in the last week of July 1914 with imminent war on the continent of Europe, was split. Five months earlier, Simon had shown where his sympathies lay: he had opposed Churchill's plans to increase naval expenditure ('unprecedented at a time of apparent international calm', as he put it in a letter threatening resignation).[81] He wrote to Asquith suggesting that he sack the First Lord and thereby strengthen the radical element in the Liberal Party. Then, as the Cabinet agonized in the last days of July over the implications of the Austrian ultimatum to Serbia, Simon kept quiet; but Asquith can scarcely have been surprised, on Sunday 2 August, to receive Simon's formal resignation: 'why should we support a country like Russia?', he asks.[82] At Monday's Cabinet, Asquith announces

[76] See the account given by Simon of his seconding the motion moved by the well-known journalist and historian J. L. Hammond: H. A. Morrah, *The Oxford Union, 1823–1923* (London, 1923), 130.

[77] MS Simon 1 contains notes on the 1908 Licensing Bill (intended to reduce the number of licensed premises and assert state control over what could be seen as a brewers' monopoly. The Bill was rejected by the House of Lords).

[78] See note 74 above. Simon believed that the Established Church had neglected the people of Wales, but he also conceded that there were significant cultural differences between the Welsh and English: the Welsh adopted practices which offended the 'loyal Churchman's sense of what is proper and decent...The dignity of episcopal methods and the solemnity of them are very easily misunderstood by that hot and impetuous population as coldness and mere formality...': Rowland Evans (ed.), *Comments and Criticisms*, 118.

[79] Simon – spurred on by his wife (see Dutton, *Simon*, 56) – remained a radical on Irish issues, writing to *The Times* in April 1921 to denounce what he described as British atrocities and condemning the Lloyd George coalition's policy as 'politically disastrous and morally wrong'; see also Rowland Evans (ed.), *Comments and Criticisms*, ch. 5.

[80] Simon most clearly articulated his political philosophy in his speeches against what he regarded as the menace of socialism. On 16 July 1923, for example (opposing a motion in support of public ownership), he urged the need to humanize industry and 'use the force of public opinion, the power of Parliament, to correct the rigours of unrestricted selfishness by putting public needs and human rights before private interests...without sapping the energies or undermining the liberties of the British people': Rowland Evans (ed.), *Comments and Criticisms*, ch. 4.

[81] See Dutton, *Simon*, 19–23.

[82] See the correspondence in MS Simon 2, ff. 17, 18.

Simon's resignation;[83] and Simon 'briefly but with much emotion, quivering lip and tears in his eyes' explains his apparently firm decision.[84] But that afternoon Asquith persuades him to change his mind, subsequently writing: 'After full reflection (in which I have in every respect had regard to your strong convictions) I am clearly of the opinion that, at such a moment as this, you have something that nearly approaches to a public duty, for the time being at any rate, to remain.' However, 'I am most anxious that whatever I ask you to do should not in any way compromise your future. In that respect, I think that I can fully safeguard you.'[85] Whatever Asquith meant by this, it worked:[86] the next day Simon 'with good will, though with a heavy heart' agrees to stay. Violation of the Belgian neutrality guaranteed by treaty in 1839 – the famous 'scrap of paper' – is the basis for the British ultimatum delivered that day in Berlin, and rejected; and this provided justification sufficient to satisfy the Nonconformist liberal conscience for armed intervention.[87]

Was Simon right to stay? Loyalty to an old colleague, upholding international treaties, even patriotism, are all laudable characteristics. But Simon had unquestionably been indecisive, perhaps indeed hypocritical;[88] and suspicions that he had been bought off lingered.

For the time being, though, all seemed well. Simon did not become Lord Chancellor: in 1915, he became Home Secretary – at a time when what Simon described as the 'horrible cruelties and barbarities' of war were increasingly engendering popular emotions threatening the liberties for which the war was said to be being fought. He was able for a time and up to a point to protect the

---

[83] Along with three other ministers (who did in fact resign).

[84] See J. Morley, *Memorandum on Resignation, August 1914* (London, 1928); Dutton, *Simon*, 29–30.

[85] Asquith to Simon, 3 August 1914: MS Simon 2, ff. 17, 18.

[86] Simon wrote in his memoirs that 'revulsion from the horrible cruelties and inevitable barbarities of war was so strong that, until the last moment of final decision' he was prepared to 'give up a political career rather than to assent'. But the Foreign Secretary, Grey, asked him to breakfast on the morning of Monday 3 August, and 'his firmness of judgment, combined with his distress that his life's work for peace should be ruined, were a great help to me'. But it was Grey's speech in the House of Commons that afternoon which was the conclusive factor. Simon claimed that for most Englishmen it was not the fear or the danger of Germany's increasing might which justified our entry into war; it was 'the promise which we had given to Belgium which compelled it': Simon, *Retrospect*, 96.

[87] Grey's speech to the House of Commons, *Official Report* (*HC*) 3 Aug. 1914, vol. 65, col. 1809, skilfully emphasized this aspect of the crisis, which had previously been almost ignored.

[88] Charles Hobhouse (1862–1941), MP for Bristol East, described Simon's behaviour as 'almost despicable because he pretended to a special and personal abhorrence of killing' in any shape or form: see E. David, *Inside Asquith's Cabinet: from the Diaries of Charles Hobhouse* (London, 1977), 180. This judgement is all the more telling because Hobhouse was generally fairly well disposed to Simon, whom he described as having 'a most attractive personality: boundless ambition with whose aims he will let nothing interfere . . . ear always on ground, and though he will not advocate principles in which he does not believe he will certainly push aside those in which he was trained if they happen to stand in the way of political advancement. In private life a very lovable character': David, *Inside Asquith's Cabinet*, 229–30.

traditional freedoms. He refused,[89] for example, to suppress the 'disgraceful and poisonous' magazine *John Bull* for urging[90] a vendetta 'against every German in Britain whether "naturalised" or not... You cannot naturalise an unnatural beast... But you can exterminate him. And now the time has come'. But however firm one's commitment to the freedom of the individual, the line has to be drawn somewhere: only weeks later Simon is seeking to justify the government's decision to take power under the Defence of the Realm Acts 1914–1915 to detain without trial persons of 'hostile origin or associations' regardless of nationality, with arguments which Professor Brian Simpson tells us 'nobody seriously committed to the rule of law could possibly accept'.[91]

But in his own mind and indeed in his actions Simon stayed firm to his principles. On 1 January 1916, only seven months after his appointment, 'under the compulsion of a conviction'[92] that the imposition of conscription exceeded the bounds of the state's legitimate power to direct the activities of its citizens, he resigned, telling the House of Commons[93] that military organization by force was the very system the country had united to destroy. It is not easy to see what he hoped to achieve by resignation. 'I am so sorry for him in his self-righteousness', wrote Asquith.[94] Simon certainly paid a high price: for the next fifteen years he was in the political wilderness.

The *Morning Post* (later absorbed in the *Daily Telegraph*, but at the time the authentic voice of one strand of Tory opinion) accorded Simon a long obituary on his 'political suicide'.[95] But the *Post* thought both Simon and Asquith were infected by the same disease: they were lawyers, and lawyers' 'cold calculating minds' habitually put argument in place of action even in the critical phases of a great war. To find a lawyer who was also a great Englishman it was (so the *Post* believed) necessary to go back to the Glorious Revolution. The cure? At all costs, to drive the 'fee-hunters' out of the temple of policy: there 'must be no rest for the wigged'. As philippics go, this is certainly not in the highest class. But perhaps the writer had a point: the very qualities which make for success in the barrister – the remorseless attention to detail, the careful calculation not so much of the strengths of the client's case as of the strengths of the other side's and above all how the strengths on each side might be countered, the refusal to become emotionally identified with the client (this last for long being seen by traditionalists as one of the advantages of

---

[89] Simon described the publication as 'disgraceful and poisonous' but thought it best to 'let this access of misdirected zeal work itself out as it will do in a very few days': see the materials cited in T. Wilson, *The Downfall of the Liberal Party 1914–1935* (London, 1966), 159 (a very helpful guide to a confused and confusing story).

[90] In its issue of 15 May 1915.

[91] A. W. Brian Simpson, *In the Highest Degree Odious: Detention without Trial in Wartime Britain* (Oxford, 1992), 13–14.

[92] Simon to Asquith, 29 December 1915, as cited in Dutton, *Simon*, 38.

[93] *Official Report* (*HC*) 5 January 1916, vol. 77, col. 962; 12 Jan. 1916, vol. 77, col. 1645.

[94] R. Jenkins, *Asquith* (London, 1964), 388.

[95] Simon kept the cutting: see MS Simon 52.

a profession divided between the solicitor and the barrister, the barrister having a certain distance from the lay client's affairs) – are not those which a modern career counsellor would put particularly high in the profile of the politician and certainly not of the conviction politician.

Simon had gone into politics as a radical; but his firm belief in the right of the individual to be free of all but the most necessary state control made him increasingly hostile to Labour. In 1923 we find him speaking forcefully in the Commons against the motion moved by Philip Snowden (soon to become Labour's first Chancellor) urging the 'public ownership and democratic control of the instruments of production': Simon had already warned the electors of the Spen Valley that such policies would involve destroying the country's industrial structure in the mere hope that it would be rebuilt and that they constituted a serious threat to the improvements in working-class life achieved by liberal governments.[96] And Labour became exceedingly hostile to him: the newly elected MP making his maiden speech in 1906 in support of legislation overturning the decision of the House of Lords – disastrous for the trade unions – in the *Taff Vale* case[97] was also the man who helped to bring down the general strike of 1926 by telling Parliament that the strike was illegal.[98] (No one seems to remember that it was the risk that vengeful employers would by legal action for breach of contract strip the thrifty artisan of his modest savings which most influenced Simon's decision to urge caution on the Unions.) Things came to a head in June 1931: he resigned the Liberal whip as a protest against the Parliamentary Liberal Party's 'pitiful exhibition' in supporting Ramsay MacDonald's Labour government's proposals for a land tax based on the 'right of the community to the ownership of land'. Two months later the Labour Government split over whether to accept bankers' demands for a reduction in unemployment benefit. MacDonald goes to the palace late on the evening of Sunday 23 August to 'throw in his hand'. King George V persuades him to lead a national government – Conservatives, Liberals, and some (some very few, as it turned out) from Labour – with a so-called 'doctor's mandate'. Simon is not at

[96] A draft of Simon's 1922 Address to the electors of Spen Valley claimed that it was the Liberals who had done almost everything which had been done for the working man. The Liberals would be sympathetic to much in Labour's programme but not if it involved pulling down the whole industrial structure in the hope that it would be rebuilt. Jacobs, Bridges, and Beckett sent him a congratulatory telegram on his election, saying that the younger fellows of All Souls College were profoundly thankful at the outcome.

[97] The House of Lords decision meant the Unions and their members were exposed to liability in tort actions for loss caused by strikes. Simon claimed that the Trade Disputes Act 1906 was no more than an 'honest and generous attempt . . . to get back to the position which the public has always understood to have been secured by the existing law': *Official Report (HC)*, 9 Nov. 1906.

[98] Simon believed his pronouncement made some contribution to bringing the strike to an end. Simon's view was that, although the Trade Disputes Act 1906 protected Unions from tort liability in respect of actions taken in 'contemplation or furtherance of a trade dispute' there was no such protection against a strike intended primarily to threaten the Government. The Labour Party's spokesman, Sir Henry Slesser, was not the only one to disagree with Simon's analysis.

that time offered office. But he accepts an invitation from twenty-seven Liberal MPs to lead a new political party: the Liberal National (subsequently National Liberal) Party pledged in the interests of 'orderly government' to support Mac-Donald even at the cost of abandoning some of what Simon now describes as 'cherished formulas' (for example, free trade). An election gives the 'National Government' an overwhelming majority with perhaps more than 550 MPs out of 615. Simon becomes Foreign Secretary.

SIMON, THE FOREIGN SECRETARY

The timing was unfortunate for Simon's future reputation. A month previously, troops of the Japanese Empire (then a power with which this country was on friendly terms) had seized the Manchurian town of Mukden, not without some claim of right. The situation, diplomatically and legally, was formidably complex. Simon tells a friend how the Foreign Secretary has to spend his days 'writing and reading about problems which nobody quite understands and which nobody is able to solve'.[99] Chamberlain was later to record Simon's inability as Foreign Secretary 'to give a lead', instead 'always asking the Cabinet to give him instructions'.[100] That is, of course, what lawyers do; and Simon saw very clearly that there were two sides to the problem. But he made no secret of his attitude: 'I am', he told the House of Commons in 1933, 'enough of a pacifist to take this view that, however we handle this matter, I do not intend my country to get into trouble about it . . . [I]n no circumstances will this Government authorise this country to be a party to the struggle' between China and Japan. In this way (some were to say) the pathway to the beaches of Dunkirk lay through the wastes of Manchuria. On 31 January Adolf Hitler had became Chancellor of Germany. Simon continued disarmament negotiations; and in 1935 went to Berlin for talks with Hitler.

It is possible to defend the international policies which British governments pursued from that time until 1939 and Simon (displaying an especial loyalty to Chamberlain) did so in his autobiography.[101] But for the purposes of this chapter

[99] In a letter to Lady Inchcape, as cited in Dutton, *Simon*, 124. Simon told her that being Foreign Secretary had the attractions of a 'really complicated crossword puzzle'.
[100] See e.g. Dutton, *Simon*, ch. 7, especially 209–10.
[101] See Simon, *Retrospect*, 239; and see *Official Report* (*HC*), 5 Oct. 1938, vol. 339, col. 337. Simon argued that there was nothing discreditable in a statesman going to great lengths in the effort to find peaceful solutions before deciding that there was nothing for it but to let millions of people be plunged into the misery of years of war, and specifically defended the Munich agreement as the means by which country and commonwealth eventually united on the necessity for war against Germany. But Simon's public image was probably irretrievably damaged by his speech in the House of Commons on 15 March 1939 when he gave the impression that appeasement was still a viable policy notwithstanding the German action in invading Czechoslovakia (i.e. those parts of the country not already ceded under the Munich agreement). He warned against giving extensive, indefinite commitments to foreign countries who would thus effectively take control of the policy which should remain the responsibility of the Westminster Parliament: see Dutton, *Simon*, 271.

the question whether the policies were right is irrelevant (even if the writer were qualified to discuss it): whatever the merits and whatever can be said of Simon's role as Foreign Secretary in formulating and carrying out the policy, he totally failed to convince others. Donald Somervell[102] (Simon's All Souls colleague and his successor as Solicitor-General) recorded in his diary the curiously formulated but apparently widespread assessment of Simon as the worst Foreign Secretary since Ethelred the Unready. Somervell (himself a man of Munich) thought Simon's defects as a minister were exaggerated. But he remained 'a colossal liability';[103] and Simon's reputation as a politician has never recovered from his time as Foreign Secretary.[104] He was of course unlucky in taking office at a time when disarmament was still the policy. He was equally unlucky in taking office as Chancellor of the Exchequer in 1937[105] and thus becoming responsible for ensuring financial prudence at a time of huge pressure for increased expenditure on armaments.[106]

SIMON: A HUMANE HOME SECRETARY

This is to anticipate. Blackshirts were not only found on the continent of Europe. In 1934 Simon gave an eloquent speech in Glasgow. He attacked the growth of private armies: keeping public order was exclusively a matter for authorities controlled by ministers answerable to parliament or elected local representatives.

Paradoxically it seems to have been Simon who insisted on an immediate declaration of war when German forces invaded Poland on 2 Sept. 1939; as A. J. P. Taylor puts it, the 'man who had been on the point of resigning in protest against the First World War gave the final push to the second': Taylor, *English History 1914–1945* (Oxford, 1965), 452. See also Green, this volume, ch. 10.

[102] Sir Donald Bradley Somervell (1889–1960), Conservative MP for Crewe from 1931 to 1945, was Solicitor-General from 1933 to 1936 and Attorney-General 1936–45. He was appointed Lord of Appeal in Ordinary in 1954. His first degree was in chemistry; and his election as a Prize Fellow of All Souls College in 1912 is thus all the more noteworthy.

[103] Somervell recorded in his diary for the 'week of the Royal Wedding' (presumably that of the Duke of Gloucester on 6 Nov. 1935) that 'a lot of people imagine that England could in fact have done things which no Foreign Sec could have done' but that it would be 'almost impossible to persuade people that what can be done is being done while he is there'. Somervell wanted to see Simon become Lord Chancellor, 'undertaking legal reform on a large scale – codification – reforming the J.P.s – ie assimilating the C.C. Judge to the Sheriff letting him sit with local J.P.s for petty criminal work...', but in fact when Simon did become Lord Chancellor wartime conditions made it difficult to undertake long-term structural reforms: see below.

[104] In a note written after the end of the Second World War Somervell made a harsher assessment of Simon's performance, claiming that he had been a 'hopeless' Foreign Secretary, who would have put the British point of view admirably if the world had 'jogged along', but in fact he was faced with problems which 'required resolution and vision neither of which he had': Somervell, *Politics* (Oxford, Bodleian Library, Somervell Papers, 19).

[105] Simon succeeded Neville Chamberlain as Chancellor when Chamberlain succeeded Stanley Baldwin as Prime Minister in the National Government on 28 May 1937.

[106] Simon's supposed 'parsimony' in relation to defence expenditure is the main charge made against him in the 'Guilty Men' indictment.

The 4,000-strong audience was impressed, treating him to a spirited rendering of 'For he's a jolly good fellow'.[107] They were not the only ones. *The Times* detected a growing feeling at Westminster that Simon's 'profound legal knowledge and power of luminous statement' made him an ideal candidate to be again Home Secretary.[108] And in 1935 to the Home Office he returned.[109]

Home Office officials saw their chance. They recognised a liberal when they saw one. In 1929 a new Factories Bill had been produced for the Labour government. But it got nowhere. Under Simon it got – all 145 pages of it – onto the statute book. On issues such as restricting working hours there had to be compromise between Labour's trade union MPs (in those days, men who knew from personal experience what life on the shop floor or in an overheated underground bakery was like) and Tories genuinely concerned that the cost of new fire escapes, industrial fencing, and washrooms would bankrupt businesses just emerging from the slump. The Parliamentary draftsman commented that Simon, speaking in disarmingly simple and candid language, with a real grasp of the background, managed to convince MPs that they were all on the same side, seeking the best solution to human problems of considerable complexity.[110] And Simon brought forward a Public Order Bill 'to prohibit the wearing of uniforms in connection with political objects' and provided a more secure legal framework for political demonstrations.[111] This legislation survived for fifty years.[112]

Simon was also a force for reform in what we now call family law. Legislation ended the virtually automatic imprisonment of men who (often on an obstinate point of principle) refused to maintain their families.[113] And, as Home Secretary, he was instrumental in getting the cabinet to allow A. P. Herbert's Matrimonial Causes Act 1937 (extending the grounds for divorce along the lines recommended

---

[107] *The Times*, 23 Feb. 1934.

[108] The comment in *The Times*, 24 Feb. 1934 (from which the quotation in the text is drawn) seems to have been influential.

[109] In September 1931 Simon accepted an invitation to become the Leader of the Liberal National Party (subsequently the National Liberal Party). Opponents regarded the National Liberals as Tories sailing under false colours, and Simon's membership of the Cabinet gave plausibility to the Government's claim to be a 'National' (rather than a Conservative) administration. Generally for a clear account of the fortunes of the Liberal Party from 1916 see Wilson, *The Downfall of the Liberal Party 1914–1935*, and note the summary in D. Butler and G. Butler, *Twentieth-Century British Political Facts, 1900–2000* (Basingstoke, 2000), 176. For a eulogistic account of Simon's role as leader of the National Liberals see G. H. Shakespeare, *Let Candles Be Brought In* (London, 1949), 138.

[110] See the illuminating account given by Kent, *In on the Act*, ch. 8.

[111] The decision to legislate was prompted by the growth of demonstrations – culminating in the so-called 'Battle of Cable Street' in the East End of London on 4 Oct. 1936 (when the Metropolitan Police Commissioner successfully used Common Law police powers to order the British Union of Fascists to disperse). Simon claimed that the Public Order Act 1936 'operated like a charm. Mosley's men looked and felt very different in ordinary clothes, and the police used their [extensive] powers of controlling processions with their usual good sense': Simon, *Retrospect*, 216.

[112] The Act was replaced, after much discussion, by the Public Order Act 1986.

[113] The Money Payments (Justices' Procedure) Act 1936. This gave effect to the *Report of the Departmental Committee on Imprisonment by Courts of Summary Jurisdiction in Default of Payment of Fines and other Sums of Money*, Cmd 4649, 1936.

by a Royal Commission a quarter of a century earlier) to be properly dealt with in both Houses of Parliament. As Herbert recorded, Simon 'seldom seems to receive due credit for anything he does; so let me say here that... within the limits of his authority he did all he could for us throughout'.[114]

Bringing forward legislation is of course an important function of government but by no means the only one. The Home Secretary has vast responsibilities, possibly at that time the most important of which was advising – in effect deciding – on the exercise of the prerogative of mercy in respect of those condemned to death. Before Simon's time Home Secretaries generally took the view that, 'as death was the penalty laid down for murder there had to be some mitigating circumstance to justify setting that penalty aside... Simon's approach seems to have been quite different... [H]e looked for some aggravating feature... but in default of some aggravating feature he was prepared to reprieve'.[115]

The Home Secretary also has departmental responsibility for relations between the executive and the monarch it serves; and as Home Secretary Simon played a central part in the events between 13 November 1936 (when the Cabinet first discussed the so-called 'King's matter') and 12 December 1936 when King Edward signified the Royal Assent to His Majesty's Declaration of Abdication Act. It was Simon who drafted Baldwin's 'supremely effective' statement to the Commons rejecting the 'utterly impracticable' proposal that legislation permit Mrs Wallis Simpson to marry the King but not become Queen. And when the King's advisors realized that the divorce decree nisi granted to Mrs Simpson might be rescinded if evidence that she had committed adultery became available it was Simon who bore the chief burden of advising on the ingenious proposal that government legislation should not only deal with the monarch's abdication but also make the Simpson divorce secure against ever being overturned. He began by advocating this solution – it would, after all, strain the traditional British sense of fair play to allow King Edward to abdicate in order to marry the woman he loved only to have King George's Attorney-General request the court to rescind her divorce and thereby make it impossible for her to marry the ex-King or indeed anyone else – but in the end the argument for constitutional propriety (that it would be unacceptable to accord Mrs Simpson and Edward a concession not available to the ordinary citizen) carried the day.[116] Simon unquestionably wobbled on this (as on other matters) but once the decision had been taken he was a master of all the complex and burdensome administrative steps which had to be taken, not least those required under the Statute of Westminster to obtain the necessary concurrence of the dominions. Sir Walter

[114] A. P. Herbert, *The Ayes Have It: The Story of the Marriage Bill* (London, 1937), 96. Simon also sponsored the Adoption Act 1949 and was often able to bring relevant factors to the attention of the Home Office because of a daughter's knowledge gained as a Justice of the Peace. His daughter the Hon. Mrs Edwards had herself adopted a child.
[115] See Heuston, *Lives of the Lord Chancellors 1940–1970*, 51.
[116] See Cretney, 'The King and the King's Proctor', 583.

Monckton admiringly recorded: 'I have seen many staff officers but none so competent';[117] and he might have added few ministers so resilient. For at the same time, in the week of the abdication, Simon was imperturbably, and with a total mastery of the smallest detail and the most difficult points of principle, taking his Public Order Act through both its final stages in the House of Commons.[118]

Simon was a progressive and humane Home Secretary. But however strong his commitment to traditional liberal values, no one could pretend that he was a man of vision: it was Winston Churchill (not Simon) who as an ambitious member of Asquith's 1908 Cabinet bombarded the Prime Minister with 'large designs' – compulsory education to 17, National Health and Unemployment Insurance, and other measures modelled on what Churchill described as 'the successful experiences of [Bismarck's] Germany';[119] it was Herbert Samuel (not Simon) who in the 1920s tried to get what remained of the Liberal Party to formulate and publicize distinctive policies on such matters as Britain's industrial future.[120]

LORD CHANCELLOR SIMON

Churchill may have appointed Simon Lord Chancellor in 1940 in order to render him innocuous; but Simon continued to show his skills in handling potentially difficult situations. He is certainly entitled to a short footnote as the only British Cabinet minister to have had discussions with a leading member of the Nazi hierarchy during the hostilities of the Second World War. To do justice to the talk between Simon (given the implausible pseudonym 'Dr Guthrie') and Rudolph Hess, recently fallen from the skies over Scotland, requires the skills of a Harold Pinter rather than the verbatim record now available; but Simon's calm matter of fact responses – Hess's threats of hunger strike are, he tells him, 'very silly' – indicate that once again he had a safe pair of hands.[121]

It is not such diversions, however, but Simon's discharge of the duties of Lord Chancellor which compel admiration: it is (the historian of twentieth-century Lord Chancellors has written)[122] 'impossible to open any volume [of the Law Reports covering Simon's period in office] without being struck by the scale and

---

[117] See Lord Birkenhead, *Walter Monckton: the Life of Viscount Monckton of Brenchley* (London, 1969), 149.

[118] *Official Report* (*HC*) 7 Dec. 1936, vol. 318, col. 1659.

[119] See Churchill's letter of 29 Dec. 1908, reproduced in Jenkins, *Churchill*, 146–7.

[120] *Britain's Industrial Future: being the report of the Liberal Industrial Enquiry* (London, 1928).

[121] Simon was accompanied to the meeting (which took place on 9 June 1941 at Mytchett Place, near Aldershot) by the Foreign Office official (subsequently Permanent Secretary) Ivone Kirkpatrick, but Hess insisted on seeing Simon alone for part of the meeting.

[122] Heuston, *Lives of the Lord Chancellors 1940–1970*, 57.

distinction of his achievement'.[123] Unhappily it is impossible in a few moments to give a lay audience any impression of this; as a reminder to the lawyers one may just list some of the more important: *United Australia, Limited v. Barclays Bank Limited*,[124] *East Suffolk Rivers Catchment Board v. Kent and Another*,[125] *Benham v. Gambling*,[126] *Mancini v. DPP*,[127] *Joseph Constantine Steamship Line v. Imperial Smelting Corporation Ltd*,[128] the *Fibrosa* case,[129] *Perrin and others v.*

[123] This judgement relates to Simon's judicial work. Heuston is less impressed by Simon's discharge of the Lord Chancellor's executive duties as the minister responsible for the court system and the civil law: the war 'provided an excuse for not undertaking a task for which Simon had no aptitude – the reform of the legal system': see Heuston, *Lives of the Lord Chancellors 1940–1970*, 57, and contrast Somervell's expectations in this respect: n. 104 above. Simon did however formulate ambitious plans for the trial of undefended divorces, but these were not adopted by the incoming Labour Government and reform was delayed for thirty years. In one respect Simon played a decisive part in improving the judicial system: he was responsible for establishing the Committee on Legal Aid and Legal Advice in England and Wales whose report led directly to the enactment of the Legal Aid and Advice Act 1949 and the creation of the Legal Aid scheme, which dramatically improved access to the courts for those of modest means. Simon was also responsible for recommending, in 1944, the appointment of A. T. Denning to the High Court bench.

[124] [1941] 1 AC 1. The narrow point to be resolved in this case was whether the fact that the Company had started proceedings against the payee of a cheque for money had and received debarred them from suing the Bank (after the payee had gone into liquidation) in the tort of conversion for collecting the cheque. Simon's Opinion goes into much detail on the history of the doctrine of waiver of a tort and concludes that the interests of justice require the Company to have a remedy. The approach of the House of Lords is encapsulated in Lord Atkin's well known statement (at p. 29) that the 'fantastic resemblances of contracts invented in order to meet requirements of the law as to forms of action which have now disappeared should not in these days be allowed to affect actual rights. When these ghosts of the past stand in the path of justice clanking their mediaeval chains the proper course for the judge is to pass through them undeterred.'

[125] [1941] AC 74: the Board (which had a mere power to remedy flood damage) was not liable for the negligent conduct of the work it did; liability only arose if the negligence had added to the damage which would have been suffered had the Board done nothing.

[126] [1941] AC 157: the damages payable in respect of loss of expectation of life when a child is killed by a defendant's negligence should be fixed at a conventional figure of £200 (perhaps £5,000 in year 2000 values). The decision was a straightforward example of judicial legislation: Simon noted that in reality the benefit would go to the infant's family who had not suffered any economic loss. He accepted that in fixing damages for the loss of a happy life, the court had to decide an issue more suitable for discussion in an essay on Aristotelian ethics than in the judgment of a court of law. In 1976 the Fatal Accidents Act adopted an approach more sympathetic to claims by bereaved parents in prescribing a fixed sum of £7,500 specifically as damages in respect of bereavement.

[127] [1942] AC 1: the provocation sufficient to render a killer guilty of manslaughter rather than of murder must be such as would have deprived a reasonable man of self-control; and the fact that the accused did in fact lose his or her self-control is irrelevant. This harsh rule was abolished by the Homicide Act 1957, s. 3.

[128] [1941] AC 154: an important case on the doctrine of frustration (i.e. the rules determining the situations in which a party to a contract is justified in refusing to perform a contract because the surrounding circumstances have changed). The House of Lords held that the defendant did not need affirmatively to prove that he had no responsibility for the events constituting the change; and Simon asserts his belief in the so-called 'implied term' theory of the doctrine.

[129] [1943] AC 32: where a contract is frustrated, the loss must lie where it falls; and any notion that the loss can be apportioned between the parties must be a matter for legislative rather than judicial action. (On the facts of the case before it, however, the House held that a deposit paid in advance of performance could be recovered under the doctrine of failure of consideration). The Law Reform (Frustrated Contracts) Act 1943 (enacted following consideration by the Lord Chancellor's Law Revision Committee: *7th Interim Report*, Cmd 6009, 1939) attempted to remedy the inflexibility of the law.

Morgan,[130] *Chichester Diocesan Fund and Board of Finance v. Simpson and others*,[131] *Crofter Hand Woven Harris Tweed Company Ltd v. Veitch*.[132] The reasoning in some of these cases certainly evidences Simon's ideological preferences: for example the justification given for the decision in *Nokes v. Doncaster Amalgamated Collieries* (coal miner not liable to a statutory penalty under an Act of 1875 for wrongfully absenting himself from work at the Hickleton Main colliery) was founded on the legal principle that his duties to his original employer had not been validly transferred to another and that in turn was based on Simon's belief that it was a 'fundamental principle of our common law that a free citizen, in the exercise of his freedom, is entitled to choose the employer whom he promises to serve'.[133] But once again there is in Simon's decisions no great sense of a vision of the great society: perhaps that is what Dr Stevens has in mind in classifying Simon as a 'substantive formalist'.[134]

Simon was able in his judicial role as Lord Chancellor to bring about a major reform in the divorce law dating from 1857 and based on the principle (reasonable enough as an abstract proposition) that only those who are themselves innocent should be entitled to the 'relief' of divorce against a guilty party. It is true that those who had fallen from grace might be allowed a divorce if the court exercised the discretion which the law conferred on it to do so; but the courts, at least until the Great War,[135] would generally refuse to do so – a fact so widely understood that on average only one person a year bothered to ask. The courts' reluctance meant that the more self-evident it was that the marriage was dead beyond prospect of repair (the case where both parties have acquired other partners and had children by them, for example) the more certain it was that the law would insist that the legal relationship be kept in being until severed by

---

130 [1943] AC 399: if a testator makes a gift of his 'money' what does that expression cover? Simon and his colleagues preferred a more flexible test than had been accepted in the past.

131 [1944] AC 341: Caleb Diplock left his substantial fortune to such charitable or benevolent objects as his trustees should select. The House of Lords held that, since the trustees could properly under such a gift have given the entire estate to objects which were not legally charitable but were considered by the trustees to be 'benevolent', and since that expression had no legal meaning, the testator had failed to dispose of his estate which accordingly passed on his intestacy. A valid will must effectively dispose of the testator's property; a testator cannot leave it to his trustees to do so.

132 [1942] AC 435: officials of the Transport and General Workers' Union in Stornoway 'blacked' imported yarn in an attempt to forward or protect the interests of the Union and its members. They were not liable in conspiracy: the fact that a number of people combined for reasons of self-interest did not of itself make them liable for the loss their actions caused.

133 [1940] AC 1014. But however justifiable the principle of freedom to choose may have been, the rule laid down in *Nokes* could cause inconvenience to workers as well as employers; and it has been modified by delegated legislation.

134 See R. Stevens, *Law and Politics: The House of Lords as a Judicial Body 1800–1976* (London, 1979), 335, for the view that there was 'something profoundly disquieting about [Simon's] Chancellorship with respect to the appellate process'. Dr Stevens's unease seems to be based on the belief that Simon and others wanted to persuade the public that the judges were not in fact taking decisions of importance; and that they preferred prestige to power.

135 See *Apted v. Apted and Bliss* [1930] P. 246: the great increase in the number of judges dealing with divorce cases may have been a factor in liberalizing the application of the law.

death. In this way, the law (so it was said)[136] promoted virtue and morality and discouraged vice and immorality. In 1943 the principles upon which the court's discretion should be exercised came before the House of Lords for the first time; and Simon succeeded in convincing his colleagues that the principles for exercising discretion should be reformulated so as to give primary importance to 'the interest of the community at large, to be judged by maintaining a true balance between respect for the binding sanctity of marriage and the social considerations which make it contrary to public policy to insist on the maintenance of a union which has utterly broken down'; and in practice, the fact the marriage had indeed broken down became so strong an element in the matter that the court's discretion came to be exercised in all but the most flagrant cases – twenty years on, exercised in nearly 4,000 cases and refused in only three – and those usually involving perjury by those concerned.[137]

This is a, perhaps extreme, example of the way in which the Lords of Appeal not only decided cases but made law; and today it seems strange that Lord Chancellors should sit in cases which might be thought to have had a political element.[138] Simon, however, thought that 'no one would dispute that it was a most important part of the Lord Chancellor's "duty as head of the Judiciary"[139] to preside in . . . appeals as much as he can',[140] and would, I think, have viewed with incredulity the suggestion[141] that no Lord Chancellor should ever sit in the highest court of appeal: for Simon, the public interest was served by a system in which the independence in legal matters (of the Law Officers as well as the Lord Chancellor) was combined with membership of the executive.[142] Even so it

---

136 *Constantinidi v. Constantinidi and Lance* [1905] P. 253, 278, *per* Stirling LJ.

137 For the change in practice, see *The Field of Choice*, Cmd 3123, 1966, p. 12, nn. 30, 32, 33.

138 The litigation following the loss of the HMS *Thetis* is the most remarkable: see below.

139 The author knows of no evidence that Simon had any judicial experience prior to taking office as Lord Chancellor. He evidently believed that on assuming office the Lord Chancellor should be seen primarily as a judge, 'notwithstanding his mixture of duties which at first sight seems so oddly combined': Simon, *Retrospect*, 260. Simon gives a full account of the chapter of accidents which led to Lord Chancellors taking a smaller part in the judicial work of the House of Lords than he had done: ibid., 258–61; and see Heuston, *Lives of the Lord Chancellors 1940–1970*, 26–7.

140 See Simon, *Retrospect*, 259–60. Simon was particularly concerned that the administration of the courts and the selection of judges should remain with the Lord Chancellor. He deplored the fact that Civil Servants were increasingly concerning themselves with matters he felt should be in the hands of the judiciary, and was strongly opposed to the creation of a Ministry of Justice.

141 Made from time to time over the years, notably by Lord Steyn in his Neill Lecture, 'The Case for a Supreme Court', *Law Quarterly Review*, 118 (2002), 382. For a full and balanced discussion of the role of the Lord Chancellor see D. Woodhouse, *The Office of Lord Chancellor* (Oxford, 2001), especially ch. 8. The Constitutional Reform Act 2005 created a Supreme Court for the United Kingdom which began to hear appeals in 2009. As first envisaged by the Blair Government, it was intended to abolish the office of Lord Chancellor, but after powerful opposition had been expressed to what was evidently an inadequately thought-out proposal it was decided to retain the office whilst redefining its characteristics.

142 The essence of Simon's view seems to have been that a Minister of Justice would be a politician heading a department staffed by civil servants, and that the appointment of judges in such a system would endanger the culture in which judges (appointed impartially by the Lord Chancellor 'with his knowledge of the law and of the Bar') are 'completely indifferent as to whether . . . he decides against the Government of the day or in its favour': see Simon, *Retrospect*, 259–60.

is strange to modern minds that he saw no reason not to sit in a case which for a quarter of a century defined what is called crown privilege, the extent of the government's right to determine conclusively whether or not to disclose documents relevant to litigation – in that case about liability to compensate the families of victims of the loss of the submarine *Thetis*.[143]

Attitudes change and there was certainly room for argument about how far the doctrine of separation of powers should be allowed to govern constitutional practice in this country.[144] But the discovery of Simon's attempt to persuade one of the Law Lords (Lord Atkin) to modify the outspoken language[145] of a judgment in which Atkin had vigorously dissented from the view of the other Law Lords that the courts had no power to investigate the grounds upon which the Home Secretary had ordered the detention without trial of a person alleged to be of 'hostile origins or associations'[146] has attracted strong criticism: indeed Dr Robert Stevens, in his magisterial 1979 study of the House of Lords as a judicial body,[147] described Simon's intervention as 'most sinister'.[148] But Simon's reason for suggesting some modification in the language Atkin had used was to avoid the risk of wounding the colleagues with whom Atkin disagreed. It is probable that a plain, simply expressed suggestion to that effect would not have attracted comment, but regrettably Simon's letter to Atkin was couched in the oleaginous prose of which, sadly for his reputation, he was a master.[149] Let me give you another example: in 1945 Archbishop Fisher had somehow come to

[143] *Duncan v. Cammell Laird & Co* [1942] AC 624: Simon, delivering the unanimous decision of a panel of seven Law Lords, upheld the decision of the courts below to refuse to order the Crown to disclose documents (including the vessel's specification) relating to the submarine HMS *Thetis* (lost on 1 June 1939, with substantial loss of life). Simon's approach was to set out factors which should influence ministers faced with a request for disclosure but to assert unequivocally that the minister's decision, once taken, was not to be questioned. The eventual outcome (which Simon conceded to be remarkable) was that the victims' relatives failed to recover any damages but he justified this by reference to the principle that 'in order to recover damages it is necessary to prove liability against one or other of the parties': *Woods v. Duncan* [1946] AC 401.

[144] The creation of the Supreme Court by the Constitutional Reform Act 2005 (see n. 141 above) was influenced by a desire to underline the separation between the legislature and the judiciary.

[145] 'In this case I have listened to arguments which might acceptably have been addressed to the Court of King's Bench in the time of Charles I.' Simon also regarded Atkin's somewhat sneering reference to Alice in Wonderland as inappropriate.

[146] *Liversidge v. Anderson* [1942] AC 206. Simon did not himself sit to hear the appeal because he had, as Home Secretary, signed similar orders under the legislation in force during the First World War: *R. v. Halliday* [1917] AC 260, HL (where the validity of the order was also upheld).

[147] Stevens, *Law and Politics*.

[148] See ibid., 333; see also Simpson, *In the Highest Degree Odious*, 376, giving further details of subsequent events (including the refusal of the Cabinet to change the law in the sense of Atkin's judgment, and a broadcast by Simon on 28 April 1942 in praise of the state of affairs in England as compared with Germany). Simpson regards Simon's talk as 'rubbish' and claims that the broadcast seems to give 'final confirmation to the view that there is no limit to the hypocrisy of which lawyers are capable'.

[149] For an account less unsympathetic to Simon see Heuston, *Lives of the Lord Chancellors 1940–1970*, 60; and *Law Quarterly Review*, 86 (1970), 33–68, particularly 45–6.

hear that the Government planned to allow court Registrars (rather than judges) to pronounce undefended divorce decrees. The Archbishop wrote to Simon to warn that the Church would oppose such an attack on the sanctity of marriage 'with all its might'. The careful detail of Simon's long and skilful reply does not matter. Nor, perhaps, does the fact that Simon urges Fisher to keep the list of those he consults 'narrow and well-selected' to avoid 'tendentious articles and hints in unauthorised quarters'. But listen to the conclusion: 'I need not tell you, my dear Archbishop, how much I hope that our first contact in the legislative field should exhibit an agreement not unworthy of the ancient traditions of the Woolsack when that awkward piece of furniture was usually occupied by a distinguished ecclesiastic, though I will not offer the instance of Cardinal Wolsey as the model of how to deal with divorce law! Yours very sincerely...' (In fact, Fisher should not have worried: the incoming Labour government, fearful of alienating Roman Catholic voters in the large industrial cities, dropped the proposal, which became law only thirty years later.)

SIMON, THE HUMAN BEING

No wonder Simon, an outstandingly gifted man, was not widely popular or indeed universally trusted. In part the explanation is political: Simon had made enemies in all three of the major political parties. For Labour, there was the legality of the general strike, and above all there was the collaboration with the traitor MacDonald. The Tories hated him as an appeaser; and they feared and despised him: too clever by half,[150] or even more. And the Liberals? He had betrayed them, or some of them, too. He was, to put it mildly, not a successful politician. But someone more adept at public relations might well have overcome these difficulties.[151] One of the many anti-Simon jests has him on his knees every night beseeching the Almighty to make him a good chap, but the Almighty never did.

In one respect, at least, Simon was fortunate. He lived before politicians felt it necessary or desirable to put themselves figuratively 'in the psychiatrist's chair'. Today, the closeness of his relationship with his mother – he published a memoir[152] of the woman who had made his childhood home a 'palace of

[150] The allegation made in 1961 by the Marquess of Salisbury against the then Colonial Secretary Iain Macleod in the context of Macleod's policy of promoting African self-government.
[151] Chamberlain, commenting to his sister on the Commons debate about the military situation in Norway (which led to his resignation as Prime Minister), confessed that he found it difficult to understand the 'personal dislike' of Simon – and his colleague Hoare – but none the less regarded it as having played a significant part in the rebellion amongst the Government's supporters: Heuston, *Lives of the Lord Chancellors 1940–1970*, 54.
[152] Simon, *Portrait of My Mother* (London, 1936). The book carries a note that any proceeds were to go to Lady Simon's 'fund for the abolition of present day slavery': see below. Simon's will made careful arrangements for the future of the two portraits 'of a beautiful old lady' he had had painted by Sir Gerald Kelly.

enchantment'[153] and sent copies as a condolence to bereaved acquaintances –
would no doubt be a source of sly comment. And there was tragedy in Simon's
life. Married to Ethel Venables, Vice-Principal of St Hugh's College,[154] in the
year he was called to the bar, only three years later he was a widower with three
children.[155] Fourteen years afterwards he remarried. His will a quarter of a
century later referred to her (in terms unusual in documents drafted by eminent
City solicitors[156]) as 'my darling Kathleen who has been to me the dearest of
wives'. But she did not appeal to everyone: perhaps the fact that she was Irish had
something to do with it – Rowse even wrote that 'being Irish, she became an
alcoholic'[157] – perhaps that she had been his children's governess (even a
governess who impressed the Asquiths by hunting with the Bicester in company
with F. E. Smith),[158] more probably perhaps that she had strong radical views: in
Who's Who she described her career – 'devoted to the cause of freedom everywhere; to Ireland, to Zionism, to assisting backward and oppressed peoples,
Chairman Shamrock Club for Irish Soldiers'.[159] Worse still, for some, she wrote
a book, *Slavery* (London, 1929), directing attention to the fact that there were
still four million slaves, and seeking (as Simon put it in the preface he wrote) to
substitute for historical complacency a stimulus to fresh action. In 1931 Simon
persuaded the government to appoint his wife a Dame of the British Empire,
refusing for himself the peerage he had been offered in recognition of his work on
the Indian Commission; but it is clear that some well-placed individuals did not
think her a suitable spouse for a Foreign Secretary. Today, as Professor Heuston
remarks,[160] she would have become a television personality but at the time she
was, in some quarters, an embarrassment. Simon deeply resented this. Sensitive
observers noted an increasing bitterness and sense of disappointment.

John Sparrow wrote (and later tried to suppress) an epigraph for Simon:[161]

This stone, with not unpardonable pride,

Proves by its record what the world denied:

Simon could do a natural thing – he died.

---

[153] Simon, *Retrospect*, 18.

[154] Her duties – defined as 'to assist the Principal in such ways as she may require' – seem to have
been comparable to those more recently discharged by College Secretaries. She also took a special
interest in the Library which she first organized; and a touching obituary in the *St Hugh's Club Paper*,
no. 10 (1903), suggests she had a considerable pastoral role in the life of the St Hugh's students. I am
grateful to the former Principal of St Hugh's College, Derek Wood CBE, QC, and to the College's
Librarian, Debbie Quare, for tracing archival material.

[155] His wife died in a Woking Nursing Home on 12 September 1902 within days of the birth of
her third child and only son, John Gilbert Simon. The cause of death was certified as 'Confinement.
Septicaemia 8 days.'

[156] Stephenson, Harwood & Tatham.

[157] Rowse, *All Souls*, 63.

[158] See Asquith to Stanley, 9 March 1914, as printed in Brock, *Asquith, Letters to Venetia Stanley*,
53. The letter records that the governess 'rules the whole establishment'.

[159] See *Who Was Who*, vol. 5.

[160] Heuston, *Lives of the Lord Chancellors 1940–1970*, 45.

[161] Nicolson, *Diaries and Letters 1939–1945*, 11 Jan. 1954.

But even in death Simon could not be entirely natural. 'I believe', he had written in his memoirs,[162] 'that Mr Gladstone, a most devoted son of Oxford, was buried in the gown of a Doctor of Civil Law'; and 'I should like to be cremated in mine, for the same reason.' Simon was devoted to All Souls and the University of which it is a part; he was indeed, I believe, a man of traditional liberal beliefs consistently applied; he was a superlative lawyer, he gave many years of his life to 'public service'. Unhappily Simon's unfortunate personality, taken with his failure as Foreign Secretary, has overshadowed what would otherwise be seen as a remarkable record of public service. It is true that no one would describe Simon as a 'good chap', but I believe he was a good man who did do a great deal of good.

[162] Simon, *Retrospect*, 227.

4

Government by a Mallardian

On the Possibility of Public Service in the Political Thought of R. H. Brand

S. J. D. Green

When Lord Brand died on 23 August 1963, *The Times* lamented the passing of a truly remarkable 'banker...statesman and...philosopher'. To justify such a rare, multiple, accolade the paper paid equal attention to his achievements in each of these fields. Dutifully noting the domestic heights – this long-time Managing Director of Lazard Brothers was also a particularly influential member of the Macmillan Committee on Finance and Industry during the 1930s – it made still more special play of the international dimensions of Brand's financial career: first, as trusted advisor to Lord Robert Cecil's Supreme Economic Council and at Versailles, in 1919; then as inspirational vice-president of the International Financial Conference of the League of Nations, held at Brussels, the following year; eventually as assiduous Treasury representative in Washington, between 1944 and 1946. But most of all, the obituary celebrated an impeccable record of public service, broadly conceived. This had begun with his seminal role in the creation of the South African constitution of 1909. It had culminated in his critical contributions to the formation of the International Bank for Reconstruction and Development and the International Monetary Fund, following the Bretton Woods and Savannah Conferences at the end of the Second World War. Finally, the Thunderer acknowledged one of the nation's 'wisest...and most realistic minds'; a long-time fellow of All Souls and a 'distinguished...economist', legendary luminary of 'The Round Table' – even a 'wise counsellor' to the old journalistic workhorse itself.[1]

---

[1] Anon., 'Lord Brand', *The Times*, 24 Aug. 1963, 8. Brand was born in 1878. He was a fellow of All Souls between 1901 and 1931 and again between 1938 and 1963. He was a member of the Editorial Board of *The Round Table* from its foundation in 1912 and a director of *The Times* from 1922. There is no full-length biography. The best biographical account can now be found in K. Burk, 'Brand, Robert Henry, Baron Brand (1876–1763)', *ODNB*.

But there was something else. Two columns of otherwise unrestrained eulogy could not entirely obscure a certain elegiac tone in this glowing notice of a great life's work. That went far beyond the normal obsequies about a once estimable colleague, now sadly departed. *The Times* also remarked upon Brand's broader significance as an 'outstanding example' of a 'dwind[ling] species'.[2] As such, his was deemed to be something of a symptomatic death. It marked the end not merely of an era but also of a type. This was of a figurative race of patrician virtuosi: rounded, civilized, and sensible guardians; wise men and excellent authorities in an age of otherwise fanatical, barbarian, and quixotic potentates. To be clear: virtuosi not dilettanti; for these were invariably tough-minded individuals who spent much of their lives running a far-flung empire. And they were astute enough to manage it on a proverbial shoe-string. But they were also highly educated persons who proved that rule did not preclude culture. That virtuosity was at least in part traceable to their complex composition. This was not an exclusively landed élite; though many of its members, like Brand himself, were drawn from ancient families. Few of its number were mere scions of business fortunes; though some might plausibly have described themselves as 'gentlemen capitalists'. Fewer still were direct descendants of the mid-Victorian 'intellectual aristocracy'; yet most were not merely adorned by lineage and wealth, but also graced through considerable academic distinction. Rather, it was an unusually able and remarkably adaptable governing tribe, curiously constituted out of an institutionally amphibian fusion of rank, property, and mind.[3] There was no better example than Brand himself: the second son of Viscount Hampden, married into the Langhorne clan, thereby connected to the Astor fortunes; also an impeccably discreet banker continually trusted with the more delicate interests of the British Empire; finally a 'brilliant...scholar', charged with reconciling the 'orthodox traditions' of the City of London to the 'liberal and progressive ideas' of John Maynard Keynes.[4]

This was not an ancient breed: not, at least, as a breed. *The Times* traced its lineage back no further than the last quarter of the nineteenth century; more precisely to the pages of Bagehot's *Lombard Street*.[5] Nor was it long-lived. Its

---

[2] *The Times*, 24 Aug. 1963, 8.

[3] For some insights into its (still largely unwritten) history, see P. J. Cain and A. G. Hopkins, *British Imperialism: Innovation and Expansion, 1688–1914* (London, 1993), ch. 3; D. Cannadine, *The Decline and Fall of the British Aristocracy* (New Haven and London, 1990), chs 6 and 9; N. Annan, 'The Intellectual Aristocracy', in idem, *The Dons: Masters, Eccentrics and Geniuses* (London, 1999), annexe; the more aristocratic dimensions of this élite are memorably captured in K. Rose, *Superior Person: A Portrait of Curzon and his Circle in late Victorian England* (London, 1969), chs 5, 8, and 12–14; the more bourgeois in R. Skidelsky, *John Maynard Keynes: A Biography*, 3 vols (London, 1983–2000), i, chs 4–7. Much related insight can be gleaned from Noel Annan, *Our Age: Portrait of a Generation* (London, 1990), ch. 2; so too, albeit in a quite different way, from T. J. H. Bishop (in collaboration with R. Wilkinson), *Winchester and the Public School Elite: A Statistical Analysis* (London, 1967), esp. chs 2 and 4.

[4] *The Times*, 24 Aug. 1963, 8.

[5] Ibid.; Walter Bagehot, 'Lombard Street', in N. St John Stevas (ed.), *The Collected Works of Walter Bagehot*, 9 (London, 1978), 45–233, esp. chs 9–11. The original book was published in 1873.

apogee is perhaps most vividly described in the mature writings of John Buchan. Indeed, its reign barely survived the end of the Second World War. During the years since, it has disappeared altogether. There has been no successor to Brand. Moreover, with the decline of power has seemingly gone much of the possibility of sympathetic understanding. Amongst the once famous of its kind, this has led to an extraordinary degree of subsequent abuse; think of Buchan's posthumous reputation.[6] For the more discreet, it meant neglect. Again, there is no better example than Brand. Home and abroad, his legacy has largely been forgotten. This would greatly have surprised his contemporaries. During the weeks immediately after his death, his old friend, Felix Frankfurter, declared himself quite 'confident' that the 'opening up' of the 'relevant . . . archives' and 'private papers', notably those of Lothian and Halifax, would establish not only the particular importance of Brand's 'wise counsel' for these two great missionaries of Empire, but also of his wider significance in the development of 'Anglo-American relations' more generally during the second third of the twentieth century.[7] That has not proved to be the case. The official lives both of Kerr and Wood make little mention of Brand's influence on their respective subjects.[8] Most modern historians of the so-called 'special relationship' count it for still less.[9]

Such ingratitude, if that is what it is, owes little or nothing to a peculiarly American forgetfulness. For Brand has also been largely written out of the history of modern Africa too. Thus Hancock's massive study of *Smuts* contains precisely two references to Brand's contribution to 'Union'.[10] Nor can foreigners generally stand condemned for a supposed small-mindedness in these

---

[6] John Buchan, first Baron Tweedsmuir (1875–1940), Governor-General of Canada, 1935–40; barrister, public servant, and writer. See especially some of his non-fiction works, e.g. *The Last Servants* (1923), *Homilies and Recreations* (1926), *Men and Deeds* (1935), *Canadian Occasions* (1940), and *Memory, Hold the Door* (1940). There is now an important study of Buchan's social and political thought in J. P. Parry, 'From the Thirty-Nine Articles to the Thirty-Nine Steps: Reflections on the Thought of John Buchan', in M. Bentley (ed.), *Public and Private Doctrine: Essays in British History, Presented to Maurice Cowling* (Cambridge, 1993), 209–35; a more detailed, but narrower, analysis of his fiction can be found in J. Kruse, *John Buchan and the Idea of Empire: Popular Literature and Political Ideology* (Lewiston, NY, 1989), *passim*. For the context, see C. Harvie, *The Centre of Things: Political Fiction in Britain from Disraeli to the Present* (London, 1991), 149–52 and 165–6; or, for a celebration, R. Usborne, *Clubland Heroes* (London, 1953), 3–4 and 15–16.

[7] F. Frankfurter, 'Lord Brand: Anglo-American Relations', *The Times*, 16 September 1963, 16; on Frankfurter and England, especially All Souls, see I. Berlin, 'Felix Frankfurter at Oxford', in idem, *Personal Impressions* (London, 1980), 83–90.

[8] J. R. M. Butler, *Lord Lothian (Philip Kerr), 1882–1940* (London, 1960), chs 14 and 15; though see ch. 2 for South Africa; the Earl of Birkenhead, *Halifax: The Life of Lord Halifax* (London, 1965), contains just three passing remarks on Brand; these on 74, 480, and 553; Andrew Roberts' more recent life, *'The Holy Fox': A Biography of Lord Halifax* (London, 1991), is similarly elusive; just two references, on 288 and 297. Kerr was the British Ambassador to Washington between August 1939 and December 1940; Wood, from January 1941 to May 1946.

[9] See, *inter alia*, A. P. Dobson, *The Politics of the Anglo-American Economic Special Relationship* (London, 1988) and R. B. Woods, *A Changing of the Guard: Anglo-American Relations, 1941–1946* (Chapel Hill, NC, 1990): massive recent studies containing barely one reference each to Brand. A more caustic account, J. Charmley's *Churchill's Grand Alliance: The Anglo-American Special Relationship, 1940–1957* (London, 1995), at least attributes none of the blame (or anything else!) to Brand.

[10] W. K. Hancock, *Smuts: The Sanguine Years, 1870–1919* (Cambridge, 1962), ch. 13, at 261–2. On Hancock see Davidson, this volume.

matters. The most recent and the most exhaustive study of British political economy and imperial policy during the climactic years between 1926 and 1932 makes no more than half-a-dozen passing remarks to the – even then – marginally interesting opinions of 'another City banker'.[11] Of course, Brand has not been entirely written out of the historical literature. He plays a part, if scarcely a central role, both in Walter Nimocks' now rather dated study of *Milner's Young Men* and in John Kendle's more recent depiction of *The Round Table*.[12] He appears as a figure of, fleetingly sane, authority in David Kynaston's haunting account of the rise and fall of the *City of London*.[13] A wise opponent of appeasement is accorded rare praise in Norman Rose's otherwise critical dissection of the *Cliveden Set*.[14] And a delightful portrait of the man emerges from James Fox's unerringly faithful evocation of the *Langhorne Sisters*.[15] Finally, at least some of his economic ideas are permitted a sympathetic hearing in Skidelsky's magisterial *Life* of Keynes.[16] But so acute is the current shortage of sustained and serious analysis of Brand's life and work, taken as a whole, that his otherwise sympathetic *DNB* chronicler was reduced to the observation that he had become 'one of those figures, puzzling to historians, whose influence with their contemporaries can be sensed but not easily charted'.[17]

What follows is an attempt to explain at least part of that influence. To explain, not to chart; this is not a potted biography. Still less is it a history of the patrician virtuosi of his time. Brand deserves a proper *Life*; the virtuosi, a fully documented narrative. The materials for both survive in abundance.[18] The present writer will be content simply to capture the broader significance of Brand's kind through a

---

[11] P. Williamson, *National Crisis and National Government: British Politics, the Economy and Empire, 1926–1932* (Cambridge, 1992), 69–70; other references to Brand can be found on 195, 232, 255, and 498.

[12] W. Nimocks, *Milner's Young Men: The 'Kindergarten' in Edwardian Imperial Affairs* (London, 1970), 80ff., 105–7, 138ff., and 179; J. E. Kendle, *The Round Table Movement and Imperial Union* (Toronto, 1975), 14–17, 27–45, 68–71, and 283–300. See also Howard, this volume.

[13] See especially vol. 3: D. Kynaston, *The City of London*, vol. 3: *Illusions of Gold 1914–1945* (London, 1999), 38ff. and 58ff. and ch. 8 *passim*.

[14] N. Rose, *The Cliveden Set: Portrait of an Exclusive Fraternity* (London, 2000), ch. 9; and for an assessment of Brand, see 210–13.

[15] J. Fox, *The Langhorne Sisters* (London, 1998), esp. chs 12, 14, 15, and 19; also pp. 14, 440–60, and 491–565. Brand was married to the fourth of these sisters, Phyllis Langhorne (1880–1937), between 1917 and 1937. Their marriage produced three children: his son James, killed in action in 1945; and daughters Virginia Ford and Dinah Bridge. James Fox is the son of Dinah Bridge.

[16] See especially vol. 2; Skidelsky, *Keynes*, i. 22–3, 118–19, 161 and 186, 266–7, 351, 361, 385, and 475.

[17] D. Watt, 'Robert Henry, Baron Brand', in E. T. Williams and C. S. Nicholls (eds), *The Dictionary of National Biography, 1961–1970* (Oxford, 1981), 130–2 at 132. For a similar, later, view, see Burk, 'Brand', at 345.

[18] Some 200 boxes of Brand's private papers have been deposited in the Bodleian Library, Oxford. These cover all aspects of his career, travels, and writings. They remain largely unused. This is not even to mention the store collected in 'Bob Brand's Trunk', held by Sir Edward Ford at

careful analysis of Brand the 'philosopher'.[19] More specifically, this is an essay about the evolution, substance, and impact of Brand's political thought, broadly conceived. Its purpose is threefold: first, to demonstrate the internal coherence and intellectual force of Brand's ideas about politics in the twentieth century; secondly, to show how Brand developed these particular doctrines strikingly early in his life and why they remained remarkably consistent throughout his subsequent career; finally, to identify the ways in which they informed his many public activities that variously influenced the life of the nation. The point of all this is not to claim for a pre-eminent man of affairs some implausibly elevated reconsideration in the tradition of political philosophy. Piercingly intelligent, profoundly literate, and deeply thoughtful man that he was, Brand was not a latter-day Salisbury. Still less was he an English Kojève. (Perish the thought.[20]) Rather, it is to pursue the more modest end of taking the fruits of his contemplative existence sufficiently seriously in order to appreciate the underlying purposes of his active life more fully. Minimally, it is to suggest that the search for both the origin and consequences of Brand's 'influence' should begin neither with the high birth that he unquestionably boasted, nor with those privileged positions which he undoubtedly held, but in an informed understanding of the practical impact of a peculiar insight, subtly conveyed. More generally, it is hoped to describe that rather special kind of public service in which Brand actually

Eydon and alluded to in Fox, *The Langhorne Sisters*, 548–9; see also 19–20. The papers of the other patrician virtuosi, many of them mentioned above, are generally as full and as easily accessible.

[19] *The Times*, 24 Aug. 1963, 8. Brand would unquestionably have eschewed the self-description of 'philosopher'. Yet he may still have deserved it.

[20] R. A. T. Gascoyne-Cecil, third Marquis of Salisbury (1830–1903): statesman and philosopher. Prime Minister of England 1885–6, 1886–92, 1895–1902; fellow of All Souls, 1853–8. Some of his thoughts are collected in P. Smith (ed.), *Lord Salisbury on Politics: A Selection from his Articles in the Quarterly Review, 1860–1883* (Cambridge, 1972); others in *Essays by Robert, Marquess of Salisbury*, vol. 1: *Biographical*, vol. 2: *Foreign Policies* (London, 1905). A detailed consideration of the statesman can be found in David Steele, *Lord Salisbury: A Political Biography* (London, 1999); of his political philosophy in the 'Introduction', Smith (ed.), *Lord Salisbury on Politics*, and in M. Bentley, *Lord Salisbury's World: Conservative Environments in Late Victorian Britain* (Cambridge, 2001), esp. chs 5 and 6. One of his contemporaries saw in Salisbury 'something ... of Pascal'; see Steele, *Lord Salisbury*, 378. None can have failed to note his curiously untriumphant guardianship of the greatest empire in the history of the world; on which see especially J. Gallagher and R. Robinson (with Alice Denny), *Africa and the Victorians* (London, 1961), 255–7.

Alexandre Vladimirovitch Kojevnikov, or Alexandre Kojève (1902–1968): bureaucrat and statesman. Counselor to the Foreign Economic Relations bureau of the French Ministry of Finance 1945–68; part-architect of the EEC, highly influential in French subscription to the GATT accords. Scholar of Hegel; see especially his *Introduction to the Reading of Hegel: Lectures on the 'Phenomenology of Spirit'*, trans. J. H. Nicholls, Jr (Ithaca, NY, 1969). His fame lies in being the principal modern theorist of the 'end of the history'; on which, see his contribution to *Leo Strauss: On Tyranny, Revised and Expanded Edition, Including the Strauss-Kojève Correspondence* (New York, 1991). He was described by Allan Bloom as 'the most brilliant man I ever met'; moreover 'both (Raymond) Aron and (Leo) Strauss said the same of him'; see A. Bloom, 'Alexandre Kojève', in idem, *Giants and Dwarfs: Essays, 1960–1990* (New York, 1990), 268–73, at 268. A cooler account, by M. Lilla, 'Alexandre Kojève', in idem, *The Reckless Mind: Intellectuals in Politics* (New York, 2001), ch. 4, refers to the distinct possibility that this long-standing servant of De Gaulle was also a lifelong Soviet double agent; see 126. No such accusations have ever been made against Lord Brand.

believed himself to have been engaged during six decades of otherwise bewilderingly heterogeneous pursuits. After all, we have powerful bankers and putative financial statesmen still. None now merits the description of a sage. Brand did. We might reasonably ponder why this was then so; similarly, by implication, why few have justified anything of the kind ever since.

This last question is important. But it needs to be carefully understood. Brand was a man of penetrating mind. Yet he lived – determinedly – according to the dictates of common sense. If he shared with Keynes at least some part of the characteristic conceit of the intellectual – that ideas rule the world – he surely suffered less than almost any of that ilk from the self-serving delusion that 'mere words', even good words, well spoken, were all that was necessary to put the lot of mankind to right; a rueful observation about the reality of things that Brand made, repeatedly, to Keynes himself.[21] Put another way, Brand was both a thinker and a doer; this because he thought that both mattered. He was never just an ivory-towered academic; similarly, he was never a mere wire-puller. In fact, he was both something less, and something more than an *éminence grise*: less in the sense that he rarely stood in direct physical immediacy to power; more, in that what he said was always intended for use beyond the narrow purposes of executive authority. To be sure, it was often designed for immediate effect. But it was also invariably crafted to survive the scrutiny of posterity. As such, its precise results may be difficult to trace. But the rewards for success in this respect will be that much the greater.

I

None of which is to underestimate the difficulties involved. Brand said a great deal and wrote much. But he published relatively little. What he did publish often appeared deceptively undemanding. It has certainly deceived some of his subsequent interpreters. Thus David Watt, a generally perceptive critic, has characterized both his books, namely *The Union of South Africa* (1909), *War and National Finance* (1921), and *Why I am not a Socialist* (1923), and his 'frequent occasional articles' as being 'a little dull'. They might, he argues, have served as 'clear [enough] statements' of 'a middle-of-the-road position' at the time. But, he insists they 'lacked [the] cutting edge'.[22] This was – and is – a superficial reading. Brand's books and articles only *looked* dull. Their author intended as much. That implied no self-conscious perversity on his part, just a knowing particularity of purpose. Brand hated writing for public consumption. As he observed to his mother: 'Whenever I see anything I have written in print I have a most depressing feeling of its badness.'[23] Consequently, he published

---

[21] Oxford, Bodleian Library, Brand Papers, MS 198, Brand to Keynes, 3 Jan. 1940.
[22] Watt, 'Robert Henry, Baron Brand', 132.
[23] Brand Papers, MS 185, Brand to Viscountess Hampden, 1 Oct. 1906.

only as a duty. Moreover, his principal duty was to persuade: commonly other businessmen, sometimes public officials, more rarely the politically informed voter. That object entailed the cultivation of a prose, and to all appearances the dissemination of a doctrine, characteristically conceived at a level above an 'obvious . . . platitude', but seemingly below the demands of a more abstract proposition. For his purpose was to convey to the audience that image of 'enlightened commonsense' which might actually persuade the interested reader.[24] Not by trickery but through a certain, calculating, modesty; thus, none took to heart more completely Milner's advice to the Kindergarten delivered just before he left South Africa for the last time:

never . . . let the spirit of Oxford in [your] minds grow dim but, if [you] wish . . . to have any influence . . . in the world . . . be sure that [your] origin[s] . . . remain in the deepest obscurity.[25]

So precise an understanding of the proper function of publication also determined much of its superficial content. This meant that the subjects of Brand's writings were invariably serious. Few can have been less tempted by the lure of the light, personal, essay. But it also ensured that the specific objects of its concern were often ephemeral (strictly understood) and always mundane (similarly so conceived). Put another way: they were confined to things which were happening in the real world, as ordinary people experienced it. Both by temperament and training, Brand had little interest in the a priori. But this was an informed detachment, not an ignorant aversion. He was acutely aware that what he called 'philosophy' (by this, he meant an academic activity of the same name) was generally conducted in an 'unintelligible language of its own'.[26] Thus intellectually excluded, he attempted no foolish approximations of the genre. By the same token, even the most theoretical of his discussions with Keynes – and during the early 1930s some of these were highly theoretical – observed a recognizable distinction between those purely conceptual models with which the erstwhile Cambridge mathematician sought 'to convince my academic colleagues' and the scarcely less formidable prose with which he engaged the technically competent, but humanistically educated, City banker.[27] That differentiation of method, in turn, implied a subtle divergence of ends. Ultimately, Keynes was striving to recast an intellectual discipline. Brand wanted to know how to increase the Gross National Product.

[24] Ibid., 28 Feb. 1903.
[25] Ibid., 19 Mar. 1905. Milner was High Commissioner in South Africa between 1902 and 1905. His more famous, public, farewell address was delivered on 31 March 1905. These and other events are related in T. H. O'Brien, *Milner: Viscount Milner of St James's and Cape Town, 1854–1925* (London, 1979), ch. 9; see also Kendle, *The Round Table Movement*, ch. 2.
[26] R. H. Brand, 'Lombard Street in War', in idem, *War and National Finance* (London, 1921), 37; this was originally published in *The Round Table: A Quarterly Review of the Politics of the British Empire*, 16 (Sept. 1914), 585–613.
[27] Brand Papers, MS 198, Keynes to Brand, 29 Nov. 1934.

Much of the same was true of Brand's political thought. From his meticulous defence of the necessary compromises entailed in the South African constitution, through to his careful dissection of the Webbs' plan for a socialist common-wealth, Brand emphasized the practical, minimized the normative, and always wrote himself out of any necessary narrative. But if he was not – or rather, if he rarely gave the impression of being – a political scientist in the modern sense of the term, Brand nevertheless spent much of his young adulthood in search of an adequate political theory; one capable, that is, both of describing and of evalu-ating contemporary developments in the realms of British, Imperial, and inter-national politics. Moreover, his understanding of each was often as much the product of his own independent intellectual labour as something derived from the writing of other, ostensibly more professional, thinkers. The unusual urgency with which he viewed this task reflected that crisis in Western civilization – no less – through which he believed himself to be living. The striking perceptiveness which characterized his efforts bore witness not only to his appreciation of the inadequacy of the materials with which he had been bequeathed but also to the remarkably fertile mind he brought to the task. In short: Brand may have harboured no burning desire to make a reputation for himself either as a political actor or as a political thinker. He was, in that sense, neither a prince nor a professor *manqué*. Instead, mere circumstances furnished a wholly sufficient motive both for his public activity and for his more philosophical reflections upon it. Yet the results of both frequently surprised their self-effacing author. Brand had a great impact on the world in spite of himself.

One aspect of the contemporary crisis was obvious enough. This was the parlous state of the late Victorian Empire, as revealed by the South African War.[28] And one part of the proposed solution has come down to us all too famously, as set out in the various schemes for Imperial Union described in *The Round Table*. Brand's long-standing association with this institution is well known, his early enthusiasm for its wider goals – of British imperial union as the vehicle of a broader, civilizing, mission – similarly so.[29] Less prominently promoted at the time and altogether less fully appreciated since was his diagnosis of the simultaneous contemporary degeneration of indigenous politics. But Brand had isolated this particular disease earlier still. Moreover, he feared its malevolent symptoms no less keenly even though he generally experienced them from afar. That was because the enthusiastic servant of empire never once took his eyes off the 'home front' after his self-imposed exile in 1902. And he liked very little of what he saw.

[28] Nimocks, *Milner's Young Men*, chs 2 and 3; see also N. Mansergh, *The Commonwealth Experience*, vol. 1: *The Durham Report to the Anglo-Irish Treaty* (London, 1982), ch. 3; and, more broadly, R. Hyam, 'The British Empire in the Edwardian Era', in J. M. Brown and W. R. Louis (eds), *The Oxford History of the British Empire*, vol. 4: *The Twentieth Century* (Oxford, 1999), 47–63.
[29] Nimocks, *Milner's Young Men*, ch. 11; Kendle, *The Round Table Movement*, ch. 3; Butler, *Lord Lothian*, ch. 3; Fox, *The Langhorne Sisters*, ch. 12. The most scholarly study is now to be found in D. Lavin, *From Empire to International Commonwealth: A Biography of Lionel Curtis* (Oxford, 1995), ch. 6. But see also Howard, this volume.

Part of Brand's exasperation expressed itself in the characteristic complaint of Edwardian expatriates. Hence his frequent tirades against the ignorant interference in early twentieth-century Imperial affairs of 'sentimental... peace-at-any price, nonconformist, faddists'. Ironically, these 'Little Englanders' (minus the dissenting sensibilities) included his own father. This made him no less critical of their kind.[30] Brand also subscribed to the popular Edwardian parlour game of belittling the politicians of his own time through their comparison with those of the recent past. Thus he mourned the substitution of the titanic figure of Salisbury by the 'cultivated but decadent' persona of Balfour. Just to emphasize his impartiality, he also bemoaned the replacement of the prodigious presence of Gladstone by a 'fatuous object like Campbell-Bannerman'.[31] But a shrewd reviewer of his first book noticed an altogether more serious – and more general – complaint. This concerned 'Mr Brand's' apparently passing observation that:

Even in Great Britain the decay of parliament is noticeable, and everywhere parliaments seem to be failing to cope effectually with the burdens imposed upon them by the growth of state socialism and the complexity of modern life.[32]

He would spend most of the rest of his life confronting those two problems; or rather, attempting to solve the overriding problem of which they were the two principal symptoms. But what, precisely, was that problem?

Some part of the underlying failure, Brand believed, was peculiar to the British situation. Long before the fateful confrontation of peers and people, he had concluded that, in the modern order, 'a hereditary legislature was... of course... patently absurd'.[33] As such, he feared that its continued significance within the Imperial régime would render the domestic parliamentary system increasingly illegitimate. But a greater part of the trouble of modern European government was generic. It was also deep-rooted. Certainly, it was not put to rights, even in Britain, by the events of 1910 and 1911.[34] This, broader, political malaise was grounded in the decline of both the ideal and practice of aristocratic 'trusteeship' in contemporary representative institutions. That was common to all liberal societies.

---

[30] Brand Papers, MS 185, Brand to Viscountess Hampden, 9 July 1906.

[31] Ibid., 13 Mar. 1904.

[32] R. H. Brand, *The Union of South Africa* (Oxford, 1909), 55; the (anonymous) review was from *The Standard*, 9 Nov. 1909.

[33] Brand Papers, MS 185, Brand to Thomas Brand, 3 Nov. 1906. On the hereditary chamber and early twentieth-century Liberalism, see A. Adonis, *Making Aristocracy Work: The Peerage and the Political System in Britain, 1884–1914* (Oxford, 1993), ch. 6; also C. C. Weston, 'The Liberal Leadership and the Lords' Veto, 1907–1910', in C. Jones and D. Lewis Jones (eds), *Peers, Politics and Power: The House of Lords, 1603–1911* (London, 1986), 489–518.

[34] The unsurpassed account remains that contained in G. Dangerfield, *The Strange Death of Liberal England* (London, 1935), ch. 5. Drier narratives include those of R. C. K. Ensor, *England, 1870–1914* (1936), 414–30 and J. D. Fair, *British Interparty Conferences* (Oxford, 1980), ch. 4. Diverging interpretations can be found in H. Cunningham, *The Challenge of Democracy: Britain 1832–1918* (London, 2001), ch. 9, and M. Bentley, *Politics without Democracy 1815–1914*, rev. edn (Oxford, 1996), 248–66.

Indeed, it was the paradoxical product of their precipitous democratization. This was because a (near) universal franchise, mass political parties, and the rise of national systems of electoral organization had effectively destroyed the inherited social basis – namely, the propertied monopoly – of representative rule. They had also undermined its traditional political justification. The presumption of prescriptive right no longer held. The ideal of disinterested service was increasingly suspect. At the same time, a revolution in public expectations ever more defined popular aspirations *against* those ancient, representative, institutions through which self-government had traditionally been defended. In that way, it not only found them specifically wanting: that is, inefficient, unimaginative, and the rest. It also impugned their essential purposes. Increasingly, they were viewed as the instruments of vested interests, pitted against the unheeded voice of ordinary citizens. As Brand put it:

There is no more curious phenomenon in modern politics than the distrust of representative government which some forms of democracy have engendered.[35]

For all that, Brand believed in both parliamentary sovereignty and representative government. Thus its contemporary trials deeply troubled him. The pathology of such dual delegitimation – Brand took it for nothing less – contemporaneously assumed its most pernicious form in the rise of an explicitly activist, extra-parliamentary, politics. With it would eventually emerge 'modern . . . democratic . . . demagogues'.[36] Mussolini, Stalin, and Hitler became in time the most appalling examples of the type. But they had their prototypes, even then. Moreover, even in England; consider his description of another, earlier villain:

This able but . . . ignorant . . . man . . . has, neglecting parliament entirely, forged a new . . . extra-constitutional form of agitation; one which appeals directly to the people. His [ambitions] . . . point to the possibility . . . of the rule of the uneducated . . . in crucial matters of public policy. If he succeeds . . . he will demonstrate the absurdity of democratic government itself.

His name? Joseph Chamberlain. His cause? Imperial Preference. His saving grace? He failed – temporarily at least.[37]

---

[35] Brand, *The Union of South Africa*, 48. On franchise reform and its contemporary impact, see N. Blewett, 'The Franchise in the United Kingdom, 1885–1918', *Past and Present*, 32 (1965), 27–56; and more controversially, H. C. G. Matthew, R. McKibbin, and J. A. Kay, 'The Franchise Factor in the Rise of the Labour Party', *English Historical Review*, 91 (1976), 723–52. On radical aspirations, see the remarks in M. Taylor, 'Labour and the Constitution', in D. Tanner, P. Thane, and N. Tiratsoo (eds), *Labour's First Century* (Cambridge, 2000), 151–90, esp. 151–6. The broader dimensions of the issue are most fruitfully discussed in W. H. Greenleaf, *The British Political Tradition*, vol. 1: *The Rise of Collectivism* (London, 1983), 201–21.

[36] Brand Papers, MS 185, Brand to Viscountess Hampden, 10 Oct. 1903. For Brand's views on parliamentary sovereignty in more extended form, see idem, *The Union of South Africa*, 46–7.

[37] Brand Papers, MS 185, Brand to Viscount Hampden, 1 Jan. 1904. For a different interpretation of these events, see J. Amery, *Joseph Chamberlain and the Tariff Reform Campaign* (London, 1969), 109–11. Note, however, Amery's otherwise neutral description of the 'demagogic

All of this pointed to something wrong beyond the mere forms of rule. Anyway, the transparent inadequacy of contemporary political institutions suggested a deeper fault in the dynamic of modern social relations. This, again, Brand believed to be true throughout the civilized world. In the speech that eventually made him famous, his vice-presidential address to the Brussels Conference of 1920, he pondered at length upon some of its causes. Curiously, perhaps, his analysis emphasized not so much contemporary economic breakdown as emerging intellectual confusion. Indeed, he explicitly celebrated the capitalist mode of production, making particular reference to the 'unprecedented . . . developments' which it had made possible during 'the past hundred years', above all, those 'new methods of wealth [creation]' which had facilitated the growth of 'population . . . capital [and] income' at a 'greater rate than ever before'. But then he pointed to some of the subtler institutional vulnerabilities of its 'profoundly complex', at times indeed barely comprehensible, 'organisation of industry and finance'. This 'vast . . . interchange of European manufactured articles and . . . non-European . . . raw materials' had made a more abundant existence possible, yet it seemingly rendered it increasingly insecure. Finally, he drew special attention not only to the obvious weaknesses of an economic order, apparently 'incapable of self-support', but also to the more pressing susceptibilities of an entire material 'civilisation', now increasingly dependent upon the 'smooth running' of 'a machine' which provided for the material well-being of 'so many millions' – yet which was barely comprehended, let alone appreciated, by most amongst them.[38]

The particular context of the Brussels speech was the aftermath of the Great War. Its peculiar purpose was to forge the necessary degree of economic cooperation between European governments that Brand believed was essential to prevent 'the sort of peace which we have now', amounting to no more than 'merely an interlude between wars'.[39] But the broader analysis that it reflected long pre-dated the events of 1914.[40] Moreover, the crisis of legitimacy which it implied extended far beyond the dubious machinations of selfish national

flavour' of the Liverpool speeches of October 1903, 496. For a context, see J. H. Zebel, 'Joseph Chamberlain and the Genesis of the Tariff Reform Controversy', *Journal of British Studies*, 7 (1967), 131–57, and, more generally, A. Sykes, *Tariff Reform in British Politics, 1903–1913* (Oxford, 1979). An important new interpretation of this episode can be found in E. H. H. Green, *The Crisis of Conservatism: The Politics, Economics and Ideology of the British Conservative Party, 1880–1914* (London, 1995), ch. 7. For Brand's later, and rather different, views on this issue, see Kendle, *The Round Table Movement*, 279.

[38] R. H. Brand, 'Europe's Economic Needs', Appendix 1, in idem, *War and National Finance*, 274–5. On Brussels more generally, see C. P. Kindleberger, *A Financial History of Western Europe* (London, 1984), 333–4; also Harold James, *The End of Globalization: Lessons from the Great Depression* (Cambridge, MA, 2000), 36–7.

[39] Brand, *War and National Finance*, 282–3.

[40] See, *inter alia*, Brand, *The Union of South Africa*, 89–91 and 109–118; also idem, 'Lombard Street and War', 1–36, esp. 7–18. This essay was originally published in *The Round Table*, no. 6 (September 1912), 246–84.

administrations, post-Versailles. In fact, it represented nothing less than what Brand perceived as the decay of moral consensus within the advanced societies. This disease extended far beyond the plight of paternalistic privilege in an era of egalitarian sensibility. (Brand could just about live with that.) It constituted nothing less than unprecedented disjunction of the economic and political realms, one which threatened the health of commercial civilization more generally. This, he believed, might one day have potentially terrible implications. Brand again:

Political power which was once... confined to those which a strong incentive to support things as they are is falling fast into the hands of those with the strongest incentive to alter things.

In principle, Brand could just about live with that transformation too. The real problem was that our 'new masters' had 'no conception of the extraordinary, complex and intricate [economic] system' which they now so eagerly 'look[ed] forward to transforming'. Bent upon profound social transformation, they were headed altogether more directly towards simple, mutual, immiseration.[41]

Brand never entirely shed his underlying scepticism about the possibilities of economic responsibility under democratic government. During the agony of the second Labour administration he even elevated such doubts into something not far short of a general theory of democratic irresponsibility in economic management. Writing to Keynes about the 'dangerous situation' developing in Britain during January 1931, he lamented that 'democracies seem constitutionally unable to make Budgets balance'. This was because it was seemingly 'impossible for candidates for parliament not to promise to spend money'. The result was that 'in country... after country... drastic economies' had only been brought about by 'suspending the constitution'. Britain had thus far escaped this unhappy fate. But he was beginning to wonder – anyway in 1931 – whether 'our time is not coming'.[42] Still, he generally refrained from attributing the worst consequences of this sorry impasse to plebeian ignorance or popular ingratitude. Nor was he content to defend the modern industrial system in its every emergent aspect. In fact, he was conscious, in the manner of every enlightened economist since Smith, of the restrictive and enervating dimensions of the division of industrial labour.[43] And he was more aware than most of that ilk not only of the implied injustice but also of the undoubted inefficiency, that is, of the measurably deleterious effect upon 'the welfare of the whole community', of the sorts of inequality entailed in the actual distribution of wealth within Edwardian England.[44] So much so that Keynes's pragmatic arguments in favour

---

[41] R. H. Brand, *Why I am Not a Socialist* (London, 1923), 3.

[42] Brand Papers, MS 30, Brand to Keynes, 30 Jan. 1931.

[43] See A. Smith, *An Inquiry into the Nature and Causes of the Wealth of Nations*, ed. R. H. Campbell and A. S. Skinner (Indianapolis, 1981), vol. ii, book 5, article 2, 781–2; cf. Brand, *Why I am not a Socialist*, 23.

[44] Brand, *Why I am not a Socialist*, 9.

of a greater equality of income outlined during the 1930s neither shocked nor dismayed a lifelong anti-socialist. He had come to similar conclusions several years earlier.[45] What did shock and dismay him was the degree to which so much of the contemporary unrest within the advanced societies seemed increasingly to be directed against the very essentials of modern, commercial, civilization itself: that is, against large-scale production and consumption of material wealth (i.e. the industrial system); against vast agglomerations of population (i.e. large cities), even against indispensable liberal, political, freedoms.

This kind of criticism suggested not merely atavistic self-deception (as if there were not more unemployed in 'former and simpler ages').[46] It also pointed to the modern pathology which equated 'greater opportunity' for the many and a 'freer life' for all with the grotesque reduction of entire peoples to the level of massed 'slaves of a bureaucratic state'.[47] That way, Brand insisted, led to madness. Moreover, the threat from such insanity was far from distant; similarly, anything but theoretical. Thus, the barbarous turn in European politics after 1917 appalled Brand. But it did not unduly surprise him. Intellectually forewarned, he also proved morally forearmed. He was certainly unusual – if not unique, then one of a small number – amongst contemporary British public figures in his immediate and absolute opposition both to Bolshevism and to Nazism; in each case, from the very moment of their respective irruptions into the world. The first he immediately condemned as no more than a perverse instrument for the reproduction of its Czarist predecessor in still more 'ruinous . . . form'. The latter he instantly derided as the ideological expression of a 'lunatic state', the abysmally appropriate embodiment of a nation passing through a 'lunatic phase'.[48]

Keen as they were, none of these insights marked Brand out as an especially original political thinker. Liberal opponents of collectivism were scarcely unknown during the inter-war years; progressive-minded critics of radical democracy similarly so. Nor were such views deemed generally incompatible with imperialist sentiment, at least until well after the end of the Second World War.[49] What was unusual, particularly for such an apparently exemplary product of the educated English

[45] Brand Papers, MS 198, Keynes to Brand, 29 November 1934; and for its more public expression, see the remarks in Skidelsky, *Keynes*, ii. 437; Brand, *Why I am Not a Socialist*, 25.
[46] Brand, *Why I am not a Socialist*, 23.
[47] Ibid., 20–1; also Brand, 'The Financial and Economic Situation', in idem, *War and National Finance*, 2034; this essay was originally published in *The Round Table*, no. 36 (September 1919), 672–705.
[48] Brand, *War and National Finance*, xii, 205, 232. Brand Papers, MS 198; typescripts of interview with Stanley Williamson, ? Feb. 1962, 1. His *contemporary* utterances on the matter are well documented in Fox, *The Langhorne Sisters*, 493–5. For an interesting parallel, see the stands taken by Josiah Wedgwood in 'Under the Red Flag', in idem, *Essays and Adventures of a Labour MP* (London, 1924), and *Memoirs of a Fighting Life* (London, 1940), 224–38. Apart from an idiosyncratic Liberalism, the two men can have had little else in common.
[49] See, *inter alia*, G. Cassell, *From Protectionism through Planned Economy* (London, 1934), T. E. Gregory, *Gold, Unemployment and Capitalism* (London, 1933), W. H. Hutt, *Economists and the Public* (London, 1935), L. C. Robbins, *The Economic Basis of Class Conflict and other Essays in*

upper classes, was Brand's conviction – early established and for ever after fervently held – that the moral and intellectual resources with which he and other members of the Edwardian governing classes had been bequeathed were inadequate to meet the challenges that they entailed. This inadequacy suggested to Brand the stark possibility that, whilst the Enlightenment promise of commercial civilization still remained the best form of life for twentieth-century man, the terms of its most efficient management had radically changed; similarly, the nature and nurture of its proper governors. That held true even at the most basic level of his being. To be sure, Brand was never ashamed of his birth. Certainly, he never apologized for his rank. Yet he became increasingly embarrassed by, and increasingly critical of, the characteristic self-understanding of his own, historic, ruling class. Indeed, by 1905 at the very latest, he had come to the view that too many of the personnel and too great a part of the characteristic ethos of British administrative life had come to seem dominated by men of the outlook of Lord Hertford: 'bucolic and extremely stupid; [that] regular kind of Englishman who thinks that if a man hunts regularly, he is fit for anything'.[50] Occasional exceptions seemed only to prove the more general rule. As a result, Brand explained his immediate affinity for Philip Kerr, later Lord Lothian: 'He is an intelligent gentleman, a combination more difficult to find than you might think.'[51]

To be fair, such shortcomings were, in Brand's sober-minded judgement, usually less a matter of faulty genetics than of an inadequate education. Especially late Victorian public-school education; indeed, he reckoned that particular passage – even in its reformed dispensation – as something 'luckily left behind' by those fortunate enough to go to Oxford.[52] As such, he insisted that Marlborough's sole, identifiable contribution to his own intellectual development has been to inflict upon him a chronic dose of malnutrition so serious as eventually to precipitate a complete physical collapse during his second year as an undergraduate.[53] Still, the enforced period of recuperation was fruitfully deployed in a round-the-world cruise which ended in the United States. The climax of this trip proved to be neither Niagara nor the Pacific Ocean, but the University of Chicago. Founded just six years earlier as an institution dedicated to 'original

Political Economy (London, 1939). For a detailed consideration of the evidence, see the debates amongst contemporary Liberals outlined in M. Freeden, *Liberalism Divided: A Study in British Political Thought, 1914–1939* (Cambridge, 1986), ch. 5 (though Brand's rather marginal position is noted on 135).

[50] Brand Papers, MS 185, Brand to Viscountess Hampden, 2 Jan. 1905. George Francis Alexander Seymour, 7th Marquess of Hertford, JP, DL (1871–1940); Lieut. 3rd Battalion Blackwatch, 1889–1904; at that time apparently on holiday in South Africa.

[51] Ibid., 25 Mar. 1905.

[52] Ibid., ? Dec. 1902.

[53] Fox, *The Langhorne Sisters*, 179. Yet Marlborough in the 1890s cannot have provided an entirely valueless education. Old Marlburian Prize Fellows of Brand's own generation included Cyril Alington (1896), Arthur McDowall (1900), and Keith Feiling (1906). They have become more noticeable for their absence in subsequent years.

research and [for] postgraduate as well as undergraduate men', that new centre of learning impressed the young Englishman not just by the peculiarity of its organization but also in the novelty of its academic pursuits. It was, he observed, a place with a 'great number of professors' and many departments, pursuing such previously neglected charges as 'pedagogy, sociology, comparative religion and even Astronomy and physical culture'.[54]

None of this made him deride the offerings of contemporary Oxford. Far from it. He was, after all, a distinguished beneficiary of one of its relatively new academic departures: the degree of Modern History.[55] Soon afterwards, he became the grateful recipient of one of its most conspicuously reformed gifts: a Prize Fellowship at All Souls College.[56] Nor were these just transitory advantages. A historical sense, enlivened by his undergraduate studies, informed all of his later theoretical work.[57] And a devotion to the spirit of his old university marked his every subsequent utterance on educational matters. But Brand's openly acknowledged debts to Oxford tended otherwise to be tantalizingly unspecific. Similarly, its most important influences upon him were more personal than institutional. Thus the facts of the matter compel a profoundly paradoxical conclusion. This is that Brand began his truly substantive education only *after* he was elected a fellow of All Souls in November 1901. More still: he achieved his desired end – that of a modern, educated, mind – in part at least, by going away from Oxford. Certainly, that is what he determined to do, and from the earliest convenient date. This was more than a matter of experiencing 'the real world'. It was a question of enhancing his intellect. As he explained to his father: 'the idea of working at Oxford is not . . . at all congenial to me. A fossilizing process sets in [there] very soon.'[58] What was remarkable was how he subsequently managed to ally so cursory a theoretical with so thorough a practical training of his crucial faculties.

II

Exactly when Brand began to teach himself economics is not clear. Nor was the immediate cause any more obvious. The revelation of President Harper's

---

[54] Brand Papers, MS 185(3), Brand to Viscountess Hampden, 21 Sept. 1898, and ?Oct. 1898.

[55] Brand gained first class Honours in this discipline in 1901. It dated, in the form in which he took it, only to 1872. See R. N. Soffer, 'Modern History', in M. G. Brock and M. C. Curthoys (eds), *Hist. Univ. Oxf.*, vii, 2, 361–84, esp. 362–3.

[56] On which, see J. S. G. Simmons, 'All Souls', in Brock and Curthoys (eds), *Hist. Univ. Oxf.*, vii, 2, 209–20, esp. at 212–15; the best description of the implications of those changes remains that contained in H. H. Henson (ed), *A Memoir of the Right Honourable Sir William Anson* (Oxford, 1920), ch. 3.

[57] See, *inter alia*, R. H. Brand, 'War and Financial Exhaustion', in idem, *War and National Finance*, 69. This essay was originally published in *The Round Table*, no. 17 (December 1914), 136–65; idem, 'Europe's Economic Needs', in *War and National Finance*, 274ff.; and idem, *Why I am Not a Socialist*, 22–4. Countless other examples might be cited.

[58] Brand Papers, MS 185, Brand to Viscount Hampden, 16 July 1902.

Chicago seems to have proved strangely unilluminating in this respect.[59] His historical studies demanded no more of him than a competent command of Mill's *Principles*. A remarkable, apparently self-constructed, inventory of the books left in Brand's library at 5 Grosvenor Gardens, following his departure abroad, reveals a striking paucity of anything even vaguely related to the subject.[60] South Africa – and its pressing problems – appear to have been the catalyst. Whether these might even then have easily been reduced to so clear a form of calculation is unclear. The only thing we can say is that this was how Brand chose to interpret his world at that time. Within the year he was specifically instructing his sister to send him new works in the field: Price's *English Political Economy* and Mirth's *Free Trade*.[61] Just a few months after that he reported triumphantly that he had 'been elected a Fellow of the Royal Economic Society', adding, with a certain double-edged modesty, that 'I suppose Edgeworth managed it for me.'[62] Whatever the reason, or its immediate consequences, Brand dated his professional involvement with the discipline from that moment. Just a few weeks later, he determined to 'read a paper on the true principles of finance and economics to the Transvaal Philosophical Society'. No doubt, they were suitably impressed.[63]

But it would scarcely have mattered if they had been politely underwhelmed. For the young colonial administrator had discovered his true intellectual vocation. Brand would be an economist. And it was as an economist that he would strive to be a wise servant to the world. This was then altogether less common a commitment than it subsequently became. Thereafter, the basic categories of that discipline coloured his every experience. Even in some of the furthest reaches of the world: recounting a trip into the Kalahari Desert, undertaken with a few close friends in 1906, Brand especially remembered that:

At one place we wanted some milk. A Bakalahari offered us a tin full for 2/-. This absurd offer we indignantly refused. We then displayed a six-penny knife, and told him he could have it if in return he bought us milk every day for a week. The bargain was closed at once. Indeed, he almost fainted with delight at the glorious prospect before him. It was an excellent object-lesson in the theory of value.[64]

[59] Brand Papers, MS 185(3), Brand to Viscountess Hampden, 21 Sept. 1898; and ?Oct. 1898. Economics was one of the few 'new' subjects Brand did *not* mention.
[60] Brand Papers, MS 185, Appendix: 'Books Belonging to R. H. Brand, in the Library at 5 Grosvenor Gardens', n. d., *c*.1902.
[61] Ibid., Brand to Alice Brand, 23 May 1903; L. L. F. R. Price, *A Short History of Political Economy in England from Adam Smith to Arnold Toynbee* (London, 1891). For a modern guide to the kind of economics Brand would have learned at that time, see A. Kadish, *The Oxford Economists in the Late Nineteenth Century* (Oxford, 1982), especially chs 6–8.
[62] Brand Papers, MS 185, Brand to Viscountess Brand, 11 July 1903. Francis Ysidro Edgeworth (1845–1926) was Drummund Professor of Political Economy at Oxford between 1891 and 1922 and a fellow of All Souls until his death.
[63] Ibid., Brand to Viscountess Brand, 18 July 1903.
[64] Brand Papers, MS 186, R. H. Brand, 'Account of a Trip to the Kalahari Desert', n. d., *c*.1906, 10.

There is no need to exaggerate the cosmic significance of one man's, intellectual, conversion in this respect. After all, Brand made no lasting contribution to the modern subject of economics. No Brand Theorem has made its way into the academic textbooks. But his soon widely acknowledged command of its arguments, at least in their peculiarly English form, not only made a considerable difference to his own existence; it also had a profound impact both upon the content, and the subsequent reception, of his broader political theory. At a personal level, it won him the respectful friendship of John Maynard Keynes: 'The only man I have ever met to whom I should unhesitatingly apply the word of genius'.[65] The two were first introduced at the Paris Peace Conference in 1919. Thereafter, they met regularly at the Tuesday Club, a society specifically formed to encourage intellectually rigorous interchange on the great issues of the day between leading 'civil servants... bankers and economists'.[66] From these informal dinners, held until February 1922 'on every second Thursday in each month' (thereafter, subsequent to gravely debated change, on 'every second Wednesday'), the two men established a long-standing correspondence. This involved the exchange of both manuscripts and ideas. From January 1930, these included the earliest drafts of what later became the *General Theory*. After November 1934, they were particularly concerned with basic questions about the problem of demand (as Keynes insisted) and the true extent of the presumed plenty of supply (as Brand qualified his argument) in the British economy.[67]

Then, there was the broader, professional, dimension. Certainly, it was Brand's 'sound views on ... finance and economics' that had first secured his employment at Lazard Brothers in 1910.[68] Moreover, these rare abilities were judged simply too valuable to waste during the subsequent Great War. Seconded to public service from 1915, Brand quickly emerged as an economic advisor to the Munitions Board of Canada. Then, for some nine months between 1917 and 1918, he served as Deputy Chairman of the British Mission in Washington, charged with the business of the Ministry of Munitions throughout the USA.[69] Peace brought promotion in the bank. In 1919, he was appointed a Managing Director; this at a guaranteed salary of £6,176 per annum, plus 7½ per cent of

---

[65] Brand Papers, MS 198, Brand to Barbara Wootton, 20 Nov. 1946. See also the remarks in Skidelsky, *Keynes*, ii. 144.

[66] Brand Papers, MS 56/2, Oswald Falk to Brand, 13 Jan. 1922; and 14 Feb. 1922. Falk (1881–1972) was a stockbroker and actuary and Keynes's closest colleague in the City. He founded the Tuesday Club in 1917. On Brand and Keynes at Versailles, see Skidelsky, *Keynes*, i. 365–9; in the Tuesday Club, *Keynes*, ii. 196–7.

[67] Brand Papers, MS 198, Keynes to Brand, 12 Mar. 1934; Brand to Keynes, 26 Nov. 1934; Keynes to Brand, 29 Nov. 1934. For an assessment of the relationship of the two men, as economists, see Skidelsky, *Keynes*, ii. 22–3, 186, 197, and 266–7.

[68] Anon., 'The Honourable R. H. Brand', *The Bankers', Insurance Managers', and Agents' Magazine*, 110, no. 920 (Nov. 1920), 529–32, at 529.

[69] Anon., 'The Honourable R. H. Brand', 529; see also Watt, 'Robert Henry, Baron Brand', at 131; also Burk, 'Brand', at 345.

the net profits of the company in excess of the annual sum of £90,000.[70] The general view in the City at the time was that he was worth it. The following year, a glowing pen-portrait in *Banker's Magazine* acclaimed his 'remarkable... command' both of the 'scientific aspects of business' and the 'practical [dimension] of the subject'.[71]

Thus a guru had been born. And the guru meant to teach. Indeed, he was determined to pass on the lessons of a wisdom which by now stretched far beyond the scientific and practical dimensions of banking. Simply conceived, economic analysis formed the basis of Brand's mature social and political thought. This made it rigorous. But it also made it controversial. This was because its teaching was both timely and stark. It began with an intellectual defence of capitalism against socialism. That was vital. For in this view egalitarian collectivism was the principal threat – the most theoretically plausible contemporary challenge – to the social and political order to which Brand remained cerebrally committed. His response was both wide-ranging and subtle. But, at the risk of a certain over-simplification, it may be reduced to two arguments. The first might be called the paradox of primitive egalitarianism. This was his contention that in a society like Edwardian England, where wealth and income were so unequally distributed, the significance of comprehensive egalitarian redistribution would actually be rather unimpressive. Using the most reliable contemporary figures, Brand arrived at the following conclusions:

If all... unearned income... were nationalised, and every earned income reduced to £160 per annum... some £200,000,000 would remain... transferable.... Accordingly, the amount due to each family would be quite small.... In fact, the average net income of a household of 4.5 would [be] £162. Yet... very nearly half the population already enjoy more than that.

In plain English, it would be necessary to destroy both the entire upper class and the whole of the middle class, similarly to lower the standard of living of a large proportion of the working classes, just to make everyone equally well-off. The implication was clear: for post-armistice Britain anyway, 'greater production per head [was] far more important than a mere redistribution of wealth' between persons.[72]

His second objection was more thoroughgoing still. Indeed, in its sheer starkness it bore a striking resemblance to von Mises's contemporaneous 'impossibility theorem'. This was the assertion that no sophisticated economy could ever be efficiently subject to a collective ownership of the means of production, distribution, and exchange. That was because the necessary information was simply not available. Nor would it ever be. Government, *qua* government, was

---

[70] Brand Papers, MS 199, 'An Agreement Made on 31 December 1919 between Lazard Bros. as Co. of the One Part and the Honourable Robert Henry Brand of the Other Part', 1–2.

[71] Anon., 'The Honourable R. H. Brand', 530.

[72] Brand, *Why I am Not a Socialist*, 6–9.

simply not – and never could be – capable of assembling and acting upon the relevant materials quickly enough. Only free markets, through the price mechanism, might hope to do so.[73] To be sure, there is no compelling evidence that Brand had actually read any of this great liberal economist's most important writing prior to the Second World War.[74] Certainly, his own arguments lacked the substantive theoretical justification that would have suggested a deep acquaintance. Yet even in such apparent ignorance there were clear rhetorical echoes. Moreover, the substance of his case presumed the significance of economic analysis. Thus Brand insisted that he had 'never seen in any book on socialism any proper consideration given to the fundamental... problems of price and interest'.[75] Indeed, when confronted by the Webbs' (apparently serious) suggestion that both prices and the rate of interest – this across all industry and services – be determined by 'a social parliament, on the recommendation of its Standing Committee on Finance', he responded in a way that would have been recognized by any member of the Austrian School:

Does anyone who really knows human nature [let alone] the immense complexity, intricacy and delicacy of national and international trade, industry and finance, actually believe [that] a government in this or any other country [could] control and guide all these infinitely multifarious actions... now [set] by supply and demand acting through the medium of prices.[76]

Most important of all, the point of all this was not to justify the status quo. That Brand took to be a historic function of the Conservative Party. He regarded himself as a lifelong – if politically unorthodox – Liberal.[77] It was to insist that the teachings of economic liberalism still pointed to the fundamental truth that 'so far as the production of material wealth is concerned', a society 'founded on private enterprise, initiative and saving' was 'wholly superior' to one predicated on 'public ownership and control'.[78] That broad generalization suggested no prospective panacea, merely the rather melancholy fact that the 'road... to social progress' was slow and that governments had 'small powers' to make it any faster. More importantly, it never meant that central authority had *no* capacity for good.

---

[73] Ibid., 12–14; Ludwig von Mises, *Die Gemeinwirtschaft* (Jena, 1922), pt. 2; this work was translated by J. Kahane as *Socialism: An Economic and Sociological Analysis* (London, 1936).

[74] Brand's principal connection with the 'Austrian School' would have been through the writings of F. A. Hayek and (to a lesser extent) Lionel Robbins, both at the LSE after 1931. The principal relevant works would have been Robbins, *An Essay on the Nature and Dynamics of Economic Science* (London, 1932), and Hayek (ed.), *Collectivist Economic Planning* (London, 1935). This latter work contained a translation of L. von Mises's seminal article, 'Die Wirtschaftsrechnung im sozialistichen Gemeinwesen', originally published in *Archiv für Sozialwissenschaften und Sozialpolitik*, 47, no. 1 (Apr. 1920).

[75] Brand, *Why I am Not a Socialist*, 14.

[76] Ibid., 13.

[77] See ibid., 2. This pamphlet was issued under the auspices of the Council of Liberal Summer Schools. Brand also attended the Liberal Industrial Inquiries of 1926 and 1927; see Skidelsky, *Keynes*, ii. 264 and Freeden, *Liberalism Divided*, 134–5.

[78] Brand, *Why I am Not a Socialist*, 4; idem, 'Introduction', *War and National Finance*, pp. xx–xxi.

It did. And this extended beyond the provisions of the 'nightwatchman state'. To be sure, Brand never reconciled himself to the collectivism of the 1940s. Against the general trend, he confessed himself appalled by the 'wild ... and unthinking' reaction to the Beveridge Report in 1942. Still, he envisaged 'a real and large share' for intelligent and limited public intervention in future social welfare.[79] Most pointedly of all, he insisted that the virtues of economic liberalism did not imply the slightest justification either for existing distributions of wealth and income in Britain or emerging patterns of leisured behaviour throughout the advanced world. Indeed on these questions, Brand was surprisingly radical. Thus he insisted, in 1923, that 'if no-one had over £5,000 per annum, we should probably hear not so much about inequality'.[80] There were just 12,000 such households in Britain at the time, Brand's emphatically one of them. No less striking, he openly deplored the 'modern development' of a class of 'simple ... money and investment owners'. These were too often men and women rich 'only by inheritance', and prone to 'luxurious expenditure ... socially damaging to themselves and others'. Many contemporaries might have described his own 'Cliveden Set' in precisely those terms.[81]

These observations reflected, anyway in part, the considerable contempt for idleness that Brand had developed, under the strain of colossal labour, during his years as a junior colonial administrator in South Africa.[82] But they were much more the reflective product of his mature insistence that such an existence, and the behaviour which it characteristically engendered, were actually 'economically harmful'.[83] This was because they diminished national savings and the stock of available investment.[84] Hence Brand was able to conclude, without contradiction, that under conditions of a rising national product, there being a worthwhile sum to redistribute, 'the welfare of the community would increase by a greater tendency towards equality'.[85] It was also why he defined himself from the very beginning of his politically active life as a 'Liberal in a good many things; and [a man] ... committed ... to ... social reform'; why indeed he might have remained an orthodox Liberal in all things if only early twentieth-century British Liberalism could have 'confined the objects of its ... moral ... vision ... to England'.[86]

[79] Brand Papers, MS 198, Brand to Geoffrey Dawson 12 Apr. 1943; Brand, *Why I am Not a Socialist*, 24–5. On that shift, see P. Addison, *The Road to 1945: British Politics and the Second World War* (London, 1975), esp. chs 6 and 8; also, K. Middlemas, *Power, Competition and the State*, vol. 1: *Britain in Search of Balance, 1940–1961* (London, 1986), ch. 3.

[80] Brand, *Why I am Not a Socialist*, 8.

[81] Ibid., 5. On Claud Cockburn, and the 'invention' of the 'Cliveden set' during the 1930s, see Rose, *The Cliveden Set*, chs 7 and 8.

[82] Brand Papers, MS 185, Brand to Katie Brand, 19 Apr. 1903; also Brand to Viscountess Hampden, 12 Mar. 1905; on other aspects of the austerity of Brand's character, see Fox, *The Langhorne Sisters*, 544.

[83] Brand, *Why I am Not a Socialist*, 5.

[84] Ibid., 5–6.

[85] Ibid., 9.

[86] Brand Papers, MS 185, Brand to Alice Brand, 26 May 1907.

But it could not, would not, and certainly did not. There was the rub. Asquithian Liberalism, so sound on 'housing the poor, Land Reform, Temperance and the rest', had simply failed to harmonize 'liberal principles in England with the efficient management of a Great Empire'. Brand knew this because of what he had learned in South Africa. Out of his South African education, he strove to forge what he called those properly 'plastic principles', that is, a truly inter-national and economically literate – and thereby politically realistic – liberalism that might yet reconcile the two.[87] Not as a convenient compromise; but as the best, the most sensible, and the most responsible expression of an old creed in the modern world.

It is important not to sentimentalize this education. To do so would actually rob it of much of its real content. To be sure, Milner's Kindergarten was real enough. Brand was deeply 'proud' of his 'membership' of it, more than 'anything else' he had done 'in [his] life', to 1907 anyway.[88] But it was not quite the hand-picked troupe of incorrigibly brilliant, impeccably selfless, *jeunesse dorée* of subsequent memory.[89] Most of its members were intellectual, if not also eco-nomic, adventurers. Like Brand himself, they meant very properly to be useful, but they were also out to 'avoid doing the usual things that younger sons do in England'.[90] Indeed, they often equated such usefulness with that very idiosyn-crasy of action they craved. For all that, many fell haphazardly into this privileged circle. Indeed, their paths were not always prepared with diplomatic red carpet. This was emphatically the case for Brand himself. To be sure, his father wrote him a letter of introduction to Lord Milner. But nothing came of it. So he went to South Africa, as he put it, 'on spec', able to assure his parents only that 'it would not be necessary [for him] to become . . . a mining engineer, or anything of that sort'.[91]

Further, early, interventions proved similarly ineffective. This was initially true even of those efforts made by fellow All Souls Kinder. A letter of recommenda-tion from Leo Amery to Sir Percy Fitzpatrick the following year came to nothing.[92] So delicate did Brand's position become that another young fellow, John Perry, found himself in the slightly embarrassing position of writing to Warden Anson in 1903, assuring him that Brand would not be expected to 'stick to his present . . . menial tasks . . . for more than a year'.[93] That proved to be the case, but only fortuitously so. Brand was appointed temporary secretary of the

---

[87] Ibid., Brand to Viscountess Hampden, 8 Apr. 1906.

[88] Ibid., Brand to Viscountess Hampden, 10 Mar. 1907.

[89] For this tendency, see Butler, *Lord Lothian*, ch. 2, and Nimocks, *Milner's Young Men*, 80ff. There is a more balanced account in Kendle, *The Round Table Movement*, ch. 1. Note, however, the derogatory *origins* of the term; see O'Brien, *Milner*, 191–2.

[90] Brand Papers, MS 185, Brand to Viscountess Hampden, 8 Dec. 1907.

[91] Ibid., Brand to Viscount Hampden, 16 July 1902.

[92] Ibid., Brand to Viscountess Hampden, 1 Feb. 1903, recording that failure.

[93] Ibid., Brand to Viscount Hampden, 15 Feb. 1903. Penry's letter to Anson was related by Brand, to Hampden, in these terms.

Inter-Colonial Council of the Transvaal and Orange River Colony in August 1903.[94] This post was actually scheduled for abolition the following January.[95] Its last-minute salvation alone enabled him to demonstrate his superior administrative abilities to an otherwise sceptical Lord Milner.[96] Even so, the position was not, in fact, made permanent until the following May.[97] Only from there did Brand eventually rise to become Secretary of the Railway Commission of the Central South African Railways.[98]

These were important jobs. But they were not glamorous appointments. Brand was never Private Secretary to H.E. Lord Milner, as his fellow collegian, Robinson, had been, nor to Milner's successor, Selborne, as another Mallardian, Malcolm, became. When enthusing, in a letter to his brother, about the presence of four young fellows from All Souls within the Imperial administration, he was not being entirely ironic in numbering amongst them 'my humble self'.[99] Shorn of any rosy reminiscence, Brand's various posts initially involved working long hours at tedious tasks in difficult conditions. Even at the time, he admitted that such a life in South Africa entailed the endurance of often 'intolerable' and invariably 'vulgar... society'; similarly an 'appalling... dearth of female beauty'. But, from the first, he 'never... regretted coming out... to this place'.[100] By 1908, the new Secretary of Transvaal delegates to the South African Convention, hand-picked by Smuts to do most of the intellectual dirty-work of constitution-making, had come to see the value of starting low before aiming high. Indeed, the junior clerk who became 'the wisest man in the Empire' soon came to doubt the value of any other form of practical and moral experience. Anyone who really wanted to run the Empire's railways, he declared, should first 'get a [university] education; then start as a porter and work his way up'.[101]

Put another way: South Africa, experienced so, taught Brand lessons he felt he could never have learned at home. As such, it is deeply ironic that much of this hard-won wisdom has subsequently come down to us in an apparently ingenuous collection of boyish enthusiasms: for a reinvigorated Empire, capable of surviving

[94] *Official Gazette of the High Commission of South Africa*, vol. 5, no. 96 (14 Aug. 1903).

[95] Brand Papers, MS 185, Brand to Viscountess Hampden, 31 Jan. 1904.

[96] Ibid., Brand to Viscountess Hampden, 13 Mar. 1904.

[97] Ibid., Brand to Viscountess Hampden, 14 May 1904; official confirmation came through on 12 June 1904.

[98] Ibid., Brand to Viscountess Hampden, 2 Feb. 1908; also, 31 May 1908.

[99] Ibid., Brand to Thomas Brand, 3 Nov. 1906. Geoffrey Robinson, later Dawson (1874–1944), civil servant, businessman and journalist, editor of *The Times*, 1912–19 and 19–1941; fellow of All Souls, 1898–1944; (assistant) private secretary to Milner 1901–5; Dougal Malcolm (1877–1955), imperial administrator, businessman and scholar; fellow of All Souls, 1899–1955. Both Robinson (Dawson) and Malcolm were lifelong friends of Brand.

[100] Brand Papers, MS 185, Brand to Viscountess Brand, 31 May 1903; Brand to Katie Brand, 19 April 1903; Brand to Viscount Brand, 15 Feb. 1903.

[101] Ibid., Brand to Viscountess Brand, 25 Nov. 1908. Fox, *The Langhorne Sisters*, 172; the phrase was invented by a contemporary newspaper.

into the distant future;[102] for a new parliamentary democracy that would 'show the way [that] Australia...should have gone';[103] for a very exclusive brotherhood, that had done 'so much...good in a distant land'.[104] This is also unfortunate. First, it is profoundly mistaken. Brand never was one of those 'dumb...instinctive, boy-masters', back-handedly celebrated in Santayana's unforgettable soliloquy.[105] He went into imperial administration a thoughtful young man and came out of it an experienced citizen of the world. He brought both an open mind and critical intelligence to his travels. And exposure to foreign parts changed his sensibilities mightily. Above all, it rid them of any last comforting illusions a privileged domestic adolescence might have sustained. Underlying the superficial euphoria of his detailed account of the 'immense work I have done here' was an altogether more sombre assessment of its real significance; not just concerning the prospects of South Africa itself, but also of the wider world for which this otherwise 'strange country' then, he believed, stood as a curiously emblematic case.[106] This, mature, judgement concerned the prospects of conflict in the twentieth century: within European civilization; between European and non-European civilizations; even against civilization itself.

For in Brand's analysis, many of the trials of South Africa merely represented the characteristic strains of Europe writ large: of capital against labour; town against country; young against old.[107] Others pointed to something newer and more sinister still. Here was a place where European nationalisms had *recently* clashed; and where Europeans had *recently* proved that they were all too capable of going to war with each other. That, in turn, pointed to 'profound differences' of 'language, tradition and ideals' between the 'nations of Europe', which might easily degenerate into an indigenous European war. Thus, the then widespread notion that Europeans were 'inherently reasonable' and therefore could be in 'no danger' of going to war with each other was, Brand insisted, no more than a 'comforting (but) vain delusion' of the times.[108] But South Africa taught him something more. Still, this was a lesson of the uttermost importance. For it pointed to the most sobering of conclusions. Characteristically, Brand chose an ironic occasion to reveal its force. At the very moment when the European powers were actually engaged in the bloodiest civil war of their history, Brand

[102] Brand, *The Union of South Africa*, 30.
[103] Brand Papers, MS 185, Brand to Viscountess Hampden, 25 Nov. 1908. By this Brand meant to praise the unitary contribution of South Africa; comparing it favourably with the Federal Constitution of Australia. See Brand, *The Union of South Africa*, 46–7.
[104] Brand Papers, MS 185, Brand to Viscountess Hampden, 29 June 1908.
[105] G. Santayana, 'The British Character', in idem, *Soliloquies in England, and Later Soliloquies* (Ann Arbor, MI, 1967), 29–32, at 32. However, see Fox, *The Langhorne Sisters*, 174, where the comparison is explicitly made. This seems to me to strike a rare false note in a book characterized elsewhere by an almost faultless social pitch.
[106] Brand Papers, MS 185, Brand to Viscountess Hampden, 12 July 1908.
[107] Brand, *The Union of South Africa*, 47.
[108] Brand, 'Lombard Street and War', in idem, *War and National Finance*, 34.

assured a distinguished American academic audience that the differences between what he called the European peoples being fiercely fought out at that moment were 'not nearly so fundamental and lasting as those which separate the European from the non-European races'.[109] In other words, there was every possibility of worse to come in a post-European world order.

Some modern critics have seized upon these and related observations as evidence of Brand's unenlightened racial views. To be sure, the record of Round Table discussions points to his reluctance to embrace a truly multi-racial concept of the British Empire.[110] But the operative word here is reluctance, not resistance. In fact, Brand made relatively little use of racial categories, as such. Moreover, he seems to have been strikingly untouched by the pseudo-scientific racism that tainted the political awareness of many of his contemporaries. The historian in him, perhaps too the Scottish economist in him, insisted upon conceiving of mankind much more in terms at least of the progressive stages of human civilization; thereby, of the theoretical possibility that all peoples might eventually reach its highest stage.[111] In this respect, he was very hopeful of India; and despite the fact that by 'race, caste, religion and language, it was even more divided than Europe'.[112] He was less sanguine for the future of South Africa; 'no other nation', he concluded, faced 'prospects . . . so perilous'.[113] It can scarcely be said that he was subsequently proved altogether wrong.

Brand's political science was accordingly defined in a delicate intellectual balance through which he attempted to reconcile the overwhelming reality of contemporary conflict – both within and between the advanced societies – with a sensible hope for a future equilibrium, similarly universalized. In domestic matters, this view invariably posited the virtues of a rather traditional liberalism against newly triumphant collectivism. In international affairs, it made for a kind of neo-realism. That might best be described as the doctrine of 'inverse Angel-lism'. Anyway, it is only just an exaggeration to observe that Brand spent the whole of his adult life repudiating the various theories of Sir Norman Angell. Before the First World War, these had pointed to the Panglossian conclusion that increased international interdependence had effectively made war between the advanced nations inconceivable. That was because there was simply too much at

---

[109] Brand Papers, MS 8, R. H. Brand, 'The British Commonwealth of Nations', unpublished paper delivered to a Joint Session of the American Historical Association, American Political Science Association, American Economic Society, and American Sociological Society, in Washington, DC, 20 Dec. 1917, 12.

[110] See, for instance, the remarks in Lavin, *From Empire to International Commonwealth*, 116. Cf. Kendle, *The Round Table Movement*, 136.

[111] Brand, *The Union of South Africa*, 108–11; idem, *War and National Finance*, 274–5; on Scottish historicism, see above all, A. Ferguson, *An Essay on the History of Civil Society*, ed. F. Oz-Salzberg (New Brunswick, NJ, 1995), pts 2 and 4. The original was published in 1767.

[112] Brand, 'The British Commonwealth of Nations', 11.

[113] Brand, *The Union of South Africa*, 27.

mutual stake.[114] This view was more widely held at the time than now seems credible. More importantly still, it was most widely held in the dominions; where, Brand feared in 1912, 'a large number of people [now] believe war is an anachronism'.[115] South Africa had taught him otherwise.

Not that Brand doubted for one moment the real, that is, the latent interdependency of modern industrial nations; nor indeed, its wide-ranging political consequences. Such interdependency had more than anything else forged a lasting peace in South Africa. As he explained:

The American monetary crisis of 1907 caused … a collapse of American credit and the paralysis of American trade … As a result … American women ceased almost entirely to buy diamonds. Hence the diamond trade, based almost wholly in South Africa, was cast into depression. With that … the finances of the Cape Colony were thrown into confusion and the Colony itself induced to unite with the other South African colonies on terms which in its days of prosperity she would never have agreed.[116]

But not all nations were modern in this sense. And not all modern nations were liberal in any sense at all. Finally, war – ancient or modern – was never just a matter of '£.s.d'.[117] As Brand, the historian insisted: 'Germany did not fight France in 1870 to make money, but to become a nation.'[118] And as Brand, the futurologist, added: 'The Germans are sore now because they did not feel [that they] have got their fair place in the world. They seek colonies … [in order] to spread German civilization.'[119] All that could be said with certainty was that war, in an interdependent industrial world, would be mutually ruinous; which is what Brand did say, in article after article, published in *The Round Table*, between 1912 and 1914.

All of which made the prevention of war imperative. However, it did not make it the only imperative. Nor did it point to the evident virtue – still less the supposed wisdom – of mutual association among nations; this conceived as the best means for the prevention of war. In that respect, Sir Norman actually erred again after the First World War. He was scarcely alone in this respect. The widespread presumption that the League of Nations, 'no super state but a purely

---

[114] See especially N. Angell, *The Great Illusion* (London, 1910), *passim*; and idem, *The Foundations of International Polity* (London, 1914), chs 2–4; on 'Angellism' more generally, see M. Ceadel, *Pacifism in Britain, 1919–1945: The Defining of a Faith* (Oxford, 1980), ch. 3 and ch. 8, esp. 141–5; also, idem, *Semi-Detached Idealists: The British Peace Movement and International Relations, 1854–1945* (Oxford, 2000), 177–85 and 300–15; finally, idem, *Living the Great Illusion: Sir Norman Angell, 1872–1967* (Oxford, 2009), chs 3 and 4.

[115] Brand, 'Lombard Street and War', in idem, *War and National Finance*, 32. More generally, see Kendle, *The Round Table Movement*, ch. 5.

[116] Brand, 'Lombard Street and War', 2. For an account of this crisis, see H. Rockoff, 'Banking and Finances, 1789–1914', in S. L. Engerman and R. E. Gallman (eds), *The Cambridge Economic History of the United States*, vol. 2: *The Long Nineteenth Century* (Cambridge, 2000), 643–84, at 665–75. For its implications, James, *The End of Globalization*, 19–20.

[117] Brand, 'Lombard Street and War', 35.

[118] Ibid.

[119] Ibid., 36.

voluntary association', could impose effective sanctions upon sovereign nations was a 'dangerous delusion'. Those words were written in 1935.[120] Brand's opposition to such mindless international associationalism became more acerbic still when confronted by the 'fixed and ossified' ideas of his erstwhile colleague, Lionel Curtis, for world government. This he denounced as 'a staggeringly simple conclusion to a vastly complex problem'. It was also, he believed, rooted in a fundamental error. As Brand observed:

The fact that...Canada and the United States do not have wars with one another is an indication that national ideals and ways of thinking have something to do with the problem as well as national sovereignties.

Those words were written in 1943.[121] It is hard to believe that they have entirely lost their relevance today. These insights critically informed Brand's complex – and pragmatic – imperialism. Initially, they had led him towards the ideal of Imperial Union, this when he conceived that the conditions for associated self-government might be met. That held true until the end of the First World War. Later, changing conditions pushed him away from the unifying imperative, as he gradually appreciated not only that 'no part of the Empire' had yet been 'ready to go' down that road. Rather, self-government in the colonies had increasingly come to be understood in terms of independent, or even nationalistic, self-assertion.[122] For a long while, they also justified – at least in his eyes – the withholding of full self-government from the non-white Commonwealth until the necessary conditions – primarily those of 'moral strength and character rather than intelligence' – had been met.[123] Yet it is at least worth recording that he regarded Indian self-government as not merely a worthy aim, but as the best test-case for the possibility of mankind's peaceful, multi-racial, future.[124] Finally, it is why he insisted that there existed a complete harmony of interests between the British and American 'commonwealths of nations'; also why, as power slowly shifted from the former to the latter, he came to attach even greater importance to the task of 'persua[ding] the people of the United States that once they understood...the true character of the British Commonwealth', they would 'realize that all its fundamental convictions were the same as their own'.[125] Bretton Woods and Savannah were, in their own ways, monuments to this profound, if ultimately mistaken, commitment.[126]

[120] Brand Papers, MS 198, Brand to Dawson (unpublished letter to *The Times*), 29 Aug. 1935.
[121] Ibid., Brand to Dawson, 18 Jan. 1943.
[122] Brand, 'The British Commonwealth of Nations', 1–2; Brand Papers, MS 12B, Brand to Sir Charles Addis, 16 Dec. 1918; Brand Papers, MS 198, Brand to Dawson, 18 Jan. 1943. See Kendle, *The Round Table Movement*, chs 5 and 8, for a modern discussion of these issues.
[123] Brand, 'The British Commonwealth of Nations', 10.
[124] Ibid., 12; see also Brand, *The Union of South Africa*, 97–9.
[125] Brand, 'The British Commonwealth of Nations', 14.
[126] Though Brand's view was considerably cooler than Keynes's; see Skidelsky, *Keynes*, i, chs 10–12, especially 343–4, 435–6, and 443–52. On the reaction of the Labour Government to the deals, see Middlemas, *Power, Competition and the State*, i. 122–6. On the realities of American policy towards the

III

Brand's was assuredly a flexible political theory. But about one thing, it was quite firm. All its arguments pointed to the clear moral superiority of the active over the contemplative life. This was because they presupposed that the fundamental political problems were best addressed through prudential statesmanship rather than by philosophical re-evaluation. Indeed, they insisted that such philosophical re-evaluation was, in general, precisely what was to be avoided. True wisdom lay in the acknowledgement of past progress and the pursuit of future gain. This was not an argument for ignorant action. Rather, it represented Brand's subtle understanding of the best use of an enlightened education. More relevantly still, it expressed his profound conviction about the best – that is, contemporary – political use of educated men. As a result, Brand envisaged returning to Oxford full-time only if 'everything else' proved 'impossible'.[127]

Yet politics in the raw never attracted him. That was least importantly because he could 'never fit himself very well . . . into' the necessary straitjacket of 'party politics'.[128] It can be explained only to some extent by the ethical sewerage that clogged up the dominant Liberal circles of his age: whether around that 'parliamentary mountebank', Lloyd George, or amongst the cronies of the 'indecent' young Winston Churchill.[129] More striking was Brand's judgement about the nature of modern political life, especially modern, democratic, political life. This was, on occasion, little more than contemptuous. Hence his belief that 'brains' could no longer 'command success' in this field, since they were now too often outgunned by the overwhelming force of 'a certain kind of thick-headedness'.[130] But at its more subtle, it pointed to an emerging disjunction of administrative and political qualities that, he believed, now counted – for both good and ill – against men like himself. Hence his curiously admiring account of the 'shrewd and capable Botha'; to be sure, 'not what you would call the Oxford type', but a man possessed of 'qualities . . . which are very useful in politics [and] which education tends to destroy'.[131]

Put another way: the attraction of Crown colony administration in South Africa after 1902 was precisely that it allowed for the unimpeded rule of the educated; thus it briefly sustained, at least in one part of the Empire, that fusion of the administrative and the political which aristocratic trusteeship had once promised. This, for Brand, was what the Kindergarten had truly been

British Empire during the Second World War, see W. R. Louis, *Imperialism at Bay, 1941–1945: The United States and the Decolonization of the British Empire* (Oxford, 1977), especially pt. 4.

[127] Brand Papers, MS 185, Brand to Viscount Hampden, 16 July 1902.
[128] Ibid., Brand to Viscountess Hampden, 9 June 1907.
[129] Ibid., Brand to Viscountess Hampden, 17 Apr. 1904; and 21 Apr. 1906.
[130] Ibid., Brand to Viscountess Hampden, 23 Sept. 1906.
[131] Ibid., Brand to Viscountess Hampden, 6 July 1907.

about. But this was an isolated event. It also described a doomed régime. From 1907, responsible government in South Africa had inevitably meant the rule – from then and into the foreseeable future – of men like Botha. In these circumstances, Brand had no intention of 'becom[ing] just . . . another . . . Transvaal civil servant'.[132] This did not mean that Brand's future necessarily lay in England. In fact, when he first joined Lazards it was with the hope that he might set up a new branch of the company in Canada.[133] What it did mean was that he increasingly came to see the possibility, indeed the desirability, of pursuing what he still construed as the possibility of disinterested public service through the apparently anomalous medium of private employment. If that necessarily meant a future conceived in terms of indirect rule, it might still enable – might indeed more probably permit – him and others like him to wield a real and beneficial influence in the world. Thus the young man who had once insisted that he would 'simply detest going into the city' decided, at the age of thirty-two, to become a banker.[134]

In fact, there was no contradiction here. Nor were events leading up to his employment at Lazards as fortuitous as received accounts generally relate.[135] On the contrary, what was most striking about Brand's behaviour at this time was how carefully he sought to avoid certain professions: the law, continually from 1902; also journalism, even after John Buchan offered him the Assistant Editorship of *The Spectator*, in December 1906.[136] He may have arrived at banking by a process of elimination. But it was also a carefully calculated decision. It was not just that he made a good living out of banking, though he certainly did that. It was not even that he considered banking to be a critical – perhaps indeed *the* critical – dimension to the development of a truly productive, an abundant, modern capitalism (*Lombard Street and War*, written in March 1912, is surely the only *moving* essay on the function of banking and the money-markets ever written).[137] It was rather that banking permitted him to do what he, by then, really wanted to do. At a time when that profession *itself* has come to seem the very epitome of selfish, private concern – even irresponsible individual action – it

---

[132] Ibid., Brand to Viscountess Hampden, 29 June 1904. This was, as the chronological discrepancy indicates, an observation *anticipating* the impact of responsible government. For his reaction to the fact, see ibid., Brand to Viscountess Hampden, 10 Mar. 1907: 'The Great Boer victory and the election has changed my mind about the future . . . I [shall] not be out here more than a year longer.'

[133] Brand Papers, MS 199, Brand to Robert Kindersley, 17 Jan. 1910; on the position of Lazard's in the pre-war City, see D. Kynaston, *The City of London*, vol. 2: *Golden Years, 1890–1914* (London, 1995), 151, 270, 313, 505, 587, and 601; on Kindersley, ibid., 313–14 and 543.

[134] Brand Papers, MS 1999, Brand to Viscountess Hampden, 8 Dec. 1907.

[135] See, for instance, the remarks in Watt, 'Robert Henry, Baron Brand', at 131; for another account, see Nimocks, *Milner's Young Men*, at 179.

[136] Brand Papers, MS 185, Brand to Viscount Hampden, 16 July 1902; ibid., 15 Feb. 1903; ibid., Brand to Viscountess Hampden, 1 Apr. 1906, for examples for avoiding the law; ibid., Brand to Viscountess Hampden, 9 Dec. 1906, on Buchan's offer and Brand's consideration (later rejection) of it.

[137] Brand, 'Lombard Street and War', in idem, *War and National Finance*, 1–36; see especially 3–6. To the extent that it actually was, see Kindleberger, *A Financial History of Western Europe*, ch. 18.

is important to be clear what Brand meant by 'being a banker'. This, for him, was a private position that enabled him to be of public service by way of moving unobtrusively, but effectively, between the private and public sectors; that to the real (and metaphorical) enrichment of both.

Above all, he meant to do good works. The conditions of his employment made this ambition clear enough. After all, Brand was hired by Lazards on account of his previous 'practical [i.e. governmental] experience', as well as advanced economic understanding.[138] Moreover, the specific terms of his contract made it similarly evident that whilst the appointment was no sinecure, and work on behalf of competitors was strictly prohibited, public service was generously permitted, subject to the permission of the partners.[139] This Brand continually sought and was always granted. Between 1914 and the end of the Second World War scarcely a year passed without his being seconded into official duties of one sort or another. To some extent, that fact just reflected the increasing significance of banking – and bankers – in the political economy of inter-war Europe. So, Brand the politician and public servant *manqué* chose his new profession well.[140] But the psychological effect was more far-reaching still. From about 1920, Brand came to re-interpret the nature of his life: similarly, to reorientate the self-conscious basis of his proper influence in the world. Increasingly, he began to conceive as a specific virtue the otherwise simple fact that he had 'spent the first half of his [adult] life in government service [and] the [second] half in private business'.[141]

So too did others. Indeed, the *Banker's Magazine* profile elevated his admirable life into a peculiarly significant typology. With no little pomposity it even opined that:

Our financial history has shown . . . that in times of difficulty, this country has never failed to produce men who, while strenuously engaged in the affairs of their daily business, have found time and energy to render services to the country by their knowledge of the principles of finance and commerce which have established our greatness in the past.[142]

Yet, bombast aside, there was a point here. By 1920, Brand had become not merely a theoretical guru but also a practical authority in the City, not least because of his presumed intellectual and political authority outside its symbolic walls. Even before the Brussels Conference, he had become the port of first call for American financiers seeking access to 'the right people' in London; this in the words of Eugene Mayer, Managing Director of the War Finance Corporation of

[138] Anon., 'The Honourable R. H. Brand', 529.
[139] Brand Papers, MS 199, 'An Agreement Made on the First Day of July 1912 between Messrs Lazard Frères . . . in the Republic of France of the one part and the Right Hon. Robert Henry Brand . . . of the other', 5–6.
[140] Kindleberger, *A Financial History of Western Europe*, ch. 18; James, *The End of Globalization*, 35–7 and 40–8.
[141] Brand, *War and National Finance*, p. xi; also *Why I am Not a Socialist*, 13.
[142] Anon., 'The Honourable R. H. Brand', 531.

Washington, DC.[143] Thereafter, his pivotal position was understood and exploited by leading European bankers too.[144] By way of return, he also became the most efficient conduit through which transient British civil servants and other public officials passed into the international banking world. By way of example, a modern British historian will be forgiven for noting his patronage after this fashion for an obscure Polish Jew, albeit a man Brand immediately identified as 'possessing very considerable ability', then temporarily employed in the Political Intelligence Office of the Foreign Office. His name was Lewis Namier.[145]

Much of this could have been described then, and certainly is now, as networking. But it could not and cannot be reduced to so instrumental an end. Rather, it reflected Brand's truly amphibious *definition* of public service. Through the instrument of the Tuesday Club, he succeeded in maintaining close contact with contemporary academic economists: not just with Keynes but also Layton, Henderson, and Robertson.[146] More importantly, he also ensured that they, in turn, gained fruitful exposure to such leading City figures as Charles Addis, Reginald McKenna, and Henry Strakosh: similarly, to Treasury officials, like Basil Blackett and Otto Niemeyer, and other public servants, such as John Anderson and Josiah Stamp.[147] This was a tiny society – membership was increased to twenty in 1922 – but it was emphatically an influential body. Indeed, it was the principal route by which Keynes's views found their way into the Treasury and the City. Yet it was never merely a place for the worship of Bloomsbury economics. In specifically inviting leading members of the Labour Party to its meetings from early 1923, it played a quite self-conscious role in attempting to persuade them, a new governing class in the making, of the merits (as well as some of the mysteries) of modern, liberal, capitalism.[148]

His fellowship of All Souls undoubtedly helped in all of this. For it conferred upon Brand a certain intellectual respectability to which the academic

---

[143] Brand Papers, MS 12A, Eugene Meyer to R. H. Brand, 1 July 1919.

[144] Fox, *The Langhorne Sisters*, 442–4.

[145] Brand Papers, MS 12A, Brand to Sir Richard Vasser-Smith, 27 Aug. 1919.

[146] Brand Papers, MS 56/2, Falk to Brand, 26 Feb. 1923; see also the comments in Skidelsky, *Keynes*, ii. 22, 40, 196–7, 282, and 436. Sir Walter Layton (1884–1966), editor of *The Economist*, 1922–1938; Hubert Henderson (1890–1952), Drummond Professor of Political Economy at Oxford and fellow of All Souls, 1934–52; Dennis Hulme Robertson (1890–1963), influential Cambridge economist.

[147] Brand Papers, MS 56/2, Falk to Brand, 29 Dec. 1922; also the remarks in Skidelsky, *Keynes*, ii. 22–3. Sir Charles Addis (1861–1945), Director of the Bank of England, 1918–25; Reginald McKenna (1863–1943), Chancellor of the Exchequer 1915–16 and Chairman of Midland Bank, 1922–43; Sir Henry Strakosh (1871–1973), leading City banker; Sir Basil Blackett (1882–1935), Controller of Finance at the Treasury, 1919–22 and Director of Bank of England, 1931; Otto Niemeyer (1883–1971), Controller of Finance at the Treasury, 1922–7, Director of Bank of England, 1938–52; John Anderson, First Viscount Waverley (1882–1958), Permanent Under-Secretary of State at the Home Office, 1922–32, later Home Secretary (1939–40), Lord President of the Council (1940–3), and Chancellor of the Exchequer (1943–5); Josiah Stamp (1880–1941), statistician.

[148] Brand Papers, MS 56/2, Falk to Brand, 14 March 1923; see also Skidelsky, *Keynes*, ii. 436.

economists paid lip service; also a kind of academic authority to which the City men at least nominally deferred. Brand made sure never to exploit this resource illegitimately. But he used it when necessary and appropriate. He always had. He was surprised and delighted to be elected at All Souls: a 'ripping thing to get' as he told his mother, three days after the result.[149] Anyway, he neither felt nor expressed any of that Olympian contempt for the 'despised All Souls' which marked Raymond Asquith's correspondence before, during, and after his successful candidacy, the following year.[150] Moreover, he treated it, from the first, as a serious honour. Patrick Shaw-Stewart's later observation that a junior fellowship felt 'rather like being a fag at Eton again' would not have amused him.[151] This meant, in turn, that he treated the College as a serious place. All Souls was never Brand's Oxford club. He envisaged for it a specific role in British public life. That vision encompassed teaching as well as administration; especially, the kinds of teaching suitable *for* modern administration. Writing to Warden Pemberton in 1918, Brand specifically urged that surplus revenue be used to:

endow... Professorships or Readerships in Political Science or Economic History, [since] I regard some knowledge in both these subjects [to be] of vital importance to a citizen of the United Kingdom and of the British Empire during the next generation [when] they will be called upon to solve the most momentous problems in both spheres.[152]

This did not mean that All Souls could not be a place of friendship too. It often was. Indeed, it was occasionally the otherwise distant occasion for deep friendship amongst young men stationed abroad during the early years of their association with the College. This was certainly true of Brand. Those All Souls gaudies on the *veld* were not a myth. They actually happened, and occasionally they left the 'young... Fellows' in 'a state that would have shocked the sedate men of Oxford'.[153] These friendships in turn truly did become networks. Brand's lifelong association with Geoffrey Robinson (later Dawson) was forged in South Africa and lasted to Dawson's death in 1944. It was a true friendship. Brand remained fiercely loyal to his friend's memory after it became fashionable to traduce Dawson's reputation during the 1950s and early 1960s; fashionable indeed, even amongst those who had not proved nearly so stout opponents of

---

[149] Brand Papers, MS 185, Brand to Viscountess Hampden, 5 Nov. 1901; Brand would later remark that 'all my good fortune came' from the passing of that examination; see Fox, *The Langhorne Sisters*, 180.

[150] Raymond Asquith to H. H. Asquith, 8 October 1901; in J. Jolliffe (ed.), *Raymond Asquith: Life and Letters* (London, 1980), 84; for other examples of this attitude, see 62, 83, 93, 139, 143, and 152. Asquith (1878–1916) was elected fellow of All Souls in 1902; he was the son of H. H. Asquith, and a barrister.

[151] Patrick Shaw-Stewart to unknown, 7 November 1910; in R. Knox, *Patrick Shaw-Stewart* (London, 1920), 75; on Shaw-Stewart's unedifying role in the non-election of Namier, in 1911, see V. Tree, *Castles in the Air* (London, 1926), 147. Shaw-Stewart (1898–1917) was elected fellow of All Souls in 1910; he became a banker with Barings. See also Louis, this volume, ch. 11.

[152] Brand Papers, MS 12B, Brand to F. W. Pember, 17 Dec. 1918.

[153] Brand Papers, MS 185, Brand to Viscountess Hampden, 4 Mar. 1950.

the policy of appeasement, or of *The Times*'s support of that policy, as had Brand himself.[154] But it was also a real *network*; as such, it worked both ways. Brand successfully leant on Dawson to get Keynes's economic views prominently published in *The Times* during the years when they were otherwise not by then quite yet respectable.[155] By the same token, Dawson edged some of Brand's more vituperatively anti-German asides towards *The Round Table*, as a way of respectfully keeping them out of his own paper.[156]

It was once common to admire this form of behaviour, even to celebrate those kinds of institution. Indeed, during the years in which Brand's influence was at its height they were both – quite explicitly – the object of a certain kind of semi-public approbation. In 1932, C. W. Brodribb issued a pamphlet concerning *Government by Mallardry: A Study in Political Ornithology*. There, he characterized All Souls as a turbo-charged inspired think-tank, benevolently dedicated to the guidance of Imperial and national affairs; its fellows, in turn, as the enlightened members of a kind of higher Rotary Club, 'condensed to its quintessence and raised to the nth power of efficiency'.[157] Such eulogistic judgements were altogether rarer thirty years later. So much so that *The Times* was unusual, even anachronistic, in its sympathetic assessment of one of those glorified do-gooders. The journalistic norm was by then different otherwise. From Bob Boothby's characteristically inaccurate condemnation of that 'disastrous...dining table' through to the subtly symptomatic sneer in Anthony Sampson's bogusly scientific *Anatomy of Britain*, a certain, knowing, condemnation of, even derision for, both the College and its latter-day fellows had become altogether more common.[158]

Yet another view is surely possible, and surely also desirable. So perhaps it might be suggested that: of All Souls and appeasement; of the 'Establishment' and its characteristic institutions; of grey men in suits and the unappetizing reality of bureaucratic democracy, much has already been written. But of a curious, passing, English type, and of its characteristic working methods during

---

[154] Brand Papers, MS 198, typescript of interview with Stanley Williamson, ? Feb. 1962, 3–4. The most notorious example was that of Robert Boothby in his 'Dawson', *My Yesterday, Your Tomorrow* (London, 1962), 131–5; for Boothby's less than consistent opposition to appeasement see Green, this volume, ch. 10.

[155] Brand Papers, MS 198, Brand to Keynes, 31 May 1939: 'Your memo should be in *The Times*...You can ask...Dawson to speak to me.'

[156] Brand Papers, MS 198, Dawson to Brand 2 Feb. 1938: 'I note your admirable and comprehensive analysis of the situation. [It] would better appear in a single article in the *Round Table* rather than a series in *The Times* [since] some passages could be taken as damning any attempt at co-operation with Germany'.

[157] C. W. Brodribb, *Government by Mallardry: A Study in Political Ornithology* (London, 1932), see esp. 4–6. Brodribb was a long-standing leader-writer, proof-reader, and general *factotum* on *The Times*. He was also a crony of Dawson's. See Anon., *The History of The Times*, vol. 4: *The 150th Anniversary and Beyond, 1912–1948* (London, 1952), 926–9; and I. McDonald, *The History of The Times*, vol. 5: *Struggles in War and Peace, 1939–1966* (London, 1984), 41, and 48–9, with Green, this volume, ch. 2.

[158] Boothby, *My Yesterday, Your Tomorrow*, 131–3; A. Sampson, *Anatomy of Britain* (London, 1962), 214–15.

the late nineteenth and early twentieth centuries, there has been strangely too little consideration. For this neglect has produced a strangely lopsided understanding of administrative and political change in Britain during that era. This is true even of otherwise sympathetic accounts. In his *Life* of Keynes, Skidelsky refers to a revolution in British government between the wars. That was expressed, he argues, in 'a return to the medieval practice of involving the clergy in the affairs of state'. Compelled by the 'greater complexity of governing an industrial, urban, society', coupled with a simple 'fear of the masses' in an age of democracy, British government increasingly found itself 'us[ing] experts', just as 'bright university men' sought 'new careers' to replace 'the reduced attractions' of the priestly and (latterly) the Imperial callings. The result was a remarkable 'merging of political and institutional authority' in post-war Britain.[159]

But that is to caricature pre-war British government. It is also to indulge in a curious nostalgia for the post-war consensus. Moreover, it is worth noting that very same shift, both for the administrative importance of so-called 'experts', and in the vocational opportunities for the educated, actually permitted an unprecedented (also unrepeated) *versatility* in the public purposes of institutional life in early twentieth-century England. Put another way: its initial impact was less that bureaucratization of the mind that Skidelsky anachronistically describes than a broadening of the practical possibilities for the indigenous intellect, which his otherwise admirable account strangely passes over. It was in this institutional space – briefly wrought but vigorously held – that the institutional amphibians came into their own. It was also the mark by which they judged their own social utility: as disinterested public servants precisely because they were neither employees of the state nor slaves to any particular learned trade. They may have been wrong. But they were not insignificant. They made a real difference to the working of British government for a generation or more after 1914.

Robert Brand was one such man. He was also the political theorist of such men. Moreover this, ultimately, was what his political theory was actually about. Thus it may have seemed internationalist in its scope. It certainly comprehended the national interest in all of its concerns. But its principal preoccupation was the role of the stateless aristocrat – the excellent man – under a democratic dispensation. It conceived of that role partly, but only partly, through the guise of expertise; much more in the talent of virtuosity. Put another way: it presumed that the technical education of the excellent necessarily created expertise, but also permitted virtuosity. That was why he chose to celebrate in the emblematic figure of Keynes not so much a peculiarly differentiating quality of mind but rather the wider expression – the real effect – of an 'extraordinary versatility'. This was certainly what he understood as the particular social value represented in that alternatively peculiar and mundane 'combination of academic man, practical

---

[159] Skidelsky, *Keynes*, ii. 23. The present author is guilty of adding to that literature himself; see Green, this volume, ch. 10.

man, the artist, the farmer and the money-maker'.[160] Brand's innate modesty
precluded any personal comparisons. But they were, and are, obvious. They have
only become clearer during the intervening years, as the 'patrician virtuosi' have
degenerated into the 'great and the good', and as administrative flexibility has
gone the way of bureaucratic rationality.[161]

[160] Brand Papers, MS 198, Brand to Barbara Wootton, 20 Nov. 1946. It may be objected that
Keynes was more 'intellectual aristocrat' than 'patrician virtuoso'; by origins perhaps, by destination,
certainly not.

[161] For some of the causes and consequences, see Annan, *Our Age*, chs 2, 6, 9, and 10; Skidelsky,
'Our Age' and 'Oxford in the 1920s', in idem, *Interests and Obsessions: Selected Essays* (London,
1993), 135–41; and M. Green, *Children of the Sun: A Narrative of 'Decadence' in England after 1918*
(London, 1977), ch. 2. For future 'progress', note the prognostications in G. Walden, *The New
Elites: Making a Career in the Masses* (London, 2006), chs 1 and 3. Burk, 'Brand', actually calls him
one of 'the great and the good', on 346. This, I think, is both anachronistic and incorrect; anyway,
inadequate.

5

Have Brain, Will Travel

W. K. Hancock and the Idea of Public Service

Jim Davidson

The association of Sir Keith Hancock with All Souls began in 1923 and extended for nearly sixty years. After an initial stint as Prize Fellow, he returned to the College frequently, most notably as Chichele Professor of Economic History from 1944 to 1949. The subjects of other chapters in this volume were all known to him – Robert Brand perhaps less than John Simon, John Simon less than Leo Amery. Hancock was also particularly attached to Lionel Curtis, to whom he acknowledged a filial bond; but in following Curtis's prompting to undertake more contemporary history, he found that research 'increased the distance between the Empire Builders and me'.[1] For Hancock the College functioned as an English home, although this did not save it from occasional flashes of Australian irreverence. He was a prime mover in playing cricket in the Codrington Library, with the statue of Blackstone as wicket – an unintended tribute to the law as the ultimate backstop.

Hancock owed All Souls much. His first chair, at Adelaide, was offered in 1924 when its Vice-Chancellor was eager to secure for his university the first Australian to be elected a fellow of the College. His next appointment was at Birmingham, and Charles Grant Robertson, the Vice-Chancellor and another fellow of the College, would have had a hand in that. Most significant of all, Hancock got wind of the projected Civil Histories of the Second World War through his All Souls connections, and went to discuss the matter with Sir Edward Bridges, fellow, and Secretary to the Cabinet; and was told, somewhat disarmingly, that the job of supervisor was his, if he wanted it. Later he was encouraged to draft his own instructions.[2] It was through All Souls, too, that Hancock published his first book: the Estates Bursar, Geoffrey Faber, had started his own publishing firm, and *Ricasoli and the Risorgimento in Tuscany* appeared

---

[1] Oxford, Bodleian Library, MS Curtis 10/146, Hancock to Curtis, 23 Sept. 1937; W. K. Hancock, *All Souls, 1923–1982: Recollections and Reflections* (privately printed, 1982), 11.
[2] W. K. Hancock, *Country and Calling* (London, 1954), 196–7.

on an early Faber list; so too would his personal testament, *Country and Calling* (1954). Clearly, All Souls was the largest single influence on Hancock's career.

What kind of man was he? Slight in build, jaunty in movement, late to age; even when he had, his white hair tumbled forward in a boyish way. His conversation was charged; the slowness in delivery was the result of an early speech defect as much as of care in choosing his words. A strategically placed grin or a puff at the pipe would provide additional punctuation. There was an element of guile there, more developed in his businessman brother; and there was also a native pugnacity. It must have been difficult to accept that the two plainest proofs of masculinity would be denied him: he was deprived of the opportunity of fighting in the First World War, while later there would be no children. More than he wished to be, he was a loner.

This condition was exacerbated by his talents: Hancock was a born scholarship boy. A close friend suggested that he might have been one of those rare people who seems to have remembered nearly everything he read. Moreover, he had a frugality of temperament and powers of concentration that pushed everything else to the margins: he had not known of Michelangelo until he was twenty-four, had not read or seen *Hamlet* until he was nearly forty, and – despite a clerical upbringing – did not attend a performance of the *Messiah* until he was seventy. The family's relative poverty and his father's ambition for his scholarly son meant that he was firmly prodded along the educational path, so that a succession of scholarships eventually brought him to Oxford.

In a well-known passage in *Country and Calling* Hancock describes the revelation that occurred when he was chatting one day with half-a-dozen Rhodes Scholars:

Everybody in that room, so it turned out – Australian, New Zealander, Newfoundlander, Canadian, Rhodesian, South African – was a parson's son. The coincidence was not quite so unusual as might be thought, for the Rhodes Scholars of those days, despite their wide diversity of geographical background, had for the most part a closely similar background of family upbringing. And from their similar families they went to schools of pretty much the same stamp. Although I did not know it, the path that I was following between the ages of nine and nineteen was little different from the paths that my contemporaries were following in the widely different landscapes of Natal, Taranaki or British Columbia. For ten years or more I was being shaped for Oxford without ever imagining that this was my destiny.[3]

'Destiny' now seems a very grand word to use, although for somebody from the other side of the world a geographical component – destination – certainly runs as strongly in it as any idea of fate. It also contains an element of singularity, and the reason it could do so was the great awareness of the possibility of participation in public life and in an imperial culture. Every deed could cast a shadow, regardless of any Christian precept. Underlying such notions, underlying a

---

[3] Ibid., 55.

great many things then, was the concept of duty: so much was this 'current coin' (Hancock's term)[4] that whole sporting teams of his contemporaries would go down to recruiting depots to volunteer for active service. The very nature of duty made its claims unambiguous. The word 'service', on the other hand, presents a problem: it has been used so widely. For the Victorians, a general in service was not an army officer, but a maid of all work. And today the word can be used to designate either the regular activity of the local vicar, or the spasmodic one of the farmer's bull. But – for an educated person of two or three generations ago – service could be seen as the application of talents to a good or designated purpose, in particular a public purpose; where the stimulation of rising to meet the challenge could eclipse any sense of personal obligation incurred on reaching office, this being replaced by responsibility – and ultimately recognition.

Apart from his being Australian, and of a later generation, Hancock differed from Amery, Simon, or even Brand in that he served government directly far less than they did. What his case usefully demonstrates is how broadly the idea of service – a word Hancock rarely used – nonetheless informed much of his thinking. What we must now consider are the following questions. What were the sources of Hancock's ideas of public service? How did he express them, and in what ways did they run congruently with his personality? How did he seek to apply them, and to what effect? And to what extent did they develop, or shift, during the course of his life?

SOURCES

The famous triad of God, king, and country were regularly invoked in the Edwardian period, when Hancock was growing up. At different stages of his life, two of the three would present some difficulty for him.

Between God and the young Keith stood Keith's father, an unusually effective clergyman who could be principled to the point of stubbornness. Fortunately William Hancock had a well-developed sense of humour to moderate his impact, but even so, coping with this overmighty parent left its mark on the son. For a time, in his undergraduate days, he appears to have abandoned Christianity altogether; but by 1930 – partly moved by attending chapel services in All Souls – he was back within the Anglican fold. Nevertheless, whereas William trusted in faith, Keith preferred reason; he was never quite sure of his ground when people seemed to be prompted by non-rational motives.

Equally important, relations with his father may have predisposed the nature of Hancock's relations with power. He was not, on the whole, interested in wielding it; he may have turned down a number of offers of vice-chancellorships in Britain after the War. More important to him seems to have been his

---

[4] W. K. Hancock, *Testimony* (Canberra, 1985), 57.

recognition by those in authority. He would preside over an alternative court of intellect, the high-powered seminar; from a position of Olympian detachment all prospective courses of action could then be laid out, their possible consequences considered. Unlike politicians, or even statesmen, one would not be exposed, delimited, or compromised by having to follow any single one of them.

Hancock's fascination with power meant that he was repeatedly propelled towards the contemporary, even as he felt a need to be screened directly from it. To a large extent this creative tension determined the shape of his writing career. In Adelaide in the late 1920s, he conceived the idea of writing a major work on the development of the armed, sovereign state. It kept on being postponed. No sooner had he arrived back in England from a Dominion city – and he himself was aware of the irony – than he became committed, not to this project, but to writing a survey of the whole Empire. Hancock did it splendidly, but viewed it as a diversion nonetheless. He had scarcely begun to think of returning to his 'Moloch book' – he thought of the state as 'greedy guts'[5] – when the conversation with Bridges led directly to his appointment as supervisor of the Civil Histories of the Second World War. When he emerged from that, in 1957, Hancock immediately applied himself to the mammoth biography of Jan Christian Smuts. This too was a commission, from Cambridge University Press and the Smuts Trust. He was aware that the British public had subscribed £150,000[6] to honour the late Field Marshall, and was aware, too, of what Nationalist rule in South Africa might mean. So an immense amount of Hancock's energy went into helping to build up and secure a Smuts archive: historians might come and go, he would cheerily say, but an archive remains forever. Fortunately, since he shared a number of interests with his subject, and had known Smuts both in England and South Africa, he found much of his double task enjoyable.

This had not been the case with the *Survey*; in 1940 he wrote to the widow of his old professor in Melbourne that 'this accursed Empire work which has been a millstone round my neck for years is almost finished'.[7] His comments as the last volumes of the *Civil Histories* appeared would be even sourer. Duty kept him to the task; indeed duty had frequently supervened, so markedly that in the case of the *Survey* he volunteered to write the second, larger volume on the economic aspects of Empire (for no fee) because he felt it was the necessary complementation of his existing political analysis.[8] Of his major books only the first, *Ricasoli and the Risorgimento in Tuscany*, and the last, *Discovering Monaro*, could be said to have been written unprompted, entirely from the imperatives of his own curiosity. Circumstances had made him a twentieth-century historian, he declared;[9] but it was also his need to engage, at one remove, with power.

[5] Hancock, *Country*, 114.
[6] *The Times*, 21 Feb. 1952, 6.
[7] National Library of Australia [NLA], MS 703/11/36–38, Hancock to Lady Scott, 25 Apr. 1940.
[8] Hancock, *Country*, 167.
[9] Ibid., 216.

Once Hancock made his own peace with God, quite unaffected by relations with his father, he could concede that one possible outcome of his early life was that he might have become an Australian bush parson. Traces of his churchy background and leanings remained in his speech and writings. No doubt there was sometimes an element of irony present, as when he wrote to Whitehall officials to describe a request as being for 'the last time of asking', but the ease with which he could also speak of a 'return to my parochial duties' indicates rather more.[10] Indeed the concept of 'calling' stayed with him strongly, becoming modulated to describe how Hancock saw his role as an historian. Calling is, in the end, a very individual perception of one's role, prompted by spiritual urgencies; it is quite the opposite of seeing history as a profession, a concept tainted in Hancock's mind by its association with galloping credentialism. In his old-fashioned way he rather liked the 'honest down-to-earth ring' of craft, and craftsman – for Hancock wrote some of his late drafts in pencil, on the kitchen table, rather like the monk Pimen in his cell. But of course there was also the necessary work with colleagues and students that was associated with academic appointments. This meant that while he was engaged in a craft, Hancock could not think of himself simply as a craftsman; he therefore countenanced the idea of the 'historians' guild'. Nonetheless, believing as he did that there was a vital 'moral element' in his studies, 'calling' remained his preferred term.[11]

Hancock discussed his idea of calling purely in relation to the way he wrote, thought, and taught as an historian. Describing himself as being 'not a seer, but a seeker',[12] he was in effect casting himself as a pilgrim – and *The Pilgrim's Progress* was one of his favourite books. But he could also be called by someone else; as already indicated, by the state. This brings us to the second of the triad God, king, and country, the one that was relatively straightforward for Hancock, if one takes 'king' to mean authority.

Even so there was a phase, his undergraduate days at Melbourne University, when Hancock would cheerily overturn almost any conservative assumption: but then the month he began there – and left home – coincided with the outbreak of the Russian Revolution. Heady times – even in the middle of a war. Characteristically, though, his new readiness to interrogate ideas, institutions, and practices was also marked by a thoroughness and moral earnestness. He soon became a prime mover in and secretary of the newly-founded Public Questions Society, a student organization which set up study groups and was determined to put both sides of contentious questions before the public. Occasionally provocative speakers were chosen, for Hancock also had a mischievous side to him, a quirky sense of humour that must have originated at home as a protest of his individuality. More usually, this Loki-like characteristic was obscured by his Palladian

---

[10] TNA, CAB 160, Hancock Personal File, Hancock to Brook, 14 Feb. 1952 and 2 Feb. 1948.
[11] Hancock, *Country*, 72–3, 212.
[12] Ibid., 177.

intellect; and, coinciding as it did with his switch from classics to history, Hancock's involvement with the PQS can be seen as a harbinger of the way he would later proceed.

Hancock was so much aware of contending views and the fluctuations in their valency that he was loath to effect closure: there must be confidence that all the evidence had been laid out for appraisal. In a critical situation it was only then, after having given up all hope of any favourable or further development, that one might move decisively. In the case of the Nazis, his sympathy with Germany arising from the harshness of the terms of the Treaty of Versailles led him to be remarkably resistant to condemning them, even though he had witnessed their decisive gains in the election of 1930 at first hand. But once Hitler occupied the Rhineland, his judgement came down like the guillotine. Partly influenced by the Abyssinian crisis, he broke with the Round Table group very soon after.

It was a commonplace of the time that those best equipped for public service were likely to be graduates with a good liberal education. It was therefore not uncommon for history and political science to be taught in the same university department. Hancock further believed that there was, moreover, a real convergence between historical understanding and good government. 'Understanding the concrete facts of a particular situation', he wrote, 'is the first task of sound historical judgement, as it is the first task of competent statesmanship.'[13] Indeed his three watchwords, attachment, justice, and span, could be applied almost as readily to one as to the other.

From the gubernatorial point of view the doubtful one of the three is attachment, and it is odd that Hancock felt it necessary to deal with the question of the historian's involvement with any given party in quite this way. Another person might have written of *de*tachment, and have recast the two other watchwords accordingly; but it was attachment that Hancock had to struggle to reach.

There were a number of reasons why this detachment was so marked; moreover – given his talents – it further equipped him for Imperial service. 'When I was a boy', he wrote, 'I used to declare that I loved places more than people.'[14] While he later doubted that this was really true, it does indicate a predisposition towards mobility. And when, at the age of fifteen, he won a scholarship to Melbourne Grammar School, this tendency became exacerbated. Although Hancock did make friends at this school, he also felt – rather as Trollope did at Harrow – ashamed of his relative poverty, evident in his case in grey flannel underwear. He was not comfortable among the Melbourne wealthy, and the city (although not the University) is surprisingly insubstantial in *Country and Calling*. But Melbourne Grammar, as a bridgehead of Imperial culture, also pointed to the world beyond. First Hancock won a scholarship to Trinity College at the University of Melbourne. At the university the links with Oxford were strong: a

---

[13] W. K. Hancock, *Professing History* (Sydney, 1976), 160.
[14] Hancock, *Country*, 127.

number of his teachers were Round Tablers, and in due course a special Rhodes Scholarship awarded for Australia at large would take him to England.[15]

This pathway indicates the manner in which Britain and Australia seemed indissolubly linked, as they would till the 1960s. For many young Australians – and a good many New Zealanders and South Africans – moving to England was merely a matter of moving to the other end of the spectrum, one offering richer possibilities. This was not only in the academy and in the arts: young graduates found few opportunities in journalism at home, while the public service specifically debarred them in favour of school-leavers.[16] So the notion of country, the last of the Edwardian triad, was far less problematic in the 1920s for many Australians (particularly if Protestant) than might have been expected. It had been English culture they had been soaked in at school, particularly if attending one like Melbourne Grammar. Until the Second World War, the Australian federal government was relatively weak, so patriotism overwhelmingly meant Empire patriotism. Attachment to Australia was essentially a regionalism within it. Hancock could even write in 1930 that Imperial patriotism could be represented 'as an extension of Australian nationalism', and that, given the degree of mixture, 'if such a creature as the average Briton exists anywhere upon this earth, he will be found in Australia'.[17] By contrast, Afrikaners knew that theirs was *die Vaderland*. For Australians there was no fatherland, only a mother country – which was England. For a time Hancock complicated things by taking Italy as a mistress; but Australia lingered in the background like an old love based in childhood, waiting to be reclaimed.

APPLICATION

Hancock's second journey to England in 1933 was not undertaken on a metaphorical escalator, like the first, but was much more a matter of deliberate choice. In Adelaide he had felt frustrated, and at one stage entertained the idea of becoming a public servant altogether, by joining the infant Australian Department of External Affairs.[18] Instead he became increasingly determined to return to Britain. Hancock was aware of the paradox, that while Australia thought of itself as a new country, it was in 'tradition-ridden centres where men are adventurously thinking'.[19] But it was also the case that the centre of the Empire was weaker than it had been, that with the rise of other powers Britain no longer ruled the waves alone. Australia – and Australians – must take greater responsibility

[15] For the Round Table, see further Howard, this volume.
[16] W. K. Hancock, 'Prizes in Education', *Advertiser* (Adelaide), 27 Oct. 1928.
[17] W. K. Hancock, *Australia* (Brisbane, 1961; first published 1930), 51, 38.
[18] Casey to Bruce, 15 Mar. 1928, in W. J. Hudson and Jane North (eds), *My Dear P. M.: R. G. Casey's Letters to S. M. Bruce 1924–1929* (Canberra, 1980), 319.
[19] Hancock, *Australia*, 245.

in its affairs.[20] In addition, Hancock was a great supporter of the League of Nations, and took the view that the cluster of communities that the British Commonwealth was evolving into and the success of the League were, in fact, intimately connected.[21] This view might seem to be a Round Table one; in fact it was equally Australocentric. When the League began in 1919, fully one-fifth of its member-states were also members of the British Commonwealth, and, until the devolution of foreign policy, Geneva was, apart from London, the only diplomatic representation in Europe that most dominions had.

Hancock had scarcely arrived in Britain when he was being considered as the prospective author for the *Survey of British Commonwealth Affairs* that Chatham House was planning, as a counterpart to Toynbee's *Survey of International Affairs*. 'Considering your origin,' Curtis told Hancock, 'training and natural capacity I do not believe there is anyone so well equipped to give it this standard as you are.'[22] Initially, Hancock was 'both attracted and repelled' by the prospect. He had, he explained to Toynbee, put some effort into *not* becoming an expert on Empire history and politics, when in Australia, and had done his best 'to keep myself "European" in feeling and thought'.[23] But he could see that with this project he would be doing for the British Empire what he had already done for Australia in the book of that name. It might also ease him into the relationship with power that he found most congenial. The independence of his own position had been recognized when he was conceded the right to express a point of view, rather than simply provide a reference book. So to become a Commonwealth man in England made good sense: it might help to relieve the incipient tension between the claims of country and calling.

Moreover, Hancock was perhaps discovering that by temperament he seemed to prefer to deal with a succession of problems, rather than a limited range of them. 'This old dog will not return to its vomit', he would say in later life, and it was true. After his visit to South Africa in 1966, a quarter of a century after his first involvement in its problems, he showed remarkably little interest in that country, and never went there again.

The *Survey* gave him a royal road around the world; and he could practice, in a slight variation of his three watchwords, attachment, judgement, acquittal. In this there was something of the briskness of an efficient Imperial officer; but along with his intellectual restlessness there was also his capacity for positive rootlessness. When Hancock travelled, he liked to change class as well as country, and by staying in cheap hostelries in places like Malta and Palestine,[24] he earthed his observations in everyday life.

[20] *Advertiser*, 22 May 1933, 9.
[21] Hancock, *Australia*, 225–6.
[22] Oxford, Bodleian Library, MS Curtis 10/6–7, Curtis to Hancock, 5 Feb. 1934.
[23] Chatham House SBCA 19/4, Hancock to Toynbee, 13 Jan. 193[4].
[24] Hancock, *Country*, 155.

There could not have been a greater contrast with Hancock's major contribution to public service, the supervision of the Civil Series of the *Histories of the Second World War*. Here he headed an establishment which, at its greatest extent in 1946, employed twenty-five people working full-time, plus twelve part-timers. There would, in the end – and Hancock would have been horrified had he been told that the absolute end would not come until 1972 – be twenty-eight volumes produced in the series, plus 239 'extra' studies deemed to contain additional useful information. Two of these – on the Anglo-French alliance and the British–American 'combination', as he termed it – were by Hancock himself, in addition to the published volume co-authored with Margaret Gowing, *The British War Economy*.[25]

Almost from the very beginning, there was an awareness that the Second World War would be very different from the First. It was much more likely to involve the work of civilian ministries, reflected the Secretary to the Cabinet Sir Edward (later Lord) Bridges in October 1939. Bridges therefore issued a directive that all departments should keep diaries, which would double as an index to important documents. These would assist historians in due course. But it soon became plain that pressure from above was needed to ensure that diaries were kept in an appropriate fashion, and that the time had come to appoint narrators across the civil ministries under an officer in charge.[26]

The question was, who? Lists were drawn up, and in the opinion of Dr E. S. Benians, then the Vice-Chancellor of 'another place', the post should go to E. A. Walker, of Cambridge, who had spent twenty-five years in South Africa and so 'would be acceptable to the Dominions'. G. N. Clark was also considered. Hancock was not the immediate candidate even of the All Souls coterie who seemed to be guiding the decision: Bridges, Grant Robertson, Richard Pares, Charles Rickett.[27] But, as both a Prize Fellow and an Australian, he had the right combination of familiarity with the establishment and some detachment from it. And, as the *Survey* demonstrated, Hancock also had a proven ability to shape contemporary history.

So far as Whitehall was concerned, it was a matter of 'funding wartime experience for government use'. Confidential prints were the immediate objective; the question of publication was left in abeyance, until such time as, following practice in the military histories, the initial narrators were replaced by fully-fledged historians. But benefits were expected to flow immediately. The Ministry of Food, for example, was converted to the cause of record-keeping when it

---

[25] *Official History of the War: Civil Series*, Report by Hancock, Cabinet Office Jan. 1957 [hereafter Hancock Report], 9.

[26] TNA, CAB 103/149, Bridges to Harold Parker, Treasury, 23 Oct. 1939; CAB 103/59, draft of letter to Permanent Heads of Departments, Sept. 1939; CAB 103/150, notes of discussion, 14 Mar. 1941.

[27] TNA, CAB 103/150, Yule to Bridges, 7 Apr. 1941; Notes of meeting between Col. Yule and Dr Benians, 12 Apr. 1941; Notes, first meeting of Committee on the Control of Official Histories, 20 Sept. 1941.

found that it was unable to ascertain the procedures adopted in 1914–18. Narrators might give assistance not only with streamlining record systems, but also with the identification and analysis of issues, which could have immediate applicability.[28]

There is a story that when Hancock, on his first reconnaissance visit, was taken to the hangar-like structure that housed the two million or more wartime files that had been accumulated by most departments, he was asked whether there was anything he particularly needed. 'Yes', he replied, 'a motor bicycle.' Undaunted by the sheer volume of material, Hancock's sense of calling now became high purpose, a 'task of national service' that he took 'all the more seriously because it seemed so peculiar'.[29] Drawing strength from the way the section was attached to the War Cabinet, although only he had an office in Whitehall, Hancock was aware that this gave him the necessary standing with the ministries.

From his privileged access to all official papers, Hancock was able to see that the War Cabinet committees had already identified the key problems for him. Their focus on manpower, finance, shipping, food, and so forth had effectively tagged the topics that would become the organizing principle of the various volumes. Moreover, Hancock wrote, 'a process of selection is operating continuously in the work of the administration itself, and to this process the work of the historian can naturally and profitably conform'. The historian (or narrator) could begin his work with these high-level documents, but it would be necessary to tackle the mass of everyday ones for the 'concrete detail' necessary for all effective historical work. Occasionally the process would be reversed, when a lead was first found at a lower level which might profitably be traced back to the memoranda of War Cabinet committees, or even to the War Cabinet itself. The important thing was dialogue between the two ends of the process, advancing by means of the most rigorous selection. And, of course, careful thought about which files to choose: otherwise the historian's work 'may be thrown out of focus at the very start'.[30]

Having hit upon this approach, and having devised a prescient plan for the series within six weeks of his appointment, Hancock was perhaps unduly optimistic about the task ahead; he was so confident of his energies that he spent at least one night a week as a member of the Fire Watch at St Paul's Cathedral. On securing the services of the economic historian M. M. Postan, Hancock gave him the direction of the War Production Series as a satrapy. It was nonetheless necessary for him to remain concerned with the overall shape of the series, and to discuss what elements needed to be drawn in at any given point. For while the move to 'task' or 'subject' histories may have clarified the vectors, it had also pluralized the sources. How very much easier it would have been to have written

[28] Hancock, *Country*, 196; TNA, CAB 104/59, Bridges to Longhurst, 23 Oct. 1939.
[29] Interview with Hugh Stretton, June 2000; Hancock, *Country*, 197.
[30] TNA, CAB 103/59, W. K. Hancock, 'The Civil Histories: A Note on Their Purpose and Method', 1; TNA, CAB 103/69 (I), Hancock draft paper, submitted to Bridges 22 July 1943, 3.

single departmental histories – but Hancock well knew that when this had been done in the recent past, there had not only been overlap, but even repudiation of one department's account of events by another. Better then to stick to the task-centred approach, even if this did involve – as in the case of Titmuss's *Problems of Social Policy* volume – being based on one ministry, Health, while extending investigations into another seven.[31]

Good relations with civil servants were essential. Bridges suggested to Hancock that he should begin by contacting the Permanent Secretary of each department; in the event, he also made sure that he met the chiefs of all the important sections or divisions. Hancock would ask three questions: What had been their main tasks in the successive periods of the war? What records remained to show how these tasks had been tackled? And, where were they? After Hancock's own survey – 'parish visiting', as he called such forays – a narrator would soon be appointed to that department. The narrator would be advised to have a preliminary conversation with the appropriate official, very much with cap in hand as he sought direction through the documentation. Then, having done the work, he would return for another conversation on more equal terms. Unlike most historians, Hancock delighted in the way 'we could cross-examine our evidence'. But rather than claim historical omniscience, he found that sometimes the civil servant's interpretation was nearer the truth than the narrator's; sometimes vice versa; and 'sometimes we found a clue to something really important that the civil servant had not himself perceived and we ourselves had not originally guessed at. We might then approach the evidence afresh from quite a different angle.'[32]

On going through the official files of the Histories one is struck by how little reference there is to the events of the war: Hancock was fully engaged in fighting one of his own, a 'combat with time', as he termed it. At the beginning, as the scale of the venture began to reveal itself, there was difficulty in recruitment. Apart from the call of the armed services, the Civil Service had already milked the universities 'pretty dry', so narrators were hard to find. Hancock had been fortunate in securing Postan early in the piece; but with one of the other crucial figures of the venture, Richard Titmuss, there was a long battle to keep him out of the clutches of the Army. This was won decisively only with the intervention of

[31] TNA, CAB 98/COH (U), memo by Hancock to Advisory Historical Committee, 14 Nov. 1941; TNA, CAB 160/3, Hancock to Bridges, 29 Apr. 1942; Hancock, 'British Civil Histories of the Second World War', in Robin Higham (ed.), *Official Histories* (Lawrence, 1970), 519; TNA, CAB 102/602, report by W. K. Hancock, Progress of Civil Histories, 14 Sept. 1944, 2; M. Gowing, 'The Civil Histories of the Second World War', 9 (unpublished paper given at the Hancock memorial seminar at the Institute of Commonwealth Studies in 1988; ANU, Hancock papers, P96/22).

[32] Hancock Report, 4; Hancock, 'British Civil Histories', 519; TNA, CAB 160/4, Note of Interview, attached to Hancock to Bridges, 11 Feb. 1942, 2; BBC Documentary Archives, Caversham, T197 665/6, Work in Progress – Hancock, 'The Civil Histories of the War', Third Programme, 22 July 1949, 6–7.

Bridges himself. Personnel would remain a problem: sometimes people moved on to more exciting work, a few proved not up to scratch, and even when someone demonstrated ability and loyalty, in a word indispensability, they might, like Margaret Gowing, find themselves unable to secure permanency in the Civil Service. For Hancock, the prospect of victory in the German War paradoxically posed an additional problem: the universities would soon require their members to return to academic duties. The commitment of many narrators to the Histories would fall to half-time, or less. And as he was well aware from his own discussions with Oxford, there was a widespread feeling in the universities that the venture 'could scarcely be regarded as "real history" '.[33]

Another factor impelling Hancock towards 'high speed' was the inevitable dispersal of evidence. To some degree this had occurred anyway, during the course of the war. But behind Bridges's initial enthusiasm for the Civil Histories lay the attraction of being able to document the activities of the 'mushroom' ministries – those such as shipping, economic warfare, supply, and food, which, having come into existence to serve the purposes of war, would be wound up with the return of peacetime conditions. Already there had been occasional panics about removal of records, but once the ministries were disbanded and personnel re-allocated, the historian's task would become impossible.[34]

The Histories were spurred on by yet another pressure: when originally conceived, the series had been spoken of as being concluded about ten years after the war. Officially – and this would remain the case until 1946 – the histories were being prepared for confidential print, not for broader publication. Into the apparent vacuum sprang a succession of proposals. In 1943 E. S. Benians, as chairman of the Advisory Historical Committee, proposed a more general three-volume history of the war, a more accessible account of each of the diplomatic, military, and civil spheres. Another proposal, incidentally, spoke of flanking key volumes of the Civil Histories with accounts of the military aspects written (with the help of narrators) by such luminaries as C. S. Forester, E. M. Forster, and – in the case of the Air Force – A. L. Rowse. Hancock had three responses to these developments. One was to discourage talk of a ten-year post-war period for the Histories. Another was to argue successfully that his own narrators needed no literary top-dressing, but having stayed the course, should themselves now be recognized and styled historians. Finally, there would be the synoptic volumes, written by himself and Titmuss and Postan, which would be

[33] TNA, CAB 103/199, draft attached to Hancock to Bridges, 22 July 1943, 1; Hancock Report, 5; TNA, CAB 106/6, Application for Deferment of a Civil Servant Liable for Military Service, 16 May 1942; TNA, CAB 160/5 (Gowing), Harris to Acheson, 17 July 1951; TNA, CAB 98/COH M/P 40–46, Hancock, Report, Progress of Civil Histories, 14 Sept. 1944, 3; TNA, CAB 160/4, Hancock to Vice-Chancellor, Oxford, 4 Oct. 1944, 2.

[34] TNA, CAB 98/COH M/P 40–46, Hancock, Report of 14 Sept. 1944, 3; TNA, CAB 103/ 150, Bridges to Col. Yule, 13 Feb. 1941.

more accessible in that together they would provide an overview of the series as a whole.[35]

The terms of reference for Hancock's own volume, which became *British War Economy* (co-authored with Margaret Gowing) fluctuated considerably. At times these included not only central institutions but also central policy, extending to elements of the strategic background, since there was some desire for a 'bridge' volume reaching across to the Military Histories. The variations and discussions of Hancock's work – whether connected with this volume or beyond – would have taxed the patience of Job. But consultation was built into the system. First a manuscript in the series had sometimes to be brought up to standard, which could involve Hancock himself in extensive redrafting. Once completed to his satisfaction, the manuscript went to the head of the department concerned for comments; then, when these had been incorporated, or noted, it was sent on to the Secretary to the Cabinet, who might effectively adjudicate on any outstanding points between the officials and the historians. Here there was an additional frustration; as Hancock put it, there could be 'months of delay while the officials screwed themselves [up] to the point of reading'. A draft would rarely get through without the need for Hancock to take part in discussion with officials from one or more departments. Later there was more direct dealing with administrators, with the Secretary to the Cabinet sending a book to press once he had been minuted by Hancock to say that all criticisms had been satisfactorily met.[36]

Other constraints were more immediate. Hancock liked to style them 'self-denying ordinances' that might help his historians, rather than hinder them, in applying their professional skills and judgement 'according to the accepted standards of their profession'. Precise, cool, expository prose was called for, the form of expression being calculated to avoid the projection of the author's own opinions. (Hancock himself came under fire here, for his implicit suggestion that an attempt to impose fuel rationing was abandoned because of the selfishness of the upper and middle classes.) In addition, historians were enjoined to respect the convention of Civil Service anonymity as far as possible when discussing policy – especially when it was found to be unsuccessful. The government was, in fact, far less concerned about Hancock's identifying temporary civil servants, since they had, and there was, less to lose. Effective, continuing governance required a margin of safety – or error; and against this basic Whitehall axiom was pitted the liberal assumption inherent in the notion of academic freedom and the rights of authorship, stated in a brief prefatory paragraph opposite the title page of all the

---

[35] TNA, CAB 103/COH M/P 40–46, Minutes 1 Feb. 1944, 2; Hancock Report, 5; TNA, CAB 98/COH (U), Benians memo, 20 Apr. 1943; TNA, CAB 102/602, R. A. Butler, Preliminary Histories of the War, 10 Jan. 1945.

[36] TNA, CAB 103/222, Brook to Laithwaite, 23 June 1945, and Hancock, Notes Signposting the Evolution of the 'Central Volume', 20 June 1945, Hancock to Brook, 21 June 1948; TNA, CAB 160/3, Hancock to Acheson, 29 July 1949; TNA, CAB 103/199, Note of Meeting, 29 Mar. 1949; TNA, CAB 160/3, Acheson, Note for Record, 21 Feb. 1952; Hancock Report, 6.

volumes. Moreover, reconciliation of these views was made more difficult by virtue of the fact that neither party was as yet accustomed to a regular release of documents once they were fifty years old. This process was set in train only by the Public Records Act of 1958.[37]

There were, in consequence, some major rows. When the Titmuss manuscript on social policy came to be circulated, a spokesman for the Treasury – which had little sympathy for the Histories – wanted it torn up and started all over again. Other senior officials also had serious reservations, feeling that it was 'seriously biased . . . the war as seen from the Ministry of Health registry'. Yet the chapters had been read by over sixty civil servants in eight different departments during its gestation. Some had been enthusiastic; the criticism of others had been assimilated. Hancock was therefore very angry to find that the Cabinet Office had not only delayed publication, but had actually recalled it from the printers. The procedures historians and officials had agreed upon had been found inadequate; Hancock strongly fought for Titmuss, and steeled himself to resign, if necessary. The book returned to the printery. Modifications might be made later, he made plain, at proof stage – with the author's consent. Relations between the Cabinet Office and the historians were redefined, and improved; together they later successfully overcame the objections of the service and supply departments, made on security grounds, to the publication of Postan's synoptic volume *British War Production*.[38]

Hancock may have fought hard for Titmuss in particular partly because he may have felt that he had not defended *British War Economy* as vigorously as he should have done. The war years and private difficulties had taken their toll, and in 1944–5 a debilitating weariness had set in. The assistance given by Margaret Gowing in writing this volume became so great that it compelled recognition as co-authorship; but the capitulations he felt it necessary to make to official pressure meant that the final volume was, in the words of Jose Harris, 'much greyer, more discreet, more anonymous, and [a] less popularly accessible work than the original draft version'. Some argued that such compromises were inherent in the very project of official history, an imputation Hancock strenuously resisted.[39]

Indeed a rare note of sarcasm emerged as he defended the venture: an involuntary response since the work had been exhaustive and exhausting, and

[37] Hancock, 'British Civil Histories', 521; TNA, CAB 103/199, Hancock to Bridges, 5 Oct. 1942; TNA, CAB 103/222, Bridges to Hancock, 11 Aug. 1948; Hancock Report, 18.
[38] TNA, CAB 103/540, P. D. Proctor to Bridges, 29 Apr. 1948; Gowing, 'The Civil Histories of the Second World War', 11–12.
[39] J. Harris, 'Thucydides amongst the Mandarins: Hancock and the World War II Civil Histories', in D. A. Low (ed.), *Keith Hancock: The Legacies of an Historian* (Melbourne, 2001), 139. For early criticism of the project of official history, see V. H. Galbraith, *Historical Study and the State: An Inaugural Lecture* (Oxford, 1948), 1–22, and H. Butterfield, 'Official History: Its Pitfalls and Criteria', in H. Butterfield (ed.), *History and Human Relations* (London, 1951), 182–224; for Hancock's response to Butterfield, see *History of Our Times* (London, 1951), 14.

had crowded in on him. More than most people, Hancock required space and room to manoeuvre. Apart from the great alternation of England and Australia, this was something he habitually sought. With the Civil Histories, he found the suspension of the question of publication liberating, since (presumably because it lessened official anxieties) it meant 'an enlargement of our freedom'. Similarly, just before the war, he had hidden the scale of his investigations in the Commonwealth by telling the South Africans he was interested in their wage structure, and people in West Africa that he was simply investigating the market price of export crops. Recognition of the need for psychic space also profitably informed his mission to Uganda in 1954. Hancock realized that the objective of getting the Baganda to agree to a reform agenda would not be achieved if he ignored their great grievance against the British, the recent removal and exile of their ruler, the Kabaka. So at the second meeting with their delegates he stilled the minute-taker, before proceeding with the business in hand, and urged them to speak their minds.[40]

The Uganda mission was important in Hancock's life as it was his one direct exercise of political power; so direct that at one point he persuaded the Governor, Sir Andrew Cohen, to attend the Namirembe Conference under his, Hancock's, chairmanship – something probably without precedent in any British colony. It was even more important in that, immediately after the Central African Federation had attempted to impose stasis on three divergent territories, and when the Mau Mau uprising had recently disrupted neighbouring Kenya, Hancock had been able to steer Uganda towards majority rule. 'It is true that I hope for a self-governing and "primarily African" state in East Africa', he told Lionel Curtis, 'and perhaps I helped this summer to lay the foundations of it; but the building is bound to be slow.'[41]

Just as Hancock had sought to master the subject matter of the various official histories in order to be able to edit them more efficiently, so he had prefaced his mission in Uganda by a series of seminars at the Institute of Commonwealth Studies. These were centred on a document he called *The Buganda Querist*, which consisted of 249 closely linked questions. In this case Hancock brought his academic skills to bear on a political problem; but just as notably – and perhaps more often – he brought the fruits of his experience of the Civil Service to academe. People were impressed with the way that, at the Institute of Commonwealth Studies, papers were circulated in advance, and spoken to briefly by the paper-giver, while notes were taken of the discussion. These were circulated too. Hancock's seminars were run rather like committees, with effective intervention from the chair. Should officials be present, Chatham House rules would prevail.

[40] TNA, CAB 103/199, Hancock to Biddle, 13 Apr. 1943; Hancock, *Country*, 170; Hancock, *Professing*, 103.
[41] Hancock, *Professing*, 105; Oxford, Bodleian Library, MS Curtis 95/174, Hancock to Lionel Curtis, 9 Dec. 1954.

Away from the seminar room, Hancock adapted another Civil Service technique
to help him through difficult situations. When there had been a serious discussion with an adversary, as with Dr Kieser of the South African Archives, he would
sometimes disarm the opposition by sending a summary of the exchange which
included a scrupulous statement of both positions.[42]

This decisive fairness may not have been without a touch of Machiavelli.
Hancock had always been fascinated by the Florentine, and Machiavellian
precept might, on occasion, not be so very far removed from Christ's injunction
to the disciples: 'be as wise as serpents and as innocent as doves'. He himself was
added to the bestiary by an ANU adversary, the second Lord Lindsay of Birker,
who dubbed him 'Sir Fox'. For Hancock knew the necessity of tactics, the
temptation of working for worldly purpose alone. Years after it had occurred,
he wrote to Anthony Low of the 'lie' that saved the Namirembe Conference in
Uganda in 1954 – and how it rose up involuntarily, totally unpremeditated.
Hancock was also aware of the need to publicize a cause: there was an invigor-
ating clarity about putting issues in the black and white of a newspaper article, he
declared. And, in the course of public service, he would willingly write propaganda. In this category must be placed his school textbook *Two Centuries of
Change* (1934), written to promote the cause of the League of Nations, *The
Modern Map* (1941), arising from BBC broadcasts during the War, and the tract
designed to educate the Americans, *Argument of Empire* (1943).[43]

SHIFTS

One of the surprises in writing my biography of Keith Hancock was to find the
strength of his attachment to Australia.[44] There are hints in *Country and Calling*:
one is that having spent his boyhood in the Australian countryside, he could
never (unlike most Australians of his generation) feel anything but a 'spectator'
when viewing the English landscape. More surprising are the remarks indicative
of a mild alienation; his recurring sense of 'they', meaning the English he was
moving among – although it should be added that he was also slow to use 'our' in
the book *Australia*, or, indeed, to acknowledge his wife in his autobiography. The
detachment of a successful son of Empire again – hidden from the people he was
moving among by a fairly free use of 'we' and 'our' at the time he was involved
with the Official Histories. The one thing that might have anchored him to

[42] Information from Anthony Low, Mary Bull, and Michael Twaddle; Killie Campbell Africana
Library, Durban, Malherbe Papers, KCM 56970 (629): Hancock, Note for Record, 6 Mar. 1955,
and A. Kieser, Chief Archivist to Hancock, 22 Mar. 1955.
[43] Matthew 10:16, King James version; Hancock to D. A. Low, 24 Dec. 1968; Hancock, 'What
Shall We Live to See?', *Advertiser*, 18 June 1932.
[44] J. Davidson, *A Three-Cornered Life: The Historian W. K. Hancock* (Kensington, NSW, 2010).

England would have been the Wardenship of All Souls, which he lost to his old tutor Humphrey Sumner in the election of 1945.[45]

To some degree, Hancock achieved a balance in the competing claims of country and calling by describing himself as being 'in love with two soils', or as 'British with a small b'. He gladly stated that he did not 'feel myself to be an exile in London, or for that matter in Oxford or Birmingham or anywhere else in Britain'. But not to be an exile is not to *belong*. Sir John Habakkuk recalled that, unlike other Australians in England – Kenneth Wheare, or Max Hartwell, for example – Hancock was anguished by his separation from his native land. Here his response was more that of the artist than the academic: one thinks of his compatriot, the painter Tom Roberts, or for that matter, of Prokofiev or Solzhenitsyn, both of whom lost impetus when far away from their homeland. Hancock, to the contrary, was prolific; but the sacrifice of country to calling disturbed him. Frequently, since he was aware of the task of nation-building to be done in Australia, he described himself as a 'deserter' – and for someone edgy about his non-participation in the First World War, that term packed a punch. So he was forever plotting his return, even as it was postponed.[46]

When, immediately after the Second World War, the Australian government proceeded to establish the Australian National University, Hancock was appointed one of its four academic advisors – it being understood that each of them would probably become director of one of the four planned schools. Since the ANU was envisaged as being essentially a research establishment, with the only students being postgraduates, the concept Hancock seems to have been working towards was of a kind of All Souls in the bush. (Since all four academic advisors were working in Britain, some of their meetings in 1947–9 were indeed held in the College.) But problems gradually emerged, arising from different assumptions.

The Australian objective was more instrumentalist than Hancock felt comfortable with. Suspicious of systemic thought and dismissive of sociology, Hancock 'shied away from the -ologies' in general. His distaste extended to the very term 'social sciences'; he preferred 'social studies', and even described himself as 'more of a social artist than a social scientist'. At the same time, his habitual hesitancy made for an incompleteness of commitment to the new institution, which was noticed and resented. He was dumped. Spanning two countries had imposed considerable strain, and in all sorts of subtle ways had meant that he had

---

[45] Hancock, *Country*, 127, 185, 245; R. Ollard, *A Man of Contradictions: A Life of A. L. Rowse* (London, 1999), 186–7.

[46] Sir John Habakkuk, interview Nov. 1999; Hancock, *Country*, 126; NLA MS 1174/1/4258, Hancock to Nettie Palmer, 26 June 1933; Chatham House SBCA 14/4, Hancock to Arnold Toynbee, 8 June 1936; NLA MS 703/11/36–38, Hancock to Emily Scott, 25 Apr. 1940; Butlin Archive, ANU, P96/23 (38), Hancock to Badger, 5 Sept. 1943. Hancock owed the 'small "b"' formulation to Fred Clarke, *Survey of British Commonwealth Affairs*, vol. 1 (London, 1937), 497, n. 1.

to prove himself twice over; perhaps ultimately, he must have thought in those dark days of 1949, without ever fully qualifying for acceptance in either.[47]

While the University of London came to his rescue by offering the directorship of the Institute of Commonwealth Studies, Hancock's thoughts still turned Australia-wards.

He was knighted; and there was a new Vice-Chancellor in Canberra – one who had read parts of *Australia* in manuscript. Then *Country and Calling* appeared – perhaps a little more shaped towards Hancock's Australian roots than might otherwise have been the case. One wry powerbroker, noting its open-endedness and perhaps the famous lack of a concluding full stop, described the book as the longest job application ever written.

The novelist Frank Moorhouse once wrote a satirical piece about Australians who, on return, are sent to a Woomera-like camp to go through a process of 'de-overseasing'. After showing continued interest despite his rejection, Hancock seems to have been deemed sufficiently de-overseased to be appointed director of the ANU's Research School of Social Sciences in 1957.[48]

Once installed, Hancock engaged in a number of nation-building projects. With his characteristic far-sightedness, he realized that Australia needed cultural infrastructure, and that a national university should be one of the leaders in supplying it. Perhaps it was his work all through this period on Smuts and South Africa, where (whatever else they had) the Afrikaners had a firm, geocentric grip on the world, that made this need clearer to him than to others. Whatever the case, he was the major force behind the establishment of the *Australian Diction-ary of Biography*; was also instrumental in the foundation of the Australian Academy of the Humanities, and indeed left it half of his estate. He was involved in the publication of documents in Australian foreign policy, in procuring sets of British confidential prints for the National Library of Australia, while he encour-aged the cataloguing of all manuscript material of Australian interest held throughout the British Isles.[49]

Once he ceased to be Professor of History, Hancock felt free as never before. An initial distaste for Canberra gradually became a strong attachment to the place and to the region. Shortly after retirement in 1965 he went trout fishing in the nearby Monaro district, and as the fish rose and was caught, the historian had a moment of epiphany: the Monaro would become his next task. After Australia, Italy, the Empire, England, and South Africa, it was time for the parish pump. This inversion was striking enough, but there followed another that was even more spectacular.

---

[47] W. Osmond, *Frederic Eggleston: An Intellectual in Australian Politics* (Sydney, 1985), 268.

[48] For a succinct account of Hancock's delayed appointment to the ANU, see S. G. Foster and M. M. Varghese, *The Making of the Australian National University 1946–1996* (Sydney, 1996), 24–5, 28–9, 127–9; F. Moorhouse, *Loose Living* (Sydney, 1995), 125–7.

[49] *Documents on Australian Foreign Policy* (Canberra, 1975–); interview with Graham Powell, NLA, July 2001; P. Mander-Jones, *Manuscripts in the British Isles Relating to Australia, New Zealand and the Pacific* (Canberra, 1972), v.

It could be said that for Hancock, even at the end of his days, the idea of public service remained strong; but now it was not only unconnected with government, but could even be opposed to it. Just before the 1972 Australian general election, he joined fifteen other notables in writing a letter carried by a number of newspapers pointing out that, in the interests of effective democracy alone, it was necessary to replace the Liberal government after its twenty-three years in power. But the Whitlam Labor government that came to office brought Hancock little joy. It was intent on building a communications tower on Canberra's Black Mountain. Hancock's native pugnacity, prompted by his new localism and an abiding interest in environmental issues, now came to the fore. He became a militant campaigner against the tower, taking part in protests and being one of those who brought the case to the highest court in the land. For two years it was his greatest obsession; but the government prevailed and the tower was built. As the 1970s turned into the 1980s, Hancock became a spokesman for another, larger radical cause: that of an armed, neutral, non-nuclear Australia. It was the American bases on Australian soil that provoked him. He had never liked the United States: an ancient, atavistic prejudice. In this vision of his country as forthright and independent – his last cause – there was more than a hint that deep down he remained British, with a small 'b'.[50]

[50] Hancock et al., *Age* (Melbourne), 23 Nov. 1972; Hancock, *Professing*, 110ff.; see also W. K. Hancock, *The Battle of Black Mountain* (Canberra, 1974); Hancock, *Testimony*, 40, 47–65, 90, 100–9. Subsequent to this publication Hancock moved further to the left.

6

All Souls and 'The Round Table'

Michael Howard

To understand the relationship between All Souls and 'The Round Table' – that group of politicians, publicists, and academics which convened in 1909 to discuss and if possible chart the future course of the British Empire – we have first to consider a third group, which drew strength from the first and was the progenitor of the second. This was the 'Kindergarten': the young men recruited by Alfred Lord Milner to help him with the reconstruction of British dominion in South Africa in the immediate aftermath of the Boer War.[1]

The main nursery from which Milner drew his disciples was not so much All Souls as New College, which provided all but two (Patrick Duncan from Balliol, and Geoffrey Dawson, né Robinson, from Magdalen) of the dozen members of the Kindergarten. But the four fellows of All Souls who did belong were seminal, both for the recruitment of the Kindergarten and for its future.

The earliest member was J. F. (Peter) Perry, a New College man who had defeated Leo Amery in the fellowship examination in 1896. He was seconded to Milner's staff from the Colonial Office in 1901 to act as his 'Imperial' secretary, dealing with relations with neighbouring British territories in Basutoland, Swaziland, Bechuanaland, and Rhodesia. He was to become the Kindergarten specialist in dealing with 'native' affairs. Perry's feeling for the College was evidently strong. 'About this time tomorrow', he wrote disconsolately in May 1901 to Geoffrey Robinson, his junior in the fellowship by two years, 'it will be bitter to think you are gathering in Hall, making salad and flocking round the Warden as he stands with his back to the fireplace.'[2] But Perry was not to remain for long in his lonely exile. Robinson, who was in London at the Colonial Office and at the time responsible for recruiting staff for Milner, was making such a good impression that Milner invited him out as his Assistant Private Secretary, and the two friends were reunited before the end of the year.

---

[1] The development and influence both of the Kindergarten and of the Round Table have been described by J. E. Kendle, *The Round Table Movement and Imperial Union* (Toronto, 1975) and W. Nimocks, *Milner's Young Men: The 'Kindergarten' in Edwardian Imperial Affairs* (London, 1970).
[2] Nimocks, *Milner's Young Men*, 52.

In 1902 a third fellow arrived: Robert Brand, yet another New College man, who had been elected to his fellowship in 1901 and who now came out to act as secretary of the new Intercolonial Council, which dealt primarily with communications and transportation. Brand was eventually to be a key figure when it came to drafting a constitution for the new Union. Three more years were to pass before the All Souls connection was reinforced; then in 1905 there arrived Dougal Malcolm, also from New College, who had been elected a Prize Fellow in 1899. Malcolm was also on secondment from the Colonial Office: the number of All Souls men who entered that department of state provides a useful indication of the interest taken in the Empire by the young Oxonian élite at the turn of the century. Malcolm came out as private secretary to Milner's successor, Lord Selborne, and so did not work with Milner himself; but by the time that Milner returned home in 1905 the Kindergarten had acquired its own momentum, and was quite capable of continuing to propagate the true faith even though their founder had left them.

A fifth name is that of Leo Amery, who had been elected to an All Souls fellowship in 1897. Amery was not himself a member of the Kindergarten but described it as 'a wonderful band of friends of which I was happy and proud to be counted informally a member'.[3] His interest and expertise in South Africa had been established during the time that he spent in that country as the *Times* correspondent during the Boer War, and in 1901 Milner had invited him to return there as his private secretary. But Amery felt that his time would be better spent at home, completing his mammoth History of the War in South Africa and pressing for the military reforms which that lamentable campaign had shown to be so necessary. When Milner returned home, however, to confront the new and highly unsympathetic Liberal government, Amery became his *homme de confiance*, and remained so until the First World War. By his activity in London, particularly on *The Times* (which was at the time edited by another Quondam fellow of All Souls, George Earle Buckle), and by his continuing influence at All Souls, Amery was able to support the activities of the Kindergarten while they remained in South Africa, and to provide more direct help when, after the establishment of the Union, they returned to London and set about proclaiming their vision to a wider audience.

That vision had been set out by Milner in a series of speeches and particularly summarized in those he made in the immediate aftermath of the South African War. It was one of the British Empire transformed from a heterogeneous collection of colonies and dependencies, scattered at random about the world, into a great superpower, 'a group of Nations spread throughout the world, united and not divided by the ocean, each independent in its own concerns, all indissolubly united for a common purpose, all free and willing subjects of the

---

[3] L. S. Amery, *My Political Life*, 3 vols (London, 1953–5), i. 178.

most ancient and august Monarchy in the world'.[4] South Africa itself he saw as a microcosm of the Empire. Here he confronted, in the aftermath of the war, two defeated and embittered Boer Republics, the Transvaal and the Orange Free State, together with a British-dominated Natal and a Cape Province of mixed race. The fact that the white inhabitants were only a thin oil-slick spread over a large helot black population was not, in his view, the major problem. There was indeed a 'race-conflict' to be reconciled, but it was that not between black and white, but between Briton and Boer. Having defeated the Boer attempt to assert their independence of the British Crown, Milner now aimed to reconcile them as loyal subjects of the Queen. 'The *ultimate* end', as he expressed it, was 'a self-governing white Community, supported by *well treated* and *justly governed* black labour from Cape Town to Zambesi. There must be one flag, the Union Jack, but under it equality of races [i.e. British and Boer] and languages . . . All South Africa should be one Dominion . . . [although] a considerable amount of freedom should be left to individual States.'[5]

The creation of this Dominion was the task that Milner bequeathed to the Kindergarten. But beyond that he saw the yet wider vision of an Empire which, as a model of free peoples governing themselves yet willingly cooperating over their common affairs, was itself 'the principal hope for the progress of mankind'. The members of this Empire, he believed, should be 'united, not in an alliance, but in a permanent organic union'. The task, he admitted in his valedictory address in Johannesburg in March 1905, was a hard one; it would be 'a race, a close race, between the manifold influences so manifestly making for disruption, and the growth of a great but still very imperfectly realised political conception'. 'But think', he urged, 'of the greatness of the reward; the immense privilege of being allowed to contribute in any way to the fulfilment of one of the noblest conceptions which has ever dawned on the political imagination of mankind!'[6]

This was the vision that he left with his disciples of the Kindergarten, and which inspired some of them throughout their lives. In particular there were two who had as yet no connection with All Souls but who in later life were to become closely associated with the College; Philip Kerr, later to become the Marquess of Lothian; and most important of all, Lionel Curtis, who became universally known as 'the Prophet' and who was to play the role of St Paul in the dissemination of the Milnerite creed.

Kerr was of a slightly younger generation of New College men, graduating in 1904 (when he competed unsuccessfully for All Souls) and going out to South Africa at the end of the year, where he was rapidly enlisted by Robert Brand as his assistant on the Intercolonial Council.[7] A cheerful, attractive enthusiast, he was

---

[4] Speech in Durban, 28 Oct. 1901. C. Headlam, *The Milner Papers*, 2 vols (London, 1931–3), ii. 287.

[5] Letter of 28 Nov. 1899, Headlam, *Milner Papers*, ii. 35.

[6] Headlam, *Milner Papers*, ii. 546–7.

[7] Lothian's career is described in J. R. M. Butler, *Lord Lothian (Philip Kerr) 1882–1940* (London, 1960). J. Turner (ed.), *The Larger Idea: Lord Lothian and the Problem of National Sovereignty* (London, 1988) contains useful studies of his ideas.

to become the workhorse both of the Kindergarten and of the Round Table. But the real dynamo of both institutions was Lionel Curtis. Curtis had volunteered for service in South Africa as soon as the war began, together with his New College contemporary Lionel Hichens, who was also to join the Kindergarten. He was thus already on the spot when he was recruited onto Milner's staff and given the task of establishing Milner's headquarters in Johannesburg when the reconstruction of South Africa began. Having had some brief experience with the London County Council, Curtis became the Kindergarten's expert on municipal government, but he rapidly established his primary role as the ideologue of the group. His enthusiasms sometimes exasperated his friends but the power of his personality was irresistible. 'At times', Brand admitted in his obituary notice of Curtis in the *Dictionary of National Biography*, 'some of his colleagues wilted under the strain, but whether they agreed with him or not, they remained his devoted friends.' Kerr said of him, 'I know no man who has so big a furnace in his belly. It is so fierce that the fumes overwhelm his brain at times. But it scorches all whom he encounters.'[8] His more practically minded colleagues were indeed to find him a bit much: Amery's references to him in his diaries became few and unenthusiastic. On one occasion when Curtis was holding forth, Amery reported with some relish, 'during one of his most eloquent passages, the bathroom pipe burst overhead and deluged him'.[9] But in South Africa, under the immediate shadow of Milner, all the young men of the Kindergarten were equally enthusiastic and united in their mission of creating, out of a deeply divided country, a single Dominion united under the British flag.

For our purposes, their object was less important than the method they used to achieve it. They first hammered out their agreed objective in informal discussions in a body that, perhaps with dim undergraduate memories of Anglo-Saxon decision-making, they christened 'The Moot'. Having agreed their objective of 'a Closer Union', they set about making it everyone else's as well. They established similar discussion groups all over the country, which they fed with information and propaganda through a journal, *The State*, which was established and edited by Philip Kerr. Curtis then drafted a document setting out their aims, which they persuaded Milner's successor, Lord Selborne, to issue under his name and which became known as the Selborne Memorandum. Simultaneously they orchestrated a popular movement of support throughout South Africa. Their efforts were crowned, or appeared to be crowned, by the establishment of the new, centralized Union of South Africa in 1910.

In fact, as later historians have shown, the success of the 'Closer Union' movement owed far more to the perception among the Boers themselves that they would eventually dominate such a Union than it did to the propaganda and

[8] Butler, *Lord Lothian*, 28.
[9] J. Barnes and D. Nicholson (eds.), *The Leo Amery Diaries*, vol. 1: *1896–1929* (London, 1980), 67.

organization of the Kindergarten.[10] Milner's hopes of a massive British immigration that would dwarf the Boer electorate were not to be fulfilled. The South African Union which the Kindergarten had laboured so devotedly to create was to become, not a pillar of the new-style British Empire, but its most fractious and dissident member. The race against the forces of disintegration had already been lost. A few of Milner's acolytes like Patrick Duncan and Richard Feetham (another New College recruit) remained in South Africa to fight for their ideal, Duncan in politics, Feetham in the judiciary, but the rest considered that their work was done and returned home, to set their sights on bigger game.

By now all were well on their way to becoming Great Men, with one exception. Peter Perry, the senior among them who had some claim to being the founder of the group, remained in South Africa for another three years before leaving for Canada, where he seems to have lost contact with his former colleagues and disappears from our screen. But of the other fellows of All Souls, Robert Brand joined Lazard Frères and began his hugely successful career as a banker. Dougie Malcolm, after a spell as private secretary to the Governor-General of Canada, became a Director of the British South Africa Company, the creation of Rhodes and the last of the great colonizing corporations; and Geoffrey Robinson, soon to change his name to Dawson, succeeded Buckle in 1912 as editor of *The Times*.[11] Leo Amery entered the House of Commons in 1911, though politics was to be only one of his innumerable activities. But the members of the Kindergarten remained closely bound together, and not only through their connection with All Souls. In London Brand, Kerr, Lionel Hichens (chairman of Cammell Laird in 1910 at the age of 36), and John Dove, yet another New College Kindergarten member, shared a bachelor establishment in London until 1917. But their basic link was the new association which they created to carry on the work they had begun in South Africa: the Round Table.

The Round Table involved a great deal more than the quarterly established under that name in 1910. It was intended to achieve for the Empire as a whole what the Kindergarten believed that they had accomplished for South Africa in creating the Union, and comprised much the same membership. The idea was already in the mind at least of Curtis while their South African operation was still in progress. 'It has always been our idea', he wrote to a friend in 1908, 'to unite South Africa and then try to make some scheme for closer Imperial Union to grow out of it'; and as he explained to Amery, in South Africa they had merely acted as 'an advance party of sappers sent out to build a vital section of the road over which the main force will travel later on'.[12] His imagination, and those of his colleagues, had been further fired by F. S. Oliver's biography of Alexander

---

[10] In particular L. M. Thompson, *The Unification of South Africa 1902–1910* (Oxford, 1960). See also K. Ingham, 'Philip Kerr and the Unification of South Africa', in Turner (ed.), *The Larger Idea*, 20–32.

[11] E. Wrench, *Geoffrey Dawson and our Times* (London, 1955).

[12] Nimocks, *Milner's Young Men*, 124, 134.

Hamilton, a work written with the deliberate intention of showing the vital need for close federation for any union, whether that of the United States or the British Empire, if it was to be politically effective. Oliver himself joined the Round Table as a founder member.

No doubt the most important influence was that of Milner himself, whose disgust with the course that British politics had taken since the Liberal landslide of 1906 only confirmed his desire to take major issues out of the hands of parochial Parliaments and entrust them to a central Imperial Council immune to the pressure of short-sighted and self-interested electorates.[13] Urged by the indefatigable Amery, with finance provided by the Rhodes Trust and later by the South African millionaire Abe Bailey, Milner presided over a series of meetings of the reconstituted Moot in the summer of 1909, whose conclusions were summed up in a memorandum by Kerr:

It was agreed that the principle of co-operation was insufficient as a means of holding together the Empire. It was thought that in the long run some form of organic union was the only alternative to disruption . . . [but] organic unity would probably only be possible when people realise that the principle of co-operation had broken down.[14]

The group appointed Curtis and Kerr as full-time employees with the immediate task of studying the problem of Imperial union and recommending the best way to solve it. In January 1910 they reported to a full meeting of the Moot: Milner, Amery, Duncan, Feetham, Hichens, Curtis, and Kerr, afforced by Oliver and one or two others. This meeting accepted that the goal was the creation of 'an organic union to be brought about by the establishment of an Imperial government, constitutionally responsible to all the electors of the Empire with power to act directly on individual citizens'. It set up an organization entrusted with 'the preparation and eventual publication of a scheme of union – if possible a constitution'; with, as a means to this, 'the promotion of public measures contributing towards the consolidation of the Empire, and the education of public opinion in the truth about Imperial affairs, and the necessity for Union'.[15] Curtis and Kerr were to be full-time officers of the organization. Kerr was to set up a London office and establish a journal which would serve the same propagandistic and informational purpose as had his earlier publication in South Africa, *The State*. Curtis was to be peripatetic, preaching the true faith throughout the Empire, collecting data, enrolling disciples, and establishing the grassroots groups from whom the thrust for organic union had to be seen to originate. He was also to prepare a document that would serve the same purpose as the

[13] For the work of the opposition leader, Lord Lansdowne, with the Round Table see A. M. Gollin, *Proconsul in Politics: A Study of Lord Milner in Opposition and in Power* (London, 1964), 164ff.

[14] Butler, *Lord Lothian*, 36.

[15] Ibid., 40.

original Selborne Memorandum. Once the soil had been thus prepared, in the words of one historian, 'the quiet conspiracy would give way to a great crusade'.[16]

It is clear that by no means all the members of the Moot were equally happy with the idea of 'organic union'. The first issue of *The Round Table*, which appeared in November 1910, skirted delicately round the subject. It did not aim, stated the editorial, 'at propounding new theories or giving voice to ingenious speculations'. They were prepared to go no further than to express 'an uneasy sense that times are changing, and that the methods of today will not serve in the competition of tomorrow. They feel that if the various communities of the Empire have common interests, they are singularly badly equipped to pursue them.'[17] Amery in particular had no time for 'organic union', especially since the Moot refused to put their weight behind his own favoured solution of tariff reform. 'The whole tendency of the movement', he wrote in his memoirs, 'was to sidetrack, or even deprecate as tainted with party controversy, the practical steps by which the maximum of effective co-operation could be brought about.'[18] None the less, Amery cooperated in finding Curtis a base in Oxford where he could recruit research assistants, preach the gospel, and recruit a new generation of young Oxonians under the Imperial banner.

Amery had already been tilling the Oxonian soil to good effect. In 1904 he had met the millionaire Alfred Beit at a dinner party and 'before we had finished the soup' he had elicited an endowment for a chair of colonial history, together with two supportive lectureships.[19] He had no difficulty in persuading Warden Anson to house the new chair in All Souls. It was filled initially by Hugh Egerton, a scholarly but uninspiring teacher who did little to popularize his subject. One of the lectureships remained vacant, and it was to this that Amery persuaded the authorities to appoint Curtis in 1911. Curtis's tenure lasted only a year, and he was not to be elected a Research Fellow of All Souls until 1921, but it began a connection with the University that was to last until Curtis's death in 1955.

Curtis's impact on Oxford is best described by Egerton himself, who wrote that he felt 'like a country rector with the prophet Isaiah as his curate'.[20] Part of the task given to him by the Moot was, as we have seen, to draft the basic text, as he had done in South Africa, which would explain and justify as well as propound the new Imperial structure that they had in mind, and his drafts of this text became the basis of his lectures. Separate sections of it were handed out as research assignments to pupils whom he then invited to stay at his home in Ledbury to discuss them. He was instrumental in founding the Ralegh Club,

[16] Nimocks, *Milner's Young Men*, 157.
[17] *The Round Table: A Quarterly Review of the Politics of the British Empire*, 1 (1910), 1.
[18] Amery, *My Political Life*, i. 270.
[19] Ibid., i. 184.
[20] D. Lavin, 'Lionel Curtis and the Idea of Commonwealth', in F. Madden and D. K. Fieldhouse (eds), *Oxford and the Idea of Commonwealth* (London, 1982), 106. See also her biography of Curtis, *From Empire to International Commonwealth: A Biography of Lionel Curtis* (London, 1995).

whose Sunday evening meetings, addressed by prominent figures from the world of politics and affairs (not least fellow-members of the Moot) became for many years a regular Oxford social fixture. Appropriate faculty members were enlisted for contributions and advice; not only fellows of All Souls like Charles Grant Robertson and W. G. Adams, but such other young scholars as Robert Rait, R. W. Seton Watson, Lewis Namier, Alfred Zimmern, and in particular Reginald Coupland.[21]

Coupland was by far Curtis's most important catch. He was at the time tutor in ancient history at Trinity, but Curtis was able to persuade him that modern empires were a more worthwhile subject for study than those of antiquity. He arranged for Coupland first to replace him as Beit Lecturer in 1913 and then to succeed Egerton on his retirement as Beit Professor in 1920: a chair he was to hold, together with his fellowship at All Souls, until 1948. Coupland became an influential member of the Moot, editing *The Round Table* briefly in 1917–19 and again in 1939–41. He became an indispensable advisor of governments on all Imperial questions, particularly those affecting the Indian Constitution. But perhaps his greatest achievement was to make Oxford the world centre of Commonwealth history and Commonwealth studies that it still remains.

Curtis was perhaps more successful in finding converts in Oxford than he was among his colleagues on the Moot. Having launched *The Round Table,* the Moot continued to hold regular meetings in such agreeable surroundings as Kerr's great house at Blickling, Oliver's establishment at Checkendon, Lord Robert Cecil's family home at Hatfield, and Cliveden, the home of a new enthusiast for imperial affairs, Waldorf Astor. The journal quickly established itself as an authoritative and influential focus for the discussion of imperial affairs at a time when the question of imperial relations was, for both military and economic reasons, forcing itself upon the public consciousness, not only in Britain but throughout the Empire. But discussion did not quite jell into prescription. When at the end of his Oxford tenure Curtis produced his draft memorandum, it was far too radical for many members of the Moot, to say nothing of being unacceptable to the 'grass-roots' groups that had now been established in Canada, Australia, and New Zealand.

Curtis could hardly have produced his 'egg', as it was known within the Moot, at a worse moment. At the Imperial Conference in 1911 the self-governing dominions had made it quite clear that they had no intention of forfeiting a single jot of their independence. So far as the British electorate was concerned, the idea of the House of Commons abdicating any of its sovereignty to another body when it had only just established its supremacy over the House of Lords was a patent non-starter. Curtis was able to keep the concept alive in the Moot until 1914, when it was overtaken by events. When his document was eventually published in 1916 as *The Commonwealth of Nations*, it took the form rather of a

---

[21] For Curtis's influence in Oxford, see Lavin, 'Curtis', passim.

lengthy scholarly rumination than of a stirring call to action. In the middle of a war in which the Dominions were establishing their right to independence on the battlefield – and acquiring little respect for the British High Command in the process – the question of 'organic union' did not have even academic interest; one suspects even for many members of the Round Table themselves. The proceedings of the Imperial War Conference in 1917 were to put an end to it for good.

Paradoxically, however, it was during those war years that the members of the Round Table reached the peak of their influence. With the co-option of Milner into the Lloyd George War Cabinet in 1917, the corridors of power were opened to his disciples. Amery joined the new Cabinet secretariat, becoming almost as influential a figure as the Cabinet Secretary, Sir Maurice Hankey, himself. Kerr became private secretary to Lloyd George, assisted by one fellow Moot member, W. G. Adams (Gladstone Professor of Government at Oxford and later Warden of All Souls) and succeeded in 1921 by another (also a New College man), Edward Grigg. As for Curtis, although appointed to no office, he reached the zenith of his career as an *éminence grise*. He threw himself first into the study of Indian affairs, proposing the system of 'dyarchy' that divided responsibility between a British-controlled central government and provinces whose ministers would be responsible to elected legislatures but advised by British officials, which was to be the core of the Montague–Chelmsford reforms. In 1918–19 he was a member of the League of Nations section of the British delegation at the Paris Peace Conference. Immediately thereafter he took the lead in the founda- tion of the Royal Institute for International Affairs, in whose anteroom at Chatham House can still be seen the round table designed, with the initials of the members of the Moot, by Sir Herbert Baker. And in 1921 Curtis was joint secretary, with Tom Jones, to the British delegation that negotiated the Anglo-Irish Treaty whereby the Irish Free State gained its independence. It was in that year that he was elected a fellow of All Souls, where he was to pass the rest of his life.

The Round Table survived the war years. Coupland took over the editorship of the journal when Kerr went to Downing Street in 1917, and in 1920 handed it on to John Dove: a founder member of the Kindergarten, who was to edit it until his death in 1934. Kerr himself returned to Oxford as secretary of the Rhodes Trust from 1925 till 1939. But although the Moot continued its regular meetings and the periodical remained an authoritative journal of Commonwealth affairs, it was no longer a single-minded pressure group, and 'organic union' had been forgotten by everyone except Curtis himself. And although Curtis continued to urge the idea in season and out of season, he had lifted his eyes to yet more distant horizons and even less practicable projects. He spent his first decade at All Souls writing his magnum opus, *Civitas Dei*, in which he charted the onward march of self-government from the Anglo-Saxons through the British Constitution and the British Commonwealth to a new World Order that would effectively be the Kingdom of God on Earth.[22]

As for the other members of the Moot, most of them had now become Very Great Men Indeed, whose interests and personalities tugged them in different directions. The development of Commonwealth relations, culminating in the Statute of Westminster of 1931, made it clear that the Empire could survive only as an instrument for free cooperation between jealously sovereign states. Those concerned with making that cooperation work, especially Amery, on whose shoulders as Secretary of State for the Colonies between 1924 and 1929 the responsibility chiefly rested, found Curtis's vaticinations particularly unhelpful. As for Coupland, enduring the necessary drudgery of establishing Commonwealth studies as a respectable academic option within the University and absorbed in the detailed work of the Peel Commission on Palestine and the Cripps Mission to India, he and Curtis ended up barely on speaking terms.

But Curtis never lost his ability to inspire the young. In the inter-war years he recruited to the Round Table such younger fellows of All Souls as H. V. Hodson, Geoffrey Hudson, Dermot Morrah (whom Geoffrey Dawson also recruited for *The Times*), and the Australian Keith Hancock.[23] Hancock he persuaded to write the Chatham House *Survey of British Commonwealth Affairs* in parallel with the wider annual survey of world affairs being written by Arnold Toynbee; and from this springboard Hancock went on to become the leading post-war academic in the field of Commonwealth studies. Hodson he 'seduced' ('he was a great seducer', commented Hodson later) to undertake a tour of the Commonwealth, notably of India, preparatory to succeeding Dove as editor of *The Round Table*. During the war Hodson was to become Constitutional Adviser to the Viceroy, and afterwards would write the authoritative account of Indian independence, *The Great Divide: Britain-India-Pakistan*.[24] The contribution of the College to the history of the subcontinent is, however, dealt with elsewhere in this volume.

Curtis's influence on the younger fellows between the wars must have been powerfully reinforced by the regular weekend visits of his colleagues from the Moot: Amery, Brand, Geoffrey Dawson, and Dougie Malcolm, not to mention the resident Reginald Coupland and, up the road at the new Rhodes House (designed by their old Kindergarten associate Herbert Baker), the continuing presence of Philip Kerr. It is not surprising that a friendly critic wrote, in 1932, that the fellows of All Souls had 'taken upon themselves no less a task than forming an unofficial committee for running, or helping to run, the destinies of the British Empire'.[25]

---

[22] 3 vols (London, 1934–7).
[23] On whom see Davidson, this volume.
[24] London, 1969.
[25] C. W. Brodribb, *Government by Mallardry: A Study in Political Ornithology* (London, 1932), with Green, this volume, ch. 2.

But whatever the contribution of individual members of the Round Table to Indian affairs, the development of British policy towards India cannot be attributed to any concerted policy or pressure from the Moot; and their influence on other developments in the Commonwealth between the wars is even harder to trace. As Professor Anthony Low reported to the Round Table 80th Anniversary Conference in 1990:

The sad fact . . . is that in the three major developments in Commonwealth history from World War I to the mid 1960s – the Balfour Report and the Statute of Westminster; the making of the London Declaration of 1949; and the changeover to a principally non-white Commonwealth by 1965 – the Round Tablers (of all people) never once played a major part.[26]

This loss of influence can be attributed to several causes. With the loss of faith in 'organic union' there was no longer any cause to bind the members of the Round Table together except a general interest in, and benevolence towards, the affairs of the Commonwealth. Although all its members remained close personal friends, they became deeply divided in the 1930s over major issues of foreign policy, as is chronicled elsewhere in this volume. And although their vision of the Commonwealth was broad enough to encompass India, the growth of the multi-racial Commonwealth of the post-war years created more dissent among them than unity. The ideals which they had so enthusiastically espoused in the Edwardian era were not in themselves enough to provide guidance in dealing with the complex problems of Commonwealth relations during the second part of the twentieth century.

Neither, after the Second World War, did the Round Table as a body maintain much contact with All Souls. Although Dermot Morrah took over the editorship of the journal in 1944, the Moot became increasingly remote from Oxford, with eventually only Morrah and Hodson as Quondams providing links with the College. The members of the original Kindergarten and their immediate successors – Amery, Curtis, Dawson, Malcolm, Brand – passed away. Perhaps more important and more significantly, on Coupland's retirement in 1948 the Beit Chair was given up to Balliol, and although Commonwealth studies continued to flourish and expand under Coupland's successors, they did so in total independence from All Souls.

Most important of all, after the Second World War the affairs of the Commonwealth and Empire no longer had the same appeal for bright young Prize Fellows as had been the case half a century earlier. Many of them regarded the surviving members of the Kindergarten as figures from an infinitely remote historical epoch. A link was re-established in 1970, however, when two fellows of the College, Robert Jackson and the present writer, were recruited to edit the

---

[26] D. A. Low, 'What Happened to Milner's Young Men: What of their Successors?', *The Round Table*, 315 (1990), 257–67.

Diamond Jubilee number of *The Round Table*, joining Hodson and Morrah as members of the Moot. The link was strengthened when the chairman of the Moot, Robert O'Neill, became the new Chichele Professor of the History of War in the University in 1987 and was elected to a fellowship of the College. O'Neill, himself an Australian, was making the Moot more reflective of the nature of the Commonwealth by broadening its national composition, and by the end of his six years in the chair nearly half of its members were non-British. Nevertheless by 1994 its British membership included four All Souls Quondams. In addition to Hodson, who was now the Nestor of the Moot, these consisted of Robert Jackson, then a Conservative junior minister and Member of Parliament; Sir Robert Rhodes-James, an historian who also sat in Parliament in the Conservative interest from 1976 until 1992; and Sir Robert Wade-Gery, whose career in the Foreign and Commonwealth Office had culminated in his tenure as High Commissioner in India from 1982 to 1987, and who had married the granddaughter of one of the original Moot members, William Marris. With this strong support, the College was able to host international conferences sponsored by the Round Table in 1990 and 1993.

No longer a base for young zealots of Imperial union, the Round Table has become a broad group of experts on whom individuals, governments, and the Commonwealth Secretariat test their ideas. It remains close to All Souls, even though it is now independent of its parental home.

7

All Souls and the War of the Professors

John Clarke

In August 1914, All Souls was still mourning the loss of its 'second founder', Sir William Anson, who had died on 4 June. The sense of loss must have been compounded by news of the tragic death of Anson's nephew and heir only a month later.[1] When Sir Denis Anson drowned on 3 July, few in Oxford imagined that Britain would soon be at war. Only a fortnight earlier, German honorands had been among the chief guests at the College's Encaenia lunch.[2] On 19 July, E. L. Woodward, a future fellow of All Souls, dined in St John's. Woodward had been staying at a rather grand hotel in the Black Forest when the news of Franz Ferdinand's assassination came through and was astounded when some of his fellow guests declared that the assassination would lead to a European war in which England would be involved. After returning to Oxford, Woodward toyed with the idea of raising the possibility of war when he dined in St John's, but decided not to do so – largely because he did not want to appear foolish. He was sure that not more than two of the fellows had given any thought whatsoever to developments in the Balkans, and, in any case, 'It would have seemed ridiculous to suggest at dessert on this quiet Sunday evening that a European war might break out in a fortnight.'[3]

---

[1] 3 July 1914. In the early morning, Sir Denis Anson, Bt, dived into the Thames at Battersea off a launch returning from a midnight excursion and was drowned: verdict (9 July) 'Accidental Death': *Annual Register 1914: Chronicle*, 21.

[2] German Honorands were Ludwig Mitteis, Professor of Law at Leipzig, the composer Richard Strauss, the Duke of Saxe-Coburg-Gotha, and Fürst von Lichnowsky, German ambassador to the Court of St James. *Oxford Magazine*, 11 June 1914. See K. M. Lichnowsky, *Heading for the Abyss: Reminiscences* (London, 1928), 33.

[3] E. L. Woodward, *Great Britain and the War of 1914–1918* (London, 1967), pp. xiii–xiv. Curiously, although writing more than fifty years after the events he describes, Woodward seems less interested in the lack of awareness about the coming war than concerned with a fear that some of his readers might conclude that, in his youth, he had been an *habitué* of 'large, cosmopolitan hotels'. He takes care to point out that his presence in such an establishment in June 1914 had been completely untypical of his lifestyle – either then or later. One might have thought such assurances unnecessary. In their wildest dreams, those who knew Woodward in old age could have never imagined him in the role of the 'lounge lizard'.

If the fellows of St John's took their news from *The Times*, edited since 1912 by Geoffrey Dawson, né Robinson (fellow of All Souls 1898), their lack of concern about events in south-eastern Europe is understandable. Until the last week of July, *The Times* gives far more attention to the Irish crisis, even to the possible links between smoking and cancer, than to the dispute between Austria and Serbia. The main item of Continental news is often the trial of Madame Cailloux – wife of a former Prime Minister of France – who was accused of the murder of the editor of *Le Figaro*. Any references to the Serbian crisis are couched in reassuring terms. On 21 July, *The Times* declared, 'The Government of Austria-Hungary has acted hitherto with comparative moderation', and the report is headed 'Settling up outstanding differences'. There was a moment of alarm on 27 July when the Balkan crisis finally received the attention of a First Leader – significantly a day when Dawson was not in his office.[4] But the next issue insisted that the situation was 'perceptibly less threatening than it was yesterday'. The basis of this renewed optimism was a report from the paper's Berlin correspondent, entitled 'Putting on the Brakes'. The report insisted that Germany was doing its best to restrain hotheads in Vienna and 'certainly and sincerely working for peace'.

Of course, thereafter, events were to move with breathtaking speed – so much so that Spenser Wilkinson (fellow 1909) was to write later that war had come 'like a thunderbolt'.[5] But surprise at the outbreak of war, in which Germany seemed to be the aggressor, was probably linked to other factors. Ignorance of European politics was often combined with a distinct sympathy for Germany. Harry Hanak reminds us that, after two wars, fought to prevent German world domination, it is difficult to appreciate the tremendous impact that Imperial Germany had made on England. People of every class had been influenced by the German example and there was widespread admiration of German achievements in all spheres of life.[6]

Admiration of Germany was particularly marked in the academic world, not least in the fields of history and theology. The Oxford theologian, W. E. Selbie, was to quote Mark Pattison, writing as early as 1857: 'The capital of world learning is in the hands of the Germans, and theirs has been the enterprise which has directed it into theological channels.'[7] German ideas dominated liberal theology and had influenced both Tractarians and Evangelicals. As the nineteenth century progressed, more and more theological students went to Germany and

[4] According to S. Morison et al., *The History of The Times*, 7 vols to date (London, 1935–), iv. 201, Dawson was involved in a minor motor accident on 26 July, which kept him away from the paper for a few days. During Dawson's absence, *The Times* was run by Henry Wickham Steed.

[5] Wilkinson to the editor of the *Springfield Republican*, reprinted in S. Wilkinson, *Great Britain and Germany* (Oxford Pamphlet no. 4; London, 1914), 28. Wilkinson himself had important links with Germany and his wife was the niece of Admiral von Holzendorff.

[6] H. Hanak, *Great Britain and Austria-Hungary during the First World War: A Study in the Formation of Public Opinion* (London, 1962), 40.

[7] W. B. Selbie, *The War and Theology* (Oxford Pamphlet no. 53; London, 1914), 4.

returned 'imbued with something of the German spirit and method; and full of admiration for teachers like Harnak and Herrman, Troeltsch and Julicher, Johannes Weiss, Seeberg, and Loofs'.[8] As events on the Continent unfolded, many who valued their links with Germany recoiled at the prospect of war with a country they believed had contributed so much to European civilization. These attitudes are reflected in a manifesto that appeared in *The Times* of 1 August 1914:

We regard Germany as a nation leading the way in the Arts and Sciences and we have all learned and are learning from German scholars. War against her in the interest of Servia and Russia will be a sin against civilization. If by reason of honourable obligations we be unhappily involved in war, patriotism might still our mouths, but at this juncture we consider ourselves justified in protesting against being drawn into a struggle with a nation so near akin to our own, and with whom we have so much in common.[9]

The list of signatories is dominated by Cambridge names, though at least one eminent Cambridge figure declined to sign. On 18 September 1914 Henry Jackson, Regius Professor of Greek at Cambridge, told Charles Cannan, Secretary to the Delegates of the Clarendon Press, that he had received a telegram from Foakes-Jackson urging him to add his name to the list. But Jackson had refused, deploring the way 'Foakes-Jackson and J. J. Thomson & Co. licked their [the Germans'] boots (or something else) in that outrageous memorial', adding 'I did *not* telegraph the obvious three words'.[10]

The 'Manifesto' received the support of two Oxford figures. Both were heads of institutions not then full colleges of the University. Manchester and Mansfield were essentially Nonconformist establishments where the traditions of Gladstonian Liberalism and 'Little England' were strong. But Selbie and Carpenter were by no means peripheral figures. Selbie, Principal of Mansfield since 1909, was a former Scholar of Brasenose. Significantly, he had been in Cambridge as Minister of the Emmanuel Congregational Chapel for seven years from 1902. He was now chairman of the Congregational Union of England and Wales. Both Selbie and Carpenter had intellectual links with Germany. Selbie's works included *Schleiermacher* (1913) and he was well acquainted with German theologians, such as Troeltsch and von Harnack, who were experts in the same field. Carpenter, a Unitarian, had been Principal of Manchester College since 1906. He had been appointed Wilde Lecturer in Comparative Religion for 1914 and was regarded as

---

  [8] Ibid., 7.
  [9] The signatories were: C. G. Browne, Professor of Arabic, University of Cambridge; F. C. Burkett, Norrison Professor of Divinity, University of Cambridge; J. Estlin Carpenter, Principal, Manchester College, Oxford; F. J. Foulkes-Jackson, Fellow of Jesus College, Cambridge; M. Latimer Jackson, Rector of Little Canfield, Essex; K. Lake, Professor of Leiden and Harvard Universities; W. M. Ramsey, Professor Emeritus, University of Aberdeen; W. B. Selbie, Principal, Mansfield College, Oxford; J. J. Thomson, Cavendish Professor of Experimental Physics, University of Cambridge.
  [10] Archives of the Oxford University Press (hereafter OUP), Walton Street, Oxford, unclassified.

the leading Oxford exponent of techniques of biblical criticism developed in Germany.

But the 'Manifesto' merely repeats ideas that had recently commanded widespread support in Oxford and elsewhere. It is tempting to suspect that the signatories were 'quoting' earlier statements to the same effect. Thus, *The Anglo-German Courier* of 13 January 1906 had declared:

For us, as between England and Germany, there is no frontier to be defended ... A war between the two powers would be a world-wide calamity for which no victory could compensate either nation.[11]

This journal was published by the Anglo-German Friendship Society, established in 1905 in an attempt to repair the damage to Anglo-German relations caused by the Boer War. Warden Anson of All Souls had been a prominent member of the committee of the Society, whose honorary president was the Duke of Argyll.[12] While the political tone of All Souls in the years before 1914 was largely Tory or, in Anson's case, Liberal Unionist, it too had close links with Germany. For many years, perhaps the best-known German figure in Oxford had been Max Müller (fellow of All Souls 1858), a friend of Wilhelm II.[13] Although Müller died in 1900, Anson played an important part in the decision of the University to award an honorary degree to the Kaiser in 1907.[14]

---

[11] Quoted in S. Wallace, *War and the Image of Germany: British Academics 1914–1918* (Edinburgh, 1988), 14. The same letter was published in *The Times* of 12 January 1906 and was signed by forty-one prominent figures, including Lord Avebury, Edward Elgar, and Thomas Hardy. This number corresponded precisely to the number of German signatories of a letter – printed in *The Times* of the same day – from equally prominent German figures stressing the absence of anti-English feeling in Germany.

[12] Wallace, *War and the Image of Germany*, 236. Anson's role in promoting good relations between Britain and Germany also involved membership of the Anglo-German Students' Committee, which organized a visit of fifty-eight German students to eight British universities, including Oxford, in the summer of 1910.

[13] Müller enjoyed the honours and decorations which he received from all over the world, and would refer to Kaiser Wilhelm II of Germany, who used to send him a congratulatory telegram whenever Oxford won the boat race, as 'my favourite emperor'. R. Symonds, *Oxford and Empire: The Last Lost Cause?* (Oxford, 1991), 106.

[14] In 1907, the Kaiser received a doctorate of Civil Laws by Diploma, a form of honorary degree conferred only on Heads of State and newly elected Chancellors of the University. Perhaps through Müller, Wilhelm had learned something of All Souls traditions. This may have had unfortunate consequences. According to College lore, at the Encaenia Luncheon, when approached by a servant bearing a decanter of wine, the Kaiser waved the man away, remarking 'I am German and in Germany we drink beer. I have heard of your famous All Souls Audit Ale. Bring me some of that.' They brought him the Audit Ale in a small silver cup, but the Emperor said, 'That is not enough; in Germany we drink beer in large steins.' Then his eyes fell upon one of the large eighteenth-century tankards used as a table decoration. He said, 'Fill that up for me.' They warned him that Audit Ale was extremely strong but he insisted. Eventually the tankard, containing at least a quart was brought to him. With his withered arm he could barely lift it, but he downed the beer in one or two mouthfuls. Shortly afterwards, before Anson's horrified gaze, he slid under the table and had to be taken to the Warden's lodgings to recover.

German violation of Belgian neutrality caused many to change their minds – not least Selbie – but there was a possibility that a degree of 'pro-German' sentiment might persist even after the outbreak of hostilities, partly in Britain itself and even more so in neutral countries. The potential consequences alarmed those academics who supported the war. One solution was to write pamphlets, explaining both the long- and short-term causes of the war from the allied point of view. But who was to provide the appropriate material? The answer was less obvious than it would have been later. In 1914, there was a marked paucity of British experts on modern European history, especially in the areas of southern and eastern Europe. The Oxford School of Modern History was dominated by medieval and early modern studies. In part, this was the result of William Stubbs's view that events that had occurred since the fourteenth or fifteenth century could not be studied with the objectivity essential to proper historical scholarship. The problem was compounded by the fact that few collections of documents – believed to be the proper basis of teaching – were available for the period after 1870. Thus, Oxford historians, like their colleagues in other British universities, were 'not well prepared for the role of semi-official apologists for the British declaration of war in August 1914'.[15]

Yet Oxford historians rose to the challenge. Perhaps they had the added incentive of being able to provide another example of Oxford's traditional loyalty to the state, in contrast to the implicit 'pro-Germanism' of the unfortunate 'Tab' Manifesto. The result was *Oxford Pamphlets 1914–1915*. When completed the series ran to eighty-seven contributions. Fellows or former fellows of All Souls account for sixteen – far more than any other college.[16] There are several reasons why All Souls should have figured so prominently. The central figure was H. W. C. Davis; although now at Balliol, Davis knew most of the fellows and Quondams of All Souls very well. Further, at least by the standards of 1914, All Souls had more fellows with 'modern' interests than was the case with other colleges – where the academic composition of the fellowship was more determined by the demands of the undergraduate curricula. All Souls provided an important point of contact with the wider world of London – politics, the press, and the Bar. There was also the urgency of the situation: most of the All Souls authors were fairly prolific. There was the nature of the Prize Fellowship examination itself, which requires candidates to write impressive essays on a variety of topics, sometimes on the basis of rather slender knowledge. Given the prevailing lack of expertise, something similar was required again. Some of the authors, Fletcher perhaps more than any other, seem to have been affected by the exhilaration of the early days of war. They may have relived the excitement of the days when they wrote essays to gain a fellowship; now they were writing essays to win a war. Significantly some of them referred to themselves as 'Sharpshooters'.

---

[15] Wallace, *War and the Image of Germany*, 60.
[16] See Appendix.

The published pamphlets do not name a general editor, but it is clear that Davis took this role. Already a distinguished medievalist, he was moving to more recent history. He was also becoming an influential figure in Oxford – a member of the General Board of Faculties in 1913 and a curator of the Bodleian Library in 1914. He had also developed a close relationship with the Clarendon Press. In 1905 he prepared an Oxford edition of Jowett's translation of Aristotle's *Politics* and in 1913 undertook a revision of Stubbs's *Select Charters* for the ninth edition.[17] Shortly before the outbreak of war Davis signed a contract with the Press to write a book on modern European history – although in the event this never appeared.

No correspondence survives at the Press about Davis's initial appointment and there is little about the 'placing' of the first pamphlets. The early contributors, who were all based in Oxford, may have been approached by word of mouth. Many had close personal links with Davis. C. R. L. Fletcher had been one of the first to appreciate his talents. When Davis was a schoolboy at Weymouth College, Fletcher marked his scripts for the Oxford Local Examinations and commented, 'This boy ought to be trained for a Brackenbury Scholarship at Balliol.'[18] Shortly before his election to All Souls, Davis had shared lodgings – at 9 Woodstock Road – with Ernest Barker.[19] During his time at All Souls he became a close friend of Charles Grant Robertson and the two travelled together in France, Germany, and Italy.[20] But personal contacts were not enough. Correspondence starts from the middle of September 1914 with Davis writing to potential contributors in Oxford and elsewhere. His letters outline his ideas on the purpose of the pamphlets as well as their intended readership. Davis wrote to the London-based Sir Valentine Chirol, an expert on Serbia, on 14 September:

The series is intended for the intelligent workingman and therefore the method of treatment is simple, even elementary... The contributors belong to very different schools of political opinion, but they are all anxious to confirm the ordinary elector in his present admirable attitude towards the war, and to warn him against the danger of making peace on terms which settle nothing.[21]

Davis continued in the same vein throughout the remainder of 1914, sometimes bracketing the intelligent workingman with elementary school teachers. We may concede that educational standards have declined since 1914, but it still seems that Davis was making heavy demands on his projected readership. Although some of the 'All Souls' pamphlets employ rhetorical flourishes inappropriate in the 'driest' of scholarly works, none could be regarded as 'populist' – with the possible exception of Fletcher's. Perhaps Davis was indulging in a little ruse,

---

[17] J. R. H. Weaver, *Henry William Carless Davis, 1874–1928: A Memoir* (London, 1933), 31–2.
[18] Ibid., 7.
[19] Ibid., 12.
[20] Ibid., 14.
[21] OUP archives.

stressing the simplicity of the level to allay the fears of potential contributors tempted to decline on grounds of ignorance. A few did, although there were none from All Souls. He may have calculated that, once authors 'got into' their task, they would produce something of a fairly high academic order. The only one to take his advice literally was Fletcher – and that threatened to cause problems. On 14 September, Fletcher told Cannan, 'I give Davis *carte blanche* to alter my tracts, only don't let him make them too judicial and fair minded. It's no time for respecting the enemy's feelings.'[22] On 18 September, however, Davis assured Fletcher that everyone in the office at the Press had enjoyed *The Germans: What they covet*, adding, 'My wife says it made her ill with laughing.'[23]

The suspicion that Davis intended a more academic readership from the start is strengthened by the initial decision on price; the pamphlets were to sell for 3d each. In his letter to Cannan, Fletcher argued that this would discourage working-class readers; even fellows of Magdalen were grumbling that 3d was too dear.[24] The price was duly reduced to 2d. This was still sufficient for the Press to regard the project as potentially profitable. Printing costs were usually about £1 2s 0d per thousand, though this fell when runs were longer. Production costs amounted to about three farthings per copy. Royalties were fixed at one eighth of a penny per dozen copies, but virtually all authors gave their royalties to the Belgian – or in Chirol's case to the Serbian – Refugee Funds. By the end of October 1914, approximately 100,000 copies had been sold.

The very success of the project created its own problems. On 22 October, Humphrey Milford, the publisher and London manager, told Cannan that all copies available had been sold outright, so that there were none left for sending out 'on sale'.[25] There are suggestions too of administrative difficulties:

The labour of dealing with pamphlets is immense, involving a vast number of entries of minute sums in the cash books and ledgers, a disproportionate amount of handling and sorting and a continual reexamination of partly executed orders to dig out items that have been out of stock... But anyhow, a shillingsworth of pamphlets undoubtedly costs us more to handle than a shilling book.[26]

There were also problems with booksellers. Some, including the Liverpool Booksellers Company and Basil Blackwell, urged Davis and Cannan to number the series to facilitate ordering. Although eventually adopted, Milford originally resisted this suggestion as 'impractical, no doubt'. Most booksellers clamoured for more and more copies, but a few were less enthusiastic. R. W. Chapman noted on 3 October that booksellers hated 'two-penny goods'; it was only the

---

[22] Ibid.
[23] Ibid. On 25 March 1912, Davis married Jennie Lindup, daughter of Walter Lindup of Bampton Grange, Oxfordshire (Weaver, *Henry William Carless Davis*, 34).
[24] OUP archives.
[25] Ibid.
[26] Ibid.

pressure of public demand that enabled the Press to get them to stock what they regarded as 'unprofitable lumber'.[27] Milford even cited cases where parcels of the pamphlets had been returned unopened.

Such attitudes led to discontented authors. After visits to Liverpool and Sheffield respectively, Arthur Hassall and Paul Vinogradoff complained that the series was not being adequately promoted in the provinces. Vinogradoff even asserted that the pamphlets were not sold energetically enough in Oxford itself. Complaints of this nature caused irritation among the hard-pressed officials in Walton Street. Cannan wrote – rather icily – to Vinogradoff on 8 October:

Dear Professor,

I am afraid that you are not the first person to find Sheffield short of books; it is not perhaps as bad as some other northern towns I could mention; but its *métier* is certainly not bookselling. I saw a heap of the pamphlets in Parkers shop as I came up this afternoon.

Despite the problems, Davis – who worked hard in 'The Tower' throughout September and October – was pleased with the progress that had been achieved. He was usually impressed by the All Souls contributions as they arrived and was especially taken with Keith Feiling's pamphlet on Italy. Yet a projected pamphlet from Charles Grant Robertson on 'Great Britain's continental policy', did not materialize and a contribution from Headlam (fellow 1885) – also a friend of Davis – was rejected.[28] Davis considered inviting the Chancellor, Curzon (fellow 1883), to write on India, but the idea was vetoed by the Press on the grounds that Curzon would probably make difficulties about royalties and typefaces. Trevelyan was the third choice for the pamphlet on India and Davis considered the result dull.

But there were more serious difficulties with contributors from other colleges. A pamphlet on Russia offered by Lewis Namier of Balliol was politely received, but Davis considered that it assumed too much background knowledge and required extensive revisions that were unacceptable to the author. On 17 November, Davis had to apologize to the Greek Minister in London for errors in a pamphlet by Morgan of Keble, assuring the Minister, 'In Oxford we are all Phil-Hellenes.' No author could be found for a projected and highly sensitive pamphlet on the United States. Although a pamphlet on the German overseas empire – Evan Lewin's *The Germans in Africa* (no. 32) – eventually appeared, Davis was reluctant to include the topic at all. On 16 September, he told

---

[27] OUP archives.

[28] Headlam, later Bishop of Gloucester, had decidedly authoritarian views. Ernest Jacob (personal conversation) thought this might be due to the fact that Headlam was descended from an illegitimate son of Peter the Great, fathered during the Czar's residence in England. According to Jacob, Headlam returned from a visit to Russia full of admiration for the Orthodox Church. When asked his reasons, he cited the alleged fact that Orthodox bishops were entitled to beat their clergy.

Herbertson, the Professor of Geography, 'Perhaps the less said about the German colonies the better. It would look as if we had gone to war to grab colonies.'[29] Cannan rejected Davis's idea for a pamphlet on German atrocities, although he added 'I do think somebody might well write, say, Louvain. T. B. Macaulay would have done it very well.'[30] The weakest pamphlet was generally considered to be W. Benet's *England's Mission* (no. 25), described by Milford as 'poor, toshy Benet'.[31] But the most worrying problem arose with D. G. Hogarth, a fellow of Magdalen and Keeper of the Ashmolean Museum. Hogarth had actually completed a pamphlet on the diplomatic preliminaries to the war, but wrote to Cannan on 4 October insisting on withdrawing it. He had not found the topic interesting and had never experienced 'such difficulty in grinding out anything in my life'. The main reason for Hogarth's decision, however, was his growing suspicion that, throughout, Grey and Asquith had been 'telling only half truths'.[32]

Apart from suggesting a certain tight-fistedness in Magdalen, Fletcher's intervention on the question of price reveals that, whatever Davis's original intentions, the series was reaching an academic readership. Perhaps, if Woodward's comments on the indifference to Continental affairs prevalent in St John's was typical of the University as a whole, fellows of Oxford Colleges needed basic information as much as any working man. But there were pressures to move the series in a more academic direction. Letters began to arrive at the Press from 'war lecturers' asking for more detailed material to help them with the preparation of their talks. On 25 October, A. H. Coombes, a schoolmaster from Hurstpierpoint College, Sussex, wrote to suggest longer pamphlets. Interestingly, Coombes compared the new Oxford pamphlets with their most famous predecessors, with *Tracts for the Times*. As the *Tracts* had begun with very short pieces and then developed into more elaborate works, so the pamphlets should now move on 'to bigger essays on such subjects as Prussia and Austria'. Cannan considered this sensible, but R. W. Chapman thought that Coombes should not be taken too seriously; his proposal for a deeper study of 'Serbs, Croats and Slovaks' suggested that he did not know the difference between Slovaks and Slovenes.[33]

Of far greater importance to the direction of the pamphlets was the recognition of their potential to influence opinion in neutral countries, especially in the

---

[29] OUP archives.

[30] This is a reference to the German destruction of the University Library at Louvain in August 1914. There is still much controversy as to official German responsibility but there can be no doubt that the destruction of a famous library caused outrage in academic circles and the events in Louvain were sometimes contrasted to the care the English Parliamentary commanders took to protect the Bodleian Library in Oxford in 1644.

[31] OUP archives.

[32] Ibid. Davis may have been irritated by Hogarth's attitude, but this did not prevent the two men working together in 1920 and 1921 on the revision of the *Dictionary of National Biography* (Weaver, *Henry William Carless Davis*, 45).

[33] OUP archives.

United States. This meant that government agencies began to take an interest. The section run by Sir C. Schuster in C. F. C. Masterman's semi-secret office in Wellington Square, London, had special responsibility for opinion in neutral countries. Curiously, like Davis, Masterman was an old boy of the then somewhat obscure Weymouth College.[34] Eventually a close relationship developed between Schuster's section and the Oxford series. Schuster proved willing to 'take' a number of the pamphlets for distribution overseas, ordering as many as 35,000 copies of Vinogradoff's *Russia, the Psychology of a Nation*.[35] It seems, however, that the contact with Schuster and Masterman came about fortuitously through Fletcher's family connections. In his letter to Cannan of 14 September, Fletcher wrote:

My brother-in-law, Sir C Schuster, seems to be in charge of a bureau (at the F.O.?) which is turning out much the same sort of tracts as ours – he has several well known writers of fiction working for him. And he has a staff of translators. He would like to have an early Copy (or a 2nd proof) of my tracts and I think you might send him the others also. We might work with his gang.[36]

Although Fletcher's suggestion was taken up, it must be stressed that Schuster never commissioned any of the Oxford series directly; that remained with Cannan and Davis. As they appeared, pamphlets were 'offered' to Schuster's office, which was then free to take or reject them. No attempt was made to alter texts and the series retained more independence than Squires implies (see below). The Press had no desire to compromise academic integrity and Chapman wrote on 11 January 1915, 'We are anxious not to give the impression that our pamphlets are propaganda or are being distributed by us except in the ordinary way of trade.'[37]

There was certainly no question of any government subsidy. Although the longer print runs resulting from Schuster's orders reduced unit costs, the price of a half penny per copy usually charged to the government would have not left much profit. Indeed, if any subsidy was paid, it was from the Press to the government. Schuster appealed to patriotism and Chapman noted on 18 September, 'S. hopes we will be generous because he has very little money.'[38] Calculations of the prices charged to Schuster excluded any royalties and Chapman commented that authors who had signed their rights away could hardly complain; the only losers would be the unfortunate Belgian refugees. Relations between the Press and Schuster's department were often strained. There appeared to be little consistency about which pamphlets were accepted or rejected. Dr Sanday's contribution, *The Deeper Causes of the War* (no. 11), was turned

[34] Weaver, *Henry William Carless Davis*, 6.
[35] OUP archives.
[36] Ibid.
[37] Ibid.
[38] Ibid.

down because it read too much like a sermon and hence was not 'hot stuff', yet, at least initially, Fletcher's works on Germany were rejected for precisely the opposite reason. Few connected with the Press had a high opinion of Schuster's staff – often referred to contemptuously as 'Schuster's myrmidons'. Milford wrote to Cannan on 14 October:

Schuster wants ten copies 'in proof' of each pamphlet that we publish, so that the various members of his inefficient staff who are responsible for feeding the various countries should have plenty of time to consider what steps they will not take.[39]

There were complaints about the slowness of Schuster's translators, so slow that pirate translations sometimes appeared in other countries before they finished their task. On occasion, the Press employed its own translators and was delighted when Mrs Penson, who translated some of the pamphlets into Swedish, or Mrs Hadow, who translated German documents into English, finished well ahead of their London rivals.[40] More seriously, despite the large orders, Schuster's office was not ensuring that enough of the Oxford pamphlets actually reached the United States – focusing its attention on Americans in Britain, who, it hoped, might take copies with them when they returned home. This gave rise to complaints from allied sympathizers in America. Miss L. W. Perkins of Concord, MA, wrote to the Press on 4 November 1914 to warn that, as far as she could see, efforts to circulate 'this wonderful series' in the United States had been sadly deficient. She received her own copies direct from London but had not seen any in American bookshops. More energetic action was needed to inform opinion and counter the activities of the German Press Bureau:

Though it may be wise for us to be a neutral government, we cannot afford at this moment to be a neutral nation in our judgement of this great issue of honour and loyalty and truth for which the allied Nations stand.[41]

Of course, if German propaganda was circulating in neutral countries, it was essential for the authors of the Oxford series to have access to it so that they could prepare proper refutations. Thus, on 16 September 1914, Chapman wrote to the Dutch bookseller, Martinus Nijhoff, thanking him for sending copies of the English version of the German *Weissbuch*. Chapman explained that the Press was finding it difficult to acquire German pamphlets published in English and intended for circulation in the United States. He asked Nijhoff to send three copies of the German theologians' *Address to Evangelical Christians Abroad* and 'anything else you think likely to interest us'. But Nijhoff replied that he had learned that 'it is forbidden to English people to import German books, also from neutral countries'. Under the circumstances, he was unable to comply with

---

[39] Ibid.
[40] Mrs Penson's husband, T. H. Penson, was later chairman of the War Trade Intelligence Department in which Davis served as vice-chairman (Weaver, *Henry William Carless Davis*, 36).
[41] Ibid., 20.

Chapman's request – unless, of course, the Press could obtain special exemption from the government ban. If permission were obtained, he would be delighted to supply – adding plaintively, 'I have many copies in stock.'[42]

In the event, appropriate arrangements were made: Nijhoff sent the German material to the British Legation in the Netherlands, which then forwarded it to England in the Diplomatic Bag. By 22 October, Cannan could report that 'a great heap of German *Hetzereien*' had come in from Nijhoff and was waiting for Davis in his box at the Press. Cannan had read the German pamphlets, but doubted if they would be of much use. Later the same day, Davis left a note for Cannan saying 'Better stop them'.[43] Although the purchases were resumed towards the end of the year, Davis was to show little enthusiasm for the decision.

Davis's attitude seems surprising and can only be explained in the light of his growing dispute with Ernest Barker of New College. By the end of October 1914, Davis and Barker agreed that the circumstances surrounding the outbreak of war had now received more than adequate coverage. But whereas Davis wanted to move to a new emphasis on the current military situation – hence his later contributions on Mons, the Marne, and other battles – Barker was more interested in the academic and cultural dimension. He wished to concentrate upon what he believed to be malign aspects of German culture, particularly on attitudes to history, philosophy, and theology. As much of the German material – produced, as in Britain, by academics – was also concerned with the cultural issues, Barker's task would have been much harder if the flow of *Hetzereien* ceased.

Barker could have argued that he was only seeking to build upon interpretations of the war advanced in earlier numbers of the Oxford series, including several by fellows or former fellows of All Souls. Behind the ostensible purpose of the series – to demonstrate that the Allies were right and the Germans wrong – there was an additional private agenda. Perhaps, in the very vehemence of their attacks on German scholars, some of the Oxford authors were seeking to prove to themselves and others that they had escaped from the German cultural orbit to which they had once belonged.[44] Their attacks have all the bitterness of quarrels between former friends. Now they set out to demonstrate that German culture as defined by German academics had become inherently dangerous and aggressive and, hence, that these academics carried a major moral responsibility for the war. To give their arguments a special piquancy, some went so far as to assert that the interpretations of the war advanced by German scholars and their supporters in the United States could be refuted by the application of the same historical

[42] OUP archives.
[43] Ibid.
[44] Curiously, the behaviour of the British academics almost exactly mirrored that of their German opposite numbers. One of the signatories of the 'pro-British' letter published in *The Times* of 12 January 1906 was the Berlin celebrity and classicist Ulrich von Wilamowitz-Moellendorff, who in October 1914 was to draw up the very 'anti-British' *Manifesto of the Ninety-Three*.

techniques that had been developed by earlier generations of German scholars. In other words, they were half suggesting that England, not Germany, was the true heir of the golden age of German historical scholarship in the first half of the nineteenth century. As the British and German armies clashed in France, another war was going on – the 'war of the professors'.

Curiously, it was the very moderation of some of the authors of the Oxford series that forced them to cast German professors in the role of villains. At a time of great excitement, it must have been tempting to place responsibility for the war on the German people as a whole. Remarkably none of the College contributors make this assertion. Although Fletcher's pamphlets, *The Germans: Their Empire and how they have made it*, and *The Germans: What they covet*, are the most 'highly coloured' of the entire series, Fletcher still insists, 'Nothing shall persuade me that the German people as a whole (I know hardly anything of the governing classes or the professional soldiers of Germany) wanted this war.'[45] He describes the Germans as a nation with 'great aptitudes for the arts of peace, and for the enjoyment of the modest pleasures of a quiet life'.[46] Faced with stories of German atrocities in Belgium, he writes 'But let us make no mistake; German officers and German privates are not acting thus because they are naturally more cruel than other soldiers.'[47] In particular, Fletcher has considerable affection for the non-Prussian elements of Germany, for the people of 'these little German states, who wanted to drink their beer, and listen to their divine music, and write their deep books on philosophy like good peaceful men'.[48] He tells an agreeable story about an elderly Saxon lady who took him for a drive around Dresden. When they came to the city walls, he asked, 'Are these the fortifications of Dresden?', and she replied, 'No, my dear, these are the fortifications of Berlin.'[49] It is the Prussians who are most to blame, but not all Prussians are bad and Fletcher has serious doubts about whether even the Kaiser can be held responsible.[50]

The trouble with the Germans is that they have been 'blown up' by their governing classes 'into a kind of madness which made them think they wanted this war'.[51] The madness has been spread by government-controlled newspapers. Not only newspapers but also schools and universities are wholly in the hands of the state. All professors and schoolmasters are salaried state-agents. All know that any promotion and even the retention of their posts depend on teaching and preaching exactly what the government wishes. The decline in religious

[45] C. R. L. Fletcher, *The Germans: Their Empire and how they have made it* (Oxford Pamphlet no. 6; London, 1914), 3.
[46] Ibid., 5.
[47] Ibid., 17.
[48] Ibid., 21.
[49] Ibid., 30.
[50] Ibid., 17.
[51] Ibid., 3.

observance in both Catholic and Protestant parts of Germany has reduced the influence of ministers of religion and priests. The German religion is now culture, but culture as defined by hireling professors.[52]

The professors' religion involved the reworking of most of the Ten Commandments. For the first, they replaced the traditional Christian God with the God of Force. For the second, they ignored the prohibition on graven images and set up 'a graven image of the German man in full armour, and thou shalt bow down to him and worship him, and shall call him the king of men, the Superman'. For the sixth, they substituted the ban on murder with 'thou shalt murder all who stand in the way of the triumph of thy New God'. For the eighth, against stealing, their version was 'Thou shalt not stick at fraud'. For the tenth, against covetousness, they simply removed the 'not'.[53]

Fletcher has no hesitation in linking this new doctrine with two important German thinkers – with Nietzsche and with von Treitschke. He says of Nietzsche:

This Superman was the special invention of a philosopher called Nietzsche, who spent his life in railing against the 'superstition' of Christianity, and against the virtues of pity, mercy and love, which are, he said, the most distinctive doctrines of that superstition. You need not remember anything else about Nietzsche, except that he went stark staring mad before he died. But while he was going mad (and it would be only charitable to suppose that he was never very sane), he contrived to bite a great many of his countrymen, and to instil a good deal of his poisonous doctrines into those he bit.[54]

According to Fletcher, ideas ultimately derived from Nietzsche informed the publications of the various patriotic leagues set up in Germany from the beginning of the 1890s – and in whose governing committees academics often played a prominent part. The Leagues sought to identify Germany's enemies as France, Russia, and England, but the greatest venom was directed against England. Here the paramount influence was the historian Heinrich von Treitschke – 'Treitschke's whole animus was directed against England to the day of his death; and Treitschke did more to form educated opinion in Germany than anyone.'[55]

The same theme of blaming scholars for the cultural climate in Germany was taken up by many of the Oxford pamphlets. The now changed Selbie criticized German theology for creating a total divorce between theology as a science and its social and religious purpose. Barker himself produced *Nietzsche and Treitschke*, which echoed Fletcher but stressed that Treitschke took 'the worship of power' to the extent that 'the only power Treitschke tolerates is the power of the collective national State', leaving decisions 'not to the scales of justice, but to the arbitrament of the sword'.[56]

---

[52] C. R. L. Fletcher, *The Germans: Their Empire and how they have made it* (Oxford Pamphlet no. 6; London, 1914), 4.

[53] C. R. L. Fletcher, *The Germans: What they covet* (Oxford Pamphlet no. 7; London, 1914), 5–7.

[54] Ibid., 5.

[55] Ibid., 19–20.

[56] E. Barker, *Nietzsche and Treitschke: The Worship of Power in Modern Germany* (Oxford Pamphlet no. 20; London, 1914), 18, 23.

One of the most interesting of the pamphlets, Spenser Wilkinson's *Great Britain and Germany*, attempts to turn German methods against the German interpretation of the road to war – in this case, however, through an examination of the pro-German American professor, John Burgess.[57] Wilkinson quotes at length from letters from Burgess published in the Springfield *Republican*, a paper widely read at Harvard. Burgess professed to be proud of his English ancestry, but insisted 'what I possess of higher learning has been won in Germany'. He had first gone to Germany in 1871 and

> almost from the first day that I took my seat in the lecture room at the university, I imbibed the doctrine that the great national and world purpose of the newly created German Empire was to protect and defend the Teutonic civilization of Continental Europe against the oriental quasi-civilization on the one side and the decaying Latin civilization on the other.[58]

Sadly, Germany's success after unification 'excited soon the jealousy, the envy and then the hostility of Great Britain'.[59] The true villain of the piece had been King Edward VII, whose efforts had brought together the three great forces working for universal war in Europe – 'namely the pan-Slavic programme of Russia, the "revanche" of France and Great Britain's commercial jealousy of Germany'.[60] Britain too increasingly looked to war as 'an opportunity to divert the mind of her people away from internal questions which were threatening to disrupt her constitution'.[61] In the recent crisis, the German Emperor had attempted to mediate between Austria and Serbia, only to be thwarted by Russia's mobiliza-tion. He then tried – once more in vain – to secure the neutrality of France. When European war became inevitable, Germany had still tried to avoid conflict with Britain. But when Britain asked Germany to promise not to use her Navy against either France or Russia and to desist from her military movement through Belgium, the German government, quite reasonably, required Britain to promise that she too would respect Belgian neutrality. Britain made no response to this fair suggestion, but simply declared war on Germany.[62]

Having established Germany's innocence to his own satisfaction, Burgess goes on to consider the likely consequences of her victory or defeat – clearly a matter of crucial concern for the United States. If Germany and Austria were to win, their triumph could 'never be so complete as to make any changes to the map of Europe'. At most, Russia would have to abandon her 'pan-Slavic' programme, French 'revanchism' would be silenced, and Britain would be unable to achieve

[57] Burgess held a chair of political science and constitutional law at the University of Columbia.
[58] John W. Burgess to the editor of *The Republican*, 17 August 1914, printed in Wilkinson, *Great Britain and Germany*, 11–12.
[59] Ibid., 13.
[60] Ibid., 17.
[61] Ibid., 18.
[62] Ibid., 20, 27.

her objective of destroying German commerce.[63] Yet, if the Allies were to win, Russia would be the mistress of Continental Europe, and the 'rattle of the sabre would then be music to our ears, in comparison with the crack of the Cossack's knout and the clanking of Siberian chains'. Britain would enjoy undisputed mastery of the sea. Faced with the giants of Britain and Russia – together with their 'oriental ally, Japan' – the United States would be compelled to shoulder an enormous burden of armaments, which would sap her wealth and even threaten the existence of her republican institutions.[64]

But Wilkinson makes short work of Burgess's case. It was nonsense to claim that German victory would make little difference to the map of Europe. If Germany were to win, the King of Prussia would be overlord of Europe. The conclusion is obvious: if Europe is to remain free, the nations Germany has challenged must defeat and disarm her and 'compel her to be content to till her own soil and mind her own business, not as the ruler of other nations but as one among the united states of Europe'.[65]

Like Burgess, Wilkinson acknowledges a considerable intellectual debt to Germany – in his case to the works of Leopold von Ranke, whose guiding light had been that historical enquiry must rest upon scrupulous examination of evidence. Wilkinson does not quarrel with that; indeed, he asserts that this was precisely the principle that informed the School of History in England whose Oxford representatives were Stubbs, Freeman, York Powell, and Firth.[66] Trained in this School himself, Wilkinson can apply von Ranke's methods to Burgess's arguments. It soon emerges that they are worthless. Thus, Wilkinson follows the approved German methodology and subjects Burgess's sentence – that Germany's mission had been to defend the Teutonic civilization of Europe from 'oriental Slavic quasi-civilization' and from 'decaying Latin civilization' – to detailed textual analysis:

Teutonic, it will be observed, is only the full dress name for German. 'The Teutonic civilization of continental Europe' is the German way of saying that such civilization as there is in Europe is the gift of Germany. German professors are very fond of this theme, which is no doubt patriotic. The doctrine then which the professor imbibed is that the German Empire stands for Germany and that Germany thinks she ought to impose herself on France, Italy, Spain and Portugal ('the decaying Latin civilization') and upon Russia, Servia and Bulgaria ('the oriental Slavic quasi-civilization').[67]

For someone who claimed to admire German methodology so much, Burgess's handling of his evidence was distinctly peculiar. Above all, it ignored the golden

[63] John W. Burgess to the editor of *The Republican*, 17 August 1914, printed in Wilkinson, *Great Britain and Germany*, 21.
[64] Ibid., 22.
[65] Spenser Wilkinson to the editor of *The Republican*, 22 August 1914, printed in Wilkinson, *Great Britain and Germany*, 10.
[66] Ibid., 23. Wilkinson asserts, 'Ranke set up, I think, the right standard of impartiality'.
[67] Wilkinson, *Great Britain and Germany*, 24–5.

rule of impartiality. Thus, at the time of the Moroccan crisis of 1905, Burgess had addressed his inquiries about British policy, not to Britain, but to Germany.[68] Later, he argued that the Ententes of Britain, France, and Russia were directed against the Triple Alliance of Germany, Austria, and Italy. Apparently it was right and proper for Germany, Austria, and Italy to be allied, but when England, France, and Russia so much as compared notes they were doing something wicked.[69]

Of course, it was inevitable that German scholars would respond to accusations against their country and against themselves. Barker was particularly distressed by the reaction of German academics to *Why We are at War: Great Britain's Case*. This book, a copy of which had been presented to the Codrington Library of All Souls by Davis on 22 September 1914, is described as written by 'Members of the Oxford Faculty of Modern History'. The actual contributors were Davis, Barker, Arthur Hassall of Christ Church, L. G. Wickham Legg of New College, and F. Morgan of Keble. There was thus a substantial overlap between this group and the subsequent contributors to the Oxford pamphlets series – although the general tone is more scholarly. Barker discovered that a number of German scholars had accused *Why We are at War* of 'poisoning intellectual wells'. *The Times* of 9 November carried a letter from Barker pointing out that 'the harnessing of history to the chariot wheels of political propaganda' is precisely what other scholars have long found so distasteful in the works of German historians. Barker probably has in mind the *Manifesto of the Intellectuals of Germany*, organized by Ulrich von Wilamowitz-Moellendorff in October 1914. The *Manifesto* proclaimed:

Have faith in us . . . believe that we shall carry on this war to the end as a civilized nation to whom the legacy of a Goethe, a Beethoven and a Kant is just as sacred as its own hearths and homes.

By this time there can have been few in Oxford who had even a residual belief in such assurances. As the pamphlet by W. G. S. Adams on *The Responsibility for the War* had argued with considerable skill, the only principle in recent German action had been to sacrifice every consideration of civilization or morality for the sake of military advantage.[70] For Adams, Germany's great crime was that, by invading Belgium, she had thrown aside all respect for international law, and several of the Oxford pamphlets, notably Barker's, stress that contempt for international law was implicit – on occasion explicit – in the works of von Treitschke.[71] Yet German scholars continued to assert that they were fighting a war for civilization. A subsequent work, *Deutschland und der Weltkrieg*, by Otto

---

[68] Ibid., 25.
[69] Ibid., 25, 30.
[70] W. G. S. Adams, *The Responsibility for the War* (Oxford Pamphlet no. 3; London, 1914), 20.
[71] Barker, *Nietzsche and Treitschke*, 24.

Hintze, Herman Onken, Herman Schmacher, and Friedrich Meineke maintained exactly this line.

Barker now began to prepare a pamphlet that he believed would destroy the German case once and for all. His pamphlet would be considerably longer than anything that had appeared in the series so far. Davis did not welcome the suggestion. Ostensibly, his argument was based upon purely commercial considerations. On 13 December, he observed to Cannan, 'I am afraid, however, that the Oxford series has already as many dissections of the German intellectual position as the public desires.'[72] Davis's reservations increased when he saw a draft of the proposed pamphlet and he wrote to Cannon on 20 December:

Barker:
I think his stuff is not worth printing. The war of the professors has already become a byword and if Barker wants to defend the Red Book [*Why We are at War*] any further, he had better do it somewhere else. I don't mind having more tracts on Austria-Hungary when opportunity occurs. But Barker would only write Seton Watson and water on that subject. I would rather have Adams if I can get him, but I would like still more to have Dillon of the *Daily Telegraph*.[73]

But Cannan's first reaction was to support Barker, or at least not upset him. Cannan wrote to Barker on 21 December:

He [Davis] appears to be nervous about the 'war of the Professors' and to put his trust in 13.5 or 15 inches instead of honest dialectical weapons and anyhow has been gibbing about replying to any criticisms or apologetics of any Germans. It may be that Sanday, you and I are the only people interested in seeing what the blessed Germans have to say, but I certainly like reading their vapourings.[74]

On 22 December, Barker sent an impassioned plea to Cannan. 'Putting aside all feelings of private pique', he begged the Delegates to print his pamphlet, stressing that recent German material continued to repeat the errors and distortions that he had exposed earlier:

If anything is worth publishing in this war, an answer to the German historians and theologians in respect to the false history they are printing *is* worth it. America is a poor place; but are we to let it swallow German lies unheeded? I mean by lies the fictions of its Press Bureau which has never had a good name.[75]

After reading Barker's work and discussing it with Sanday, however, Cannan concluded that Davis was right; the whole effect was scrappy. But Cannan still wished to avoid a confrontation; on 23 December he told Davis that Barker was very hurt at the rejection of his pamphlet and urged a meeting over Christmas in

[72] OUP archives.
[73] Ibid.
[74] Ibid.
[75] Ibid.

the hope of a reconciliation. Cannan may have feared that 'the war of the professors' was about to degenerate into a civil war between Oxford 'professors'. A meeting between Davis and Barker did take place and it seems that a partial reconciliation was effected, although relations remained strained. Davis continued as editor and, for a time, both 'military' and 'cultural' pamphlets appeared. Yet the impetus behind the series was faltering. In part, this was due to the fact that Davis had increasingly urgent additional calls upon his time. He was becoming involved in war work at the Admiralty – and this may explain his growing interest in military matters and his seeming indifference to more academic issues.

Davis may have been right about the decline in public interest for pamphlets of the sort Barker wanted, but his own alternative was hardly more promising. In reality, of the later pamphlets, neither the 'military' nor the 'cultural' variety sold particularly well. On 12 January 1915, the OUP American branch reduced its order to two hundred copies of any new pamphlet, adding 'The Market on this side has been so flooded with war literature that people are surfeited with it and there is no longer the active demand for these pamphlets that there was formerly.' On 18 January, Milford admitted to Cannan that recent pamphlets were not selling as well as the 'first shoots'. He hoped that this might prove only a temporary problem – 'it takes time to get each new one known – remember your disappointment at the slow start of the first issues'. But the expected improvement did not occur. By 11 March, Milford could conclude that the situation in Britain now resembled that in the United States because the home market too was showing 'distinct signs of saturation'. He was inclined to 'finish up the series and close down, except for any pamphlets that are already arranged'. On 29 March, the Delegates took the decision to discontinue; Davis then moved to a full-time job at the Trade Clearing House. Despite the decision to close, the Press continued to receive suggestions for further pamphlets throughout 1915. These proposals usually received scant sympathy. On 16 October, J. Johnson wrote to Arthur Hassall, who had forwarded a pamphlet from a Mr Mellors, 'There seems no place nowadays for Mr Mellors' *Slav v Teuton*. Moreover there seems to be little knowledge behind the pamphlet but a great deal of hyperbole is coupled with rather tiresome attacks on individuals.'[76]

There is still something puzzling about Davis's determination not to continue with 'the war of the professors', especially as this obviously involved an unpleasant dispute with his old friend Ernest Barker. Perhaps the real clue as to what was happening is to be found in the first line of the preface to *Why We are at War* – 'We are not politicians, and we belong to different schools of political thought.'[77] While such differences may have seemed unimportant in the first days of the war, they were probably beginning to reappear by the end of 1914. It is striking that in

[76] Ibid.
[77] E. Barker, *Why We Are at War* (Oxford, 1914), 5.

addition to his quarrel with Barker, Davis regarded Adams – arguably the most effective of the earlier contributors – as only his second choice for the proposed pamphlet on Austria-Hungary. In the early pamphlets, Adams and Barker had gone furthest in identifying the allied cause with democracy. Adams, in particular, focused on the Germans' contempt for small states and argued that one of the chief reasons why countries like Belgium, Holland, Denmark, and Switzerland had to be preserved against German expansionism was precisely because in such small states 'the democratic spirit is strongly developed'.[78]

It is unlikely that Davis would have been attracted to this line and that may have made him reluctant to accept another pamphlet from Barker. It is true that he agreed with Adams about the value of small states – but not because they tended to be democratic. Davis had visited Belgium in 1901 and 1902; on the second occasion he had been accompanied by Grant Robertson and Hensley Henson.[79] His pamphlet *What Europe Owes to Belgium* stresses that without the delay afforded by Belgian resistance, 'it is hard to see how the Germans could have been kept out of Paris'.[80] But what most impressed Davis about Belgium were its cultural achievements – writers like Maeterlinck and Verhaere, and above all, the school of Flemish painters represented by the Van Eycks and Hans Memling.[81]

Davis's lack of enthusiasm for democracy may be deduced from his whole philosophy of history. Following his appointment as Regius Professor, he delivered his inaugural lecture on 'The Study of History' on 4 November 1925. Davis is scathing about 'those self-styled social historians' who think they can find 'the quintessence of our common humanity in the life of the common man':

They tell us that what we need to know about any civilization of the past is what its poorer and more illiterate members thought and did. How the social order affected the welfare of these people is indeed a momentous question, but the historians of the commonplace have in their minds a confused doctrine of the wisdom of the humble, which has been eloquently expounded by imaginative writers, and has overflowed from their works into certain schools of historical research. I can find no justification for the belief that what the masses think today society as a whole will infallibly believe tomorrow; that religions, philosophies, political ideas rise like exhalations from the cottage, the workshop, and the market place. On the contrary, it would appear from what we know of the history of new ideas that, even if they do not fall like the rain from heaven, they make their first appearance somewhere near the summit of the social fabric and percolate downwards, not infrequently suffering adulteration or corruption in the process. Our common humanity is best studied in the most eminent examples that it has produced of every type of human excellence.[82]

[78] Adams, *The Responsibility for the War*, 19.
[79] Weaver, *Henry William Carless Davis*, 27.
[80] H. W. C. Davis, *What Europe owes to Belgium* (Oxford Pamphlet no. 36; London, 1914), 12.
[81] Ibid., 14, 22.
[82] H. W. C. Davis, *The Study of History*, reprinted in Weaver, *Henry William Carless Davis*, 77–8.

Davis's obituary, in *The Times* of 29 June 1928, observes that his historical orthodoxy 'was shot through by an almost wayward impatience of the verdict of the crowd, and his severe intellectual serenity submitted to a native sympathy for men destined to bear the responsibility of life and death decision'.

It would be wrong to suggest that Davis's unashamed elitism in any way reduced his commitment to the Allied cause in 1914; a belief in democracy was not the only or even the most cogent reason for supporting war against Imperial Germany – especially as one of Britain's main allies was Czarist Russia. Yet Davis's attitude to Germany and to German scholarship in particular does raise interesting questions. Davis clearly had a profound knowledge of and respect for the works of several major German historians. Soon after his election to All Souls, he told Grant Robertson of 'his determination to master the technique of historical method and sound scholarship'. In the context of the 1890s, that was tantamount to saying German scholarship. During his time at All Souls, Davis visited Germany twice. In 1897, he went to Dresden 'in order to perfect his German and to make acquaintance with Opera'.[83] He returned to Dresden in the summer of 1899 – on this occasion with Grant Robertson – seeing 'something of the Saxon mountains and more opera'.[84]

Although Davis effectively vetoed Barker's proposed pamphlet, that did not mean that he had lost all interest in the German intellectual tradition. On the contrary, towards the end of 1914, he published – with Constable of London – *The Political Thought of Heinrich von Treitschke*. It is true that Davis's work was aimed at a more academic readership than the artisans and elementary school teachers who were supposedly the intended target of the Oxford pamphlets, but we are bound to speculate about Davis's motives. It is surely unlikely that he would have been so petty as to seek to make a 'corner' in the subject himself. Two possibilities present themselves. Davis might have argued that while the public as a whole had lost interest in German academics, the scholarly community had not. But the scholarly community was unlikely to be impressed with the commentary and hostile interpretation that had characterized the pamphlets written by Fletcher and even Barker. It would probably prefer to read what von Treitschke had actually said – if not in the original then at least in translation – and then make up its own mind. In other words, von Treitschke's works should be treated as historical documents – that is in the tradition of von Ranke and, indeed, of Stubbs.

Perhaps the best way of discrediting the German historians among the academic community in Britain and elsewhere in the English-speaking world would be to allow them to condemn themselves with their own words. This may indeed have been Davis's intention. In what little commentary he does provide, there are some decidedly 'loaded' words and phrases. Thus he talks of 'the political

83 Ibid., 14.
84 Ibid., 20.

philosophy now in vogue in Germany' and asserts that von Treitschke's *Politik* 'seems so inexplicably one sided to the foreign reader'. If this interpretation is correct, then the sole difference between Davis and Barker appears to be one of strategy: both men want to discredit the German historians but Davis thinks he can achieve this more effectively through subtlety than through direct denunciation. The other possibility is that Davis does not want to discredit von Treitschke at all – or at any rate only partially – and that he is reluctant to be associated with another furious attack on the memory of a scholar for whom he still retains considerable affection. It is tempting to conclude that the Oxford pamphlets series was brought to an end as much for the tensions inside Davis himself as for purely commercial reasons.

It is instructive to compare Davis's inaugural lecture with his book on von Treitschke. Davis's dismissal of 'social historians' echoes von Treitschke's attack on the precepts of sociology in his doctoral dissertation of 1857.[85] In his 1914 book, Davis stresses that von Treitschke 'believed in the rights of individual conscience' and had a profound respect for Kant – still generally regarded as a 'good' German. Davis gives considerable attention to *Die Freiheit* of 1861, originally composed as a review of J. S. Mill's *On Liberty*. Davis claims that it is hardly surprising that von Treitschke rejected Mill's Utilitarianism, but he also asserts 'it is surprising how much of humanism and of Liberalism he has retained in his revolt from the lines of thought then fashionable in the smaller German states'.[86] While he concedes that von Treitschke's Liberalism may seem strange to English readers, he still believes that it 'has undeniable nobility'.[87] Above all, Davis insists that he has not written the book with 'any controversial purpose' in mind and that criticism had not been his main object.[88] The last chapter of the book contains – with almost no comment – selections devoted to English history from *Deutsche Geschichte im Neunzehnten Jahrhundert*. As Davis notes, the most striking feature of the extracts is von Treitschke's firm belief 'that England has been decadent since 1832'.[89] The work concludes with an extract from *Deutsche Kämpfe*:

The fallacious security of insular life has bred in the English State and people an arrogant disregard for the feelings of foreign nations, such as no continental nation could venture to indulge. The tone of the English press, in discussing foreign affairs, exhibits a similarity to those arrogant utterances which marked the newspapers of the declining republic of the Netherlands at the beginning of the eighteenth century; in each case the nation attempts to console itself for a loss of power by morbidly exaggerated self confidence. It seems altogether to escape the observation of these serenely self-satisfied islanders, that gradually their fundamental contempt for all progress in international law, and the professional bias

---

[85] H. W. C. Davis, *The Political Thought of Heinrich von Treitschke* (London, 1914), 7.
[86] Ibid., 9.
[87] Ibid., 17.
[88] Ibid., preface, p. v.
[89] Ibid., 227.

of the British authorities against all foreign ships, are working upon the public opinion of the whole of Europe, and that by degrees an immense hatred and disdain for England has accumulated on the Continent. Of the sense of justice of the British people one more edifying example has just been afforded in the annexation of the Transvaal Republic, an absolutely flippant proceeding, which had not the excuse of any sort of reasonable motive. Towards the weak John Bull still shows invariably that same disposition which once prompted the bombardment of Copenhagen; before the strong he humbles himself, and sighs dolefully with his minister, Cardwell: 'The English alliance has little value for other nations, since we have nothing to offer them save our sincere love of peace'.[90]

Davis's prime purpose was not to judge but 'to explain how the thought of Treitschke was influenced by the events of his own lifetime'. *The Political Thought of Heinrich von Treitschke* is best regarded as an example of an Oxford academic's determination to be fair to the scholars of another country, even though that country is at war with Britain. But Davis's stance is only an extreme example of a phenomenon visible in the Oxford pamphlet series. Thus A. V. Dicey's *How We Ought to Feel about the War* insists 'it is our clear duty to entertain equitable feelings – I do not say kindly feelings towards the Kaiser and his subjects'.[91] He urges his readers 'to form an historical view of the war . . . to look upon the war from something like the point of view from which it may probably be regarded by a fair minded historian in A.D. 2000'.[92]

Although some of the 'pamphleteers' – including Fletcher – argue that the militarist ravings of General von Berhardi are only too typical of German opinion as a whole, this analysis is rejected by Spenser Wilkinson, who doubts 'whether any responsible person, except for General von Berhardi, who is a retired officer and speaks only for himself, has openly advocated a policy of aggression'.[93] Adams's *The Responsibility for the War* produces a remarkably even-handed list of possible long-term causes, including industrial unrest in Russia, Serbian agitation in the Slav provinces of the Austrian Empire, the recovery and pressure of Russian political and military policy, and 'even the political crisis over the Irish question in England'.[94] There is certainly no demand for a vindictive peace. Fletcher, on most counts the most anti-German of the authors, still insists:

We must show ourselves Christian soldiers and Christian gentlemen; we must let the penalty for the war fall in full measure only on those who made it, only the German government, not on the German people, or on the venerable monuments of German antiquity.[95]

[90] Ibid., 287–8.
[91] A. V. Dicey, *How We Ought to Feel about the War* (Oxford Pamphlet no. 55; London, 1915), 4.
[92] Ibid., 5.
[93] S. Wilkinson, *August 1914: The Coming of War* (Oxford Pamphlet no. 36; London, 1914), 17.
[94] Adams, *The Responsibility for the War*, 4.
[95] Fletcher, *The Germans: Their Empire and how they have made it*, 17–18.

The Oxford pamphlets series has attracted the notice of a number of historians. D. Squires's *British Propaganda at Home and in the United States from 1914 to 1917* has no hesitation in identifying the series as propaganda, if of a superior kind. Squires acknowledges that, on the whole, the pamphlets were 'distinguished by authentic information' but claims that 'the authors were able to give a patriotic bias to the apparent objective presentation of the material'.[96] Squires links the series to various 'unofficial propaganda' initiatives, such as the publications of the Atlantic Union, the Overseas Club, and the Victoria League, and portrays the Oxford pamphlets as essentially a front for the British government.

S. Wallace's *War and the Image of Germany: British Academics 1914–1918* makes several criticisms of the series. He argues that one of the chief failings is the authors' 'passion for documents', documents which they are 'too ready to take at their face value'.[97] They tend to concentrate on the British White Paper and similar allied documents and to underplay the significance of longer-term trends and such things as the pre-war military discussions between Britain and France, for which documents were not available. Wallace further claims that the pamphlets place too much emphasis upon Germany's attack on 'poor little Belgium'. 'Belgium' was a godsend for the Asquith government and provided lifelong Liberals with an excuse for supporting a war which went against their long-proclaimed principles.[98] All the time the pamphlets conveniently ignore Britain's cavalier treatment of the rights of smaller states in the past and never face up to the question of what Britain would have done if the French rather than the Germans had first violated Belgian neutrality.[99] When it suits them they appeal loudly to concepts of morality and international law, but apply their appeals with remarkable selectivity.[100] Wallace does acknowledge, however, that some of the Oxford pamphlets do show remarkable prescience about the role of expansionist leagues inside Germany. Indeed, what were probably only guesses in 1914 have been substantially validated by the subsequent discovery of documents by historians such as Fritz Fischer.

It would be foolish to deny that Squires and Wallace – Wallace in particular – make some valid points. Of course, these writers view the series by rigorous standards of historical scholarship. It cannot have been easy for men who wanted to serve their country with their pens – especially at a time of tremendous national excitement – to resist the temptation to an occasional sleight of hand. Yet taking the series as a whole, and especially the All Souls contributions, the remarkable thing is how little the authors compromised their academic integrity

---

[96] J. D. Squires, *British Propaganda at Home and in the United States from 1914 to 1917* (Cambridge, MA, 1935), 17.
[97] Wallace, *War and the Image of Germany*, 60.
[98] Ibid., 61.
[99] Ibid.
[100] Ibid.

and how far they were prepared to go to be fair to the enemy. They may have indulged in the odd half-truth, but they were genuinely convinced that prime responsibility for the war did rest with Germany. Despite the enormous amount of scholarship devoted to the question since 1914, their basic position still retains a substantial measure of academic credibility. Although they may – or may not – have been writing for the intelligent working man, the All Souls writers were probably also undergoing an experience of self-discovery. At the lowest level there must have been a realization that admiration and respect for German scholarship did not carry with it an obligation to admire all things German.

Although All Souls contributors figure prominently in the Oxford pamphlet series, it is important to stress that they were drawn from the academic rather than the 'London' element of the College. It is now clear that the period 1914–1945 should be viewed as a whole; many of the negative observations made about Imperial Germany in the Oxford pamphlets could have been applied with even greater force to Germany of the Third Reich. This is important to the later history of the College. In *All Souls and Appeasement*, A. L. Rowse argued that, by and large, academic fellows were more likely to oppose appeasement than London fellows. As Simon Green shows elsewhere in this volume, this generalization is open to exception, but, in the case of the academics, the experience of writing for Davis's series may have provided a basis for later doubts about the wisdom of appeasing Hitler's Germany.

Perhaps the strongest inspiration behind appeasement was the belief that Germany had been falsely accused and thus unjustly punished for starting a European war in 1914. The authors of the pamphlets may have tried to be fair to Germany but they had no doubt that Germany was in the wrong. Yet the same men who believed that Germany was wrong could not hide their admiration for many of the achievements of Imperial Germany – and this may have led them or their successors towards appeasement. But at least the academics had to learn some contemporary history. In some cases the lines of development are clear. The tone of Dawson and *The Times* only a few days before the outbreak of the First World War anticipates their later attitude to Hitler. But for the most part, the implications are more complex. Appeasement itself is hard to define, but in so far as the concept retains some validity, the Oxford pamphlets could be seen as pointing either to appeasement or to anti-appeasement, though more to the latter than to the former. Both had their roots in Anson's All Souls.

APPENDIX

All Souls authors of Oxford pamphlets

W. G. S. Adams (Gladstone Professor of Political Theory, fellow 1910)
  The Responsibility for the War (no. 3)

Spenser Wilkinson (Professor of Military History, fellow 1909)
  Great Britain and Germany (no. 4)
  August 1914: The Coming of the War (no. 26)

C. R. L. Fletcher (fellow 1881, later fellow of Magdalen)
  The Germans: Their Empire and how they have made it (no. 6)
  The Germans: What they covet (no. 7)

Keith Feiling (fellow 1906, later Student of Christ Church)
  Italian Policy since 1870 (no. 10)

H. W. C. Davis (fellow 1895, later fellow of Balliol)
  French Policy since 1871 (no. 11) [with F. Morgan of Keble]
  The Retreat from Mons (no. 27)
  The Battle of the Marne and Aisne (no. 28)
  What Europe owes to Belgium (no. 36)
  The Battle of Ypres-Armentières (no. 65)

H. E. Egerton (Beit Professor of Colonial History, fellow 1905)
  The British Dominions and the War (no. 21)
  Is the British Empire the Result of Wholesale Robbery? (no. 23)

Sir Ernest Trevelyan (fellow 1903)
  India and the War (no. 24)

Charles Grant Robertson (fellow 1893)
  Germany: The Economic Problem (no. 34)

A. V. Dicey (Vinerian Professor of Law, fellow 1882)
  How We Ought to Feel about the War (no. 55)

8

All Souls and India:*

The 1920s

Sarvepalli Gopal

There have been quite a few fellows of All Souls in the twentieth century who have had links with India. Apart from those, British and Indian, who happened to have been born in that country, there are three Viceroys of the British period as well as a President of free India, several judges, civil servants, and scholars, even a novelist. Some, without having served in India, have played a role in formulating British policy towards it. To go through this list would be interesting enough; but in these two chapters I shall consider a general issue. The main development in India from the 1920s until 1947 was the growing force of Indian nationalism under the general leadership of Mahatma Gandhi and the Indian National Congress. The question before British policy-makers was how to deal with this problem. Should one try to thwart, arrest, defeat, even crush the nationalist sentiment or should one work with it, especially as Britain was committed from 1917 to the progressive realization of responsible government? And what were the attitudes in All Souls during these years to this question?

In the early years of the last century some fellows of the College were members of Milner's Kindergarten in South Africa and they worked on the premise that the greatest contribution they could make to the world was to maintain the British Empire and develop it on what they regarded as the right lines. There was for a long time almost a faith that the British Empire was a part of the Divine Order. Indeed, Leo Amery went so far as to comment, 'The empire is not external to any of the British nation. It is something like the Kingdom of Heaven within ourselves.'[1] But the specific interest of this group in India really stems from the ideas and work of Lionel Curtis, who was frequently spoken of in Oxford as the ancient mariner of All Souls. But Curtis had thought out and expounded his

* A shortened conflation of this and the following chapter was published in *The Journal of Imperial and Commonwealth History*, 27 (1999), 86–106, with acknowledgement to the Warden and Fellows of All Souls College for permission to do so.

[1] Quoted in W. Studdert-Kennedy, *British Christians, Indian nationalists and the Raj* (Delhi, 1991), 195. On the Kindergarten and Lionel Curtis, see further Howard, this volume.

views even before he became associated with All Souls. He believed that Britain and the 'white' Dominions were the custodians of the 'highest civilization' yet evolved, and were therefore justified in imposing restrictions on the immigration of people of Asian origin. Though honest enough to recognize that this smacked of racism and was a violation of human rights, he asserted that these Dominions had no other option if they were not to be swamped by 'the more backward and more numerous societies' of mankind. Active in the enforcement of this policy in South Africa, he came into contact and into conflict with Gandhi, then organizing the Indian community to assert their rights as equal citizens; and this did not make Curtis popular with Indians.

Curtis, however, was not concerned only with South Africa. Throughout his life he was an advocate of the idea of a world state, but in these early years he combined it with a justification of empire, on the ground that only those should participate in government who had proved themselves capable of doing so; and it appeared to Curtis that, with the possible exception of the Japanese, the peoples of European origin had alone shown themselves equal to the task of self-government. Among the peoples of Europe the British were to Curtis pre-eminent and he considered it providential that the task of ruling vast communities, which he believed could not as yet govern themselves, had been accepted by Britain, a country which was mainly identified with the principle of self-government.[2]

For the British Empire in India in particular Curtis put forward a novel justification. From the sixteenth century India had been overrun by European adventurers and the rulers and institutions of Indian society had been powerless to resist them. They could only be controlled by fellow Europeans who represented the 'moral forces' of a 'higher civilization'; and of these forces the British were to Curtis the best, because they understood better than others the meaning of freedom. As contacts with Europe had rendered the Indian people unable to govern themselves in the way they had been doing until then, inclusion in the British Commonwealth, where the rule of law was better understood and observed than in any European state, was the best alternative open to them.[3]

So, according to Curtis, Britain had established an empire in India in order to protect Indians from European marauders. But he believed in freedom as not just a Western but a human ideal, and he was sure that Britain's empire could not endure unless it fulfilled what Curtis defined as the principle of its being, which was self-government. The contradiction between dominance and liberty he sought to surmount by thinking in terms of training Indians to govern themselves, a process which he expected to need for completion not years or decades but centuries. He toured India in the winter of 1916–17 and drafted proposals which won the approval of Edwin Montagu, the Secretary of State for India, and later of the Viceroy, Lord Chelmsford, himself a former fellow of All Souls and

---

[2] L. Curtis, *The Problem of the Commonwealth* (London, 1916), 200.
[3] L. Curtis (ed.), *The Commonwealth of Nations* (London, 1918), 159–62, 180.

years later the Warden. Curtis's scheme, while leaving the central government undisturbed and under unqualified British control, suggested the transfer in the provinces, to Indian ministers answerable to the legislatures, of certain subjects which were deemed peripheral to the maintenance of British authority, such as education, sanitation, and local self-government. This seemed to Curtis the proper first step on the very long road to freedom. The rationale he offered was that Indians, working side by side with British officials who continued in charge of the crucial portfolios like law and order, would gain experience of administration, while Indian voters would know how the persons they had elected were functioning and whether they merited the confidence of the electorate.

This was the system of dyarchy, as it was known, which was introduced into India by statute in 1919. It operated in the provinces for eighteen years, until 1937, and thereafter was informally adapted to the central government. Though later Austen Chamberlain and Sir William Duke, a retired Indian civil servant, each claimed the credit for having first thought of it, there is no doubt that dyarchy in its complete form was the brainchild of Lionel Curtis. It was not popular with anybody. The British governors of the provinces disliked it as cumbrous. They preferred a unitary government under their tight control rather than an unwieldy two-tier combination. Lord Ampthill, who had once been governor of Madras, denounced Curtis in Parliament as 'a globe-trotting doctrinaire with a positive mania for constitution-mongering',[4] while Lord Sydenham, who had served as Governor of Bombay, wrote of 'the disastrous Mr Lionel Curtis', who was the author of 'one of the most crazy constitutions ever concocted'.[5] Nor was Indian opinion more favourable. Dyarchy had the appearance of a swamp in which nationalist aspirations would be bogged down for an incalculable time to come; and transfer of certain subjects which were regarded by both British and Indians as relatively insignificant seemed to serve little purpose. It has been reported that in Burma during these years, if anyone wished to abuse another, a general term of vituperation was 'you are a dyarchy'.[6]

It must be said in fairness to Curtis that the results might have been better, and his efforts would certainly have been more appreciated in India, if, along with the principle of dyarchy, Montagu and Chelmsford had adopted some of the other suggestions of Curtis. He had regarded the development of awareness among Indian voters as even more important than the political education of Indian ministers by association with British administrators. He wanted the Indian electorate to grow over time, in size and in responsibility; and for this reason he wished to see greater use in public life of the Indian languages. Reading today

---

[4] Quoted in L. Curtis, *Dyarchy* (Oxford, 1920), xxviii.

[5] Lord Sydenham, *Studies of an Imperialist* (London, 1928), quoted in Studdert-Kennedy, *British Christians*, 224.

[6] M. Collis, *Into Hidden Burma* (London, 1953), 165.

his writings of over seventy years ago, one is struck by his prophetic insight on many matters. He envisaged the indefinite continuance of British rule in India; but he also recognized that a great obstacle to the effective extension of popular government in India was the practice of conducting business in the English language. He was aware of the weaknesses of Indian society but he added that the British had themselves become another caste. India was full of chasms which divided one class from another, but the most dangerous of all chasms was that which divided British officials from educated Indians. Engrossed in administration, these officials were apt to forget that governance was at best a means to an end. The British had made themselves unlovable in India and the first step towards mending their ways was frankly to accept that they needed mending.

Above all, Curtis appealed to Montagu and Chelmsford to revoke the decision of John Morley and Lord Minto ten years earlier to create separate electorates, whereby only Muslim voters exercised their franchise to elect Muslim candidates. Curtis realized that separate constituencies based on religious divisions would, more than anything else, hamper and delay the development of responsible government in India. It would lead to Muslims depending on artificial protection instead of catching up with the rest of the Indian community; and he therefore regarded the decision of Morley and Minto to be 'the greatest blunder ever committed by the British government in India'. He added, with what one can only term penetrating foresight, that separate electorates would eat into the unity of Indian nationhood and in the end would require civil war for their eradication. So he urged 'that we shall be guilty of an unpardonable crime against India if we fail now to make provision whereby these fetters, in which we have allowed her to bind herself, can be loosed'.[7] Had the governments of India and Britain at that time set aside immediate prospects of selfish advantage and paid heed to the warning of Curtis, the later history of India might have been very different.

Over the years, Curtis's thought developed in stages. He hoped that the British Empire would broaden into a commonwealth of the self-governing 'white' Dominions, with an Imperial Parliament and Cabinet. Other European countries and the United States could also join; and Curtis was prepared to consider the entry into this federation of territories under British authority when, at some remote period, they attained full self-government. The ultimate goal, lying far in the future, was a world state. Curtis strove, throughout his life, to win over public opinion in Britain, the 'white' Dominions, and the United States to the acceptance of these objectives; and strength and purpose were lent to his crusading instincts by his conviction that he was in fact seeking to build the Kingdom of God on earth. He had no doubt that this was the best way to carry out the teachings of Jesus Christ. The plan to transform the British Empire into a Commonwealth leading on to the elimination of national sovereignty throughout the world was, in Curtis's eyes, the translation of the Sermon on

---

[7] Curtis, *Dyarchy*, 441.

the Mount into political terms. The Christian Church appeared to him to lay too much emphasis on the salvation of the individual soul; but the best way to carry out the Divine Purpose was to build up a system of human relations based on the law of God, which stressed the duty of each person to all humanity. 'My own conclusion is that if we could now ask the founder of Christianity to say whether in any degree his idea of the Kingdom of Heaven had been realised he would surprise us by pointing to the sphere of the state rather than of the church.'[8]

A devout Christian who believed that Christianity was the real force not only behind Western civilization but behind all civilization truly so called, it would have been logical for Curtis to have been an advocate of evangelization and missionary activity. Indeed, Gilbert Murray thought it necessary to point out to him the dangers of such a step. To argue that such principles as justice, cooperation, and the brotherhood of man were worthless unless they were combined 'with a belief in the divinity of Jesus, the Virgin birth and Lord knows what other bizarre and speculative beliefs' was not just, wrote Murray, essentially irrelevant; it was 'pernicious rubbish, leading straight to the renewal of the wars of religion and the persecution of heretics'.[9] But Curtis was careful not to tread such a narrow road. Though the ultimate values were to him Christian values, he did not insist on others accepting these values only for this reason. But believing Christians, more than others, could be expected to act on them. So when Edward Wood, a fellow of All Souls who had shared rooms with Curtis, a man of Christian dedication but with a commitment, expressed in his maiden speech in the House of Commons, to maintaining the position and fulfilling the functions of 'a superior race', was appointed Viceroy of India in 1926, the anticipation that these values which were regarded as Christian would be applied to the sustenance of empire was keen.

The selection of Wood to go out to India as Lord Irwin was, to British public opinion, a surprise. He had no obvious qualifications for the job but in a general consideration of possible choices his name had floated to the surface. 'How much better in life', observed Birkenhead, the Secretary of State for India, 'and how much more paying it is to be blameless than to be brilliant, and it certainly pays in such a connection never to have attacked anyone.'[10] The urgent issue at this time in India appeared to be not the working of dyarchy or the meaning to be attached to the British acceptance in 1917 of the progressive realization of responsible government as the objective of their rule or the pace at which this commitment should be implemented. It was the growing tension between sections of Hindus and Muslims which seemed to dominate the scene, and Irwin's first speech as Viceroy, devoted to this topic, enabled him to show India

---

[8] Curtis to Olaf Carse, 15 Sept. 1932. Oxford, Bodleian Library, Curtis MSS, box 9.

[9] Gilbert Murray to Curtis, 10 Feb. 1939. Oxford, Bodleian Library, Curtis MSS, box 13.

[10] Earl of Birkenhead, *Frederick Edwin, Earl of Birkenhead*, vol. 2: *The Last Phase* (London, 1935), 250.

how deeply religious a person he was and what religion meant to him. He appealed for toleration not only in the name of Indian national life but also that of religion, because he said he could appeal to nothing nobler, and because religion was the language of the soul and it was a change of soul that India needed. All religions assumed a sense of personal deficiency in the mind of the individual, a consciousness of failure to apprehend more than a fraction of life's mystery, leading to an irresistible yearning to reach out for higher things. Achievement was hard and the attempt would result in a wide tolerance of the deficiencies of others. There could be no greater tragedy than that religion, which should be the expression and the support of man's highest instincts, should be prostituted by an alliance with actions through which these instincts were distorted and disgraced.[11]

This was no definition of religion in any narrow, denominational sense. Though, as Penderel Moon later commented, Irwin was 'a Christian who really believed in Christianity',[12] in this speech he gave utterance to broad aspirations and values which would appeal to men and women of religious feeling whatever their particular creeds. While the speech had little immediate consequence, Irwin had presented his credentials to the Indian public as a Viceroy who was concerned with more than mere execution of policy and management of the administration.

However, the good that this speech may have done was soon overlaid by a decision taken in 1927 for the substance of which Irwin himself bore the major responsibility. Trust in British declarations about their role in India had been destroyed by General Dyer's wanton slaughter in Amritsar in 1919 and, even more, by the widespread support in Britain for his action. Could Irwin start the process of rebuilding that trust? The chance came in 1927. The Government of India Act of 1919 had laid down that a commission should be appointed after ten years to enquire into the working of the act and recommend what, if any, further steps should be taken. But the British government decided not to wait until 1929 but to appoint a commission in 1927 itself – primarily to prevent the decision being taken by a possible Labour government. Irwin advised the British government to exclude Indians from the commission because their presence would make the body unwieldy and probably result in two separate reports; it would be far better to confine the choice to Members of Parliament, thereby making the exclusion of Indians seem not a deliberate decision but a fortuitous circumstance. Irwin had as yet little knowledge of India and no imaginative comprehension of her people, their problems, and their attitudes; and he was guided by officials with limited experience. It should be added that Curtis also was for a commission consisting only of Members of Parliament, because he believed that the practice

---

[11] Speech at Simla, 17 July 1926. Lord Irwin, *Indian Problems* (London, 1932), 231ff.

[12] P. Moon, *Gandhi and Modern India* (London, 1968), 125. For Moon, see further Gopal, ch. 9, this volume.

prevalent in the days of the East India Company of Parliament securing its own information rather than being dependent on others should be resumed.[13]

Accepting Irwin's advice with some misgivings, Birkenhead appointed as chairman of the statutory commission his friend and colleague at the Bar, Sir John Simon, whom Birkenhead knew to share his view that India would and should remain for long, if not forever, under British rule. Simon had visited India a year earlier and had returned, according to Leo Amery,[14] very much with the conviction that the Indian was not really adapted to parliamentary government. Now Simon took up the chairmanship, confident that he would have the cooperation of the Viceroy, if only because he and Irwin were both fellows of All Souls and belonged, as Simon later described it, to 'a band of brothers'.[15] He might in a sense be said to have deserved the support of the Viceroy, for it was Irwin's preference for a wholly British commission that led to general resentment in India and to a widespread boycott of Simon and his colleagues. But Irwin believed that the boycott would die out for lack of momentum. 'I think', he wrote in 1929, a year after the commission's first arrival in India, 'it is really very much like a child refusing to eat its supper. There comes a point when it is no good preaching or reproaching any longer and when, if its tempers are ignored, it may return to eat it on its own.'[16] Of the Congress Party Irwin had no great opinion and, as for Gandhi, Irwin, after his first meeting with him in 1927, shared the assessment of Curtis, who had known Gandhi in South Africa and had met him again in India in 1916, that 'the smart young Johannesburg lawyer had completely vanished in the typical ascetic of the East'.[17]

However, the boycott held. Simon lacked the personality and the political flair to weaken the ostracism. As Irwin described him, Simon was accustomed to 'keeping all his personality within locked doors while inviting other people to disclose theirs'.[18] We have had several assessments of Simon. Lord Blake has written that he was a clever cold fish who was 'indefinably unlikable',[19] and Lord Jenkins has described him as 'ingratiating and unctuous'.[20] Lord Hailsham, however, has reminded us that there was another side to Simon and has quoted Lord Attlee, who, as a member of the commission, knew Simon well, as saying that there was always 'a little pink quivering Simon struggling to get out'.[21] But this more human aspect of Simon, if it did exist, was not discerned in India. His

[13] Curtis to T. B. Sapru, 31 Dec. 1927. Curtis MSS, box 3; Curtis, *Civitas Dei*, vol. 2 (London, 1937), 271–2.
[14] J. Campbell, *F. E. Smith, First Earl of Birkenhead* (London, 1983), 750. On Simon, see also Cretney, this volume.
[15] Simon, *Retrospect* (London, 1952), 38.
[16] Quoted in Lord Birkenhead, *Halifax* (London, 1965), 255.
[17] Foreword of Curtis to a book on South Africa. Curtis MSS, box 10.
[18] Irwin to Neville Chamberlain, 15 April 1929, quoted in A. Roberts, *'The Holy Fox': A Biography of Lord Halifax* (London, 1991), 23.
[19] *The Times*, 21 May 1992.
[20] *The Observer*, 31 May 1992.
[21] Lord Hailsham, *A Sparrow's Flight* (London, 1990), 86.

bitterness at the humiliation of the boycott deepened his dislike of India and Indian politicians. India did not appear to him in any sense a nation[22] and he thought Indians were lacking in courage 'and moral courage most of all – there is more of it in Kathleen's little finger than in three hundred millions of people in India, and this is what will be their undoing'.[23] But Simon was disappointed in his hope that the Viceroy would give him full backing. Irwin had little personal regard for Simon and ironically, on the one occasion in these years when fellows of All Souls held two of the highest posts in Indian affairs, they could not get on with each other. Irwin also gradually realized that he had erred in excluding Indians from the commission and in underrating Gandhi and the Congress Party. So the government of India carefully distanced themselves from the commission and in Simon's view the most successful demonstration against him and his colleagues was in Delhi, where it had been handled 'about as badly as it could be'.[24] He later complained that Irwin had joined the boycott and was talking to Gandhi and the Congress even while the commission was being stoned.[25]

It was too much, however, for Simon to expect that Irwin's government would suspend all operations on the political front until his commission had submitted its report. Events in themselves made this impossible. In a part of Gujerat, in the then Bombay presidency, the provincial government ordered an enhancement of the land revenue without a proper investigation, and the peasant proprietors under Congress leadership refused to pay anything until the enhancement had been cancelled. The case of the Bombay government was weak and if the Viceroy failed to intervene, the official rigidity, coming in the wake of the inept decision about the composition of the commission, would take the viceroyalty beyond the point of no return into the desert of mindless repression. So, before it was too late, Irwin directed the Bombay government to reach a compromise. He thereby got his administration back on the road and, two years after his arrival in India, started moving towards an answer to the key question of how Britain could regain the trust of Indian opinion.

By now also Irwin, though he had not given up hope of building up loyalist parties as a counter to the Congress, recognized that as yet there was no alternative to it. But the Congress was no monolithic body. A committee presided over by Motilal Nehru produced a report in the summer of 1928 asserting that Dominion status was the immediate objective. The secretary of the committee was Jawaharlal Nehru. He signed the report with reluctance, for a few months earlier, at a session of the Congress in December 1927, he had pushed through a resolution declaring the goal of the Indian people to be complete independence. He was aware that there was no substantive difference

[22] To F. W. Hirst, 19 Mar. 1929. Oxford, Bodleian Library, MS Simon 62.
[23] Simon's note on his talk with Ramsay Macdonald, 1 May 1930. MS Simon 64. Kathleen was Lady Simon.
[24] Simon to Ramsay Macdonald, 11 Dec. 1928. MS Simon 62.
[25] Simon to J. L. Garvin, 17 Sept. 1930. MS Simon 66.

in practice between Dominion status and independence; but he attached importance to the mental attitudes which these two concepts indicated, and was eager that India should break completely with the past and with the British connection. Gandhi and other senior Congressmen did not take the independence resolution seriously; but its significance lay not in itself but as a reflection of the non-compromising stance of the younger elements in the party.

To Irwin and his advisors this seemed to open up prospects of dividing the Congress and weakening the section which was unqualifiedly hostile to the Raj. Official expectation that the Congress would split in 1929 was defeated by the compromise which Gandhi effected in December 1928. It was resolved that if the British Government did not accept by 1929 the Nehru report seeking Dominion status, then the Congress would initiate a campaign of civil disobedience in order to gain independence. Irwin promptly and publicly replied that the British Parliament could never agree to being reduced merely to endorsing the opinions of others. But in contrast to Simon, who rejected the Nehru Report out of hand as 'a very empty performance' and 'a shoddy piece of work',[26] Irwin saw in the emphasis placed by the Nehru Report on Dominion status an opportunity to be exploited. Motilal Nehru told Geoffrey Dawson, the editor of *The Times*, then on a visit to India, that what was really wanted was an assurance that Dominion status was on the way;[27] and Gandhi told Irwin that if India had the predominant voice in constitution-making, she would astonish Britain by showing how much she would desire to leave in British hands through lack of self-confidence.[28] Dominion status with reservations, while logically contradictory, was clearly the immediate aspiration of the larger part of Indian public opinion. It sought a firm recognition of full rights to come rather than a major constitutional advance at once; and this, Irwin felt, required consideration.

In Britain on leave in the summer of 1919, the Viceroy found his authority increased by a change of government. Labour was now in office and the Prime Minister, Ramsay Macdonald, was committed publicly to India becoming a Dominion within months. But the government was weak and preferred to leave the initiative to a Conservative Viceroy who could rely on the personal support of Baldwin, the Leader of the Opposition. Irwin proposed that, to redress the affront caused to Indian opinion by the composition of the Simon commission, a conference of British and Indian delegates be convened to consider India's constitutional future; and that it be clearly affirmed that Dominion status was the goal. There was considerable opposition to this in the Conservative and Liberal parties and Baldwin, on learning that Simon had not been consulted, withheld the support of the Conservative party and cabled to the Viceroy, by now

[26] Simon to Ramsay Macdonald, 11 Dec. 1928 and note of 24 April 1929. MS Simon 62.
[27] Dawson's memorandum, 25 Mar. 1929. E. Wrench, *Geoffrey Dawson and Our Times* (London, 1955), 272.
[28] Irwin to Lord Peel, Secretary of State for India, 21 Feb. 1929. London, British Library, Oriental and India Office Collections, Halifax papers, MSS Eur. C 152, vol. 5.

back in India, not to make any public statement on these lines. Nevertheless Irwin made the announcement on 31 October 1929, with the approval of the Labour government and in defiance of the leadership of his own party. Simon blamed Wedgwood Benn, the Labour Secretary of State, for this 'light-hearted folly',[29] but in fact it was Irwin's decision.

The Declaration in itself from the British viewpoint surrendered no ground. It committed the British government merely in the sphere of ultimate purpose. The objective was Dominion status but no immediate transfer of any measure of authority was contemplated. Indeed, Irwin was confident that the declaration would ensure that the essential mechanism of power would remain in British hands as long as one could foresee and with the support of the Congress except for those few members who advocated independence. But it was more than a mere reaffirmation of earlier British statements about their objectives in India. Coming as it did after Balfour's definition of Dominion status in 1926, it was taken by Indian opinion as a more precise commitment than any made before by the British government, and this reading was underlined by the criticism of Irwin in Britain, especially by Simon, Reading, and Birkenhead. 'Refusal', wrote Irwin sharply to Reading, 'to make our purpose plain affords ground to our enemies to say that we intend India to occupy a permanently subordinate place in an Empire of white nations.'[30]

It was in fact the reaction in Britain which led Gandhi and the Congress to retreat from their immediate positive response and to feel that little purpose would be served by relying on a single individual, however sincere, with the support of a weak government in London. Irwin, in his memoirs published many years later, conceded that the situation had chilled and hardened under the impact of the unfriendly debates in Parliament.[31] The Congress now pledged itself to the goal of independence and a campaign of civil disobedience under the leadership of Gandhi. With this mandate, Gandhi set out in March 1931 from Ahmedabad in western India to the seashore in order to challenge the imposition of a tax on salt. Irwin thought that the issue was so trivial and the incidence of the tax so minimal that Gandhi should be allowed to become a figure of ridicule rather than be converted by arrest into a martyr. This attitude again showed a deficiency in imaginative understanding, for in fact Gandhi's march to the sea has a high place in the history of the Indian freedom movement and indeed of freedom in the world. Irwin himself seems to have realized, as Gandhi's march proceeded with public interest not evaporating and with no popular resistance developing to civil disobedience, that he might have been mistaken in taking no

[29] Note of Simon, 1 May 1930. MS Simon 64.
[30] Irwin's note to Reading enclosed with letter to Wedgwood Benn, 14 Nov. 1929. Halifax papers, vol. 5.
[31] Lord Halifax, *Fulness of Days* (London, 1957), 145.

action. For there is a tinge of frustration as well as an element of banter in his report to the Secretary of State:

The will power of the man must have been enormous to get him through his march, which must have been a very severe physical strain. I was always told that his blood pressure is dangerous and his heart none too good, and I was also told a few days ago that his horoscope predicts that he will die this year, and that this is the explanation of this desperate throw. It would be a very happy solution.[32]

Ultimately Gandhi was arrested and, to smother the campaign of civil disobedience, Irwin virtually set aside the ordinary law and ruled by ordinance, imposed tight control of the press, and placed about 60,000 political workers in prison. But he was surprised and impressed by the influence in the country, which the campaign had revealed, of Gandhi and the Congress; and this convinced him that it was necessary to bring the Congress into the constitutional discussions. Logically, he told Benn, there were only two alternatives, to govern without consent or to make terms with Gandhi; and the concept of the knock-out had become futile.[33]

The basis for such constitutional discussions would normally have been the Simon Commission's report, which was published in the summer of 1930. But in assuring both the King and Simon that this would be so, the Viceroy, as Penderel Moon has written, was being 'untruthful'.[34] The Declaration of October 1929, which Simon had so disliked, had in fact left him high and dry. When some members of the commission had at that time threatened to resign, Simon had held his group together by securing the King's intervention; and he now produced an unanimous report by tailoring the recommendations to fall in line with the views of the most reactionary members – a process no doubt made easier by the fact that he himself shared those views. No mention was made of Dominion status, it was doubted if parliamentary government was suited to India, no changes were suggested in the central government, a step back was taken by proposing indirect elections for the central assembly, and in the provinces dyarchy was sought to be replaced by autonomy with heavy safeguards. This 'very obvious and deliberate' refusal, in Irwin's words, of Simon 'to take the bandage off his eyes' robbed the report of all relevance.[35] It presented a clear survey of the history of British administration in India without taking any notice of the growth of nationalist sentiment in the country. So the report was dead before it was born and Irwin made clear to the Indian public, within three days of its publication, that he would take no notice of it. Knowing this, Simon appealed to the British members of the Viceroy's executive council to have the report

---

[32] Irwin to Wedgwood Benn, 7 Apr. 1930. Halifax papers, vol. 6.
[33] Irwin to Wedgwood Benn, 5 Sept. and 3 Nov. 1930. Halifax papers, vol. 6.
[34] P. Moon, *The British Conquest and Dominion of India* (London, 1989), 1044.
[35] To Wedgwood Benn, 20 June 1930. Birkenhead, *Halifax*, 287.

circulated in India under the auspices of the government.[36] This too leading to no response, Simon turned to All Souls for help. He complained to the Warden about Irwin, requested Geoffrey Dawson to cable to the Viceroy suggesting that he give the report more respectful attention, and asked Reginald Coupland to write to *The Times* supporting the report.[37] But the Warden did not react and the others politely shied off. The crowning blow was when the Labour government, on Irwin's advice, refused to invite Simon and the members of the commission to the conference of British and Indian delegates which met later that year.

The path Irwin took on his own initiative during the last months of his term in India was that of direct negotiations with Gandhi; and by now he knew the right approach. Banking on his reputation as a deeply religious person he publicly, on 17 January 1931, while deploring Gandhi's policy, recognized the spiritual force impelling him, thought that Gandhi would be as willing to recognize that the British were sincere in their attempt to serve India, and suggested that ultimate purposes differed little, if at all. The Prime Minister, Ramsay Macdonald, followed this up two days later by offering full provincial autonomy and a central executive responsible to a federal legislature; some safeguards would be required but only for a period of transition and in the interests of the minorities. And then, to cap it all, Gandhi and his chief colleagues were released unconditionally.

Gandhi in reply, after some hesitation, sought an interview, 'to meet' as he wrote, 'not so much the Viceroy as the man in you'. Irwin agreed, and set out not to convince Gandhi on any subject but to gain his confidence. He succeeded in that Gandhi came back from their first meeting with the feeling that Irwin's sincerity was beyond doubt. Thereafter they had seven more sessions and talked in all for a little less than twenty-four hours. At this time, unlike in December 1929, Gandhi did not worry about the sharp attacks on Irwin by Churchill and his supporters in Britain. Indeed, the 'change of heart' to which Gandhi attached much importance and which he thought he discerned in the Viceroy was sufficient for him not to insist on any of the fundamentals of the Congress programme. He put forward no demands on the constitutional issue and accepted responsibility with safeguards or, as he preferred to call them, adjustments, provided they were in the interests of India and could be discussed with Britain on equal terms. The talks moved to the verge of a breakdown on the question of an inquiry into the alleged excesses of the policy while combating civil disobedience in 1930; but finally Gandhi gave way when Irwin said that the government could not afford to weaken the morale of the police for the Congress might resume civil disobedience and then the police would be needed again. On picketing and the manufacture of salt Irwin made minor conces-

[36] Simon to Sir George Schuster, Finance Member, and to Sir William Birdwood, Commander-in-Chief, 25 June 1930. MS Simon 64.

[37] Simon to the Warden of All Souls and to Geoffrey Dawson, 30 June 1930, and to R. Coupland, 1 July 1930. MS Simon 65.

sions; but on all other points the government had their way. By transforming the conversations with Gandhi from parleys between implacable political opponents into discussions between two spiritually sensitive individuals, Irwin had gained the advantage on most issues.

After the settlement had been reached, Gandhi asked Irwin, as 'a great Christian', to commute the death sentences which were to be carried out that week on three men held responsible for the murder of a police officer. This would have made it easier for Gandhi to secure ratification of the settlement by the Congress. Irwin replied that he could find no grounds for a reprieve and to postpone the hangings until after the session of the Congress would be dishonest. So the three men were hanged, making Gandhi's task at the session more difficult than expected; but he said publicly, in accordance with his promise to Irwin, that while he had pleaded with the Viceroy in the language of the New Testament that 'charity never faileth', he could not see what other course Irwin, from his point of view, could have taken.

Simon, while refraining from public comment, was in private a severe critic of Irwin's policy. He blamed the Viceroy for letting matters 'slide and glide' without taking a stand *somewhere*. He had allowed himself to be surrounded by persons who told him that he was the only saviour of India. Irwin was being rapidly turned into 'a British Gandhi', and in his desire always to agree with what any Indian politician said had descended to 'the depths of shivering apology'.[38] That Irwin had dealt with Gandhi on almost equal terms upset not only diehard opinion in Britain but also many British officials in India, and after Irwin's departure in April 1931, the government of India rapidly, and with relief, reverted to their traditional policy of confrontation with Indian nationalism. But Irwin contended that he was not compromising with nationalist forces but planning to weaken them by adopting a more sophisticated approach. He told the Conservative party that the day was past when India could be held by Churchill's 'possessive instinct... That conception of imperialism is finished and those who try to revive it are as those who would fly a balloon that won't hold gas... The thing just won't work.'[39] Later, on his return to London, he claimed at a private meeting of the Conservative party that his settlement would ensure the loyalty to Britain of Gandhi and the older politicians and that it had built a breakwater against the dangerous agrarian forces which were being harnessed by Jawaharlal Nehru and would cause the serious problem of the future.[40] Dividing the Congress was an objective of which Irwin never lost sight.

Irwin had an earnest, unspeculative, and unimaginative mind. He never doubted the indispensability of empire and he had no far-sighted vision of the

---

[38] Simon to Lord Linlithgow and to R. Coupland, 1 July 1930; MS Simon 65. Simon to J. L. Garvin, 17 Sept. 1930; MS Simon 66.

[39] Irwin to J. C. C. Davidson, quoted in J. Charmley, *Lord Lloyd and the Decline of the British Empire* (London, 1987), 41.

[40] Lord Butler, *The Art of the Possible* (London, 1971), 41.

relations between the British and the Indian peoples. On first coming to India he made grave mistakes. But he grew in the job and gradually realized that he had to deal with the Congress and particularly with Mahatma Gandhi. He saw that it was in Britain's interest to win Gandhi over; and in dealing with Gandhi he was helped by the emphasis he laid on the fact that both of them were devout believers. Gandhi, and hence Indian opinion, accepted Irwin as an honest Viceroy with decent impulses. Testimony to his impact was the proposal by the Congress in December 1931 that he be asked to give a ruling, which they would accept, as to whether it was the government or the Congress who were violating the settlement. The most important aspect of Irwin's years in India was perhaps the improvement in the atmosphere of relations between India and Britain. Even when bitterness and conflict returned, the memory of its assessment of Irwin's term of office was not wholly erased from the Indian mind.

Irwin began negotiations with Gandhi on grounds of expediency and with the wider purpose of strengthening British rule in India. But as the conversations proceeded, they gained for the Viceroy personal significance. He warmed to Gandhi's personality and spiritual strength and was struck by his force of character, his immensely active and acute mind, and his singularly winning directness, which was accompanied by a subtlety of intellectual process which the Viceroy had sometimes found disconcerting.[41] When, while the talks were in progress, a senior British official asked Irwin if Gandhi had been tiresome, the Viceroy replied, 'Some people found Our Lord very tiresome.'[42] Finally, on 6 March 1931, after the settlement had been reached, Irwin wrote to Gandhi a letter which must be unique in viceregal correspondence:

Dear Mr Gandhi,

I want to write you a personal note of my own very great thanks to you for all you have done, while we have been working together during these last difficult days.

It has been a great privilege to me to be given this opportunity of meeting and knowing you; and I hope that, either before I leave India or in England, you will give me the pleasure of seeing you again.

I do pray—as I believe—that history may say you and I were permitted to be instruments in doing something big for India and for humanity.

Believe me, with again much thanks and with deep understanding,

Yours very sincerely,
Irwin[43]

---

[41] Irwin to the King, 13 Mar. 1931; H. Nicolson, *King George the Fifth* (London, 1952), 507–8; Halifax, *Fulness of Days*, 146.

[42] Birkenhead, *Halifax*, 299.

[43] Halifax papers, vol. 26.

9

All Souls and India:

The 1930s and After

Sarvepalli Gopal

At the end of the 1920s, two schools of imperialist doctrine could be found at All Souls: what one might term the Christian approach favoured by Curtis and Irwin, and the diehard rigidity symbolized by Simon. Curtis saw in Irwin the successor to Milner, providing moral and intellectual leadership to promising young men so that they would devote themselves to serving the Empire.[1] But it was the Simon approach which was gaining ground in the College. When in 1929 some fellows proposed that the College spend part of its surplus income on studying the problems of the Empire, including 'problems connected with the government of subject races', the scheme was struck down by a majority in the College, and one reason advanced was that All Souls was already being criticized for, to a large extent, identifying itself with a particular school of imperialist thought.[2] This school was clearly the one of extreme conservatism.

But in the thirties All Souls was not as prominent in policy-making for India as it had been in the years of Irwin and Simon. Its chief link with that country was Maurice Gwyer, the main draftsman of the Government of India Act of 1935, which was not negotiated with Indian leaders as had been planned in 1931 but was imposed on India and as such did not commend itself to much of Indian opinion. Even Penderel Moon, at this time a junior civil servant in the Punjab, did not approve of the method,[3] while H. V. Hodson later described the Act as being far behind the times for which it was legislating.[4] Gwyer came out to India in 1937 as the first Chief Justice of the federal court, to keep a judicial eye on the implementation of the Act. In that capacity Gwyer did not hesitate on occasion

---

[1] See draft letter (probably not sent) of Curtis to Irwin, 3 June 1931. Oxford, Bodleian Library, Curtis MSS, box 5.

[2] All Souls College archives, 'Minute Book, 1936–46', vol. 1, memo IV of October 1929 and record of subsequent discussions.

[3] Moon to his mother, 3 Aug. 1932. London, British Library, Oriental and India Office Collections, Moon MSS (MS Eur. F 230).

[4] H. V. Hodson, *The Great Divide* (London, 1969), 60.

to strike down executive decisions. His legal knowledge was respected and his impartiality was never doubted. Gandhi accepted Gwyer's arbitration in a dispute between himself and a petty ruler in Gujerat. Gwyer also, not having much judicial work, took on in 1938 the Vice-Chancellorship of Delhi University, and, after retirement from the court in 1943, stayed on in India for another seven years, primarily because he was crippled by arthritis and the climate of the country suited him. But, throughout his long stay in India, Gwyer remained, to the Indian people, a somewhat remote figure; and he cannot be said, despite twelve years as Vice-Chancellor of Delhi University, to have made any major contribution to India's system of higher education.

Gwyer himself never at any time felt fully at home in India. His term as Chief Justice ended with acrimonious correspondence with the Viceroy, Lord Linlithgow. He was piqued at not having been consulted about the choice of his successor and was outraged that the India Office should have selected not an Indian but a Conservative backbencher with no great reputation in the British courts of law. Gwyer wrote to Linlithgow that he was no longer as convinced as he had been that the British government were sincere in their desire to grant India the equal status that she coveted.[5] Nor did conditions in India lighten Gwyer's sense of gloom. The British seemed to him to have lost interest, heart, and faith, while India had yet to acquire the stable foundations for a sovereign state.[6] So Gwyer watched from the sidelines with increasing pessimism as India stumbled through rioting and bloodshed to partition and independence. The only relieving factor to Gwyer was Gandhi's courageous stand against this general drift to savagery. Gwyer had not at the start been drawn to Gandhi but was converted by the time Gandhi was assassinated in January 1948. 'I found myself at the end feeling a real affection for him and his like will not be seen again.'[7]

It is with the appointment of Leo Amery as Secretary of State for India in the Churchill government of 1940, and his continuance in that office until the end of the war, that the College once again comes prominently into the Indian picture. Amery was a good All Souls man. It is not necessary for me to deal in detail with Amery for William Roger Louis, in his Chichele Lectures of 1990, provided a comprehensive survey of Amery's view and policies.[8] By contrasting them with Churchill's crude imperialism, Louis suggests that Amery had a radical outlook with a firm commitment to the freedom of India. He certainly never failed in his pronouncements during the war years to state that he envisaged a time when Britain would withdraw from India. But in fact he believed in an enduring Empire and regarded All Souls, as Louis brings out so clearly, as representing the almost spiritual essence of the British Empire. In interpreting that essence,

---

[5] Sir M. Gwyer to the Viceroy, 4 Nov. 1942. India Office Collections, File L/PO/8/89.
[6] Gwyer to Moon, 12 June 1943. Moon MSS, file 28.
[7] Gwyer to Moon, 16 Feb. 1948. Moon MSS, file 29.
[8] Published as W. R. Louis, *In the Name of God, Go! Leo Amery and the British Empire in the Age of Churchill* (New York, 1992). See also Louis, this volume, ch. 11.

Amery leant heavily on the side of Simon, and had a poor opinion of Irwin, whom he described, long before the years of appeasement, at a time when the Viceroy was probing for a settlement with Gandhi, as 'a dignified exterior who says nothing'.[9] He was willing to accept Dominion status as the objective for India provided its attainment was indefinitely postponed. As Secretary of State, he regarded Irwin's settlement with Gandhi in 1931 as a precedent to be rejected. He refused to act on the basis that the Congress under the leadership of Gandhi was the main protagonist in Indian politics and he was all for the policy of a knock-out blow to the party which sought to secure the end of British rule.

In defence of this change of tack, it was argued that the situation in India had changed considerably during the thirties. Elections to the provincial assemblies had been held in 1936 and the Congress, while opposed to the Government of India Act of 1935, had contested the elections and won clear majorities in seven of the then eleven provinces. The Muslim League, claiming to represent the interests of the Muslim voters, fared less well and, even in the constituencies with separate electorates, won many fewer seats than it had expected. So the Congress, rejecting the League's offer to form coalition ministries, formed governments on its own. It asserted that it was a national and not a Hindu party and had many Muslim members; and several Muslim Congressmen took office as ministers. But it was easy to conflate two facts, that the Congress had won substantial majorities and that the Hindus formed a substantial majority in India, and to contend that the Congress was a Hindu party. British governors later testified that the Congress, while in office in the provinces from 1937 to 1939, had been careful to respect the interests of religious minorities. But changes were made, and it was believed that Muslims were being oppressed and Islam was in danger; and tension between Hindus and Muslims took on a deeply political tinge.

As Secretary of State, Amery was careful not to emulate his Prime Minister, Winston Churchill, who stated explicitly that tension between Hindus and Muslims was the mainstay of British rule in India, for if the Hindus and Muslims got together they would join in showing Britain the door. But Amery accepted the conventional understanding of British officials in India that India was a plural society divided by religion and that this division was age-old and deep-seated. Hindus and Muslims were thought to be, and always to have been, fiercely opposed to each other, with the animosities of centuries never ceasing to smoulder beneath the surface. So the Congress and Gandhi were not treated by Amery, as Irwin had treated them, as the most important factors on the Indian scene, but only as bit-players along with several others. Nor did Amery regard nationalist aspirations as forming the main issue in Indian politics. It was the Hindu–Muslim conflict that to him was the crux of the Indian problem. So the fact that the Congress could win majorities by electoral process was to Amery

---

[9] Amery, MS diary, 9 Nov. 1930, Churchill College, Cambridge.

irrelevant. Sensitiveness to public opinion was acceptable only in a homogeneous society, which, to Amery, India was not. She could only be governed democratically on the basis of agreement between Hindus and Muslims. The appeal of the Congress to secular parliamentary traditions had to be resisted vigorously, for to Amery this outlook was at bottom totalitarian. Amery recognized that the expectation of the Congress, as the largest and most effectively organized party in India, to govern would be normal in any democratic society; but in India he regarded the claim as untenable. The adoption by the Muslim League in March 1940 of a resolution demanding the creation of a separate state of Pakistan, consisting of those provinces in India with Muslim majorities, strengthened Amery's conviction that the Congress would have to be put down firmly.[10]

So while, immediately after assuming office, Amery told the Viceroy that he was considering how best to bring Jawaharlal Nehru, with his known sympathy for the Allied cause, into closer association with the government, his first public statements were a clear rejection of the Irwin approach. Stress was laid on the rift between the Hindus and Muslims and the Congress charged with being unrepresentative of Indian opinion as a whole. In August 1940 Amery announced the offer of the British government to appoint a few 'representative Indians' to the Viceroy's executive council and to arrange for the framing of India's future constitution by a small body 'representative of the principal elements in India's national life'; and these elements would include the Princes and British commercial interests. The Muslims were assured that power would not be transferred to their disadvantage; and it was made clear that any decision of the body framing the constitution would be subject to the fulfilment of Britain's 'obligations' in India.

This offer, not surprisingly, satisfied no section of Indian opinion and H. V. Hodson, at that time an official in the Ministry of Information in London, found it difficult to explain it to the press. He later commented that in the offer there was hardly a sentence without a qualifying or balancing clause, creating the general impression of taking as much with one hand as was given with the other. The note of boldness or imagination or generosity was wholly absent.[11] Yet Amery defended the offer as very far-reaching and going a long way to meet the hopes of Indian nationalism, and contended that the Congress had rejected it because the party wished to seize power immediately so as to be able to control future constitutional developments.

Thereafter the purpose of Amery was to thwart the Congress and conciliate the Muslim League. Louis has suggested that he was one of the key figures within the British government favouring the tilt towards a separate Muslim state. When Churchill, in a sudden, startling, change of mood in 1942 offered to fly out to

---

[10] Amery's speeches: 14 Aug. 1940, 21 Nov. 1940, 22 April 1941: L. S. Amery, *India and Freedom* (Oxford, 1942); also Amery's letters to Reginald Coupland, 10 Aug. 1942 and 8 Feb. 1943: Coupland MSS, Oxford, Bodleian Library of Commonwealth and African Studies at Rhodes House, MSS Brit. Emp. s. 403, box 5. On Coupland see also Howard, this volume.

[11] Hodson, *The Great Divide*, 86.

Delhi or at least to broadcast to the Indian people in an effort to reach agreement, Amery, supported by the Viceroy, headed Churchill off for fear that he might take a position sympathetic to the Congress. Instead, Stafford Cripps went out to Delhi with a declaration which, as Churchill explained to Amery, was essentially a pro-Muslim and reasonably Conservative policy. It offered no more than, for the present, collaboration in defence and, for the future, Dominion status with possible partition of the country. It was Amery who was responsible for the clause which gave provinces the right to secede. But even this declaration Amery did not wish to see accepted, and was relieved when the Viceroy, with Churchill's backing, ensured that Cripps failed in his mission. 'I ... feel', Amery wrote in his diary, 'like someone who has proposed for family or financial reasons to a particularly unprepossessing damsel and finds himself lucky enough to be rejected.'[12]

The Congress and the British government were now on a collision course and Amery, who believed that nothing could be of greater benefit to India than that the Congress should disintegrate,[13] wholeheartedly approved the decision to arrest Gandhi and other leaders of the Congress and wished them to be kept in custody until the end of the war. His positive suggestions veered between declaring India, still largely run by officials, a Dominion as soon as the war was over and the convening of a conference without the participation of the Congress and the Muslim League to frame proposals for a future constitution. The first suggestion was rejected as unrealistic by the Cabinet and the second, for the same reason, by the government of India. The inspiration behind both proposals was a desire to ignore the Congress, even if it meant bypassing the League as well.

Amery planned to build up a Kindergarten of his own and chose fellows of All Souls to wander about India and suggest what should be done in the way that Milner's young men had promoted the cause of empire in South Africa.[14] Reginald Coupland went out in the autumn of 1941 to study the constitutional problem and H. V. Hodson was appointed Reforms Commissioner, leading Lord Linlithgow to comment that any further All Souls influence might lead the next Viceroy, his successor, if new to India, straight up the garden path. Coupland kept in close touch with Amery and his report, published in 1944, bears the imprint of Amery's views. He thought that Irwin's declaration in October 1929 about Dominion status being the objective should have been made much earlier and he believed that the faults of the Raj had been mainly negative: an insular

[12] J. Barnes and D. Nicholson (eds), *The Empire at Bay: The Leo Amery Diaries, 1929–1945* (London, 1988), 794.
[13] Amery to Linlithgow, 28 May 1942. N. Mansergh (ed.), *The Transfer of Power 1942–7*, 12 vols (London, 1970–82), ii, document 95.
[14] See Amery's remarks to L. Curtis in August 1940. Barnes and Nicholson (eds), *Empire at Bay*, 661.

aloofness, insensitiveness, and want of imagination. The most regrettable feature of British rule was the difficulty white men often found not to feel and to betray a sense of superiority to coloured persons. Too many Englishmen had claimed from Indians a deference inconceivable on any grounds but those of race and, even worse, they had sometimes enforced the claim with unpardonable insolence.[15] But to Coupland, as to Amery, the major and urgent issue was not Britain's attitude to Indian nationalism but the differences between Hindus and Muslims. No two philosophies of thought and conduct could be more discordant, in his view, than those of Hinduism and Islam, and the clashes between the followers of these two religions was the outcome of two sharply contrasted faiths and of the social systems and ways of life that they had inspired.

If this long-standing tension had recently acquired a political colouring, Coupland held the Congress wholly responsible. He agreed with the contention of Curtis many years earlier that the creation of separate electorates had been a flagrant breach of democratic principle; but he felt that the Muslims had a strong case to justify such a breach. Britain had not lit the fire of rancour between Hindus and Muslims or done the devil's work of stoking it. He accepted Amery's description of the Congress as totalitarian, and it was this totalitarianism, along with what Coupland called the dictatorship of Gandhi, which to Coupland was responsible for rousing the fears of the Muslims in India and transforming the idea of Pakistan from an empty slogan into a real possibility. He acknowledged that the Congress ministries, which had functioned in the provinces from 1937, had on the whole done well and had established that the Congress party could perform constructively and was more than an organization for resistance. But he accused these ministries of creating the impression of the Congress being the natural successor to the Raj, of being responsible to the central executive of the party rather than to the provincial legislatures, and of being unable to break away from the personal authority of Gandhi. Even worse than the ministers seemed to Coupland to be the backbench supporters of the party, who were said to strut around the villages claiming to be wielders of authority and sometimes even talking in terms of raising a private army.

Coupland, writing in 1944, did not suggest that what he described as the totalitarian mentality of the Congress party was akin to that of the Nazi and Fascist parties; but he argued that the essence of totalitarianism was not in its methods but in its principle, and the Congress was following the totalitarian principle of one-party government by refusing to form coalitions with the Muslim League. To the contention that one-party governments are a normal feature of democracies in the Western world, Coupland's reply, like that of Amery, was that these countries were homogeneous societies with educated electorates. In India, where caste and illiteracy impeded democracy from taking

---

[15] R. Coupland, *The Constitutional Problem in India*, Part 3: *The Future of India* (Madras, 1944), 175; Coupland, *India: A Re-Statement* (London, 1945), 68.

root and religion created a deep cleft in public life, attempts to run governments on Westminster lines would only result in aberrations of democracy. The charge of the Muslim League that the Congress was not a secular but a Hindu Party was accepted. It followed that to Coupland parliamentary government, or government by political parties securing a majority of the votes, was not acceptable in India; it would always have to be government by coalition and compromise between parties which, whatever their professions, in fact (in Coupland's view) represented religious communities.

Coupland in his report, therefore, elaborated on the lines of Amery's thinking, and his interpretations were at the time endorsed by Hodson. He too was of the view that the Congress party, which Irwin had recognized as the main vehicle of Indian nationalism, had arrested the processes of democratic functioning by making the provincial governments answerable to a party executive which itself was under the thumb of Gandhi, whom Hodson characterized as a 'man of remarkable personality and nihilistic outlook'.[16] In his book written many years later Hodson toned this down and distanced himself from the criticism. The Congress, he wrote, was a tightly disciplined national organization, and its structure, combined with its claim to represent all Indians, gave rise to charges, both in India and abroad, of dictatorship and totalitarianism. These were particularly dirty words in democratic countries in the thirties, but if they did apply to the Congress they applied in a fundamentally different sense from the totalitarian dictatorships of Europe, for the Congress ethos, if not always its practice, was essentially democratic. But Hodson still blamed the Congress for debasing provincial autonomy as envisaged in the Act of 1935 and for implying that in the future majority rule would be Congress rule exercised from the centre, which would be dominated by the Hindu majority through an organization which brooked no opposition and refused to share its power.[17]

There was, however, one fellow of All Souls who had come out to India on his own long before those sent out by Amery. Penderel Moon had been elected a Prize Fellow in 1927 and was described by Curtis some years later as the most brilliant of the young men elected since the war, with a mind naturally mature but flexible.[18] Encouraged by Curtis and Coupland, Moon joined the Indian Civil Service and reached India in 1929 with the twin aspirations of doing what he could for the poor and facilitating the transition to full self-government. The officials at the India Office in London regarded such idealism as misplaced and told Moon that the British remained in India to safeguard the £1,000 million of capital invested in that country and not to teach Indians how to govern themselves. Disregarding this advice, Moon proved himself an outstanding district officer in the Punjab, touring extensively and concerning himself with the details

---

[16] Hodson's review of the second volume of Coupland's report, *The Spectator*, 7 March 1943.
[17] Hodson, *The Great Divide*, 63–4, 75.
[18] Curtis to A. D. Bell, September 1933. Curtis MSS, box 9.

of administration. But such total involvement brought with it its own sense of disillusion. He became convinced that the British, whatever the hopes of the best of them in the nineteenth century and whatever the good work they might have done, had by the 1930s become, in the phrase of Lord Ellenborough, a Governor-General of the mid-nineteenth century, 'strangers in India', creators of parasite classes and themselves parasitic, obstructionists because they stuck to the ruts and resisted new ideas. The revenue, taxation, and judicial systems were all cumbrous and wholly unsuited to India and were smothering her.[19] Nor could India afford these gigantic structures. Travelling, on his first arrival in India, from Bombay to Lahore by train, Moon was struck by the sterility of the country. 'I am surprised', he wrote to his mother, 'not at the poverty of Indians but at their continued existence.'[20] This first impression was confirmed by his later experiences. India was basically a poor country and the British were doing hardly anything to change this. They seemed to have neither the will nor the ideas to initiate even the beginnings of an economic transformation, such as the promotion of industrialization or cooperative farming. It could even be that such changes were beyond the capacity of an alien government; if so, it was all the more reason for hastening the day of Indian independence.

Indeed, Moon believed that British rule in India had continued too long and should have ended at least fifteen to twenty years before it was withdrawn in 1947. He had no use for Simon's lifeless report, supported fully Irwin's policy and described as an amazing stroke of luck the selection by the Conservative party of such a comparatively rational man as Viceroy.[21] But Moon would have liked the British government to have acted promptly on Irwin's declaration about Dominion status rather than to lose themselves in the 1930s in the interminable process of seeking a constitutional provision for every possibility and thereby postponing full self-government. Moon's explanation for this was that the British were in two minds: they had promised India self-government but did not really want to relax their hold and did not have much faith in the form of self-government that was being considered. This made the British seem untrustworthy; it had certainly led to Indians losing faith in them.[22]

Moon had no respect for the men in high places in Lahore and Delhi in the late 1930s and made no attempt to conceal his contempt. He also had little regard for most Indian politicians, especially those who became ministers in the provincial governments in 1937. British officials in India had become no more than 'mercenaries' in an administration which was, in Moon's opinion, daily getting more and more shady and in another five years would be wholly

---

[19] Moon to his mother, 23 Feb. and 25 June 1930. Moon MSS, file 1; P. Moon, *Strangers in India* (London, 1944), 22ff.

[20] 2 Dec. 1929, Moon MSS, file 1.

[21] To his mother, 13 Aug. 1930. Moon MSS, file 2.

[22] Moon, *Strangers in India*, 165.

corrupt. The British 'mercenaries' would then have no alternative but to pocket their pride and their honour along with their pay.[23]

After a long discussion with Coupland in India in the spring of 1942, Moon reported that they were in agreement as to the main lines on which a solution should be sought.[24] It is true that they were both thinking at this time in terms of satisfying the demands of the Muslim League without shattering the unity of India by grouping provinces together with a weak government at the centre. They both had their doubts about parliamentary government for India, and they agreed that much economic progress could not be expected under foreign rule. But on other major issues Moon's position was very different from that of Coupland. Moon was of the view that Irwin's policy of dealing with the Congress and Gandhi should continue. So strongly did Moon feel about this that it led to his leaving the service in 1943. While fully supporting the action taken by the government in arresting the leaders of the Congress, he wrote to the Punjab government condemning the harsh treatment, 'which smacks of the concentration camp', of Congress workers in prison. 'I really think', he commented to his father, 'that old Hitler has more excuse for his various atrocities in the occupied territories than we have for our barbarities out here.'[25]

But it was not just the contrast to the principles of freedom for which the British were supposed to be fighting the war that worried Moon. To him ill-treatment of members of the Congress was also poor policy, for, despite the strengthening of the Muslim League after 1937, the Congress represented India more nearly than any other party and when, after the war, the Indian problem was again considered, it would be impossible to ignore the Congress. It was the party of the future, bound to come again to the front as the active leaders of the country, and wisdom required that if its members had to be interned, this should be done with the minimum of harshness. So the Punjab government's reply to Moon's protest, that Congressmen deserved to be shot as traitors and would have been in a free country, so angered Moon that he passed on the government's reply to an Indian friend, describing it as a shameful story. The letter was intercepted by the censor and the Punjab government, supported by the government of India, proposed to get rid of Moon, whom they had always found difficult and never loath to taunt senior officers. Amery, who knew Moon's family and had met him frequently in All Souls, tried to find employment for him outside the Punjab, but Linlithgow, the Viceroy, refused to consider this; nor were the officials of the India Office willing to accommodate Moon in London. Moon, who had from 1938 been toying with the idea of leaving India and going into politics in Britain, now resigned, unapologetic, and refusing to apply for a proportionate pension or to claim all the leave to which he was entitled.[26]

---

[23] To his father, 10 Apr. 1938. Moon MSS, file 13.
[24] To his father, 1 Mar. 1942. Moon MSS, file 13.
[25] To his father, 15 Nov. 1942. Moon MSS, file 17.
[26] India Office Collections. File L/SG/6/3601, of 1943.

On the Hindu–Muslim problem the viewpoints of Moon and Coupland also differed sharply. Moon held that the desire for posts and power, which had developed in recent years, formed the basic cause for differences between Hindus and Muslims. The divergent beliefs and ways of life stretching back for centuries, on which Coupland laid stress, no doubt existed; yet, despite these differences, the fact was that Hindus and Muslims were closely intermingled, lived and worked side by side, and were hardly at all distinguished by race; and those belonging to the same area spoke the same language and shared a common provincial patriotism. The British had not created the divisions, but their mere presence had kept these differences alive, and both consciously and unconsciously the British had made use of them for their own purposes.[27] In particular, he regarded the continuation of separate electorates to have been a very grave mistake;[28] but this opinion which he held in the thirties and forties he changed towards the end of his life in the light of the deteriorating situation and considered separate electorates to be a regrettable but necessary evil.[29]

However, he adhered consistently to the view that it was the responsibility of the British to make some efforts to bring about agreement between the Hindus and the Muslims; and when the Muslim League adopted the Pakistan resolution in 1940 Moon was in favour of encouraging leaders in the Congress and the League known for their moderation to get together and bypass both Gandhi and Jinnah, the uncompromising leader of the Muslim League. At that time secretary to the governor of the Punjab, Moon persuaded the governor to write to the Viceroy on these lines; and he also joined a group of British civil servants in the Punjab who wished to wait upon the Viceroy to urge the same approach. But Linlithgow was following a policy, once the war broke out, of strengthening the League in order to weaken the Congress; and he therefore refused to take any steps to promote agreement between the two parties and frowned on all attempts to induce Muslim leaders to disown Jinnah. To Coupland the Viceroy's attitude was understandable and the Congress was to be blamed for the deadlock which lasted throughout the war years;[30] and to Hodson Linlithgow ranks in history as an outstanding Viceroy.[31]

But to Moon Linlithgow's attitude seemed, even at the time, indefensible. He became a severe critic and described Linlithgow as 'probably the most unpopular Viceroy there has been for nearly a century. I don't know which speak worst of him, Indians or English.'[32] He had played an easy hand so amazingly badly that he had driven Gandhi and the Congress, who were eager to support Britain in the war, into opposition; and by his ineptitude he had forced the Hindu–Muslim problem, which need never have been raised at all, into the forefront. On the

---

[27] Moon, *Strangers in India*, 103; Moon, *The Future of India* (London, 1945), 23.

[28] To his father, 17 Aug. 1932. Moon MSS, file 5.

[29] P. Moon, *The British Conquest and Dominion of India* (London, 1989), 953.

[30] Coupland, *India: A Re-Statement*, 197–8.

[31] Hodson, *The Great Divide*, 109.

[32] Moon to his father, 23 Feb. 1941. Moon MSS, file 16.

other hand, had the cooperation of the Congress been secured at the start of the war, a national government would have come into existence of its own accord and Hindu–Muslim questions and the demand for Pakistan would have melted away. Thanks to the Viceroy, the chance of a settlement between moderate members of the Congress and the League had been lost. The only course now left for the British was to go all out for the strong support of the Muslims, leading either to the establishment of the Muslims as unquestionably the dominant political power in India or to the division of India.[33] To avoid this Moon, after his resignation, advocated the imposition of a settlement by the British, even if need be by force. The Hindu–Muslim conflict was still open to the influence of human will and effort; for few even of the leaders had really decided in their own minds the minimum demands which they had in all circumstances to obtain and the maximum concessions which they could make and beyond which they could in no circumstances surrender.[34]

While Moon saw an element of artificial contrivance in the Hindu–Muslim problem and did not share Coupland's view that it was solely a product of history, he agreed that it had in recent times been allowed to develop such proportions as to make parliamentary government in India a mockery. Asserting that democracy in India did not have to be on the basis, best known in Britain, of elected governments answerable to legislatures, Moon was inclined, like Gandhi, to think in terms of autonomous village communities and a chain of councils from the village upwards with indirect elections. But he did not see why self-government need mean democratic government. In All Souls during the inter-war years and after, there was a strong streak of sympathy for the monarchical principle in India and much support for the Indian Princes. Rushbrook Williams was their staunchest champion and for six years had the odd designation of Foreign Minister of one of the minor states—odd because these states had no foreign relations at all. Amery thought in terms of strengthening these Princes by improving their bloodstock. 'If India', he wrote to the Viceroy,

is to be really capable of holding its own in the future without direct British control from outside, I am not sure that it will not need an increasing infusion of strong Nordic blood, whether by settlement or intermarriage or otherwise. Possibly it has been a real mistake of ours in the past not to encourage Indian Princes to marry English wives for a succession of generations and so breed a more virile type of native ruler. Perhaps all that may yet come about.[35]

He also suggested to Coupland that in any future settlement the States could form a Dominion of their own, for no Secretary of State could ever inform Parliament that these states were being handed over to anyone else against their

---

[33] Moon to his father, 5 and 19 Nov. 1939, Moon MSS, file 14; 31 Jan. and 13 Oct. 1940, file 15; and 3 Dec. 1942, file 17.
[34] Moon, *Strangers in India*, 87; *The Future of India*, 27.
[35] 1 Oct. 1943, Linlithgow MSS, India Office Collections, MSS Eur. F 125, vol. 12.

will.[36] But on this point Coupland did not follow Amery's lead and, while listing the advantages which might have accrued if the British had retained the monarchical tradition in India, did not favour a Dominion consisting of the Princely States, and advised them to adapt themselves to the progress of democracy and seek constitutional arrangements with the rest of India.[37] Irwin, as Viceroy, was firm in dealing with the Princes but he too believed that the sentiment for monarchy was strong in India and suggested to Attlee, the Prime Minister, in 1947 that the King and Queen should go to Delhi to say goodbye formally – a proposal which Attlee sensibly brushed aside.[38]

Moon, too, surprisingly, thought that the Princes could have a major role to play in the future. The absorption of the States into the rest of India seemed to him to be out of the question, and attempts to force their ruling families, several of whom were well established in the affections of the people, would only result in Hindu–Muslim clashes and convulsions which were unlikely to succeed. Far better to leave the Princes to adapt themselves to the times and to draw on their political wisdom, which Moon believed other parts of the country, under the influence of Western ideas and institutions, to have lost. Even the least powerful of the Princes could, as a pensioned and titled nobility, continue to be influential members of a recognized and respected ruling class – a class which Moon thought India badly needed. Moon went further and suggested that the States should absorb the provinces under British rule rather than the other way round, and that the Princes should take the place of British governors as heads of the provinces. So he concluded that 'in the backward obsolete states, the objects of so much misplaced scorn, there perhaps lies the secret of India's future and her best hopes'.[39]

With the departure from India of Linlithgow in 1943, it was possible to steer Moon back into direct concern with Indian affairs. He first worked at Chatham House on Indian problems and then, early in 1946, returned to Delhi on a contract as secretary of the Development Board. The grounds for his resignation earlier were by now well known in India and ensured his general popularity. No other British official, after several years in pre-independent India, served first Pakistan and then India in various capacities and was well regarded by both countries. But by the time he returned in 1946 the situation had so developed as to leave all his speculations about the future of India far behind. The scheme with which he had been associated in 1938, linking some provinces together with a weak central government, and Coupland's scheme of 1944, of four regions, two with a Hindu majority and two with a Muslim majority, with an inter-regional centre, clearly influenced the plan of the Cabinet Mission which came to India in

[36] Amery's note on the future of the States. Coupland MSS, box 5.
[37] Coupland, *The Future of India*, 150–4; *India: a Re-Statement*, 79, 279.
[38] Halifax to Attlee, 12 June 1947, and Attlee's reply, 15 June 1947. Mansergh, *The Transfer of Power*, vol. 11, no. 222, enclosures.
[39] Moon, *Strangers in India*, 65–7 and 164; *The Future of India*, 36.

the summer of 1946. The idea of sections and groups for provinces was taken up but, unlike in Coupland's scheme, there would be a central government responsible to a legislature and not merely an executive which would by statute be a coalition chosen by the head of state. But this plan too fell to the ground and the creation of Pakistan appeared unavoidable.

Moon, whose years of service in the Punjab had convinced him that the unity of that province should not be broken, was keen that the Sikhs, who formed a large minority in this Muslim majority area, should be given sufficient assurances to make them feel secure in Pakistan; and to this end he tried to bring together Sikh and Muslim leaders and also, in 1947, got in touch with Lord Mountbatten's staff.[40] But this hope of a united Punjab within Pakistan proved illusory and Moon, watching the massacres and migrations which followed the bisection of the province by Cyril Radcliffe, blamed equally Gandhi, Jinnah, and the British for the lack of wisdom and statesmanship which had led to the tragedy. The Congress, obsessed by the desire to get rid of the British, had given insufficient attention to the growing menace of Muslim separatism; Jinnah had given hardly any thought to the consequences of creating Pakistan and to the need to win over Sikh opinion; and the British should have hastened to transfer power, made it clear that they would never consider the division of the country and above all, as Moon saw it, had not thought in terms of parliamentary democracy in India.

The divergent approaches of Halifax and Simon to India continued until the end of the Empire and even beyond. In February 1947 Halifax spoke in the House of Lords supporting the plan for the transfer of power. He said he was not prepared to condemn the Labour government's policy unless he could honestly recommend a better solution. This speech changed the temper of the debate and infuriated Churchill. Two years later, when it was decided that India would continue, as a republic, to be a member of the Commonwealth, Amery, after initial hesitation, accepted the position. But Simon was even less enthusiastic. 'The truth is', he wrote to Churchill, 'that Nehru and Cripps have won. The agreement may be the best way out but the fact remains that Cripps has attained his ambition to "dissolve the British Empire" and Nehru, like Costello, gets all the advantages without any of the responsibilities.'[41] However, despite Simon's advice, Churchill wholeheartedly supported the decision.

'Between all that is best', wrote Curtis in 1920, 'of the British in India and of Indian nationalism there remains no wall but only the phantom of a wall, which will presently vanish.'[42] A comment in similar vein was made in Delhi many years later, in 1954 by Sarvepalli Radhakrishnan, who said that history is not

---

[40] Moon to Lord Ismay, 27 June 1947, Mansergh, *The Transfer of Power*, vol. 11, no. 371; Moon, *Divide and Quit* (London, 1961), 84.

[41] Amery's letters to Churchill, 14 and 29 April 1949, and Simon's undated note but obviously of April 1949. Churchill College, Cambridge, Churchill Archive, CHUR 2/44. J. A. Costello was the Prime Minister of Ireland.

[42] L. Curtis, *Dyarchy* (Oxford, 1920), p. xxxiv.

what we remember but what we choose to remember; and India remembered the positive aspects of British rule and elected to forget the rest. Radhakrishnan had been elected a fellow of All Souls in 1940 and lived there for two terms every year from 1945 until 1952, when he took up full-time assignments in India and was elected an Honorary Fellow. The connection with the College was of special importance to him. To Zhou En-Lai in 1954, for example, he spoke with a touch of mischief of the delights of All Souls common room. 'The last subject', reported *The Times* correspondent in Delhi, 'is said to have confused the Chinese Prime Minister.'[43] As for the College, its first Indian fellow was a philosopher of religion, who could have been expected to be concerned almost wholly with matters which had nothing to do with everyday life.

Yet Radhakrishnan was not, and had never been, a secluded philosopher. He was always fully involved in the world even if not in the rough and tumble of political life. His early writings are set in the context of British rule in India, with Christianity appearing as an ally of imperialism and an alien ideological force and with many European scholars writing off the thought of India as a crass combination of the crude and the fatuous with nothing positive to contribute to the world. In reply, Radhakrishnan set himself the task of interpreting Indian thought in terms which related it to the Western tradition so that it could be seen as a bright chapter in the history of the human mind, become a part of every person's heritage, and enter into the bloodstream of world culture. His attempt to establish that Indian thinkers had grappled with the basic problems and formulated theories which had not lost their value helped Indians, smarting under foreign rule, to recover their intellectual self-esteem. But Radhakrishnan also made clear to Indians that this long and rich tradition had been arrested and required innovation and further evolution. While he elucidated Hinduism at its highest levels and renewed its dignity, he stressed that it had to cast off much that was corrupt and abhorrent.

The commitment to society, the crusading tone even in his scholarly writings, the modern note in his interpretation of classical texts, and his intellectual resistance to the deforming pressures of colonialism gave Radhakrishnan by the 1930s a distinct public image both in Britain and in India. He was convinced that even non-political endeavour could not thrive in the absence of political freedom. Foreign rule could not evoke any living response from the people. Intellectual sterility in India was to no small extent due to the shame of subjection. No nation could be trusted with the charge of another. It was Britain's duty to grant freedom to India, and if she did so with intelligent sympathy the friendship between Britain and India would be enduring. To speak of Hindu–Muslim differences as the obstacle was to accept the deficiency of British rule, for, in Radhakrishnan's view, it was the government which had promoted this rift among a generally harmonious people.

[43] 3 July 1954.

Not surprisingly, Radhakrishnan approved of Irwin's settlement with Gandhi in 1931, for he saw in Gandhi a leader armed with the strength of the spirit, who was developing non-violence as the moral equivalent of war. He missed no opportunity, even when Gandhi was in prison, to speak and write explaining Gandhi's work and thought. In 1922, when the synod of bishops of the Church of England in India denounced Gandhi's non-violent resistance as unchristian and called on Christians in India to obey the government unquestioningly, Radhakrishnan replied in a series of articles that Christ had called on his followers to resist evil but to do so, as Gandhi did, in a non-violent manner. The bishops would do better spending their time promoting a reconciliation between India and Britain. When Gandhi was murdered, Radhakrishnan, addressing the memorial meeting held in the Codrington Library, spoke of the faith in humanity which had made Gandhi the leading prophet of the moral and spiritual revolution without which the world would not find peace.

With India free, the priorities in Radhakrishnan's intellectual objectives shifted. His position now moved closer to that of Curtis, but he was more interested in promoting a world community rather than a world state. He did not share Curtis's vision of the British Empire as the nucleus of a world federation; and he saw the basis for a world community not in Christian teaching but in human values and inter-religious understanding. He criss-crossed the world asserting that to regard one's own country as the centre of the universe was an outmoded idea and one should learn to admit the possible worth of values and ways of life which were not acceptable to oneself. Appointed India's ambassador in Moscow in 1949, he saw his task, at the height of the cold war, as one of seeking a better understanding of each other's viewpoint, without compromising on principles or weakening his own commitment to democracy and the freedom of the individual.

Irwin was the first fellow of All Souls to live in the Viceroy's house built by Lutyens in New Delhi; and Radhakrishnan, nearly forty years later, was the second. By then both the name of the house and the designation of the occupant had been changed. But these were more than mere changes in nomenclature. They reflected a change in the basis of the relations between Britain and India. In turn, over these years, the nature and spirit of the Indian connection of All Souls had also been transformed.

10

Appeasers and Anti-Appeasers: All Souls and the International Crisis of the 1930s

S. J. D. Green

It is to cast not the least aspersion on a doubtless admirable institution to observe that we still lack – and in all probability will long yet be denied – either scholarly treatise or polemical tract on the grave matter of 'Brasenose and Appeasement'.[1] But of the critical role of All Souls in that fateful foreign commitment, there seems to be no end of books, chapters, and articles in sight. Amongst only the most recent additions to the genre, Norman Rose's study of *The Cliveden Set* includes a detailed analysis of Mrs Astor's College connections.[2] So does James Fox's elegiac account of the vanished world of *The Langhorne Sisters*.[3] Some of this work has achieved significant new insights into broader questions of real historical importance. Sidney Aster's *Appeasement and All Souls* stands ahead of the rest of the field in this respect.[4] Much of the rest merely regurgitates the tired pieties of righteous hindsight. Lynn Olson's *Troublesome Young Men* is a good example of that easily recognizable type.[5] But inherited memories are possibly

---

[1] J. M. Crook, *Brasenose: The Biography of an Oxford College* (Oxford, 2008), offers a spirited new account of this society. See esp. ch. 7; it makes no mention of 'appeasement'.

[2] N. Rose, *The Cliveden Set: Portrait of an Exclusive Fraternity* (London, 2000). See esp. ch. 3; also particular accounts of Leo Amery, 46–7, 61, 71–8, 95–6, and 186; Bob Brand, 29–32, 45–9, 78, 187, and 211–15; and, finally, Geoffrey Dawson, 45–9, 68–80, 96, 106, 120, 131, 169, 181, and 189–203.

[3] J. Fox, *The Langhorne Sisters* (London, 1998), offers the most detailed account yet published of the marriage between Bob Brand and Phyllis Langhorne, also of its wider repercussions. Brand's (always caustic) views on Nazi Germany are detailed on 451, 458, 488, and 493.

[4] S. Aster (ed.), *Appeasement and All Souls: A Portrait with Documents, 1937–1939*, Camden Society, Fifth Series, 24 (Cambridge, 2004). See esp. Aster's 'Introduction: Appeasement and All Souls', 1–19. Amongst his other works, *Anthony Eden* (London, 1976), esp. ch. 2, and *1939: The Making of the Second World War* (London, 1973), esp. chs 1 and 2, also constitute important contributions to the debate.

[5] L. Olson, *Troublesome Young Men: The Rebels Who Brought Churchill to Power in 1940 and Helped to Save Britain* (London, 2007); see esp. 113, 122, and 174–5 for an account of the College, and 111 and 133–4 for an uncritical rendering of Amery's supposed 'anti-appeasement stance'. D. Faber, *Munich: The 1938 Appeasement Crisis* (London, 2008), is in much the same vein; see esp. 1–7, chs 7, 8, and 14. The author is the grandson of Harold Macmillan.

revised slowest of all. Consider Alan Ryan's British Academy 'Obituary' of Stuart Hampshire, published only in 2007:

He arrived...at All Souls...in 1936...at a time when the College...was deeply implicated in the policy of appeasement pursued by the Conservative Government of the day. [T]here he could observe at first hand the 'servility of the Conservatives in the face of fascism'.[6]

Perhaps. What any young Prize Fellow of that vintage cannot have failed to notice was that All Souls between the wars was not like Brasenose. It was a very unusual Oxford college. It was something of an academic society. It housed many considerable scholars, who produced much serious work during these years. The pre-1939 labours of its research fellows, particularly Oman and Pollard but also Henderson and Pares, and amongst the Professors, of Coupland, Clark, and Radcliffe-Brown, even, in his own way, of Holdsworth, stood comparison with those of anyone else, whether within the university or the wider world beyond.[7] But its peculiar fief was public affairs. During the years immediately leading up to the outbreak of the Second World War, possibly half of its strength was either directly or indirectly involved in their administration.[8]

Moreover, a fair proportion of those fellows was intimately involved in the British government's increasingly forlorn efforts to secure lasting agreement in the critical matter of common relations with Nazi Germany.[9] Most prominent amongst these Mallardians were Halifax and Simon, respectively Foreign Secretary and Chancellor of the Exchequer under Chamberlain.[10] More marginally involved, though still of considerable weight, was Donald Somervell. He was

---

[6] A. Ryan, 'Stuart Newton Hampshire', *Proceedings of the British Academy*, 150: Biographical Memoirs of Fellows, 6 (2007), 107–23, at 109. These observations are themselves based on the autobiographical recollections related in S. Hampshire, 'Introduction', *Innocence and Experience* (London, 1989), 1–19, at 5–6.

[7] See S. J. D. Green, 'All Souls and the Study of History in Twentieth-Century Oxford', *The Oxford Historian*, 7 (2009), 24–7; also idem, *The Exceptional College: All Souls c. 1850–1950* (forthcoming), ch. 8.

[8] J. S. G. Simmons, 'All Souls College: A Chronological List of Fellows, 1438–1988, with Additional Lists, Tables and an Index', unpublished, Oxford, 1988, 3–69; see esp. 55–9. A. L. Rowse, 'All Souls (1945)' in idem, *The English Past: Evocations of Persons and Places* (London, 1951), ch. 1; see esp. 13ff.

[9] P. Neville, *Hitler and Appeasement: The British Attempt to Prevent the Second World War* (London, 2006), offers the best up-to-date survey of the origins, ends, and consequences of this policy. See esp. chs 2–4 and 7–9. N. Thompson, *The Anti-Appeasers: Conservative Opposition to Appeasement in the 1930s* (Oxford, 1971), 27–31, furnishes a number of important *contemporary* definitions of the term.

[10] The Earl of Halifax, *Fulness of Days* (London, 1957), ch. 5; cf. A. Roberts, *'The Holy Fox': A Biography of Lord Halifax* (London, 1991), chs 10–18. Viscount Simon, *Retrospect* (London, 1952), chs 10–13; cf. D. Dutton, *Simon: A Political Biography* (London, 1992), chs 7–10, with Cretney, this volume. Both Halifax's and Simon's memoirs are notably elusive concerning these great events. These later, biographical, accounts are amongst the most illuminating.

Attorney General from 1936.[11] Leo Amery, the former Secretary of State for the Colonies, was by then confined to the backbenches.[12] This scarcely made him less vocal: first as a supporter, increasingly after Munich as a critic of the National Government.[13] Then there was Quintin Hogg, elected as a Chamberlainite MP for Oxford, in October 1938.[14] Quondam Fellows Edward Bridges and Eric Beckett served His Majesty's purposes unobtrusively as Cabinet Secretary and Legal Advisor to the Foreign Office.[15] Young 'prizeman' Con O'Neill laboured as Third Secretary in Berlin from 1938. He resigned in protest against Henderson's understanding (and implementation) of government policy in 1939.[16] Geoffrey Dawson, ubiquitous editor of *The Times*, invariably argued the Prime Minister's case in the court of public opinion during these troubled years.[17] His underling, Dermot Morrah, occasionally did some of the necessary writing-up for him in the Thunderer's influential first leaders of those days.[18] Harry Hodson coordinated Commonwealth perspectives on this vital question through the pages of *The Round Table*.[19] Lionel Curtis took care of Chatham House, and Archbishop Lang ensured that the nation never forgot the spiritual perspective on ostensibly secular issues.[20]

Whether or not this made All Souls a genuinely influential institution in the formulation and execution of inter-war British foreign policy is quite another matter. The conclusions reached below will be for the most part negative. But one thing can be said, and quite categorically, at the outset. Whether or not All Souls ever was an 'unofficial committee' for the fortunes of the British Empire, it

---

[11] Evershed, rev. M. Brodie, 'Somervell, Donald Bradley, Baron Somervell of Harrow (1889–1960)', *ODNB*, at p. 601. On Somervell's (remarkable) All Souls success, see Green, this volume, ch. 2, 53–4.

[12] J. Barnes and D. Nicholson (eds), *The Empire at Bay: The Leo Amery Diaries, 1929–1945* (London, 1988), chs 1–7, is the essential source. D. Faber, *Speaking for England: Leo, Julian and John Amery – the Tragedy of a Political Family* (London, 2005), chs 13–16, offers a sympathetic modern account. See also Louis, this volume, ch. 11.

[13] Barnes and Nicholson (eds), *The Empire at Bay*, chs 6 and 7; cf. Faber, *Speaking for England*, ch. 17. See also W. R. Louis, *In the Name of God Go! Leo Amery and the British Empire in the Age of Churchill* (London, 1992), ch. 2.

[14] Lord Hailsham, *A Sparrow's Flight: Memoirs* (London, 1990), ch. 17, recalls the event; G. Lewis, *Lord Hailsham: A Life* (London, 1997), ch. 5, recounts it.

[15] R. A. Chapman, 'Bridges, Edward Ettingdene, First Baron Bridges (1892–1969)', *ODNB*, at p. 581; I. Brownlie, 'Beckett, Sir (William) Eric (1896–1966)', *ODNB*.

[16] R. Denman, 'O'Neill, Sir Con Douglas Walter (1912–1988)', *ODNB*.

[17] E. Wrench, *Geoffrey Dawson and Our Times* (London, 1955), chs 30–2, offers an essential narrative. P. Neville, 'Dawson (formerly Robinson), [George] Geoffrey (1874–1944)', *ODNB*, at pp. 553–4, is an updated version. There is no modern biography of Dawson, a major gap in the literature of the period.

[18] C. Monteith, 'Morrah, Dermot Michael Macgregor (1896–1974)', *ODNB*, at p. 246.

[19] R. Wade-Gery, 'Hodson, Henry Vincent (1906–1999)', *ODNB*, at p. 513, with Howard, this volume.

[20] D. Lavin, *From Empire to International Commonwealth: A Biography of Lionel Curtis* (Oxford, 1995), esp. ch. 13. Note also the observation of Neville, *Hitler and Appeasement*, 11: 'If appeasement needed an intellectual forum, Chatham House provided it.' J. G. Lockhart, *Cosmo Gordon Lang* (London, 1949), esp. chs 33–4.

made surprisingly little impact on popular consciousness at the time, either for
good or ill.[21] Few then counted the College as a fifth estate within the realm.
Fewer still either praised or castigated its contribution to contemporary Anglo-
German understanding. Appeasement was for long a popular policy. But the
nation never voted All Souls any unofficial thanks for its gratuitous *sagesse* in
planning the Prime Minister's alternative to war.

No less significantly, contemporary scandalmongers never pointed in its
direction as an example of illegitimate, undemocratic, influence either. That is
surely interesting. For as government policy became increasingly controversial
during the weeks leading up to, and in the months after, the Munich settlement,
scurrilous journalists, motivated by dubious allegiances (alternatively, concerned
citizens anxious to uphold parliamentary accountability), assiduously searched
for evidence of potentially nefarious agencies at work in the land. This was how
Claud Cockburn found such a juicy morsel in the supposed activities of the so-
called 'Cliveden Set'.[22] His repeated accusations of pro-German influences,
orchestrated amongst elevated company in that agreeable place, had such a scan-
dalous effect as to force Nancy Astor to defend herself – and her household – in the
pages of *The Saturday Evening Post*.[23] Similar rumours moved Geoffrey Dawson to
track down all references to the 'sheer legend' of that unpatriotic association, this
across virtually every paper published throughout the Commonwealth.[24] He even
exploited his good offices with the *Johannesburg Star* to persuade them to publish a
refutation of this 'tissue of falsehoods', given fresh publicity in *The Primary
Producer*, a periodical then irregularly issued by 'an association of [socialist] cooperative societies' in pre-war South Africa. In truth, there cannot have been many
of these. But Cockburn never mentioned All Souls.[25]

Nearly two years later, and immediately after the fall of France, another set of
'scurrilous journalists' (and/or 'concerned citizens') took up their pens in furious
denunciation of the so-called *Guilty Men*.[26] Furthermore, 'Cato' defined his
public purpose very clearly. In his own words: 'the use of recriminating about
the past is to enforce effective action at the present'. He could say it with

---

[21] C. W. Brodribb, *Government by Mallardry: A Study in Political Ornithology* (London, 1932),
3–7.

[22] C. Cockburn, '*The Times* Scandal', *The Week*, 8 Sept. 1938, 1; Oxford, Bodleian Library,
Dawson Papers, MS 80, f. 38; Rose, *The Cliveden Set*, 178–80 and 189.

[23] Anon. [Nancy Astor], 'The Cliveden Set: The Origins and History of a Harmful Political
Legend', *Saturday Evening Post*, 13 May 1939, 7; Rose, *The Cliveden Set*, 182–3.

[24] Dawson Papers, MS 80, ff. 156–8, Dawson to John Martin, 16 Apr. 1939; Martin to Dawson,
25 Apr. 1939.

[25] Dawson Papers, MS 81, fol. 9, Dawson to John Martin, 6 July 1939; Cockburn, '*The Times*
Scandal'; Rose, *The Cliveden Set*, 74–6 and 155–9.

[26] 'Cato', *Guilty Men* (London, 1940). The book was first published in July 1940. It went
through twelve editions in that month alone. 'Cato' was conceived in the wake of Dunkirk by
Michael Foot (then of the *Evening Standard* and subsequently leader of the Labour Party, 1980–3),
and Frank Owen (editor of the *Evening Standard*, 1938–41, and the *Daily Mail*, 1947–50), finally,
P. Howard (columnist on the *Express* papers, 1933–41, and thereafter a farmer).

impunity too. For these were precisely the words of Winston Churchill, from 28 May 1936. And by July 1940, Churchill was Prime Minister.[27] Blessed with bipartisan indulgence, 'Cato' now felt free to identify this inglorious cast by name.[28] His infamous list included two Mallardians: Halifax and Simon.[29] Yet they were scarcely singled out in his opprobrium. He was very keen to denounce other incriminating connections too: the National Government (obviously); the Tory Party (by extension); finally, Big Business and the Banks (this was a socialist document after all).[30] But the College never got a look in.[31]

In fact, the very idea of such conspiratorial complicity at All Souls, more specifically, of the College as the intellectual *fons et origo* of appeasement, was wholly an invention of the post-war imagination. If it ever had any serious origins, these lie in Henry Fairlie's contemporary delineation of an English 'Establishment'. By that term, probably first coined in 1955, Fairlie meant to identify a system of small and mysterious (though strictly secular) circles of interlinked and unrepresentative bodies of public administration, similarly purveyors of social influence and manufacturers of élite opinion. This unelected network and its luminaries, so Fairlie insisted, actually governed Britain's ostensibly democratic régime in the post-Atlee era.[32] He eventually identified All Souls College amongst these institutions.[33] Anthony Sampson's *Anatomy of Britain* subsequently mapped the precise position of the College, albeit at the very fringes of this system of unaccountable authority.[34] Contemporary critics took it as axiomatic that 'The Establishment' governed England badly as well as unconstitutionally. Men with scores to settle now suggested that it (and they) had always done so. One of the most prominent amongst their number was the maverick Tory MP, Robert Boothby.[35] He also seems to have been the first specifically to

---

[27] 'Cato', *Guilty Men*, 5.

[28] Ibid., 6, 'Cast': Mr Neville Chamberlain, Sir John Simon, Sir Samuel Hoare, Mr Ramsay MacDonald, Lord Baldwin, Lord Halifax, Sir Kingsley Wood, Mr Ernest Brown, Captain David Margesson, Sir Horace Wilson, Sir Thomas Inskip (Lord Caldecote), Mr Leslie Burgin, Lord Stanhope, Mr W. S. Morrison, and Sir Reginald Dorman Smith.

[29] Simon featured prominently in chs 3, 4, 8, 9, and 11. Halifax, interestingly, had no chapter devoted to his peculiar contribution. Note the absence of Dawson altogether.

[30] 'Cato', *Guilty Men*, esp. chs 16–20.

[31] It is not mentioned once in the text, not even by way of connection with Simon or Halifax.

[32] H. Fairlie, 'Political Commentary', *The Spectator*, no. 1639 (23 Sept. 1955), 379–81. The subsequent history of this term is thoughtfully considered in Fairlie, 'Evolution of a Term: The Establishment', first printed in *The New Yorker* for 15 Oct. 1968 and reprinted in J. McCarter (ed.), *Bite the Hand that Feeds You: Essays and Provocations by Henry Fairlie* (New Haven, 2009), 68–91.

[33] E.g. H. Fairlie, 'Are We Ruled by the Sparrow Minds?', *Daily Mail*, 25 Oct. 1958, 8. But even Fairlie took a while to turn his sights on All Souls. It was not one of his initial bugbears.

[34] A. Sampson, *Anatomy of Britain* (London, 1962), 214–15, under 'Oxbridge and Politics'. But it was fading fast. By the time of Sampson's *Anatomy of Britain Today* (London, 1965), All Souls is already 'a [less] important place . . . than Nuffield College', anyway, in terms of 'close links with Downing Street and Lambeth'.

[35] R. J. Graham, Baron Boothby (1900–86); ed. Eton College and Magdalen College, Oxford; pass degree in Modern History; member of parliament for East Aberdeenshire, 1924–58; parliamentary private secretary to Winston Churchill, then Chancellor of the Exchequer, 1926–9; lover of Dorothy Macmillan, 1929–66; under-secretary at the Ministry of Food, May–October 1940,

have connected 'The Establishment', All Souls, and the (by then, universally acknowledged) pernicious policy of 'appeasement'.[36] An initial salvo to *The Spectator*, written in response to John Sparrow's defence of Foreign Office recruiting methods against Fairlie's vague charges of elitism and subterfuge, set the tone. Expressing 'no surprise' at Warden Sparrow's 'complacent attitudes' in this matter, Boothby also observed in passing that

All Souls [was] the headquarters of the establishment [and] the intellectual H.Q. of appeasement... during the decade preceding the Second World War and it would be difficult to overestimate the damage then done to this country at that disastrous dining table.[37]

Quite why Boothby chose to highlight this *particular* link is far from clear. He had no personal connection with the College. Indeed, he knew very little about All Souls, either before or after the war.[38] Moreover, his own record on 'appeasement', anyway according to the most elevated standards of post-war purity, was far from unblemished.[39] Still, by the mid-1950s, he lacked neither for grievances nor in vanity. What had become the palpable failure of his own political career was something that needed to be explained – anyway, by him. The idea of his having been denied so many rightful rewards as a result of an unbreakable commitment to principle made agreeable sense of it all – anyway, to him.[40]

resigning after a select committee of the House of Commons found his activities in relation to émigré Czech financial claims 'contrary to the image and derogatory to the dignity of the House'; junior staff officer with RAF Bomber Command; liaison officer with the Free French; Légion d'honneur, 1950; KBE, 1953; life peerage, 1958; Rector of St Andrew's University, 1958–61; regular broadcaster and commentator on national affairs in the 1950s; associate of the Kray twins in the 1960s, who probably procured homosexual escorts for him. Twice married, first to Diana Cavendish, 1935–7, secondly to Wanda Senna, 1967–86. There is an airbrushed life of him by R. Rhodes James, *Bob Boothby: A Portrait* (London, 1991). It passes over the spat with Sparrow except for a fleeting reference on p. 11. Ironically, Rhodes James was himself a Junior Research Fellow of the College between 1964 and 1968.

[36] R. Boothby, *I Fight to Live* (London, 1947), an early essay in 'autobiography', made no mention at all of this connection. It therefore cannot have been construed, even by Boothby himself, much before 1955. See also next note.

[37] R. Boothby, 'The Establishment', *The Spectator*, no. 6641 (7 Oct. 1955), 448, responding to John Sparrow, 'Burgess and Maclean', *The Spectator*, no. 6640 (30 Sept. 1955), 418.

[38] Boothby, *I Fight to Live*, passes over his Oxford career in one page (16), though he does furnish an account of sorts in A. Thwaite (ed.), *My Oxford* (London, 1977), ch. 2. Rhodes James, *Bob Boothby*, ch. 2, fills in some of the gaps. His ignorance of All Souls, before and after the war, is unwittingly reaffirmed in his *Recollections of a Rebel* (London, 1978), at p. 25, and implicitly corroborated by Rhodes James in *Bob Boothby*, at p. 16.

[39] Thompson, *The Anti-Appeasers*, 153–4 and 161–70, long ago established how Boothby supported Chamberlain against Eden in February 1938 and government policy against its critics at the time of the Anschluss. For his even more curious behaviour at the time of Munich, see n. 139 below. His abandonment of Katherine Atholl during her anti-Chamberlainite by-election campaign of November 1938 is documented in R. A. C. Parker, *Churchill and Appeasement* (London, 2000), at 200–1. David Dilks makes the no less important point that Boothby's vacillations over Anglo-German relations in 1938 could easily have counted to his credit – if only he had not subsequently denied them (private communication to the author).

[40] For the substance of these grievances, compare Rhodes James, *Bob Boothby*, chs 8, 11, and 14 with J. Grigg, 'Boothby, Robert John Graham, Baron Boothby (1900–1986)', *ODNB*, at p. 640.

Having once initiated so grave a polemical charge, Boothby stuck manfully to his metaphorical guns. On being challenged to make clear what it was he was alleging, he wrote a second, longer letter, this time listing the All Souls 'Establishment' men. These included Lang, Halifax, Dawson, Simon, Curtis, Somervell, and Brand.[41] It might be observed in passing that anyone including Brand amongst that number had long since given up trying to distinguish appeasers from anti-appeasers.[42] No matter. Boothby's far-reaching critique of this caricature of erstwhile ill-governance quickly moved beyond the confines of recoverable evidence, or indeed the ascertainable significance of the College's collective eating habits. In his own words:

[T]hey had no need to dine together in order to achieve their ends. They were in telepathic as well as telephone communication with each other.[43]

That proved too much for some of the nation's saner souls. When Boothby repeated the same charge, in relation to much the same subject, this time during Associated Rediffusion's televised documentary about 'The Establishment' broadcast in 1958, the redoubtable Violet Bonham Carter put him forcibly to right. As she recalled:

I followed him and said that . . . it was not because of the Cliveden Set or All Souls that we had then pursued a disastrous policy but because the PM of the day believed in it and so did his Cabinet and they were supported by the House of Commons.

She also pointed out:

That Bob, who alleged that all through his career he had bumped up against the Establishment with results disastrous to himself, was [actually] plastered with decorations: that indeed titles, knighthoods or life peerages [had] rained down on him.

So much so that what really stuck in the craw was the way in which:

he emerges drenched and drowned from the Fount of Honour and then shakes himself like a dog getting out of dirty water.[44]

---

[41] R. Boothby, 'The Establishment', *The Spectator*, no. 6643 (21 Oct. 1955), 528. 'I have since been asked, "Which of them gathered at All Souls?".'

[42] Ibid.: 'I cannot say, because I do not know which side each of them took on the great controversial issues of the day, but it is not difficult to imagine the desperate and losing postprandial actions that must have been conducted by Mr Amery.' In fact, Leo Amery was out of fellowship after 1912. He returned to All Souls as a Distinguished Fellow in October 1939. See *Recollections of a Rebel*, 25. A generation on, and Boothby apparently was now informed. Only Amery, Rowse, and Salter distinguished themselves as anti-appeasers. The rest, seemingly represented by Quintin Hogg (later Lord Hailsham), were appeasers.

[43] Ibid. This was, he announced, to be his 'final word' on the matter. That proved far from the case. Damning portraits of Halifax and Dawson were subsequently sketched in his *My Yesterday, Your Tomorrow* (London, 1962), at 127–31 and 131–5, respectively. The more general allegations were repeated, wholesale, in *Recollections of a Rebel*, 25.

[44] M. Pottle (ed.), *Daring to Hope: The Diaries and Letters of Violet Bonham Carter, 1946–1969* (London, 2000), 206–7, 'Diary' for 19 Aug. 1958. The same incident is recounted, from another

A prudent man would perhaps have left it there. But no one ever accused Dr A. L. Rowse of being merely a prudent man. Outraged by Boothby's underhand claim that the absence of any rebuttal from All Souls somehow confirmed his charges, Rowse dutifully set about supplying a suitably robust refutation. This eventually emerged as an essay some 40,000 words long. *All Souls and Appeasement* was published in April 1961.[45] It took no account of the revisionist school in appeasement studies inaugurated by A. J. P. Taylor's *Origins of the Second World War* that year. Indeed it may be doubted whether Rowse's (uncharacteristically) delayed response would have been altered by Taylor's subtly subversive argument, even had he read it.[46]

The learned doctor happily accepted Boothby's portrait of an 'influential institution'. And he condemned even more forcibly the 'policy of appeasement'. In fact, his denunciation of Halifax, Simon, and Dawson was harsher still.[47] But his point – one which he did not hesitate to reiterate throughout the text – was that only a fraction of the then College was properly tarred by Boothby's blackening brush. For the 'Guilty Men' were not representative of the whole College. Least of all had they represented him. To the contrary, there had been many anti-appeasers in All Souls: a few amongst the seniors (such as Brand), even the odd professor (for instance, Salter), but, above all, within the body of the young (led by you know who). They had denounced the policy from the first. They had actively opposed it. They had, indeed, done everything reasonably within their powers to change government policy and influence public opinion towards a necessary confrontation of German aggrandizement and Nazi thuggery.[48] Simple historical truth, as well as subsequent fair-mindedness, now demanded proper acknowledgement that, in the matter of 'All Souls and Appeasement' there had

perspective, in D. R. Thorpe, *Supermac: The Life of Harold Macmillan* (London, 2010), at 419–20. Thorpe also makes the point that Boothby had been raised to the peerage on 24 July 1958. This tirade was broadcast on 19 Aug. that year. No wonder Violet Bonham Carter, who had to wait until 1964 for a similar honour, was *quite* so piqued.

[45] A. L. Rowse, *All Souls and Appeasement: A Contribution to Contemporary History* (London, 1961); see esp. p. 1; note again, Boothby, *Recollections of a Rebel*, 25. Interestingly, Rowse entitled the American edition of his work *Appeasement: A Study in Political Decline, 1933–1939* (New York, 1961). Subsequently, he came to prefer this title, for reasons that will perhaps become apparent below.

[46] A. J. P. Taylor, *The Origins of the Second World War* (London, 1961). Taylor's book is generally regarded as the pioneering work of 'revisionist history' in relation to Munich and appeasement. For a sense of the stink that it caused, see the various essays in W. R. Louis (ed.), *The Origins of the Second World War: A. J. P. Taylor and His Critics* (London, 1972). J. Joll, 'The Ride to the Abyss', *The Spectator*, no. 6930 (21 Apr. 1961), 561–4, represented a truly heroic effort to review Rowse's and Taylor's books together. His clear preference for Taylor over Rowse demonstrates the way in which the academic winds were beginning to shift, even then. Rowse's ever-increasing anxiety in the face of this trend is amply demonstrated in his 'Foreword' to M. George, *The Hollow Men: An Examination of British Foreign Policy in Britain between 1933 and 1939* (London, 1965), 7–11, esp. at 11.

[47] Rowse, *All Souls and Appeasement*, see *inter alia*, 6–13, 16–23, 27–9, 76ff. But almost anywhere will do.

[48] Rowse, *All Souls and Appeasement*; on Brand, see 142ff; on Salter, 43–4, 59–62 and 80–1; on Rowse (and the young), see 22–9, 50–1, 72–5, and 113ff.

been just as many (if not more) on the side of honour and justice as had been true of the country at large: amply proved (in both cases) by their collective response to Churchill's revolution (and national redemption) in May 1940.[49]

I

Rowse meant this 'Contribution to Contemporary History' to settle the matter once and for all. He could scarcely have been less successful. His massive missive in retrospective self-vindication enabled Boothby's resentful conceit to achieve an intellectual half-life far beyond anything that either historical truth or reasonable fair-mindedness would otherwise have allowed.[50] The idea of 'the Establishment' ran out of steam years ago. Fashionable scribblers alternatively celebrate or excoriate the significance of 'new élites' these days.[51] All Souls does not so much as rate a mention in Sampson's most recent investigations into *Who Runs This Place*.[52] But the myths and falsehoods surrounding the activities of the College and the policy of appeasement still thrive.[53] This is doubly unfortunate: first, because the hoary myth conceals a much more interesting truth; secondly, because the basic falsehood of Boothby's lazy accusation is easily exposed. Indeed, it has long since been definitively demolished. In an unpublished lecture, delivered nearly two decades ago, Charles Wenden finally showed it up for the nonsense it always was.[54]

It is worth repeating some of Wenden's most remarkable findings. Let us begin with the basic assumption that All Souls was indeed *the* place where the great and the good then wined, dined, and persuaded each other about such grave matters of policy. The surviving evidence – anyway about the issue of

[49] Rowse, *All Souls and Appeasement*, 106–7. See also A. L. Rowse, 'Mr Churchill and English History', in idem, *The English Spirit: Essays in History and Literature* (London, 1946), 1–22.

[50] Boothby, *Recollections of a Rebel*, 25, insisted that this was because his allegations remained 'uncontradicted' twenty-five years later. That cannot be an adequate explanation. See below.

[51] Two devastating contemporary critiques of the concept can be found in A. Macintyre, 'The Straw Men of the Age', *The New Statesman*, 58, no. 1490 (3 Oct. 1959), 433–4; and B. Williams, 'Fairlie, the Establishment and the BBC', *Encounter*, 13, no. 5 (November 1959), 63–5. These put a stop to any further – serious – discussion of the idea. G. Walden, *The New Elites* (London, 2006), shows how it can be revived. Fairlie's retreat in 'Evolution of a Term', shows why this is such an error.

[52] A. Sampson, *Who Runs This Place? The Anatomy of Britain in the Twenty-First Century* (London, 2004); note the diminished role of academia more generally in ch. 14 of this work. In fact, All Souls seems to have fallen off Sampson's radar as early as his *The New Anatomy of Britain* (London, 1971), where it is mentioned only in relation to Winchester College. It disappeared altogether in *The Changing Anatomy of Britain* (London, 1982).

[53] M. Gilbert and R. Gott, *The Appeasers* (London, 1963), 49, 73, 76, 83, 86, and 93–4, was also influential in this respect; see also nn. 2 and 3 above.

[54] All Souls College archives, D. J. Wenden, 'Appeasement and All Souls', 24 pp., Chichele Lecture, 1990. It is much to be regretted that Mr Wenden (1923–92), Bursar of All Souls, 1970–92, and Research Fellow of the College, 1990–2, died before he could revise this lecture in a form suitable for publication. My debt to his work is profound. That – scarcely less – of Professor Sidney Aster is acknowledged in his *Appeasement and All Souls*, at 2, n. 4.

appeasement – suggests otherwise. Neville Chamberlain visited the College just
once: this for Encaenia luncheon after accepting an honorary degree from the
University, in 1933. That award drew him no closer to Oxford. A worthy
graduate of Mason College, he adopted the University of Birmingham for his
own and sent his son to Cambridge.[55] Nor did Churchill find much succour
there, even amongst Rowse's vigorous, anti-Nazi, youth. He also visited All Souls
just once, in October 1935. Characteristically, he both lunched and dined there
that day. In between, he unveiled a plaque to T. E. Lawrence at the City of
Oxford Boys School.[56] None of this should surprise us. Certainly none of it
reflected badly on either Chamberlain or Churchill. The College during those
years was altogether more of a fellows' haunt than an outsider's delight. Before the
war, there were no regular guest nights. But there were gaudies. These were famously
raucous get-togethers of continuing and former fellows. No doubt, little effort of
the imagination is required to presume that this was when Halifax, Simon, and
Dawson also got together and talked of buying off Hitler. If so, the ordinary
imagination fails us once again. College kitchen books faithfully record that the
three coincided at dinner just *twice* between January 1933 and 3 September 1939:
first on the occasion of Warden Adams's elevation; then after the election of O'Neill
and Woozley to Prize Fellowships on 2 November 1935.[57] More strikingly still,
they show that during those six-and-a-half years Halifax visited the College on just
ten occasions in total. Simon made twenty-two visits, adding up to twenty-eight
days in residence. Only Dawson, with seventy-eight days from fifty-one visits, was
in any sense a 'regular' during the 1930s.[58]

To be sure, All Souls' grandees did not have to meet in order to communicate.
There was a remarkably good postal service in those days. However, Dawson's
papers actually reveal how little he corresponded with either Halifax or Simon.
Still, they could talk. Friends often do. But these three were friendly only to a
very limited degree. Neither Halifax nor Dawson was close to Simon. To be fair,
few of his contemporaries were. Simon was not a man who inspired much
intimacy amongst those who knew him.[59] There was another problem. Halifax
(quite unambiguously) and Dawson (anyway, by Simon's standards) were men of

---

[55] Wenden, 'Appeasement and All Souls', 21; R. Self, *Neville Chamberlain: A Biography*
(London, 2006), 21, deals cursorily with Chamberlain's education; D. Dilks, *Neville Chamberlain*,
vol. 1: *Pioneering and Reform, 1869–1929* (Cambridge, 1984), 23–4 and 26–34, is a little more
informative. Frank Chamberlain (1914–65), Neville's second child and only son, was educated at
Winchester (not Rugby) before university.

[56] Wenden, 'Appeasement and All Souls', 21; M. Gilbert, *Winston S. Churchill*, vol. 5: *1922–
1939* (London, 1976), 789. Interestingly, he had a 'friendly talk...with Geoffrey Dawson' that
evening, 3 Oct. 1935.

[57] Wenden, 'Appeasement and All Souls', 6. The original materials on which Wenden based this
account have since disappeared. But there is no need to doubt the veracity of his findings.

[58] Wenden, 'Appeasement and All Souls', 6; Wrench, *Geoffrey Dawson*, 382, makes the point that
his 'frequent visits' to Oxford in 1938 were as frequently visits to Magdalen as to All Souls.

[59] Compare Cretney, this volume. Dutton, *Simon*, ch. 13, offers a chapter-length exploration of
this theme, with comments from Halifax (p. 324) and Amery (p. 325) along the way. Amery's

rank and estates. Simon was neither. He did not join them at shooting parties on the Dales. By the same token, both Halifax and Dawson were devoted fellows of Eton. They were also parents of pupils at that august institution. Indeed, they met more frequently there than at All Souls.[60] Simon was a scholarship boy from Fettes; his children were educated elsewhere.[61] Moreover, Halifax had no particular reason to seek out his Chancellor's company, other than when strictly necessary. Their rather unhappy earlier experience as colleagues, particularly over Indian matters, suggested that this might be very rarely indeed. So it proved. Dawson had no need of Simon's society at all. Until 1937, he was a close friend of the Prime Minister. And in Halifax, he had a collegiate colleague and clubland comrade.[62]

Yet Halifax's relations with Dawson were never quite as close as some reckoned. Unsympathetic critics took Dawson for Halifax's poodle. Wenden quotes Oliver Harvey remarking, early in 1938, that Dawson 'will do whatever H[alifax] tells him'. This was not true. Indeed, it proved dramatically false during September that year. But Harvey's observations were not merely mistaken. They reveal a very poor understanding of the man. Dawson undoubtedly respected Halifax. But he was not in the least overawed by him. It is quite impossible to conceive of him, as Harvey imagined, 'eat[ing] out of [the Foreign Secretary's] hand'.[63] Dawson may have been Halifax's social inferior. He was, of course, less politically prominent. He was scarcely uninfluential. No one had better contacts. And in their small world where these things mattered, he was the former Viceroy's academic senior. He was also more conventionally learned than his fellow Mallardian. Dawson was a distinguished classicist; Halifax a mere modern historian. There was one final difference, more important than all the others. Dawson was a protégé of the Kindergarten. In common with all his fellow Milnerites, he bowed to just one man in his life: first to the near numinous presence and then to the revered memory of H. E. himself. He acknowledged no one else in such terms.[64] Loyalty to the brotherhood demanded nothing less.[65]

'Memorial Address' is collected in P. Fraser (ed.), *The Memorial Addresses of All Souls College, Oxford* (Oxford, 1989), 18–22.

[60] Wenden, 'Appeasement and All Souls', 8.

[61] Lovingly described in Simon, *Retrospect*, at 24–31; see also Dutton, *Simon*, 6–7.

[62] See Halifax's 'Foreword' to Wrench, *Geoffrey Dawson*, 11–13; also Halifax, *Fulness of Days*, 176ff. For a modern version, see R. Cockett, *Twilight of the Truth: Chamberlain, Appeasement and the Manipulation of the Press* (London, 1989), 12–13.

[63] Wenden, 'Appeasement and All Souls', 7; J. Harvey (ed.), *The Diplomatic Diaries of Oliver Harvey, 1937–1940* (London, 1970), 115 and 140, entries for 12 Mar. 1938 and 19 May 1940. Perhaps he was only willing to eat out of the Prime Minister's hand. For one instance, anyway interpreted as such, see D. Dilks (ed.), *The Diaries of Sir Alexander Cadogan, 1938–1945* (London, 1971), 146, entry for 31 Jan. 1939.

[64] Wrench, *Geoffrey Dawson*, ch. 4, also pp. 461–3. For another perspective, see J. Marlowe, *Milner: Apostle of Empire* (London, 1976), ch. 10; compare also Howard, this volume.

[65] Wenden, 'Appeasement and All Souls', 8. Ironically, that loyalty was long unsympathetically interpreted as another reason for Dawson's alleged 'pro-Germanism'; see A. J. P. Taylor, *English*

If Boothby was just cavalier and ignorant, Rowse was more subtly self-deceiving. *All Souls and Appeasement* purported to be a memoir. It was no such thing. It constituted a subtle rewriting of history. More to the point, it projected a subtle rewriting of Rowse's personal history. This is not to suggest that it was merely a fantasy. Of *his* frequent presence in All Souls during the relevant years, there can be not the slightest doubt. The Kitchen Books for 1934–9 reveal that only his (then) fellow bachelor Salter was resident more often in College during those years.[66] Whether this made him a reliable witness to what went on within its walls at that time is a quite different matter. Whether it induced him to give a faithful account of his role in those proceedings is another matter again. Commenting on the scholarly foundations of *All Souls and Appeasement*, Wenden observed that some three-quarters of the footnotes in a lightly annotated work referred to just five works: Tom Jones's *Diary with Letters*; *The History of the Times, 1921–1948*, pt. 2; Wrench's *Life* of Dawson; Halifax's slim autobiography, *Fulness of Days*, and the third volume of Leo Amery's *My Political Life*.[67] But none of those was (or is) an especially fruitful source for this subject. Consequently, Rowse's account relied mainly on his own diary. This was then wholly unreferenced, and anyway unavailable. Other historians long had to take its supposed riches on trust. What that meant was that they had to trust the fidelity of Rowse's subsequent selections from the wealth of material it ostensibly furnished.[68]

This was even true of Wenden. Rowse's diaries were not open to him at the time of his writing.[69] Had he been able to consult them, he might have been surprised at some of their contents. He might also have found answers to questions that have long puzzled other thoughtful readers of Rowse's strident account. For it is, in truth, a very strange history of 'All Souls and Appeasement'. Indeed, it scarcely furnishes any narrative at all for the years 1933 to 1939. This is true not just of the College. From a man not naturally given to reticence, it is also rather oddly unspecific about Rowse's own activities, especially in relation to the policy of appeasement. About committees organized, meetings attended, speeches given – similarly, of tracts published, conversations recalled, thoughts committed

---

History, 1914–1945 (Oxford, 1965), 417–18. For once, Taylor's otherwise salutary scepticism seems to have failed him.

[66] Wenden, 'Appeasement and All Souls', 13. Salter belatedly married in 1940. Rowse remained single. Some of the reasons why were hinted at in A. L. Rowse, *Homosexuals in History: A Study of Ambivalence in Society, Literature and the Arts* (London, 1977). See esp. 'Preface', p. xi, para. 1.

[67] Wenden, 'Appeasement and All Souls', 2–3; a point earlier made by Joll, 'The Ride to the Abyss', at 564.

[68] Above all, through its deployment in Rowse's running autobiography. See, esp. A. L. Rowse, *A Cornishman at Oxford* (London, 1965), ch. 9; idem, *A Cornishman Abroad* (London, 1976), esp. chs 2–4, 8, and 9; finally, his *A Man of the Thirties* (London, 1979), *passim*.

[69] Wenden's lecture was delivered in 1990. He died in 1992. Rowse (1903–97) outlived him. His diaries were bequeathed to Exeter University Library on his death. Good sense on the difficulties involved in their use is conveyed by P. Payton, *A. L. Rowse and Cornwall* (Exeter, 2005), pp. ix–x.

to memory – there is remarkably little in the text. There is a reason for these omissions. Rowse led no one in the battle against appeasement. More: he never even tried to do so. With the exception of a few letters to *The Times* and other newspapers between 1935 and 1939, he took little or no part in the public debate over appeasement. Indeed, he was effectively inactive in public affairs for much of the relevant period.[70]

This is odder than it may first seem. For anyone who knew Rowse only in his later years, it can come as a surprise to learn that he was the official Labour Party candidate for Falmouth at the General Elections of 1931 and 1935. Indeed, he remained its Prospective Parliamentary Candidate until 1943. He would have won in 1945. He always insisted that Ernest Bevin had putatively offered him a place in a future Labour cabinet. It might be best not to ponder that possibility.[71] It is, however, important to recall the kind of political figure that Rowse had become by the time of the publication of *All Souls and Appeasement*. In 1961, he was a thoroughgoing 'Churchillian'. Once a Marxist, long a Labour party supporter, he had come during the war and after to a view of English history and society which self-consciously paralleled that of Sir Winston Churchill himself. This was Whig by way of long-term analysis, imperialist in its contemporary concerns, and transatlantic for future aspiration.[72] It made Rowse politically conservative in a way that would have been unthinkable prior to 1945. Indeed it rendered him something of a reactionary in an age of decolonization, especially after Suez. Above all, it compelled him to assume a specifically anti-Baldwinian view of the international politics of the 1930s. For all practical purposes, this transformation left Rowse politically 'high and dry' thirty years later, an increasingly absurd anachronism in the age of 'Cool Britannia'. Historically, it created if anything an even greater problem still. For what he had

---

[70] A. L. Rowse, 'Abyssinia and Italy', *The Times*, 1 Oct. 1935, 10; idem, 'The Future of British Foreign Policy', 17 July 1936, 10; idem, 'British Foreign Policy: A Labour View', 23 Aug. 1937, 15; idem, 'British Foreign Policy: Mr Rowse's Reply', 3 Sept. 1937; idem, 'The Spanish Civil War: a Plea for Intervention', 16 Mar. 1938, 10. The views expressed in these letters are of considerable interest in themselves. It is less clear that they represented the whole truth of Rowse's opinions at this time. Hence the extensive use made of his contemporary diaries below.

[71] A. L. Rowse, *All Souls and Appeasement*, 22–3 and 70, offers a few hints for those capable of reading between the lines.

[72] R. Ollard, *A Man of Contradictions: A Life of A. L. Rowse* (London, 1999), 72, 86, 90, 277, 283, and 298. Payton, *A. L. Rowse and Cornwall*, 154, however, makes clear his ambivalent attitudes – that is, the degree to which he had already become a 'Churchillian' – by 1945. On the broader theme, compare Rowse, 'Mr Churchill and English History', with idem, *The Early Churchills: An English Family* (London, 1956), esp. 'Preface', p. vii; and also idem, *The Later Churchills* (London, 1958), 'Preface', pp. vi–ix and chs 11–15, esp. 15. The connection between these two books and *All Souls and Appeasement* is very clear, but rarely commented upon. Rowse's developing transatlanticism is well brought out in his Trevelyan Lectures for 1958, published as *The Elizabethans and America* (London, 1959). See esp. the 'Preface', at pp. vii–viii, and also chs 1–2. Churchill's philosophy of history is summarized in J. H. Plumb, 'The Historian', *Churchill: Four Faces and the Man* (London, 1969), 117–51, and dissected in A. Valiunas, *Churchill's Military Histories: A Rhetorical Study* (Lanham, MD, 2002), esp. chs 3–6.

become bore little resemblance to what he had been. Worse still, it made precious little sense of what he had once done. It also made precious little sense of what he had done and said during the fateful decade of 'appeasement'. A bit of creative rewriting was thus in order. This was what he attempted in *All Souls and Appeasement*.

So the self-conscious anachronism of his later persona belied the man of action during the 1920s. In the same way, the 'contemporary historian' of the early 1960s carefully covered the tracks of his political past. The older man now posed as a left-wing Churchillian of the 1930s. *All Souls and Appeasement* is, above all, a Churchillian treatise. It argues the Churchillian case against British policy during those years. That was then perfectly plausible. It also insists on Rowse's sympathy with that case during these years. This is largely false. But the book is no simple pack of lies. The improbable reinvention of himself that it entailed was rendered paradoxically plausible by Rowse's effective political disengagement after 1935. He was able to rewrite his own, personal, history of appeasement precisely because there was relatively little in the contemporary record to revise. Most of it could just be filled in with subsequent self-justification. Rowse had indeed been a highly active figure both in Labour Party politics, and international socialism more generally, up to that date. He entered active parliamentary politics shortly after becoming a Prize Fellow of All Souls, in 1925.[73] But disappointment and illness gradually sapped his enthusiasm for active politics. This was perhaps not obviously apparent. Only by reading his diaries – or rather by consulting the motley collection of notebooks and other jottings that represent his 'diary' for those subsequent years – can the historian become aware of this abrupt depart-ure. Ollard's careful editing of the published version covers over the most obvious ruptures in his social commitments.[74] But it also makes next to nothing of their underlying cause. This was clear enough, all the same. It should be bluntly stated: Rowse's famous and frequent repudiation of the 'idiot people' began with their 'foolish' rejection of him: first in 1931, then again in 1935.[75]

Let us leave all the various psychological explanations for that reaction to one side. We are interested here only in their political consequences. These were strange enough. By 1935, Rowse had come to combine a continuing intellectual commitment to Marxism with an ever-increasing anti-populism. The first he had consciously acquired shortly after his election to All Souls.[76] The latter crept up

---

[73] Payton, *A. L. Rowse and Cornwall*, 102–6.

[74] R. Ollard (ed.), *The Diaries of A. L. Rowse* (London, 2003), 61–116.

[75] Exeter University Library [EUL], MS 113/2/1/9, A. L. Rowse, 'Diary in Notebook', 23 Mar. 1929–28 Dec. 1935; an entry for 4 Nov. 1932 refers to 'my increasing disillusionment with politics . . . and the people . . . poor fools; half of them voted for the National Government. I have never forgiven them for that; nor shall I.' EUL, MS 113/2/1/10b, Rowse, MS diary, March 1935–April 1939, entry for 28 June 1939: 'What is to be done with a people of idiots? They have . . . ruined my pleasure in politics.'

[76] EUL, MS 113/2/1/5b, Rowse, MS diary, October 1925–November 1925, entry for 18 Nov. 1925: 'I am going to read Marx's *Capital* during the vac; I intend to make myself a proficient Marxist . . . during the next five years.'

on him as a result of continual electoral frustration.[77] The two converged in the years immediately prior to the outbreak of war.[78] The curious effect was not always made clear in his few public pronouncements after that date. Even Ollard's otherwise judicious selections of the material never quite do justice to the product of this striking combination. But it was only through their concurrence that Rowse was able to insist that it was 'international ... capitalism' which had caused the 'irruption of Nazism in Europe' (note the generality of that observation); simultaneously, to berate 'the bloody fools of the working classes' who had been taken in, alternatively by 'it' or 'them' (seldom actually specified).[79] These fairly typical commentaries on current events date from March and April 1935, respectively. Their importance for our purposes cannot be overstated. For it was also through what might be called the political theory of democratic centralism as applied to international politics – he was a combative apologist for Lenin throughout – that Rowse was able to interpret *both* German aggression and British defensiveness during the late 1930s to his own, self-evident, satisfaction.[80]

This is crucial. It illuminates much that would otherwise remain deeply obscure. First, it establishes what it was that Rowse took himself to be witnessing *at the time*. That he took to be what he called the painful 'passing of appeasement' [sic] throughout the industrial world. Note the term. Like many of his generation, Rowse then used 'appeasement' non-pejoratively. In later years, when he revisited his diary, he often crossed out the offending word, usually to be found between 'moderate' and 'civilisation' or some such other admirable epithet – and invariably attributed to worthy souls only – in order to replace it with the word 'peace'. But he did so only in later years. His contemporary, that is, his pre-1939 presupposition was that 'appeasement' (or peace) was a good thing.[81] However, it was also, he believed, a very rare thing. Indeed, he insisted that it was possible only under conditions of 'true internationalism', more specifically, as a result of 'socialism'.[82] This, to Rowse at least, was something that might actually have been possible between 1929 and 1931.[83] Europe, he then argued, might have

[77] EUL, MS 113/2/1/10b, Rowse, MS diary, March 1935–August 1939, entry for 17 June 1936: 'The National Government is a government of fraud, by fraud, for frauds.'

[78] EUL, MS 113/2/1/10b, Rowse, MS diary, March 1935–August 1939, entry for 11 Apr. 1935: 'This is what we have come to ... This is the world they have made for us to live in. The bloody upper classes, the bloody middle classes, the bloody fools of the working classes who have been taken in by them ... We have been defeated by them: they now have things their way.'

[79] EUL, MS 113/2/1/10b, Rowse, MS diary, March 1935–August 1939, entries for 23 Mar. 1935; 11 Apr. 1935.

[80] EUL, MS 113/2/1/10b, Rowse, MS diary, 1933–4 (actually, 1933–8), entry for 28 Jan. 1936: 'Lenin made the revolution ... embody[ing] the hopes and aspirations of his people.'

[81] EUL, MS 113/2/1/10b, Rowse, MS diary, March 1935–August 1939, entry for 23 Mar. 1935: 'The monied rule the world ... They have defeated and crushed, in practically every country, the people who [like me] believed in moderation, appeasement and civilisation.'

[82] Ibid.

[83] EUL, MS 113/2/1/9, Rowse, Diary in Notebook, 23 Mar. 1929–28 Dec. 1935, entry for 4 Dec. 1932: '1929–1931 was a chance for some of us.'

come together as a whole and in peace through a rapprochement between left-leaning governments in the West and the great Marxist experiment in the East. By 1935 at the very latest, he had come to the view that this opportunity was now finally gone. In Britain, a Labour government had been illegitimately removed from power.[84] In Germany, a liberal republic had been allowed to fall.[85] And, for the West generally, the lifeline of a Soviet alliance had seemingly been lost forever.[86]

What now remained was a world of 'sovereign capitalist states'.[87] The logical and final consequence of their natural rivalry was war. ('Come, come', Wood-ward once responded, 'none of those bad jokes of the 1890s').[88] What in the interim flowed from their continued and egregious existence was something that Rowse defined as 'the internationalism of the governing classes'.[89] By it, he meant to identify the reassertion of a narrow-minded, bourgeois, rule in the liberal democracies. This was bad enough in itself. But it also entailed craven conces-sions to Hitler and Mussolini and the other dictators. That, he believed, was perpetuated in the vain hope of sustaining anti-socialist régimes throughout Europe. Yet it had – or soon would have – the certain consequence of making war – and with it defeat, more particularly defeat for the British Empire – much more likely. As a result, Rowse supported British 'rearmament' from 1937 onwards. This was, he acknowledged 'probably necessary'.[90] But he did so only in recognition of it as the superficial treatment for a malignant disease. The real cure to the underlying problem, he insisted, still lay in international socialism; this would be, in his own words, the 'only formulation for peace'.[91] War would follow, as night followed day, if, contrary to all logic and every hope of progress, the people continued to opt for the rule of 'their governing classes, their capitalists, their fascists'.[92]

The problem, of course, was they repeatedly had done just that. This both dismayed and infuriated him: 'I have never forgiven them for that; nor shall I.'[93]

---

[84] EUL, MS 113/2/3, Rowse, Pocket Notebooks, 1920s–1940s, entry for Good Friday, April 1938: 'The British governing classes . . . kicked the Labour Party out in 1931.'

[85] Ibid., entry for 27 Oct. 1938: 'International collaboration [might] have made it possible for a decent Germany to survive. But now there is an internationalism of the governing classes making every concession to Hitler and Mussolini.'

[86] Rowse, 'Future of British Foreign Policy'; idem, 'British Foreign Policy: A Labour View'; idem, 'British Foreign Policy: Mr Rowse's Reply'.

[87] EUL, MS 113/2/1/10b, Rowse, MS diary, March 1935–August 1939, entry for 5 Mar. 1937.

[88] EUL, MS 113/2/1/10b, Rowse, MS diary, March 1935–August 1939, entry for 5 Mar. 1937; cited in Aster (ed.), *Appeasement and All Souls*, at 69.

[89] EUL, MS 113/2/3, Rowse, Pocket Notebooks, 1920s–1940s, entry for 27 Oct. 1938.

[90] EUL, MS 113/2/1/10b, Rowse, MS diary, March 1935–August 1939, entry for 5 Mar. 1937; see also Rowse, 'British Foreign Policy: A Labour View'.

[91] EUL, MS 113/2/1/10b, Rowse, MS diary, March 1935–August 1939, entry for 23 Mar. 1935.

[92] EUL, MS 113/2/1/10b, Rowse, MS diary, March 1935–August 1939, entry for 5 Mar. 1937.

[93] EUL, MS 113/2/1/9, Rowse, Diary in Notebook, 23 Mar. 1929–28 Dec. 1935, entry for 4 Nov. 1932.

It also explains his response to the events of 1935 and beyond. What he did was to pronounce his increasing detachment from the collective fate of both the pre-war ruling classes and their ever more supplicant populations. By the outbreak of war, this self-conscious exercise in internal exile had come very close to completion. Indeed, during the Oxford by-election of October 1938, Rowse declined to campaign for Lindsay against Hogg. As he put it: 'Thank God that I at any rate didn't waste any time trying to persuade an idiot vote.'[94] Naturally, 'Quintin's (hollow) victory' only reminded him, 'as if I were ever likely to forget – that people are always and everywhere fools'.[95]

Not content simply to observe the fact, he now set himself the more intellectually demanding task of understanding the broader phenomenon. As early as 1936, this idiosyncratic project had already acquired some rather striking dimensions. That very year he turned to the study of anthropology: 'since people are the idiots they are it is just as well to study them in the raw'. This academic flight of fancy eventually wrought surprisingly beneficial – indeed pioneering – consequences for his later, historical, studies of sixteenth-century religion and popular reactions to the Reformation in *Tudor Cornwall*.[96] Whether it made for a sensible understanding of the events of the 1930s must still be doubted. There is no need to sympathize with Woodward's rather complacent put down in order to question Rowse's grip on contemporary events. More sympathetic observers than the hated 'Abbé' increasingly came to the conclusion that Rowse was describing a very different world from the one they could actually see.[97] Indeed, his self-conscious detachment from mundane realities not only deprived him of much of the political prescience he subsequently claimed. It occasionally entailed contemporaneous error of truly heroic proportions. Observing the accession of Edward VIII in January 1936, Rowse remarked only that: 'Personally, it pleases me to have a king who like Herr Hitler is a bachelor...no nonsense about marriage.'[98]

II

Boothby's superficial slights and Rowse's contemporary self-absorption long blinded later chroniclers to most of what actually did go on in All Souls during

[94] EUL, MS 113/2/3, Rowse, Pocket Notebooks, 1920s–1940s, entry for 27 Oct. 1938.
[95] Ibid.
[96] EUL, MS 113/2/1/10b, Rowse, MS diary, March 1935–August 1939, entry for 29 Apr. 1936. For the finished product, see Rowse, *Tudor Cornwall: Portrait of a Society* (London, 1941), esp. chs 8–9, 11–12, 14, 16.
[97] EUL, MS 113/2/1/10b, Rowse, MS diary, March 1935–August 1939, entry for 5 Mar. 1937. Even Rowse's own diary records a similar reaction from Salter, with whom Rowse maintained cordial relations at the time; see Ollard (ed.), *The Diaries of A. L. Rowse*, 110–11. Nor should Rowse's lifelong antipathy to Woodward pass unchallenged. For a more sympathetic view, see R. Butler, 'Sir Llewellyn Woodward', *Proceedings of the British Academy*, 57 (1971), 497–511.
[98] EUL, MS 113/2/1/10b, Rowse, MS diary, 1933–4 (actually, 1933–8), entry for 23 Jan. 1936.

the crucial years after 1937. Not so Wenden. He succeeded in piecing together an account of Professor Arthur Salter's 'Foreign Affairs Seminar', which ran in All Souls during the winter and spring of 1937–8.[99] This was a genuinely important contemporary exercise in the interpretation and influence of international relations. Yet it is only briefly mentioned in the Gladstone Professor's memoirs.[100] It also features in Liddell Hart's autobiography.[101] But until Wenden stumbled on a significant batch of surviving papers, first seemingly preserved by Harold Nicolson, and then anonymously deposited in the archive at King's College, London, it had defied all attempts at serious historical investigation.[102] Wenden's pioneering labours remain sadly unpublished. They have since been superseded by Sidney Aster's detailed reconstruction of the whole episode. His *Portrait with Documents* furnishes an admirably scholarly account.[103] No attempt will be made here to reproduce its arguments, still less to match their illustrative corroboration.[104] What might still be of value is to place these discussions into some sort of College context. After all, there would have been no seminar – certainly not what became affectionately known as 'Salter's Soviet' – but for Salter and, by extension, for All Souls.[105]

Sir Arthur Salter was appointed Gladstone Professor of Political Theory and Institutions at Oxford in 1934. His chair was attached, ex officio, to the College.[106] An excellent classicist as a young man, Salter's career up to that point had been pursued almost entirely as a civil servant, latterly as a distinguished international administrator.[107] For all that, his preferment occasioned less surprise than might subsequently have been the case. The Gladstone Chair, certainly as then conceived, presumed an intimate connection between academic activity and public service. This made Salter a respectable, if not a universally popular, appointment.[108] Both his previous and subsequent published work were

---

[99] Wenden, 'Appeasement and All Souls', 14–21.

[100] A. Salter, *Slave of the Lamp: A Public Servant's Notebook* (London, 1967), ch. 10, esp. pp. 130–2. Interestingly, it is all but omitted from his earlier book, *Memoirs of a Public Servant* (London, 1961).

[101] B. Liddell Hart, *Memoirs*, vol. 2 (London, 1965), 150. The episode passes completely unrecorded – Salter is absent even from the index – in A. Danchev, *Alchemist of War: The Life of Basil Liddell Hart* (London, 1998).

[102] Wenden, 'Appeasement and All Souls', *passim*; Aster (ed.), *Appeasement and All Souls*, 2–3.

[103] Aster (ed.), *Appeasement and All Souls*; see esp. 1–3 and 243–4 on his collection and organization of this material. I have attempted to quote from this source, wherever possible, below.

[104] In any case, these were anticipated by his own ' "Salter's Soviet" ' in M. Graham Fry (ed.), *Power, Personalities and Policies: Essays in Honour of Donald Cameron Watt* (London, 1992), 117–39.

[105] Liddell Hart, *Memoirs*, ii. 150: '[I]t embraced a wide range of views, specialist and political – even though Arch-Conservatives called it "Salter's Soviet", while others criticized it, with more justice, for not including anyone of definitely left-wing views.'

[106] Salter, *Memoirs of a Public Servant*, 238ff.; idem, *Slave of the Lamp*, 129ff.; Denis Rickett 'Salter (James) Arthur, Baron Salter (1881–1975)', rev., *ODNB*.

[107] Salter, *Memoirs of a Public Servant*, chs 7–10; idem, *Slave of the Lamp*, chs 6–8; A. L. Rowse, *All Souls in My Time* (London, 1993), 110–11.

[108] H. Hardy (ed.), *Isaiah Berlin: Flourishing, Letters 1928–1946* (London, 2004), 125 and 199, and Rowse, *All Souls in My Time*, 110–11, offer contemporary and subsequent evidence of a certain condescension in All Souls against one so practically minded.

of largely a practical bent.[109] He also combined his professorial duties with the office of Member of Parliament for Oxford University after 1937.[110] From the start, he was intent not simply upon teaching politics in Oxford but also influencing events as they unfolded, both home and abroad. In this respect at least, he had certain advantages. He was both well-connected and genial. He was also a good organizer. Most important of all, he was rarely deterred by failure. The idea of the foreign policy seminar originated in his so-called 'Next Five-Year Group': a standing conference organized specifically for the purpose of bringing academic and non-academic figures together, in All Souls, to discuss public affairs. The first series concentrated almost entirely on domestic matters. Its professed goal was to forge a 'New Deal' for British politics, albeit one conceived very much after an English, parliamentary, fashion. It even published a report, in 1935, edited by Salter and supported by over a hundred leading luminaries including Clifford Allen, Norman Angell, Geoffrey Crowther, Julian Huxley, and Harold Macmillan. Like most of its kind, this came to nothing.[111]

No matter. Salter continued his labours. More shrewdly, he also redefined them. Concerned by the deteriorating international situation in 1936 and 1937, he now invited his friends to turn their thoughts to Europe: more specifically, to formulate credible views about how Britain should deal with the dictators.[112] A select few first convened in All Souls on 18–19 December 1937.[113] What became 'the Group' subsequently met on nine occasions, twice in London, but more usually in College, until 15 May 1938.[114] Two further meetings, planned for 5–6 June and 16 July that year, were cancelled.[115] Salter invariably acted as a convenor. Clifford Allen served as his chairman.[116] The first party included Curtis, Hodson, Hudson, and Radcliffe-Brown from the College; also Norman Angell, Basil Liddell Hart, Harold Macmillan, Gilbert Murray, Harold Nicolson, and Arnold Toynbee, drawn from the wider world. A young Guy Wint acted as Salter's informal secretary; so informally, that he seemingly kept no official

---

[109] Post-1934, these included: *World Trade and Its Future* (Philadelphia, 1936), *Security: Can We Retrieve It?* (London, 1939), and *Personality in Politics: Studies of Contemporary Statesmen* (London, 1947).

[110] Salter, *Memoirs of a Public Servant*, ch. 13; B. Harrison, 'Politics', in idem (ed.), *Hist. Univ. Oxf.*, viii, ch. 14, at 379–80.

[111] Salter, *Slave of the Lamp*, 130–1; H. Macmillan, *Winds of Change, 1914–1939* (London, 1966), 374–6.

[112] Salter, *Slave of the Lamp*, 131–2; Aster (ed.), *Appeasement and All Souls*, 2–3.

[113] Aster (ed.), *Appeasement and All Souls*, 21–8 (Liddell Hart Papers, LH5/1; locations of manuscript collections drawn on by Aster are given in his Acknowledgements).

[114] Specifically, on: 15–16 Jan. 1938, 6 Feb. 1938, 26 Feb. 1938, 8 Mar. 1938, 16 Mar. 1938, 23 Mar. 1938, 31 Mar. 1938, 24 Apr. 1938, 15 May 1938.

[115] Aster (ed.), *Appeasement and All Souls*, 17. This paper was circulated, however: 'Memorandum on Czechoslovakia', 8 June 1938, and 'Memorandum by J. A. Spender', January 1938, enclosures in Christina Hole to All Souls Group, 29 June 1938 (Liddell Hart Papers, LH5/1).

[116] Aster (ed.), *Appeasement and All Souls*, 2–6; David Howell, 'Allen, (Reginald) Clifford, Baron Allen of Hurtwood (1889–1939)', *ODNB*.

minutes. Certainly no formal record of its business survived. Hence the delay in historical investigation of its significance.[117]

Whatever else, it was, 'Salter's Soviet' was no collection of Chamberlainite sycophants. To the degree that it was initially remembered at all – largely through the self-serving recollections of participating members – it came to be understood as something close to the opposite.[118] But that was not really true. In neither organization nor ethos was the group ever cast in explicit, or even implicit, opposition either to the government of the day, or indeed to the public activities of the College's grandees.[119] This was for the simple reason that neither was then conceived of in disreputable terms. There was no reason why they should have been. Recall that it was Dawson's crushing leader that, perhaps more than anything else, had brought down Samuel Hoare, and with it the Hoare–Laval pact, in December 1935.[120] By the same token, All Souls' imperialists were by no means opposed to Chamberlain's way of thinking about Anglo-German relations *before* Munich. Amery, for one, regarded the Premier's repudiation of the doctrine of collective security in the wake of Eden's resignation in February 1938 as a positively admirable departure: 'the first breath of fresh air on the government bench for many long years'.[121]

Indeed, what struck most contemporaries about Chamberlain's foreign policy from 22 February 1938 onwards was not its timidity but rather its boldness.[122] The majority of analysts both within and beyond Salter's group saw it as constituting a clean break with earlier ideas about collective security.[123] That made it controversial.[124] But few, anyway before September 1938, regarded it as remotely pusillanimous.[125] Discussion at All Souls usually concentrated on the considerable risks involved in Chamberlain's insistence upon bilateral relations, with both Mussolini and Hitler.[126] Some of the group tended to favour this

[117] Aster (ed.), *Appeasement and All Souls*, 2–3; Wint achieved considerable (posthumous) fame as the joint author (with Peter Calvocaressi) of *Total War: Causes and Consequences of the Second World War* (London, 1972).

[118] Macmillan, *Winds of Change*, 374–6; Liddell Hart, *Memoirs*, ii. 150; Rose, *The Cliveden Set*, 185–6.

[119] Aster (ed.), *Appeasement and All Souls*, 3ff. and 70–80; Salter, 'Notes on Foreign Policy', 8 Mar. 1938 (Liddell Hart Papers, LH5/1).

[120] Leader, 'A Corridor for Camels', *The Times*, 16 Dec. 1935, 15; Wrench, *Geoffrey Dawson*, 325–7, recounts the rest of the story.

[121] Barnes and Nicholson (eds), *The Empire at Bay*, 457, entry for 22 Feb. 1938. Amery specifically referred to 'Collective security . . . as [now] dead and . . . a dangerous sham.'

[122] Ibid., 457–8.

[123] Aster (ed.), *Appeasement and All Souls*, 56–62; Foreign Affairs Group, 26 Feb. 1938 (Liddell Hart Papers, LH5/1).

[124] Ibid. This may have been overstated. For a more 'evolutionary' interpretation of events, see D. Dilks, '"We Must Hope for the Best and Prepare for the Worst": The Prime Minister, The Cabinet and Hitler's Germany', *Proceedings of the British Academy*, 73 (1987), 309–52, at 323ff.

[125] Aster (ed.), *Appeasement and All Souls*, 104–5; Lord Allen, 'Foreign Policy Now' (Liddell Hart Papers, LH5/1), offers the fullest statement of this view.

[126] Aster (ed.), *Appeasement and All Souls*, 55ff.; Harold Nicolson Diaries (Nicolson Papers), 26 Feb. 1938; Foreign Affairs Group, 26 Feb. 1938 (Liddell Hart Papers, LH5/1).

departure. Others were more cautious.[127] In that way, its discussions self-consciously reflected the full range of reasonable opinions concerning Britain's foreign relations during the 1930s. All of these arguments embraced some dimension of what would now be called appeasement. That should not in the least surprise us. This was because 'everyone was an appeaser somewhere'.[128] No one wanted war simultaneously with all the Axis powers. When it did befall the British Empire at the end of 1941, it proved fatal.[129] Moreover, everyone was an appeaser *somehow*. No one advocated immediate and unconditional hostilities against any foreign power, not even Nazi Germany. For all that, every serious student of Britain's foreign relations also took cognizance of the possible necessity for resistance, the need for rearmament, and the fine line to be drawn between settlement and disagreement.[130] Indeed, it is often very difficult to distinguish amongst so many academic and political practitioners, expressing so many different opinions, simply by dividing the protagonists between those who would subsequently be considered as 'appeasers' and those who would be granted retrospective laurels as 'anti-appeasers'. It may even be a mistake.[131]

This was true of the politicians. It was certainly true of *all* the mainstream politicians. No one, not even Churchill, eventually boasted a more consistent record of opposing Chamberlain's policies than 'Bobbety' Cranborne.[132] He, almost alone, advocated an American alliance and the repudiation of *all* the dictators from late 1937.[133] He, largely unaided, engineered Anthony Eden's (actually rather reluctant) resignation, following Chamberlain's rapprochement with Mussolini, in February 1938.[134] Finally, he delivered what was by far the most damning contemporary indictment of Munich.[135] Yet it is worth

---

[127] Aster (ed.), *Appeasement and All Souls*, 64ff.; Allen to Curtis, 1 Mar. 1938 (MS Curtis 12, ff. 36–8), notes the differences and his (Allen's) own proposal for a 'transitional' policy, somewhere between the two. See also Rose, *The Cliveden Set*, 185–6.

[128] I owe this phrase to Professor David Dilks. See also his ' "We Must Hope for the Best and Prepare for the Worst" ', at 318ff. Neville, *Hitler and Appeasement*, ch. 5, offers a succinct account of the Italian and Japanese dimension to the problem. The whole issue is unforgettably treated in J. Gallagher, *The Decline, Revival and Fall of the British Empire* (Cambridge, 1982), 129–41.

[129] Taylor, *English History*, 540: 'In England, 10th December 1941 was the darkest day of the war.'

[130] W. N. Medlicott, *Britain and Germany: The Search for Agreement, 1930–1937* (London, 1969), 32; Dilks, ' "We Must Hope for the Best and Prepare for the Worst" ', 318ff.

[131] Medlicott, *Britain and Germany*, 32; Wenden, 'Appeasement and All Souls', 4; Aster (ed.), *Appeasement and All Souls*, 18–19.

[132] Simon Ball, *The Guardsmen: Harold Macmillan, Three Friends and the World They Made* (London, 2004), chs 4–6, offers the best account of Cranborne's evolving views on the matter. There is still no life of 'Bobbety' Cecil, fifth Marquis of Salisbury. This constitutes a major gap in modern British historiography. In the interim, see D. Goldsworthy, 'Cecil, Robert Arthur James Gascoyne – fifth Marquess of Salisbury (1893–1972)', *ODNB*, at p. 759. Whether either or both of these accounts establish that even Cranborne was entirely consistent in this matter is a different question. I am grateful to Professor Vernon Bogdanor for suggesting an appropriate scepticism in this matter.

[133] Ball, *The Guardsmen*, 164–5.

[134] Ibid., 163–8.

[135] Ibid., 156–7.

reminding ourselves of what he actually said on that crucial occasion. In the very same breath that he denounced the agreement as a 'wicked mockery', and Chamberlain's diplomacy as 'an abiding source of shame', Cranborne reiterated his view that 'wider appeasement is the honest and sincere desire of us all'.[136] To this very dutiful Cecil, it was the manner – much more than the substance – of Munich that really mattered. There was, he insisted, an appeasement of weakness and an appeasement of strength. For Cranborne, Chamberlain's failure flowed from his unwillingness, on this vital occasion, to demonstrate British strength: 'if we had mobilised the fleet earlier and shown that we meant business, the last agonizing day would not have been experienced'.[137] Yet he abstained when the time came to vote. So too did Churchill.[138] Bob Boothby hedged his bets more subtly still.[139] Amongst senior ministers, only Duff Cooper actually resigned over Munich.[140] All the while, everyone acknowledged – most full-throatedly too – the 'honest and sincere desires' that underlay the Prime Minister's actions at this time.[141]

That, detached but sympathetic, view of the contemporary British dilemma similarly characterized the discussions of Salter's group. Still more than the politicians, these men were 'appeasers'; that is, they were concerned citizens of the world anxious to create 'some new kind of pacific confederacy amongst the nations'.[142] This made most of them initially more disposed to collective security through the League than to particular agreement by direct negotiations.[143] Many of them, however, changed their minds on that question during 1938. Few, with the possible exception of Harold Nicolson, advocated consistent opposition to German policy aims, anyway as directed eastwards.[144] By the same token, fewer

[136] Ibid., 187.

[137] Ibid.

[138] N. Nicolson (ed.), *Harold Nicolson: Diaries and Letters, 1930–1939* (London, 1966), entry for 6 Oct. 1938: 'our group decide that it is better for us all to abstain than for some to abstain and others vote against'. Amongst the abstainers were Eden, Cooper (bizarrely), Churchill, Amery, Cranborne, Wolmer, Richard Law, Bob Boothby, Jim Thomas, Duncan Sandys, Ronald Cartland, Anthony Crossley, Brendan Bracken, and Emrys-Evans.

[139] Thompson, *The Anti-Appeasers*, 189, notes that Boothby split his vote, siding with the government against the amendment but abstaining in the confidence vote. However, on 1 Nov. 1938, he also claimed that 'Munich was something to be profoundly thankful for and I agree with the Prime Minister that it is nothing to be ashamed of.'

[140] J. J. Norwich (ed.), *The Duff Cooper Diaries, 1915–1951* (London, 2005), 270–2, 30 Sept. 1938: 'The Prime Minister explained the differences between the Munich and the Godesberg terms – and they are really greater than I had understood...I felt it my duty to offer my resignation.' For a sympathetic account, see Faber, *Munich*, 419–20 and 422–3; for the opposite opinion, J. Charmley, *Chamberlain and the Lost Peace* (London, 1989), 139 and 145.

[141] Barnes and Nicholson (eds), *The Empire at Bay*, 576–8 (entries for 5 and 6 Oct. 1938); Self, *Neville Chamberlain*, 331–2.

[142] Aster (ed.), *Appeasement and All Souls*, 143; Lord Allen, 'Foreign Policy Now', n. d. (Liddell Hart Papers, LH5/1).

[143] Aster (ed.), *Appeasement and All Souls*, 47ff.; Lord Allen, 'Document C' (Liddell Hart Papers, LH5/1), esp. at p. 49.

[144] Aster (ed.), *Appeasement and All Souls*, 42: Curtis to Dawson, 17 Jan. 1938 (MS Curtis 12, ff. 10–13); cf. 43–55, 'Nicolson's suggested additions to Wint's redraft of Document C' (Liddell Hart Papers, LH5/1).

still expressed any great admiration, still less affection, for Hitler's régime. Perhaps only Gilbert Murray was unwise enough to confess that he harboured 'no particular bias against Nazi ideology as such'. Moreover, even he insisted that, such enlightened tolerance notwithstanding, he remained absolutely opposed to the 'war ideology which [all] the dictator states possess[ed]'.[145]

Such broad theoretical boundaries also permitted the consideration of wide-ranging practical possibilities. Two points emerge most strikingly from the substance of these debates. First, how critical collective conclusions tended to be about government policy towards war-torn Spain; and secondly, how receptive 'Salter's Soviet' was to almost any suggestion that might have facilitated the peaceful dismemberment of Czechoslovakia. In fact, they were genuinely nervous about Spain. Predicting as early as March 1938 that this 'camouflaged European war' might soon be decided 'in favour of Italy and Germany', Liddell Hart insisted that

if events . . . in Spain . . . were simply allowed to take their course, these two powers would [thereby] obtain an advantage of such magnitude as in all probability to prove decisive in any subsequent [continent-wide] conflict.[146]

But concerning Czechoslovakia, they were almost blasé. Indeed, Curtis spent most of the first three meetings of the group outlining the advantages of a 'German Commonwealth' of Eastern European states (albeit subject to League mandates), including a settlement of the 'Czech problem' through the establishment of Sudeten German cantons on the Swiss model.[147] Salter effectively endorsed both propositions, at least down to September 1938.[148]

The fundamental difficulty facing the group was that it had no direct influence over government policy. Moreover, it sought strictly to avoid partisan commitments. To that extent, it was just a talking shop. What is interesting, in retrospect, was how even so innocent an activity as that quickly produced sharp division amongst otherwise like-minded men.[149] Yet disagreements within 'the Soviet' generally followed less on account of long-standing differences of opinion, and much more often as the unavoidable consequence of their different reactions to fast-moving events. Sometimes the result was something close to rupture. Eden's resignation grievously split the group. But it was perhaps all the

---

[145] Aster (ed.), *Appeasement and All Souls*, 69–70; the whole episode passes unrecorded in D. Wilson, *Gilbert Murray, OM, 1866–1957* (Oxford, 1987); see esp. ch. 26.

[146] Aster (ed.), *Appeasement and All Souls*, 91–2, citing Liddell Hart, 'Aide-mémoire on Spain' (Liddell Hart Papers, LH5/1), March 1938.

[147] Aster (ed.), *Appeasement and All Souls*, 29–43: Curtis to Brand, 20 Dec. 1937 (MS Curtis, 11, f. 168–70); Curtis to Geoffrey Dawson, 17 Jan. 1938 (MS Curtis, 12, ff. 10–13).

[148] Aster (ed.), *Appeasement and All Souls*, 70–81; Salter, 'Notes on Foreign Policy', 8 Mar. 1938 (Liddell Hart Papers, LH5/1).

[149] Aster (ed.), *Appeasement and All Souls*, 47ff.; Lord Allen, 'Document C' (Liddell Hart Papers, LH5/1): 'The proposals are intended to represent the kind of policy we should like to see followed by the British government in foreign affairs.'

more disruptive since it coincided with Rowse's introduction into the discussions. Salter had meant him to act as a catalyst. He succeeded only too well. Recoiling from the effect, Curtis bitterly condemned his 'fanaticism'; an objection he also then levelled at Hudson.[150] About the young historian at least, the 'ancient mariner of All Souls' did not complain alone. Allen agreed, expressing much regret that Salter had 'brought in Rowse' without previously consulting him.[151] This was particularly unfortunate, he insisted, since 'groups such as [ours] require a combination of intense sincerity... and a capacity for restrained expression'.[152] All of which was seemingly lost on the young tyro: 'a man no doubt intellectually alive', but largely motivated by a 'desire to batter [his] opponent into submission', and seemingly possessed by a curious desire 'to prove other people either fools or knaves'.[153] To be fair, Rowse recorded no such righteous triumph for himself. In his diary he noted only 'feeling weak... losing [my] way in argument', and departing with a sense of 'fearful humiliation'.[154]

Perhaps as a result, Salter's energies were increasingly directed to avoiding similar such divisions amongst his discussants. Rowse's deteriorating health (and absence from All Souls) during the early months of 1938 may have made his task easier.[155] It certainly coincided with a remarkable shift in the tone of the group's private discussions. These became ever more directed towards the need for an agreement with Germany. In March Salter circulated a major paper, or 'Memo', probably written by Wint, but carrying his own unambiguous imprimatur. Acknowledging Western weakness generally and British impotence to deal with Hitler particularly, it advocated defensive negotiation, tempered only by rearmament.[156] War, Salter insisted, was inconceivable, at least in the short-term. Democracy's best hope, for now anyway, lay in encouraging internal splits within the Nazi régime.[157] Brand, on reading the memorandum, expressed general agreement with its conclusions. He even added, in a letter to Dawson, that he found it 'pathetic' that Salter had not reached such obvious truths many years previously.[158]

The Anschluss concentrated this kind of thinking wonderfully. Within days of Germany's conquest of its neighbour, Hudson (having undergone something of a conversion in this respect) issued a position paper all but advocating the

[150] Aster (ed.), *Appeasement and All Souls*, 63–4; Curtis to Allen, 28 Feb. 1938 (MS Curtis, 12, ff. 33–4).
[151] Aster (ed.), *Appeasement and All Souls*, 64–6; Allen to Curtis, 1 Mar. 1938 (MS Curtis, 12, ff. 36–8).
[152] Ibid.
[153] Ibid.
[154] EUL, MS 113/2/1/10b, Rowse, MS diary, March 1935–August 1939, entry for 19 Jan. 1938.
[155] Wenden, 'Appeasement and All Souls', 10; Rowse, *All Souls and Appeasement*, 70.
[156] Aster (ed.), *Appeasement and All Souls*, 70–80; Salter, 'Notes on Foreign Policy', 8 Mar. 1938 (Liddell Hart Papers, LH5/1), esp. 75–7.
[157] Ibid., 79–80.
[158] Ibid., 79.

abandonment of Czechoslovakia.[159] Two subsequent meetings of 'the Soviet' (on 24 April and 15 May) were dedicated to developing this idea further. Within that remit, the group made surprisingly good progress. Increasingly, Czechoslovakia was dismissed as a misconceived reaction whose complete disappearance might reasonably be countenanced (Chamberlain, interestingly, never went that far).[160] It was also agreed to report to Halifax with concrete proposals to this effect. Whether these documents were ever sent we do not know.[161] But a draft 'Peace Policy for the Immediate Present' did appear on 10 May.[162] Wint, Hudson, and J. A. Spender were the principal contributors. Its critical argument must have been by now thoroughly familiar to all. Czechoslovakia was an error; it was not worth fighting for; negotiations should proceed upon other, more mutually agreeable, lines.[163] Allen and Salter worked hard to press this draft against opposition from Arnold Toynbee and Gilbert Murray. They failed. It was never formally adopted.[164] With that, very inconclusive, conclusion, the group and its association with All Souls faded away. Salter resurfaced just four months later in the company of Winston Churchill, Anthony Eden, and all the other anti-Chamberlain associates.[165]

III

This apparent change of tack did not point to any development of great moment in itself. Salter's journey initiated just one man's path to personal enlightenment.[166] That was something made, in much the same way, by many of the other grandees during the months that followed. For the most part, these were odysseys undertaken to similarly inconclusive – indeed, often incoherent – effect. This should not surprise us. Thoughtful observers changed their minds more than

---

[159] Aster (ed.), *Appeasement and All Souls*, 94–9, esp. at 98–9; G. F. Hudson, 'Notes on the European Situation', 18 Mar. 1938 (Liddell Hart Papers, LH5/1).

[160] Aster (ed.), *Appeasement and All Souls*, 149–84, see esp. 150 and 183; Foreign Affairs Group, meeting of 24 Apr. 1938 (Liddell Hart Papers, LH5/1); Harold Nicolson Diaries, Sunday, 15 May 1938 (Nicolson Papers).

[161] Aster, 'Introduction', 18–19.

[162] Aster (ed.), *Appeasement and All Souls*, 159–80; Allen to members of the Foreign Affairs Group, 10 May 1938 (Allen Papers, box 17, manuscripts, speeches, etc.).

[163] Ibid., see esp. 166–8.

[164] Aster (ed.), *Appeasement and All Souls*, 183–4; Harold Nicolson Diaries, 15 May 1938 (Nicolson Papers); Toynbee to Allen, 16 May 1938 (Allen Papers, box 15, correspondence, 1937–8).

[165] A. Salter, 'A Foreign Affairs Committee', *The Times*, 29 Sept. 1938, 8: 'Parliament should at once appoint a Foreign Affairs Committee [representing] different parties and sections ... pending [the] reconstruction of the government on a wider basis.' Dawson Papers, MS 1/42, Geoffrey Dawson, diary for 1938, 21 Sept. 1938: 'Lunch with ... Salter who talked an immense amount of pompous nonsense (Neville was doomed in any event – Attlee, Greenwood, Snowdon, Winston etc. must be brought into the government: a solid front with Russia and France against the Dictators etc. !).'

[166] Salter, *Slave of the Lamp*, ch. 11.

once on the merits of government policy at this time. Indeed, between February 1938 and March 1939 possibly just two significant political players, Chamberlain and Cranborne, succeeded in maintaining a consistent line of argument in considering Britain's relations with Germany. Chamberlain has famously come down to us as the principal advocate of an audacious gamble subsequently derided as the craven policy of 'appeasement'. It is perhaps better understood as the determined pursuit of bilateral agreement.[167] Cranborne was perhaps the most ardent 'anti-appeaser'. Yet his views are probably better conceived within the (equally bold) doctrine of honourable – but limited – resistance.[168]

The rest, Amery, Churchill, and Cooper included, more commonly found themselves stranded somewhere between their hopes for peace and their fears of war.[169] This often made them sound much more belligerent than they ever truly were. Moreover, in their considered judgements upon government policy, it usually left room only for specific criticism tempered by general acquiescence. Collective wisdom in these matters began to shift only as broader criticism progressively eclipsed long-standing acquiescence; above all, as it did so beyond the ranks of the obviously disaffected.[170] That meant only a very reluctant conversion – which it was in the overwhelming majority of cases – to an aggressive understanding of national obligations. Some passed through this tortuous process more quickly than others. But such clarification of mind as it

---

[167] W. N. Medlicott, *The Coming of War in 1939*, Historical Association Pamphlet (London, 1963), 9–10, provides what remains as good and succinct a summary of Chamberlain's 'aims for appeasement, c. 1937–9', as any. D. Dilks, '"We Must Hope for the Best and Prepare for the Worst"', is also important. Self, *Neville Chamberlain*, chs 13–14, furnishes the fullest and most up-to-date account. Its interpretation can be supplemented from the documents cited in R. Self (ed.), *The Neville Chamberlain Diary Letters*, vol. 4: *The Downing Street Years, 1934–1940* (London, 2005), ch. 6, *passim*.

[168] Ball, *The Guardsmen*, chs 4–6, supplies a useful narrative. The phrase, however, is my own.

[169] Barnes and Nicholson (eds), *The Empire at Bay*, chs 6 and 7, illustrates the sheer variety of Amery's views on this matter, no less his extreme caution in opposing government policy either in the solution of the Czech problem or in relations with Germany. See, e.g., 499–500 (entry for 24 Mar. 1938), 502–3 (20 Apr. 1938), 506 (30 May 1938), 508 (26 July 1938), 509–10 (16 Sept. 1938), 510–11 (19 Sept. 1938), 520–2 (28 Sept. 1938), 522–4 (30 Sept. 1938), 524–5 (3 Oct. 1938), 526–7 (5 Oct. 1938), 527–8 (6 Oct. 1938), 541 (31 Dec. 1938), 542 (31 Jan. 1939), 548 (15 Mar. 1939). Cooper's vacillations to 1 Oct. 1938 are (inadvertently) recorded in Norwich (ed.), *The Duff Cooper Diaries*, 241–3 (20 Feb. 1938), 244–5 (27 Mar. 1938), 251 (10 July 1938), 255–6 (30 Aug. 1938), 259 (13 Sept. 1938), 260–1 (17 Sept. 1938), 262–3 (21 Sept. 1938), 265–7 (25 Sept. 1938), 267 (26 Sept. 1938), 269–70 (28 Sept. 1938), 270–2 (30 Sept. 1938). Churchill kept no diary, but his ambivalent attitudes and reactions were noted at the time by Amery. See Barnes and Nicholson (eds), *The Empire at Bay*, esp. 521 (28 Sept. 1938), 525 (3 Oct. 1938), and 549 (21 Mar. 1939). These issues are discussed at length in Parker, *Churchill and Appeasement*, 192–202 and 210–12. He particularly comments on Churchill's deafening silence at the time of the occupation of Prague. P. T. Marsh, *The Chamberlain Litany: Letters within a Governing Family from Empire to Appeasement* (London, 2010), 316, rightly challenges the whole notion of his being in 'opposition' to the government, even in October 1938. He wanted to *join* the government (and most of his contemporaries knew as much).

[170] It should be emphasized that this group never necessarily included Amery, Churchill, or Eden. It did, perhaps, include Cooper after Munich and Harold Macmillan, Ronald Cartland, and other members of the 'Awkward Squad', all along. See Thompson, *The Anti-Appeasers*, chs 11–13.

wrought was often as much the product of political calculation, carefully conceived, as the result of chivalrous sensibility, ultimately aroused.[171] Of course, it eventually proved decisive. That was what did for the Prime Minister's subtle wager. Still, amongst the so-called 'anti-appeasers' only Simon can properly be described as 'Chamberlain's mugwump' (Brand's word for him).[172] Halifax (much to his chief's dismay) and Dawson (ultimately to the Prime Minister's still more considerable cost) in the end broke with Chamberlain. Their actions fatally undermined first his policy and then his premiership. But just as there had been no 'Mallardian league' to appease the Axis powers, so there was no All Souls conspiracy to replace Chamberlain either. Events (and individuals) counted for everything at the end.[173]

Dawson's motives in this respect are not always easily recoverable. This was not least because he remained – to and beyond a fault – a Victorian man of duty. His fundamental impulse was always to subordinate personal preference for what he took to be the national (and Imperial) interest.[174] He was also a subtle and skilful political animal, long used to playing his cards close to his chest. However, it is important to remember that he was a close friend of Baldwin, not of Chamberlain.[175] Certainly, it was clear that by the summer of 1938 at the latest, he was beginning to have doubts about the new Prime Minister, albeit less on account of his policies than of his personality. This was why he described Chamberlain to Rab Butler as 'a difficult man to run with'. He especially came to deplore the manner in which 'Chamberlain . . . quite needlessly [and] provocatively . . . assaulted the opposition to his plans'.[176] Halifax proved slower to judge, but quicker to strike. As was his wont, he invariably maintained good relations with

---

[171] M. Cowling, *The Impact of Hitler: British Politics and British Policy, 1933–1940* (Cambridge, 1975), pts. 2 and 3, *passim*.

[172] Dawson Papers, MS 81, ff. 1–2, Brand to Dawson, 28 June 1939.

[173] Roberts, '*The Holy Fox*', chs 13–21; Wrench, *Geoffrey Dawson*, chs 32–4.

[174] Wrench, *Geoffrey Dawson*, 373–6 and 454ff.; S. Ball (ed.), *Parliament and Politics in the Age of Churchill and Attlee: The Headlam Diaries, 1935–1951* (Cambridge, 1999), 430, entry for 8 Nov. 1944. Cuthbert Headlam, a friend of Dawson's from his Magdalen days, emphasized Dawson's 'Round Table-ish mind' at the time of his death, part in praise and part in criticism.

[175] P. Williamson and E. Baldwin (eds), *Baldwin Papers: A Conservative Statesman, 1908–1947* (Cambridge, 2004), 5, 93, 117–18, 133–4, 164, 211–12, 215–16, 252, 266–7, 297, 330–1, and 358, furnishes a considerable body of evidence to this effect. P. Williamson, *Stanley Baldwin: Conservative Leadership and National Values* (Cambridge, 1999), 72, 80, 88, 159, and 162, offers some analysis of the causes.

[176] Emmanuel College, Cambridge, Private Archive of Elisabeth van Houts, Geoffrey Faber's Diary, 2 July 1938; Rab Butler, reporting Geoffrey Dawson's words, to Geoffrey Faber. I am immensely grateful to Dr van Houts for drawing my attention to this previously unexploited source, currently in her keeping. There is no biography of Faber. In the interim, see C. Monteith, rev. C. T. Taylor, 'Faber, Sir Geoffrey Cust (1889–1961)', *ODNB*. Faber was a fellow of the College from 1919 until his death, and Estates Bursar after 1923. He founded the publishing firm that became Faber and Faber in 1925. He was a close friend of R. A. Butler. They corresponded and spoke frequently during the period 1938–40.

Chamberlain, throughout 1938 and indeed 1939.[177] But he always acted quite self-consciously on behalf of His Majesty's Government, never in the interest of one man's administration. Insofar as he had any other concerns, he was intermittently anxious about the fortunes of the Conservative Party in the upcoming General Election of 1940.[178] Most important of all, he enjoyed a certain freedom of action, gratuitously bequeathed to him by both the fact and manner of Eden's resignation in February 1938.[179] Put simply, Chamberlain could not afford to lose a Foreign Secretary quickly. And Halifax knew it.[180]

It was, of course, *The Times*'s leader of 7 September that year, suggesting the use of a plebiscite as a way out of the Sudeten *impasse*, which first alerted Claud Cockburn to the supposed existence of nefariously pro-German influences at work in high places.[181] Ironically, the paper of record was then more usually assumed, both in Germany and beyond, to be the semi-official mouthpiece of the British government.[182] As such, it was widely assumed that the whole thing had been got up by Dawson and Halifax, as a kind of *ballon d'essai*, prior to the publication of the Runciman Report. In fact, Dawson's diary makes it clear that, on this occasion anyway, the editor wrote wholly on his own initiative.[183] His motive seems to have been a long-standing desire to reflect what he took to be

[177] Halifax, *Fulness of Days*, 227–32, offers a fascinating (if subsequent) appraisal. Roberts, '*The Holy Fox*', 86, 131–3, and 140, reflects the mixture of ever-present politeness and growing distance that marked the relations of the three men at this time. Harvey (ed.), *The Diplomatic Diaries of Oliver Harvey*, 213, entry for 12 Oct. 1938, offers some contemporary evidence.

[178] Cowling, *The Impact of Hitler*, 273–83, offers a wonderful portrait.

[179] Self-servingly recounted in the Rt Hon. Earl of Avon, *The Eden Memoirs: Facing the Dictators* (London, 1962), ch. 14. For a different view, see D. Carlton, *Anthony Eden: A Biography* (London, 1981), esp. 123–31. Chamberlain's case is best followed in Self (ed.), *The Neville Chamberlain Diary Letters*, 301–4: letters to Hilda, 13 Feb. 1938 and 27 Feb. 1938. Eden's isolation at the Cabinet meeting of 19 Feb. 1938, no less the significance of his actions at the time, were both caught in the disparaging observations of Duff Cooper. See Norwich, *The Duff Cooper Diaries*, 242–3, entry for 20 Feb. 1938: 'On Friday...at Cabinet...the Prime Minister [insisted] on our urgent need of reaching an agreement...with Italy...his views were not shared by the Foreign Secretary [but] Eden...did not...state his case very well, and I felt that everyone who had not already made his mind up must have been convinced by the Prime Minister. [Still] everybody realized what a tremendous blow [his resignation] would be for the Government. It might even bring about the Government's fall.' Eden resigned later that evening.

[180] Roberts, '*The Holy Fox*', 85–6. Halifax, *Fulness of Days*, 195–6, puts it in a very different way.

[181] Dawson Papers, MS 80, ff. 38 and 52–3, Dawson memoranda on *The Week*; Cockburn, '*The Times* Scandal', 1. Moreover, this view was scarcely unique to *The Times*. It was shared by Kingsley Martin at *The New Statesman*. See B. Morris, *The Roots of Appeasement: The British Weekly Press and Nazi Germany during the 1930s* (London, 1991), 130–4 at 132. I am grateful to Professor Vernon Bogdanor for drawing this point to my attention.

[182] Cockett, *Twilight of Truth*, 12–13, repeats the charge. G. Martel (ed.), *The Times and Appeasement: The Journals of A. L. Kennedy, 1932–1939*, Camden Society Fifth Series, 16 (Cambridge, 2000), 'Introduction', 1–15, at 9–12, describes a more complex reality.

[183] Dawson Papers, MS 1/42, Geoffrey Dawson, Diary of 1938, entry for 7 Sept. 1938. R. Rhodes James (ed.), *Chips: The Diaries of Sir Henry Channon* (London, 1967), 164–5, entry for 10 Sept. 1938.

Commonwealth opinion on the matter.[184] The Foreign Office was less than pleased by his efforts.[185] Still, he and Halifax lunched together that day in the Travellers Club. There was no bad blood between them. The Foreign Secretary merely made it clear to his fellow Mallardian that he was himself 'as much in the dark as everyone else' about what would 'happen next'.[186]

In the event, nothing much did. So, Dawson (his own views notwithstanding) was happy to publish an apparently contrary letter from Eden, just five days later. There, the former Foreign Secretary exhorted the government to reach a peaceful solution to the problem. Then he noted how much the Czechs 'had already conceded on the issue'. Finally, he emphasized that if any conflict did break out (as a result of anyone's false move) it would be most unlikely to remain localized. To some, this sounded critical, both of *The Times* and of government policy. Actually, it was no such thing. The text in draft had been approved by both Chamberlain and Halifax.[187] Ironically, the Prime Minister interpreted it as tacit support for his own policy. This was, after all, the most he could hope for in the circumstances. It was very possibly also the most he actually wished for under any circumstances. He certainly did not want Eden back in his Cabinet. Moreover, he had a trick up his sleeve. On 14 September he announced to Cabinet his intention to negotiate with Hitler. Even erstwhile critics applauded this move. Detached observers found real hope in its possibilities. One of the latter was Geoffrey Faber, Bursar of All Souls. He had 'longed . . . for war' at the time of the 'Austrian Anschluss'. But he found 'the news' of direct and peaceful contact freshly 'heartening'.[188]

What has subsequently become known as the 'Munich Agreement' resulted from these negotiations. For all that, it is important to understand that 'Munich' was never merely a bilateral agreement.[189] It is scarcely less vital to appreciate that it did not emerge overnight.[190] Indeed, its progress was anything but smooth. This was scarcely surprising. For Hitler, as we now know, had no intention of pursuing a peaceful path to the resolution of the Czech crisis. He wanted a war

---

[184] A view shared with Malcolm Macdonald, the Dominions Secretary. For an account see S. Wilkinson, 'Perceptions of Public Opinion: British Foreign Policy Decisions about Nazi Germany', unpublished DPhil thesis (Oxford, 2000), ch. 6, esp. at p. 244; also R. Ovendale, *Appeasement and the English-Speaking World: Britain, the United States, the Dominions and the Policy of Appeasement* (Cardiff, 1975), 142–3.

[185] Dawson Papers, MS 1/42, Geoffrey Dawson, Diary of 1938, entry for 7 Sept. 1938: 'F. O. went up through the roof.'

[186] Ibid., entry for 7 Sept. 1938: 'Not so the Foreign Secretary.'

[187] Ibid., entry for 11 Sept. 1938; A. Eden, 'The British Mind', *The Times*, 12 Sept. 1938, 13.

[188] Geoffrey Faber's Diary, 15 Sept. 1938. Self (ed.), *Neville Chamberlain Diary Letters*, 345–9; Chamberlain to Ida, 19 Sept. 1938. This became known as 'Plan 2'. On Chamberlain's fait accompli to Cabinet, see Norwich (ed.), *The Duff Cooper Diaries*, 259–60, entry for 14 Sept. 1938.

[189] Marsh, *The Chamberlain Litany*, ch. 10, best sets out Chamberlain's views and achievements at this time.

[190] I. Kershaw, *Hitler, 1936–1945: Nemesis* (Harmondsworth, 2000), 108–25, gives a good sense of the multiple dynamics at work during these weeks.

S. J. D. Green

over the Sudetenland.[191] That was why he specifically rejected the principle of self-determination put to him by Chamberlain in Bad Godesberg, on 22 September. However, he did not particularly want a war against Britain: not at that time, anyway.[192] He proposed, instead, that German forces should occupy designated territories prior to their integration into the Reich. Initially angered by such an obvious display of bad faith, Chamberlain formally resisted that provocation.[193] Yet his concerns were much more about the modalities of the transfer than its substance. This became clear in his report to Cabinet on 24 September. At that point, Halifax carefully distanced himself from his boss.[194] The following morning, 25 September, he argued – against Chamberlain – that Hitler was dictating the terms of the putative agreement almost as if he had already won a war. But this was not true. And acting as if it were was quite unacceptable. Naturally, he wanted the Czechs to agree to a proposal for the peaceful transfer of Sudeten territories to the Reich. However, he did not think that Britain should force them to do so.[195] The cabinet concurred. Two days later, Horace Wilson dispatched Chamberlain's famous memo to Hitler. Its obvious implication was war.[196]

It is at least arguable that this event – let us call it Halifax's crucial quibble – was a more important moment in the evolution of British foreign policy towards Nazi Germany than that declaration of 'peace in our time' which followed Chamberlain's visit to Germany at the end of the month. True, the break it marked is easily missed. It was certainly long forgotten. This is because the image of 'Munich' that still dominates common comprehension presumes a simple division of the political nation into those self-deceiving 'doves' that dominated government and a few far-sighted 'hawks' sprinkled around the backbenches, pitted against each other in unequal conflict for the hearts and minds of an otherwise credulous and ignorant people. But this is a caricature of reality. Revisionist historiography has long since done for much of the (supposed) 'realism' of Chamberlain's political opponents at the end of September 1938.[197] It has perhaps made less of the significance of much uncommitted

[191] G. L. Weinberg, *The Foreign Policy of Hitler's Germany: Starting World War II, 1937–9* (Chicago, 1980), chs 10 and 11.

[192] Medlicott, *The Coming of War in 1939*, 15–16.

[193] Ibid., 16; Self, *Neville Chamberlain*, 216–17; Wilkinson, 'Perceptions of Public Opinion', 262–3.

[194] Self, *Neville Chamberlain*, 317, notes that the colleague who first spotted the problem was, ironically, Simon.

[195] Ibid., 318–19, makes it clear how great a surprise this apparent change of view was to Chamberlain. Wilkinson, 'Perceptions of Public Opinion', 270–1, provides a blow-by-blow account.

[196] Dawson Papers, MS 1/42, Geoffrey Dawson, Diary of 1938, entry for 25 Sept. 1938. The Cabinet's concurrence with Halifax's view was relayed to Dawson by Hoare. Self, *Neville Chamberlain*, 321–2, outlines the origins and implications of Wilson's mission.

[197] Medlicott, *Britain and Germany*, 31–2, though ostensibly only dealing with events up to 1937, was a truly pioneering work in this respect. Important recent studies include R. A. C. Parker,

but intelligent opinion that observed those events from a distance. This was not without either good sense or reasonable concern. For many, what emerged at Munich was, in Geoffrey Faber's words, 'good news that seemed bad'.[198] By that he meant to acknowledge what was a necessary agreement. But he was far from willing to herald it as gallant action. This, perhaps very typical, reaction induced a kind of detached but disgusted acquiescence in the movement of events. It was a response that was perfectly captured by Llewellyn Woodward's letter to *The Times* of 4 October 1938. There he declared himself:

prepared to trust the judgement of our rulers that our ultimate victory would have been of less value to the preservation of liberty in Europe than our present policy [whilst insisting] that this was not a moment in which we in England should be singing 'Rule Britannia' in our streets [or] ringing church bells for the saving of peace.[199]

When detached but disgusted acquiescence finally translated itself into serious suggestions about an alternative policy, it invariably did so under the guise of 'military preparedness'.[200] Suddenly, everyone outside the government began talking in such terms. Salter may have played no small part in the process, subjecting his fellow countrymen to a series of 'blood-curdling' homilies about the 'likely impact of air-raids'.[201] Such views were not long confined to 'opposition' spokesmen either. From within the administration, Inskip soon admitted to 'gaps in our defences'.[202] Even Dawson took up the challenge.[203] This subtly different apprehension – of war as imminent and in the necessity of preparing for it – dictated common interpretation of unfolding events far more decisively than those supposedly great divisions of opinion revealed in the Oxford by-election of 1938 (in which Quintin Hogg stood for the government but other fellows of the College took surprisingly little interest).[204] It also counted for far more in the

Chamberlain and Appeasement: British Policy and the Coming of the Second World War (Houndmills, 1993), 183–6; Charmley, *Chamberlain and the Lost Peace*, 145–8; Neville, *Hitler and Appeasement*, 114–15; and Self, *Neville Chamberlain*, 330–2.

[198] Geoffrey Faber's Diary, 30 Sept. 1938.

[199] E. L. Woodward, 'To the Editor of *The Times*', 4 Oct. 1938, 10. Halifax's prescient sense of just how brittle public support actually was for Munich and its provisions is well brought out in Self, *Neville Chamberlain*, 29; also Roberts, *'The Holy Fox'*, ch. 14.

[200] Harvey (ed.), *The Diplomatic Diaries of Oliver Harvey*, 211–12, entry for 11 Oct. 1938 and following; also Macmillan, *Winds of Change*, 583; finally, Liddell Hart, *Memoirs*, ii. 175. This is not to suggest that 'rearmament' was ever far from Chamberlain's mind from 1937 onwards. For an important correction to a common misconception in this respect, see Marsh, *The Chamberlain Litany*, 282ff.

[201] Geoffrey Faber's Diary, 2 Oct. 1938.

[202] Geoffrey Faber's Diary, 5 Oct. 1938; Anon., 'Europe Saved from Armageddon', *The Times*, 7 Oct. 1938, 6–8.

[203] Geoffrey Faber's Diary, 7 Oct. 1938, also 8 Oct. 1938; Leader, 'The Nation's Spirit', *The Times*, 8 Oct. 1938, 13.

[204] Harvey (ed.), *The Diplomatic Diaries of Oliver Harvey*, 215–16, entry for 27 Oct. 1938, and Macmillan, *Winds of Change*, 205–6, try to convey some sense of a great conflict. M. Ignatieff, *Isaiah Berlin: A Life* (London, 1998), 72–3, shows how it was possible, even then, to treat the whole thing as a joke.

stiffening of collective resolve than that final exposure of the evil of the Nazi régime laid bare by the enormity of *Kristallnacht* (about which fellows of All Souls staged distressingly little protest).[205]

There was something else too. Munich had real consequences amongst the principal players in Chamberlain's government. Once both the cheering and the jeering had died down, the truly lasting significance of the events of 29 and 30 September was that they broke the moral unity of the Cabinet. That rupture shifted the weight of its authority away from the Prime Minister and towards his Foreign Secretary. When Hitler finally occupied the whole of Czechoslovakia early the following year, the terms of the guarantees Britain then felt compelled to give to Poland reflected his thinking, not Chamberlain's.[206] The 'Holy Fox' acted out of real conviction on this occasion. But he did so convinced that the others were also moving in the same direction. These included many of his fellow Mallardians. Indeed, he was specifically encouraged to take such a stand by Amery. Still, this can scarcely have been decisive.[207] More importantly, Dawson began to report of significant alterations in public opinion at much the same time. This may also have reflected a subtle change in his own mind: by now, groping towards a view which no longer saw any contradiction between 'calmness' and 'firmness' in Britain's relations with Germany. It certainly pointed to the gradual emergence of a consensus on the matter that had effectively been achieved by the early summer of 1939. This may have come about by default. It was no less effective for all that.[208]

Not least because it affected *The Times* too. Many had considered its stance admirable at the time of Munich. Some came to think of its position as compromised in the wake of the agreements of 29 and 30 September.[209] Dawson was far from oblivious to this shift in the national temper. To be sure, he

[205] Dawson Papers, 1/42, Geoffrey Dawson, Diary of 1938, entry for 10 Nov. 1938: 'A pogrom of the Jews all over Germany.' Ninety-one Signatories, 'Preservation of the Jews', *The Times*, 22 Sept. 1938, 10: 'We want to record our solemn protest, before the conscience of civilization, against the persecution of the Jews in Germany.' Just two were fellows of All Souls: Cyril Radcliffe and Charles Grant Robertson.

[206] Self (ed.), *The Neville Chamberlain Diary Letters*, 393–9, Chamberlain to Hilda, 19 Mar. 1939, and to Ida, 26 Mar. 1939, demonstrate the Prime Minister's ambivalence about the matter; Self, *Neville Chamberlain*, 301–8, offers an interpretation. Roberts, 'The Holy Fox', ch. 16, is the clearest account. S. Newman, *March 1939: The British Guarantee to Poland* (Oxford, 1976), ch. 9, remains the most balanced interpretation. Leader, 'A Stand for Ordered Diplomacy', *The Times*, 1 Apr. 1939, 15; Martel (ed.), *The Times and Appeasement*, 286, entry for 4 Apr. 1939.

[207] Barnes and Nicholson (eds), *The Empire at Bay*, 548–9, entries for 15 and 16 Mar. 1939; Roberts, 'The Holy Fox', 143–4.

[208] Geoffrey Faber's Diary, 22 Jan. 1939: 'had a talk with Geoffrey Dawson . . . he admitted the Nazi regime was not moved by rational considerations [and] did not consider war . . . at all impossible.' Cf. Martel (ed.), *The Times and Appeasement*, 283–4, entry for 17 Jan. 1939, and 288, entry for 5 Apr. 1939.

[209] Dawson Papers, MS 80, f. 91, W. S. G. Adams to Dawson, 7 Oct. 1938: 'Just . . . a line to say how splendid *The Times* has been through this crisis in leader after leader.' Oxford, Bodleian Library, Berlin Papers, MS 281, John Sparrow to Isaiah Berlin, 7 Oct. 1938: 'my loyalty to *The Times* has been strained to breaking point during the last few weeks and beyond'.

remained formally loyal to Chamberlain's régime right up to 3 September 1939. Indeed, he explicitly supported the logic of keeping Churchill out of government for so long as a peace remained even the vaguest possibility (no less, of bringing him back when it ceased to do so).[210] But a noticeable change in the tone of *The Times*'s pronouncements about the conduct of British foreign policy was clear to all who read the paper carefully during the spring and early summer of 1939. Whether by cause or in effect, Dawson's friend, Brand, began to write more regularly to the editor. Both in private and in public, he now sought to dispel any remaining myths about German deprivation. He also urged the paper (and the public) to get serious about 'the Polish guarantee' and finally he argued for a broadening of the basis of the national government in order to make it a truly representative administration.[211] These were not novel arguments. What was new was Dawson's willingness to afford them so much respectable publicity. Moreover, after 3 September, he ceased to act by stealth. The editor's very first wartime leader warmly commended Chamberlain's swift change of personnel. But it was highly critical of the Prime Minister's failure to reconstitute the government; that is, fundamentally to alter the structure of the administration for the purpose of conducting a very modern conflict.[212] This may have sounded self-contradictory. It was actually very thoughtful. Indeed, it became the basis upon which Conservative leaders would eventually agree to replace Chamberlain as Prime Minister just nine months later.[213]

Not everyone appreciated the true significance of the change involved. Thus Dawson received a letter the very next day from Amery, 'much encouraged' by his criticism of Chamberlain's hybrid War Cabinet. Just in case he might have missed the point, the ex-minister went on to observe how the editor's *volte face* on Churchill's inclusion in the government made perfect sense according to a logic that 'applied equally to myself'. More than equally, in fact: for whilst 'I am just senior to Winston in actual years . . . I remain . . . a good deal junior in body and [am] not yet fossilized in mind.'[214] Dawson proved a somewhat less than amenable patron on this occasion. But Amery's hopes of preferment were undimmed. They went on rising as the influential editor became ever increasingly more critical of government economic policy during the first months of

---

[210] Leader, 'The War Cabinet', *The Times*, 4 Sept. 1939, 9.

[211] Dawson Papers, MS 80, ff. 102, Brand to Dawson, 28 June 1939; Bodleian Library, Brand Papers, MS 198, Brand to Geoffrey Dawson, 21 July 1939, and Geoffrey Dawson to Brand, 31 July 1939. Dawson urged Brand to publish these thoughts in 'Oxford pamphlets' so that he could quote them in his leading articles.

[212] Leader, 'HITLER'S WAR' and 'The War Cabinet', *The Times*, 4 Sept. 1939, 9. Note especially the content and tone of the last paragraph of the second section of this latter article; and see Cockett, *Twilight of Truth*, 244–5.

[213] Neville, 'Dawson', 654, emphasizes the shift in Dawson's opinions at that time. Indeed, the noted military correspondent, B. H. Liddell Hart, was actually forced to leave *The Times* in October 1939 because of his perceived defeatism. See also Cockett, *Twilight of Truth*, 145–6.

[214] Dawson Papers, MS 81, ff. 13–15, Amery to Dawson, 4 Sept. 1939.

the war. Indeed, when Dawson made oblique reference to the as yet untapped coordinating skills of 'ex-ministers' in a leader of 11 January 1940, his fellow Mallardian had no doubt 'that he was referring to me'.[215] As a matter of fact, the editor's thoughts were almost certainly directed elsewhere.

By March 1940, Dawson had come to the conclusion that 'it was [now] essential that we should have a proper War Cabinet'.[216] What he really meant was that he too was contemplating a change of Prime Minister.[217] That view became something like common wisdom amongst thinking Conservatives in the spring of 1940. It predated the Narvik fiasco.[218] It was rooted in growing frustration at Chamberlain's – principled, considered, and far from self-evidently stupid – unwillingness actually to fight the war he had nominally declared on Germany so many months earlier.[219] Chamberlain believed that the war would most likely be won if it was least vigorously waged.[220] Narvik seemingly gave the lie to that view. Yet its lamentable outcome scarcely pointed to the obvious advancement of Churchill.[221] All sensible opinion pointed to the impeccable claims of Halifax.[222] Except Dawson: he now increasingly doubted whether 'Halifax would make a suitable PM'; or indeed, 'whether he would take [the post], if offered it'.[223]

This represented a doubly unfortunate turn of events for Cranborne's 'Watching Committee'.[224] It had been set up in early 1940 with the explicit purpose of organizing 'respectable conservatives' (i.e. people other than Churchill) for the purpose of 'exercising pressure on the cabinet' (that is, engineering the removal of Chamberlain). Hotel Cecil was at that time still nominally committed to the candidacy of Eden.[225] But the Committee was not established to achieve any such purpose. Indeed, in some ways, it marked the virtual abandonment of that long preferred goal. This may not have been entirely evident at the time. After all,

[215] Barnes and Nicholson (eds), *The Empire at Bay*, 580, entry for 12 Jan. 1940.
[216] Ibid., 584, entry for 14 Mar. 1940.
[217] Dawson Papers, MS 81, ff. 35–37, Amery to Dawson, 16 Apr. 1940.
[218] Ibid.; Self, *Neville Chamberlain*, ch. 17; see also J. Ramsden, *A History of the Conservative Party*, vol. 4: *The Age of Balfour and Baldwin* (London, 1978), 370–2.
[219] Self, *Neville Chamberlain*, ch. 16, offers the best account of this line of thinking. It is documented in Self (ed.), *The Neville Chamberlain Diary Letters*, 445ff.
[220] Self, *Neville Chamberlain*, 398–403.
[221] S. Lawlor, *Churchill and the Politics of War, 1940–41* (Cambridge, 1994), ch. 1, furnishes the fullest account of the many reasons why.
[222] Self (ed.), *The Neville Chamberlain Diary Letters*, 504–6, Chamberlain to Ida, 2 Mar. 1940, demonstrates that this was Chamberlain's *own* view, at least at the time. See, however, the remarks in n. 240 below.
[223] Barnes and Nicholson (eds), *The Empire at Bay*, 581, entry for 14 Mar. 1940.
[224] Ball, *The Guardsmen*, 207–13, 226, 229, 255, and 351–2, now furnishes the best modern account of this body. See also Self, *Neville Chamberlain*, 392–3.
[225] Ball, *The Guardsmen*, 207–8: 'The Watching Committee was run entirely on Cecil lines . . . Men did not choose to join, they were invited to join . . . The committee was not a pro-Eden body. Eden was not consulted about its formation, was kept in ignorance of its operation and was irrelevant to its plans . . . [It] was committed to the destruction of Neville Chamberlain.'

Cranborne had spent much of his political capital on promoting the case of the younger man. He had hoped, in turn, for the Foreign Office as his reward.[226] But by the spring of 1940, he was beginning to have doubts about the 'glamour boy'.[227] Eden had proved too often weak-kneed when it really mattered.[228] His return to government had perceptibly weakened his position, in both the party and the country.[229] Halifax increasingly appeared to be the most likely beneficiary of any short-term change in the administration.[230] This was very much a second-best outcome for the Cecil faction. Indeed, Halifax's attempt at the end of that month to keep Italy out of the war very nearly turned Cranborne against him. This was, he believed, 'idiotic [diplomacy]: appeasement in its most vicious form'.[231] Note the change in language. Still, the group made contact on 29 April. Cranborne's father, the fourth Marquis of Salisbury, led the delegation to see Halifax in order to discuss the deteriorating situation. In effect, they were offering him the premiership. The meeting was a disaster. Paul Emrys Evans (Secretary to the Committee) concluded, pregnantly, that, '[h]e understands the situation but does not seem to have any idea about [how] to deal with it'.[232] Harold Macmillan commented, laconically, that it 'all reminded him of a dinner' at All Souls. Perhaps he still had Salter's seminars in his head at the time. Perhaps this was the source of Boothby's subsequent fantasy. We shall probably never know.[233]

What we can say is that it was in this profoundly confused context that Amery rose to denounce Chamberlain in the House of Commons on 8 May 1940.[234] Whether that great peroration really was decisive in sealing the Prime Minister's fate may reasonably be doubted.[235] What is beyond question is that it had an

[226] Ibid., 144–5, 151, 162, 165–6, 168, 195, 197–8, 204, 211–15, 226–7, 248–9, 280–1, and 311.

[227] R. Rhodes James, *Anthony Eden* (London, 1986), 202, refers to a group of younger Conservatives, know to the Whips as 'the Insurgents' or 'the Glamour Boys' and led – from time to time – by Eden, after February 1938. Carlton, *Eden*, 135, refers to an 'Eden Group' of between twenty and thirty Members of Parliament, including Cranborne and Thomas, also Macmillan, Nicolson, Mark Patrick, Paul Emrys-Evans, Richard Law, E. L. Spears, Anthony Crossley, and Ronald Cartland, whose 'importance and coherence may well have been exaggerated'.

[228] Ball, *The Guardsmen*, 208ff.

[229] Carlton, *Eden*, 153–63. D. R. Thorpe, *Eden: The Life and Times of Anthony Eden, First Earl of Avon, 1897–1977* (London, 2003), 235–43, offers an alternative account.

[230] Harvey (ed.), *The Diplomatic Diaries of Oliver Harvey*, 331–3, entry for 24 Dec. 1939. Roberts, *'The Holy Fox'*, 189ff.

[231] Cranborne to Paul Emrys-Evans, 20 Apr. 1940, with a postscript dated 1 Apr. 1940; Emrys-Evans Papers, cited in Ball, *The Guardsmen*, 210.

[232] Emrys-Evans to Cranborne, 5 May 1940; Salisbury Papers cited in Ball, *The Guardsmen*, 210.

[233] Ibid. H. Macmillan, *The Blast of War, 1939–1945* (London, 1967), 69ff., simply passes over the incident. Perhaps he had forgotten by then.

[234] Barnes and Nicholson (eds), *The Empire at Bay*, 610–11, entry for 8 May 1940, relates the scene with touching modesty. L. S. Amery, *My Political Life*, vol. 3: *The Unforgiving Years, 1929–1940* (London, 1955), 360–5, sets it out in more detail, possibly emboldened by the passing of the years.

[235] Wenden, 'Appeasement and All Souls', 23–4, makes the case, but Self, *Neville Chamberlain*, 423, emphasizes the retrospective nature of this judgement. What is true is that it was an

ulterior motive. By it, Amery meant to advance his own candidacy for the soon to be vacant position. He seriously believed that he could still become Prime Minister. This was not a wholly self-deceiving aspiration. Amery's credentials as an 'anti-appeaser' (1940 definition) were at least as good as Churchill's. Following Eden's appointment to the War Office, he had effectively become leader of the group in parliament that still bore the former Foreign Secretary's name. Moreover, he had been on good terms with the 'Watching Committee' from the start. For a few hours that evening, anything – even this strange outcome – seemed plausible.[236] But in the clear light of the next day that outlandish possibility passed. The wider difficulty – what caused the crisis that confronted 'every respectable Conservative' just two days later – was that no one really acknowledged anybody else's candidacy either. The 'Watching Committee' may have slain the Prime Minister. But it had effectively slaughtered the other candidates too. Certainly, the issue of the accession no longer lay in its gift.[237]

For the Labour Party now had a significant say in the eventual outcome. It was, of course, ostensibly otherwise engaged at the time. But the following day, *The Times* published a letter from a certain A. L. Rowse, arguing for 'A Broader Alternative Government'. This was sent – actually on 7 May – not from a fellow of All Souls but rather from the Labour candidate for Penryn and Falmouth. As such, it almost certainly had official approval. That was probably why Rowse first argued the case for Herbert Morrison: 'the man with imaginative vision ... capable of inspiring the people [to victory]'. Acknowledging that this otherwise admirable outcome might not 'be immediately possible', Rowse conceded 'the Labour movement would serve under Lord Halifax'. He also pointed to the perhaps greater attractions of a 'truly national government', with 'Mr Churchill in the charge of the conduct of the war and Mr Morrison directing "the home front" '. He made clear only that:

> The Labour movement [would] never serve under ... Mr Chamberlain, Sir John Simon and Mr Samuel Hoare [whose] disastrous course [has] landed us where we are.[238]

That closed down several options. But it suggested an intriguing alternative.

What actually happened in the discussions between Chamberlain, Churchill, and Halifax has long been debated by historians. The fact is that Churchill

---

unexpectedly good speech – neither long nor boring (as was Amery's wont) – but succinct and stirring (thus to considerable effect).

[236] Barnes and Nicholson (eds), *The Empire at Bay*, 611–12, entry for 9 May 1940, sets out Amery's own (coy) version. This is repeated in Amery, *My Political Life*, iii. 369–71. Macmillan, *The Blast of War*, 70–1, offers a tantalizing hint. On Amery and the 'Eden Group' after 3 Sept. 1939, see Ramsden, *The Age of Balfour and Baldwin*, 371–2 and 374. For Amery and the 'Watching Committee', see G. Stewart, *Burying Caesar: Churchill, Chamberlain and the Tory Party* (London, 1999), 407.

[237] Ball, *The Guardsmen*, 211–15.

[238] A. L. Rowse, 'A Broader Alternative Government', *The Times*, 9 May 1940, 7. Rowse's own, almost apologetic, account of the episode is recorded in his *All Souls and Appeasement* at 107.

became Prime Minister on 10 May 1940 because he was the only man both willing and able to assume this thankless task at such an inauspicious moment. This was, as he knew only too well, his last chance to achieve that office and fulfil a lifetime's ambition.[239] Others hesitated. It was not that they did not want the job. It was rather that they did not want it just then.[240] Their equivocation had bitterly construed consequences. Frustration at his failure, attempted 'earnestly and at ... length', to persuade Halifax 'to accept the Premiership' led Rab Butler famously to denounce 'this ... sudden ... disaster[ous] and unnecessary ... coup', a grave misfortune which had, at one stroke, put an end to:

the good clean tradition of English politics, of Pitt as opposed to Fox and ... sold the pass ... to the greatest political adventurer in modern history ... a half-breed American [whose] main support was amongst those inefficient and talkative people [such as] Lady Astor and Ronnie Tree.[241]

Only the openness of his rancour was remarkable. The sense of shock was quite general. For '[t]he events of May 1940 turned the [British] political world upside down'. No 'serious politician' during the 1930s had been 'a Churchillian'.[242] Proof of his long-standing irrelevance lay in the bizarre nature of the praetorian guard he brought with him to Downing Street. This was a motley collection of outsiders and amateurs: Max Beaverbrook, or 'been a crook', the man who had seemingly long since met his nemesis in Baldwin; Brendan Bracken, the former schoolmaster turned dodgy City press-lord; 'Prof' Lindemann, Salter's defeated opponent as MP for the University of Oxford in 1937 and possibly the rudest man in contemporary academic life; Duncan Sandys, the old man's son-in-law and not much else; finally, Edward Louis Spears, Conservative MP for Carlisle, half-French, half-soldier, of whom, in Duff Cooper's immortal words:

---

[239] M. Gilbert, *Winston S. Churchill*, vol. 6: *1939–1941* (London, 1983), 313; J. Charmley, *Churchill: The End of Glory; A Political Biography* (London, 1993), 395. Carlton, *Eden*, 161–2, points to the constitutionally unsatisfactory nature of what took place that day, and advances the intriguing possibility that Chamberlain actually wanted Churchill to succeed him in 1940, leaving open the possibility of his own return to the premiership at a later stage, an outcome that would probably have been rendered impossible by Halifax's preferment at that point. But see also next note.

[240] Roberts, 'The Holy Fox', 199, and A. Clark, *The Tories: Conservatives and the Nation State, 1922–1997* (London, 1998), 174, between them advance the possibility that Halifax was playing a 'waiting game' on 10 May 1940, i.e. waiting for Churchill to fail and his own opportunity to succeed uncontested. There is no evidence to substantiate this suggestion. But there is no evidence against it either.

[241] J. Colville, *The Fringes of Power: Downing Street Diaries, 1939–1945*, rev. edn (London, 2004), 96–7, entry for 10 May 1940. An observation endlessly quoted in the relevant secondary literature. Less often remarked upon is what came immediately before: 'Alec [Dunglass] and I went over to the F. O. to explain the position to Rab and there, with Chips [Channon] we drank in champagne the health of the "King over the Water" (not Leopold, but Mr Chamberlain).' Of course, the King over the Water was (still is?) supposed to return.

[242] I owe this wonderful phrase to Ball, *The Guardsmen*, 216. J. Colville, *Footprints in Time* (London, 1976), 75–8, conveys a real sense of the drama involved.

if the word SHIT...had...been written on his forehead [nothing] would be more apparent than is...already...clear...now.[243]

This was important. Churchill's sheer lack of plausible allies left him profoundly vulnerable to the surviving Chamberlainites, including Chamberlain himself.[244] That was why, amongst the arch-appeasers, only Simon paid a speedy price for supposed errors of earlier judgement. He was immediately banished from the Exchequer, albeit to the wartime sinecure of the Lord Chancellorship.[245] Others were removed more slowly and surreptitiously in the months and years that followed. But removed they surely were. All the while, this veteran political steeplechaser plotted to settle his many and various scores. Chamberlain's early and fatal illness afforded him a quite unexpected bonus. After his death, Halifax was dispatched to America.[246] Hoare was sent to Spain.[247] Eden was kept under control, first at the War Office, then as Foreign Secretary. He was specifically denied the weightier burdens of Defence.[248] Lesser fry, like Hore-Belisha or Butler, were alternatively cast into darkness or demoted.[249] Even friendly rivals, such as Amery, were denied the preferment they presumed as their right. He was marginalized in India.[250] Other troublesome creatures shuffled surreptitiously off the stage, whether by their own accord or through God's hand. Dawson retired, broken in health, in 1941. He died in 1944.[251] Lang went voluntarily, and in slightly better stead, in 1942. He too died in 1945.[252]

[243] Ball, *The Guardsmen*, 177 and 216ff.; Cooper on Spears is quoted in M. Egremont, *Under Two Flags: The Life of Major-General Sir Edward Spears* (London, 1997), 137. J. Colville, *The Churchillians* (London, 1981), chs 3–5 and 8–9, offers a kinder view of Churchill's clique.

[244] Gilbert, *Churchill*, vi. 326ff., acknowledges this only implicitly; Charmley, *Churchill*, ch. 35, is explicit. A. Roberts, *Eminent Churchillians* (London, 1994), ch. 3, is trenchant; Self, *Neville Chamberlain*, 431–4, is more subtle. See also Lawlor, *Churchill and the Politics of War*, ch. 4. For their short-lived but, in many ways, amicable cooperation, see above all, D. Dilks, 'The Twilight War and the Fall of France: Chamberlain and Churchill in 1940', *Transactions of the Royal Historical Society*, Fifth Series, 28 (1978), 61–86, esp. at 85–6.

[245] Simon, *Retrospect*, ch. 14 (see esp. p. 255), provides a deadpan account; cf. Dutton, *Simon*, ch. 11, esp. p. 301, which outlines the bitter truth.

[246] Halifax, *Fulness of Days*, 235, formally attributed this move to 'Providence operating through Churchill', but on 236 recognized the realities behind it. Roberts, *'The Holy Fox'*, chs 29–31, offers a full account, both of the fact and of his unexpected success in the role.

[247] Viscount Templewood (the Rt. Hon. Sir Samuel Hoare), *Nine Troubled Years* (London, 1954), 433, records this episode in one, short, paragraph – the last of the book. J. A. Cross, *Sir Samuel Hoare: A Political Biography* (London, 1977), 317–30, relates the episode in rather more detail. Churchill's *animus* is made clear on 326.

[248] W. S. Churchill, *The Second World War*, vol. 2: *Their Finest Hour* (London, 1949), 505, speaks of his 'return to the Foreign Office like a man going home'. Charmley, *Churchill*, 433–4, tells a different story.

[249] Gilbert, *Churchill*, vi. 120ff.; cf. I. R. Grimwood, *A Little Chit of a Fellow: A Biography of the Rt. Hon. Leslie Hore-Belisha* (Sussex, 2006), ch. 13; Lord Butler, *The Art of the Possible* (London, 1971), 86–91; A. Howard, *RAB: The Life of R. A. Butler* (London, 1987), 107–11.

[250] Barnes and Nicholson (eds), *The Empire at Bay*, 617, entry for 13 May 1940; Charmley, *Churchill*, 397; Ball, *The Guardsmen*, 214 and 219–20.

[251] Wrench, *Geoffrey Dawson*, ch. 37.

[252] Lockhart, *Cosmo Gordon Lang*, 453–4; see also A. L. Rowse, 'Archbishop Lang of the Abdication', in idem, *Friends and Contemporaries* (London, 1989), 157–81, esp. 180–1.

IV

It was, of course, no conscious part of Churchill's grand strategy to denude the Mallardians of their long-assumed access to the higher offices of the realm. Still, it had that effect. None of the College grandees returned to public prominence after 1945. None of them has ever really returned there since. With the exception of the office of the Lord Chancellor, no fellow of All Souls has filled any of these positions subsequently: nor, indeed, that of Attorney General, vacated by Somervell in 1945.[253] This is not the place seriously to consider why that has proved to be the case. We might merely observe that in this, as in so many other respects, the Second World War proved a watershed in modern British history. It signalled not merely the end of *Pax Britannica* but also of a system of social relations, even of a recognizable body of cultural assumptions, that might be conceived of as the sum of Victorian England.[254] Anson's All Souls may not have been the most significant of its victims. Nor was its passing perhaps quite so directly connected to the events of 1940–45. But it was a very Victorian institution. It was also something of a casualty of that later conflict. No one really noticed this change at the time. No one understood why it had happened for long after. But the glory days of 'the exceptional college' were gone forever.[255]

[253] Evershed, 'Somervell', 601.
[254] Taylor, *English History*, 600, puts it into poetry. A. Marwick, *Britain in the Century of Total War: War, Peace and Social Change, 1900–1967* (London, 1968), ch. 6, reverts to prose.
[255] Rowse, 'All Souls (1945)', 2–3 and 13ff., contemporaneously offered not so much as a hint: either of any sense of its imminent general eclipse or of his disapproval of the recent record of some of its recent fellows – including Dawson, Halifax, and Simon – in public affairs. Indeed, he allowed himself the amusing suggestion that perhaps the best form of national war memorial might be 'to found a Cambridge All Souls' (p. 3).

11

Leo Amery and the Post-War
World, 1945–55*

Wm. Roger Louis

This chapter assesses Leo Amery's place in the history of the post-war world, more specifically the post-war colonial world, during the last decade of his life. In 1945, at the age of 71, he lost his Parliamentary seat and never again held office. This was a time of reflection and writing, but he nevertheless continued as actively as ever to try to influence the course of national and international affairs. From the beginning to the end of the decade, Amery was preoccupied with economic issues of post-war reconstruction in Britain, the economic relations between Britain and Europe, and above all the economic ties between Britain and the Empire and Commonwealth. Another dominant intellectual concern is in the title of his Chichele Lectures in 1946, 'Thoughts on the Constitution', which in turn were the subject of a series of lectures in 1997 at All Souls by Lord Beloff.[1]

Amery's Chichele Lectures probably represented the zenith of his intellectual influence. His appearance to his audience in the University Examination Schools would have been striking because he was very short, only five foot four, but brimming over with vitality. At his first lecture he attracted an audience of four hundred, which diminished only slightly for the remainder of the series. From 1946 he continued to play an active part in the life of All Souls as a Distinguished Fellow. During this decade Amery published three volumes of his autobiography, but the fourth and last volume had yet to be completed at the time of his death

---

* An earlier version of this chapter was published in *The Journal of Imperial and Commonwealth History*, 30 (2002), 71–90, with acknowledgement to the Warden and Fellows of All Souls College for permission to do so.

[1] L. S. Amery, *Thoughts on the Constitution* (Oxford, 1947); 'More Thoughts on the Constitution', lectures delivered by Max (Lord) Beloff on 6, 13, and 20 February 1997 (typescript, All Souls College archives). Useful recent works on Amery include D. Faber, *Speaking for England: Leo, Julian and John Amery – The Tragedy of a Political Family* (London, 2005); and S. Onslow, 'Julian Amery and the Suez Operation', in S. C. Smith (ed.), *Reassessing Suez 1956: New Perspectives on the Crisis and its Aftermath* (Aldershot, 2008), 67–77.

in 1955.[2] There is no forewarning in the autobiography, which stops in 1940, of the tragedy of Leo's son, John, who was executed for high treason in December 1945.

His other son, Julian, increasingly became Leo's partner, taking over and continuing his father's work for a greater Commonwealth in which the Dominions and Colonies would be drawn together not only in economic recovery but also in self-defence against external challenges, especially from the United States. Julian had a Parliamentary career from 1950 that spanned nearly five decades, and he held high office, but the consensus among political observers is that he did not realize his full potential, and that in later years he became a caricature of a Tory imperialist. His later reputation has obscured his earlier achievement.

The use of the familiar names Leo and Julian, in part for clarity, seems natural enough because I became friends with Julian during the last decade of his life. I spent much time with him discussing his father's career and the partnership forged between him and his father as they worked together in an attempt to reverse the trend of allowing the Empire to disintegrate, for example, by the closing down of the great military base at Suez. Julian never objected to anything I said or wrote, and took for granted that historical accounts must be accurate and comprehensive as well as truthful. He was amused rather than offended, for instance, at the description of Leo by Sir Maurice Hankey, the Secretary of the War Cabinet during the First World War, as 'a scheming little devil' plotting intrigue and conspiracy.[3] There is, however, one problematic point about the family's history that has arisen since Julian's death because of the meticulous research of Professor William Rubinstein. Leo concealed, or at least never revealed, the Jewish identity of his mother.[4] It is hard to gauge how Julian would have responded to this revelation, though it would probably have been along the lines that he suspected as much. Indeed one would be surprised if Julian had not known the true details of his family's history. In any event, this discussion deals with Julian as well as Leo, and it picks up the story where my 1990 Chichele Lectures left it, at the end of the Second World War.[5] This account is based on a rereading of the Amery diaries, Julian's as well as Leo's, but also on a broader study of archival and other sources to place Leo and to some extent Julian in the context of the post-war colonial world.

---

[2] L. S. Amery, *My Political Life*, 3 vols (London, 1953–55). Some eight months before his death, Amery noted on New Year's Eve that he had completed volume 3 and hoped to complete volume 4 'before the middle of 1956': Diary, 31 Dec. 1954. All references to 'Diary' refer to the diaries of Leopold Amery unless otherwise specified, e.g. Julian Amery's Diary will be referred to as Julian Amery Diary. The Amery Papers, including the Diary, are accessible at Churchill College, Cambridge.

[3] Louis, *In the Name of God Go! Leo Amery and the British Empire in the Age of Churchill* (New York, 1992), 63.

[4] See W. Rubinstein, 'The Secret of Leopold Amery', *History Today*, 49 (February 1999), 17–23; and the more detailed version of the same article in *Historical Research*, 73 (June 2000), 175–96.

[5] Lectures published as Louis, *In the Name of God Go!*

I

The key to the personalities of Leo and Julian is that they were both patriots. This is a point worth emphasizing while reviewing some of the main aspects of Leo's life. He was born in 1873, a year before Churchill. Their careers ran parallel. They were intellectual equals, though Churchill was the more grandiloquent. Amery was one of the few contemporaries Churchill could not browbeat. They were schoolboys together at Harrow, and in the last stage of his career Amery served as Churchill's Secretary of State for India 1940–45. But even though they were closely associated, they were never intimate friends. On India and other matters Amery held quite different views from Churchill. For instance, Amery helped to prepare the way for India's independence, though it must not be assumed that he did so entirely for liberal reasons. He believed that independence and equality rather than continued subjugation would be the only way to keep India within the British Imperial system. In this regard there is a consistent thread that runs through his thought. Whether at the time of the Boer War or the Second World War, Amery saw that the Colonies or Dominions, or for that matter nations generally, would cooperate only on the basis of free association. He championed the cause of national independence. This is why he was held in high esteem by one of the great historians of the British Empire at All Souls, Sir Keith Hancock (discussed elsewhere in this volume by Jim Davidson). Hancock identified Amery's purpose as his own. He believed that he could have a dual loyalty to both Australia and Britain. Amery upheld this principle, but it is useful to inquire into his underlying or ultimate motive. As with most things about Amery, there was a certain logic. Amery believed in the cause of the Empire and Commonwealth, in Britain's place in the world, and in the capacity of the Empire and Commonwealth to sustain British power and influence.

Amery was elected to All Souls in 1897. His experience at the College was the paramount influence on both his personality and his career. He took advantage of the opportunity to widen his intellectual horizons and he used his college connections. In every sense he was a good college man. Throughout his life, he took college responsibilities seriously, he came to All Souls whenever possible on weekends, he viva'd or interviewed candidates, he befriended younger members, and he relished the banter and conversation. In public speeches as in government committees or other meetings, he could be tedious. But in conversation he was quick and amusing. In this sense there were two Leo Amerys, one the public bore, the other the college personality. And here William Rubinstein's research raises a question. Would Amery have won an All Souls Prize Fellowship had it been known that his mother was Jewish? Throughout his life, and in his memoirs, he referred to his mother simply as Hungarian.

The evidence of Amery's Jewish ancestry has been firmly established in synagogue records. Amery himself always gave his name as Leopold Charles

Maurice Stennett Amery. His third name at birth, however, was 'Moritz', as recorded on his baptismal form in India. When preparing a legal document at the time of his mother's death in 1908, he used the name Moritz.[6] There is no doubt that he was fully aware of his Jewish ancestry. Why then did he conceal it? Anti-Jewish sentiment at All Souls would not necessarily have doomed him to defeat. Concealment of Jewish origins was not by any means regarded as a serious offence in Oxford circles of the time. But Lewis Namier failed in his quest for an All Souls fellowship in 1911 and anti-Jewish sentiment did play a part in the decision.[7] In the event, the first Jew – Amery's case aside – to be elected to All Souls was Isaiah Berlin in 1932.[8]

Amery apparently thought that his Jewish ancestry might have damaged his chances. He always regarded his All Souls election as close. As late as 1945 one of his rivals speculated that, had he not been forced to withdraw from the examination because of illness, he, not Amery, would have been elected.[9] So keen was the competition that Amery probably believed that knowledge of his Jewish origins would not have helped him and might have hurt him. There is also a psychological dimension. Once something has been concealed, especially early on, then it becomes increasingly difficult to reveal it. Even during his school days at Harrow there was no mention of Amery as Jewish. Might his mother's Jewishness have prevented him from entry to Harrow as well as All Souls? Again, possibly, though not necessarily. Harrow would probably have been mainly interested in whether or not he would attend chapel. Conformity was the key point. But we will never know. All this is worth bearing in mind because Amery had a reputation for absolute honesty. The question about his Jewish ancestry would surely have caused him anguish if it had been raised in his lifetime.

Some things were too painful for Amery to mention in his diary. There is virtually no reference to his son John before the end of the Second World War and John's imprisonment at Wandsworth on grounds of high treason at the end of July 1945. The outbreak of the war in 1939 had found John in France, where he lived as an expatriate after having participated in the Spanish Civil War on the fascist side. It appears that John Amery may have become a Spanish citizen. Though the circumstances are controversial, this was the legal point on which Leo and Julian hoped to base John's defence. In the autumn of 1945 Julian – seven years younger than his brother[10] – went to Spain to acquire evidence of

[6] See Rubinstein, 'The Secret of Leopold Amery', *Historical Research*.

[7] According to Patrick Shaw-Stewart, who had been elected a fellow in the previous year: 'by the strenuous efforts of me and one or two others, the election of a Polish Jew from Balliol, much the strongest candidate really, was prevented.' Quoted in M. G. Brock, 'The Oxford of Raymond Asquith', in M. G. Brock and M. C. Curthoys (eds), *Hist. Univ. Oxf.*, vii, 2, 802. Namier failed in a second attempt in 1912.

[8] See M. Ignatieff, *Isaiah Berlin: A Life* (New York, 1998), 61: 'As Isaiah was to learn later, another fellow, the Bishop of Gloucester, objected to the very idea of electing a Jew to a fellowship.'

[9] Diary, 20 Nov. 1945. Amery referred to Sir Arthur Robinson, a distinguished civil servant.

[10] Julian was born in 1919, John in 1912.

John's Spanish citizenship. If he had been a Spanish citizen, then he could not be tried for British treason. Or so the case could be made. But the evidence did not hold up for technical reasons concerning the certified copies of the naturalization certificate.

In November 1945 Amery had to face the prospect that the only way to save John's life would be an appeal to the Home Secretary for a reprieve on grounds of insanity or perhaps near insanity. But this would be difficult to argue because John in ordinary conversation was rational and could be charming. The writer Rebecca West, who followed the case, probably summed it up best: 'He was, judged by any accepted standard, not mad, but he was not sane.'[11] Leo's own judgement, the idea that runs through his diary at this time, was that John suffered from 'moral instability'.

Amery believed that if the facts of John's 'psychopathic' and profligate life were established, then it would at least be obvious that he was not a dangerous enemy of the state and thus did not deserve execution. At the age of sixteen John had been diagnosed by a psychiatrist as lacking any sense of moral responsibility. A few other points help to establish the context of erratic and irresponsible behaviour. In 1927 he ran away from Harrow to become a film director – perhaps not a bad career choice but he also pursued a dissolute life. In 1936 he was forced to declare bankruptcy. He led what was then called the life of a playboy. He had a taste for wine, women, fast cars, and gambling. Leo had repeatedly helped him financially. In Amery's own words, John was 'a psychopathic case who if he had not been my son and always bailed out by me would long ago have been shut up in an institution'.[12] After fighting on Franco's side of the Spanish Civil War by helping to smuggle arms across the Pyrenees, John fell into ill health, which in 1939 drove him to a sanatorium in the south of France. After he regained his strength, he collaborated with the Germans and from 1942 toured British prisoner-of-war camps to recruit a 'Legion of St George' to fight along with German troops against the Russians. In his view the true enemy was not Nazi Germany but the Soviet Union. He made broadcasts for the Nazis in an attempt to persuade Britain to change sides.[13] These facts, Leo noted in his diary, were not in dispute. His son was a traitor. John saved his family the anguish of a prolonged public trial by admitting his guilt. On 28 November 1945 he stated to the judge: 'I plead guilty to all counts.' But unless the Home Secretary offered a reprieve, death would be certain. For treason there could be no other sentence.

Leo first visited John in prison in late November, after John's admission of guilt. The diary entry reads:

[11] R. West, *The Meaning of Treason* (first published 1949; London, 1952), 197.

[12] Diary, 6 Dec. 1945.

[13] See especially M. R. D. Foot, 'Amery, John (1912–1945)', *ODNB*; A. Weale, *Patriot Traitors: Roger Casement, John Amery and the Real Meaning of Treason* (London, 2001); West, *The Meaning of Treason*.

I had not felt able to see Jack before – he has made us all suffer so terribly – but I felt I must do so now. He was delighted to see me, cheerful and full of talk on the big political issues, all most intelligently and ably put. He has grown into a real man and a personality and no longer a play boy... [14]

Leo spent the rest of that day reflecting on John's courage in entering a plea of guilty, thus accepting the responsibility for his actions, and knowing that it would lead to his execution. Leo began to write a statement explaining John's behaviour. John was a misguided English patriot. He fought on the side of the Germans not because he was anti-British but because of a misconceived idea that it was imperative to rally British troops against the Russian Communists. This was the basis of the pamphlet circulated privately by Leo after John's execution. [15] One has the feeling that it is Leo's rather than John's rationale, especially in its coherence, but there can be no doubt from the diary that Leo believed it – or wanted to believe it.

The Home Secretary refused to recommend a reprieve. On 17 December 1945 the Amery family learned that the law would take its course. In one sense the news came as a relief. Once reconciled to the inevitability of execution, Leo believed that it was better to have died a noble death than to have lived a life in prison or, if granted a reprieve, to have reconstructed a life that had been, in Leo's view, worthless. 'Reprieved he would have been an object of contemptuous pity...' [16] By all accounts John conducted himself with dignity and honour. Members of his immediate family went to see him for the last time at Wandsworth on 18 December. According to Leo's diary:

He took charge of us all for an hour, full of charm and gaiety and whimsical humour and philosophic detachment... Once he said in passing, 'la vie est belle', but with no touch of sentimentality, and his whole attitude was that he had done his work and that it might be recognised afterwards... It [his heroic confession of guilt] has blotted out all memory of his many sad vagaries in the one recollection of the man of finest steel whom big experience and the supreme test have forged, hammering out all the dross.

Amery reflected a couple of weeks later, on New Year's Eve 1946, summing up this excruciating episode in his life: 'the one consoling aspect is that after a sorry life Jack rose at the end to a height of courage and dignity which atoned for all and made him a happy and even proud memory'. [17] Leo's diary reveals another thought, which intensifies the element of human drama. Beneath the new courage of his lost son, Leo detected in the 'cheery naturalness' a trace 'of the old Jack' who had never been capable 'of realizing that he had done anything wrong and never felt a shadow of shame or remorse'. [18]

[14] Diary, 30 Nov. 1945.
[15] L. S. Amery, *John Amery: An Explanation* (privately published, London, 1946).
[16] Diary, 19 Dec. 1945.
[17] Diary, 31 Dec. 1945.
[18] Diary, 30 Nov. 1945.

II

The drama of Jack's execution preoccupied the Amery family for much of the autumn and winter of 1945–6. The episode reveals Amery's human qualities that have sometimes been overlooked by historians dealing with his public life. There was a surprising hostility towards him vented by a few critics when they reviewed my Chichele Lectures published in 1992. Some of the reviewers took the opportunity not to comment on the book so much as to attack Amery. With friends like Amery, concluded the review in *The Times Literary Supplement*, did the Empire need any enemies?[19] Amery is out of fashion. He espoused the cause of the Empire and the Commonwealth, he spoke in the racist vernacular of the time, referring to 'Jews', 'Niggers', and 'Chinks' (though certainly far less than Churchill and many others of the era). He represented elitism, in that the public associated him with All Souls College and its legendary contacts and influence. Amery's reputation declined at the same time that All Souls came under criticism for not making a sufficient contribution to the life of the University. This was not a coincidence. In the two decades after his death in 1955, the popularity of the British Empire reached its nadir. To his critics, Amery represented not only the idea of exploitation and the racism of the Empire but also the small group of people who controlled it and manipulated much of British public life as well.

There is an element of truth to all that. Amery by present-day standards was politically incorrect. He did, along with Churchill and others born in the Victorian age, hold racial and other stereotypes, he did represent British imperialism, and he did believe that All Souls was and should remain an elite institution. Looked at from the outside, it is easy to see how All Souls resembled a sort of conspiracy, and why some of Amery's critics regarded him as manipulative. More positively put, he had a talent for making things happen behind the scenes. Amery was what today would be called a networker or facilitator. One is struck in reading his diaries of the post-war era by how much of his time was dedicated simply to helping others as well as to promoting his own ideas. He was militant and aggressive, but this should not deflect attention from the extent to which he assisted others to achieve things that otherwise would have been beyond their reach. As for All Souls, Amery died before its time of troubles in the 1960s and 1970s. But the pattern of his College participation suggests that he certainly would have backed the response of All Souls to the criticism of 'infirmity of purpose' by creating the programme of Visiting Fellows.

In the autumn of 1945, even though he was preoccupied with Jack's fate, Amery campaigned against the conditions attached to the American loan to the British government for $3.75 billion. Amery was also much concerned with the

---

[19] Andrew Porter in *The Times Literary Supplement*, 25 Dec. 1992.

health of his wife, 'Bryddie' or 'B' as she was known within the family, who never fully recovered from the ordeal of the execution. He was very much a family man, but he never lapsed in his public duty. What is remarkable in this case is that he completed his book, *The Washington Loan Agreements*, during the time of family troubles.[20] This short work is remarkable as a polemic against 'irresponsible American capitalism'. According to Amery himself, it failed to influence the outcome of the negotiations or to bring about a general reconsideration of the issues. Still, the book is of interest because it so sharply restates his views at the beginning of the post-war era. To Amery, the United States posed a vicious challenge to the bedrock principles of Imperial Preference, by which he meant the tightly integrated economic system that would strengthen economic union with the Colonies and Dominions while safeguarding British industry from foreign competition, maintaining a high level of employment, and raising revenue for social reform.

Leo Amery carried the standard of Joseph Chamberlain, who inspired the idea of an Imperial economy at the turn of the century. Julian in turn continued to champion Chamberlain's cause. In 1946 Julian was invited to carry on with J. L. Garvin's unfinished three-volume biography of Joseph Chamberlain. This was a compliment to Julian's reputation as a serious writer. The biography, which he completed in three volumes, analysed, with subtlety and stylistic flair, the protectionist measures of Britain's economy.[21] Julian as well as Leo not only studied the complexity of the system but caught its spirit. The basic idea was to build a wall of tariffs around the British Empire, within which there would be a self-sufficient common market. It would withstand the vicissitudes of the world economy, not least the upheavals of American capitalism. This was a sophisticated, flexible, and complicated system, among other reasons, because there were no uniform tariffs but intricate bilateral agreements designed to regulate – to mutual and collective advantage – the flow of foodstuffs, raw materials, and manufactured goods. The Dominions, for example, fixed their own tariffs to protect domestic industries, while giving preference to other Dominions as well as Britain in other sectors.

Imperial Preference had reached its high water mark with the Ottawa tariffs of 1932, though Ottawa to Leo represented only a partial victory. Britain and the Dominions negotiated bilateral agreements on timber, metals, tobacco, wheat, beef, mutton, lamb, bacon, sugar, cocoa, coffee, fish, and apples.[22] These arrangements did not constitute a uniform system. Amery wanted to forge an Imperial economy by developing a common agricultural and industrial community as well as a single currency. The Ottawa agreements fell far short of those

---

[20] The subtitle is: *A Critical Study of American Foreign Economic Policy* (London, 1946).

[21] Julian Amery, *The Life of Joseph Chamberlain*, vol. 4: *At the Height of His Power, 1901–1903* (London, 1951); vol. 5: *Joseph Chamberlain and the Tariff Reform Campaign, 1901–1903* (London, 1969); vol. 6: *Joseph Chamberlain and the Tariff Reform Campaign, 1903–1968* (London, 1969).

[22] See Louis, *In the Name of God Go!* 106–8.

goals, but the extravagant claims made by him and others had the effect of convincing the United States government that the British were sealing off the Empire behind a scaffolding of tariffs to the detriment of American trade. After the outbreak of the Second World War, the Americans pressed time and again for the abolition of Imperial Preference. Amery was outspoken in his criticism of American motive, which he regarded as a naked reach for economic dominance. In 1946, as earlier, he emerged as the unrelenting critic of what he believed to be the American bid for hegemony by reducing Britain to an economic satellite. The test came in July 1947 when sterling became convertible in accordance with the Loan agreements. The British economy could not withstand the strain. The Americans quickly allowed the British to re-establish sterling controls rather than see the collapse of the British economy. Amery felt that he had been vindicated, though it was a hollow victory. 'How sadly right I have proved [to be]', he wrote in his diary.[23] He upheld the principle, as he had throughout his career, that a closed economic system would be the only way to promote British recovery and prosperity, and that the British economy needed shelter from the rapacious thrusts of American capitalism.

Britain's economic crisis of July 1947 coincided with Amery's own financial crisis. In the same week that sterling became convertible, he learned that a principal source of his income had been cancelled. This was a contract with the *Sunday Times* worth £2,500 a year (roughly £50,000 today). Amery's annual income was less than £4,000 a year (Churchill's income by comparison was £12,000 yearly). With other losses, three-fourths of his annual income had been eliminated within a few weeks.[24] He pondered giving up the house in Eaton Square and the prospect of 'becoming homeless'.[25] He anticipated a period of sacrifice and privation, though he continued to have faith in his own ability for hard work and ingenuity. Perhaps with luck he would pull through. This was a period of acute anxiety for Amery, but within a month the South African financier Sir Ernest Oppenheimer offered him a seat on a company board, Rhokanna, and restored £2,000 of the missing income.

The prospect for improving the British economy also appeared on the horizon in 1947 with the discussion of how best to respond to the initiative of Secretary of State George Marshall and what became known as the Marshall Plan. Amery continued to believe that Britain must break free from the trammels of American economic domination, accepting the responsibility for her own debt, and restoring a balanced economy by thoroughgoing reforms in agriculture and industry and by the systematic development of the Empire's resources. Amery's mind was moving in the same direction as those within the British government who were beginning to devise an elaborate system of currency controls and development

---

[23] Diary, 7 Aug. 1947.
[24] Diary, 7 July 1947.
[25] Diary, 7–8 July 1947.

plans for cocoa in West Africa and groundnuts in East Africa. He regarded the Marshall plan as an opportunity to develop a coordinated European economic policy that would complement Britain's economy. This was one point on which Amery and Churchill agreed. They were both Europeans in the sense that they wanted to see Germany re-established as an equal and prosperous country and a participant in a European economic union. They were not Europeans in any sense of wanting to join a European political union. But they were not hostile to it. Amery in particular saw the future of the world as developing in economic blocs. There was no reason why Europe's economy could not prosper along with Britain's with the two interacting or combining to counter American economic influence. Britain would remain a world power holding the balance between the United States and the Soviet Union.

III

The danger was that the British Empire might disintegrate in the process of restructuring the post-war world. Amery and many others in the winter and spring of 1946–7 believed India to be on the verge of civil war. His views on India bore a close similarity to those of Lord Wavell, the Viceroy, with whom Amery had worked in the latter part of the war to move India forward towards independence. Both had been frustrated by Churchill, and both were now critical of the Labour government's partiality, so they believed, towards Jawaharlal Nehru and the Indian National Congress with, in their view, the malevolent figure of Gandhi in the background. Wavell had a fixed antipathy towards the leaders of the Congress, especially Gandhi, as did Amery. The Muslims, they believed, had genuine grievances. 'I must admit I feel grave disquiet at the handing over of almost unlimited power to Nehru and his crowd without the steadying counter-influence of the Moslems', Amery wrote in his diary.[26] He thought that Wavell made a major advance when he secured, so it seemed at the time, the cooperation of Mohammed Ali Jinnah, the Muslim leader, in late 1946. But by then Wavell was heading towards a collision with his political masters in London as well as with Nehru. 'Nehru is talking most mischievously against Wavell because of Jinnah's attitude', Amery recorded.[27] In November 1946 he posed the question of how the Labour government would respond to the crisis:

The question is whether if it comes to civil war or near it the Government here will order Wavell to support Nehru with British or British officered troops or will face the alternative of either falling back on the Moslem provinces and the States with the Army, or else reverting for the time being to direct Viceroy Government.[28]

[26] Diary, 1 Oct. 1946.
[27] Diary, 21 Nov. 1946.
[28] Diary, 23 Nov. 1946.

In other words, would the British government revert to emergency rule over all of India, the Indian states as well as the provinces, in a last-ditch effort to preserve India's unity? Alas, Amery concluded, Britain no longer possessed the military power to do so: 'The Civil Service and Police are demoralised and even the Army cannot be relied on indefinitely to prevent civil war.'[29] The British now had neither the resources nor the will power to prevent further deterioration. Amery had an informed opinion because he talked directly with Wavell when the latter came to London in December 1946.[30] A few weeks later Wavell was sacked. Amery rightly suspected that one of the reasons lay in Wavell's hostility towards the Congress and his underlying sympathy with at least some of Jinnah's aims. There is a recurrent theme of indignation in Amery's diary at the lack of gratitude demonstrated by the Labour government towards Wavell. Amery believed him to be one of the great viceroys of India who had not only stood up to Churchill but had challenged the Labour government to deal fairly with the Muslims and not to load the dice in favour of the Congress. Amery rightly suspected that Wavell's political courage was one of the reasons for his dismissal – or, as he later described it in his diary, the 'parting kick to poor Wavell'.[31]

Amery and Wavell had a convergence of views on one point that went to the heart of the problem of partition as well as on one of the preoccupations of Wavell's successor, Lord Mountbatten. Amery no less than Wavell believed that Gandhi was essentially a Hindu nationalist. Whatever his claim to sainthood, his influence on British rule and the fate of the Muslims and other minorities had been entirely pernicious. Amery wrote about the period up to independence:

He was, I daresay, a genuine saint. But he used his sanctity to the full as an instrument of dictatorial power. And he was, in fact, if not in intention a good bit of a humbug. From our point of view he sabotaged every attempt to advance Indian self-government... He was for all or nothing... He won his power by being as essentially Hindu as Winston was British or Hitler lower middle class German. But in winning it he made Congress all the more repulsive to the Moslems.[32]

This judgment on Gandhi's essential Hinduism led Amery to conclude that Gandhi himself was in large part responsible for the partition of India and the subsequent massacres. After Gandhi's assassination in January 1948, Amery refused to take a sentimental view. 'Whether he did more mischief as a politician or he did good as a preacher of non-violence', Amery wrote, 'will always be an open question.' But in contrast to Wavell, Amery recognized the spiritual dimension of Gandhi's greatness. He believed that in time 'the more purely

---

[29] Diary, 4 Dec. 1946.
[30] Wavell recorded his own view of Amery at this time: 'His views on India are not up to date with the pace things have been going, and are still tinged with Imperialism, but he has plenty of common sense about it all.' P. Moon (ed.), *Wavell: The Viceroy's Journal* (Oxford, 1973), 395.
[31] Diary, 3 June 1947.
[32] Diary, 5 Sept. 1947.

spiritual significance of the man' would transcend his political accomplishments. 'Exactly the proportions between true saintliness and political astuteness and love of power may never be determined.'[33]

Amery habitually claimed credit for at least having a hand in large political developments. Though he did not suggest to anyone in the Labour government that Mountbatten be appointed Viceroy in 1947, he had proposed him rather than Wavell as Lord Linlithgow's successor during the war.[34] Mountbatten was appointed in February 1947. By early summer of that year Amery entirely agreed with him about the necessity of partition. When Mountbatten returned to London in May to consult with members of the Labour government on setting the date for independence two months later, Amery was among those he consulted. Amery cheered him on, in part because of the constitutional part of the problem. Independence would now be granted before the completion of final constitutional arrangements. 'That means following the line I have always myself advocated of transferring power under the existing constitution and letting them enjoy it while they are framing their own constitution.'[35] It is interesting that as a constitutional authority Amery despised, in his phrase, 'constitutional pedantry'.[36] He wanted first and foremost a political settlement. This was the part of Mountbatten's solution that appealed to him the most, as it did to Churchill, because India as well as Pakistan would remain a Dominion. Mountbatten had achieved what only a few months previously had seemed to be virtually impossible. Britain would withdraw on friendly terms with the two successor regimes. Promising Mountbatten that he would do all he could to steady Tory opinion, Amery also gave his blessing to the plan of partition with 'the greatest goodwill'.[37] On the date of independence, 15 August 1947, Amery wrote to Mountbatten that the achievement was 'so much better than one dared to hope at one time, at least so far as Anglo-Indian goodwill is concerned'.[38] India as well as Pakistan would remain within the British system.

If Amery thought that the British had managed reasonably well in India, he believed the situation in Palestine to be a disaster, in his phrase, a 'scuttle'. Amery's connection with Palestine went back to the Balfour Declaration in 1917 when he worked in the Cabinet secretariat and had a hand in the drafting of the declaration itself. Amery was careful never to claim original authorship of the declaration, but in this as in many other instances he did not hesitate in his diary to describe his influence in bringing about seminal developments. In the earlier case of South Africa, for example, he reflected that he had helped to create the band of disciples of Lord Milner known as the Kindergarten: 'I seem to have

[33] Diary, 31 Jan. 1948.
[34] P. Ziegler, *Mountbatten: The Official Biography* (London, 1985), 354.
[35] Diary, 27 May 1947.
[36] Diary, 17 May 1946.
[37] Diary, 27 May 1947.
[38] Diary, 15 Aug. 1947.

been responsible for most of M.'s Kindergarten, for I planted Lionel Curtis . . . on to him and he brought out his whole train of New College friends . . . [including] Bob Brand and Philip Kerr.'[39] On the Balfour Declaration, he wrote carefully in his memoirs:

Milner . . . showed me one or two alternative drafts which had been suggested, with none of which he was quite satisfied. Could I draft something which would go a reasonable distance to meeting the objectors, both Jewish and pro-Arab, without impairing the substance of the proposed declaration? I sat down and quickly produced the following . . . [40]

– which proved to be identical to the Balfour Declaration itself in final form. This is a theme that appears repeatedly in the diaries. To give a much later example about Palestine, he remarked on the partition plan devised by the United Nations Special Committee on Palestine in 1947: 'the U. N. O. recommendation is almost identical with the partition scheme I put before the Cabinet Committee during the war'.[41] What is one to make of this? There can be no doubt that Amery, always modest in conversation, exaggerated in his diary. Yet his influence existed to some degree. Perhaps it was not always so direct or as seminal as he suggested, but for a full half century, in and out of government, Amery was close to many of the events he described. He held emphatic views, and he conducted a voluminous correspondence. There is a revealing passage in the diary for 1946 on how Amery addressed himself to this point: 'I am not so sure that when my chapter is finally closed the most useful part of it may not have been what I have through my talks and letters induced others to do, rather than the things I have actually been credited with myself.'[42] On Palestine, he consistently pleaded the Zionist cause.

In no other case, perhaps, did the idealistic and Machiavellian parts of Amery's personality find such an intricate balance. Whether or not his knowledge of his mother's Jewishness contributed to his Zionism, it is true that he regarded the Balfour Declaration as an idealistic statement. He believed that the Jews were entitled to a national home and that this might be accomplished in harmony with Arab aspirations. At the same time, he wrote that the Jews could be put to work to help build the Empire in the same way as the Scots. This was the manipulative side of Amery's character, which also had a strategic preoccupation. Palestine would become the lynchpin of British communications in the eastern Mediterranean with superb opportunities for the Royal Navy, the Army, and the Royal Air Force to construct permanent bases. Amery thus watched with unmitigated

[39] Diary, 5 Aug. 1947. On the Kindergarten see also Howard, this volume.
[40] L. S. Amery, *My Political Life*, vol. 2: *War and Peace, 1914–1929* (London, 1953), 116.
[41] Diary, 4 September 1947.
[42] Diary, 31 May 1946. Or, as he later pursued this line of thought: 'I daresay I may have done far more in the world for my ideas by getting them into the heads of others than by my own public advocacy.' Diary, 3 Oct. 1948.

dismay the action of the Labour government after 1945, in particular that of the Foreign Secretary, Ernest Bevin. Amery and Bevin held antithetical views. Bevin wanted the Jews to be reintegrated into European society. He believed that the creation of a Jewish state would lead to lasting tension with the Arabs that in turn would poison Britain's relations with the Arab world. In Palestine itself, Bevin supported the solution of a bi-national state in which the Jews and Arabs would have autonomy as well as constitutional guarantees for religious and other rights. Amery believed that the Jews had a right to a state of their own, especially in view of their suffering during the war, and that a sharp and clear partition was the only solution. He had held this view at least since the mid-1930s and he espoused it all the more vehemently after 1945.

When Amery pondered the problem of Palestine, he was troubled by the memory of Ireland, where terrorism and civil war had led to partition. Though a committed Zionist, he had no sympathy with what he called the 'fanatical Jewish terrorists'. 'One is haunted by the unpleasant thought that, as in Ireland, the terrorists may achieve their end.'[43] If fanatical Jews managed to seize control of a new state, and if it became expansionist in the sense of conquering more and more Arab territories, then they would create an Arab resistance that might lead to the destruction of the Jewish state itself. Amery wanted a compact Israel mainly along the coast that would be able to defend itself while creating the minimal amount of Arab opposition. This was an idea not far removed from the concept of the rump Jewish state embraced in British official circles as the best outcome of an increasingly desperate situation. Amery did not know the inner thought of the Colonial Office or Foreign Office, but he was offended at the failure to guide the lines of partition or indeed to accept the responsibility for the events leading to all-out civil war. It was beyond his comprehension that a British administration would simply throw up its hands – 'just walking out without handing over such elementary things as water works, Police, etc., to somebody'.[44] To repeat his phrase, this was a 'humiliating scuttle'.[45] What would be the consequences? After the declaration of the state of Israel in May 1948, Amery feared that the new Jewish state would be even smaller than the one anticipated by the Peel Commission in the 1930s, mainly along the lines of coastal strips where there were Jewish settlements. At one point he pessimistically thought that the Jews 'may be forced in the end to abandon their state and in some sort accept Arab sovereignty'.[46] In one of the remarkable military and political developments that he admitted he failed to predict, the Israelis not only held their own but successfully defended the desert area of the Negev extending to the Gulf of

---

[43] Diary, 17 Sept. 1948.
[44] Diary, 20 Oct. 1947.
[45] Diary, 11 May 1948.
[46] Diary, 29 May 1948.

Aqaba. What Amery had underestimated, and what he joyfully acknowledged, was 'the immense superiority of the Jews in fighting spirit'.[47]

IV

One of the last great episodes of Amery's life was his role in the origin of the Suez crisis, and in this political drama Julian played an equal part.[48] From July 1945 to about 1950 Leo had hoped to regain a seat in the House of Commons. His quest was thwarted in part because of his increasing deafness. He occasionally responded to speeches at dinners when he did not fully understand what the speaker had said. His remarks thus sometimes created a certain bemusement on the part of his audience. In any event he accurately sensed that the Conservative Party preferred a younger man. He might have gone to the House of Lords, but he refused to be considered for a peerage because after his death Julian would inherit the title, which would mean the end to a career in the House of Commons. Leo wanted to do nothing to damage Julian's political prospects. Though Leo was involved from the late 1940s onwards in discussions with Churchill and others about creating Life Peerages, this innovation in the House of Lords occurred only in 1958, three years after his death.[49]

Julian entered the House of Commons in 1950, the same year he married Catherine, the daughter of Harold Macmillan. Julian never made it to Cabinet rank, but he did eventually serve as Colonial Undersecretary (1958–60), Minister for Aviation (1962–4), and later Minister of State at the Foreign Office (1972–4). His principal achievement in colonial affairs was in 1960, when he negotiated with Archbishop Makarios the terms of independence for Cyprus and secured two British sovereign bases on the island. In the period from 1950 he – along with Leo – opposed the British withdrawal from Suez. Both had many other issues with which they were concerned, but the base at Suez was the paramount problem. Julian referred to Suez as the nerve centre of the British Empire, or in another striking phrase that he used in a newspaper article, as 'The Clapham Junction of the Commonwealth'.[50] If the British lost Suez, they would lose much more than the sea and air routes to India and Australia. It is difficult to convey to a present-day readership the emotional as well as the political significance that Julian attached to the eclipse of the Empire. He believed that the

[47] Diary, 27 Aug. 1948.
[48] See further Louis, this volume, ch. 12.
[49] In late 1951 at Harrow Churchill drew Amery aside, 'and asked me whether I would like to go to the House of Lords'. The diary entry continues: 'He realised my difficulty about Julian but thought that presently the House of Lords would be reformed and Hereditary Peers given the right to opt for the House of Commons. But he was quite vague when I asked when that was likely to be.' J. Barnes and D. Nicholson (eds.), *The Empire at Bay: The Leo Amery Diaries, 1929–1945* (London, 1988), epilogue, 1050–1.
[50] *Everybody's*, 21 Nov. 1953, news cutting, Julian Amery Papers.

British would not only lose their place in the world but also their sense of national purpose and indeed their common national identity.

The Amerys believed that the Egyptians were systematically undermining the British position. Julian's words have a resonance that sounds familiar in the context of the present-day problem of terrorism in the Middle East and elsewhere. He stated in 1951:

[The Egyptians] have deliberately encouraged xenophobia, and, in this process, have unleashed terrorist forces which they can no longer control. For six years now, the whole Middle East has been in the grip of an epidemic of terrorism. The list of assassinations and attempted assassinations is formidable. At least a dozen of the leading men of Syria, Egypt, the Lebanon, Jordan and Persia have been struck down ... The killings of moderate leaders are not just mad outbursts of fanaticism. They are acts of deliberate policy and it is very hard to believe that they are not all part of a common design.[51]

The Egyptian revolution of 1952 persuaded neither of the Amerys that the Egyptian government, whether of King Farouk, General Mohammed Neguib, or later Colonel Gamal Abdul Nasser, had changed in its hostility towards Britain. If anything the animosity had merely gained momentum as it shifted to the left with General Neguib and to the revolutionary left with Nasser. Yet the Amerys believed that the Egyptian people themselves remained friendly to the British because of the benefits of economic and social reform brought to Egypt, in Julian's words, by 'the work of Milner and Cromer'. There was nothing wrong with the Egyptian people. The problem was with their leaders.

The great, ongoing national drama of Suez was one of the closing episodes in Leo's life. During his last four years, he finally reconciled himself to the role of a political observer when Churchill failed to invite him to become a member of the Conservative government of 1951. Yet Leo continued to play an important part in advising the 'Suez Group' of Conservatives in the House of Commons who rebelled against 'appeasement in Egypt'. His diary remains an important source of information. For example, it has often been assumed that the British in 1956 had no coherent plan in attempting to oust Nasser. Who would take his place? According to Leo, writing in 1953, the goal would be 'a temporary occupation of Cairo and [the] formation of a friendly government'.[52] The purpose would be not only to provide stability in Egypt but to reassert Britain's position in the Middle East. In Amery's view, radical Egyptian or Arab nationalism presented only one obstacle to a revival of British sway. There were also external dangers. Amery thought that the United States as well as the Soviet Union wanted to

51 *Parliamentary Debates* (Commons), 30 July 1951, cols. 1020–1.
52 Diary, 6 Oct. 1953. The comment reflected a conversation with Sir Walter Smart, the former Oriental Minister in the British embassy in Cairo. According to Julian, the pro-British Egyptian government would be constructed mainly around the former Prime Minister Nahas Pasha. Julian had MI6 contacts who would assist – this part of the story remains obscure – but he believed that Nahas and others represented a genuine alternative government and would not be British puppets.

destroy the British Empire in the Middle East and elsewhere. Whether consciously or not, the United States, Amery believed, aimed 'to break up the British
Commonwealth'.[53] 'Suez', which was often a shorthand expression for Egypt,
had an overarching symbolic as well as a military and economic significance. By
holding fast the British would demonstrate to the Americans as well as the
Egyptians and colonial peoples throughout the world that the spirit of the
Empire remained unbroken. 'If only we stand firm now it may be a turning
point in the whole psychology of the Empire.'[54]

Amery was certainly right about the psychological dimension of the Suez crisis,
but he did not live to see the outcome. He died in September 1955. During the
next year – the year of the climax of the Suez crisis – Julian established his
reputation as the champion of British imperialism of his generation. It was the
formative event in his career. In the House of Commons, he had emerged,
despite his youth, as one of the leaders of the Suez Group of about forty fellow
MPs who wanted to maintain Britain's position at Suez. After Nasser nationalized
the Suez Canal Company in July 1956, Julian felt that public sentiment in
Britain had shifted decisively in their favour. At first, the country was united in
outrage at Nasser's takeover of the Canal. Aneurin Bevan, the Labour leader who
later led the attack against Anthony Eden, tapped Julian on the shoulder and
said, 'I'm sorry to say, Julian, you've been right after all.'[55] The members of the
Suez Group felt vindicated by the strong current of anti-Nasser sentiment. They
drank champagne together. But the euphoria did not last long. Eden quickly
seemed to revert to true form, Julian believed, by caving in to both the Egyptians
and the Americans. Instead of a quick and decisive military action to restore the
canal under British and French control, the Suez crisis seemed destined to peter
out in endless international discussion.

Julian detested Anthony Eden. He believed Eden to be weak, indecisive, and
entirely unreliable when it came to matters concerning the Empire. When the
Suez crisis drifted into the faint-hearted negotiations at the United Nations,
Julian despaired. Later on, he could hardly believe his eyes when he read in the
newspapers on 1 November that Israeli troops had attacked the Egyptians and
were moving through the Sinai peninsula towards Suez.

> The morning papers announced an Israeli attack on Egypt. My immediate reaction was
> that this was the heaven-sent opportunity for armed intervention. My next thought, that
> Eden would never have the guts to do it... The more I thought about it, the more sure
> I became that we must intervene and the more doubtful whether we would.[56]

Julian's diary reflected pessimism because he thought the British would fail to
act. His spirits soared when he learned that British troops had entered the Canal

[53] Diary, 25 Feb. 1953.
[54] Diary, 12 May 1953.
[55] S. I. Troen and M. Shemesh, *The Suez-Sinai Crisis: 1956* (London, 1990), 117.
[56] Julian Amery Diary, 1 Nov. 1956.

Zone. He then dropped into profound despondency when Eden called off the expedition under the pressure of the United States. Reflecting on the course of events, he wrote:

I can't help feeling that Eden going to war against Nasser... was out of character. Eden's basic approach to the Middle East had been one of appeasement. When suddenly he turned round and decided to smash Nasser, he had no more idea how to play the hand than Chamberlain had when he turned against Hitler in 1939.[57]

Julian's own reputation developed from this point on as a diehard, and he emerged from the Suez crisis itself as one of Eden's most persistent and eloquent critics in the House of Commons.

Leo's death in 1955 represented the end of an era. He died still believing that Britain was a great world power, and that the Empire and Commonwealth would continue to play a critical part in the world's history in the second half of the twentieth century. The consequences of Suez were fatal to that vision. To Julian, Suez was a spectacular defeat for the British Empire, above all because it revealed a loss of will. The British Empire thereafter began to collapse with a rapidity that no one previously had foreseen. Virtually all of Britain's African dependencies became independent within the next decade, often, Julian believed, with deplorable consequences, as for example in Uganda. Julian fought a rearguard action. At the Colonial Office in 1958–60, he unsuccessfully tried to slow the pace of decolonization. He believed that the British Empire could revive and could still exert both direct and indirect influence through an arc of bases extending from Gibraltar to Cyprus to Aden to Singapore. Despite the catastrophe at Suez, he hoped that the British Empire would continue to exist as a world power. He fought for a losing cause, but so also did his father. Julian in every sense inherited his father's mantle and will rank as one of the leading Conservative figures in the era of decolonization. The two of them provide a continuity in the intellectual history of the Empire for nearly the entire century.

[57] Ibid., 11 Nov. 1956.

12

All Souls and Suez*

Wm. Roger Louis

On the evening of 3 November 1956, when television was still a novelty, Sir Anthony Eden addressed Britain on the crisis in the Middle East. Of all his speeches over a long career, this one proved the best in his political life and became ingrained in public memory. He described himself as a man of peace, working throughout his life as a League of Nations man, as a United Nations man. His voice rang with sincerity when he expressed his deepest feelings that the decision to invade Egypt would stand the test of history as the right course at the right time: 'There are times for courage, times for action and this is one of them.' The Egyptian dictator had to be stopped.

Eden's speech produced radically different reactions. In London, the chairman of Reuters, Sir Christopher Chancellor, hurled his whisky glass at the television screen.[1] At All Souls, at least in one group, the response was subdued and reflective. In 1956 there was only one television set in the College. It happened to be in the Warden's lodgings. A group of four or so watched the broadcast together. They included the Warden himself, John Sparrow; a young Prize Fellow, Keith Thomas; the publisher Geoffrey Faber; and the Chancellor of the University, Lord Halifax. At the end of the speech, the Warden turned off the television set. There was silence. Finally Halifax said: 'The trouble about Anthony is that he's always had a thing about dictators.'

Halifax is far more significant in the history of All Souls than in the history of the Suez crisis, and he gives point to the argument of this chapter. In 1956 the College more closely resembled the All Souls of 1936 than that of 1976. There was, however, one major difference. By 1956 there were far fewer grandees at All Souls than there were in 1936, at least those with influence in national affairs. Grandees there certainly were: Halifax above all, but also Lord Brand, Lord

---

* An earlier version of this chapter was published in W. R. Louis (ed.), *Penultimate Adventures with Britannia* (London and New York, 2008), 245–58, with acknowledgement to All Souls College.

[1] Keith Kyle, *Suez* (London, 1991), 432.

Bridges, and Lord Salter. Yet by the time of Suez, the mystique of the College had begun to fade. It no longer seemed to be a nexus of power and intellect. From the 1930s onwards, there were widespread suspicions that All Souls in one way or another had been responsible for the policy of appeasement.[2] No one has ever held All Souls accountable for Suez.

I

The purpose of this chapter will be to establish the meaning of the Suez crisis for All Souls, and for Oxford more generally, by commenting on Suez as a moment in the history of the British people, part of Our Island Story – I know that I am being presumptuous by using the word 'our,' but I have lived with the story for so long that I feel a part of it. I was in Cairo in 1956 during the initial phases of the crisis.

I shall pursue the direct involvement of three members of the College: Roger Makins, Patrick Reilly, and Quintin Hogg (Lord Hailsham). They were of the same generation, Makins elected to All Souls in 1925, Hailsham in 1931, and Reilly in 1932. Makins was ambassador in Washington when Gamal Abdel Nasser nationalized the Suez Canal Company on 26 July 1956 – the salient point being that it was the nationalization of a company, not the canal, which lay within Egyptian sovereign territory. Reilly was working in the embassy in Paris. He returned to the Foreign Office to become Deputy Undersecretary at a critical stage of the crisis. Hailsham was First Lord of the Admiralty. All three were critical of Eden and believed his handling of the crisis to be disastrous, though Hailsham came closer than the others to sympathizing with the purpose of British intervention. In broad strokes, Makins and Reilly were anti-Suez while Hailsham was pro-Suez, though he objected, violently, to the Prime Minister's methods and behaviour.

Reflect for a moment on the year 1956 as a point in time. It was still the world of the bowler hat, a symbol of stability and status. Hailsham, a formidable cyclist throughout his life, even in old age, always wore a bowler while cycling. One member of the Foreign Office recalls going to lunch in St James's Park with sandwiches and hard-boiled eggs. Since there were no litter bins, he put the eggshells under his bowler until he got back to the Foreign Office. The challenge to such decorous and quaint behaviour, the challenge to the bowler itself, came in May 1956 with the production of John Osborne's play *Look Back in Anger* and what one critic of All Souls has described as 'the rude entry of Jimmy Porter'.[3] The anger and the iconoclasm of the play represented attitudes that erupted subsequently at the peak of the Suez crisis. Michael Howard, who later played a

---

[2] See Green, this volume, ch. 10.

[3] D. Caute, 'Crisis in All Souls', *Encounter*, 36.3 (March 1966), 15.

significant part in the history of All Souls, remembers going to Trafalgar Square to join the crowd of thirty thousand people protesting against the invasion of Egypt. He felt alienated from fellow demonstrators: 'The crowd consisted mainly of people who could have worn demonstration campaign medals ... who were really to come into their own a few years later with the foundation of the Campaign for Nuclear Disarmament.'[4] Comparable protest did not exist at All Souls. But by 1956, almost invisibly, social and political attitudes had altered during the previous decade. The change was most apparent, perhaps, in the attitude of the post-1945 generation towards the British Empire and Common-wealth. In the inter-war years, whatever one thought about the Empire, there could be no doubt that it played an important part in college affairs. L. S. Amery and Lionel Curtis, stalwarts of the Empire in different ways, both died in 1955. Their deaths can be seen as closing the chapter on Empire at All Souls.

Reflect on Oxford in 1956. In April, in the spirit of the post-Stalin era, Khrushchev and Bulganin visited London and Oxford. Students chanted 'Poor Old Joe' to the tune of the 'Volga Boat Song'. Oxford, in the view of the public, made up part of the 'Establishment', but students themselves wanted to tweak the Establishment and keep it on the hop as much as to be a part of it. In the sense that the word caught on in the 1950s, the Establishment consisted of people with power and influence who ran the country. In the first edition of Anthony Sampson's *Anatomy of Britain* (1962), Oxford and Cambridge occupy an entire section, but his comments focus on All Souls, by then having lost its national influence and possessing no particular academic function other than to elect two or so new fellows each year.[5] This view of the College coincided with the outlook of both A. J. P. Taylor and Hugh Trevor-Roper, the two prominent Oxford historians in the 1950s, who disagreed on almost everything but the ossified nature of All Souls. In the context of Suez, Taylor and Trevor-Roper provide a perspective that runs parallel with the divide within the College. Taylor denounced the Suez operation and held views similar to those of A. L. Rowse, while Trevor-Roper detested the Prime Minister but was pro-Suez in the same way that Hailsham was pro-Suez. All Souls revealed the same fault-lines that ran through Oxford itself.

Within the College, Isaiah Berlin is a figure of particular interest, not only because, as will be seen, he changed his mind about Suez, but also because of his connections. He remained on good terms with both Taylor and Trevor-Roper, for example, though he shared gossip much more freely with the latter. But one is also struck by the missing voices, and it is important to remember that in late 1956 there was a dual emergency. The crises of Suez and the Hungarian revolution coincided. I had hoped to be able to report on the view of All Souls' historian of Hungary, C. A. Macartney, but, alas, his papers at the Bodleian

[4] M. Howard, *Captain Professor: A Life in War and Peace* (London, 2006), 155.
[5] A. Sampson, *Anatomy of Britain* (London, 1962), 214–15. See also Green, this volume, ch. 10.

Library are mute on these questions. (Macartney is of interest in college lore because he thought Hitler was not such a bad chap after all, and I believe this to be true and not a slander.) Nor can I say much about his friend Geoffrey Hudson, whose potential for a great book that was never written rivals anyone else's at All Souls. (Among those who never wrote their great book he ranks with Hugh Trevor-Roper.) By 1956, Hudson was already director of the Far Eastern Centre at St Antony's College, but he still moved within college circles and was as much a hawk then as he was later, on Vietnam. Sadly there are no Geoffrey Hudson papers. Nor on the other side of the divide is there any written evidence about the views of the Professor of Social Anthropology, E. E. Evans-Pritchard, though in college lore he ranks among the most vehement critics of the Suez operation. I mention these silent voices – silent because of the lack of documentary evidence – because I think it important to be clear that much of what I have been able to piece together about the response to Suez at All Souls is based on oral testimony and is by no means a complete record. But it is possible to detect changes of mood. In 1957, Max Beloff arrived as the Gladstone Professor of Public Administration. As David Butler has pointed out, no cause was truly lost until Max espoused it. Perhaps this helps explain why the balance of college sentiment finally became anti-Suez.

Nothing succeeds like success, and in the case of Suez, nothing failed like failure. It is also possible that the college mood shifted in the aftermath of the crisis not because of personal influences but because of the forbidding reality of a botched operation that had divided the nation and jeopardized Britain's relations with both the United States and the United Nations. The Suez operation might have succeeded, at least in a limited sense, if the Canal Zone had been reoccupied and the issue of withdrawal then used as a weapon to extract concessions from Nasser on the management of the canal. The stopping of the troops midway down the canal carried great symbolic importance. Britain could no longer conduct a major military operation independently of the United States. The outcome of the Suez crisis thus came as a revelation: Britain no longer ranked with the Soviet Union and the United States as a world power. In the early 1950s Goronwy Rees, when he was Estates Bursar at All Souls, represented the view that Britain was in decline and that the Establishment concealed the truth.[6] From the time of the Suez invasion onwards, the issue of 'collusion' raised doubts – profound doubts – about the integrity of the British government. It was not until the opening of the archives, in the 1980s, that evidence revealed conclusively the details of the secret arrangements among Britain, France, and Israel to invade Egypt. But to many at the time, not least to the All Souls figures directly involved, it was clear what had happened. To Makins, Reilly, and Hailsham, England's honour had been tarnished.

[6] N. Annan, *Our Age* (London, 1990), 228.

II

The chronology of the Suez crisis, for purposes of this chapter, can be described as the beginning, or Roger Makins phase; the middle, or Patrick Reilly phase; and the end, or Hailsham phase. The first part of the crisis occupied the last weeks of Makins's ambassadorship in Washington. The Eden government agreed to a maritime conference and to the creation of a Suez Canal Users Association. Sir Robert Menzies of Australia went to Cairo to try to reason with Nasser. He reported that Nasser remained impervious to common sense and would roll his eyes upward in response to practical suggestions. In September 1956 Harold Macmillan, then Chancellor of the Exchequer, visited Washington and met with President Eisenhower. Makins was present at the meeting. As is obvious from his papers in the Bodleian, the Suez affair greatly preoccupied him then and forever after.

The second phase, Patrick Reilly's, lasted from late September to the beginning of the military operations in late October. During this time, negotiations at the United Nations nearly succeeded in reaching a peaceful solution, but in the meantime the Prime Minister made commitments to the French and Israelis. The Treaty of Sèvres coordinated military action for the invasion of Egypt, in effect, collusion. Reilly indirectly witnessed these events; his analysis of the complex interplay of personalities, written later, is preserved in his papers in the Bodleian. Like Makins, Reilly regarded Suez as an event that had burned itself into his soul.

In the last phase, Israel invaded Egypt on 29 October. The British and French attacked Egyptian airfields and dropped paratroops in the Canal Zone. These events coincided with the revolt in Hungary. At the United Nations, the General Assembly on 2 November voted 65:5 for an immediate ceasefire and the withdrawal of troops from Egypt; of the five, three of course were Britain, France, and Israel. Only Australia and New Zealand sided with them against the resolution. In the Canal Zone, military operations suddenly came to an end when Eden, under unprecedented and extreme pressure from Eisenhower, halted the advance of the troops. Hailsham had become First Lord of the Admiralty in early September, but he was not allowed access to the secret plans for the invasion until late in the day. He bitterly resented his exclusion. In his memoirs he describes his part in the Suez operation as 'absolute agony'.[7]

III

When Roger Makins was elected a fellow of All Souls in 1925 at the age of 21, he stated that he had never known 'such perfect satisfaction'. The son of a

---

[7] Lord Hailsham, *A Sparrow's Flight* (London, 1990), 292.

brigadier-general, who later became a Conservative MP, he was educated at Winchester and Christ Church. He arrived at All Souls in the same year as A. L. Rowse. In his own words, 'the College gulped heavily before electing Rowse, and then, having done that, they looked for the most conventional candidate in sight'.[8] The word 'conventional' is not quite right, though it reflects his sense of modesty. Makins was among the most able of his generation. He spent much of his career in the United States, beginning in 1931 in the embassy in Washington. He married an American, Alice Davis, the daughter of Dwight Davis, who was a former governor of the Philippines and who is best known for endowing the great prize in American tennis, the Davis Cup. Makins later believed that one of the problems underlying the Suez crisis was that neither Anthony Eden nor Sir Ivone Kirkpatrick, the permanent Undersecretary at the Foreign Office, had much understanding of the United States. Eden had a genteel anti-Americanism characteristic of his generation. Kirkpatrick had devoted most of his career to Germany and never visited America.

Makins himself strengthened his familiarity with certain leading American personalities, including Eisenhower, while working on Harold Macmillan's staff in Algiers during the Second World War. Macmillan became one of Makins's patrons, a point of interest in view of later trends in historical interpretation. In the 1990s, it became fashionable to denounce Macmillan for having plotted or schemed to bring about the downfall of Eden so that Macmillan himself could become Prime Minister. Imagine my astonishment when I found in the Makins Papers a memorandum entitled 'Note of Conversation with Professor Roger Louis'.[9] The reason for the memorandum was that we both agreed that there had been no conspiracy. I stand by that judgement. Macmillan became Prime Minister through a combination of luck, skill, and opportunism, which is not the same thing as active scheming.

After 1945 Makins rose through the ranks of the Foreign Office. His involvement in the Persian oil crisis of the early 1950s gave him a knowledge of economic issues that later served him well at the Treasury. His tenure as ambassador in Washington, 1952–6, is remarkable for many things, but two will serve the purposes of this chapter. First, he took an interest in Eden's health. It was Makins who made the arrangements in Boston in 1954 for a famous American surgeon, Dr Richard Cattell, to repair damage from a previous operation on Eden's bile duct, when the scalpel had slipped and Eden had nearly died. Makins believed that Eden was never the same person, and that his later swings in mood, which sometimes approached hysteria, could be traced to these medical misfortunes. Whatever the truth of that, Makins got first-hand accounts of Eden's health during the crisis of 1956. He had no doubt that the Prime Minister was frequently doped,

---

[8] Memorial service addresses by Sir Peter Ramsbotham, Sir Jeremy Morse, and Lord Carrington (All Souls College, 1997).
[9] Makins papers, Oxford, Bodleian Library, MS Sherfield 957, dated June 1993.

his eyes dilated, his mood plunging from excitement and emotional instability to a Dunkirk attitude of quiet and fatalistic determination. This was Makins's firm and considered verdict.

The other point is Makins's clear and consistent judgement on Eisenhower and Dulles and their attitude towards the possible use of force. Makins got on well with John Foster Dulles. Apart from his ponderous and tedious moralism, Makins found him willing to engage in argument and to be a good companion who enjoyed his bourbon. But Makins was emphatic that it was Eisenhower who controlled matters of importance. Dulles always took care to square things with Eisenhower before making important pronouncements: 'It was Eisenhower, not Dulles, who made the decisions.'[10] Makins thought that Eden had allowed himself to become obsessed with Dulles while failing to see the identity of outlook between the President and the Secretary of State on the point of transcendent importance: the United States would not condone the use of force. In Makins's view, this point was so clear and so vital that he would have jumped on the first airplane to London if he believed anyone held otherwise. He thought no one could have failed to get it.

Yet when Makins returned to London, he became the equivalent of a political leper. No one wanted to see him; no one would discuss with him the crisis in Egypt. He finally learned from Sir Ivone Kirkpatrick about the plans for invasion. 'I was astounded,' he wrote in his unpublished memoir. 'It had never occurred to me that we would go to war without full American support, and I at once realised that there would be a disaster, for which I began mentally to prepare myself.'[11] Why had his advice been ignored? Why did his sharp and cogent view of Eisenhower and Dulles fail to impress? The answer is to be found in the perceptive biography of Eden by D. R. Thorpe: Eden believed that Makins had gone native.[12]

One of Makins's last acts in Washington had been to accompany Macmillan on his visit to Eisenhower. They entered through a side door to the White House so as not to attract attention. The President and the Chancellor greeted each other as old comrades-in-arms. They enjoyed each other's company. They talked, so it seemed to Makins, about everything under the Anglo-American sun but avoided, to his astonishment, discussing Suez. Eisenhower believed he had made his view so clear that the subject was a closed book. Macmillan thought that Eisenhower, by skirting the topic, had implicitly endorsed the British plan to topple Nasser by force if necessary. In Macmillan's phrase, which became infamous, Ike would 'lie doggo', or in other words lie low. Makins thus witnessed one of the great misunderstandings of the twentieth century. Nor was it any easier to

[10] MS Sherfield 957, Makins to Sir Donald Logan, 2 Aug. 1978.

[11] Makins, 'Sidelights on Suez', MS Sherfield 957.

[12] D. R. Thorpe, *Eden: The Life and Times of Anthony Eden* (London, 2003), 496; William Clark Papers, Bodleian Library, Box 160.

follow the pattern of Macmillan's thought after Makins returned to London. Makins was now at the Treasury, an appointment made at the initiative of Macmillan, though he now seemed to give Makins the cold shoulder. Perhaps sensing opposition, Macmillan refused to see him until the troops disembarked. He then sent an 'urgent summons' for Makins and said, 'Now that the expedition has sailed, I can talk to you.' Makins immediately raised the issue of how the Americans would respond; Macmillan 'reacted like a man coming out of a trance'.[13] This is an extraordinarily revealing line about Macmillan, and entirely consistent with Makins's overall interpretation of his intricate personality. A few days later, just as Britain and France announced conditions for a ceasefire on 3 November, Makins was elected a Distinguished Fellow at All Souls. The circumstances of Suez made his satisfaction with life a little less than complete.

Patrick Reilly's career in the diplomatic service was the mirror image of Makins's but with a French reflection. While Makins was associated forever with the United States, Reilly served three times in France, the last as ambassador in the 1960s. He was born in India, in a family that had served the British Raj for four generations. After a lonely childhood, he attended Winchester and New College before being elected to All Souls in 1932 – the same year as Isaiah Berlin and Richard Wilberforce. A. J. Ayer commented that Reilly's election 'astounded Oxford', a remark referring to his modesty and low-key personality. Reilly was a man of complete and unassuming integrity. He was self-deprecating. He once told me how Lionel Curtis wounded him by remarking that he talked so little that he contributed nothing to the College. Most people would have disregarded such a comment or would have viewed it as ironic in view of Curtis's own volubility. I was interested to see in Reilly's papers how he morosely mulled this over. He was an extraordinarily sensitive man. His part in the Suez crisis is of interest because he was in Paris at the time of Nasser's nationalization of the Suez Canal Company but returned to the Foreign Office when the crisis reached its climax. He was thus able to assess the French origins of the Suez crisis as well as the dynamics within Whitehall.

To Reilly and others at the time, the plan for an Anglo-French strike force had a 'made in Paris' imprint to it. The French held Nasser responsible for the troubles in Algeria. In their view, Nasser was an octopus whose tentacles extended throughout the Middle East and North Africa: lop off the head, and the tentacles would wither. But the French needed British military assistance as well as use of the airfields and harbours in Cyprus to be able to attack. The question was, to change the metaphor and to use Aneurin Bevan's earthy language, would Marianne be able to seduce John Bull? Though Reilly became Deputy Undersecretary when he returned to the Foreign Office in late August 1956, he heard only rumours about British conversations with the French. He believed that the Prime Minister would seek a peaceful solution. But one day in late August or

---

[13] Makins, 'Sidelights on Suez'.

early September (the exact date is not clear) the veil was lifted from his eyes. It happened by mistake. Kirkpatrick placed a telegram in Reilly's box that should not have been there: 'One morning I was astounded to find ... a telegram on which was written in pencil in the Prime Minister's unmistakable handwriting: "Foreign Secretary, perhaps this will give us the pretext for which we are looking" ... I sat and looked at the telegram for a long time.' It came as a revelation: 'Eden was deeply committed to military intervention.'[14] Marianne may have seduced John Bull, but it was Reilly's view that Eden wanted to be seduced.

Reilly became aware of the extraordinary lengths to which the Prime Minister would go to keep plans for the military operation as secret as any of the secret operations of the Second World War. Eden's wartime experience gave him both the inspiration and the knowledge of how to manipulate the government machine. Only a handful of officials in the Foreign Office knew of the plans. The key figure was Kirkpatrick. Here I am grateful to Patrick Reilly for putting me right years ago, on an important issue. I had believed Kirkpatrick to be the guiding genius behind the operation. He was intelligent, deft, and bellicose – wholly convinced of the danger of Nasser. He said at one point:

The PM was the only man in England who wanted the nation to survive; that all the rest of us have lost the will to live; that in two years' time Nasser will have deprived us of our oil, the sterling area fallen apart, no European defence possible, unemployment and unrest in the UK and our standard of living reduced to that of the Yugoslavs or Egyptians.[15]

But Kirkpatrick had his doubts about the Suez operation. He continued to perform his duties out of loyalty to Eden and because he was a scrupulous civil servant, not because he believed it to be a good plan. He paced the corridors of the Foreign Office wringing his hands and exclaiming to himself that it was a daft idea. It was Eden himself, according to Reilly, who must bear the responsibility for the consequences – and they were catastrophic. Conspiracy had involved British ministers 'in deceit and lies'. Dishonesty had penetrated into the heart of the British government and could be summed up in the word 'collusion': 'it undermined the moral basis for our military intervention'.[16] In Reilly's judgement – his words are inscribed in my memory and he used phrases carefully – Britain's reputation for ethical conduct had been irrevocably damaged.

Hailsham's part in the Suez crisis can be related more briefly because more of it is already in the public record. Like Makins and Reilly, Hailsham believed the Suez expedition to be a shambles, but for quite different reasons. Reflect for a moment on Hailsham's defiant toughness and pugnacious courage. A photograph

---

[14] Unpublished memoir by Reilly. Oxford, Bodleian Library, MS Eng. c. 6921, Reilly Papers. I am indebted to Jane Reilly for permission to use and quote from her late father's papers.
[15] Quoted in W. R. Louis, *Ends of British Imperialism* (London, 2006), 637–8.
[16] Unpublished memoir by Reilly.

from the 1950s shows him wading into a freezing sea in a baggy old swimsuit, perfectly capturing an uncompromising Tory determination. Much later, when the IRA bombed the Old Bailey in 1973, Hailsham decided immediately to visit the site. Since his official car would cause further problems for the security forces, he arrived on his bicycle (wearing, of course, his bowler). He became the longest-serving Lord Chancellor in the twentieth century. By the time of the Suez crisis, he had long established a reputation for bold, even if not always original, legal judgement – which was often spiced with a trace of brilliance for its own sake, something not unexpected from an All Souls Prize Fellow. In the case of Nasser's nationalization of the Suez Canal Company, Eden's most tenacious legal critic, Sir Gerald Fitzmaurice of the Foreign Office (who later became a judge of the International Court at the Hague), held that Egypt possessed sovereign rights over the canal and that Nasser had merely taken over a company. The shareholders in the company could expect reasonable compensation but little more. Hailsham would have nothing to do with this argument. In his view, which was unoriginal but reflected popular sentiment at the time, Nasser had behaved recklessly and violated international law. Hailsham became one of Eden's more effective defenders. Within the government, he was among the most belligerent, though in a particular sense. He was appalled by the plans for invasion but, once in, he wanted to fight on to the end.

Hailsham had served during the Second World War in a tour of duty that took him, briefly, to Egypt, Syria, and Palestine. He became familiar with the deadly force that naval bombardments might have on civilian populations even if the targets were exclusively military. As First Lord of the Admiralty in the Suez crisis, he was acutely aware that he would be held publicly responsible for civilian deaths in Egypt. He also faced unprecedented internal revolt. Lord Mountbatten, the head of the professional navy, threatened to resign. Hailsham met this challenge head on: he told him that as First Lord he himself was responsible for the good name of the Royal Navy and gave Mountbatten a written order to stay on duty. Hailsham acquitted himself very well.

A note of disclosure: I never especially liked Hailsham or warmed to him. One evening at dinner when I was sitting next to him, he looked at me quizzically and said in a clear and rather loud voice, 'Play it short, play it up, play it noisy.' I was mystified, but Tony Honoré came to the rescue by explaining that this was one of Hailsham's campaign slogans in the 1950s – I remain flummoxed as to why he said it to me, though I am glad to have collected a Hailsham aphorism. I have come rather to like him as a historical figure, and I find his position on Suez significant. Hailsham had been anti-Zionist, believing the creation of the state of Israel to be a mistake. But once Israel had taken its place in international society, then it was morally incumbent on Britain, the United States, and all other law-abiding nations to protect Israel from Arab aggression. He had no doubt that Nasser aimed to bring the Arab states into an alliance to destroy Israel. Hailsham believed that Israel could strike first in self-defence under Article 51 of the United

Nations Charter. He despised what he considered Eisenhower and John Foster Dulles's pusillanimous attitude: 'Their behaviour throughout this unhappy affair seems to me to be both misguided and quite incomprehensible.'[17] As for Eden, Hailsham had no use at all for the 'hypocrisy' of the secret operations. Keith Thomas remembers him in the Common Room declaiming – playing it loud and certainly not short – his resentment at being misled and deceived. This is the only instance during the Suez crisis that I can find that bears resemblance to the debates on appeasement at All Souls in the 1930s.

IV

In assessing the meaning of Suez for All Souls, and for Oxford, it helps to think briefly about the Warden, John Sparrow, who later became, to critics of the College, the personification of reaction. But not in 1956. Sparrow had been elected in 1952, in part because he would have, it was hoped, a healing effect after a period of bitterly divisive college politics. At the time of Suez, he was still in his early period of popularity. It is useful to bear in mind that he was of the same generation as Maurice Bowra, Cyril Connolly, Anthony Powell, and Evelyn Waugh. Like them, he had an interest in human foible. At All Souls, he could be charming, witty, and kind when he wanted to, though he was devastating on sloppy thinking and academic pretension. He held strong views about Nasser and considered the Suez expedition a jolly colonial war to stop the rot. He had aesthetic objections to Nasser. He kept a photograph of the Egyptian dictator on his desk and would summon visitors to his office to gaze at it and contemplate Nasser's ugliness. His views on Nasser's grotesque physical appearance, his own impression at least, perhaps anticipated the John Sparrow of the 1960s and the attacks on the bearded and unkempt student generation that he detested – 'filthy young things'. Or, in his delicious phrase, 'revolting students'. In any event his reaction to the Suez crisis indicated, as Robin Briggs has written in his perceptive essay on Sparrow in the *ODNB*, how he failed, totally, to perceive the immense changes that would overtake All Souls, as well as Oxford and the country itself in the next decades. Nevertheless, at the time of the Suez crisis, Sparrow himself probably best summed up the mood at All Souls by saying that the College was a hotbed of cold feet.

In Oxford generally, the Suez crisis caused the same divisions as in All Souls, though probably at a higher pitch. Sparrow's sentiments resembled those of the famous scholar and classicist Gilbert Murray, who led the pro-Suez group at Oxford. Despite championing the League of Nations, Murray believed that the United Nations consisted of a horde of barbarous nations, one of which had

---

[17] Hailsham, *A Sparrow's Flight*, 285.

broken an international agreement. Murray took a public stand in support of Eden against Nasser.[18] He led the Oxford pro-Suez petition, which was signed by eight heads of house, two former heads, fifteen professors and readers, and seventy-five fellows of colleges – and supported the men of Brasenose singing 'Rule, Britannia'.[19] The protest against the Suez venture was led by Alan Bullock, whose views were identical with those of A. L. Rowse and David Astor. I mention David Astor as part of the national background because he penned in the *Observer* the most famous of all anti-Suez declarations: 'We had not realised that our government was capable of such folly and crookedness.'[20] Emotions ran as high as on any other issue in living memory. Alan Bullock's anti-Suez petition was signed by 10 heads of house, 20 professors and readers, and 235 fellows of colleges. The total was thus 265 anti-Suez versus a pro-Suez count of 100. The same proportion would have held true for All Souls, perhaps with a slightly higher figure for the pro-Suez cohort. But there are no solid figures, because people altered their views. Isaiah Berlin, for example, wrote to Clarissa Eden after Nasser's nationalization of the Suez Canal Company that Egypt should be punished. But he changed his mind after he pondered the consequences for Britain of another prolonged occupation of Egypt and the possibility of an expansionist Israel. In a highly complex play of emotions, his anti-colonialist convictions clashed with his pro-Zionist sentiments.[21]

I began this chapter by calling for reflection on Suez and the year 1956 as a point in time, and for a comparison of the College then with the All Souls of 1936. To recapitulate: the College in 1956 more closely resembled the College of twenty years earlier than that of twenty years later. The key year was 1966. The anti-Suez demonstration at Trafalgar Square had become institutionalized in the Campaign for Nuclear Disarmament. The hippies whom John Sparrow detested were in the ascendancy. All Souls was under siege, challenged by a University Commission for infirmity of purpose. Yet the College survived – and in fact entered into a period of renewed purpose. There is great irony that this change took place under John Sparrow, whose aim in life had become to keep the College in exactly the same state, if not where it had been when he was a Prize Fellow in the 1920s, then at least in its condition from the day before yesterday. Sparrow rose to the challenge of the University Commission by acquiescing in the plan for Visiting Fellows. For him, it was merely the best among bad alternatives, one of which, amalgamation with St Antony's, would have created, according to Geoffrey Hudson, a new Oxford institution called St Antony's and Other Souls.

---

[18] F. West, *Gilbert Murray: A Life* (London, 1984), 244.
[19] *Hist. Univ. Oxf.*, viii. 408.
[20] Quoted in Louis, *Ends of British Imperialism*, 23.
[21] M. Ignatieff, *Isaiah Berlin: A Life* (London, 1998), 237.

The Visiting Fellowship programme was viewed by some at the time as Sparrow's double-cross, a way of keeping the College the same but camouflaging it with visitors. It proved otherwise. At one stroke All Souls was transformed from an Oxford college that had ceased to have a public function, and was becoming academically insignificant, into an international intellectual institution that began again to flourish by attracting distinguished academic talent from throughout the world. In 1966, ten years after Suez, the British were beating a retreat from the southern Arabian peninsula at Aden and were about to wind down the Empire once and forever more. At Oxford, All Souls was still more than a decade away from Warden Sparrow's retirement, in 1979, and still some fifteen years away from an event perhaps as significant as the creation of the Visiting Fellows programme. In 1981, All Souls elected a female Fellow, exactly twenty-five years after the Suez crisis and what now seems a remote era.

13

G. M. Young: The Last Victorian?

J. Mordaunt Crook

Early in 1956 Rupert Hart-Davis sent George Lyttelton a set of Young's selected essays. Lyttelton was grateful. 'His writing gives me enormous pleasure. [But] what does he look like? That is very important'. Back came a telling pen-portrait.

G. M. Young is tallish and thin, with a long thin-pointed nose. Very little hair and that quite flat on his scalp, so that... he looks like a judge who has mislaid his wig and is feeling the cold. I think in fact that he *does* feel the cold, probably has a bad circulation, and in winter wears an enormous astrakhan overcoat which he purchased in Tsarist Russia.[1]

To this we can add one or two more details: an anaemic complexion, a humorous eye, a strategic cough, and a halting, over-cultivated mode of speech. All part of a calculated persona: formal dress, quizzical gaze, valetudinarian habits, plus a stock of attitudes and terms of reference already consciously antique. That was how Noel Annan remembered him: a 'fine old codger... Victorian and proud of it'.[2]

It took him quite a time to acquire that patinated image. Politics, education, government, diplomacy, banking, journalism, historical research: he tried them all. Only the last brought him serious success. But the prize was worth the wait. By the time of his death in 1959, 'G. M.' was widely regarded as England's finest historical essayist. In particular, he had made himself master of a genre peculiarly his own: the social history of ideas.

The origins of George Malcolm Young were fairly obscure. Born in 1882, his father was a ship's pilot on the Thames, at Greenhithe in Kent. But his early years were dazzling. Scholar and Captain at St Paul's, Scholar at Balliol, a first in Classical Moderations, a Prize Fellowship at All Souls (in 1905), and swift promotion to the upper echelons of the Civil Service. The only chink in his

---

[1] R. Hart-Davis (ed.), *The Lyttelton Hart-Davis Letters*, vols 1–2: *1955–1957* (London, 1985), 130: 9 May 1956; 131–2: 15 May 1956.

[2] N. Annan, *Our Age: Portrait of a Generation* (London, 1990), 126. 'Like a survivor of his own Victorian Age', R. Ollard (ed.), *The Diaries of A. L. Rowse* (London, 2003), 145: 14 Feb. 1950.

armour was a second in Greats. But then he had little patience with the Hegelianism taught at Balliol in the 1890s. And it didn't hold him back. By 1906 he was tutoring in Ancient History at St John's and mixing with the *jeunesse dorée* of Oxford Tories, notably Viscount Wolmer, the future Earl of Selborne. By 1907 he was touring southern Africa like a potential recruit to Milner's Kindergarten, and actually planning a career in politics on the side of Joe Chamberlain's Liberal Unionists.[3] But he couldn't face the commitment, or the compromises. In July 1908 one of his Oxford friends, H. N. Dickinson, sensed that Young wasn't made of the right stuff: 'There is one fundamental thing wrong with him', he wrote; 'which I should seem a prig if I explained.' The cloven hoof of the sybarite? The egoism of the intellectual? Both, probably. Anyway, Young took refuge on the moral high ground: 'One must believe in God furiously', he wrote, 'before politics can become tolerable.'[4] In any case, he couldn't afford it. By living at All Souls and teaching at St John's he could save £300–400 per annum. But an election campaign might cost £800, and defeat would reduce him to penury; even victory would condemn him to a life of journalism. In those Oxford days he dreamed of a moralized system of government: municipal socialism mitigated by governmental parameters. But he lacked the stomach for a fight. Unfortunately he also 'hated the thought of lecturing... to unselected undergraduates'. The status, the leisure, the security of Edwardian Whitehall suited him better. In August 1908 he plumped for the Board of Education.[5]

It must have been the former Parliamentary Secretary to that department, Sir William Anson, then Warden of All Souls, who introduced him to its administrative head Sir Robert Morant. Now Morant was a man who made enemies,

[3] Young joined the Canning Club in 1906. With the future third Earl of Selborne, he also set up the New Tory Club ('What I want is a sort of spiritual Canning': Oxford, Bodleian Library, MS Eng. Hist. c. 1005, ff. 189–91, Young to Wolmer: 20 May 1907, and c. 1006, ff. 44ff. Also d. 480, ff. 11–12, 55–7). Young's tour took him to Cape Town, Pretoria, Rhodesia, Natal, Transkei, and Kimberley ('I am on the Veld... we are living in a railway carriage in stately isolation on the line, and spend the day looking at dams and ostriches': Oxford, Bodleian Library, MS Eng. Hist. c. 1006, ff. 11–13, Young to Wolmer: ? July 1907). At this stage Young espoused adult suffrage – 'get it done with' – and proportional representation: 'no more tampering with the franchise for party purposes' (Oxford, Bodleian Library, MS. Eng. Hist. c. 1005, ff. 174–5, Young to Wolmer: 30 March 1907). Like L. S. Amery and A. S. McDowell, also of All Souls, he joined the Tariff Reform League (ibid., f. 145). For his income in Oxford, see Oxford, Bodleian Library, MS. Eng. Hist. c. 1005, f. 196, Young to Wolmer: 23 May 1907.
[4] Oxford, Bodleian Library, MS. Eng. Hist. c. 1005, ff. 158–9, Young to Wolmer: 6 July 1908. 'Politics are growing more infamous every day... Licensing Bill. The Sievier Case... And I can't even earn a decent living' (ibid., ff. 156–7: 28 July 1908).
[5] National Library of Scotland, Edinburgh, Dover Wilson MSS, 14319, f. 188, Young to Wilson: 25 Oct. 1943. He also toyed with the idea of becoming a *Times* leader-writer. 'As for Young... we shall *never* really be sure what he is going to do next. He will hover on the brink of affairs – and may plunge in one day... Leave him, and give him a glimpse of politics a year hence, and see if he is not fearfully jealous of those who are still in the exciting fold' (Oxford, Bodleian Library, MS. Eng. Hist. d. 479, f. 33: 18 June 1908, and f. 38: 8 July 1908, Dickinson to Wolmer).

notably Sir Michael Sadler.[6] Beatrice Webb called him 'a strange mortal, not altogether sane', but 'the one man of genius in the Civil Service'.[7] More than anyone, it was he who steered through the considerable improvements in the provision of secondary education and national health care achieved during the decade or so before the First World War. But it was a bumpy ride. In August 1911, Morant was dramatically dismissed from Education, only to reappear – just as dramatically – a few weeks later, as Chairman of the National Insurance Commission, in effect as master of the future Ministry of Health.[8] The implications for Young's career were serious. Faced with the prospect of losing the protection of his 'old friend and master', he toyed with the idea of a return to Oxford. He went in for the Arnold Prize in History. But he avoided the suggested topic and no award was made.[9] Fortunately, Morant had secured his future. In that same year, 1911, Young became the first Secretary of the Joint Standing Committee for Universities, and thus the first Secretary to the Treasury's University Grants Committee (U.G.C.).

There he might have stayed, and the development of the English university system might have been different. But with the outbreak of war he found himself catapulted into a rather more public position. In May 1915 he became private secretary to the President of the Board of Education. And this new President was a Labour minister, Arthur Henderson. When Henderson joined the War Cabinet in December 1916, Young went with him as Civil Secretary to the Cabinet Secretary, Lord Hankey.[10] At the age of 34 he was suddenly close to the centre of

---

[6] In 1895 Sadler became Director, and Morant Assistant Director, of the Office of Special Inquiries, an independent 'think tank' operating under the aegis of Sir William Anson and the education department of the Privy Council. Together they edited an important series of comparative educational studies (*Special Reports on Educational Subjects*, *PP* 1897, XXV etc.). Bitter disagreements precipitated Sadler's replacement by Morant as Permanent Secretary to the new Board of Education in 1903 (*The Times*: 11 June, 1903, 10; 3 July 1903, 12, and 14 July 1903, 10). See also R. Lowe, 'Sadler, Morant and the Structure of Education in England', in R. Aldrich (ed.), *In History and in Education* (London, 1996), 98–116.

[7] She added, 'he certainly does not want social democracy – he is an aristocrat by instinct and conviction'. M. Cole (ed.), *Beatrice Webb's Diaries, 1912–24* (London, 1952), 98.

[8] Violet Markham, like Young and Mona Wilson a protégé of Morant, remembered these episodes well: 'No Civil Servant has been at once more attacked and more admired, more vilified by his enemies and more upheld by his friends' (*Return Passage: The Autobiography of Violet R. Markham* (London, 1953), 146); Morant became 'an offering on the altar of ignorance, intrigue and political passion' (*Friendship's Harvest* (London, 1956), 189). Young regarded Morant as 'the greatest public servant . . . our age has known' (Young, *Ourselves*, Signpost Booklets (London, 1944), 9).

[9] Young received special mention, with an essay on Roman Auxilia (Oxford, Bodleian Library, MS Eng. Lett. c. 766, f. 107, Young to R. W. Chapman: 4 Aug. 1950; G. Kitson Clark, intro. to Young, *Portrait of an Age: Victorian England* (London, 1977), 3. Young remained a fellow of All Souls until Nov. 1912; he was re-elected as a 'Fifty-Pounder' in 1913, resigning finally in 1916.

[10] In preference to Sir Arthur Steel-Maitland, also formerly of All Souls (S. Roskill, *Hankey: Man of Secrets*, 3 vols (London, 1970–4), i. 344–5). For the Civil Service background, see G. K. Fry, *Statesmen in Disguise: The Changing Role of the Administrative Class of the British Home Civil Service, 1853–1966* (London, 1969).

power. And when Henderson went to Russia in the summer of 1917, to parley with Kerensky, Young went with him again: he had a ringside seat at one of the turning points of modern history.

Those four weeks in Russia, from 20 May to 23 July 1917, are as complicated as a plot by Pirandello. Each of the key participants was playing a double role. Henderson was trying to serve two masters, Lloyd George and the Labour Movement. Kerensky, it was said, 'had two souls – one as the head of the [Provisional, and Coalition] Government and a patriot; the other as a Socialist and an Idealist'.[11] Ambassador Buchanan was trusted by Kerensky and distrusted by Lloyd George; he liked Henderson and he loathed the Bolsheviks.[12] Lloyd George was determined to keep Russia in the war, and avoid a compromise peace; at the same time keeping Henderson in the Cabinet but out of the Socialist International. And what of G. M. Young? He was trying to keep both Buchanan and Henderson on board while warning Lloyd George – via telegrams to Hankey – that Henderson's head might well be with the Allies but his heart was dangerously close to the Mensheviks.[13] In the People's Palace, Petrograd, Henderson was carried away with the applause of five thousand Soviet workers. Lenin was not impressed.[14] Young reported back to Hankey with ominous predictions of Bolshevik Revolution.[15] The end result – after three more months of confusion – was predictable. Henderson was forced out of the Cabinet; Kerensky lost out to the Bolsheviks; Russia dropped out of the war; and Young's advice that border plebiscites be employed as a method of holding the Alliance together was forgotten.[16] The only winner in this game of telegraphic chess was Lloyd George. By the time Young

[11] Reported to the Foreign Office, 21 Sept. 1917; G. Buchanan, *My Mission to Russia and Other Diplomatic Memories*, 2 vols (London, 1923), ii. 186.

[12] Young ('most helpful in many ways', ibid., 145) was involved in discussions on the prospective international socialist conference at Stockholm. For context see H. Meynell, 'The Stockholm Conference of 1917', *International Review of Social History*, 5 (1960), 1–25, 202–25.

[13] Young regarded the idea that Henderson was 'a man of sterling honesty' as 'one of the most inexplicable of popular delusions' (London, Parliamentary Archives, Lloyd George Papers F/83/1/ 20: Aug. 1917, quoted in Roskill, *Hankey*, i. 419–20).

[14] 'Whoever extends his hand to Henderson or to [Albert] Thomas [the French Socialist], extends it as well to Lloyd George and [Alexander] Ribot [the French Finance Minister, and] to the English and French bankers' (*Pravda*, trans. J. M. Winter, in *Historical Journal*, 15 (1972), 762). For Trotsky's view, see his *History of the Russian Revolution*, 3 vols (London, 1932–3), i. 374. For Henderson's speech, see [Robert Wilton's] report in *The Times*, 18 June 1917, 8.

[15] Quoted in Roskill, *Hankey*, i. 416. For international context, see R. P. Bowden and A. F. Kerensky (eds), *The Russian Provisional Government, 1917: Documents*, 3 vols (Stanford, CA, 1961), ii. 1050–1, 1115–16, 1173–4, 1183–7. For Young's views on Russian foreign policy, see *The New Europe*, 25 (1920), 271–4.

[16] Young's view was that nearly all problems to which Russia and Austria were parties (Transylvania, Bosnia, Galicia, Trieste and Trentino) were 'of a kind to which the method of plebiscite might be applied'. He 'appeared to be working on [Henderson] to lead the socialists without leaving office, and without necessarily abandoning our war aims' (quoted in Roskill, *Hankey*, i. 400–1, 416–17). For Henderson's mission and resignation, see *Hansard* xcvi, col. 2183: 1 Aug. 1917; xcvii, col. 23: 6 Aug. 1917; xcvii, cols. 909–34: 13 Aug. 1917. Also D. Lloyd George, *War Memoirs*, 6 vols (London, 1933–6), iv. 1881, 1891–8, 1900, 1903–24.

returned to Whitehall, the Welsh Wizard was already plotting the formation of a progressive post-war coalition.

One step in that process, the creation and dissolution of a Ministry of Reconstruction, is now a forgotten episode. It was not forgotten by G. M. Young. This Ministry was set up by Lloyd George in July 1917 on the basis of two Committees of Reconstruction created by Asquith in March 1916 and by Lloyd George himself in March 1917. In effect it was charged with the cultural reconstruction of England after the war: 'We are at a turning point in our national history'; we must prepare for 'a better England... a better world'.[17] An expert secretariat was set up. There was a staff of 140, serving eighty-seven committees, partly housed in a gargantuan hotel near Victoria Station. One of the two Joint Secretaries, promoted from the Cabinet Office by Lloyd George, was G. M. Young, C.B. By this move his salary was increased from £1,300 to £1,500 per annum. That was a considerable sum in autumn 1917. The House of Commons was not entirely pleased.

James Hogge MP: 'Why is it necessary to give such large increases to men who write... [and] such... a small increase to men who fight?'[18]

Worse was to come. Several of those involved – Seebohm Rowntree, Beatrice Webb, R. B. Haldane, A. L. Smith, R. H. Tawney, W. H. Beveridge – still ring significant bells today. Several reports of around this time – on further education, libraries and museums, language teaching, and the structure of government – remain seminal documents.[19] Here were the makings of a progressive manifesto. But the public was suspicious. Backbench MPs were contemptuous.

All these great brains... what [are] they doing? [They include] several ladies of extremely Socialistic proclivities... [In any case there are] too many academics and too few practical people... The country at large regards... many [of them as] intelligent cranks.[20]

What in the end would taxpayers see for their money? Mostly a series of twopenny pamphlets. One was entitled *The Classics in British Education* (1919). Was this G. M. Young's first published essay?

Col. Charles Yate MP: 'Who is the author of this pamphlet? Is he a classical educational idealist or is he a practical working man?'

---

[17] *Parliamentary Papers* [*PP*], 1918, IX, 246; *PP* 1918, XIII, 29ff.; *PP* 1918, XIV, 397, 597ff.; *PP* 1919, XXX, 453ff. See also *The Times*, 11 Jan. 1917, 9; 3 March 1917, 7; 16 March 1917, 6; 19 March 1917, 9; 20 March 1917, 7; 21 April 1917, 3; 3 Nov. 1917, 7. For aims and organization, see C. Addison, *Politics from Within, 1911–1918, Including Some Records of a Great National Effort*, 2 vols (London, 1924), i, appendix 1, 607–12; K. and J. Morgan, *Portrait of a Progressive: The Political Career of Christopher, Viscount Addison* (Oxford, 1980), 70–82.

[18] *Hansard* xcv, 3, col. 2300: 8 Nov. 1917.

[19] E.g. Adult Education (*PP* 1918, IX, 319ff. and 1919, XXVIII, 453–67); Modern Languages (*PP* 1918, IX, 381–470); Machinery of Government (*PP* 1918, XII, 1–80); Libraries and Museums (*PP* 1918, IX, 363ff.).

[20] *Hansard* xcvi, cols. 1618–81: 27 July 1917, and col. 2441: 2 Aug. 1917.

Sir Auckland Geddes MP: [He is] 'a very hard-working man!'[21]

By the summer of 1919, project utopia was being 'wound up'. Its remnants were absorbed into the Ministry of National Service. Its influence on future welfare policy was not negligible. But from the perspective of Young's career, it was a blind alley. He had scented influence, then seen it evaporate. But there was one private compensation: Mona Wilson.

Mona Wilson was a free spirit. She came from a sceptical, broad church background. Her father had been a progressive Headmaster of Clifton. In youth she seems to have combined a deadly earnestness with a deathly radiance. Thomas Sturge Moore called her 'the lady with the terrible eyes'. 'Her ethereal beauty', noted her *Times* obituary, 'might well have proved a model for Sir Edward Burne-Jones.'[22] But there was nothing ethereal about her social commitment. From Newnham, Cambridge, she became in 1899 Secretary of the Women's Trade Union League, and then in 1912 a National Health Insurance Commissioner. Like Young, she was one of Morant's protégés. She first made her name with pioneering investigations into slum conditions in West Ham and Dundee.[23] By the start of the First World War, with a salary of £1,000 per annum in her early forties, she was the highest-paid woman in the British Civil Service. Then in 1917 she was seconded, as Assistant Secretary, to Reconstruction.

With the demise of that department – and the early death of Morant in 1920 – the moment of optimism passed. Mona Wilson retired to Wiltshire. G. M. Young went off to Vienna. Here his task, initially at any rate, was to administer a special Treasury relief fund. Officially he was Secretary to Sir Francis Lindley, a sporting diplomat with whom he had worked well in Petrograd and Archangel. It was Lindley and Wolmer – both Wykehamical Tories – who seem to have engineered Young's election, in 1918, to Brooks's. At that time the club was very much a focus of political power: in Campbell-Bannerman's first ministry of 1905 no fewer than twelve out of twenty-five cabinet ministers were members of Brooks's. It was probably also the most aristocratic club in London.[24] From Greenhithe to St James's: Young's social ascent had been impressive. He was now

[21] 'Reconstruction Problems, no. 21' (*Hansard* cxv, cols 741–2: 6 May 1919; *Times Educational Supplement*, 15 May 1919, 234, and 22 May 1919, 246). Nos. 1–2 were on 'Aims of Reconstruction' and 'Housing in England and Wales' (*The Times*, 2 Sept. 1918, 4). Nos. 22–3 were on Science and Modern Languages. For the end of the Ministry, see *The Times*, 29 May 1916, 16; *Hansard* cxvi, cols. 1208–9: 28 May 1919. During the following year Young toyed with the idea of setting up a School of Foreign Affairs at London University (*The New Europe*, 14 (1920), 289–94, 135–6; *The Contemporary Review*, 118 (1920), 51–6).
[22] *The Times*, 30 Oct. 1954, 8; S. Legge, *Affectionate Cousins: T. Sturge Moore and Marie Appia* (Oxford, 1980), 193; and London University Library, Sturge Moore MSS, cited in *ODNB*.
[23] Described pseudonymously [as 'Monica Moore'] in *The Story of Rosalind Retold from her Diary* (London, 1910).
[24] See D. Seward and P. Ziegler (eds), *Brooks's: A Social History* (London, 1991). Young gives his address as Bundeskanzel, Vienna (*T LS*, 13 July 1922, 460). An 'untiring sportsman with both rod and gun', Lindley ended his days fishing at Weir House, Alresford, Hants. See *ODNB*.

the perfect mandarin. When a fellow Cabinet Secretary, Thomas Jones, first encountered him in Whitehall, he noted: Young is 'a distinctly able but also "superior" person... I realized acutely that I had not been to Oxford'.[25] In 1921 Lindley was transferred to Athens but Young stayed on in Vienna, broadening out his employment to include investment activities with the newly created Anglo-Austrian Bank in that city and in Prague. It was in Vienna that he got to know Geoffrey Madan, 'the handsomest man of his generation', son of Falconer Madan of the Bodleian. They would remain friends for life.

But Young's heart was never in banking. He had already started reading seriously on the nineteenth century. By 1925 he too had retired, and settled down as a man of letters. And he had hit upon an ideal retreat: a house called the Old Oxyard at Oare in Wiltshire, a nest of converted farm buildings situated in a fine setting between Marlborough and Pewsey. Young's ancestors had once lived just six miles away at Mildenhall. Mona Wilson acquired the property on her retirement, presumably at Young's suggestion. The site formed part of the estate of a mutual friend, Sir Geoffrey Fry, private secretary to Bonar Law and Stanley Baldwin. Several houses were built or converted, and leased to literary acquaint-ances. Fry's architect was Clough Williams-Ellis of Portmeirion; and it was Williams-Ellis who 'Cloughed up' the Pennings at Oare to create the Old Oxyard. Virginia Woolf christened it 'Wilson's folly'.[26] G. M. and Mona turned it into a rustic salon.

Young's private life, Rupert Hart-Davis recalled, 'was unusual'. He lived with Mona Wilson for twenty-five years. 'There was', he continues,

so far as I know, no just cause or impediment why they shouldn't have married, but they just didn't. I'm sure their relationship was entirely intellectual and companionable, without any sexual feelings – indeed I wonder whether either of them ever had much sex-life of any kind. Miss Wilson (as he always referred to her) was ten years older than he – a little hunch-backed old lady when I knew her [in the 1940s], rapidly going blind (her cooking was terrible: since she couldn't *see* what she ate, the food was either raw or

---

[25] T. Jones, *A Diary with Letters: 1931–1950* (London, 1954), 8.

[26] Letters to Molly MacCarthy (N. Nicolson and J. Trautman (eds), *Letters of Virginia Woolf,* 6 vols (London, 1975–80), ii. 407: 4 Dec. 1919, and iv. 284: 30 Jan. 1931). Woolf's friends formed a small colony there: Sydney and Margery Waterlow took a 28-year lease of Parsonage House, Oare, in 1918 (A. O. Bell and A. McNeillie (eds), *The Diary of Virginia Woolf,* 5 vols (London, 1977–84), i. 155); Desmond and Molly MacCarthy took the Old Bakery opposite from 1919 (ibid., 238). In 1922 Geoffrey Fry lent Oare House to Maynard Keynes (ibid., ii. 197–8). Lady Katherine Rollo lived at Cold Blow, i.e. The Dower House (*Country Life,* 53 (1923), 195–6; R. Randall Phillips, *Small Country Houses of Today,* vol. 3 (London and New York, 1925), 43–7). Young knew the area well: 'My great-great-great grandfather, a churchwarden at Mildenhall... had an Elizabethan bell recast and signed it "Gulielmus Young custos sacrarum"' (Oxford, Bodleian Library, MS Gilbert Murray, 116, ff. 123–8, Young to Murray: 10 July ?). For buildings at Oare by Clough Williams-Ellis, see J. Jones, *Clough Williams-Ellis: The Architect of Portmeirion* (Bridgend, 1996), 76–8; L. Weaver, *Cottages: Their Planning, Design and Materials* (London, 1926), 142; C. Hussey, *Country Life,* 53 (1928), 334–41; and R. Haslam, *Clough Williams-Ellis* (London, 1996).

cindery). She smoked a little pipe, which he lovingly filled for her... The house was very dirty and untidy, full of books and papers, but they were charming together.[27]

On fundamentals they were in agreement. In religion, both could best be described as post-Christian rationalists. Mona Wilson's father had been the first Anglican ordinand who openly suspended judgement about all physical miracles.[28] Young's own religion was really Shaftesbury's religion of all sensible men: sensible men never tell. But his instincts are implicit in his writing. He had no time for the Oxford Movement, though he admired Newman's style. And on the controversy surrounding *Essays and Reviews* (1860) he was damning. 'There are times', he wrote, 'when the reader of Victorian apologetic... is nauseated by the taint of sophistry and false scholarship.' But historically he saw the value of a Neo-Christian code of conduct sanctified by Parliament in symbolic form: the sort of rationalized Via Media hammered out by the mid-Victorians – Evangelical, Arnoldian, and Tractarian – reconciling 'the spiritual demands of humanity with the... cosmic indifference of Evolution'.[29]

As to relations between the sexes, both G. M. and Mona assumed that by the 1920s the principle of equality had been settled; its implementation was something which time alone would solve. The Victorian family, Young acknowledged, had been responsible for 'much falsehood and much injustice, much suffering and much cruelty'. But its stability was the key to the age: it supplied 'the clue to the Victorian paradox – the rushing swiftness of its intellectual advance and the tranquil evolution of its social and moral ideals'. In a rare footnote he adds: 'If any one chooses to substitute [for the word "family" the phrase] "monogamic idealism about sex", he may.' When it came to women authors, he was generally encouraging – except for Virginia Woolf. Ultimately, Young was on the side of George Meredith: 'to whom a society with women on a secondary plane, without, therefore, the collisions from which the purifying spark of comedy flies, is a society half finished'. Meanwhile, down at the Oxyard, it was incumbent on the new clerisy to enlarge what Young called 'the sexless sphere of disinterested intelligence'.[30]

---

[27] *Lyttelton Hart-Davis Letters*, 132–3: 15 May 1956. In 1937 Young did admit to a certain 'curiosity' as to Eileen Power's marriage to her pupil, Michael Postan: an 'unexpected survival [of interest] from a less austere period of my intellectual life' (All Souls College archives, Young to Madan: 28 Dec. 1937). See also correspondence between Power and Young, Oxford, Bodleian Library, MS Eng. Lett. d. 183, ff. 77–80.

[28] O. Chadwick, *The Victorian Church*, 3rd edn, 2 vols (London, 1971), ii. 145. Similarly, Young's approval of Gibbon's theism: 'a polite recognition of a moral order', which – as with Shaftesbury, Pope, and Voltaire – excluded the miraculous (Young, reviewing S. T. McCloy, *Gibbon's Antagonism to Christianity* (London, 1933), in *TLS*, 13 April 1933, 259).

[29] Young, *Portrait*, ed. Clark, 116–17, 123, 125, 127, 354–5. Young's correspondents included Sir Ray Lankester, a freethinking, radical zoologist, author of *The Kingdom of Man* (London, 1907). 'Between the wars [he] was taken to see the last of the old agnostic stalwarts, Edward Clodd' (*The Listener*, 14 July 1949, 57–60). At the end of his life he noted: 'Victorian England is best understood as the *Ancien Régime* of an agnostic, scientific, humanitarian society' (Young, reviewing J. Laver, *Victorian Vista* (London, 1954) in *TLS*, 26 Nov. 1954, 757).

[30] Young, *Portrait*, ed. Clark, 100, 151, 153–4, 156, 371; Young, *Today and Yesterday* (London, 1948), 58. Woolf regarded Wilson as a formidable opponent: 'no one can better correct, contradict

With G. M. very much a public figure, Mona was content in her retirement to deal with the mundanities of country living. She did produce half a dozen books of her own: *William Blake* (1927) *Philip Sidney* (1931), *Queen Elizabeth* (1932), *Queen Victoria* (1933), *Jane Austen* (1938), *Dr Johnson* (1950). They are by no means negligible. Her *Jane Austen and some Contemporaries* (1938) can still be read with profit. But much of her time in the 1930s and 1940s must have been spent making life comfortable for 'my friend Mr Young'. Such agreeable pleasures, he recalled:

The pleasure of brushing one's teeth with soda water and then drinking a glass – a small glass of beer – before breakfast. The pleasure of having one's trousers warmed on a cold morning . . . [31]

Picture their literary set in its heyday, say 1937. Young's *Portrait of an Age* had just been published, to widespread acclaim. 'Brilliant' (*TLS*); 'brilliant' (*The Times*); 'brilliant' (*History*); 'brilliant' (*New Statesman*).[32] Its author was reviewing regularly for both the *Sunday Times* and the *TLS*. Academics from Oxford; publishers from London; gentry from Wiltshire: all curious for invitations to the Old Oxyard. Young was happy to lecture to local antiquaries on the origins of the West Saxon kingdom; he was equally happy guiding public figures like Stanley Baldwin round Avebury Ring; and happier still dining with neighbouring grandees like the Frys or the Herberts.[33] G. M. and Mona would walk over to parties at Savernake Lodge: Robert Byron might be holding court. Byron's *Road to Oxiana* was the new sensation: he actually read Young's glowing review of it in the *Sunday Times*, while staying with Harold Macmillan.[34] Thanks in part to Young, the book was awarded a *Sunday Times* gold medal.[35] The

and amplify than she' (Bell and McNeillie (eds), *Diary*, v. 163: 22 Aug. 1938). For Young praising books by Dorothea Sharp, Mona Wilson, Helen Waddell, and Agnes Ramsay, see Young, *Daylight and Champaign* (London, 1937), 158–9. In a broadcast discussion with Elizabeth Bowen and Phyllis Vallance – 'Do Women Think Like Men?' – he took the view that men think in generalities, women in particularities (*The Listener*, 30 Dec. 1941, 593).

[31] Young, reviewing Rose Macaulay, *Minor Pleasures of Life* (London, 1934), reprinted in *Daylight and Champaign*, 208.

[32] *TLS*, 12 Dec. 1936, 1025; *The Times*, 15 Dec. 1936, 10; *History*, 21 (1936–7), 376; *New Statesman*, 12 Dec. 1936, 986.

[33] Young, *The Origin of the West-Saxon Kingdom* (Council for the Preservation of Rural England lecture, Wilton House: 17 July 1934; reprinted in Young, *Last Essays* (London, 1950), 112–29). 'I spent yesterday morning taking Lord Baldwin over Avebury, which we [C. P. R. E.] are now trying to preserve on a grand scale' (Oxford, Bodleian Library, MS Johnson c. 28, Young to John Johnson: 2 Sept. 1937).

[34] 'My dear G.M. . . . you saw what I was trying to do . . . to convey an attitude of mind . . . other reviewers seem to think I was trying to convey the state of my liver' (All Souls College archives, Sparrow MSS, Box 67, Byron to Young: 26 April 1937). Young's review in the *Sunday Times* – praising this 'last and finest fruit of the insolent humanism of the 18th century' – was reprinted in *Daylight and Champaign*, 31–8. Byron thought Macmillan 'a man of really remarkable intelligence'; he suggested that his publishing firm might poach Young from Oxford University Press.

[35] L. Butler (ed.), *Robert Byron: Letters Home* (London, 1991), 5; J. Knox, *Robert Byron* (London, 2003), 290, 362–3. Byron's sister Lucy later married Rohan Butler of All Souls. For Young's obituary tribute to Byron – 'he absorbed history as a dry sponge takes up water' – see *Today and Yesterday*, 9–15 (BBC, 30 Dec. 1946).

Guinnesses – that is Bryan Guinness and Diana Mitford – would drive over sometimes from Biddesden. Lord Berners was often there: 'Praise the Lord, he was seldom bored.' And Nancy Mitford, and Edith Sitwell, and Roger Fulford, and Henry Yorke, and Violet Wyndham. The epigrams flowed free. And on occasion the Old Oxyard would buzz with expectation: John Sparrow is coming to stay. G. M. writes to tell him 'the epic tale of H. G. Wells's [recent] descent upon the Oxyard, supported by Lady Juliet Duff'. Could he, perhaps, bring over from All Souls 'a happy rendering into Greek of the name of Lytton Strachey... for a projected essay on Sappho. If slightly improper, all the better.'[36]

That gives us a clue to the Oxyard's allegiance. G. M. Young had made his reputation by exposing Lytton Strachey's 'preposterous misreading' of Victorian attitudes. He was the first historian to take the Victorians seriously. Bloomsbury never forgave him. When, in 1938, he reviewed Virginia Woolf's *Three Guineas* for the *Sunday Times*, he readily admitted its author's mastery of language: 'in prose... perhaps our greatest practitioner'. But he dismissed the content of the book as outdated 'Edwardian feminism'; an exercise in 'belated sex-egoism'. Woolf was not amused.

I'm glad to see [she wrote] that I raised the hackles of that mincing old pedant, that omniscient but altogether meretricious, lapped in book-dust humbug: G. M. Young... I can't help feeling that he's packed his egg – I mean head – too full of facts and it's addled... But do tell me how he and Mona carry on.[37]

Back at the Oxyard life did indeed carry on. Another week, another dinner party. 'The company', Young reported to Sparrow on one occasion in 1937, was

somewhat anxious – Gilbert Scott's nephew; a composer whose Oratorio had been fiercely slated in *The Times*; a young man whose features seemed so familiar that I only just didn't say to him: Tell me, weren't you a Hoare? And a sculptress of great talent but unfortunately deaf and dumb. This was at the Behrens's. Next Sunday we dine at Upper Upham, and if you could give me a line on Algernon Cecil or Sir John Farmer, [Miss Wilson and I] should be grateful... religion: divorced or not etc. Would you like to give me lunch on Monday, when I am passing through [Oxford]...? Incidentally [I am] having my portrait drawn off to be put in the papers. I know – but one must dwell on these alleviations, these salves of wounded self-esteem and frustrated ambitions. That is why I am so particular in my account of my social round. [By the way], how does one react to Nuffield College? And Nuffield? There is something rather wilful about him, I feel ...[38]

---

[36] Sparrow MSS, Box 67, Young to Sparrow: 2 Oct. 1937.

[37] Nicolson and Trautman (eds), *Letters of Virginia Woolf*, vi. 247, to Ethel Smyth: 26 June 1938; 251: 4 July 1938; and 392, to Margaret Llewelyn Davies: 6 April 1940. Also *Diary*, vol 5 (1984), 153–4. *Three Guineas* was hailed as 'the book of the year' by Theodora Bosanquet in *Time and Tide*, 4 June 1938, 788–90. For Young's review, see 'Women in the Modern World'... 'Sex and the Air Raid' (*Sunday Times*, 19 June 1938, 7).

[38] Sparrow MSS, Box 67, Young to Sparrow: 14 Oct. 1937. One of two pencil drawings (c. 1935 and 1938) by Henry Lamb, National Portrait Gallery. Another, by S. Botsarvis (1938), is at All Souls (illustrated in *The London Mercury*, 38 (1938), 308a).

Beneath the badinage, that exchange is revealing. By the later 1930s, Young already sensed he was wasting his talent in trivialities. John Sparrow understood. By the early 1950s both men knew that their promise had hardly been fulfilled. In 1952 Young confesses to Sparrow that he rather enjoys writing reviews to order: that way there is 'no time spent in debating what I should do, or when'; it just has to 'catch the post'. Perhaps Sparrow should do the same, he suggests; or else announce that he has a specific 'subject in view and in hand' – a monograph on Anthony Wood, maybe – thus countering 'the objection that your scholarship, like mine, is of an antique and unproductive kind'.[39]

During the 1930s Young continued to dazzle his Sunday morning readers, and no doubt infuriated quite a number of authors. Where did Young England discover Coleridge? He suggests George Smythe (Disraeli's *Coningsby*), who was taught at Hurstmonceaux by Julius Hare, 'the first Englishman (I think) to quote Hegel . . . It is not for an ignorant man like me to wish he had been the last. [Nor to regret that Coleridge's thought was obscured by] the negligent exuberance of his own production'.[40] A youthful art historian from Cambridge named Anthony Blunt suggests that in Soviet Russia 'every artist has the right to create freely and independently'. 'Quite freely?' asks Young; 'Quite freely, Mr Blunt?'[41] John Buchan dares to write a biography of the Emperor Augustus. 'An able work' concedes the sage of Pewsey; but would it not be wiser 'if you could curb a certain habit of facile picturesqueness; of laying unseasonable tributes on the grave of Walter Pater?'[42]

All Sunday morning fun. But any commitment to major literary work was forestalled by the outbreak of the Second World War. Young found himself suddenly in public demand, a regular pundit on the BBC, broadcasting his opinions to millions around the globe. In discussion groups he was frequently paired with Harold Laski: right wing versus left.[43] He was even paid £200 per annum to check the BBC's news bulletins for style. He did not object to celebrity. On 27 September 1939, for example, Harold Nicolson lunched at 19 Lord North Street with Sybil Colefax, hostess and interior decorator. There, to his great satisfaction, Nicolson found H. G. Wells, Jan Masaryk the Czech patriot, Victor Cazalet – who was soon to die with the Polish hero Sikorsky in a

---

[39] Sparrow MSS, Box 67, Young to Sparrow: 28 Jan. 1952.

[40] Young, reviewing R. J. White, *The Political Thought of Samuel Taylor Coleridge* (London, 1938), *Sunday Times*, 3 July 1938, 9.

[41] Young, reviewing C. Day Lewis (ed.), *The Mind in Chains: Socialism and the Cultural Revolution* (London, 1937), *Sunday Times*, 25 July 1937, 6.

[42] Dover Wilson MSS, 14319, f. 154: 8 Jan. 1938; 'A Reconstitution of Augustus', *Sunday Times*, 7 Nov. 1937, 7.

[43] E.g. on compulsory state insurance (*The Listener*, 21 Jan. 1943, 77–8); on Russia as an ally (ibid., 9 July 1942, 43–4); on America in the war (ibid., 13 Aug. 1942, 205–7); on Germany after the war (ibid., 8 Oct. 1942, 461–2, 467).

mysterious plane crash in Gibraltar – and finally, the Duke and Duchess of Windsor, and G. M. Young.[44]

Clearly, not all the lights were going out. In deepest Wiltshire, Young appears, most improbably, as a Platoon Commander in the North Wiltshire Home Guard: truly 'one of the strangest militias ever raised'.[45] But in London there were still glimpses of Society. There was always Lady Colefax. In June 1943 Chips Channon noted in his diary, 'drove [with Field Marshall Wavell from the War Office] to Kemsley House, to lunch with His Lordship of that name . . . G. M. Young, the writer and thinker [was there, and] Arthur Bryant, and Deneys Reitz [the South African High Commissioner, and author of the Boer War classic, *Commando*] . . . a brilliant party, I must admit [adds Channon], though I arranged it myself'.[46] Such episodes kept Young in too many drawing rooms, and out of too many archives. Too much energy was diverted into letter writing. And, significantly, his most intimate correspondent over a period of twenty years was Geoffrey Madan, that paragon of inconsequential learning.[47]

Still, the letters are entertaining. Young's correspondence between the 1930s and 1950s – with for example, John Sparrow, Gilbert Murray, and John Dover Wilson – is peppered with classical references and teasing bons mots. The one-upmanship is relentless. In 1935 he sends an SOS to Sparrow: 'I have mislaid my Longinus . . . it is probably the only one in [Wiltshire]. Doubtless you have one by your bedside . . . '[48] In 1950 he twice laments – to Dover Wilson and R. W. Chapman – that he only knows half a dozen languages: 'I am always annoyed that I can't read Provencale . . . though I can make my way through Catalan'.[49] And so on. In 1951 we find him discussing with Gilbert Murray some arcane corres-pondence between Gladstone and the eighth Duke of Argyll over descriptions in ancient Greek authors relating to the singing of nightingales in evergreen shrubberies. Young adds for good measure: 'Apollonius Rhodius is the only Greek poet of any consequence that I have not read.' Or again: 'What a world of bad writing we should have been saved if Socrates had never lived. I always think of him as the Fra Bartolomeo of prose, or the man who was too clever by half, and not half clever enough.'[50]

---

[44] N. Nicolson (ed.), *Harold Nicolson: Diaries and Letters, 1939–45* (London, 1967), 38, 224: 27 Sept. 1939; and 248: 8 Oct. 1942.

[45] 'P. F.' [? Peter Fleming], *The Times*, 24 Nov. 1959, 15; Oxford, Bodleian Library, MS Eng. 3174, f. 28: 8 May [? 1944].

[46] R. Rhodes James (ed.), *Chips: The Diaries of Sir Henry Channon* (London, 1967), 363: 3 June 1943.

[47] J. Gere and J. Sparrow, *Geoffrey Madan's Notebooks: A Selection* (Oxford, 1981); [Beatrice Brocklebank], *Geoffrey Madan, A Memoir* (privately printed, 1984); R. Ollard (ed.), *The Diaries of A. L. Rowse* (London, 2003), 146–7.

[48] Sparrow MSS, Box 67, Young to Sparrow: 3 Oct., 7 Oct. [1935].

[49] Dover Wilson MSS, 14319, f. 238: 21 May 1950; Oxford, Bodleian Library, MS Eng. Lett. c. 766 f. 105, Young to Chapman: 7 July 1950.

[50] Oxford, Bodleian Library, MS Gilbert Murray (102), f. 68: 2 April 1951 and (116), ff. 129–31: 29 Dec. 195[?].

Trivial stuff, no doubt. But it was banter like this that consolidated Young's friendships with 'the people who counted'. From 1937 he was a Trustee of the National Portrait Gallery; from 1938 a member of the Standing Commission on Museums and Galleries; from 1947 a Trustee of the British Museum, and a member of the Royal Commission on the Press; from 1948 a Member of the Historical Manuscripts Commission: all five posts held simultaneously. This nexus of influence was confirmed in 1944 by his election to the Athenaeum. His nomination paper survives. It reads like a *Who's Who* of public service: education, journalism, law, government, and the arts.[51] With Brooks's and the Athenaeum – a rare double – Young was now strategically placed: socially, intellectually, politically.

Young's politics are easy to caricature. In later years he rather enjoyed his blimpish image. 'So glad', he wrote to Gilbert Murray in 1948, that 'Existentialism has been put on the Index' by the Pope. 'I don't know what it is, but the name is enough.'[52] In practice he was a political centrist, a Butlerite Tory. He was never a party member; he never belonged to the Carlton. In his Civil Service days he worked well enough with both Lloyd George and Bonar Law. In the later 1930s he supported Churchill's call for rearmament. But by 1944 he was openly doubtful as to the great orator's suitability as a peacetime Prime Minister. And when it came to the election campaign of 1945 – Churchill's ill-judged 'Gestapo' broadcast – his comments were vitriolic. In a private letter to Geoffrey Madan he wrote:

One cannot conceive Balfour or Asquith or Campbell-Bannerman descending to such a level ... It was the Winston of the Abdication, reckless, unscrupulous, and utterly ignorant of the way people think ... Winston the American ... the rat of 1903 ... The body politic has evacuated him. I approve.[53]

---

[51] Education (Alan Barlow, W. Reeve Wallace, Fitzgibbon Young, Willard Connely); journalism (Cyril Lakin, Douglas Woodruff, J. W. Welch); law (Cecil Carr, J. C. B. Gamlen); government (Thomas Jones, Henry Snell, Derick Heathcote Amory); the arts (Ian MacAlister, D. S. MacColl, Thomas Armstrong, A. P. Oppé, Ivor Bulmer Thomas, F. J. E. Raby). See Athenaeum club archives, candidates' book, no. 13545. Young had previously been a member of the Savage Club (founded 1857 in memory of Richard Savage, d. 1745), and later frequented meetings of the Johnson Club in Gough Square.

[52] Oxford, Bodleian Library, MS Gilbert Murray (99), f. 134: 10 Nov. 1948.

[53] All Souls College archives, Young to Madan: 30 July 1945; *London Mercury*, 38 (1938), 308–16. Young 'wants a "Left" Government in after the war with a strong, intelligent and tolerant "Right" Opposition. He doesn't think Winston could be a post-war leader – or that he would command votes as such' (M. Pottle (ed.), *Champion Redoubtable: The Diaries and Letters of Violet Bonham Carter, 1914–45* (London, 1988), 305: 12 June 1944). 'A Liberal revival is both likely and desirable ... if only [the *Manchester Guardian*] could get the self-righteous men out of their system, which they inherit from the Victorian non-conformists' (Young to Laurence Hammond, Oxford, Bodleian Library, MS Hammond, 27, f. 120: 9 Feb. 1943). 'If only [Churchill] would take warning by L. G. and shed his preference for "low men and crooked ways"! But he is rather too old to turn good' (Oxford, Bodleian Library, MS Eng. 3174, f. 25: Young to Lady Colefax: ? 1948).

In 1953 Young did feature as a contributor to one Conservative manifesto, *The Good Society*. Its motto appealed to him: 'Give opportunity to the strong and protection to the weak'. But there was always a healthy strain of Whiggery about him. 'The most useful function of a governing class', he once wrote, 'is not to govern, but to prevent anybody governing too much.'[54] Nor did he trust the market implicitly. He liked to paraphrase Peel's sentiment in the Factory Act debates of 1843–4: 'Think a little less of the economics of wealth and a little more of the economics of welfare.'[55] 'I feel very acutely, very sadly, and very humbly', he wrote in 1944, 'the limitations of the Tory mind'. But by 1950 – in a polarized political climate – he was faced with a stark choice: conservatism or socialism. There could be only one option. He was a democrat, not an egalitarian.[56] What he looked back to was the fundamental liberalism 'common to all parties' in England during the years of his youth. Hence his reluctant interest in Anglo-American relations: they 'do after all belong to the Habeas Corpus bloc, the Russians to the Firing Party bloc'.[57] By 1950 all he could hope for – and this is curiously prophetic – was the emergence of a 'European mind', historically informed, humanistically inclined; some kind of 'new Liberalism reformulated to meet the circumstances and requirements of an impoverished state, nominally equalitarian, but in fact authoritarian to a degree which our ancestors, indeed our fathers could barely have conceived... Some form of European union', he concludes, 'is desirable, and, unless it is prevented by some violent impact from the East, is indeed inevitable.'[58]

---

[54] *The Good Society: Oxford Lectures 1952* (London, 1953), 17. Also Young, reviewing Hilaire Belloc's *An Essay on the Nature of Contemporary England* (London, 1937); reprinted in *Daylight and Champaign*, 237. 'Are socialism and parliamentary methods really compatible?' – Young, 'The Liberal Mind', *The Listener*, 29 May 1948, 813–14; reprinted in H. Grisewood (ed.), *Ideas and Beliefs of the Victorians: An Historic Revaluation of the Victorian Age* (London, 1949).

[55] Young, *Ourselves*, 12. Similarly, 'I have very little regard for Fabian philosophy, but a great respect for Fabian statistics' (ibid., 17). In 1919–24 he had been not unsympathetic to Labour's view on Europe (*The Nation*, 33 (1923), 737–8, and *The Contemporary Review*, 116 (1919), 523–31; 124 (1923), 556–64; 125 (1924), 416–24).

[56] Young, *Ourselves*, 26. 'One of the chief lures of Socialism is the unlimited prospect it opens of safe employment as Planners and Deputy Planners, Inspectors and Sub-Inspectors' (ibid., 21). See his review of *Men without Work: A Report made to the Pilgrim Trust* (Cambridge, 1938), in *Sunday Times*, 1 May 1938, 9. 'I cannot conceive a time when no one will be more alert, more inventive, more sensitive or more refined than the run of his fellows, and I think these four qualities between them account for most of the improvements in social civilisation in all ages... Therefore our goal... a steady progress towards equality... is an endlessly receding one – the rainbow's end. [In any case], the way... runs through the home; and the process of improvement is surely the interchange of habits, tastes and standards between people living side by side and so improving one another. And as this is the ground of all civilisation, so it must be the ground of education, which is simply the civilising of the young' (Young, *Ourselves*, 18).

[57] Oxford, Bodleian Library, MS Eng. 3174, f. 33. With Lady Colefax he planned an Anglo-American club at Benjamin Franklin's House in Craven Street, Strand.

[58] Young, *The Good Society*, 14, and *Last Essays*, 10, 13, 15. In the 1940s he chaired the editorial committee of the *British Survey*, published by the British Association for International Understanding.

Young's approach to political theory was always deeply sceptical. He had a horror of German linguistics and Germanic abstraction.[59] His thinking was historically pragmatic: the governmental ethic of Sir Robert Peel; the reformist ethic of Edwin Chadwick; the paternalist ethic of Sir Robert Morant. Before the First World War he welcomed the Education Act of 1902 and the Insurance Act of 1911. Educational reform – a process of training in County Colleges between the ages of 15 and 18, with a new tripartite formulation: Administrative, Executive, Industrial – emerges as the key motivation of his Civil Service years. Not the theory of education – 'Education with a big and gloomy E', as he once called it – nor the psychology of education, still less 'the accelerating efficiency of modern scholarship'. That was not what he meant by the transmission of culture. What he longed to encourage was the growth of 'disinterested intelligence'; and with it the shaping of language as 'the primary mode of communication between minds'. After all, 'in any people professing to be self-governed, good speech... must be deemed the first political art'; 'conversation is our bond of cohesion'.[60] Like Morant, he began by thinking that these qualities might be inculcated by ministerial diktat. In retirement he came to realize that educationists, like politicians, are fallible creatures. Close contact with government had given him, and Mona too, a sense of disillusion. The key to civility, he came to see, must lie closer to home, in the evolving conventions of neighbourhood and family. Literature must have come to seem less and less a public good, more and more a private pleasure.

Still, those were 'golden' days, he later recalled. The days between the wars, when the higher journalism paid well; when two Civil Service pensions went a long way, and there was time to read and think. Writing to Gilbert Murray in 1947, he blamed the pressures of the 1940s – the war and the age of austerity – as the reason for his failure to produce a single satisfactory work of research. No servants, no taxies; trains full of A.T.S. girls 'crooning' and 'sucking peardrops'.[61] Actually, the reasons went deeper than that. During the early 1940s Young was flattered by Stanley Baldwin into undertaking that Prime Minister's biography.

[59] 'I was glad to have done... Hegel [at Balliol], because it showed me where Marx came from, but the αὐτος ἐφα of the Hegelians merely exasperates me' (Oxford, Bodleian Library, MS Gilbert Murray, 99, f. 206, Young to Murray: 17 April 1949, and ff. 211–12: 27 April 1949). 'The advance of the noun at the expense of the verb is a sign of linguistic decay... [From it stems] a habit of abstraction, generalisation and vagueness' (Young, *Basic* (Oxford, 1943), 35). Will our 'language have to surrender... to German-American [jargon]... as if we had been cradled in Marburg and reared in Michigan'? (Young, *Daylight and Champaign*, 135).

[60] Young, *Last Essays*, 13; *Today and Yesterday*, 7–8; 'Newman on Education', *Sunday Times*, 8 Aug. 1937, 6; *New Statesman*, 7 Nov. 1936, 738 (reviewing H. J. Rose, *Handbook of Latin Literature* (London, 1936)); *Today and Yesterday*, 5, 7; *Ourselves*, 22–3, 27. 'No political problem is incapable of solution by patience and the open mind in discussion' (Young, *The Government of Britain* (London, 1941), 22). See also *The Listener*, 28 Aug. 1941, 307, and 9 Oct. 1941, 491–2.

[61] Oxford, Bodleian Library, MS Gilbert Murray (98), f. 155: 6 Aug. 1947. 'English civilisation... the clerisy... [depended] on the Domestic Servant and the Spare Room' (Oxford, Bodleian Library, MS Eng. c. 3174, ff. 13, 24, 30: Young to Lady Colefax).

This might have been his most significant work. Perhaps he imagined a spell of agreeable reading in a country house archive. The reality was rather different. Baldwin kept little or nothing in the way of personal political papers.[62] And G. M. was hardly the man for coalface research at Colindale or in the Public Record Office (now the National Archives). More important, Young and Baldwin turned out to have little in common except a love of the English countryside, an appreciation of English prose, and a sense of the cohesion of English society: that 'habit of common happiness', as Young liked to think of it, 'the friendliness of English eyes . . . the quietness of English voices'.[63]

Baldwin's 'domestic psychology', he told Gilbert Murray in 1945, 'was very strange. He took very little interest in his children, at any age . . . His affections grew warmer as obligation or responsibility grew less, and only reached a real glow when he was speaking [on the wireless] to vast audiences with whom he had no personal relations at all. Robert Browning would have written a superb monologue [on him] in three sections: the Part, the Player, the Man.'[64] In 1948, in another intriguing letter to Murray, Young explains some of the consequences of Baldwin's empathetic deficiencies. A politician with blunted antennae, he implies, will find difficulty in seeing into the minds of his own voters.

It was perhaps at once [Baldwin's] strength and weakness [Young suggests], that he understood the feelings of others better than their ideas. 'When a thing gets difficult, Baldwin's attention flags in three minutes'. So Lloyd George said. And the pacifism of the thirties was an emotion he understood but could not handle – usually because he had no alternative idea.[65]

Hence, he assumed, Baldwin's tactical successes – the General Strike and the Abdication – as well as his failures: principally his apparent vacillation over

---

[62] 'I could put them all in my breast pocket and there would be no bulge. Except the heads of a communication to his Cabinet in Dec. '36 (and even there one can sense he had lost interest half way through), there is literally nothing' (Oxford, Bodleian Library, MS Murray, 99, ff. 8–9: 26 June 1945).

[63] Young, 'Epilogue to the Coronation', *Sunday Times*, 23 May 1937, 9; reprinted in *Daylight and Champaign*, 301–5. For Young lamenting the 'destruction of rural values', and criticizing land developers 'living on capital', see his review of C. Williams-Ellis (ed.), *Britain and the Beast* (London, 1937), in *Sunday Times*, 13 June 1937, 9, and his introduction to *Country and Town: A Summary of the Scott and Uthwatt Reports* (New York, 1943). For Young on the country house, see 'Domus Optima', in E. Blunden (ed.), *The Legacy of England* (London, 1935), reprinted in *Last Essays*, 136–61; on the manor house, see J. Lees-Milne (ed.), *The National Trust* (London, 1945), 55–60; and on the village, see his intro. to H. Pakington, *English Villages and Hamlets*, 2nd edn (London, 1934), reprinted in *Last Essays*, 162–9. Young was by no means a sentimental conservationist: 'I am very doubtful about all Councils for Turning Rural England into Jam. The beauty of England is functional . . . I am not sure that I do not prefer a universal suburb to a schedule of Potted Villages and Cliffs (Do not touch).' See Oxford, Bodleian Library, MS Hammond (24), ff. 152–4: 19 Sept. 1937.

[64] Oxford, Bodleian Library, MS Gilbert Murray (99), ff. 8–9: 26 June 1945.

[65] Ibid., f. 45: 5 March 1948. Young trenchantly supported Churchill's arguments for rearmament (*London Mercury*, 38 (1938), 308–16).

rearmament. Young's sensitivity to the nuances of politics might well have resulted in a remarkable book, had the commission come earlier and in different circumstances. As it was, the result was doubly unfortunate. His 'interim' study, published in 1952, did less than justice to a misunderstood Prime Minister; and nothing at all to enhance its author's reputation as an historian.[66]

After the Second World War, things were indeed different. By 1952 Young was permanently bronchitic, Mona Wilson effectively blind and deaf. There would be no more rowing on the river at their 'beloved' Lechlade.[67] She died in a Putney nursing home in 1954. 'The golden age of the Oxyard', he wrote to Sparrow, 'is closing in gloom ... Have you by chance in college a scout's widow, country-bred and intelligent, who would like the post of housekeeper [here] ... You can hardly see me in the post of chef-manciple-scout, can you?'[68] Well no: All Souls became his refuge. Outside, in the wider world of letters, Young realized he was swimming against the collectivist tide. Like many of his generation, he was driven further to the right by the arrival of the socialist cuckoo in the radical nest. But he accepted the Attlee Government's welfare system as an 'accomplished fact', then waited for the pendulum to swing. By July 1950 he sensed that 'the levelling process has gone far enough'. What was needed by that date, he felt, was not more penal taxation but less financial regulation. Not further redistribution of the fiscal cake but a fruitful multiplication of its slices: 'the widest possible diffusion of wealth'. That and a recovery of the community's innate historical sense. In a radio programme in the run-up to the 1950 election, he summoned up all the resources of this neo-Burkian argument: 'the vital principle of Conservatism [is] the sense of continuity between the past and the future ... We are what our ancestors have made us. And you cannot disfranchise the dead.'[69]

In practice, Young's politics are inseparable from his instincts as an historian. His Leslie Stephen lecture of 1949 set out the fundamentals. These can be summarized as follows. Culture is not a state but a process: change is built into its evolutionary flux. But civilizations disintegrate when they alter too fast, when they lose interest in their roots. History supplies the cohesion, the behavioural

[66] 'No Prime Minister in our history has been hit so hard by a biographer who knew him and who had been invited to describe him' (*TLS*, 14 Nov. 1952, 1). See also *The Times*, 14 Nov. 1952, 7, 17. The book did win the James Tait Black Memorial Prize, and was given balanced treatment by C. L. Mowat in *Journal of Modern History*, 27 (1955), 169–74; but it was ignored by the *English Historical Review*. For a considered assessment see P. Williamson, *Stanley Baldwin* (Cambridge, 1999).
[67] 'Rowing on the river at Lechlade in heavenly weather...the landscape a blend of William Morris and the Scholar Gipsy' (Dover Wilson MSS 14319, f. 2–8: 14 June 1947, and f. 229: 7 May 1948). 'I rowed a nice easy 15 miles without pain, but not without beer' (Oxford, Bodleian Library, MS Eng. 3174, f. 21; Young to Lady Colefax: June 1947?). After their autumn visit in 1951, Young developed bronchitis and Wilson pneumonia (ibid., f. 241: 19 Oct. 1951, and f. 243: 11 Jan. 1952).
[68] Sparrow MSS, box 67 [1952]. More 'trouble over Baldwin proofs. That misery never ends'.
[69] *The Listener*, 14 July 1949, 57–60 (Third Programme), reprinted in *Last Essays*, 47–68.

norms, the web of inter-generational references, without which life shrivels into an amnesiac nightmare. Hence the role of the historian. 'Historians', he concludes, are 'the high priests of continuity'. And the ancient universities – those repositories of 'social knowledge' – are uniquely qualified to mediate between the past and the present. Here – and at this point he writes as a newly re-elected fellow of All Souls – here 'learning and public service . . . [have been] integrated as . . . nowhere else in the world'.[70]

Whistling in the dark. Beyond Oxford, beyond the gates of All Souls, he looked out on what he saw as a blighted intellectual landscape. In 1948 he admitted that contemporary levels of public discourse had thrown him into a 'state of bewildered despair . . . Mentally – in its capacity for formulating, apprehending, and exchanging ideas – our Sovereign Plebs is living in the slums . . . On this theme I have written myself out.'[71] Even All Souls wasn't quite what it had been. 'You will find', he warned Dover Wilson in 1949, 'the water hot, the food passable, and the wine adequate. The conversation is anecdotal rather than scholastic, but quotations are still recognised as such, even if they can't always be placed.'[72]

By the late 1950s, Young was reported to be 'pretty well gaga'.[73] 'This Parkinson', he told Dover Wilson, 'is the very devil . . . I am trying to keep it at bay by reading Othello.'[74] One dinner-time conversation has passed into All Souls folklore.

'How are you tonight, GM?'
'Oh, going downhill, I'm afraid . . . Would that the slope were steeper.'[75]

'Poor old boy', noted Hart-Davis in April 1959, 'it isn't whisky but melancholia that has [really] got him down. He has to have a male nurse in All Souls, and I think Sparrow and the other birds would be much relieved if they could ship the old polymath off to a nursing home – or even to Paradise – for he is a great nuisance to them.'[76]

That was unkind. Several of the younger fellows – Fraser, Huxley, Habbakuk, and Dummett, for example – valued his company. They even went to his funeral – bleak and sparsely attended – at the Oxford Crematorium.[77] When Sparrow gave

---

[70] *Last Essays*, 48, 67. Young was re-elected to a 'Fifty-Pound' Fellowship in Nov. 1948; this was renewed in Nov. 1955.

[71] Young, *Today and Yesterday*, 6–7.

[72] Dover Wilson MSS, 14319, f. 234v: 20 Sept. 1949.

[73] *Lyttelton Hart-Davis Letters*, vols. 1–2, 261: 24 Feb. 1957, and vols. 3–4 (London, 1986), 234: 11 April 1959.

[74] Dover Wilson MSS, 14319, f. 250: Feb. [?1955].

[75] An oblique reference to Tennyson's *In Memoriam*, xxii. 'I am deaf in the left ear, but I have learned the strategy of surditude and contrive to sit either at the bottom [corner] of the table . . . or on the Warden's right' (Dover Wilson MSS, 14319, f. 235: 26 Sept. 1949).

[76] *Lyttelton Hart-Davis Letters*, vols 3–4, 230: 5 April 1959.

[77] Others included John Sparrow, Kathleen Ross (cousin), Hon. H. R. C. Balfour, Rev. V. J. K. Brook (Chaplain, All Souls), Dr Max Grunhut, W. D. Handcock, R. A. Nisbett, B. F. Watson, and

the memorial address at All Souls, there was a good audience. Longevity should be the historian's trump card. But the years were not kind to G. M. Young. Geoffrey Madan had once called him 'not a polymath but a pantomath'.[78] Sparrow christened him 'the omniscient G. M. Young'.[79] But by his later fifties, the dynamo was running down. Even in 1939 he seemed already an old man.[80] His memory had once been prodigious. That was both a strength and a weakness: he rarely verified his references.[81] By the later 1950s, his handwriting was shaky, and his hold on recollection shakier still. But he put a good face on it. 'Loss of memory', he assures Sparrow, 'is very productive . . . one can read books for the first time, over and over again.'[82] Never exactly gregarious, he became increasingly solitary. Just before the war his aged father had died; in 1940 his sister. 'My next of kin', he tells Sparrow, 'is now a cousin, last seen in 1892, and believed to be in Canada. There is something very satisfactory in being alone.'[83] He died in a nursing home at Goring in November 1959.[84]

Young was never, in the professional sense, an historian. In Oxford he is commemorated by a Lectureship in English Literature. He was a Fellow of the Royal Society of Literature, never a Fellow of the British Academy, though he lectured there three times: on Tennyson, on Burke, and on Shakespeare.[85] When he was elected to the Athenaeum, neither Trevelyan nor Namier signed his nomination paper. He seldom consulted archives. He never bothered with reference notes. But he could correspond, almost as an equal, with Gilbert Murray on Greek poets, with R. W. Chapman on biblio-criticism, and with John Dover Wilson on Shakespeare's sources.[86] W. B. Yeats remarked that just

J. Fillingham (*The Times*, 24 Nov. 1959, 14). He thought the younger fellows 'great pets and good scholars' (Oxford, Bodleian Library, MS Eng. Lett. c. 766, f. 112, Young to Chapman: 16 June 1954?). 'He had a notable capacity for making a junior feel, with a kind of fearful joy, that he was being treated as an equal by a senior whose whole range of knowledge and experience was at his disposal' (Stuart Piggott, *The Times*, 25 Nov. 1959, 15).

[78] *Lyttelton Hart-Davis Letters*, vols 1–2, 134: 15 May 1956.

[79] Sparrow MSS, Box 67, Sparrow to Young: 31 Aug. 1952.

[80] 'Old G. M. Young' (C. Lycett Green (ed.), *John Betjeman: Letters*, 2 vols (London, 1994–5), i. 226, 237, Betjeman to K. Clark: 14 April 1939).

[81] 'When I re-issued G. M.'s old books I started . . . to verify his quotations, and found they were all slightly wrong . . . Fancy having all that in one's head!' (*Lyttelton Hart-Davis Letters*, vols 1–2, 133: 15 May 1956).

[82] Sparrow MSS, Box 67, Young to Sparrow: 6 March 1957.

[83] Ibid., Box 69, letters misc. ii: 2 July 1940. Young's father lived at Beach Brow, Greenhithe; later at Blackheath, where he died aged 99.

[84] He left £24,435 10s. 3d., entirely to All Souls (*The Times*, 17 March 1960, 14).

[85] Young, 'The Age of Tennyson' (Warton Lecture, 1939), *Proceedings of the British Academy*, 25 (1939), 125–42, reprinted in *Today and Yesterday*, 43–63, and in Young, *Victorian Essays* (London, 1962), 46–62; 'Burke' (Mastermind Lecture, 1943), *Proceedings of the British Academy*, 29 (1943), 19–36, reprinted in *Today and Yesterday*, 83–109; 'Shakespeare and the Termers' (Shakespeare Lecture, 1947), *Proceedings of the British Academy*, 38 (1947), 81–99 (reprinted in *Today and Yesterday*, 279–306). Young's 'Scott and History' (*Essays by Divers Hands*, 25 (1950), 70–86) was reprinted in *Sir Walter Scott Lectures* (Edinburgh, 1950), and in *Last Essays*, 17–40.

[86] Both Young and Wilson fell under Morant's spell. When Wilson's proposals – in the 1918 Education Act – for the teaching of humanities in further education were abandoned in 1921, he felt

one of Young's articles 'taught me more about prosody than I have ever known'.[87] He knew about archaeology too: in Wiltshire he won the admiration of the young Stuart Piggott. In time, he became a polished public lecturer as well, happy to embroider his text as he spoke.[88] And he could write. Ruskin he admired enormously, though he knew he could never match that avalanche of 'pictorial prose'. And Dean Swift: that patrician intellect, 'the almost noiseless purr of his prose'. And Gibbon: his style 'has the exalted solidity of the Roman aqueduct'. But above all Erasmus: 'There for the first time I realised what makes good prose: not colour, not eloquence, not glamour or cry or thrill: but exactness, economy, form.' In later years Young's style became increasingly lapidary: the phrases pared down to a minimum, boxed in by colons and semi-colons.

Of course there is a good deal of artifice in it: he had no truck with 'the cult of under-writing'.[89] To the end, he believed in the discipline of classical form: spontaneity was the enemy of wisdom. Sometimes the formality is constrictive. But whatever the occasion there is always a limpid economy of phrase, a dazzling range of reference. He had his blind spots. He thought Gerard Manley Hopkins led English poetry astray.[90] He had no ear for music. He had no special interest in architecture, although he did admire the nobility of Lutyens' later work. Even as a writer, he found difficulty in focusing his energies. He published no book till he was 50, and then it was a slim essay on *Gibbon* (1932; revised 1948).[91] He was perhaps over-conscious of form: he rather fancied the title of Professor of Prose.[92] More often he described himself, simply, as an 'author'. An author who happened to write history.

---

the same sense of betrayal that Young experienced with the collapse of the Ministry of Reconstruction in 1919. See Wilson's autobiography, *Milestones on the Dover Road* (London, 1969), and his obituary in *Proceedings of the British Academy*, 59 (1973), 383–418 (by H. Jenkins).

[87] Sparrow MSS, Box 67: 23 Sept. 1935.

[88] 'Send a shorthand writer, because my methods of composition are such that no mortal printer can possibly reduce them to type' (e.g. his lectures on Scott delivered in Edinburgh; see Dover Wilson MSS, 14319, f. 188: 25 Oct. 1943; f. 213: 5 Jan. 1946; and f. 229: 7 May 1948).

[89] Young, reviewing B. Dobrée, *Modern Prose Style* (Oxford, 1934), reprinted in *Daylight and Champaign*, 125; Young, *Gibbon* (London, 1932), 87–8. For Young on Ruskin and Erasmus, see *Last Essays*, 12; on Swift, see *Daylight and Champaign*, 216. 'To make spontaneity, and not excellence in its own kind, the canon of merit, is to abrogate reason, silence judgement, and to deliver literature to the wantonness of conflicting egoisms...So far from bringing the "ordinary man" to his own, Romantic spontaneity peopled the world with monsters' (Young, reviewing Mary Colum's *From These Roots* (London, 1938), *Sunday Times*, 12 June 1935, 9).

[90] 'For Hopkins as a poet I have the greatest admiration, but his theories on metre seem to me to be as demonstrably wrong as those of any speculator who has ever led a multitude into the wilderness to perish. Unfortunately, they have been used as a justification for the cacophonies which naturally result when the metrically deaf write verse, and the metrically deaf are a very large class' (Young, *Daylight and Champaign*, 197, 202, 205).

[91] 'Gibbon is the only one of my opuscles which I pronounce to be good. "What an intellect I had"...I mean the second edition 1948 with its preface' (Oxford, Bodleian Library, MS Eng. Lett. c. 766, f. 109, Young to Chapman: 18 Aug. 1954). In fact it is little weightier than his *Charles I and Cromwell* (London, 1936; 1950).

[92] Oxford, Bodleian Library, MS Gilbert Murray (99), f. 134: 10 Nov. 1948. 'All Souls is doing me the transcendent honour of re-electing me and I think I shall ask the Professor of English to let

Now a great historian – in the modern era at least – must have two strings to his bow: the microscopic and the macroscopic; the specialist study and the broad-brush sweep. Young had only one of these. He was a communicator, not a technician. In effect, he was only an essayist; but an essayist of genius. Read him till you hear him speaking. Read him until you pick up the pitched intonation, the poised antitheses, the 'slow sadness' – Harold Nicolson's phrase – 'the slow sadness of his style'.[93]

Ultimately, he will stand or fall by one book: *Victorian England: Portrait of an Age*. Although it remained essentially an essay, it was an essay expanded and rewritten six times over. First it was a strident review in *Life and Letters* (1931), exploding the superficialities of Lytton Strachey and Esmé Wingfield-Stratford.[94] Then it became a cooler, more moderate essay, in a short-lived series edited by Humphrey Milford (1932).[95] This was refashioned into a virtuoso chapter in Young's multi-authored, two-volume *Early Victorian England* (1934).[96] And this in turn was expanded into the finished *Portrait of an Age*, first published in 1936, without notes and without an index; then reissued, with a new preface and an index, but still no references, in 1953. This was then reprinted seven times, as it stood, in paperback between 1960 and 1973. And it was this popular version which was finally re-edited with a new index and an impressive battery of notes and references by George Kitson Clark – though minus its chronological appendix – in 1977.[97] All but the first of this long sequence of thirteen incarnations was produced by the same publisher, Oxford University Press. 'Being published by OUP', he once remarked, 'is rather like being married to a Duchess: the honour is almost greater than the pleasure.'[98] Throughout all those editions, his approach remained unchanged. Thematically, it was the same essay.

How did he set about it? The foundation was an intensive study of a single primary printed source, the inexhaustible reservoir of Victorian periodical

me lecture on PROSE' (Dover Wilson MSS, 14319, f. 232: 1 Nov. 1948). He dreamed of the creation of an Oxford Chair of Prose (Oxford, Bodleian Library, MS Eng. Lett. c. 766, f. 96, Young to Chapman: 3 Jan. 1945).

[93] Dust cover, *Today and Yesterday*, from a *Daily Telegraph* review.

[94] The critical acclaim (*TLS*, 23 Oct. 1930, 845) for Wingfield-Stratford's *The Victorian Tragedy* (London, 1930) made him wonder 'whether in history we had any critical standards left at all ... I have got little from it beyond an occasional glimpse of moonshine through a flying rack of fustian. The style is a compost of the sort of declamation which our ancestors called rant, and the sort of irony which they called Sadler's Wells sarcasm ... One crass generalisation follows another till the tub gapes under the thumping' (*Life and Letters*, 6 (1931), 125–6). For Wingfield-Stratford's reply – 'not cricket' – see ibid., 322.

[95] H. Milford (ed.), *Selected Modern English Essays*, vol. 2 (London, 1932), 261–77.

[96] G. M. Young (ed.), *Early Victorian England, 1830–1865*, 2 vols (London, 1934). 'The Captain has put himself in last and has played a Captain's innings.... A masterpiece' (D. C. Somervell, *History*, 20 (79) (1935–6), 282).

[97] 'Historical narrative at its best', balancing 'the contingent, the possible, the conditional' (J. Clive in *TLS*, 20 Jan. 1978, 50–2). Published in hardback at £16.50, a price then beyond most students. The 1936 edition cost 7s 6d.

[98] *Lyttelton Hart-Davis Letters*, vols 1–2, 122.

literature.⁹⁹ What did he find? His central postulate was threefold: first the
creation of an integrated Victorian culture in the 1830s and 1840s; secondly
the high meridian of that culture – culture in equipoise – between the 1850s and
the 1870s; and thirdly its slow disintegration during the last quarter of the
nineteenth century. The pivotal year was 1859–60: *Essays and Reviews*, Darwin's
Origin of Species, FitzGerald's *Omar Khayyam*, Samuel Smiles's *Self Help*, Ruskin's
Unto This Last.

'In 1850 we are in the past', Young explains.

> In 1870 we are in a world continuous with our own. Between...lies the Victorian
> Revolution, the insular parallel to a turn in the European mind as decisive as the
> [Renaissance]...There ought to have been a debacle, and there was none: the moral
> fabric held...This is what puzzled Lord Acton...He was inclined to attribute it to
> George Eliot. So was George Eliot.

Still,

> the controversies of the mid-Victorian age, its science, its experiments in legislation and
> administration, are the first trial flights of the modern English mind. That is what
> Victorian history is made of...[Alas] England in 1900 [was] altogether unworthy of
> England in 1870...What failed in the late Victorian age was not the succession of
> great men, but a great public...The plutocracy going up passed the aristocracy going
> down...[Demographically, politically, intellectually] the clerisy was...watered
> down...[So] the historian of Victorian England must be something of a moralist,
> because his topic is how inward greatness was attained and lost...[In effect, it is the
> story of] the waning of a great civilisation.¹⁰⁰

Of course the argument is tendentious. But there is a persuasive grandeur in its
conception. In effect, it was an apology for the bourgeois values of the mid-
nineteenth-century English political class: written from the inside, by an author
whose ideals – evolutionary liberalism, representative democracy, national loyal-
ties, family ties, serious debate – remained confessedly Victorian. 'I am one of the
very few now living', he wrote in 1947, 'who can not only write but think
Victorian...my *Portrait of an Age* differs from most other works on that oceanic
theme in that it was written wholly from the inside'.¹⁰¹

The insider is not always right. By 1953 critics were already asking: 'But is this
really enough?'¹⁰² Young's indeterminate judgements – history as past opinion –

---

⁹⁹ E.g. *The Athenaeum*, 'an inexhaustible repertory' (Oxford, Bodleian Library, MS Hammond,
23: 5 May 1931). See also Young's review of M. Goodwin, *Nineteenth-Century Opinion*
(Harmondsworth, 1952), in *The Listener*, 8 May 1952, 758–9.
¹⁰⁰ Young, 'Victorian History', *Life and Letters*, 6 (1931), 123, 137–9, 141–3; 'Victorian History'
in Milford (ed.), *Selected Modern English Essays*, ii. 270, 274–6; *Portrait*, ed. Clark, 159–60, 162–3,
183. Young's periodization follows E. Halevy, *The Growth of Philosophical Radicalism* (London,
1928).
¹⁰¹ Young, *Today and Yesterday*, 1.
¹⁰² 'There is a two-way traffic between past and present, the present being moulded out of the
past, yet constantly re-creating the past. If the historian makes history, it's equally true that history
has made the historian' (*TLS* leader, 19 June 1953, 382, 397).

came dangerously close to the sort of relativism he himself denounced in Benedetto Croce.[103] In any case, Young's emphasis on the clerisy – Coleridge's term for the opinion-forming, articulate classes – was clearly a limiting factor.[104] Later research would have more to say, much more. Still, this is cultural history of a high order. Nobody has wrestled more effectively with what Young called the 'anfractuosities' of the Victorian mind. And his influence on successive cohorts of students cannot have been inconsiderable. In the decades after his death, however, his image did begin to fade. The old master had begun to lose his audience. In 1979, therefore, Sheldon Rothblatt set out to reclaim Young's reputation from the enormous condescension of the progressives. He did this by placing him in the historiographical context of Burckhardt and Huizinga. 'G. M.' emerged from this exercise as a rarity among English writers: a practitioner of *Kulturgeschichte* who could explain past thinking in structural terms; in terms of 'ideas, opinions and beliefs...caught and re-expressed through institutions'; in terms, that is, not static but dynamic.[105] A. J. P. Taylor and Asa Briggs rallied to this view. And more recently Simon Schama has canonized *Portrait of an Age* as 'an immortal classic...the greatest long essay ever written'.[106]

Well, the ghost of Macaulay might disagree. But Schama's suggestion is by no means absurd. To reread Young's *Portrait* after thirty years, after forty years, after fifty years – that is, for anybody who studied modern history at any university in the English-speaking world during the mid-twentieth century – is to explore the mental archaeology of several generations, including one's own. The epigrams greet us like old friends. Ruskin is there: 'All dogma and no system... Endowed with every gift except the gift to organise the others'.[107] And Tennyson: 'The natural laureate of an age morally conservative and intellectually progressive'; speaking 'like an archangel assuring the universe that it will muddle through'.[108] And the Peelites, moving 'to and fro across the stage [making] Conservatism a little less Tory, and Liberalism a little less Whig'.[109] And Young England: playing 'King Richard to somebody else's Wat Tyler has always been a Tory fancy'.[110]

---

[103] Young's critique of Croce's *History as the Story of Liberty*, trans. S. Sprigge (London, 1941) – 'pseudo-philosophic phrase-making'; 'idealism...inflated with verbal alembications' – was reprinted in *Last Essays*, 41–6. 'It is a bad sign when a man, professing to write on history, speaks contemptuously of Ranke: he is, and always must be, the Head of the Profession.'

[104] Young, *Portrait*, 25.

[105] S. Rothblatt, 'G. M. Young: England's Historian of Culture', *Victorian Studies*, 22 (1979), 413–29.

[106] Schama, cited without reference in Wikipedia, 'G. M. Young', accessed 12 Sept. 2010. In 1960, A. J. P. Taylor called it 'masterly...one of the very few successful attempts at unified history, fusing events and ideas, laws and opinions' (Taylor, *Politicians, Socialism and Historians* (London, 1980), 50).

[107] Young, *Portrait*, 118.

[108] Ibid., 86. A 'shadowy...metaphysic...a philosophy of Somehow, wavering between a hopeful doubt and a doubtful hope' (*Today and Yesterday*, 62).

[109] Young, *Portrait*, ed. Clark, 92.

[110] Ibid., 52.

And Oxford and Cambridge: breaking 'the fall of the aristocracy by civilising the plutocracy'.[111]

So many times, he gets it absolutely right. 'Early Victorian England ... was poised on a double paradox ... Its practical ideals were at odds with its religious professions, and its religious belief was at issue with its intelligence.'[112] Or again, on the shift from Mill to Darwin: 'As Early Victorian thought is regulated by the conception of progress, so the late Victorian mind is overshadowed by the doctrine of evolution.'[113] Or again, on the fragmentation of mid-Victorian culture: 'We leave behind us the world of historical ironmasters and banker historians, geological divines and scholar tobacconists ... And through the gateway of the Competitive Examination we go out into the Waste Land of Experts.'[114]

The judgment of R. C. K. Ensor – no slouch as an historian of late Victorian England – is worth pondering. *Portrait of an Age* is

analytical [in method] not narrative; it is not history but a historical essay. But within its chosen sphere it is wonderfully good. So flashing and frequent are its epigrams, that quite trivially-minded people might read it for amusement. So wide and accurate is its knowledge, so fair and temperate, yet so penetrating and subtle, are its fundamental judgements, that the most serious scholar must take off his hat to it.

Ensor did however doubt the book's philosophical underpinning. Young used to make fun of what he called Germanic 'hypostatisation of methodological categories'.[115] Yet here he is objectifying the Victorian mind, doing a little hypostatizing of his own. Still, Ensor does find room for comparisons of the highest order: the objectivity of Thucydides, the impressionism of Herodotus, the empathy of Maitland ... [116]

Young finishes his *Portrait*, in fact, with a tribute to Maitland – 'that royal intellect' – for which we can forgive him even a touch of hypostatic theory. Maitland had explored the mental hinterland of English common law. Young set out to explain – allusively, evocatively – the working of the Victorian mind.

No ... English writer, except Maitland, has so perfectly apprehended the final and dominant object of historical study: which is the origin, content and articulation of that objective mind which controls the thinking and doing of an age or race, as our mother-tongue controls our speaking; or possessed, in so full a measure, the power of entering into that mind, thinking with its equipment, judging by its canons, and observing with its perceptions. Capacity like that is no more imitable than the capacity which hung the dome of St Paul's in the sky ... [117]

---

[111] Ibid., 104.
[112] Ibid., 34.
[113] Ibid., 115.
[114] Ibid., 160. Young himself, like Morant, had been directly recruited into Education without passing through the open examination system.
[115] Ibid., 182.
[116] *Spectator*, 25 Dec. 1936, 1130.
[117] Young, *Portrait*, ed. Clark, 182–3, 400; *Last Essays*, 46.

In other words, to get inside the Victorian mind we must aspire to the mind of Maitland. In particular, Maitland's capacity to understand the thinking of our ancestors, 'their common thoughts about common things'.[118]

In later years Young admitted that he 'was never quite satisfied with the notion of the Objective Mind'. What he ultimately preferred was a combination of subjective and determinist methods. Instead of Objective Mind he should really have used the phrase Collective Unconscious. 'Historic forces', he eventually decided, 'act through the minds of men': they reveal themselves in common notions of right and wrong, common thoughts of common things.[119] And so the historian has to aim at a double level of explanation: not just what happened, or how it happened, but 'what people felt about it when it was happening'.[120] And the value of that doubly explanatory process has to lie in the training of a generalized historical sense. Hence Young's lifelong emphasis on history's educative role. History, he believed, must always be the bedrock of the humanities, the spine of the pedagogic process. In form 'an unceasing conversation'; in practice a key to the operation of an informed democracy.[121] Hence the aim of any education worth its salt: the acquisition of 'the historian's eye'. 'Is it worth acquiring?' he asks, at the end of *Portrait of an Age*. 'Is it worth acquiring? I think it is.'[122]

---

[118] F. W. Maitland, *Domesday Book and Beyond* (Cambridge, 1897), 520.

[119] Young, *Daylight and Champaign* (1948 edn), 172, 175, 271–7.

[120] Young, *Portrait*, ed. Clark, 10.

[121] 'Today, the highest and most necessary duty of the historian [is] to infuse into the popular judgement of current events the integrity with which the historic judgment pronounces on the past' (Young, reviewing G. M. Trevelyan, *An Autobiography and Other Essays* (London, 1949), *TLS*, 5 Aug. 1949, 504; reprinted in *Last Essays*, 72–3, 76–7). Future historians of Victorian England will have to trace 'the interplay, the interpenetration of persons and events . . . Swerve to the right, and history becomes a bundle of biographies: to the left a vague expatiation over tendencies, and movements and climates of opinion, the path all cluttered up with fragments of an exploded Zeitgeist' (Young, reviewing A. Briggs, *Victorian People* (London, 1954), *TLS*, 17 Dec. 1954, 818).

[122] Young, *Portrait*, ed. Clark, 183.

Index

ASC = All Souls College

Adams, W. G. S. 163, 183, 186, 189
All Souls College:
  and appeasement, *see* appeasement and ASC
  anti-Jewish sentiment at 266
  finances of 7–8, 29–30
  law and history studied in 1, 37–8, 47–8, 52
  model for institutions at Harvard, Princeton, and ANU 5, 151
  reputation of 226–7
  see also fellows (ASC), fellows, 'fifty-pound' (ASC); fellows, life (ASC); Fellows, Prize (ASC); fellows, professorial (ASC); Fellows, Research (ASC); fellows, thesis (ASC); Fellows, Visiting (ASC)
Amery, John 264, 266–9
  executed for high treason 264, 267–8
Amery, Julian 264–5, 270, 278–80
Amery, Leo:
  and appeasement 248
  and Imperial Preference 161, 270–1
  as contemporary and intellectual equal of Churchill 265
  as fellow of ASC 66, 69, 263
  as good college man (ASC) 265
  as member of Kindergarten 35, 156
  as patriot 265
  as 'scheming little devil' 264
  as Secretary of State for India 208–11
  as Zionist 276
  Chichele Lectures of (1946) 263
  criticizes Gandhi 273
  denounces Chamberlain (8 May 1940) 257–8
  hopes for preferment in aftermath of Munich 255–8, 260

  imperial principles of rated highly by Hancock 265
  Jewish ancestry of 264–6, 275
  likens British Empire to Kingdom of Heaven 193
  loses Parliamentary seat in 1945 263
  on independence for India 265
  on Palestine 274–6
  on partition of India 274
  on *The Washington Loan Agreements* 270–1
  plans Kindergarten for India 211
  posthumous reputation of 269
  preoccupation with post-war economic issues 263–80
  role in post-war colonial world 263–80
  Suez crisis, role in origin of 277–9
  views on India 272–3
  vision of ASC and British Empire 36, 208–9
Anson, Sir William 296
  and Anglo-German Friendship Society 170
  as patron of Workers Educational Authority 5
  as 'second founder' of ASC 1–2, 27
  funeral of 74
  passing of his All Souls 261
Apostles, Cambridge 61–3
appeasement, changing meaning of term 237
appeasement and ASC 191, 223–261
  connection invented c. 1955 227
  historiography of 223–4
  lack of contact among supposed appeasers 232–3
  see also Foreign Affairs Seminar; Munich Agreement; Simon, Sir John
Australia, patriotism in 141

Australian Dictionary of Biography
152
Australian National University
(ANU) 151

Barker, Sir Ernest 172, 178, 180,
183–5, 187
Berlin, Sir Isaiah 32, 46, 266, 283
Bonham Carter, Lady Violet 229
Boothby, Robert (R. J. Graham, Baron
Boothby) 227–31, 244, 257
identifies ASC as headquarters of
appeasement 228–9
bowler hat, as status symbol 282
Brand, Robert, Lord 101–3
and Imperial Union 126
and South Africa 103–4
as banker 128–30, 159
as economist 106–21
as fellow of ASC 130–33, 281
as member of Kindergarten 35, 104,
107, 121–5, 127–8, 156
as patrician virtuoso 102, 133–4
as political thinker 108–14
as sage 105–6
as supposed appeaser 229–30
at time of Munich Agreement 255
on hereditary legislature 109
reputation of at death 101
Bridges, Sir Edward (Lord Bridges) 143,
145–6
British Commonwealth, *see*
Commonwealth, British
Brodribb, C. W. 13, 43–8, 132
Buchan, John 69–70
Butler, Sir Harold 33–4, 63–4

Chamberlain, Neville:
foreign policy of 242–3,
248–52
Chelmsford, Lord (Frederic John Napier
Thesiger) 194–6
Church of England:
as reactionary force in India 221
see also Lang, Archbishop Cosmo
Gordon

Churchill, Sir Winston 209, 211, 219,
227, 231–2, 244, 247–8, 258–9,
265, 269
Churchillians (1930s) 259
Cliveden Set 226, 229
Commonwealth, British 142, 162,
164–5
as Kingdom of God on Earth 164
Cooper, Duff 248, 259–60
resigns over Munich 244
Coupland, Reginald 162–3, 211–18
Cranborne, 'Bobbety', Marquess of
Salisbury (Robert Arthur James
Gascoyne Cecil):
as opponent of Munich 243–4,
248
and 'Watching Committee' 256–8
Curtis, Lionel 36, 126, 135, 142, 149,
158–64, 193, 207, 219, 221, 225,
245, 288
as supposed appeaser 229–30
Christian values and mission of 196–7
vision of British Empire 194–7
Curzon, George Nathaniel, Lord 28, 35,
68, 174
on ASC 1–2

Davis, H. W. C. 32, 171–4, 178, 184–9
admires Heinrich von
Treitschke 187–9
lacks enthusiasm for democracy 186
Dawson, Geoffrey (Geoffrey
Robinson) 35, 37, 43–4, 131–2,
159, 168, 225–6, 242, 253, 260
and *Times* leader (7 September
1938) 250
at time of Munich Agreement 253–6
as member of Kindergarten 233
as supposed appeaser 229–30
motives of for break with
Chamberlain 249–51
relations with Lord Halifax 232–3
Dicey, A. V. (Albert Venn) 4, 189

Eden, Anthony 281, 286, 289, 291
educational mobility 40

Empire, British:
  ASC as Imperial Institute 31
  theology of 193, 196–7
'Establishment, The' 227, 231

Faber, Geoffrey 281
fellows (ASC):
  and appeasement, *see* appeasement
    and ASC
  and British Empire 35–6, 45, 102, 122,
    164, 208–9; *see also* Empire, British
  and India, *see* India, fellows of ASC in
    government of
  and interwar British foreign policy 225
  as Viceroys of India 221
  books as ruin of 17
  drinking habits of 29, 34
  in journalism 36–7
  nobility of 16, 33, 58
  political influence of 44–6, 281, 283
  see also Suez crisis
fellows, 'fifty-pound' (ASC) 7, 9, 28–9
fellows, life (ASC) 28–9
Fellows, Prize (ASC) 3
  age of at election 56–7
  and holy orders 38, 44
  as adventurers and travellers 4, 45,
    66–8, 142
  as men of letters 65–6
  in public service 2, 37–8, 65, 74, 224
  careers of, academic 39
  careers of, non-academic 69
  education of 4, 32–3, 58–9
  Founder's Kin 15–17, 21–3
  lack of fun and games among 62
  post-1850 3–6
  social origins of 59–60
fellows, professorial (ASC) 31, 224
Fellows, Research (ASC) 7, 9, 31, 38, 224
fellows, thesis (ASC) 31
Fellows, Visiting (ASC) 269, 292–3
Fellowship, Prize (ASC):
  and meritocracy 24–5, 45
  elections to 13–15
  obligations of 67
  reform of (1850s) 22

reputation of 6, 39–41, 46–7, 70–1
  stipend of 4, 38
Fellowship examination, Prize (ASC) 24,
  26, 30, 50, 53–4
  colleges of applicants for 57–8
  'fellowship standard' in 50–1
  one-word essay in 50, 55
  numbers of candidates for 49
  success and failure in 55–6
Fletcher, C. R. L. 172–3, 175–7,
  179–80, 189
Foreign Affairs Seminar (ASC
  1957–8) 240–2, 244–7
Forester, C. S. 146
Forster, E. M. 146
Fremantle affair 22–3, 25

Gandhi, Mahatma 193–4, 199–206, 209,
  212, 216, 221
  appreciation of by Radhakrishnan 221
  criticism of by Amery 272–4
  non-violent resistance of denounced as
    unchristian by Anglican bishops 221
  warmed to by Irwin (Halifax) 206
Germany, admiration for among
  academics 168–70
Government by Mallardry, *see*
  Brodribb, C. W.
Gowing, Margaret 143, 147
Greene, Wilfred, Lord 5
Gwyer, Sir Maurice 207–8

Hailsham, Lord (Quintin Hogg) 282,
  285, 289–91
Halifax, Lord (Edward Wood; Lord
  Irwin) 35, 37, 67, 219, 260
  as biographer of Keble 4
  as Foreign Secretary under
    Chamberlain 224, 227, 249–58
  as Viceroy of India 197–206, 221
  Christian convictions of 197–8, 207
  lack of contact with ASC in
    1930s 232–3
  on Eden's 'thing' about dictators 281
  relations with Geoffrey Dawson 232–3
  warms to Gandhi 206

Hancock, W. K. (Sir Keith) 135–53
  agrees with Amery on principles of
    British Empire 265
  and the Australian National
    University 151
  and the Round Table 164
  as candidate for Wardenship of
    ASC 151
  as director of the Institute for
    Commonwealth Studies 152
  as spokesman for Australian
    neutrality 153
  association of with ASC 135–6
  attachment to Australia 150
  ideas of public service 137–41
  on mission to Uganda 149
  plays cricket in ASC library 135
  supervises Civil Series of official
    histories of World War II 143–49
Headlam, Arthur (Bishop of Gloucester):
  as descendent of illegitimate son of Peter
    the Great 174 n. 28
Henson, Herbert Hensley (Bishop of
    Durham) 2, 4, 27, 33, 38–9,
    59–60, 64
Hodson, H. V. 164, 166, 207, 211, 213,
    225
Hogg, Quintin *see* Hailsham, Lord
Hope, Anthony 68
Hudson, Geoffrey 284

India:
  Church of England bishops as
    reactionary element in 221
  Civil Service in 20, 30, 213
  dyarchy system in 195
  fellows of ASC in government of 35,
    193–221, 233
  Government of India Act (1919),
    Commission on 189–9, 203
  Government of India Act (1935) 207,
    209
  Hindu-Muslim relations in 209–19, 220
  Indian National Congress (Congress
    Party) 200–2, 209–17, 219, 272
  intellectual tradition in 220

Muslim League 210, 215–16
  partition of 274
  Princes and Princely States 217–18
  Viceroys of, generated by ASC 68–9,
    193, 221

Jackson, Robert 165–6
Jinnah, Mohammed Ali 216, 219,
    272–3

Kerr, Philip (Marquess of
    Lothian) 157–8, 160, 163–4
Kindergarten, Milner's 4, 35, 70, 155–9,
    193, 233, 296
Kirkpatrick, Sir Ivone 289

Lang, Archbishop Cosmo Gordon 38, 260
  as supposed appeaser 229
  outspoken on public affairs 225
Lawrence, T. E. 232
League of Nations 142
Linlithgow, Marquess of (Victor Hope)
    208, 211, 215–16, 218
Lloyd George, David 298–9

Macartney, C. A. 283
  opinion of Hitler 284
Macaulay, Thomas Babington 17–18
Macdonald, Ramsay 201
Macmillan, Harold 287
Makins, Roger (Lord Sherfield) 282,
    285–8
Malcolm, Dougal 156
Marshall Plan 271
Masterman, C. F. C. 176
Mill, John Stuart 20
Milner, Alfred, Lord 54, 155–60, 233
  see also Kindergarten, Milner's
  vision of British Empire 156–7, 160
Montagu, Edwin 194–6
Moon, Sir Penderel 36, 198, 207
  and India 213–19
Müller, Max 170
Munich Agreement 251–4
  political consequences of in
    Britain 254–5

Namier, Sir Lewis 130, 162, 174, 266
Nasser, Col. Gamal Abdul 278
Nehru, Jawaharlal 200–1, 205, 210, 219, 272

open competition 17–20
  for Oxford fellowships 20–1
Oxford by-election (1938) 239, 253
Oxford, University of:
  and Asquith Commission (1919–22) 6, 8–9, 71
  and Royal Commission (1850–2) 2, 14, 20–2
  and Selborne Commission (1877) 2–3, 26, 30, 47
  Literae Humaniores in 52–3
  prize fellows in 3, 48–9, 54
  zenith of Greats in 52
Oxford Pamphlets 1914–1915 171–92
  role of ASC in 171, 178, 192

Perry, J. F. (Peter) 155
Postan, M. M. (Sir Michael) 144–6, 148
Prize Fellowship (ASC), *see* Fellowship, Prize (ASC)

Radhakrishnan, Sarvepalli 219–21
  political and cultural philosophy of 220
  praises ASC common room to Zhou En-Lai 220
Rees, Goronwy 46
Reilly, Sir Patrick 34–5, 37, 39, 282, 285
  diplomatic career 288–9
Rhodes Scholars 136
Round Table, the 5, 140–2, 159
  ASC and 155–66
  waning influence of 165–6
Round Table, The
  Commonwealth perspectives expressed in 225
  launch of 162
Rowse, A. L. 30, 33, 35, 46, 59, 146, 191, 230–39, 286
  and appeasement 230–1, 234
  and Suez crisis 292

  argues for alternative government (May 1940) 258
  changing usage of 'appeasement' by 237
  diaries of 234–5
  from Marxist to Churchillian 235–9
  introduced into Foreign Affairs Seminar 246
  on Edward VIII as bachelor 239
  studies anthropology 239
  repudiates 'idiot people' 236, 238–9
  rewrites own intellectual history 234–6

Salisbury, third Marquess of 16 n. 19, 37
Salter, Sir Arthur (Lord Salter) 240–2, 245–7, 253, 282
  and 'Salter's Soviet' 241–2, 245–7
Shaw-Stuart, Patrick 61–4
Simon, Sir John 73–99
  and Abdication crisis 91
  and India 199–200, 203–5, 207, 219
  appeasement, involvement in 78, 227, 229–30
  as advocate 79–82
  as 'Chamberlain's mugwump' 249
  as Chancellor of the Exchequer under Chamberlain 224
  as Home Secretary 85, 89–92
  as Lord Chancellor 92–7
  as pacifist 84
  as reformer of family law 90
  as Subwarden of ASC 73
  as 'worst Foreign Secretary since Ethelred the Unready' 88–9
  education of 59
  high offices held by 76–7
  Manchester origins of 75
  meets Rudolph Hess 92
  personality and reputation of 78–9, 199, 232–3
  political career of 83, 85–8, 260
Simon Commission, *see* India, Government of India Act (1919), Commission on
Smuts, Jan Christian 138
Sneyd, Lewis 14, 16, 22–3, 28, 32–3

Somervell, Donald 53–4, 89, 224–5, 261
  as supposed appeaser 229–30
South Africa, attempts to unify under British rule 157–9
Sparrow, John 98, 228, 281, 291
Spear, Edward Louis 259–60
Stubbs, William 171–2
Suez crisis, divides ASC and Oxford 281, 283–4
  ASC as 'hotbed of cold feet' over 291–2

Taylor, A. J. P. 283
Thomas, Sir Keith 281, 291
Trevor-Roper, H. R. 283–4

Uganda 149

Wenden, D. J. (Charles) 231–2, 234, 240
Wilhelm II, Kaiser, inebriated at Oxford Encaenia 170
Wilkinson, Spenser 181–2, 189
Wilson, Mona 300–3, 311
Woodward, E. L. (Sir Llewellyn) 6, 30–2, 238–9, 253

World War I, outbreak of 167–8
World War II, Civil Histories of 135, 138, 143–9

Young, G. M.:
  as commander in Home Guard 306
  as essayist of genius 315
  as historian 311–12, 319
  as polymath 313–14
  calculated persona of 295
  civil service career of 296–301
  decline and death of 312–13
  elected to Brooks's 300
  family circumstances of 59, 295
  leaves academia 38
  literary style of 314, 317
  politics of 307–9
  publications by 299, 305
  Portrait of An Age by 303, 315–19
  relentless one-upmanship of 306
  tours South Africa 296
  Virginia Woolf's estimation of 304